KINGDOM OF PRIESTS

A History of
Old Testament
Israel

Eugene H. Merrill

BAKER BOOK HOUSE
Grand Rapids, Michigan 49516

Copyright 1987 by
Baker Book House Company

Second printing, July 1988

Printed in the United States of America

Library of Congress Cataloging-in-Publication Data

Merrill, Eugene H.
  Kingdom of priests.

  Bibliography: p.
  Includes index.
  1. Bible. O.T.—History of Biblical events.
  2. Jews—History—To 70 A.D. I. Title.
  BS1197.M45 1987   933   87–30853
  ISBN 0–8010–6220–9

Contents

Illustrations

Chronological Tables

Maps

Preface

The title of this work—*Kingdom of Priests*—suggests at once the peculiar nature of a history of Israel: It cannot be done along the lines of normal historical scholarship because it relies primarily upon documents (the Old Testament) that are fundamentally nonhistoriographic in character. The Old Testament is first and foremost theological and not historical literature; this means that theological and not historical approaches must be brought to bear if its underlying purpose and message are to be discerned.

Contrary to much contemporary scholarship, however, we must assert that just because the Old Testament is by definition "sacred history," it does not thereby surrender its claim to authentic historicity as that term is commonly used. It is indeed the record of Yahweh's covenantal relationship with his special people Israel, a record that constantly calls attention to the divine interpretation and even prediction of events, but always it presupposes that those very events actually occurred in time and space. The theological message, in other words, is grounded in genuine history.

The purpose of this study is not so much to interpret the meaning of the underlying events—a task more properly in the province of biblical theology—as it is to discover the historical data themselves and by every resource at our disposal (including the biblical text, extrabiblical documents, and archaeology) to reconstruct the history of Israel along the lines of ordinary historiographical method, that is, to the extent that such a goal is possible, given the unique nature of the material. Any success in this endeavor will be of importance to the search for a true understanding of Israel's Old Testament past—a worthy objective in itself—and to the establishment of the historical factualness of the Old Testament record, the truthfulness of which is

11

absolutely critical if the religious and theological message is to have any effect. Whether or not we have succeeded must be determined by the reader.

The completion of a project that has brought so much personal satisfaction to its author requires that those who made its accomplishment possible be recognized and thanked. It was in the course of a sabbatical kindly granted by Dallas Theological Seminary in 1983–1984 that the major part of the work was achieved, so I want to express my appreciation for this generous and enlightened policy. Moreover, the seminary made its word-processing facilities available. The typing was undertaken by the gifted hands and enthusiastic spirit of Marie Janeway. To Baker Book House and particularly Allan Fisher and Ray Wiersma I pay special homage for their patience, expertise, and painstaking attention to every detail of the project. Finally I must thank my dear wife Janet and daughter Sonya for putting up with my absences, aberrations, and frequent demands and for their constant encouragement to see this through to the end.

Abbreviations

AASOR	*Annual of the American Schools of Oriental Research*
ADAJ	*Annual of the Department of Antiquities of Jordan*
AfO	*Archiv für Orientforschung*
AJA	*American Journal of Archaeology*
AS	*Assyriological Studies*
ASOR	*American Schools of Oriental Research*
AUSS	*Andrews University Seminary Studies*
BA	*Biblical Archaeologist*
BAR	*Biblical Archaeology Review*
BASOR	*Bulletin of the American Schools of Oriental Research*
BES	*Bulletin of the Egyptological Seminar*
Bib Sac	*Bibliotheca Sacra*
BTB	*Biblical Theology Bulletin*
BWANT	*Beiträge zur Wissenschaft vom Alten und Neuen Testament*
BZAW	*Beihefte zur Zeitschrift für die alttestamentliche Wissenschaft*
CAD	*Assyrian Dictionary of the Oriental Institute of the University of Chicago*
CAH	*Cambridge Ancient History*
CBQ	*Catholic Biblical Quarterly*
EQ	*Evangelical Quarterly*
GTJ	*Grace Theological Journal*

HTR	*Harvard Theological Review*
HUCA	*Hebrew Union College Annual*
IEJ	*Israel Exploration Journal*
Interp.	*Interpretation*
JANES	*Journal of the Ancient Near Eastern Society*
JAOS	*Journal of the American Oriental Society*
JBL	*Journal of Biblical Literature*
JCS	*Journal of Cuneiform Studies*
JEA	*Journal of Egyptian Archaeology*
JETS	*Journal of the Evangelical Theological Society*
JJS	*Journal of Jewish Studies*
JNES	*Journal of Near Eastern Studies*
JNSL	*Journal of Northwest Semitic Languages*
JSOT	*Journal for the Study of the Old Testament*
JSS	*Journal of Semitic Studies*
JTS	*Journal of Theological Studies*
KJV	King James Version
LexTQ	*Lexington Theological Quarterly*
NEASB	*Near East Archaeological Society Bulletin*
Or	*Orientalia*
OTS	*Oudtestamentische Studiën*
PEQ	*Palestine Exploration Quarterly*
RA	*Revue d'assyriologie et d'archéologie orientale*
RSV	Revised Standard Version
TD	*Theology Digest*
Tyn Bull	*Tyndale Bulletin*
UF	*Ugarit-Forschungen*
VT	*Vetus Testamentum*
WTJ	*Westminster Theological Journal*
ZAW	*Zeitschrift für die alttestamentliche Wissenschaft*

Introduction

The History of Israel and Historiography

Preliminary Considerations

Any scientific enterprise must take its point of departure from a set of assumptions, no matter how tentative, which provide it with a rationale and viability. This is true of history writing more than most disciplines since it must be conceded that events transpired in the past, that their facticity and meaning can be recovered (if only partially), and that it is possible to integrate and synthesize them into some kind of construct that will be credible and understandable to the modern reader.

When that history is the story of a people enshrined in holy literature, the nature of the task becomes much more complex and the assumptions much more predictive of the outcome. One's view of the integrity and authority of that literature affects one's very approach to the task, to say nothing of methodological procedure and conclusions.

A history of Israel must depend for its documentary sources almost entirely upon the Old Testament, a collection of writings confessed by

15

both Judaism and Christianity to be Holy Scripture, the Word of God. The degree to which historians are willing to submit to that claim inevitably must affect the way they think about their task. Skeptics will view the sources as nothing more nor less than a collection of myths, fables, legends, poetry, and other texts of relative reliability created and transmitted by an ancient people. Believers will be persuaded that they hold in their hands an absolutely unique literary creation, a book that professes to be divine revelation. As such it cannot be approached as one would approach any other ancient texts. It must be addressed as the Word of God, with all that implies concerning its worth and authority as historical source.

Regarding the Old Testament as the Word of God radically alters the task of writing the history of Israel by raising it to the level of a theological activity. If we grant that the writing of Israel's history and the writing of the history of any other people are on entirely different planes precisely because, in the former case, history and theology cannot be separated, we must be willing to admit that the kind of healthy skepticism that is a necessary part of conventional historiography has no place in our work. By virtue of our confession that we are under the authority of the very sources we are investigating, we have already surrendered our right to reject what we cannot understand or what we find difficult to believe.

This does not mean, however, that a modern-day history of ancient Israel can be nothing more than a retelling of the biblical story. The very fact that the Old Testament relates ancient events as sacred history, as primarily theological rather than social or political phenomena, is enough to justify repeated attempts to reconstruct the story along the lines of normal historiography. This book represents such an effort. Our purpose is to understand the history of Israel as an integration of political, social, economic, and religious factors, and to do so not only on the basis of the Old Testament as Scripture, but also with careful attention to the literary and archaeological sources of the ancient Near Eastern world of which Israel was a part.

Problems Faced in the Production of a Modern-Day History of Ancient Israel

The Question of Inerrancy

A corollary to a high view of the Old Testament, that is, the view that it is the very Word of God revealed to humans, is its inerrancy. While virtually all conservative evangelical scholars admit that this inerrancy pertains only to the *autographa*, the original texts, they also maintain that the Old Testament in its pristine form is wholly inerrant. This means that not only is it theologically free of error, but it also speaks accurately and authoritatively of matters of science and history wherever it is its intent to do so. Admittedly, this view of the Old Testament as an inerrant witness to the history of Israel is problematic for many scientifically oriented people, for it is grounded on a theological assumption: the very texts being used as historical documentation are of divine origin and nature and have been supernaturally preserved.

The Absence of Pre-Mosaic Documents

While there may be some evidence that Moses used documents in his composition of Genesis—the so-called *tôlĕdôt* ("genealogies") being often cited—their existence on the whole is without proof. This suggests, then, that he either depended on an infallible, unbroken oral tradition covering thousands of years or received his data by direct revelation. The latter possibility is, of course, rejected by most scholars on dogmatic grounds, while the suggestion of an oral tradition suffers from lack of analogy. The ancient Near East does attest to a remarkable transmission of tradition through oral channels, but never on such a scale or with such integrity as implied in the case of Genesis.

Historical Selectivity

It is inevitably necessary in history writing to include certain events and exclude others, usually on the bases of the availability of data and the special interests and concerns of the historian. This selectivity is eminently discernible in the Old Testament account of Israel's history because the Author (and authors) had particular objectives in mind. The real thrust of the Old Testament is theological. Those facts relevant to the grand themes of the divine purpose, for example, redemption, are retained while others are excluded. The history of Israel surely involved more than the record indicates. Indeed, frequent references to noncanonical documents such as the "Book of Jashar" and the "Book of the Chronicles of the Kings of Israel [or Judah]" tantalize the modern student with the extrabiblical information they must have contained. For reasons no longer clear, however, their contents did not become a part of the historical record.

The problem for the historiographer, then, is the selective nature of the Old Testament. It is not primarily a history in the chronicling, political sense of the term, but a descriptive, tendentious account of God's work in human affairs. It is *Heilsgeschichte* and not *Historie*.

The Present Approach to the History of Israel

Acknowledgment of the Revelatory Character of the Old Testament

This history of Israel approaches the task with the frank confession that the Old Testament is the revelation of God in written form. This confession, of course, presupposes its inspiration as the Word of God and asserts its inerrancy in every area, including history. This does not mean that one can write a history of Israel without facing difficulties—sometimes insurmountable—but one can do so with full recognition that the problems vis-à-vis the sources are not inherent in them, but are due to the historian's human inability to integrate and interpret them. The record may be incomplete; accordingly, it can often be profitably supplemented by extrabiblical data. It is never wrong, however, when it is fully understood.

Recognition of the Biblical Method

In line with the point just made, this volume recognizes the process of selectivity at work in the canonical text and therefore does not expect the Old Testament to say more or less than it does about the facts of history. This process of selectivity should not surprise us, for it was operant as well in various other records written at the same time. For example, some prominent Old Testament events are not recorded in secular histories even when one might expect otherwise. Conversely, many crucial events in the outside world are not mentioned in the Old Testament. It is strange indeed that Egyptian (or, more surprising, Hittite) texts make no mention of Israel's exodus while the Old Testament remains silent about the mighty Hammurabi. The only explanation for such omissions is a highly selective and (by modern standards) unorthodox historiography. The modern historian must accept the situation for what it is and go about the work at hand accordingly. It is not the historian's business to suggest what the sources should or should not have included; one can only work with them and do one's best to understand them.

Recognition of the Biblical Purpose

A burden assumed by anyone who seeks to write a history of Israel is to accept the Old Testament on its own terms. It is a book of history, indeed, but it is far more—it is a progressive revelation of the mind and purposes of the Lord, and so it must be read and interpreted theologically. Though the totality of the facts makes up a corpus of historical information, each fact, each event, each person of the Old Testament has special meaning when seen against the backdrop of the whole. The exodus, for instance, is far more than an exciting episode laying the groundwork for the nationhood of Israel. It is a paradigmatic event that typifies the Lord's salvific actions for his people Israel and indeed for the whole world. To see it as such does not vitiate its literal historicity. To fail to see it as such, on the other hand, is to fail to see that the Old Testament is a work of history that infinitely transcends the bounds of ordinary historiography.

1   Origins

Israel at Moab

At the close of the fifteenth century before Christ[1] a multitude of people known as Israel—a race unique among all nations before or since—assembled on the plains of Moab preparatory to an invasion

---

1. The rationale for the basic chronological structure adopted in this work is elaborated on pp. 66–79.

21

and conquest of Canaan, directly to their west across the Jordan River. Moses, their venerated leader for more than forty years, was about to die and, in fact, had already transferred the reins of authority to his younger colleague Joshua. This moment was uniquely significant. Formerly a disorganized slave people, Israel had been miraculously emancipated from earth's mightiest power, Egypt, and had encountered Yahweh, God of heaven and earth, at Sinai. There they had entered into covenant with him and had been made his own special people, his vassal slaves. Now, after a hiatus of forty years, they had arrived east of Jericho, poised to bring to pass the promise of their covenant God that Canaan would be their homeland.

But a host of perplexing questions demanded answers. It is true that Moses and many of his forebears had learned of the purposes of God either by direct revelation or by oral tradition and that they had communicated these divine intentions to their contemporaries in a variety of ways. Nevertheless, up till now there had been no systematic elaboration of the historical and theological building blocks that had resulted in the structure of a people united in covenant with God and charged with the awesome privilege and responsibility of functioning as his people in line with his redemptive design. Who, indeed, were these people? What was the meaning of Israel? How had Israel come to be? What, specifically, was she to achieve as one member among the family of peoples and nations? Beyond all that, what was the meaning of creation? Of the heavens and earth? Of humankind? What object did the Creator have in view for his creation, and, if Israel was a sovereignly elected servant people, how was that servanthood to be employed in implementing the great saving purposes of God?

The Purpose of Torah

Universal Jewish and Christian tradition clearly and unequivocally teaches that Moses, the covenant mediator and spokesman for Yahweh to his people, set out to answer these very questions as the last great ministry of his long and productive life.[2] The form which these answers took is what is known to Judaism as the Torah and to Christians as the Pentateuch, the five books of Genesis, Exodus, Leviticus, Numbers, and Deuteronomy. Though commonly described as "law," these

2. The rise of skeptical higher criticism in the so-called Enlightenment period of the eighteenth century issued in denial of the Mosaic authorship of the Pentateuch, which was regarded instead as a compilation of several documents written long after the traditional dates for Moses. For a history of this movement and a response to it see Roland K. Harrison, *Introduction to the Old Testament* (Grand Rapids: Eerdmans, 1969), pp. 3–82.

writings are more properly history, but history in a highly qualified sense.[3]

Genesis

The purpose of Genesis is to document the fact that the God of Israel is Creator of all things and to trace the history of the human race from creation to the time of Israel's development as a special people. Genesis reveals God's cosmic intentions, describes humanity's sinful refusal to conform to the divine purposes, and introduces those covenant arrangements and promises by means of which God would ultimately achieve his objectives despite human disobedience. This involves the selection of Abraham, who, through his innumerable offspring, would become the fountainhead of blessing to the whole world.[4]

Exodus

Exodus traces the Abrahamic descendants from their deliverance from Egyptian oppression to their constitution as the people of God in the Sinai wilderness. It shows Israel to be an unworthy object of grace which, for reasons known only to God, was elected to enter into a solemn contract with him for the purpose of serving as both a repository of his saving truth and the vehicle through which that truth would be communicated and eventually incarnated in the divine man, Jesus Christ. The principal themes of the book revolve around this covenant. The historical exodus is climaxed by the making of the covenant, the full text of which appears in Exodus 20–23. There then follow cultic prescriptions concerning the mode by which the vassal must approach the majestic person of the sovereign (sacrifice and ritual) and the place where he must be approached (the tabernacle).

Leviticus

The third section of the Torah provides standards of holiness incumbent on those who would establish and maintain access to the infinitely holy covenant Lord. These standards pertain not only to the people as a whole, but particularly to the priests, who must serve as intercessors in the structure of public worship.

3. See pp. 18–19.
4. Gerhard von Rad, *Genesis: A Commentary*, trans. John H. Marks (London: SCM; Philadelphia: Westminster, 1961), pp. 154–56. The purpose of the patriarchal stories in particular is well described by John Goldingay, "The Patriarchs in Scripture and History," in *Essays on the Patriarchal Narratives*, ed. A. R. Millard and D. J. Wiseman (Winona Lake, Ind.: Eisenbrauns, 1983), pp. 1–34.

Numbers

The Book of Numbers describes the migration of Israel from Sinai to the plains of Moab, a journey fraught with a succession of rebellions against the Lord and his theocratic administrators and climaxed by the death of the adults of the exodus generation. There was a consequent need for at least a partial restatement of the covenant legislation appropriate to the new generation anticipating settlement in Canaan. Much of Numbers, like Exodus and Leviticus, is therefore prescriptive in nature and technically not historical narrative. By and large, however, Numbers recites the significant historical events of the period between the giving of the covenant at Sinai and the arrival of Israel at the plains of Moab, a period of about thirty-eight years. It thus qualifies as history writing and makes its own special contribution to an understanding of preconquest Israel.

Deuteronomy

Deuteronomy is the least overtly historiographical of the books of the Pentateuch, for in its entirety it is an address by Moses to the covenant community on the eve of the conquest. From a literary standpoint this address is largely a massive covenant text with all the elements that are characteristic of such documents attested elsewhere in the ancient Near East.[5] The purpose of the book is to repeat, with amendment and clarification, the basic covenant message of Exodus 20–23, a repetition necessary in light of the historical circumstances which had transpired in the nearly forty years since the Sinai revelation. The adult generation with whom the Sinaitic covenant had been made was dead or dying, so the younger generation needed to hear for themselves and to respond to Yahweh's covenant claims. In other words, there had to be a covenant reaffirmation, as was the custom throughout the eastern Mediterranean world with the passing of a generation of a vassal people.[6] Furthermore, the Sinaitic covenant—as well as its adumbrations in Numbers—was particularly designed for the temporary needs of a nomadic society moving toward permanent sedentary life in Canaan. At last the tribes had arrived at the very threshold of Canaan, and so a modification of the covenant was necessary in anticipation of the greatly altered conditions in which Israel would soon find herself. Deuteronomy is Moses' farewell covenant address in which he reminds his people of who they are, whence

5. Meredith G. Kline, *The Structure of Biblical Authority* (Grand Rapids: Eerdmans, 1972), pp. 9–14.

6. Peter C. Craigie, *The Book of Deuteronomy*, New International Commentary on the Old Testament (Grand Rapids: Eerdmans, 1976), pp. 28, 30–32.

they have come, and what their mission must be from that day forward as they claim the land of promise and work out their mediatorial role among the nations.

The Story of the Patriarchs

The history of Israel does not begin with Moses and the events of exodus and covenant, but the first comprehensive and systematic account of Israel's origins, task, and destiny was certainly prepared on the plains of Moab where Moses the prophet demonstrated his consummate skills of historiography. As both eyewitness and researcher, he had collected and organized raw materials documenting the past, and thus he created the literary masterpiece now known as Torah. It is a history book, yes, but it is far more—it is a theological treatise whose purpose is to show that God the Creator will, through an elect nation Israel, sovereignly achieve his creative and redemptive purposes for all humankind.[7]

Abraham: Ancestor of the Nation

The origins of Abram

A history of Israel must properly begin with the call of Abram to be the father of the chosen nation. At the end of the genealogical list commencing with Shem, son of Noah (Gen. 11:10–26), appears the name of Terah, father of Abram, Nahor, and Haran. Terah lived in Ur of the Chaldees (v. 28), the famous Sumerian city located by the Euphrates River, about 150 miles northwest of the present coast of the Persian Gulf.[8] The most satisfactory reconstruction of biblical chronology places the birth of Abram at 2166 B.C.,[9] a time when Ur had fallen under the control of a barbaric mountain people known as the Guti.[10] As just suggested, Ur was a Sumerian city, the central hub of

7. For the patriarchal stories as nuanced historiography see, *inter alia*, John T. Luke, "Abraham and the Iron Age: Reflections on the New Patriarchal Studies," *JSOT* 4 (1977): 35–47, esp. p. 47.

8. For the excavation of Ur see C. Leonard Woolley, *Ur of the Chaldees* (New York: Norton, 1965).

9. This chronology will be elaborated on pp. 66–79. That the patriarchal era falls roughly in the Middle Bronze I–II period (ca. 2000–1800) is shown by John J. Bimson, "Archaeological Data and the Dating of the Patriarchs," in *Essays on the Patriarchal Narratives*, ed. A. R. Millard and D. J. Wiseman (Winona Lake, Ind.: Eisenbrauns, 1983), pp. 53–89; see also John Bright, *A History of Israel*, 3d ed. (Philadelphia: Westminster, 1981), p. 85.

10. C. J. Gadd, "The Dynasty of Agade and the Gutian Invasion," in *Cambridge Ancient History* (*CAH*), 3d ed., ed. I. E. S. Edwards et al. (Cambridge: Cambridge University Press, 1971), vol. 1, part 2, pp. 454–61. Gutian control extended from around 2240 to 2115.

one of a great number of city-states populated by the highly cultured Sumerians from at least as early as the mid-fourth millennium. The Ur of Terah and Abram was, however, quite cosmopolitan, for non-Sumerians such as Abram's own Semitic ancestors lived there and mingled their intellectual and cultural traditions with those of the Sumerians.[11] Since by that time Sargon (2371–2316)[12] had created the Semite-dominated Akkadian Empire at Agade, nearly 200 miles northwest of Ur, Abram was almost certainly bilingual, commanding both the Sumerian and Akkadian languages. Where Abram's ancestors originated and how they happened to settle in Ur are not addressed in the historical account. The intermingling of Semitic and Sumerian ethnic elements in the third millennium is well attested in lower Mesopotamia, however, so there is no need to seek for an Ur other than the one traditionally associated with Abram.[13]

The principal deity worshiped at Ur was the Sumerian moon god Nannar, known in Akkadian as Sin. It is certain that Abram and his family were faithful devotees of Sin and his coterie of fellow deities, for Joshua 24:2 speaks of them as having served other gods beyond the river (i.e., the Euphrates). Moreover, some scholars identify the name *Terah* as a form of the Hebrew word *yārēaḥ* ("moon"), so that his very name may testify to his religious orientation.[14] When Terah and his family left Ur, they resettled in Haran, another major center of the worship of Sin.

11. Dietz Otto Edzard, "The Early Dynastic Period," in *The Near East: The Early Civilizations*, ed. Jean Bottéro et al. (New York: Delacorte, 1967), pp. 86–87; Thorkild Jacobsen, "The Assumed Conflict Between Sumerians and Semites in Early Mesopotamian History," *JAOS* 59 (1939): 485–95.

12. The extrabiblical dates for this chapter are those of the *Cambridge Ancient History*, 3d ed.

13. Cyrus H. Gordon has proposed that Abram be connected not with Ur of the Chaldees, but with an Ura' in Syria, a location much closer to Haran and, in his view, more compatible with the stories of Isaac and Jacob, whose wives came from Abram's kinfolk in Aram or upper Syria. See his "Abraham of Ur," in *Hebrew and Semitic Studies*, ed. D. Winton Thomas and W. D. McHardy (Oxford: Clarendon, 1963), pp. 77–84. More recently it has been alleged that a northern Ur is attested in the Ebla texts, but, as Paul C. Maloney points out, the cuneiform signs for that Ur are different from those used to spell the name of the Sumerian Ur ("The Raw Material," *BAR* 6.3 [1980]: 59). For a strong defense of the view that Ur of the Chaldees refers to the southern city see H. W. F. Saggs, "Ur of the Chaldees," *Iraq* 22 (1960): 200–9. The descriptive phrase "of the Chaldees" is without doubt a late explanatory gloss since the Chaldeans and Kaldu (i.e., Chaldea) are not known until the ninth century B.C. Its purpose, of course, is to distinguish the southern Ur from many other cities of the same name.

14. William G. Dever and W. Malcolm Clark, "The Patriarchal Traditions," in *Israelite and Judaean History*, ed. John H. Hayes and J. Maxwell Miller (Philadelphia: Westminster, 1977), p. 127. The name more likely is to be traced to the Akkadian *tarḫu* ("ibex"). See Claus Westermann, *Genesis 1–11: A Commentary*, trans. John J. Scullion (Minneapolis: Augsburg, 1984), p. 564.

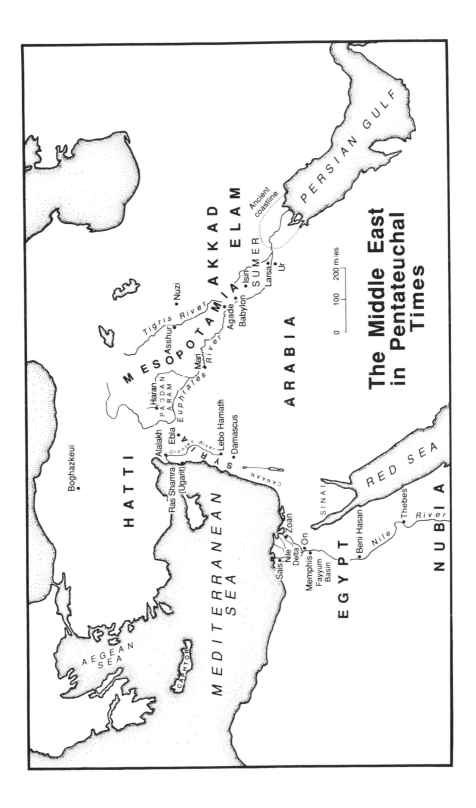

The Middle East
in Pentateuchal
Times

PERSIAN GULF

Ancient
coastline

ELAM

AKKAD

MESOPOTAMIA

SUMER

Ur
Larsa
Isin
Babylon
Agade

ARABIA

Tigris River
Nuzi
Asshur
Mari
Euphrates River

Haran
PADDAN
ARAM

HATTI

Boghazkeui

Lebo Hamath
Hamath
Damascus

Alalakh
Ebla
Orontes River

Ras Shamra
(Ugarit)

MEDITERRANEAN
SEA

CANAAN

SINAI

RED SEA

Zoan
On
Nile
Delta
Sais
Memphis
Fayyum
Basin

EGYPT

Beni Hasan
Thebes
Nile River

NUBIA

AEGEAN
SEA

CAPHTOR

0   100   200 miles

The matter of Abram's birth into paganism in light of his direct descent from the chosen line of Shem is of interest but cannot be considered here in detail. It is clear, however, that the genealogy which connects Shem and Abram must not be viewed as comprehensive but as selective only. That is, those names which do appear are representative of perhaps a great many others which, for reasons that cannot now be determined, were not retained in the record.[15] If Shem and Abram were contemporary, as a strict interpretation of the genealogy would require,[16] it is difficult to understand how Abram's immediate ancestors could have become paganized or indeed why Abram would have been called at all to his sacred mission since believers were already available for the purpose God had in view. Moreover, if Shem and Abram were contemporary, the fact that Abram died at 175 years, "at a good old age, an old man and full of years" (Gen. 25:8), is difficult to reconcile with the statement that Shem died at the age of 600, an age even considerably younger than that of his father Noah (950 years). Clearly, Shem preceded Abram by many more years than a strict reading will permit, and thus there was sufficient time for the knowledge of Yahweh to have disappeared from the line of Shem and for a need to have arisen for Yahweh to reveal himself to pagan Abram.

The journey to Canaan

It is impossible to know precisely when Abram left Ur for Haran. He was old enough to have been married and yet young enough to be under the patriarchal authority of his father. Despite the fact that his name is mentioned first in the genealogy, he was the youngest of Terah's three sons.[17] Haran died in Ur, and so only Nahor and Abram

15. For the form and function of genealogies in the Old Testament and the ancient Near East, see Robert R. Wilson, *Genealogy and History in the Biblical World* (New Haven: Yale University Press, 1977); Jack M. Sasson, "A Genealogical 'Convention' in Biblical Chronography," *ZAW* 90 (1978): 171–85; Gerhard F. Hasel, "The Meaning of the Chronogenealogies of Genesis 5 and 11," *Origins* 7 (1981): 53–70.

16. A strict interpretation, that is, one which holds that the genealogical lists omit no generations, would require that Noah died in 2168, a mere 2 years before Abram's birth, and that Shem died in 2016, predeceasing Abram by only 25 years! See Genesis 9:28; 11:10–11; 25:7. (We are assuming here that Terah was 130 when Abram was born. See note 17.)

17. This is clear from the fact that Abram was 75 when he left Haran (Gen. 12:4), a departure which took place only after Terah's death (Acts 7:4) at the age of 205 (Gen. 11:32). Abram was, therefore, born no earlier than Terah's 130th year. That Terah was 70 when he begot Abram, Nahor, and Haran (Gen. 11:26) means only that his first son was born then. Abram is listed first because he is most important in the narrative to follow.

One cannot a priori reject the great ages of the patriarchs simply because they have no modern parallels. Objective analysis of the only data we have requires that the figures be taken at face value unless contradictory historical evidence is found. It

and Haran's son Lot left with their wives and children to follow Terah to the great city of Haran, six hundred long miles northwest of Ur. Why Terah and his family abandoned Ur cannot be determined, but it might well be that the political and cultural upheavals in Sumer caused by the Guti conquest played a major role. There would have been no way for Terah to know that the barbaric Guti would be expelled by 2115 and that the glorious Ur III dynasty would be established under Ur-Nammu. By then, in fact, Terah and his family must have been in Haran, and within twenty-five years thereafter Abram departed from Haran for Canaan (Gen. 12:4; cf. Acts 7:4).

In the years in and around Haran, a commercial and business center populated mainly by a race known to the Sumerians as MAR.TU and to the Akkadians as Amurru (biblical Amorites), Abram must have become conversant in the Amorite Semitic dialects spoken there and must have imbibed the more nomadic lifestyle with which he would become intimately familiar in Canaan.[18] The Amorites by this time not only occupied the major cities of northwest Mesopotamia but had begun to expand, primarily for commercial reasons, to the southeast and southwest.[19] There eventually was a sufficient population in central Mesopotamia to give rise to Amorite city-states such as Isin, Larsa, and most importantly Babylon. Hammurabi himself (1792–1750), the most illustrious ruler of the Old Babylonian Empire, was a descendant of these Amorites. The southwesterly movement of the Amorites is of more importance to biblical history, however, for it involved the penetration and occupation of Syria and Canaan and extended even to the northeastern borders of Egypt. These Amorites, though erroneously characterized at one time as pure nomads, were technically seminomads at most and were more often than not thoroughly urbanized.[20] Archaeological research at numerous sites in Syria and Canaan

might be helpful to note that Sargon of Akkad is credited with a reign of fifty-five years, Rim-Sin of Larsa with sixty, Rameses II of Egypt with sixty-eight, and Phiops II of Egypt with ninety-four! See, respectively, William W. Hallo and William K. Simpson, *The Ancient Near East* (New York: Harcourt Brace Jovanovich, 1971), p. 55; *CAH* 1.2, p. 641; 2.2, p. 232; 1.2, p. 195. All but Rameses were roughly contemporary with the period of the patriarchs. In addition, the Sumerian King List, while greatly exaggerating, speaks of ancient kings who reigned for hundreds or even thousands of years. Surely this longevity rests on some genuine historical basis. See Thorkild Jacobsen, *The Sumerian King List*, Assyriological Studies 11 (Chicago: University of Chicago Press, 1939).

18. For the MAR.TU or Amurru of upper Mesopotamia in the early second millennium see Jean Bottéro, "Syria During the Third Dynasty of Ur," in *CAH* 1.2, pp. 562–64.

19. Ignace J. Gelb, "An Old Babylonian List of Amorites," *JAOS* 88 (1968): 39–46.

20. For the "dimorphic" character of the Amorite lifestyle see Michael B. Rowton, "Urban Autonomy in a Nomadic Environment," *JNES* 32 (1973): 201–15; M. Liverani, "The Amorites," in *Peoples of Old Testament Times*, ed. D. J. Wiseman (Oxford: Clarendon, 1973), p. 114.

has, in the view of many scholars, yielded conclusive evidence that the indigenous populations were supplanted in the latter part of the Early Bronze Age (2200–2000) by peoples usually described as Amorites.[21]

Table 1   **The Sequence of the Bronze Age**

Early Bronze	3000–2000
Early Bronze I	3000–2800
Early Bronze II	2800–2500
Early Bronze III	2500–2200
Early Bronze IV	2200–2000
Middle Bronze	2000–1550
Middle Bronze I	2000–1900
Middle Bronze II	1900–1550
Late Bronze	1550–1200
Late Bronze I	1550–1400
Late Bronze II	1400–1200

The biblical historian relates that Yahweh told Abram to leave his country (Haran by then) and to go to a place that he would progressively reveal to him. It is tempting to suppose that Abram did not move in isolation but that he became part of the Amorite migration that was under way at that very time.[22] It is true, of course, that Abram is never called an Amorite in the Bible, though the designation "Abram the Hebrew" might indicate that he was thought to be associated with certain migratory peoples.[23]

21. This so-called Amorite hypothesis was popularized by and found major support in the work of Kathleen Kenyon, *Amorites and Canaanites* (London: Oxford University Press, 1966), esp. pp. 76–77. There has lately developed a strong reaction against this hypothesis, however. Representative of this reaction is C. H. J. de Geus, "The Amorites in the Archaeology of Palestine," *UF* 3 (1971): 41–60. It is still safe to say that many scholars accept the hypothesis and that it provides the best explanation for the free movement of the patriarchs in Canaan in precisely this period and best reflects the settlement patterns described by the Old Testament itself. See Eugene H. Merrill, "Ebla and Biblical Historical Inerrancy," *Bib Sac* 140 (1983): 302–21, esp. pp. 306–8; Benjamin Mazar, "Canaan in the Patriarchal Age," in *World History of the Jewish People,* vol. 2, *Patriarchs,* ed. Benjamin Mazar (Tel Aviv: Massada, 1970), pp. 169–87, 276–78.

22. J. Kaplan, "Mesopotamian Elements in the Middle Bronze II Culture of Palestine," *JNES* 30 (1971): 293–307, esp. 305–6. The Amorite hypothesis is, of course, not essential to the historicity of the patriarchal narratives in any way. Abram could well have moved independently from upper Mesopotamia to Canaan.

23. William F. Albright has pointed out that Abram must be seen not so much as a nomadic shepherd but as a caravaner or merchant, that is, as a seminomad at most ("From the Patriarchs to Moses: I. From Abraham to Joseph," *BA* 36 [1973]: 11–15). On the designation *Hebrew* see pp. 100–2.

Table 2 **The Patriarchs**

Birth of Terah	2296
Birth of Abram	2166
Abram's departure from Haran	2091
Abram's marriage to Hagar	2081
Birth of Ishmael	2080
Reaffirmation of the covenant	2067
Destruction of Sodom and Gomorrah	2067
Birth of Isaac	2066
Death of Sarah	2029
Marriage of Isaac	2026
Birth of Jacob and Esau	2006
Death of Abraham	1991
Marriage of Esau	1966
Death of Ishmael	1943
Jacob's journey to Haran	1930
Jacob's marriages	1923
Birth of Judah	1919
End of Jacob's fourteen-year labor for his wives	1916
Birth of Joseph	1916
End of Jacob's stay with Laban	1910
Jacob's arrival at Shechem	1910
Rape of Dinah	1902
Marriage of Judah	1900
Selling of Joseph	1899
Joseph imprisoned	1889
Joseph released	1886
Death of Isaac	1886
Beginning of famine	1879
Brothers' first visit to Egypt	1878
Judah's incest with Tamar	1877
Brothers' second visit to Egypt	1877
Jacob's descent to Egypt	1876
Death of Jacob	1859
Death of Joseph	1806

The settlement in Canaan

When Abram arrived in Canaan, he found himself in a land which had undergone clearly perceivable changes because of the cultural adjustments just described. For more than a thousand years the major ethnic element of the land had been Canaanite.[24] Who the Canaanites

24. Though until recently one could not find the term *Canaan* or *Canaanite* in extrabiblical texts earlier than the mid-second millennium (see Sidney Smith, *The Statue of Idri-Mi* [London: British Institute of Archaeology in Ankara, 1949], p. 15; Michael C. Astour, "The Origins of the Terms 'Canaan,' 'Phoenician,' and 'Purple,'" *JNES* 24 [1965]: 346–47), there is no reason to doubt that the indigenous population of Palestine in the Early Bronze Age was Canaanite. As Roland de Vaux says, "Since there was no change of race or of culture in the course of the third millennium, the 'Canaanites' may be regarded as the founders of the Early Bronze Age" ("Palestine in the Early Bronze Age," in *CAH* 1.2, p. 234). Moreover, it is now pointed out that an Ebla text a thousand years older than the reference from Idri-Mi (Alalakh) refers to "the lord of Canaan" (*dbe ka-na-na-im*). See Giovanni Pettinato, *The Archives of Ebla* (Garden City, N.Y.: Doubleday, 1981), p. 253.

of Abram's time were is unclear, though the Old Testament links Canaan originally with Ham, son of Noah. Whether or not they were ethnically Semitic, they spoke a Semitic language roughly comparable to what Abram must have known from Haran.[25] Recent excavations at Tell Mardikh (ancient Ebla), less than 150 miles southwest of Haran, have yielded thousands of clay tablets written in a language so similar to Canaanite that most scholars designate it Proto-Canaanite.[26] Most significantly, these inscriptions were composed as early as 2500 B.C. Even before Abram's time, then, there was a remarkable affinity amongst the languages of northwest Mesopotamia and Syria (and presumably Canaan).[27] Being conversant in Amorite, Abram would easily have assimilated the Canaanite dialects of his new homeland.

One of the effects of the Amorite occupation of Canaan was the restriction of the Canaanites primarily to the Mediterranean coastal plain, the Valley of Jezreel, and the Jordan valley (see Num. 13:29). The Amorites tended to settle in the great central hill country, undertaking a largely pastoral and agricultural way of life.[28] Abram, too, limited his areas of settlement to the hills and to the northern borders of the Negev Desert to the south. The first place in which he encamped in Canaan was Shechem (Gen. 12:6), a name no doubt later given to the site since there was no town there in Abram's day.[29] There he built an altar and settled down, apparently with no opposition whatsoever. The land was open before him and was his for the taking. The enig-

25. Sabatino Moscati, *An Introduction to the Comparative Grammar of the Semitic Languages* (Wiesbaden: Otto Harrassowitz, 1964), pp. 3–8; William L. Moran, "The Hebrew Language in Its Northwest Semitic Background," in *The Bible and the Ancient Near East*, ed. G. Ernest Wright (Garden City, N.Y.: Doubleday, 1965), pp. 59–64.

26. Pettinato, *Archives*, p. 56; for the excavations and other archaeological data see Paolo Matthiae, *Ebla: An Empire Rediscovered*, trans. Christopher Holme (Garden City, N.Y.: Doubleday, 1981).

27. For a cautious but informative overview of the relevance of Ebla to questions about the history, social life, religion, and language of ancient Syria, especially as it forms a cultural bridge, see Lorenzo Vigano and Dennis Pardee, "Literary Sources for the History of Palestine and Syria: The Ebla Tablets," *BA* 47 (1984): 6–16.

28. Kenyon, *Amorites*, pp. 76–77; William F. Albright, "The Jordan Valley in the Bronze Age," *AASOR* 6 (1926): 68; Norman K. Gottwald, *The Tribes of Yahweh* (Maryknoll, N.Y.: Orbis, 1979), p. 452. This need not imply nomadism or tent dwelling, however, as D. J. Wiseman shows in respect to the patriarchs ("They Lived in Tents," in *Biblical and Near Eastern Studies*, ed. Gary A. Tuttle [Grand Rapids: Eerdmans, 1978], pp. 195–200).

29. William G. Dever, "Palestine in the Second Millennium BCE: The Archaeological Picture," in Hayes and Miller, *History*, p. 99; Joe D. Seger, "The Middle Bronze II C Date of the East Gate of Shechem," *Levant* 6 (1974): 117. Shechem was established as an urban center by about 1900, almost two hundred years after Abram's arrival in Canaan (ca. 2100). The narrative does not even hint that there was a town in Abram's time. To the contrary, he appears to have built his altar at an unoccupied site which later became Shechem.

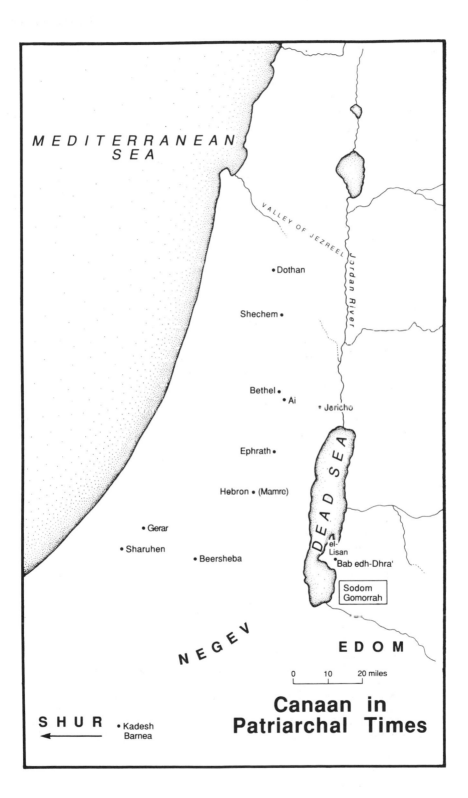

MEDITERRANEAN
SEA

VALLEY OF JEZREEL

Jordan River

• Dothan

Shechem •

Bethel • Ai
• Jericho

DEAD SEA

Ephrath •

Hebron • (Mamre)

• Gerar

• Sharuhen

• Beersheba

el-Lisan

• Bab edh-Dhra'

Sodom
Gomorrah

NEGEV

EDOM

0   10   20 miles

SHUR

• Kadesh
Barnea

Canaan in
Patriarchal Times

matic references to the Canaanites being then in the land (Gen. 12:6;
13:7) do not contradict this general picture, but may be merely notations of Moses to the effect that whereas in his own day the Canaanites were urbanized (i.e., lived in city-states), in Abram's time
they had become dispossessed and were "in the land" in the sense of
being forced to a more agrarian life.[30]

Moving on to a hill between Bethel and Ai, both of which only later
received these names,[31] Abram and his clan again encountered no
resistance. And so the pattern continued on their journey south through
the entire length of the hill country. With the Canaanites effectively
contained in the plains and valleys and the Amorites (among whom
Abram lived) pursuing at least a form of nomadism, the patriarch
moved about and settled down as he chose, unimpeded by claims of
priority or threat from indigenous populations.

The journey to Egypt

Sometime after Abram's arrival in the Negev the land was struck
by drought, and he and his family were forced to turn to Egypt for
relief. Because of the unfailing overflow of the Nile which irrigated the
rich farmlands, Egypt from most remote antiquity was the bread-
basket of the eastern Mediterranean world. The easy access of Abram
to Egypt was by no means unique to him, for the Egyptians had regularly shown the most courteous hospitality to Semitic peoples.[32] There
were, to be sure, certain prejudices and warnings concerning these
bearded foreigners, but for the most part the welcome mat was out,
particularly if the Semites were bent on merchandising.[33] Abram's
visit to Egypt occurred toward the end of the First Intermediate Pe-

30. This seems particularly the case in Genesis 13:7, which speaks of tension between Abram and Lot over pastureland. Because the Canaanites were "in the land,"
there was little room for Abram and Lot.

31. See, respectively, Genesis 28:19 and Joshua 8:28 (since the name *Ai* means
"ruin," it undoubtedly was given to the site only after the Israelite conquest). The
former name for the site of Bethel, Luz, is otherwise unattested, but it is clear that it
was established as early as Early Bronze times. See J. L. Kelso, *The Excavation of
Bethel 1934–1960*, AASOR 39 (1968). Ai cannot be located today with certainty. For a
complete review of the problem see John J. Bimson, *Redating the Exodus and Conquest*
(Sheffield: JSOT, 1978), pp. 215–25.

32. Cyril Aldred, *The Egyptians* (New York: Praeger, 1961), pp. 103–4. This state of
affairs continued throughout the First Intermediate and Middle Kingdom periods as
shown by O. Tufnell and W. A. Ward, "Relations Between Byblos, Egypt and Mesopotamia at the End of the Third Millennium B.C.," *Syria* 43 (1966): 165–241, esp.
pp. 221–23.

33. See the interesting text, "The Instruction for King Meri-ka-Re," in James B.
Pritchard, *Ancient Near Eastern Texts Relating to the Old Testament*, 2d ed. (Princeton:
Princeton University Press, 1955), pp. 414–18, esp. 11. 91ff.: "Lo, the wretched Asiatic. . . .
He does not dwell in a single place, (but) his legs are made to go astray."

riod, probably during Dynasty 10 or 11. By the time he arrived to gaze upon the great pyramids near Memphis, these monuments of the Old Kingdom era had been in place for more than four centuries. But that glorious age had ended with Dynasty 5, and for three hundred years Egypt had been in decline, primarily because of the rising power of the nomarchs or rulers of local districts. Since Abram arrived in Canaan in 2091 B.C. and must have gone to Egypt not much later, the king to whom he lied about Sarai his wife was most likely Wahkare Achthoes III (ca. 2120–2070) of Dynasty 10, the probable composer of the famous "Instruction for King Meri-ka-Re."[34] This piece of advice for his son concerning the treachery of the "Asiatics" may well be related in some way to Abram's duplicity.

The separation of Abram and Lot

Despite Abram's treachery in Egypt the Lord blessed him there, and the patriarch returned eventually to the Negev and then on with great riches to the vicinity of Bethel and Ai. So affluent in flocks and herds had he and Lot become that they found it impossible to coexist in the same pasturelands. In addition, of course, there was the likelihood of nonsedentary Canaanite elements that were also competing for the open space. To alleviate the increasing tensions that such crowding was beginning to create, Abram proposed that he and Lot separate. Again, the impression is clear that the land was freely available to them, that there were no landowners whose properties had to be purchased or from whom permission to settle had to be obtained. All this comports remarkably with what is known of settlement patterns in Canaan at this period.

Looking with covetous eyes to the east, Lot decided to seek his fortune in the verdant plain of the Jordan, probably the lower Jordan valley from east of Bethel to the Dead Sea.[35] Cultural history indicates that this region had been occupied by indigenous Canaanite peoples who suffered the same depredations at the hands of the Amorites which their brethren in the hill country had experienced.[36] Some scholars argue that the infamous cities of the plain, including Sodom, are to be located in this region north of the Dead Sea.[37] More likely,

34. William C. Hayes, "The Middle Kingdom in Egypt," in *CAH* 1.2, pp. 466–68. See also note 33.

35. Yohanan Aharoni, *The Land of the Bible* (Philadelphia: Westminster, 1979), pp. 133–34.

36. Jericho, the leading city of the area, had, according to Kenyon (*Amorites*, p. 9), been destroyed around 2300 and resettled by "a numerous but nomadic" population (p. 33). This Early Bronze–Middle Bronze culture survived until about 1900 (p. 35). The nonurban nature of the area would explain why Lot (ca. 2090 B.C.) was able to choose the "plain of the Jordan" as his allotment.

37. Willem C. Van Hatten, "Once Again: Sodom and Gomorrah," *BA* 44 (1981): 87.

however, they were to the southeast of the sea as long-standing tradition has held and recent exploration appears to demonstrate.[38] If so, Lot must have first entered the Jordan valley and then continued south until he arrived at the outskirts of Sodom (Gen. 13:12).

As for Abram, from his vantage point on the heights of Bethel he could look in all directions at the land which God had promised to give to him and his descendants. The command to "walk through the length and breadth of the land" (Gen. 13:17) implies Abram's possession and domination of the whole area.[39] And so Abram took his first steps, journeying with his family and flocks to the encampment at Mamre, which was named after an Amorite chieftain (cf. Gen. 14:13) and would someday be the city of Hebron (Gen. 13:18). We know that the reference to Hebron is a Mosaic explanatory notation since, according to Numbers 13:22, the city was not built until seven years before the construction of Zoan, a major Hyksos city of the eastern Delta of Egypt. This would place the date of the founding of Hebron at about 1727, or three hundred years after Abram.[40]

The kings of the east

The patriarchal narratives at this point take on an entirely different character. Up till now they have been essentially personal vignettes which are more biographical than anything else and which are difficult if not impossible to relate to the larger international scene.[41] In

38. See particularly the ongoing work of Walter Rast and Thomas Schaub, "Survey of the Southeastern Plain of the Dead Sea," *ADAJ* 19 (1974): 5–53; "Bab edh-Dhra' 1975," *AASOR* 43 (1978): 1–60; "Preliminary Report of the 1979 Expedition to the Dead Sea Plain, Jordan," *BASOR* 240 (1980): 21–61; "The Dead Sea Expedition Bab edh-Dhra' and Numeira: May 24–July 10, 1981," *ASOR Newsletter* 4 (1982): 4–12.

39. The divine promise of land and other blessings (Gen. 12:1–3; 15:18–21; 17:1–8) is in the form of a covenant known technically in ancient Near Eastern studies as a "covenant of grant." It was made at the initiative of the granter and often with no preconditions or qualifications. See Moshe Weinfeld, "The Covenant of Grant in the Old Testament and in the Ancient Near East," *JAOS* 90 (1970): 184–203; Samuel E. Loewenstamm, "The Divine Grants of Land to the Patriarchs," *JAOS* 91 (1971): 509–10.

40. Zoan is identified as Avaris or (more likely) as Hyksos Tanis, twelve miles from Avaris. Some scholars further identify Zoan and Tanis with Per-Ramesse. See Jacquetta Hawkes, *The First Great Civilizations* (New York: Knopf, 1973), p. 315. Whether Zoan is Avaris or Tanis little affects the chronology since both Hyksos sites were constructed at about the same time (ca. 1720). See William C. Hayes, "Egypt: From the Death of Ammenemes III to Seqenenre II," in *CAH* 2.1, pp. 57–58.

41. This is not to suggest that the patriarchal narratives, just because they are narrative—and biographical at that—are not to be regarded as historical in genre. It is increasingly recognized that narrative is an effective way of recounting genuine history. See Luke, "Abraham and the Iron Age," *JSOT* 4 (1977): 37; Lawrence Stone, "The Revival of Narrative: Reflections on a New Old History," *Past and Present* 85 (1979): 3–24; " 'Disillusioned' with Numbers and Counting, Historians Are Telling Stories Again," *The Chronicle of Higher Education*, 13 June 1984, pp. 5–6.

Genesis 14, however, Abram encounters kings and chieftains who are not only named, but whose territories and military associations are spelled out in detail. Practically all scholars concede the historiographical nature of the narrative, but practically all likewise despair of identifying the protagonists and relating them to any series of events known from extrabiblical sources.[42] The result is either an extreme skepticism which sees the account as a historical fabrication or an equally erroneous attempt to identify each of the kings with some known individual of the ancient Near East. For example, at one time Amraphel king of Shinar was thought to be Hammurabi of Babylon. Shinar indeed is a biblical word for Mesopotamia (see Gen. 10:10; 11:2), but Hammurabi (1792–1750) lived three hundred years after the best date for Abram. Besides, Amraphel can in no way be philologically equivalent to Hammurabi. Similarly, attempts to see Arioch of Ellasar as Arriyuk or Arriwuk of Mari, Kedorlaomer as Kudur-lagamar of Elam, or Tidal as Tudḫaliyaš I of Hatti all fail because of chronological or linguistic reasons. It is most prudent to say at this time that though the story bears every earmark of historical credibility, the kings of the east cannot be identified.[43]

As for the chieftains of the cities of the plain, however, a little more certainty is possible. It is argued by some scholars who have had access to the recently discovered Ebla tablets that the cities of the plain are listed there and that the names of their kings also appear, some of which agree with those of the biblical story.[44] Until the relevant texts are published and thus made available to the general public, such claims cannot, of course, be proven. There is nothing in the biblical account, on the other hand, which has been disproved by the

42. So, e.g., Ephraim A. Speiser, *Genesis*, Anchor Bible (Garden City, N.Y.: Doubleday, 1964), pp. 108–9; Niels-Erik A. Andreason, "Genesis 14 in Its Near Eastern Context," in *Scripture in Context*, ed. Carl D. Evans et al. (Pittsburgh: Pickwick, 1980), pp. 60, 62–65.

43. See the helpful discussion of Kenneth A. Kitchen, *Ancient Orient and Old Testament* (London: Tyndale; Chicago: Inter-Varsity, 1966), pp. 43–44. Kitchen points out that though the names of Genesis 14 cannot as yet be linked to specific individuals of extrabiblical history, the names are very much at home in the Middle Bronze period. S. Yeivin goes even further: dating the patriarchal period from the eighteenth to the sixteenth centuries—three hundred years later than our chronology—he identifies the kings with known rulers ("The Patriarchs in the Land of Canaan," in *World History of the Jewish People*, vol. 2, pp. 215–17).

44. David Noel Freedman, "The Real Story of the Ebla Tablets," *BA* 41 (1978): 143–64. Giovanni Pettinato, who first made this assertion, has subsequently retracted it for reasons that are not altogether clear. See his *Archives*, p. 387, for evidence of at least Sodom and Gomorrah in the Ebla texts. That one must be wary of ascribing too much importance to the Ebla finds vis-à-vis the Old Testament is worth noting. See the cautions of Robert Biggs, "The Ebla Tablets: An Interim Perspective," *BA* 43 (1980): 82–83, 85.

newly found documents, nor is there anything inherently improbable about the set of circumstances described. The invasion of Canaan by four (presumably) major powers need not imply that the full might of these kings was employed. It is entirely likely that these were tentative, exploratory raids which produced the unexpected result of bringing the cities of the plain under vassalage (Gen. 14:4).

After twelve years the cities rebelled. Consequently the eastern kings returned, put down the rebellion, and took prisoners and booty. When he learned that his nephew Lot was among the prisoners, Abram, with his confederates Mamre, Eshcol, and Aner, gave chase and finally overtook the enemy at Hobah, north of Damascus. That with only "318 trained men" Abram was able to rescue all the goods and Lot is not incredible since his Amorite neighbors also took their troops, the total of which could have run into the thousands, and there is no indication that Kedorlaomer and his allies had come with a vast host to begin with.

Abram and his culture

Reference to Abram as "the Hebrew" (Gen. 14:13) is of special interest both because this is the first use of the term in the Old Testament and because, in characteristic fashion, the word appears on the lips of a non-Israelite. Seldom did the chosen people call themselves Hebrew, especially in early times. The reason for this no doubt was the fact that though the ethnic designation *Hebrew* must find its origin in Eber, the ancestor of Abram (Gen. 10:21, 25), the similar name '*apiru* (or *Ḥabiru*) led Abram's contemporaries as well as later generations to confuse the two.[45] That is, though the Hebrews clearly distinguished themselves from the peoples known as 'apiru, others were not so careful to understand or recognize this distinction as they pejoratively referred to Abram and his descendants as Hebrews. This in turn led the Hebrews to use some other term with which to identify themselves, the usual being, in later times at least, "Israelites."

Certain peculiar actions of Abram and his wife in Genesis 15 and 16 require some attention to ancient Near Eastern custom and law, especially a few Hurrian practices attested in the Nuzi tablets. These documents, excavated and published more than fifty years ago, consist primarily of the records of important Hurrian families who lived in about 1500 B.C. and later at Nuzi (modern Yorghan Tepe), about fifty miles southeast of Asshur in Assyria.[46] They pertain to matters such

45. Full discussion of the 'apiru and their relationship to the Israelites must await our treatment of the conquest of Canaan (pp. 100–8). For now see Moshe Greenberg, *The Ḥab/piru* (New Haven: American Oriental Society, 1955); Michael B. Rowton, "Dimorphic Structure and the Problem of the 'Apiru-'Ibrim," *JNES* 35 (1976): 17–20.

46. For an account of the excavation and publication of the texts see Ephraim A. Speiser, *New Kirkuk Documents Relating to Family Laws*, AASOR 10 (1928–1929): 1–73.

as inheritance and property rights, slavery, adoption, and the like. It was noted by earlier scholars that the documents of Nuzi dealt with social and family matters in a way reminiscent of the patriarchal stories. They were then used to explain biblical customs which until that time had been very unclear at best. One of the problems to which evidence from the Nuzi tablets was applied was Abram's protest that the divine promise of an innumerable seed would be impossible since he had no heir except Eliezer of Damascus, whom he described as "a servant in my household" (Gen. 15:3). The implication here is that Eliezer was an adopted son, a point also made by Yahweh, who says that Eliezer would not be Abram's heir, but "a son coming from your own body will be your heir" (v. 4). Tablets from Nuzi appear to address this very situation: a slave could become the heir of a childless couple by being adopted by them. Another example is Sarai's barrenness and the steps she took to ensure offspring in spite of it (Gen. 16:1–6). She simply offered her slave girl Hagar to Abram as a surrogate mother, and the child of that union, Ishmael, came to be regarded as the son of Abram and Sarai. This, too, is paralleled by Nuzi texts which describe the same remedy for a similar situation.[47]

More-recent scholars have drawn attention to the facile way the Nuzi materials have been used to illuminate patriarchal custom and even to "prove" the historicity of the patriarchal period.[48] For one thing, the patriarchs by the traditional biblical chronology antedate the Nuzi texts by four or five hundred years. So serious was this problem that Cyrus Gordon chose to lower the patriarchal era to the Late Bronze Age (ca. 1550–1200) just to accommodate it to the Nuzi evidence.[49] This is subjectivism at its worst. The most reasonable position is that the Nuzi tablets reflect customs which were not initiated there but had already been prevalent for centuries. In fact, customs similar to those at Nuzi are attested from many earlier sites, and these continue to be helpful in understanding the patriarchal way of life.[50] In

47. For these and other parallels see Cyrus H. Gordon, "Biblical Customs and the Nuzi Tablets," *BA* 3 (1940): 1–12; Speiser, *Genesis*, esp. pp. xl–xliii; Samuel Greengus, "Sisterhood Adoption at Nuzi and the 'Wife-Sister' in Genesis," *HUCA* 46 (1975): 5–31.

48. Thomas L. Thompson, *The Historicity of the Patriarchal Narratives* (Berlin; de Gruyter, 1974); John Van Seters, *Abraham in History and Tradition* (New Haven: Yale University Press, 1975); Thomas L. Thompson, "The Background of the Patriarchs: A Reply to William Dever and Malcolm Clark," *JSOT* 9 (1978): 2–43.

49. Cyrus H. Gordon, "Hebrew Origins in the Light of Recent Discovery," in *Biblical and Other Studies*, ed. Alexander Altmann (Cambridge: Harvard University Press, 1963), pp. 5–6.

50. See M. J. Selman, "Comparative Customs and the Patriarchal Age," in *Essays on the Patriarchal Narratives*, ed. A. R. Millard and D. J. Wiseman (Winona Lake, Ind.: Eisenbrauns, 1983), pp. 91–139; Tikva Frymer-Kensky, "Patriarchal Family Relationships and Near Eastern Law," *BA* 44 (1981): 209–14.

any case, there is nothing in the two incidents cited which necessitates a date later than that required by biblical considerations, nor do these incidents appear as unique events without contemporary analogues.

The destruction of Sodom and Gomorrah

The story of the cities of the plain does not end with their dramatic rescue by Abram and his colleagues. Some time after that event the Lord appeared to Abram (now Abraham—Gen. 17:5)[51] and announced his intention to destroy the cities because of their unrepented wickedness. Though Abraham interceded on their behalf, he was unable to deter the wrath of God; and except for Lot and his two daughters, all five cities and their inhabitants perished. The destruction evidently was the result of some kind of volcanic eruption or petroleum explosion which threw into the heavens vast quantities of magmatic materials which then rained down upon the earth.[52]

Since this narrative is set between the promise to Abraham and Sarah that they would have a son within the year (Gen. 18:14) and the birth of Isaac (Gen. 21:2), an event which took place in 2066 B.C., the judgment of the cities must have occurred in about 2067 B.C.[53] It has already been pointed out that the Ebla inscriptions evidently mention at least Sodom and Gomorrah. Since these documents are no earlier than 2500 B.C., Sodom and Gomorrah could not have been destroyed before that date. On the other hand, recent excavations at Bab edh-Dhra' and other sites on and near the el-Lisan peninsula at the southeast end of the Dead Sea have revealed the remains of at least five ancient urban complexes, the latest of which is apparently earlier than 2000 B.C.[54] One is tempted to suppose that some or all of these are the biblical cities of the plain since both their locations and dates are compatible with the witness of the Old Testament. It is impossible to be dogmatic on this point in light of the absence of extrabiblical literary attestation from these sites, though clearly the patriarchal history does seem to have more corroboration than ever before.[55]

---

51. Abram = "exalted father" and Abraham = "father of multitudes." For the provenience and theological significance of these names see D. J. Wiseman, "Abraham Reassessed," in *Essays on the Patriarchal Narratives*, pp. 158–60.

52. Excavators of the area attribute the destruction of the urban sites to an earthquake. See Michael D. Coogan, "Numeira 1981," *BASOR* 255 (1984): 81.

53. For the line of argument in support of these dates see Eugene H. Merrill, "Fixed Dates in Patriarchal Chronology," *Bib Sac* 137 (1980): 242–43.

54. Rast and Schaub, "Bab edh-Dhra' 1975," *AASOR* 43 (1978): 2; van Hatten, "Sodom and Gomorrah," *BA* 44 (1981): 89.

55. Albright, "Jordan Valley," *AASOR* 6 (1926): 62, goes as far as to say, "It is hardly possible to separate the abandonment of Bab ed-Dra' from the destruction of the Cities of the Plain."

Abraham and the Philistines

Shortly after the overthrow of the cities of the plain Abraham jour-neyed south and west from Mamre to the area between Kadesh Barnea and Shur, somewhere in the northern Sinai peninsula. There he dwelt for a time with a certain Abimelech, king of Gerar. At Gerar Abraham told his wife to pretend to be his sister, a ruse he had previously em-ployed in Egypt. This subterfuge has led critical scholars to assume a duplicate account of the same event.[56] Similarly, Isaac's lie to Abim-elech about his wife Rebekah, calling her his sister, is alleged to be a doublet of the Abraham-Abimelech story or perhaps even a triplet with the Abraham-Pharaoh account.[57] But besides the fact that all three narratives differ in detail and share only the lie about the wife, there is no reason why Abraham would not repeat a ploy which had worked reasonably well once before, and surely Isaac might well have learned at least this much from his father.[58]

Of greater historical interest and difficulty is the identification of Abimelech as a Philistine (Gen. 21:32, 34; cf. 26:1). It is generally as-sumed that this identification is anachronistic at best because the Phi-listines, as part of the Sea Peoples migration, did not enter and subdue lower coastal Canaan until 1200 B.C. or later.[59] Moreover, the name *Abimelech* is Semitic, not Philistine.[60]

The second of these two problems will be addressed first. The name *Abimelech* means "my father is the king" and could well be a title rather than a personal name.[61] The fact that Isaac dealt with a Philis-tine king of the same name many years later would support this con-tention. In later times Joshua defeated Jabin of Hazor, a Canaanite king, and at least a hundred years after that Deborah and Barak vanquished a king of Hazor also known as Jabin. Although a personal name is here in view, this case at least illustrates that different rulers of the same place did in fact have the same name. More relevant, perhaps, is the use of terms like Pharaoh and Czar in such a way that they almost became personal names rather than titles. One cannot, then, determine the ethnic character of either Abimelech, since a Phi-

---

56. John Skinner, *A Critical and Exegetical Commentary on Genesis* (New York; Scribner, 1910), p. 315.

57. Ibid., pp. 364–65.

58. Gleason L. Archer, Jr., *A Survey of Old Testament Introduction* (Chicago: Moody, 1964), pp. 120–21.

59. Van Seters, *Abraham*, p. 52.

60. Roland de Vaux, *The Early History of Israel*, trans. David Smith (Philadelphia: Westminster, 1978), pp. 503–4.

61. Kitchen, *Ancient Orient*, p. 81; idem, "The Philistines," in *Peoples of Old Tes-tament Times*, ed. D. J. Wiseman, pp. 56–57; D. J. Wiseman, "Abraham in History and Tradition. II: Abraham the Prince," *Bib Sac* 134 (1977): 232–33.

listine could have borne a Semitic title or indeed could have become sufficiently assimilated into a Semitic culture to have assumed a Semitic name.

The problem of the presence of Philistines in Canaan nearly a millennium before the arrival of the Sea Peoples is more perplexing but not insoluble. A number of texts from Mari, Ras Shamra, and elsewhere refer to the people of Kaptara, whose place of origin was Crete or somewhere else in the Aegean world.[62] And the Bible associates the earliest Philistines with the Caphtorim, whose home was Caphtor or Crete (Deut. 2:23; Jer. 47:4; Amos 9:7; cf. Gen. 10:14). The Kaptara and Caphtorim where clearly one and the same, and their widespread travels, as attested in the extrabiblical documents, could well explain their existence in Canaan in the Middle Bronze Age.[63] The arrival of the Sea Peoples later on would have augmented the Philistines already in the land. This hypothesis, in addition to supporting the historicity of the patriarchal encounters with early Philistines, would also account for Israel's decision not to take the way of the sea en route to Canaan from Egypt, "though that was shorter" (Exod. 13:17), for it would have meant certain and disastrous opposition from the Philistines. One of the main supports for a late date for the exodus (ca. 1250) and a corresponding date for the conquest (after 1200) is the reference to the Philistines. If, however, Philistines were living in Canaan in patriarchal times, the traditional date for the exodus (1446) can be allowed to stand.

Following Isaac's birth in 2066 B.C. Abraham and Abimelech found themselves at odds over pasturage and water rights, and so they decided to enter into a covenant whereby they would pledge respect for each other's boundaries and wells. A similar contract was later enacted between Isaac and another Abimelech (Gen. 26:26–33). In both stories the site of the treaty is Beersheba, a place which took its name ("well of the oath") from the covenant making which occurred there. Archaeological evidence suggests that Beersheba was not founded until well after the Middle Bronze period, and so it is likely that Abraham and his family did not occupy the area in a permanent way, but only as a pilgrimage shrine and campsite in their seasonal migrations.[64] There is nothing in the biblical narratives, in fact, that explicitly identifies Beersheba as an urban center until the time of the conquest (Gen. 21:14, 31–33; 22:19; 26:23, 33; 28:10; 46:1; cf. Josh. 15:28). It was an

62. de Vaux, *Early History*, p. 504.

63. If a later Assyrian text concerning the empire of Sargon of Akkad is reliable, references to the Kaptara may extend as far back as his time (ca. 2350 B.C.). See Gadd, "Dynasty of Agade," in *CAH* 1.2, pp. 429–30.

64. Yohanan Aharoni, "Excavations at Tel Beer-Sheba," *BA* 35 (1972): 111–27; "Excavations at Tel Beer-Sheba," *Tel Aviv* 2 (1975): 146–68.

important dwelling-place of the patriarchs, but did not at that time develop in such a way as to yield archaeologically observable remains.

The search for a wife for Isaac

Sarah died at Hebron in 2029 B.C. (Gen. 23:1–2; cf. 17:17). Within three years after her burial in a grave site purchased from Ephron the Hittite, Abraham undertook steps to obtain a wife for his son Isaac, who by then was close to forty years of age (see Gen. 25:20). Eager for him to marry within the clan, Abraham sent his servant back to Aram Naharaim (upper Mesopotamia—Gen. 24:10) whence Abraham himself had come to Canaan.[65] His brother Nahor had sired many children including "Kemuel (the father of Aram)" (Gen. 22:21) and Bethuel, father of Rebekah and Laban (Gen. 22:23; 24:29). Thus the Old Testament indicates that the Arameans as well as the Israelites can be traced to Terah, father of Abraham.[66] (While Aram is described in Gen. 10:22 as a son of Shem, he was a son only in the sense of a descendant.)

Abraham's servant journeyed to the city of Nahor (Gen. 24:10). This is likely only a way of describing the dwelling-place of Nahor, Abraham's brother, though there was a city by that name, as is shown by Akkadian references to Naḫur(u). Since these references are much later than the time of Nahor, however, this city is probably not the one visited by Abraham's servant.[67] In any event, Bethuel and Laban agreed that Rebekah should be given to Isaac, so when all the customary obligations were met, she returned with the servant to Isaac's home in the Canaanite Negev.

Abraham now remarried and by his wife Keturah became forefather of such clans as Jokshan, Midian, and Dedan (Gen. 25:2–4; 1 Chron. 1:32–33). The Midianites would play an important part in the subsequent history of Israel. They, with the other clans, took up a nomadic lifestyle and eventually ranged throughout the vast Syro-Arabian peninsula. Abraham died at the age of 175 (1991 B.C.) leaving his two principal sons, Isaac and Ishmael, as his heirs. The offspring of Ishmael settled in the deserts east and south of Edom and, like Israel, developed into a federation of twelve tribes. Their relationship to the Midianites is unclear, though the terms *Ishmaelites* and *Midianites* appear to be almost interchangeable at times (see Gen. 37:25, 27–28, 36).

65. Terry J. Prewitt, "Kinship Structures and the Genesis Genealogies," *JNES* 40 (1981): 92.

66. For a defense of this tradition see Merrill F. Unger, *Israel and the Aramaeans of Damascus* (Grand Rapids: Baker, 1980 reprint), pp. 8–10.

67. William F. Albright, *From the Stone Age to Christianity* (Garden City, N.Y.: Doubleday, 1957), pp. 236–37. Naḫur(u) seems not to be attested earlier than 1750 B.C. whereas Nahor, Abraham's brother, would have settled in his city by 2100 or so. It is possible, of course, that the city name eventually reflected that of its founder.

Jacob: Father of the Nation

The blessing and exile

Isaac, of course, was the covenant son of Abraham, the one through whom God mediated the redemptive promises concerning a nation and a land (Gen. 12:1–3; 15; 17:1–14; 25:21–24). Though Isaac was forty years old when he married, it was another twenty years before Rebekah bore him twin sons in fulfilment of the promise (Gen. 25:20, 26). Abraham was then 160 and so within fifteen years of failing to see God's faithfulness with his own eyes.[68] Esau, the expected covenant heir, lost both his birthright and covenant privileges and had to be content with his role as father of the Edomite tribes. Jacob, though resorting to personal manipulation and assistance from his mother, nevertheless experienced the favor of the Lord in gaining the privilege of fathering the chosen nation.

The result of Jacob's machinations was alienation from Esau and flight to Paddan Aram[69] (northwest Mesopotamia) both to escape his brother and to find a wife among his own kinfolk. Jacob was by then seventy-six years old (ca. 1930 B.C.) and must have appeared destined to remain without descent.[70] Heading straight to his mother's home, he was reinforced and encouraged along the way by his encounter with the Lord at Bethel, a place known formerly as Luz but now given a new name because Jacob regarded it as the "house of God." There God renewed the covenant promises he had made to both Abraham and Isaac (Gen. 28:13–15).

At last Jacob arrived at the house of Laban. After much deliberation it was decided that Jacob should marry Laban's daughter Rachel, but only after seven years of service to Laban. It may well be that this service involved something akin to old Babylonian herding contracts whereby a herdsman would be employed for a stated period of time in return for a specified share of the increase and profits. It was possible for a crafty herdsman to use such a contract for his own advantage, even to the point of acquiring most of his employer's property. This seems to have been the situation between Laban and Jacob, for later on in the narrative Laban's sons see Jacob as a threat to their

68. For these figures see Merrill, "Fixed Dates," *Bib Sac* 137 (1980): 243–44.

69. The term comes from Akkadian *paddanu* ("road") + Aram, that is, "the road of Aram." Since this place is identified with Aram Naharaim ("Aram of the two rivers") in Genesis 24:10 (cf. 28:2) and, further, with Haran in 27:43 and 28:10, it may be that the name signifies nothing other than Haran. It is interesting to note that the Akkadian term *ḥarrānu* also means "road." See *CAD*, *Ḥ*, pp. 107–13.

70. This figure is based on the facts that Joseph was born about fourteen years after Jacob reached Paddan Aram and that when Jacob went down to Egypt he was about 130 and Joseph 40.

inheritance rights.[71] Rachel's theft of the household images was perhaps an attempt of a zealous and loving wife to retain for herself and her husband the legal claim to the lion's share of her father's estate (Gen. 31:19).[72]

Be that as it may, Jacob found to his sorrow that Laban was more treacherous than he and that after seven onerous years of service he had Leah, the elder daughter, and not Rachel as wife. He could have Rachel, he learned, only by committing himself to seven more years. When the fourteen years had passed, Laban prevailed on Jacob to remain six more years, for a total of twenty (ca. 1930–1910 B.C.), since it was clear that Jacob was a source of great economic benefit to him.

In the course of these years Jacob had eleven sons and at least one daughter by his two wives and their two maidservants. These sons together with Benjamin, who was born in Canaan, were the forefathers of the twelve tribes of Israel. According to most tradition critics, the story of Jacob and the twelve sons is a legend whose purpose is to establish a common origin and set of traditions for the twelve tribes who made up the postconquest confederation known as Israel.[73] Nevertheless, a straightforward reading of the narrative creates no insuperable historical problems. There are miracles in the story, indeed, not least of which is the direct intervention of the Lord in behalf of Jacob and his wives. The integrity of the account, however, can be denied only by a positivistic reading of history. Yet if God be absent from this story, then there is no way to see his hand anywhere, and the Old Testament becomes here and everywhere a mere work of fiction no matter how pious its intent.

The birth of the eleven sons in seven years is not as serious a problem as is sometimes argued. The first four, born of Leah, may have come in the first four years (Gen. 29:31–35). Rachel, in the meantime, envious because she did not have children, urged Jacob to take her slave girl Bilhah, much as Sarah had arranged for Abraham to father Ishmael by Hagar. The two sons of Bilhah, Dan and Naphtali, could have been born also in the first four years (Gen. 30:1–8). After Bilhah's two sons were born, Leah, believing she could have no more sons, asked Jacob to use her slave Zilpah as a substitute. Zilpah then bore two sons in years five and six (Gen. 30:9–13). Leah had become preg-

---

71. The view that the arrangement between Jacob and Laban reflects Hurrian pseudoadoption practices is rightly rejected by most scholars today. The parallels to old Babylonian herding contracts have, however, been clearly shown. See, e.g., Martha A. Morrison, "The Jacob and Laban Narrative in Light of Near Eastern Sources," *BA* 46 (1983): 156–60.

72. Ibid., pp. 161–62.

73. Martin Noth, *The History of Israel*, 2d ed. (New York: Harper and Row, 1960), pp. 121–27.

nant again, perhaps in year five, and gave birth to two more sons, Issachar and Zebulun, in years six and seven (Gen. 30:17–20). Finally, Rachel had a son of her own, Joseph, in year seven (Gen. 30:22–24). Though all this is hypothetical, it is not impossible and serves well to illustrate the kind of solutions to biblical problems that open-mindedness may be able to achieve.

The return to Canaan

After twenty years in Paddan Aram Jacob returned to Canaan. Along the way he made peace with his father-in-law Laban (Gen. 31:43–55) and his brother Esau (Gen. 33:1–17) and then arrived at Shechem. Most scholars agree that Shechem was founded at about this time (ca. 1910 B.C.),[74] but it is unlikely that it bore this name in Jacob's day. Without doubt it was named for the son of Hamor (Gen. 33:19), the head of the clan that lived in the area, but this name would almost certainly not have been given within the lifetime of Shechem himself. Moreover, it is possible that the clause "Jacob . . . arrived safely [in peace] at the city of Shechem" (v. 18) should be understood as "Jacob arrived at Shalem, that is, at the city of Shechem."[75] This would mean that the city of Jacob's time was called Shalem and was later renamed Shechem in honor of the young man of the biblical story.

At Shechem Jacob bought some property on which he dug a well and established a dwelling-place for several years. At first all went well between Hamor and Jacob, but one day Shechem, Hamor's son, seized Dinah, the daughter of Jacob, and raped her. Dinah's brothers Levi and Simeon avenged her humiliation by slaying all the males of the town, including Hamor and Shechem. Fearful of repercussions from the neighboring Canaanites, Jacob left the area and traveled south to Bethel. There he experienced the presence of Yahweh in theophany and heard once more the promises of Yahweh concerning land and seed. Again Jacob named the place Bethel, the house of God, for he had seen the presence of God in a remarkable way.

While Jacob and his family were pressing still farther south toward Ephrath (or Bethlehem), Rachel died in giving birth to her second son,

---

74. It is attested already as Skmimi in the Egyptian execration texts of around 1850 B.C. See Walter Harrelson, "Shechem in Extra-biblical References," *BA* 20 (1957): 2. Dever argues that the occupation of Shechem began in the Middle Bronze IIA period, which he dates at 2000–1800. A middle date of 1900 is in line with the biblical chronology ("The Patriarchal Traditions," in *Israelite and Judaean History*, p. 99; cf. p. 84).

75. This was suggested already by the Septuagint, the Syriac versions, Eusebius, and Jerome, cited in Franz Delitzsch, *A New Commentary on Genesis* (Minneapolis: Klock and Klock, 1978 reprint), vol. 2, p. 215. The Hebrew *šālēm* in the Masoretic text could be an adjective meaning "safe" (Francis Brown, S. R. Driver, and Charles A. Briggs, *A Hebrew and English Lexicon of the Old Testament* [Oxford: Clarendon, 1962], p. 1024), but the normal way of rendering this idea would be *bĕšālôm*.

Benjamin. After setting up a memorial stone, Jacob moved on to his father's home at Hebron. Isaac was still living but would die within fifteen years at the good old age of 180. Within a year or two of his arrival at Hebron, Jacob sent his sons back to Shechem to seek seasonal pasturage for their sheep. He then sent his favorite son Joseph to check on the welfare of his brothers and the flock. Not finding them at Shechem, Joseph inquired as to their whereabouts and learned that they had gone toward Dothan, some fifteen miles north-northwest of Shechem. When his brothers saw him approaching, they decided at first to kill him, but instead they delivered him over to a band of Ishmaelites headed for Egypt. Thus Joseph found himself a slave in Egypt at the tender age of seventeen (in 1899 B.C.).

Judah's marriage

Judah, the fourth son of Leah, had married a Canaanite woman who bore him three sons. This marriage outside the clan, particularly to a Canaanite, was reprehensible to patriarchal sensibilities as is clear from the careful efforts of both Abraham and Isaac to secure wives for their sons from among their own kinfolk (Gen. 24:3; 27:46). The refusal of Jacob and his sons to permit Dinah to marry Shechem, even after he had violated her, also reveals this spirit (Gen. 34:14). There was doubtless a tendency at work for Jacob's sons to be assimilated to Canaanite culture and religion, an assimilation which would certainly be accelerated by intermarriage. This must have alarmed Jacob, particularly since something of the Canaanite lifestyle had already been imbibed by his eldest son Reuben, who had violated one of the most cherished of patriarchal taboos, that against incest, by cohabiting with Bilhah, his father's concubine (Gen. 35:22).[76]

But Jacob's concern was insignificant compared to that of Yahweh, who had called the patriarch and his fathers to be a people set apart from all other nations. That radical uniqueness of Israel was now being threatened by the syncretistic tendencies represented by Judah's marriage. It is clear, therefore, that Joseph was sent to Egypt not as an act of punishment, but as a blessing of divine providence, for Yahweh was using him to prepare the way for a period of incubation in which the nation of Israel would grow and mature in Egypt and become a suitable servant people (Gen. 50:19–21). The selling of Joseph, then, should be viewed as a divine reaction to the marriage of Judah.[77]

---

76. Stanley Gevirtz points out that Reuben usurped his father's connubial rights ("The Reprimand of Reuben," *JNES* 30 [1971]: 98). Reuben's act was typical of a Canaanite lifestyle, and especially of the purported lifestyle of their gods. See Charles F. Pfeiffer, *Ras Shamra and the Bible* (Grand Rapids: Baker, 1962), pp. 31–32.

77. For other reasons for the placement of Genesis 38 see Judah Goldin, "The Youngest Son or Where Does Genesis 38 Belong?" *JBL* 96 (1977): 27–44.

The descent to Egypt

It is appropriate at this juncture to discuss briefly the chronological issues related to the selling of Joseph, the marriage of Judah, and the descent of Jacob and his family into Egypt, all against the backdrop of Egyptian history, the main outline of which, at least, can be reconstructed reasonably well. On the basis of an 1876 B.C. date for the commencement of the Egyptian sojourn, we know that the birth of Joseph occurred in 1916 B.C.[78] Joseph was seventeen when he was sold to the Egyptians (Gen. 37:2), so his arrival in Egypt was in 1899. Judah, who as Leah's fourth son could not have been more than three years older than Joseph (see pp. 45–46), must not, it seems, have married much earlier than 1900, when he would have been nineteen. If his marriage provided the impetus for Yahweh's allowing Joseph to be sold to Egypt, as seems most plausible, then that marriage may be dated around 1901 or 1900, that is, shortly after Jacob and his family moved from Shechem to Hebron.

In 1876, when Jacob was 130 years old (Gen. 47:9), Joseph had already been in Egypt for twenty-three years. He had worked in the household of Potiphar for about ten years and then for perhaps three more had languished in Pharaoh's prison on trumped-up charges of violating Potiphar's wife (Gen. 40:1, 4; 41:1). Finally, when he was thirty years old (1886 B.C.), he was released and began to serve as Pharaoh's minister of agriculture or in some similar capacity (Gen. 41:46). At that time the seven years of bountiful harvest commenced (1886–1879) following which were seven years of famine (1879–1872). The first visit of Jacob's sons to Egypt to acquire grain would have come about the second year of famine (1878). The second visit would then have been in 1877 (Gen. 43:1; 45:6, 11). Jacob and his entire family moved to Egypt in 1876, right in the midst of the famine period (Gen. 46:6). Joseph by then was forty years old and his brother Judah forty-three.

Included in the list of those who accompanied Jacob to Egypt were Perez and Zerah, who were the sons of Judah by his illicit union with his daughter-in-law Tamar, and even his grandsons Hezron and Hamul (Gen. 46:12). Perez and Zerah were twins who were not born until after Judah's third son, Shelah, was fully grown (Gen. 38:14). Given the early ages at which even men were married in ancient Israel, it is entirely possible that Judah was married by age eighteen, that his first two sons were born within the first two years, and that Shelah came along two or three years later. This would place the marriage of Judah in 1901, Er's birth in 1900, and Onan's in 1899. Shelah was born per-

---

78. Full discussion of and support for these dates may be found in Merrill, "Fixed Dates," *Bib Sac* 137 (1980): 241–51.

haps no later than 1896. When Shelah was denied to Tamar, she disguised herself as a prostitute and became pregnant no earlier than 1880 (probably later), giving birth to Perez and Zerah about nine months later. Even this contracting of dates makes it impossible that Perez could have taken sons to Egypt in 1876, two or three years later. Perhaps the intent of the list of Genesis 46 is to catalogue those who actually traveled to Egypt as well as those, like Hezron and Hamul, who did so *in potentia*.[79] The fact that Joseph's sons Ephraim and Manasseh are included among the seventy who entered Egypt, when in fact they had been born there, shows that the list must not be pressed too literally.

The Story of Joseph

The setting

The story of Joseph is frequently taken to be a wisdom composition with little or no historical basis.[80] Yet the Old Testament itself presents as genuine history the events surrounding his life and career. Among those who accept the historicity of the Joseph narratives there exists deep division as to the milieu in which they appear. Some, arguing on the basis of a 215-year sojourn in Egypt, maintain that Joseph served in the court of the Hyksos kings, who were in power in the period from about 1661 to 1570.[81] Proponents of this position point out that a Hyksos king is far more likely to have installed a Semite like Joseph in a position of high responsibility than would a native Egyptian ruler. Against this position, however, is the fact that no case can be made at all for a 215-year sojourn (see pp. 75–78). Moreover, everything in the narrative points to a native Egyptian rather than Hyksos background.

According to the chronology adopted in this work, Joseph was born in 1916, entered Egypt in 1899, rose to power in 1886, and died in 1806 (Gen. 50:22) at the age of 110. His whole lifespan was contemporaneous with the magnificent Dynasty 12 of Middle Kingdom Egypt, a dynasty which commenced in 1991 and ended in 1786. Though the chronology of this period is notoriously difficult to reconstruct, the *Cambridge Ancient History* dates used here cannot be far off. By this system of reckoning Joseph was sold into Egypt in the closing years of the reign of Ammenemes II (1929–1895).[82] His was a peaceful reign

79. Delitzsch, *Genesis*, vol. 2, p. 340.

80. Gerhard von Rad, "The Joseph Narrative and Ancient Wisdom," in *The Problem of the Hexateuch and Other Essays* (Edinburgh: Oliver and Boyd; New York: McGraw-Hill, 1966), pp. 292–300.

81. G. Ernest Wright, *Biblical Archaeology*, abridged ed. (Philadelphia: Westminster, 1960), pp. 35–37; Pierre Montet, *Egypt and the Bible* (Philadelphia: Fortress, 1968), pp. 7–15.

82. For his life and times see G. Posener, "The Middle Kingdom in Egypt," in *CAH* 1.2, pp. 502–4.

Table 3   **Dynasty 12 of Egypt**

Ammenemes I	1991–1962
Sesostris I	1971–1928
Ammenemes II	1929–1895
Sesostris II	1897–1878
Sesostris III	1878–1843
Ammenemes III	1842–1797
Ammenemes IV	1798–1790
Sobkneferu	1789–1786

characterized by an improved agricultural and economic life and by the fostering of close relationships with western Asia. Joseph would not be unwelcome on the basis of his ethnic background. His imprisonment would have occurred under Sesostris II (1897–1878), about a decade after his arrival in Egypt (i.e., in 1889); it was Sesostris whose dreams he interpreted and whom he served as a high government official. It is significant that Sesostris II was in power at the time the nomarch of Beni Hasan welcomed the Semitic chieftain Abisha to his city, an event celebrated in the famous murals of Beni Hasan. Sesostris also imported and employed great numbers of Asiatic slaves and mercenaries, a policy which shows anything but an anti-Semitic bias.[83] Most striking of all perhaps were the massive land-reclamation and flood-control projects undertaken under the administration of this enlightened monarch. A principal feature of these was a canal dug to connect the Fayyum basin with the Nile, a canal whose ruins to this very day bear the name *Bahr Yusef* ("River of Joseph").[84] Can it be that this name survives as a testimony to the contribution of Joseph to the public-works projects of Sesostris II? The biblical text reveals that the predicted seven-year famine was preceded by a seven-year period of abundant harvests. This obviously began immediately upon Joseph's release from prison and continued for the next seven years (1886–1879). Though one dare not press the point because of the inexactness of Egyptian chronology, one cannot help but note that, given the system accepted by the *Cambridge Ancient History,* Sesostris II died precisely at the end of the period of prosperity, and his successor Sesostris III (1878–1843) inaugurated his reign coincidentally with the period of famine.

Sesostris III, one of the major figures of the Middle Kingdom, would have been the ruler who invited Jacob and his sons to settle in the eastern Delta, the garden spot of ancient Egypt. Among his early problems was an increasing assertion of power by the local nomarchs, a

83. Ibid., pp. 541–42. Posener remarks, "The biblical story of Joseph brings to mind the slave trade" (p. 542). See also Posener, "Les Asiatiques en Egypte sous les xiie et xiiie dynasties," *Syria* 34 (1957): 145–63.
84. Posener, "Middle Kingdom," in *CAH* 1.2, pp. 505, 510–11.

fact to be explained perhaps by the desperation of the people because of famine and a lack of confidence in the central government to provide a remedy. This uprising was effectively put down, and Sesostris, perhaps with the guidance of Joseph, divided the land into three parts or "departments," each headed by an official known as a "reporter." The reporters in turn were under the vizier, in effect the prime minister.[85]

Something of this policy may be reflected in Genesis 47. At the time of famine Joseph sold the grain which had been stored up in the years of plenty; before long he had accumulated all the money of the land into the treasury (vv. 14–15). He then accepted livestock as payment for grain (vv. 16–18); when the livestock were exhausted, he appropriated even the lands and the people themselves except for the properties of the priests (vv. 19–23). When all this was done, he gave the people seed and commanded that at harvest 20 percent of their crops should go to Pharaoh as tax and the rest they could keep for themselves. Thus Joseph enabled the king to control his people and land as perhaps never before. Such wise administration would also have fostered the development of middle classes; and, in fact, all kinds of artisans and tradespeople arose precisely in the time of Sesostris III.

Sesostris was not occupied exclusively with domestic concerns, however. He strengthened the hold of Egypt upon Nubia to the south and also undertook at least one campaign into Palestine where he claims to have visited Sekmem (probably Shechem). More importantly, the so-called execration texts, which were produced at this time, show unusual interest in and understanding of Palestine and Syria. Among the names contained in the texts are those of numerous cities and towns mentioned also in the Old Testament.[86]

Joseph died in 1806, toward the end of the reign of the last great king of Dynasty 12, Ammenemes III (1842–1797).[87] Nothing is known of Joseph during this time, but Ammenemes was busily engaged in exploitation of the Sinai turquoise mines, in continued reclamation of the Fayyum, and in ambitious building programs. He enjoyed widespread influence, but with his death the mighty Middle Kingdom entered its last days.

The cultural flavor

It is quite evident that, from a historical and chronological standpoint, the stories concerning Joseph are at home in Middle Kingdom

85. Ibid., pp. 505–6; for further indication that Sesostris III is the pharaoh in view see James R. Battenfield, "A Consideration of the Identity of the Pharaoh of Genesis 47," *JETS* 15 (1972): 77–85.

86. See Pritchard, *Ancient Near Eastern Texts*, pp. 328–29.

87. Posener, "Middle Kingdom," in *CAH* 1.2, pp. 509–12.

Egypt. It now remains to demonstrate that the cultural milieu reflected in Genesis 37–50 comports best with Egyptian, not Hyksos, domination.[88] If this can be shown, the arguments for a 215-year sojourn lose practically all their force.

One should note first of all that the personal names encountered in Genesis are Egyptian and not Hyksos.[89] Admittedly, few Hyksos inscriptions have survived, but personal names are attested in rather considerable numbers. It is on the basis of these names, as well as other criteria, that scholars such as John Van Seters identify the Hyksos as Semitic, specifically Amorites.[90] Manetho suggested that the term *Hyksos* itself means "shepherd kings," but more-recent study indicates the meaning "rulers of foreign lands" or something similar.[91] In any case, the Hyksos were certainly not Egyptian, and their traditions, customs, and lifestyle were as different from those of the Egyptians as were their names.

The first foreign name in the Joseph narratives is that of Potiphar, overseer of Pharaoh's elite guard and Joseph's master. Besides being described specifically as an Egyptian (Gen. 39:1), his name is Egyptian through and through (P'-dy-p'R', "he whom Re gave").[92] Joseph himself married Asenath, daughter of Potiphera the priest of On (or Heliopolis). Her name means "belonging to Neith" (an Egyptian goddess) while her father's name is simply a variation of Potiphar. Joseph's name was changed, following his marriage (?), to Zaphenath-Paneah, possibly meaning "the one who furnishes the nourishment of life." One might concede that Joseph could have served an Egyptian nobleman even in Hyksos times. However, it is incredible that his good Semitic name would have been changed to an Egyptian name under a Hyksos ruler, and equally difficult to understand how he would have married the daughter of a native Egyptian priest serving at the cult center of Heliopolis, which was to the south of the center of Hyksos political control.

In the next place, various customs and prejudices support an Egyptian background rather than a Hyksos. When Joseph first appeared before Sesostris II following his release from prison, he shaved himself lest he offend the king. This is precisely what the Egyptian exile Sinuhe did when he returned to Egypt after living for years among the Sem-

88. The Hyksos were a Semitic people who filtered into the Egyptian Delta in the eighteenth century and eventually gained political control over most of Lower Egypt for 150 years (1720–1570). See Donald B. Redford, "The Hyksos Invasion in History and Tradition," *Or*, n.s. 39 (1970): 1–51.

89. Montet, *Egypt*, pp. 14–15.

90. John Van Seters, *The Hyksos* (New Haven: Yale University Press, 1966), pp. 194–95.

91. Ibid., p. 187.

92. For a helpful discussion of these names see Montet, *Egypt*, pp. 14–15.

ites of Syria.[93] For Joseph to have shaved prior to appearing before a bearded Hyksos king would, of course, have been an insult rather than a concession. When Joseph's brothers came to him to request grain, not yet having learned his true identity, he set them apart at dinnertime because "Egyptians could not eat with Hebrews" (Gen. 43:32). If Joseph had been representing himself as a Semitic official of a Hyksos king, it is strange that he would have segregated himself from fellow Semites. That he was acting in accordance with long-standing Egyptian tradition proves beyond question that the story has nothing to do with the Hyksos.

Another detail which betrays Egyptian prejudice even more clearly is Joseph's statement that shepherds were an abomination to the Egyptians (Gen. 46:34). If the Hyksos were anything, they were shepherds; they would not have despised the Hebrews for being shepherds. Finally, the embalming of and mourning for Jacob conform to well-known Egyptian practice (Gen. 50:2–3).[94] Though Hyksos funerary custom may not be well understood today, it certainly differed from that of the Egyptians who, uniquely among all peoples of the ancient world, followed the procedures described in Genesis.

Last of all is the matter of language. On their first trip to Egypt Joseph's brothers, under the assumption that he was an Egyptian, began to speak to one another in Hebrew (Gen. 42:23). Careful not to disabuse them of their misapprehension, Joseph carried on his part in the conversations with them in the Egyptian language. Surely if they had supposed for a moment that Joseph was a Hyksos, they would have realized the futility of speaking Hebrew in an attempt to prevent him from understanding them. Whatever ethnic stock comprised the Hyksos peoples, they certainly spoke Semitic dialects and would therefore have understood Hebrew.

In conclusion, it is overwhelmingly evident that Joseph lived and held administrative office in a period of Egyptian rather than Hyksos control. This absolutely precludes a 215-year sojourn given the traditional date of the exodus (1446), though, to be sure, a late date for the exodus (ca. 1260) coupled with a 215-year sojourn would allow us to place Joseph in a post-Hyksos Egyptian dynasty.

From Joseph to the Exodus

The Hyksos domination of Egypt falls in the period between the death of Joseph and the birth of Moses, a time concerning which the

93. Pritchard, *Ancient Near Eastern Texts*, pp. 18–22. According to Alan Gardiner, *Egypt of the Pharaohs* (London: Oxford University Press, 1961), p. 130, this tale must be dated to the period of Sesostris I (1971–1928).

94. John Ruffle, *The Egyptians* (Ithaca, N.Y.: Cornell University Press, 1977), pp. 197–210; Van Seters, *Hyksos*, pp. 45–48.

Old Testament is completely silent. It is reasonable to assume that Hyksos-Hebrew relationships were amicable, an assumption that gains some favor if the enemies referred to in Exodus 1:10 are the Hyksos. Otherwise, all that is necessary to note is that the Hyksos held effective control of Lower Egypt (the Delta) for about 150 years (1720–1570). They took and rebuilt the city of Avaris in about 1720, a fact attested to by the so-called four-hundred-year stela found at the site of Avaris by August Mariette in 1863.[95] This monument was erected in about 1320 B.C. by Seti, vizier of the Egyptian king Horemheb, to mark the four-hundredth anniversary of the (re)building of the city, a fact whose authenticity need not be suspect. The Hyksos domination began during Egyptian Dynasty 13, which, under the pressure of the Hyksos, was forced to withdraw south and maintain itself at Memphis. When Memphis eventually fell to the Hyksos, the dynasty moved farther south and finally came to an end in about 1633.[96]

Meanwhile, an Egyptian dynasty, the fourteenth, remained in control of the western Delta until about 1603. Centered around Sais (Xois), this line of kings managed to hold out against the Hyksos almost to the end. Dynasties 15 and 16 were contemporaneous Hyksos ruling elements which commenced with the fall of Memphis (1674) and continued until their expulsion from Egypt in 1567.[97] Though culturally inferior, the Hyksos learned well and adopted Egyptian arts and sciences.[98] They also identified their deities with those of Egypt, in particular equating them with Ba'al, Resheph, or even Teshub.[99] More positively, they apparently introduced or popularized in Egypt the use of the horse and chariot[100] as well as the composite bow.[101] Some of the more prominent Hyksos kings of Dynasty 15 were Salitis (Sharek); Khyan, who called himself "son of Re" (Rameses?); and Apophis I, whose daughter married a Theban prince and who also called himself a "son of Re."[102] It was he who first encountered major resistance from the Egyptians of Thebes and who was eventually driven out of Upper Egypt back to the Delta. This Egyptian revival was under the leadership of Seqenenre II of Dynasty 17 (1650–1567), whose son Kamose

95. See p. 36, n. 40.

96. Hayes, "From the Death of Ammenemes III," in *CAH* 2.1, pp. 44–54.

97. Ibid., pp. 54–64.

98. Ronald J. Williams, "The Egyptians," in *Peoples of Old Testament Times*, ed. D. J. Wiseman, p. 87.

99. Van Seters, *Hyksos*, pp. 171–80.

100. Jack Finegan, *Archaeological History of the Ancient Middle East* (Boulder, Col.: Westview, 1979), pp. 254–55.

101. Roland de Vaux, *Ancient Israel* (New York: McGraw-Hill, 1965), vol. 1, p. 243.

102. The appearance of the Re (or Ra) element in the names of Hyksos kings is of significance for the early dating of the exodus. See p. 70.

initiated the expulsion of the hated Hyksos not only from Upper Egypt, but eventually from the Delta itself.

In his third year (1575) Kamose launched an attack on Apophis, king of th. Hyksos, but died before he could finish his mission. His goal was accomplished by his brother Amosis (1570–1546), founder of Dynasty 18 (1567–1320), who, through his general Ahmose, retook Memphis and then Avaris. Ahmose was not satisfied merely to drive the Hyksos out of Egypt, however; he pursued them to Sharuhen (ca. 1563) and thus ensured that they never again would trouble Egypt.[103]

Dynasties 18 and 19 (1567–ca. 1200) make up the bulk of the third and final period of Egyptian greatness in the ancient Near Eastern world, the New Kingdom (1567–ca. 1100). Since the exodus, conquest, and much of the era of the judges fall during this time, it is important that its course be traced in some detail, especially where it touches upon the Old Testament narrative.

---

103. For this whole era see T. G. H. James, "Egypt: From the Expulsion of the Hyksos to Amenophis I," in *CAH* 2.1, pp. 289–96.

2 The Exodus: Birth of a Nation

The Meaning of the Exodus

The exodus is the most significant historical and theological event of the Old Testament because it marks God's mightiest act in behalf of his people, an act which brought them from slavery to freedom, from fragmentation to solidarity, from a people of promise—the Hebrews—to a nation of fulfilment—Israel. To it the Book of Genesis provides an introduction and justification, and from it flows all subsequent Old Testament revelation, a record which serves it as inspired commentary and detailed

57

exposition. In the final analysis, the exodus served to typify that exodus achieved by Jesus Christ for people of faith so that it is a meaningful event for the church as well as for Israel.[1]

The Historical Setting of the Exodus

The Egyptian New Kingdom

According to 1 Kings 6:1, the exodus occurred 480 years prior to the laying of the foundations of Solomon's temple. This Solomon undertook in his fourth year, 966 B.C., so the exodus, according to normal hermeneutics and serious appraisal of the biblical chronological data, took place in 1446. Before we give detailed support for this contention, however, let us look at the eighteenth dynasty of Egypt, which, according to the traditional dating, was the setting in which the exodus occurred.

Table 4   **Dynasties 18 and 19 of Egypt**

Dynasty 18	
Amosis	1570–1546
Amenhotep I	1546–1526
Thutmose I	1526–1512
Thutmose II	1512–1504
Hatshepsut	1503–1483
Thutmose III	1504–1450
Amenhotep II	1450–1425
Thutmose IV	1425–1417
Amenhotep III	1417–1379
Amenhotep IV (Ikhnaton)	1379–1362
Smenkhkare	1364–1361
Tutankhamon	1361–1352
Ay	1352–1348
Horemheb	1348–1320
Dynasty 19	
Rameses I	1320–1318
Seti I	1318–1304
Rameses II	1304–1236
Merneptah	1236–1223

As noted in chapter 1, Dynasty 18 was founded by Amosis, the expeller of the Hyksos. It may be he who is described in Exodus as the new king who did not know Joseph (1:8).[2] This is not to suggest that

1. See, e.g., Claus Westermann, *Elements of Old Testament Theology* (Atlanta: John Knox, 1982), pp. 217–18; Elmer Martens, *God's Design* (Grand Rapids: Baker, 1981), p. 256.

2. William F. Albright, "From the Patriarchs to Moses: II. Moses Out of Egypt," *BA* 36 (1973): 54.

he did not know Joseph personally, but only that his sympathies no longer lay with the Josephites, that is, the Hebrews. He had, after all, just defeated the Hyksos, a people ethnically akin to the Hebrews, and might be concerned that the populous and rapidly multiplying Hebrews could become a threat to his newly established authority. Either he or his successor Amenhotep I (1546–1526) was responsible for the repressive policies which followed. These included the reduction of the Hebrews to slave labor in construction of public-works projects (Exod. 1:11–14),[3] a plan most likely implemented by Amosis; when that failed, there followed an edict of genocide requiring the slaughter of all newly born Hebrew males (1:15–16). This would have been issued by Amenhotep or, more likely, Thutmose I according to the reconstruction advanced here.

Granting for now a 1446 date for the exodus, we can establish the birth date of Moses, a fact of greatest interest at this juncture. The Old Testament tells us that Moses was 80 just prior to the exodus (Exod. 7:7) and 120 at his death (Deut. 34:7).[4] Since his death was at the very close of the wilderness period, it occurred in 1406. Simple calculation yields a birth date of 1526. Thus Moses was born in the very year of Amenhotep's death. It must be reemphasized that absolute precision cannot be hoped for, but our dates for New Kingdom chronology, like the dates we use elsewhere, are those of the *Cambridge Ancient History*, a publication produced by impartial scholars and recognized as impeccable authority.[5] Adjustments in dates a few years one way or the other would not seriously affect the argument set forth here.

3. Though Kenneth A. Kitchen accepts the late date for the exodus, he cites abundant evidence for slave labor, including Semites, in the manufacture of brick in the period of Dynasty 18. See his "From the Brickfields of Egypt," *Tyn Bull* 27 (1976): 139–40.

4. The sectioning of the life of Moses into periods of forty years each—he was 40 when he slew the Egyptian, 80 when he returned from Midianite exile, and 120 when he died—suggests to many scholars a certain artificiality. It is argued that forty years represents an ideal generation so that Moses would have enjoyed three times as long a life as the normal full generation. See, for example, J. Alberto Soggin, *A History of Ancient Israel* (Philadelphia: Westminster, 1984), p. 383. This would apply as well to the forty-year reigns of Saul, David, and Solomon, the forty- (or occasionally twenty-) year judgeships and periods of rest in the era of the judges; and various other uses of forty. It is, of course, possible and, indeed, likely that these periods are to be taken literally and that they reflect not so much an artificial or even coincidental occurrence of forty as a deliberate ordering of history according to this pattern by the Lord himself. The number forty, in other words, may well have symbolical and typological value in itself, and God may have arranged historical events accordingly. See John J. Davis, *Biblical Numerology* (Grand Rapids: Baker, 1968), pp. 52–54. Davis, however, sees only the number seven as having symbolical value (p. 124).

5. For the dates of Amenhotep (Amenophis) I, see T. G. H. James, "Egypt: From the Expulsion of the Hyksos to Amenophis I," in *Cambridge Ancient History*, 3d ed., ed.

Amenhotep was succeeded by Thutmose I (1526–1512), a commoner who had married the king's sister. He was probably the author of the decree of infanticide, for though Moses was in imminent danger of death, Aaron, born three years earlier (Exod. 7:7), appears to have been exempt. One must assume that the king who promulgated the policy came to the throne after the birth of Aaron and before that of Moses. The biblical evidence, then, points directly at Thutmose I.

Thutmose II (1512–1504) married his older half-sister Hatshepsut. He died young under mysterious circumstances. Sensing no doubt his impending demise, he had named his son Thutmose III (1504–1450) as coregent and heir. This energetic ruler, the most illustrious and powerful of the entire New Kingdom, distinguished himself in many ways. His beginnings were not promising—he was the son of a concubine and married his own half-sister, the daughter of Hatshepsut and Thutmose II—but he eventually went on to achieve notable victories in surrounding lands, including some sixteen campaigns to Palestine alone. The first twenty years or so of his reign, however, were dominated by his powerful mother-in-law, Hatshepsut. Forbidden by custom to be pharaoh, she acted out the part nonetheless and by all criteria was one of the most fascinating and influential persons of Egyptian history.[6] Without question she pulled the strings in the early years of Thutmose III, a relationship which he detested but was powerless to oppose. Only after her death did he show his contempt by expunging every inscriptional and monumental reference to her.

The general picture of Hatshepsut leads us to identify this bold queen as the daughter of Pharaoh who rescued Moses. Only she of all known women of the period possessed the presumption and independence to violate an ordinance of the king and under his very nose at that! Though the birth date of this daughter of Thutmose I is unknown, she was probably several years older than her husband, Thutmose II, who died in 1504 while in his late twenties.[7] She may have been in her early teens by 1526, Moses' birth date, and therefore able to effect his deliverance.

Thutmose III was a minor when he came to power in 1504 and thus

I. E. S. Edwards et al. (Cambridge: Cambridge University Press, 1973), vol. 2, part 1, p. 308. For Thutmose (Tuthmosis) I, Thutmose II, Hatshepsut, Thutmose III, and Amenhotep II see William C. Hayes, "Egypt: Internal Affairs from Tuthmosis I to the Death of Amenophis III," in *CAH* 2.1, pp. 315–21. For alternative dates for Dynasty 18 (ca. 1533–1303) see William W. Hallo and William K. Simpson, *The Ancient Near East* (New York: Harcourt Brace Jovanovich, 1971), pp. 300–1. The *CAH* dates (1546–1319) are accepted by George Steindorff and Keith C. Seele, *When Egypt Ruled the East* (Chicago: University of Chicago Press, 1957), pp. 274–75.

6. An engrossing if somewhat imaginative account of her life and reign may be found in Evelyn Wells, *Hatshepsut* (Garden City, N.Y.: Doubleday, 1969).

7. Steindorff and Seele, *When Egypt Ruled the East*, pp. 39–40.

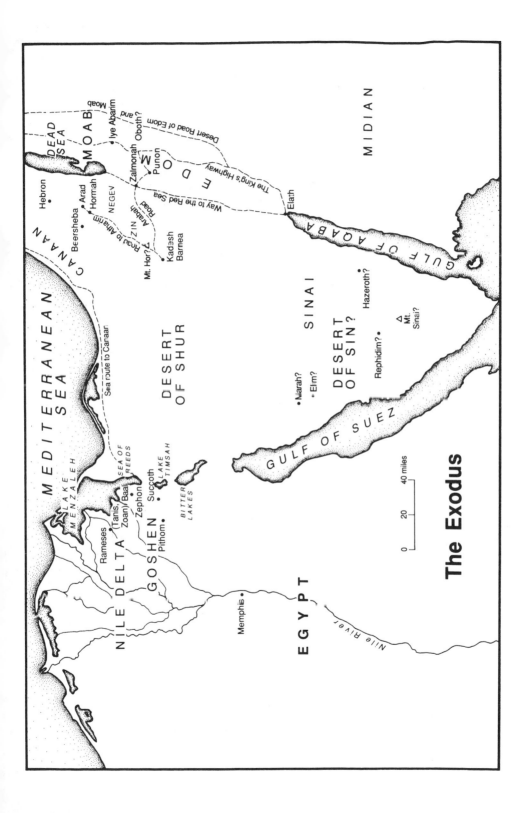

The Exodus

was younger than Moses.[8] If, indeed, Moses had been reared as the foster son of Hatshepsut, there is every likelihood that he posed a real threat to the younger Thutmose since Hatshepsut had no natural sons. That is, Moses may have been a candidate for pharaoh, only his Semitic origins standing in the way. There appears in any case to have been genuine animosity between Moses and the pharaoh. This is evident in the fact that Moses, having slain an Egyptian, was forced to flee Egypt for his life. That the pharaoh himself took note of what would otherwise have been a relatively minor issue suggests that this particular pharaoh had more than casual interest in ridding himself of Moses. Moses' self-imposed exile took place in 1486, when he was forty years old (Acts 7:23). Thutmose III had been in power for eighteen years; and the aged Hatshepsut, who died three years later, was no doubt no longer able to interdict the will of her son-in-law/nephew.[9]

For forty long years Moses remained a fugitive from Egypt, having found a home among the Midianites of the Sinai and Arabia. One of the reasons for such a long exile was the fact that the pharaoh from whom Moses had fled continued to live and reign all that time; it was only after his death that Moses felt free to return to Egypt (Exod. 2:23; 4:19). Thutmose III died in 1450 and was succeeded by his son Amenhotep II (1450–1425). According to the chronological patterns accepted throughout this discussion, it was Amenhotep who was the pharaoh of the exodus.

Before leaving Thutmose III, however, it is important for us to note that the biblical narrative requires a rule of almost forty years for the pharaoh who sought Moses' life, since the king who died at the end of Moses' sojourn in Midian was clearly the same one who had threatened him nearly forty years earlier. Of all the rulers of Dynasty 18 only Thutmose III reigned long enough to qualify. In fact, he was the only pharaoh at any period during which the exodus could have occurred who reigned that long except for Rameses II (1304–1236). But Rameses, who is associated with the exodus by most critical scholars, is usually identified as the pharaoh of the exodus and not the pharaoh whose death made Moses' return to Egypt possible. If Rameses' death had brought Moses back to Egypt, the exodus would have to have taken place after 1236, a date too late to satisfy anybody.[10]

8. Thutmose III was appointed vice-regent late in the reign of Thutmose II, probably no earlier than 1508. See Hayes, "Internal Affairs," in *CAH* 2.1, pp. 316–17.

9. Thutmose III succeeded Hatshepsut in 1483. He tried then to expunge her very memory from the land by defacing her monuments and slaying her public officials. See Hayes, "Internal Affairs," in *CAH* 2.1, p. 319.

10. The implications of this line of reasoning are devastating to the theory of a late date for the exodus; see pp. 68–69.

The Pharaoh of the Exodus

When Moses finally returned to Egypt, he and Aaron began to negotiate with the new king, Amenhotep II, concerning permission for the people of Israel to leave Egypt to worship Yahweh and eventually to leave permanently. This powerful and militaristic monarch conducted a major campaign in Canaan in his third year (ca. 1450) and another in his seventh (ca. 1446).[11] His seventh year coincides with the traditional date of the exodus, 1446, so one cannot help but wonder if the decimation of Pharaoh's army at the Sea of Reeds might not have followed this second campaign and had such demoralizing impact as to discourage further immediate adventurism, especially to the north.[12]

Our identification of Amenhotep II as the pharaoh of the exodus is supported by two other considerations. First, although most of the kings of Dynasty 18 made their principal residence at Thebes, far to the south of the Israelites in the Delta, Amenhotep was at home in Memphis and apparently reigned from there much of the time.[13] This placed him in close proximity to the land of Goshen and made him readily accessible to Moses and Aaron. Second, the best understanding suggests that Amenhotep's power did not pass to his eldest son, but rather to Thutmose IV, a younger son. This is at least implied in the so-called dream stela found at the base of the Great Sphinx near Memphis.[14] This text, which records a dream in which Thutmose IV was promised that he would one day be king, suggests, as one historian says, that his reign came about "through an unforeseen turn of fate, such as the premature death of an elder brother."[15] It is, of course,

11. Alan Gardiner, *Egypt of the Pharaohs* (London: Oxford University Press, 1961), pp. 200–2. Most historians posit a coregency between Thutmose III and Amenhotep II of between three and six years. Given the generally accepted date of 1450 for the former's death, his son would have coreigned from 1453 (or even 1456) to 1450. It seems best to interpret the first campaign as having occurred in the coregency and the second in the sole regency, thus, 1450 and 1446 respectively. See Donald B. Redford, "The Coregency of Tuthmosis III and Amenophis II, *JEA* 51 (1965): 107–22; William J. Murnane, "Once Again the Dates for Tuthmosis III and Amenhotep II," *JANES* 3 (1970–1971): 5.

12. Gardiner, *Egypt*, p. 202, describes a campaign of year nine (ca. 1444) as being "on a smaller scale" than that of year seven. It is tempting to see this reduction as a fallout from the exodus experience.

13. Hayes, "Internal Affairs," in *CAH* 2.1, pp. 333–34. It was customary for the kings of Dynasty 18 to assign the governance of Memphis to the crown prince. See Donald B. Redford, "A Gate Inscription from Karnak and Egyptian Involvement in Western Asia During the Early 18th Dynasty," *JAOS* 99 (1979): 277.

14. For the text see James B. Pritchard, *Ancient Near Eastern Texts Relating to the Old Testament*, 2d ed. (Princeton: Princeton University Press, 1955), p. 449.

15. Hayes, "Internal Affairs," in *CAH* 2.1, p. 321.

impossible to prove, but one cannot help but speculate as to whether this premature death was not caused by the judgment of Yahweh who, in the tenth plague, struck dead all the firstborn of Egypt, who were unprotected by the blood of the Passover, "from the firstborn of Pharaoh, who sat on the throne, to the firstborn of the prisoner, who was in the dungeon" (Exod. 12:29).

The Ten Plagues

Before continuing our integration of the history of Dynasty 18 with the exodus narratives, it is necessary to give some attention to the stories of Moses' return to Egypt from Midian, the ten plagues, and the exodus event itself. Moses had fled from Egypt in his fortieth year (1486) and had found sanctuary in the land of Midian (Exod. 2:15). The Midianites, descendants of Abraham through his wife Keturah (Gen. 25:2), lived in the Arabian peninsula, probably directly east of the Sinai peninsula, across the Gulf of Aqaba.[16] Moses presently became acquainted with a Midianite priest, Jethro (or Reuel), who evidently also became a worshiper of Yahweh (Exod. 18:11).[17] Moses then took one of Jethro's daughters, Zipporah, as his wife and by her begot two sons, Gershom and Eliezer (Exod. 18:3–4). Near the end of Moses' forty years in Midian Yahweh appeared to him at Sinai in a burning bush and identified himself as the God of Abraham, Isaac, and Jacob. He told Moses that at long last the time had come for the people of Israel to leave their land of bondage and inherit Canaan, the land of promise. To Moses fell the privilege and responsibility of leading them out.

Probably within a few months of this revelation Moses and Aaron encountered the pharaoh, most certainly Amenhotep II. They first requested permission to undertake a pilgrimage to the desert to worship Yahweh, but the request was met only by an intensification of the bitter labor forced on the Israelites. This in turn led the Israelites to challenge the authority of Moses, and so Moses turned again to Yahweh for an affirmation of his call. Once more Yahweh pledged to redeem his people (Exod. 6:6), to make them by covenant his special treasure (v. 7), and to see them safely into the land he had promised to the

16. For a helpful discussion of the identity and location of the Midianites see Roland de Vaux, *The Early History of Israel* (Philadelphia: Westminster, 1978), pp. 330–38.

17. Though the account (Exod. 18:1–12) does not present Jethro as a convert to exclusive Yahwism, it does suggest that he came to embrace Yahweh as supreme among the gods. See Umberto Cassuto, *A Commentary on the Book of Exodus* (Jerusalem: Magnes, 1967), pp. 216–17. For a traditio-historical analysis of alleged sources for Moses' marriage and vocation in Midian see George W. Coats, "Moses in Midian," *JBL* 92 (1973): 3–10.

patriarchs (v. 8). There followed a succession of interviews with Pharaoh, all of which failed to secure his permission for the people to worship in the wilderness. Without doubt he knew (as did they) that the real intent was not to go on a pilgrimage, but rather to leave Egypt entirely, never to return. To prove his authority, Moses performed signs and wonders before Pharaoh. The first sign involved Aaron's rod becoming a serpent and swallowing up the rods-become-serpents of the magicians of Egypt. The next ten were judgmental: plagues which followed every stubborn refusal of Pharaoh to let the people go. The last of these was the death of the firstborn, a plague which affected the family of Pharaoh himself.

It is impossible, of course, to understand precisely what happened in the case of each plague, particularly since Egyptian sources, not surprisingly, provide no attestation. It is evident, however, that each plague entailed an aberration of nature, an anomaly affecting the weather, animals, the waters, or the like. Moreover, they appear to have been polemical in intent. Each plague was an assertion of the sovereignty of Yahweh over the deity (or deities) responsible for the area of nature particularly under attack. Skeptical scholarship views the plagues as greatly exaggerated accounts of perfectly understandable, albeit unusual, natural phenomena.[18] But a serious appraisal of the narratives will not permit such cavalier dismissal of the catastrophic dimensions of the plagues. They must be understood for what they were—unique but genuinely historical outpourings of the wrath of a sovereign God who wished to show not only Egypt but his own people that he is the Lord of all of heaven and earth, one well able to redeem his people from the onerous slavery they knew under Pharaoh and to make them, by covenant, his own servant people.

When the last plague fell and Yahweh had undermined all human self-confidence, Pharaoh relented and entreated Moses and Israel to leave (Exod. 12:31–32). But when they did in fact leave, Pharaoh had second thoughts and undertook pursuit. It had dawned on the king that in his grief he had rashly let go the major source of slave labor essential to his ambitious public-works programs. By then, however, the two million[19] Israelites had left Rameses (i.e., Goshen; see Gen. 47:6, 11) and had arrived at Succoth,[20] just west of Lake Timsah. From there they went north, evidently intent upon entering Canaan by the

18. For a history of interpretation of the plagues see Brevard S. Childs, *The Book of Exodus* (Philadelphia: Westminster, 1974), pp. 164–68. An often overlooked study which views the plagues as "natural phenomena" and historical events is Greta Hort, "The Plagues of Egypt," *ZAW* 69 (1957): 84–103; 70 (1958): 48–59, esp. pp. 58–59.

19. The matter of the enormous exodus population will be considered on p. 78.

20. Perhaps *t-k-w* (i.e., Tell el-Maskhûtah), just west of the Bitter Lakes. See Yohanan Aharoni, *The Land of the Bible* (Philadelphia: Westminster, 1979), p. 196.

great Mediterranean coastal route. They were certain to encounter Philistines if they continued on that route, however, so Yahweh led them south, apparently after they crossed the Reed Sea.

The Route of the Exodus

The precise point at which Israel crossed the Reed Sea cannot now be determined, but clearly it was not at the Red Sea, the modern-day Gulf of Suez. That was too far south to fit the biblical itinerary. Moreover, the Hebrew term to describe the water crossed, *yam sûp* ("reed sea"), is totally inappropriate to the Red Sea. The translation "Red Sea" of many English versions is based on the Septuagint, which evidently assumed that the Sea of Reeds was the ancient name of the Red Sea.[21] The Mosaic record states that Israel found itself at a point near Pi Hahiroth (site unknown), between Migdol (unknown) and the sea. More specifically, they were "directly opposite Baal Zephon" (Exod. 14:2), a place identified with Tell Dafanneh, just west of Lake Menzaleh, a southern bay of the Mediterranean Sea.[22] The evidence available today suggests that this is the Sea of Reeds through which Israel passed. Though some dredging has been done there in the course of building and maintaining the Suez Canal, Lake Menzaleh was always deep enough to preclude crossing on foot under any normal circumstances. The crossing of Israel, which immediately preceded the drowning of the Egyptian chariotry, cannot be explained as a wading through a swamp. It required a mighty act of God, an act so significant in both scope and meaning that forever after in Israel's history it was the paradigm against which all of his redemptive and saving work was measured. If there was no actual miracle of the proportions described, all subsequent reference to the exodus as the archetype of the sovereign power and salvific grace of God is hollow and empty.[23]

The Date of the Exodus

Before the wilderness journey is recounted, it is appropriate that the vexing but crucially important question of the date of the exodus

21. For the view that *yam sûp* means "distant sea" or "sea of extinction"—thus referring to the Red Sea in a mythopoeic way—see Bernard F. Batto, "The Reed Sea: *Requiescat in Pace,*" *JBL* 102 (1983): 27–35.

22. Tell Dafanneh may be the same place as Tahpanhes (Jer. 2:16; 43:7–8; 44:1). See *Oxford Bible Atlas*, ed. Herbert G. May, 2d ed. (London: Oxford University Press, 1974), p. 58. The third edition (1984) does not identify Baal Zephon with Tell Dafanneh, however.

23. For an example of an approach which attempts to maintain a historical core for the event while denying the details recounted in the biblical text, see Brevard S. Childs, "A Traditio-Historical Study of the Reed Sea Tradition," *VT* 20 (1970): 406–18.

be examined. The question is crucial not only because the exodus is itself a central historical and theological event, but also because our interpretation of both antecedent and subsequent history will be greatly affected by the date we assign to the exodus.

Internal Biblical Evidence

The year 1446 has already been proposed as the date of the exodus. On this basis proceeded our discussion of the Hyksos and New Kingdom periods as well as the setting of the Joseph narratives. Since the integrity of what has been said up to this point is dependent on an early date rather than the later one to which most scholarship subscribes, it is vital that a careful case be made for the early date.

There are two principal biblical data which directly touch on the problem. The first is the statement of 1 Kings 6:1 that the exodus preceded the founding of Solomon's temple by 480 years. Granting for now that Solomon began to build in 966,[24] we calculate that the exodus took place in 1446. But for a variety of reasons this date is almost universally rejected in favor of a date sometime in the thirteenth century, generally about 1260.[25] To accommodate this desire for a later date, the figure 480 is not taken at face value, but is thought to be a cryptic way of describing twelve generations (forty years, it is said, being an ideal generation). Since, however, an actual generation is closer to twenty-five years, the time between the exodus and the initial work on the temple is held to be really 300 (25×12) years, and so the exodus is held to have occurred in about 1266.[26] If it could be demonstrated that ancient Israelite (or any other) chronological computation took this approach and that 1 Kings 6:1 is an example of the application of such a method, the case would appear to be settled.[27] Unfortunately there is no proof. The inescapable conclusion is that to

24. Edwin R. Thiele, *The Mysterious Numbers of the Hebrew Kings* (Grand Rapids: Eerdmans, 1965), p. 28; see also pp. 29, 55. We are accepting as our basic starting point Thiele's authoritative reconstruction of the chronology of the divided monarchy.

25. John Bright, *A History of Israel*, 3d ed. (Philadelphia: Westminster, 1981), pp. 123–24.

26. Ibid., p. 123; John Gray, *I & II Kings* (Philadelphia: Westminster, 1970), pp. 159–60.

27. Kenneth A. Kitchen compares the 480-year datum to the misleading totals which ancient Near Eastern scribes arrived at by excerpting selected figures from fuller records. The 480 years, then, would be an aggregate total which, in actuality, should be only about 300 years. Unfortunately, Kitchen provides no solid evidence that such a practice is at work in 1 Kings 6:1 (*Ancient Orient and Old Testament* [London: Tyndale, 1966], pp. 74–75).

factor 480 in such a way as to reduce it to 300 and thus satisfy subjective requirements is an example of special pleading unworthy of any historian or Bible scholar. Surely the burden of proof is on the critic who would view the biblical historian's chronological information in any but a literal way.

The second unambiguous support for the 1446 date appears in a communication of Jephthah the judge to his Ammonite enemies. He argues that they have no grounds for their hostility against Israel since for the three hundred years following Israel's defeat of Sihon the Ammonites have never contested Israel's rights to the Transjordan. Even a casual reading of this lengthy memorandum (Judg. 11:15–27) makes it clear that Jephthah is referring to that period of Israel's history just prior to the conquest, which began forty years after the exodus. Jephthah's defeat of the Ammonites occurred at the end of the twelfth century (i.e., ca. 1100 B.C.), a date which is widely acknowledged. So, then, he is referring to events which came to pass around 1400 B.C.

It is obvious that the figure three hundred cannot be factored into ideal generations with satisfying results (i.e., 300 is not exactly divisible by 40), so proponents of a late date for the exodus are forced to other measures. Typically they postulate a divided conquest, maintaining that Jephthah is referring not to the Israelite conquest as a twelve-tribe confederation, but to an earlier, preexodus occupation of the Transjordan by a tribe or tribes which only later associated themselves with those few tribes of Israel which had an exodus tradition.[28] The conquest of the Transjordan, by this re-creation of Old Testament history, preceded the conquest of Canaan by well over a century. All this despite the fact that the message of Jephthah unequivocally connects the conquerors of Sihon with the Israel that came out of Egypt (Judg. 11:13, 16). Again, only a drastic resort can explain away the self-evident case for 1446 as the date of the exodus.

In addition to specific chronological data, the Old Testament provides sufficient description of the preexodus and exodus milieus as to make an early date most acceptable. It has already been shown that the account of Moses best suits the dates and circumstances of Dynasty 18 of Egypt. To the contrary, the late date, which is always associated with Rameses II, is impossible if any credibility at all be granted to the biblical witness. Moses did not return to Egypt from Midian until the pharaoh who had sought to slay him was dead. Moses' return was delayed for nearly forty years, so the king in question must be one who reigned at least that long. In Dynasty 19 only Rameses II, who reigned from 1304 to 1236, satisfies that requirement, but he

28. T. J. Meek, *Hebrew Origins* (New York: Harper and Row, 1960), pp. 30–31, 34–35.

cannot be the pharaoh of the exodus since the point precisely is that that particular pharaoh followed one who had a lengthy tenure.

The late date requires Merneptah (1236–1223) to be the ruler during the humiliation of the exodus. But even if it occurred in his first year, a forty-year sojourn in the wilderness would mean the conquest began in 1196. The judges of Israel would then have to be compressed into the period between the beginning of their administration (ca. forty years after the beginning of the conquest or 1156) and the death of Samson, the last judge (except for Samuel, who lived under the monarchy as well), in about 1084. No manipulation of the evidence can squeeze the obviously long period of the judges into seventy or even one hundred years. Besides, Merneptah himself led a campaign into upper Canaan in his fifth year (1231) in the course of which he claims to have met and defeated Israel.[29] It is obviously impossible for Israel in the course of but five years to have escaped Egypt, spent time at Mount Sinai, wandered in the wilderness, conquered Sihon and Og, and entered and established herself in Canaan! Advocates of the late date must disregard all normal and accepted historiographical method and rearrange and reinterpret the only available documentation—the Old Testament itself—if their case is to be made.[30]

The Evidence for a Late Date

Lack of sedentary settlement of Transjordan

There are three major arguments advanced in support of the late date for the exodus, two of which are substantial and the third of dubious value even to those scholars who seek to maintain it. This argument will be considered first. For many years Nelson Glueck, the eminent explorer and archaeologist, argued on the basis of pottery finds on the surface and on the slopes of mounds throughout the Transjordan and the Negev that these areas had no sedentary populations between 1900 and 1300 b.c.[31] Practically all Old Testament authorities accepted this judgment and therefore concluded that references to settled peoples encountered by Moses and Joshua necessitated a date after 1300 for the wilderness journeys. It follows that the exodus also could not have been much earlier than that date. Glueck's surface

29. For the text of the so-called Israel stela see Pritchard, *Ancient Near Eastern Texts*, pp. 376–78.

30. This is precisely what is done by critical scholars. For a detailed example of this approach see H. H. Rowley, *From Joseph to Joshua* (London: Oxford University Press, 1950), esp. pp. 129–44.

31. Nelson Glueck, "Explorations in Eastern Palestine and the Negev," *BASOR* 55 (1934): 3–21; *BASOR* 86 (1942): 14–24.

explorations have been followed up by scientific excavation of many of the allegedly late sites with the findings that many of them were settled throughout the Late Bronze Age and even earlier.[32] Some of the very places integral to the Moses-Joshua stories were asserting themselves powerfully in 1400.

Israelite construction of the city of Rameses

A second basis for the late date is found in the biblical text itself. Exodus 1:11 points out that the Israelites, when they were reduced to slavery, constructed certain cities for Pharaoh, including Pithom and Rameses (or Raamses). These cities were originally known as Pi-Atum and Per-Ramesse respectively, and in any case were not built but rebuilt by the Israelites.[33] The contention that this verse is relevant to the date of the exodus rests on the assumption that the city Rameses was named for Rameses II, the famous king of Dynasty 19. That he did build or rebuild a city by this name (Per-Ramesse) and that he did so with the use of 'apiru slave labor may be conceded (though the papyrus to which appeal is always made does not expressly make this assertion).[34] It is nonetheless tenuous to try to prove by this that the city of Exodus 1:11 is the same as the Per-Ramesse of Rameses II or that the 'apiru are the Israelites. William Albright showed years ago that the Ramessides did not originate in Dynasty 19 and that, in fact, they could be traced back to Hyksos ancestry.[35] Could it not be that the Israelites rebuilt a city called Rameses long before the kingship of Rameses II?

It has recently been proposed by certain conservative scholars that Exodus 1:11 is an anachronism. That is, the Israelites rebuilt a city known at the time perhaps as Tanis, and sometime later an inspired editor

32. John J. Bimson, *Redating the Exodus and Conquest* (Sheffield: JSOT, 1978), pp. 67–74; James R. Kautz, "Tracking the Ancient Moabites," *BA* 44 (1981): 27–35; Gerald L. Mattingly, "The Exodus-Conquest and the Archaeology of Transjordan: New Light on an Old Problem," *GTJ* 4 (1983): 245–62.

33. See E. P. Uphill, "Pithom and Raamses: Their Location and Significance," *JNES* 27 (1968): 291–316; *JNES* 28 (1969): 15–39.

34. For the text (Leiden 348) see Moshe Greenberg, *The Ḫab/piru* (New Haven: American Oriental Society, 1955), p. 56, no. 162.

35. William F. Albright, *From the Stone Age to Christianity* (Garden City, N.Y.: Doubleday, 1957), pp. 223–24. Gleason L. Archer, Jr., cites a wall painting of the period of Amenhotep III (1417–1379) in which the name of Ramose, the famous vizier, appears. As Archer points out, this shows that names like Rameses antedate Dynasty 19 and that the city name of Exodus 1:11 need not be dated as late as Rameses II ("An Eighteenth-Dynasty Rameses," *JETS* 17 [1974]: 49–50). Archer is incorrect in saying that this painting has not been cited in the literature, however, for it appears in Hayes, "Internal Affairs," in *CAH* 2.1, pp. 342, 405.

changed the name in the text to Rameses since the original name was no longer used and was therefore meaningless to later readers.[36] While this is a distinct possibility and other examples may be cited, it seems unnecessary if the name *Rameses* can be shown (and it can) to have been in use before the early date proposed for the exodus.

Another factor strangely overlooked by those who maintain that the city Rameses was named after Rameses II is the very evident passing of much time between the building of the cities and the exodus itself. The passage says that the Israelites were forced to work on the project, but that the more the Egyptians mistreated them, the more they multiplied and filled the land. There is clearly the impression of generation following generation. Furthermore, when all else failed, the pharaoh initiated his policy of infanticide, an event which must be dated at the time of Moses' birth. Unless one is prepared to disregard the biblical information concerning Moses' age at the time of the exodus, another eighty years passed before the exodus. If Rameses II was the pharaoh of the exodus and the city of Rameses was named for him, his reign included the years of construction, the years between the building of the cities and the infanticide decree, and the first eighty years of Moses' life. A total of well over one hundred years is clearly in view. Even if Moses had been only forty at the time of the exodus, Rameses' reign of sixty-eight years would still be inadequate. But, of course, no biblical tradition allows Moses to have been that young at that time. If the Old Testament witness has any credibility at all, then, the city Rameses cannot possibly have been named for Rameses II previous to the exodus.

Evidence of thirteenth-century conquest

The third and by far most commonly adduced argument in support of a thirteenth-century date for the exodus is archaeological evidence of a massive and widespread devastation of the cities and towns of central Canaan during that period. Since there appears to be incontrovertible attestation of such destruction and since, so the argument goes, the only known historical event anywhere near that time which could account for it is the Israelite conquest, the conclusion is drawn

36. So, for example, Charles F. Aling, "The Biblical City of Ramses," *JETS* 25 (1982): 136–37. Aling himself points out, however, that the name *Ramses* or a variant is attested as early as Dynasty 12 (p. 133). To assume that the name in Exodus 1:11 must point to Rameses II is extremely gratuitous, though admittedly the city most likely was named after some royal person of that name. The assumption of an anachronism here requires one also in Genesis 47:11. There Jacob and his family are allotted "the district of Rameses" as their dwelling-place. A theory which entails a double updating seems somewhat tenuous.

that the conquest was in fact the cause of the destruction and that the exodus therefore must have been only slightly earlier.[37]

There are major problems with this interpretation of the archaeological data, however. First of all, there is not a scrap of extrabiblical inscriptional evidence from any Canaanite sites of the mid-thirteenth century, to say nothing of any which might identify the invaders. The alleged signs of cultural transition are greatly debated and in any case do not and cannot identify the new elements as Israelite.[38] One should note, in fact, that the only extant texts which describe political upheaval and military conflicts even remotely similar to the biblical account of the conquest are the Tell el-Amarna Letters. These relate in a graphic eyewitness manner the intercity strife of the Canaanite states and also refer repeatedly to the 'apiru who take different sides at different times.[39] The era described by these letters to the Egyptian pharaohs Amenhotep III and Amenhotep IV (Ikhnaton) is approximately 1380 to 1358, precisely the time of the traditional date of the conquest! Though one should not hastily equate 'apiru with Hebrew, the case is persuasive enough that some advocates of a late date for the exodus suggest that the Amarna Letters reflect an early conquest by certain tribes, perhaps the so-called Joseph tribes of Ephraim and Manasseh, in approximately 1375, and that the conquest by the exodus tribes occurred more than a century later.[40] Requiring Joshua to antedate Moses by a century or more, a view that obviously disregards strong and consistent biblical tradition, this reconstruction fails to make any kind of a convincing case as it tries to accommodate both archaeological data and extrabiblical inscriptional evidence to the biblical record.

This raises the question of the meaning of the thirteenth-century destruction layers and the lack of such evidence from the early fourteenth century.[41] We will begin with the latter. First, though all scholars agree that the Amarna Letters are genuine and present a realistic view of the tumultuous conditions in Canaan in the early fourteenth century, they concede that all this civil war and mistreatment at the hands of the 'apiru and others have left few visible marks of invasion

---

37. This is the view of liberal and conservative scholars alike. See, for example, Harry T. Frank, *Bible, Archaeology, and Faith* (Nashville: Abingdon, 1971), p. 95; Kitchen, *Ancient Orient*, pp. 61–69; Roland K. Harrison, *Old Testament Times* (Grand Rapids: Eerdmans, 1970), pp. 175–76.

38. Kathleen Kenyon, *Archaeology in the Holy Land* (New York: Praeger, 1960), pp. 208–10.

39. For the most important letters see Pritchard, *Ancient Near Eastern Texts*, pp. 483–90.

40. Meek, *Hebrew Origins*, pp. 23–25. Meek dates the exodus and conquest as late as 1200 B.C.

41. For the whole problem see Eugene H. Merrill, "Palestinian Archaeology and the Date of the Conquest: Do Tells Tell Tales?" *GTJ* 3 (1982): 107–21.

or conquest which are susceptible to archaeological research.[42] Is it not possible, then, that the Israelite conquest also is unattested archaeologically? Second, and far more important, there is no archaeological sign of an early-fourteenth-century conquest precisely because the Canaanite cities and towns, with few exceptions, were spared material destruction as a matter of policy initiated by Moses and implemented by Joshua. In other words, signs of major devastation in the period from 1400 to 1375 would be an acute embarrassment to the traditional view because the biblical witness is univocal that Israel was commanded to annihilate the Canaanite populations, but to spare the cities and towns in which they lived. And the record explicitly testifies that this mandate was faithfully carried out. The only exceptions were Jericho, Ai, and Hazor. Jericho has so suffered the ravages of weathering and unscientific excavation that scholars are completely divided as to the chronology involved, a fact which tends to cause one to discount the site as having any relevance to the debate at all.[43] The very location of Ai is in question, and until that can be established the date of its destruction is a moot point.[44] As for Hazor, Yigael Yadin, excavator and principal publisher of the site, at first argued that it suffered a terrible conflagration around 1400—a calamity he associated with the conquest—but he later lowered the date to the thirteenth century.[45] Regardless of what may have prompted his reevaluation, many scholars are convinced that his original date must be accepted.[46]

The reason fourteenth-century conquests lack archaeological con-

42. Kenyon, *Archaeology*, pp. 209–12; George E. Mendenhall, "The Hebrew Conquest of Palestine," *BA* 25 (1962): 72–73. Shemuel Ahituv cites evidence of destruction at Egyptian hands but gives no examples from interior Canaan later than Thutmose III (1504–1450) and earlier than Seti I (1318–1304). Moreover, not one city or town conquered by Joshua is cited by Ahituv as having been destroyed by either internal 'apiru attack or Egyptian campaigning! Thus the Canaanite hill country remained virtually unscathed in the Amarna period, the very period of the biblical conquest ("Economic Factors in the Egyptian Conquest of Canaan," *IEJ* 28 [1978]: 93–96, 104–5). Thutmose IV, who was pharaoh at the time of the wilderness wandering (1425–1417), made only one campaign to Canaan, in which he took Gezer; and neither Amenhotep III (1417–1379) nor Amenhotep IV (1379–1362)—the rulers during the conquest era—made a single foray into Canaan. See James M. Weinstein, "The Egyptian Empire in Palestine: A Reassessment," *BASOR* 241 (1981): 13–16. Michael W. Several goes as far as to argue that the Amarna age was a time of unparalleled peace, a condition he attributes to solid Egyptian control ("Reconsidering the Egyptian Empire in Palestine During the Amarna Period," *PEQ* 104 [1972]: 128–29). The Amarna Letters attest anything but peace, however.

43. Roger Moorey, *Excavation in Palestine* (Grand Rapids: Eerdmans, 1983), pp. 116–17.

44. Bimson, *Redating*, pp. 215–25.

45. Yigael Yadin, "The Rise and Fall of Hazor," in *Archaeological Discoveries in the Holy Land*, Archaeological Institute of America (New York: Crowell, 1967), pp. 62–63; "Excavations at Hazor, 1955–1958," in *The Biblical Archaeologist Reader*, ed. Edward F. Campbell, Jr., and David Noel Freedman (Garden City, N.Y.: Doubleday, 1964), vol. 2, p. 224; "The Fifth Season of Excavations at Hazor, 1968–69," *BA* 32 (1969): 55.

46. Bimson, *Redating*, p. 194.

firmation, then, is that there is nothing to confirm in this manner. Moses had said that the Lord would give Israel cities they had not built, houses full of good things which they had not gathered, cisterns they had not dug, and vineyards and olive trees they had not planted (Deut. 6:10–11). And Joshua was able to say, after the conquest, that the Lord indeed had given them a land on which they had not labored, cities which they had not built, and vineyards and olive trees which they had not planted (Josh. 24:13). Thus the assumption by many scholars that there was violent overthrow in the land simply flies in the face of the biblical tradition itself. The silence of archaeology vis-à-vis an early-fourteenth-century conquest is itself a powerful witness in support of such a date.

What, then, may one make of the obvious destruction of the Canaanite cities of the thirteenth century? First, it should be noted that if, as we have argued, the Israelite conquest occurred in the early fourteenth century, these cities would for the most part not be Canaanite any longer but Israelite. There is no way presently available to distinguish Late Bronze Canaanite from Late Bronze Israelite cultural phenomena. Second, there may be ways other than the Israelite conquest to account for the destruction. The Book of Judges makes it very clear that Israel was overrun time and time again by enemy peoples from both within and outside the land. At no time was this more devastating to Israelite life than in the thirteenth century, that is, at precisely the time in which advocates of a late date for the exodus set the conquest. Traditional chronology requires the judgeship of Deborah during this period and that of Gideon shortly thereafter. Though details concerning the extent of damage caused by the respective foes, the Canaanites and Midianites, are lacking in the narratives, the facts that Jabin of Hazor "cruelly oppressed" Israel for twenty years (Judg. 4:3) and that many of the tribes were rallied under Deborah and Barak in order to break the Canaanite stranglehold (Judg. 5:12–18) suggest widespread military engagement which could have inflicted tremendous physical damage on Israel's cities.[47] The Midianite oppression does not appear to have affected Israel in quite the same way, consisting mainly in overrunning agricultural lands, but warfare can hardly have been avoided in the seven-year period of Midianite harassment. Moreover, the civil strife which followed Gideon's expulsion of the Midianites involved material destruction: Gideon's son Abimelech, who had proclaimed himself king, reduced the city of Shechem to rubble (Judg. 9:45) before he was slain in an unsuccessful siege of Thebez.[48]

There is nothing by which to determine the agent of the thirteenth-

47. Bright, *History*, p. 176; Kenyon, *Archaeology*, p. 238.
48. Edward F. Campbell, Jr., and James F. Ross, "The Excavation of Shechem and the Biblical Tradition," *BA* 26 (1963): 16–17.

century destruction of Palestinian urban sites except the Old Testament record itself. Only it is unambiguous. A carefully constructed chronology based on a legitimate hermeneutic requires that this destruction be explained on the basis of something other than the conquest. The best alternative is the oppression of Israel by Canaanites and Midianites and the redressing of that oppression by the heroic efforts of the judges.

It should be evident that the arguments usually marshaled in support of a late date for the exodus and conquest are individually and collectively unconvincing and, in fact, run counter to every objective analysis of the biblical data. The Old Testament insists on 1446; denial of that fact is special pleading based on insubstantial evidence.

The Dates and Length of the Egyptian Sojourn

The Problem

The establishment of 1446 as the date of the exodus now permits a reconstruction of the earlier chronologies. We will consider first the question of the length of the Egyptian sojourn and then the major dates of patriarchal history. As was intimated in chapter 1, the length of the sojourn of Israel in Egypt has crucial ramifications for a proper understanding of the patriarchal and Joseph narratives. A 215-year sojourn, for example, places Joseph in a Hyksos milieu whereas a 430-year sojourn places him in a native Egyptian dynasty. The implications are profound. Similarly, a 215-year sojourn sets the dates of Abraham and his immediate successors 215 years later than the traditional chronology, thus requiring a rethinking of their relationship to what are presented in the narratives as contemporaneous events, for instance, the destruction of the cities of the plain.

The Revelation to Abraham

The beginning point of our discussion is the revelation by Yahweh to Abraham that his seed would be sojourners in a foreign land for four hundred years and that there they would endure affliction (Gen. 15:13). In the fourth generation, however, they would be brought out of that bondage by Yahweh and resettled in Canaan (Gen. 15:16). The juxtaposition of "four hundred years" and "fourth generation" strongly suggests that generation here is to be understood as a century.[49] A

---

49. William F. Albright argues the Hebrew word *dôr* ("generation") meant "lifetime" in early Hebrew, and so Gen. 15:16 is referring to four lifetimes of one hundred years each (*The Biblical Period from Abraham to Ezra* [New York: Harper, 1963], p. 9). The cognate Akkadian *dāru* also has the meaning "lifetime." See *CAD*, *D*, p. 115. For the view that the sojourn was in fact four hundred years long see Harold Hoehner, "The Duration of the Egyptian Bondage," *Bib Sac* 126 (1969): 306–16.

greater difficulty is the characterization of the sojourn as a time of affliction generally, when in fact only the latter part of that period, following the appearance of the "new king, who did not know about Joseph," was actually unpleasant.[50] The resolution, no doubt, lies in the fact that subsequent generations of Israelites who reflected on the Egyptian experience would have remembered it on the whole not as a place of gracious incubation, but as one of oppression and slavery. The exodus, after all, followed on the heels of unbearable persecution.

Evidence for a Long Sojourn

In support of a long sojourn is the explicit statement of Moses that Israel remained in Egypt 430 years: "at the end of the 430 years, to the very day, all the LORD's divisions left Egypt" (Exod. 12:40–41). This would place the descent of Jacob and his sons to Egypt in 1876 (the exodus in 1446 + a 430-year sojourn), a date which would appear to be certain on biblical grounds. A problem arises, however, in both the Septuagint reading of Exodus 12:40–41 and Paul's apparent use of that reading in Galatians 3:17. The Septuagint says that the length of time the Israelites lived "in Egypt and Canaan" was 430 years; Paul seems to support this understanding when he speaks of the Mosaic law as having come to Moses 430 years after the promise made to Abraham concerning a seed. It indeed is true that the period from the call of Abraham to leave Haran to the descent of Jacob to Egypt is 215 years. This would leave 215 years for the sojourn if Paul (and the Septuagint) intends to say that the 430 years refers to the entire era from Abraham's call to the exodus.

The chronology of the Septuagint is difficult to sustain, however. Besides the clear statement of a 430-year sojourn, there is the obviously Egyptian (rather than Hyksos) background to the Joseph stories (pp. 49–53). Moreover, Paul's reference to the period between the Abrahamic promise and the Mosaic covenant does not unequivocally point to the first time the promise was made. It was in fact affirmed and reaffirmed several times to Abraham, Isaac, and Jacob, the last occasion being precisely on the eve of Jacob's departure for Egypt (Gen. 46:3–4). Paul may be speaking not of Abraham per se, but of that Abrahamic promise, the last expression of which was to Jacob exactly 430 years before the exodus.

---

50. This is why Leon J. Wood, for example, maintains that the "new king, who did not know about Joseph," must be a Hyksos rather than Egyptian ruler. The Hyksos' rise to power around 1720 would allow nearly 280 years of oppression until the exodus of 1446 (*A Survey of Israel's History* [Grand Rapids: Zondervan, 1970], p. 37). Two hundred eighty is not four hundred, however, and so the problem of four hundred years of oppression is not solved.

Evidence for a Short Sojourn

The theory of a 215-year sojourn is attractive to many scholars because it accommodates more easily the "fourth generation" of Genesis 15:16 and the apparent total of four generations from Levi to Moses (Exod. 6:16–20). One can understand how the span from Levi to Moses might occupy 215 years, but how could only four generations fill 430 years?[51] The meaning of the "fourth generation" in Genesis 15:16 has already been addressed—generation, in effect, is synonymous with century. The answer to the genealogy question is a little more complex.

Levi was about 44 years old when he personally descended to Egypt with his father Jacob.[52] Exodus 6:16 records that Levi was 137 when he died; so he lived in Egypt for about 93 years. His son Kohath lived all (or almost all) his life in Egypt and died at 133. Amram, who spent all his days in Egypt, lived to be 137. Moses, his son, left Egypt at the age of 80. The total that all four spent in Egypt (including Moses' years in Midian) is 443, a figure not greatly in excess of 430. The four generations—Levi, Kohath, Amram, Moses—thus represent an artificial total of approximately 430 years, artificial because the overlapping of generations is not taken into account. This way of calculation is obviously at variance with modern notions of chronology, but one cannot on that account deny that such a method may have been used for literary purposes.[53]

Moreover, Kenneth Kitchen has suggested that the structure of Exodus 6:16–20 reflects not immediately successive generations, but tribe (Levi), clan (Kohath), family (Amram), and individual (Moses).[54] A parallel structure is found in Joshua 7:16–18, where tribe (Judah), clan (Zerah), family (Zimri), and individual (Achan) appear. There Achan, though in the family of Zimri, is specifically identified as the son of Carmi. Moses, therefore, may not have been the son of Amram directly, though Exodus 6:20 seems to suggest that he was.

In support of the idea that the genealogy of Exodus 6:16–20 is se-

---

51. Rowley, *From Joseph to Joshua*, pp. 70–73.

52. See Eugene H. Merrill, "Fixed Dates in Patriarchal Chronology," *Bib Sac* 137 (1980): 244.

53. A well-known example of a chronology which appears to be diachronic but in fact is largely synchronic is the Sumerian King List. The dynasties listed therein are apparently in succession, but contemporary records show that they are frequently parallel. See Thorkild Jacobsen, *The Sumerian King List*, Assyriological Studies 11 (Chicago: University of Chicago Press, 1939), pp. 161–64. The same method appears to be involved in the chronology of the judges (see pp. 150–51). Perhaps, then, the four generations of Levi through Moses were selected because the total years involved approximate 430.

54. Kitchen, *Ancient Orient*, pp. 54–55.

lective—and therefore the sojourn was of long duration—are the following considerations. Bezalel, one of the artisans who oversaw the construction of the tabernacle (Exod. 31:2–5), was a contemporary of Moses and yet was the seventh generation from Jacob (1 Chron. 2:1, 4, 5, 9, 18–20) while Moses was only the fourth. Elishama, the leader of the tribe of Ephraim at the time of Israel's journey from Sinai (Num. 1:10), was the ninth generation from Jacob though still contemporary with Moses (1 Chron. 7:22–26). Even more remarkable, Joshua, Moses' assistant, was the eleventh generation from Jacob (1 Chron. 7:27). Though these eleven generations can conceivably be contained within the limits necessitated by a sojourn of 215 years, the point being made here is that one cannot then use the four generations of the Levi-Moses genealogy to argue for a short sojourn, since it is almost certain that the names in the Levi-Moses genealogy would be only representative and not comprehensive.

A final objection to the theory of a short sojourn lies in the difficulty of understanding how the seventy (or seventy-five) persons of Jacob's family at the time of the descent to Egypt multiplied in only 215 years to six hundred thousand men, to say nothing of women and children (Exod. 12:37). Even 430 years is too short a time in normal circumstances. The biblical narrative expressly declares, however, that this remarkable growth occurred as a result of providential blessing and protection. Mathematically one can show how, over ten or twelve generations, 430 years would be adequate for this explosive population boom, but 215 years is clearly staggering to the imagination.[55]

We conclude that the notion of a longer sojourn is to be preferred. It best accommodates the biblical chronological requirements, and it suits the Egyptian historical background in a much more satisfactory way as well.

Patriarchal Chronology

The establishment of dates for the exodus and sojourn leads to considerable precision in determining the dates of the patriarchal period. And yet these dates will be accepted only if one is prepared to accept the facticity of the information contained in the Genesis account itself. If one argues, on whatever grounds, that the long life-spans of the patriarchs are impossible or that the narratives themselves report nonhistorical, legendary episodes, then clearly one cannot say anything

55. For the mathematical evidence see Carl F. Keil and Franz Delitzsch, *Biblical Commentary on the Old Testament*, vol. 2, *The Pentateuch* (Grand Rapids: Eerdmans, 1951), pp. 28–29.

very meaningful about either the chronology or history. To reject the only data available is to reject any realistic hope of reconstructing early Hebrew history. In line with the historiographical principles followed in this book, the biblical record stands on its own merits unless there are unassailable external factors which militate against it.

According to Genesis 47:9 Jacob was 130 years old when he first arrived in Egypt and appeared before the king. His date of arrival, as has been demonstrated, was 1876, and so Jacob was born in 2006. His father Isaac was 60 years old at that time, an indication that he was born in 2066 (Gen. 25:26). Abraham, of course, was 100 when Isaac was born (Gen. 21:5), and so was himself born in 2166. However one chooses to view these facts and figures, it is increasingly recognized that the patriarchal stories fit best the Early Bronze–Middle Bronze period of the ancient Near East. It may never be possible to prove to everyone's satisfaction that the patriarchs were flesh-and-blood persons, but it is becoming more and more difficult to remain skeptical about the essential compatibility between the Genesis account of the patriarchs and what is known about the times and places in which the Bible locates them.

The Wilderness Wandering

From the Reed Sea to Sinai

With this larger historical matrix in view, let us now retrace the steps of Moses and Israel after leaving Egypt. Having crossed the Reed Sea the tribes, in almost military formation (Exod. 12:51), traveled for three days through the Desert of Shur and arrived at Marah, where the bitter waters were made sweet. From there they went on to Elim and entered the Desert of Sin some forty-five days after leaving Egypt (Exod. 16:1). There they were first supplied with manna. Moving on to Rephidim,[56] they were attacked by the Amalekites (Exod. 17:8–16). These warlike, nomadic tribes are of uncertain origin, though the Amalek born to Timna, concubine of Esau's son Eliphaz, may be the

---

56. These first five place names—Shur, Marah, Elim, Sin, and Rephidim—are mentioned only in the Old Testament and cannot be tied to modern sites. Shur was a desert extending across the west central Negev (Gen. 16:7; 20:1; 25:18; 1 Sam. 15:7; 27:8). Marah appears only in the accounts of the desert itinerary (Exod. 15:23; Num. 33:8–9) as does Elim (Exod. 15:27; 16:1; Num. 33:9–10). Sin is the desert between Elim and Rephidim (Exod. 16:1; 17:1; Num. 33:11–12). Rephidim lay between Alush (Num. 33:14) and Mount Sinai (Exod. 17:1, 8; 19:2). For possible locations of these places see the map on p. 61.

eponym of the tribe (Gen. 36:12, 16). If so, the attack on Israel was all
the more reprehensible since it involved brother against brother. No
wonder Amalek was placed under the *ḥērem* of God (Exod. 17:14).[57]
Israel next met them when she attempted to penetrate Canaan from
the south (Num. 14:39–45). Later on the Amalekites joined both the
Moabites (Judg. 3:13) and the Midianites (Judg. 6:3) in their raids
against Israel in the time of the judges. Saul failed to annihilate them
as he was commanded (1 Sam. 15:1–9), but David attacked and destroyed many of them in his desert expeditions (1 Sam. 27:8; ch. 30).
They died out at last, the final reference to them coming from Hezekiah's time (ca. 700 B.C.) (1 Chron. 4:41–43).

With Joshua in command, Israel defeated the Amalekites and at last
arrived at the holy mountain in the Desert of Sinai in the third month
after the exodus (Exod. 19:1). Though the traditional view locates this
mountain in the southern part of the Sinai peninsula, recent scholars
have suggested either a northern or more central location.[58] Since
most (if not all) of the place names in this part of the itinerary can no
longer be identified, it is impossible to be sure. Nor does it really
matter. The main thing is that Israel met Yahweh there, and the two,
sovereign and vassal, entered into covenant.

The Sinaitic Covenant

It is outside the immediate interest of this study to deal with the
theological implications of the so-called Mosaic or Sinaitic covenant.
Suffice it to say that by this instrument Yahweh confirmed his work
of redeeming his vassal people from the overlordship of Egypt by making them his own servants, "a kingdom of priests and a holy nation"
(Exod. 19:6). Their role thenceforth would be to mediate or intercede
as priests between the holy God and the wayward nations of the world,
with the end in view not only of declaring his salvation, but providing
the human channel in and through whom that salvation would be
effected.[59]

Historically what must be affirmed is that all twelve tribes of Israel
were present at Sinai to participate in covenant with Yahweh. This

57. The Hebrew term *ḥērem* refers to the act of devoting someone or something to
God for his exclusive use. It might (as in this instance) involve the annihilation of the
object so devoted. See Leon J. Wood, *ḥērem*, in R. Laird Harris, Gleason L. Archer, Jr.,
and Bruce K.Waltke, eds., *Theological Wordbook of the Old Testament* (Chicago: Moody,
1980), vol. 1, pp. 324–25.

58. For a discussion of various views see Siegfried Herrmann, *A History of Israel
in Old Testament Times*, trans. John Bowden (Philadelphia: Fortress, 1975), pp. 71–73.

59. Walther Eichrodt, *Theology of the Old Testament* (Philadelphia: Westminster,
1961), vol. 1, pp. 36–45, 481–85.

affirmation is contrary to the view of Martin Noth and other scholars that the Sinaitic traditions, like those of the exodus, were originally the property of one or two of the tribes, who then shared their understanding of their past with the others until each tribe's heritage became the heritage of all.[60] We can easily see that one of the intentions of the exodus-covenant narratives is to assert that all Israel took part in the exodus and all Israel met Yahweh at Sinai. Only a skeptical approach founded on unproven and unprovable critical hypotheses can possibly read into the canonical text anything but a twelve-tribe participation in this very watershed of Israel's sacred history.

Of historical relevance also is the fact that the literary form in which the Sinaitic covenant text (Exod. 20–23) appears is strikingly similar to that of ancient Near Eastern, particularly Hittite, suzerain-vassal treaties of the same general period.[61] The similarity is even more readily apparent in the Book of Deuteronomy, which, in effect, is one long covenant appropriate to the younger generation of Israelites who were about to enter Canaan.[62] As George Mendenhall, Meredith Kline, Kenneth Kitchen, and other scholars have shown, both Exodus 20–23 and Deuteronomy follow the structure and contain the essential elements of classic suzerain-vassal treaties attested most abundantly in the Hittite royal archives at Boghazkeui, Turkey (ancient Ḫattušaš). Since these texts date from the Late Bronze Age for the most part, one might presume that the biblical texts which resemble them so closely also come from this period, that is, from the period which has traditionally been regarded as the Mosaic age. In the interest of defending a much later date for Deuteronomy, however, many scholars prefer to connect the form and content of Deuteronomy to Neo-Assyrian treaties of the seventh century.[63] But a careful comparison of these treaties and the biblical texts reveals insurmountable problems for this interpretation. For example, blessing formulae are an integral part of both the Late Bronze treaties and the biblical texts, but are unattested in the Assyrian documents.[64] On balance it is clear that Moses adopted treaty

60. Martin Noth, *History of Pentateuchal Traditions,* trans. Bernhard W. Anderson (Englewood Cliffs, N.J.: Prentice-Hall, 1972).

61. George E. Mendenhall, "Covenant Forms in Israelite Tradition," in *The Biblical Archaeologist Reader,* ed. Edward F. Campbell, Jr., and David Noel Freedman (Garden City, N.Y.: Doubleday, 1970), vol. 3, pp. 38–42; Klaus Baltzer, *The Covenant Formulary in Old Testament, Jewish, and Early Christian Writings* (Philadelphia: Fortress, 1970).

62. J. A. Thompson, *Deuteronomy: An Introduction and Commentary* (Leicester: Inter-Varsity, 1974), pp. 14–21.

63. Moshe Weinfeld, *Deuteronomy and the Deuteronomic School* (Oxford: Clarendon, 1972), pp. 59–157; R. Frankena, "The Vassal Treaties of Esarhaddon and the Dating of Deuteronomy," *OTS* 14 (1965): 122–54.

64. Moshe Weinfeld, "The Loyalty Oath in the Ancient Near East," *UF* 8 (1976): 397.

patterns well known in the fifteenth and fourteenth centuries and composed the biblical texts after these models.[65]

Why Moses did this is equally clear. He could, of course, have created a new literary form with its own peculiar elements; but since his intent was to be instructive rather than creative, he used a vehicle with which the people would already have been familiar. In other words, as a good teacher Moses was aware of the pedagogical principle that students learn best when they can proceed from the known to the unknown. To clothe the profound theological truths of the Yahweh-Israel covenant relationship in the familiar garb of the form of international treaties was of inestimable value in communicating all that the covenant implied.

From Sinai to Kadesh Barnea

The giving of the covenant, the accompanying ceremony of ratification, and the institution of the priesthood and other elements essential to the newly formed theocratic community took the better part of nine months (Exod. 19:1; 40:17). By the first month of the second year after the exodus (ca. 1445) the tabernacle was erected, and exactly one month after that preparations were made for the tribes to move out of the Sinai region on their way north to Canaan (Num. 1:1). The actual journey commenced twenty days later, on the twentieth day of the second month of the second year (Num. 10:11–12). This means that Israel had settled at Sinai for nearly one full year. It is impossible to know much about daily life during that period except that it was essentially nomadic and pastoral. There are significant oases and grazing lands in the southern Sinai, but these could not possibly have provided adequate water and food for the immense human and animal populations involved. The biblical account suggests, however, that the whole enterprise from beginning to end—from Egypt to Canaan—was an unending series of miraculous acts whereby God redeemed, sustained, and delivered his people. Modern readers can do as they will with the account, of course. They may reject it out of hand as an embellished exaggeration of singers of tales eager to glorify their otherwise very modest and normal past, or they may accept it as a recitation of sober and serious historiography notwithstanding their inability to comprehend its manifold mysteries. Such judgments lie in the realm of religious faith and not in that of scientific verification of historical hypotheses.

At last Israel did move on, pressing inexorably though with great

65. Kenneth A. Kitchen, "Ancient Orient, 'Deuteronism,' and the Old Testament," in *New Perspectives on the Old Testament*, ed. J. Barton Payne (Waco: Word, 1970), pp. 1–24.

difficulty ever to the north. Most of the places mentioned in the itineraries of Numbers and Deuteronomy can no longer be located, so
the exact route is uncertain.[66] The first encampment, Taberah (Kibroth
Hattaavah—Num. 11:3, 34), was only three days' journey from Sinai
(Num. 10:33), but its site cannot be identified. Hazeroth (Num. 11:35)
likewise is unknown today, but the major place of the Israelites' encampment throughout the forty years—Kadesh Barnea—is certainly
to be identified with Tell el-Qudeirat, which is located in the Desert
of Zin nearly fifty miles south-southwest of Beersheba (Num. 20:1).[67]
From Kadesh the twelve spies penetrated Canaan, traveling north all
the way to Rehob, probably the same as Beth Rehob, just west of Dan
and twenty-five miles due north of the Sea of Galilee. If "the entrance
to Hamath" (Num. 13:21) is to be understood as the place-name Lebo
Hamath (modern Lebweh), their reconnoitering may have taken the
twelve as far north as the headwaters of the Orontes River, one hundred
miles north of the Sea of Galilee.[68] In the course of their travel they
also visited Hebron, inhabited by the Anakim, a giant race, and they
plucked a huge cluster of grapes at Eshcol ("cluster"), so called because
of that event. By then Hebron had been in existence for nearly three
hundred years (Num. 13:22; see p. 36), though the same site may
earlier have been known to the patriarchs as Mamre or Kiriath Arba
(Gen. 13:18; 23:2; Josh. 14:15).

When the scouts returned to Kadesh Barnea, the majority report
was that Canaan was populated by giants who lived in cities with
impregnable walls. Though Joshua and Caleb argued otherwise, the
people believed the worst and decided to reject Moses' leadership. As
a result Yahweh condemned that generation of adults to an aimless
wandering in the deserts of the upper Sinai. This they did for thirty-
eight years until at last that generation died except for Joshua and

66. It is not for that reason unhistorical, as is maintained by, among others, G. I.
Davies, who sees the itineraries as the Deuteronomist's embellishments of mere "turn-
ing-points" in the old narrative source and P (the supposed source of the priestly
legislation in the Pentateuch) into a genuine journey which would give hope to the
exilic community ("The Wilderness Itineraries and the Composition of the Pentateuch," VT 33 [1983]: 12–13).

67. For the view that the site may be as ancient as Middle Bronze I see Rudolph
Cohen, "The Excavations at Kadesh-barnea (1976–78)," BA 44 (1981): 104. Cohen advances the novel theory that the destruction of Middle Bronze I sites in the Negev and
elsewhere, which is attributed to the Amorites by other scholars, should be explained
as the maraudings of Israelite tribes on their way north from Egypt. This would place
the exodus as early as 2000 B.C. ("The Mysterious MB I People," BAR 9 [1983]: 16–29)!
What is associated with patriarchal activity in the traditional view must then be
associated with the Israelite conquest.

68. Yohanan Aharoni, The Land of the Bible (Philadelphia: Westminster, 1979),
pp. 72–73.

Caleb. The conquest of Canaan which could have commenced within two years of the exodus actually began forty years later, in 1406 B.C.

In the meantime the people determined to circumvent the sentence Yahweh had pronounced against them, and they launched an attack against the Amalekites and Canaanites of the southern hill country of Canaan. Moses had opposed this ill-advised venture and had refused to permit the ark of the covenant, the tangible and symbolical evidence of the presence of Yahweh the warrior, to accompany them. Predictably, the Israelites suffered humiliating defeat and were pursued as far south as Hormah (modern Tell el-Mishash),[69] about eight miles east of Beersheba. Apparently this lesson sufficed for there is no further record of attempts to enter Canaan prematurely.

From Kadesh Barnea to the Plains of Moab

The encounter with Edom

In the fortieth year Moses made plans to resume the march to Canaan. This time the strategy called for a penetration from the east across the Jordan and up the mountain pass near Jericho. To achieve this Moses knew he must cross Edomite and Moabite territory, for the most accessible route north from Kadesh and east of the Dead Sea traversed the very heart of these two nations. And yet this route, the so-called King's Highway, could also be easily defended at the points where it went through narrow mountain passes. Travel along it therefore required the permission of those who controlled these checkpoints.

Moses first sent messengers to remind the king of Edom of the historical and familial relationship which bound Edom and Israel together.[70] The Edomites consisted mainly of descendants of Esau, who had occupied the land following his estrangement from his brother Jacob (Gen. 32:3). The biblical tradition indicates that the original inhabitants of Edom, formerly known as Seir, were the Horites, no doubt to be connected with the Hurrians of ancient Near Eastern texts. These Esau dispossessed both by his own strength and as a gracious act of Yahweh (Deut. 2:12, 22; see also Gen. 36).

Moses' appeals to common roots fell on deaf ears, however, as did both his recital of Yahweh's deliverance of Israel from Egypt and a solemn pledge to stay strictly on the roadway and refrain from making use of Edom's food and water. Frustrated, Moses nevertheless set out from Kadesh and made camp in the hill country of Hor where Aaron

---

69. Ibid., p. 201.

70. For a general overview of the identity and history of the Edomites and Moabites see John R. Bartlett, "The Moabites and Edomites," in *Peoples of Old Testament Times*, ed. D. J. Wiseman (Oxford: Clarendon, 1973), pp. 229–58.

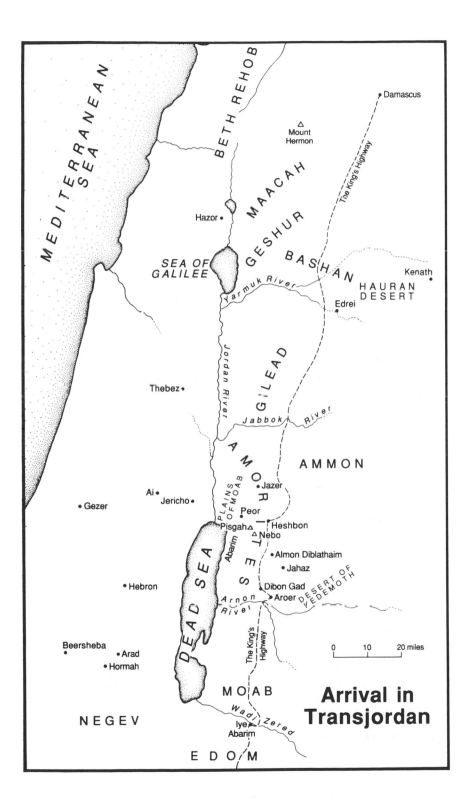

Arrival in Transjordan

died (Num. 20:28–29). This mountain, yet to be identified, was probably northeast of Kadesh "along the road to Atharim."[71] Meanwhile, the king of the Canaanite city-state of Arad learned of Israel's proximity and launched a preemptive attack against Israelite contingents. It is impossible to know as yet which Arad is in view, though it is likely Tell el-Milḥ rather than Tell 'Arad since the latter appears not to have existed in pre-Solomonic times.[72] Tell el-Milḥ is about twelve miles east of Beersheba and sixty miles northeast of Kadesh. The king of Arad was concerned because his intelligence perceived that Israel was approaching his city "along the road to Atharim," a valley which joined Arad to Kadesh. This would suggest that Moses, having had to abandon the plan to follow the King's Highway, was once more determined to enter Canaan from the south. In any event, Yahweh gave him victory over Arad at Hormah, the same place Israel had suffered crushing defeat thirty-eight years earlier.

The encounter with the Amorites

The Canaanite resistance nevertheless discouraged Moses, so he turned south again with the intent of bypassing Edom to the east. This would involve the long trek of more than one hundred miles to Elath on the Red Sea (Gulf of Aqaba) and two hundred miles back north to the plains of Moab. It is very difficult to reconstruct the itineraries followed by Israel because the information is sparse and many of the place-names can no longer be identified. By piecing together the narrative of Numbers 21 and the list of encampments in Numbers 33, however, we can reconstruct the general route.[73]

After leaving Hor the Israelites went east to Zalmonah (es-Salmaneh?) within Edom's borders (Num. 33:41). From there they went about eighteen miles southeast to Punon (Feinân), an area of copper mines and perhaps the location of the episode of the bronze serpent.[74] Oboth, the next place mentioned in both lists (21:10; 33:43), cannot

71. Aharoni, *Land of the Bible*, pp. 201–2.
72. Ibid., pp. 215–16.
73. For suggested routes see Yohanan Aharoni and Michael Avi-Yonah, *Macmillan Bible Atlas* (New York: Macmillan, 1968), map 52. The essential unity and integrity of the various itinerary lists are stressed by Albright, "Moses Out of Egypt," *BA* 36, pp. 58–59. Z. Kallai, however, drawing upon traditio-critical hypotheses, argues that Numbers 33 is a stylized summary based on a stock of wandering traditions ranging from Exodus to Numbers 21. Numbers 20–21 is, however, a narrative version adapted from Numbers 33. Finally, Deuteronomy 1–2 is a "refined version of the concept that moulded the adaptation of Num. 20–21" ("The Wandering-Traditions from Kadesh-Barnea to Canaan: A Study in Biblical Historiography," *JJS* 33 [1982]: 183–84). The problem with this hypothesis is that it rests upon an undiscriminating acceptance of traditio-critical assumptions.
74. Aharoni, *Land of the Bible*, p. 204.

be located with any precision, but, contrary to the view of most scholars, probably is to be placed east of Edom.[75] If so, a route from Punon south toward the Red Sea and then up to Oboth is not mentioned at all in Numbers. However, Deuteronomy 2:1–8 indicates that Israel set out from Hor along the route to the Red Sea and then turned north, not on the Arabah road or the King's Highway, but "along the desert road of Moab," thus bypassing to the east the major Edomite population centers. Next after Oboth was Iye Abarim on the Moabite border, which then consisted of the Wadi Zered, a perennial stream flowing from the eastern plateaus into the southeast corner of the Dead Sea.[76] From there Israel went north across the Arnon River (Num. 21:13) and set up camp in Amorite territory at Dibon Gad (Dhiban), less than forty miles from their destination of the Jordan.

Israel had successfully passed through the eastern fringes of Edom and the very heart of Moab without incident. Though the Moabites could not possibly have resisted Israel even if they tried, Yahweh instructed Moses to do them no harm, for he had given this land to Moab (Deut. 2:9). The Moabites had originated in the incestuous relationship between Lot and his elder daughter (Gen. 19:37) and so were kinfolk to Israel. They had replaced the indigenous populations of the high eastern plateau and had carved out a kingdom whose southern border was the Zered River. The northern border varied from the Arnon to a line running due east from the upper end of the Dead Sea. The earlier inhabitants are described as the Emim, a subgroup, like the Anakim, of a race called Rephaim. These were apparently a giant people whose name means "terrible ones," but whose origins are completely unknown.[77]

Having arrived at Dibon Gad, Israel found herself confronted by hostile Amorites who at that time controlled all the Transjordan between the Arnon and Jabbok except for Ammonite holdings to the east. These Amorites were most likely descendants of that early migration of Amurru to Canaan of which, as we proposed earlier (p. 30), Abraham may have been a part. From the earliest period they had forced the native Canaanites out of the hills and had themselves settled there and undertaken a seminomadic and, later, urbanized way of life. This situation prevailed into Moses' day, as the report of the twelve spies makes clear (Num. 13:29). Even the eastern plateaus had succumbed to the Amorites with the result that both the Moabites and Ammonites had had to retrench and be satisfied with greatly reduced territory

75. Martin Noth, *Numbers: A Commentary*, trans. James D. Martin (Philadelphia: Westminster, 1968), p. 245.

76. Iye Abarim has been tentatively identified as el-Medeiyineh, twenty miles southeast of the Dead Sea (Aharoni, *Land of the Bible*, p. 202).

77. Conrad L'Heureux, "The Ugaritic and Biblical Rephaim," *HTR* 67 (1974): 265–74.

(Num. 21:26–30).[78] Though sensing impending conflict Moses decided to follow a route through the Amorite lands to Beer (site unknown), Mattanah (unknown), Nahaliel (unknown), Bamoth (unknown), and finally to Pisgah at the edge of the high plateau overlooking the Dead Sea. This route passed very near the Amorite capital of Heshbon and so would doubtless provoke Amorite interdiction. Moses therefore requested permission from Sihon the Amorite king to continue on the way. This request, made while Israel was in the desert of Kedemoth (Deut. 2:26), was denied; and Sihon launched an attack on Israel at Jahaz (Khirbet el-Medeiyineh?), only twenty miles south of Heshbon. Israel prevailed and within a very short time had taken Heshbon, slain Sihon, and occupied all the Amorite lands from the Arnon to Jazer, northeast of Jericho.

The order of events as well as the route taken is very obscure since the different accounts list different places.[79] The primary narrative—Numbers 21:13–32—appears to summarize the itinerary briefly (vv. 16–20) and then records the communication with Sihon, his recalcitrance, and his defeat at Jahaz and elsewhere (vv. 21–32). The place from which the initial request for passage was made, the desert of Kedemoth, is not named in Numbers, but appears in Moses' resumé of the Transjordanian conquest in Deuteronomy 2:26. This probably was the first encampment after Dibon Gad and prior to that at Beer. The encampment list of Numbers 33 does not mention any of the places named in Numbers 21:13–20, but it adds to them Dibon Gad, the first stop north of the Arnon (see 21:13); Almon Diblathaim (Khirbet Deleilat esh-Sherqiyeh), about twelve miles north of Dibon Gad;

78. Though equivocating on the historical accuracy of the texts referring to Transjordanian Amorites, M. Liverani acknowledges that in Israelite tradition the Amorites constituted the preconquest population of Transjordan. He fails to show that that tradition rests on anything but good historical bases ("The Amorites," in *Peoples of Old Testament Times*, ed. D. J. Wiseman, pp. 125–26).

79. See Eugene H. Merrill, "Numbers," in *The Bible Knowledge Commentary*, ed. John F. Walvoord and Roy B. Zuck (Wheaton, Ill.: Victor, 1985), vol. 1, pp. 239–40. John Van Seters attempts to harmonize the accounts of Numbers 21:21–35, Deuteronomy 2:26–37, and Judges 11:19–26 by positing deuteronomistic sources (Deut. 2:26–37; Judg. 11:19–26) on which the Numbers version is based. The "writer-redactor" of Numbers inserted into the narrative a taunt-song against Moab (Num. 21:27–30), the "cryptic and artificial" account of the conquest of Jazer, and finally the story of the war against Og, an episode he took from Deuteronomy 3:1–7 ("The Conquest of Sihon's Kingdom: A Literary Examination," *JBL* 91 [1972]: 195). A variation of this—that Numbers 21:21–25 is the source of the other two accounts of the Sihon campaign—is suggested by John R. Bartlett, "The Conquest of Sihon's Kingdom: A Literary Re-examination," *JBL* 97 (1978): 347–51. This is truer to the biblical tradition itself, though even Bartlett, by denying Mosaic authorship of Numbers and Deuteronomy, fails to see the possibility of a single writer recounting the same event with different emphases.

and the "mountains of Abarim, near Nebo" (33:47). These mountains are probably a range of which Pisgah (21:20) and Nebo (Deut. 32:49) were prominent peaks. It was likely from there that Israel sallied forth to capture Heshbon, Jazer, Aroer, and all the other towns controlled by the Amorites.

To the north of the kingdom of Sihon lay that of another Amorite ruler, Og of Bashan. His jurisdiction extended from Jazer to far north of the Yarmuk River and between the Jordan to the west and the Ammonite kingdom to the east. Technically, Bashan lay north of the Yarmuk, but it appears that at the time of Israel's conquest Og controlled the area south of the Yarmuk as well, the region known as Gilead. Both Bashan and Gilead consisted of well-watered plateaus with verdant forests, pasturage, and farmlands. They were so highly regarded by the Israelites that Reuben, Gad, and half the tribe of Manasseh decided to settle there rather than cross the Jordan to Canaan.

Israel's march north toward Bashan was so rapid that Og could not intercept them until they had come to his capital city Edrei, about thirty miles east-southeast of the Sea of Galilee. There the giant king was defeated and slain (Num. 21:35), and his sixty cities were taken (Deut. 3:4). Israel thus controlled all the Transjordanian Amorite lands from the Arnon valley in the south to Mount Hermon in the north, a distance of nearly 150 miles.

The encounter with Moab

When it became apparent to Balak, king of Moab, that Israel was in firm control of all the Transjordan north of his kingdom, he feared that his territory was next to fall. On the other hand, the overthrow of Sihon had at last removed the Amorites from the lands north of the Arnon, territory to which Moab had traditionally laid claim. Acting then both to remove the Israelite threat and to repossess the region east of the Dead Sea, including the plains of Moab, Balak engaged the services of Balaam, an internationally renowned diviner from Pethor. This city, probably the Pitru mentioned in Akkadian texts,[80] was located somewhere near the Euphrates River, most likely in upper Mesopotamia (see Deut. 23:4). Cuneiform texts from the important Amorite city-state of Mari document the existence of a complex guild of prophets who were expert in a variety of skills including divination.[81] These documents date mainly from about 1700 B.C., but the types of prophets

---

80. William F. Albright, *Yahweh and the Gods of Canaan* (Garden City, N.Y.: Doubleday, 1969), p. 15, n. 38.

81. Herbert B. Huffmon, "Prophecy in the Mari Letters," *BA* 31 (1968): 101–24; John F. Craghan, "The ARM X 'Prophetic' Texts: Their Media, Style, and Structure," *JANES* 6 (1974): 39–58.

and prophetic techniques described are attested throughout the eastern Mediterranean world for hundreds of years on both sides of that date. Thus the role and function of Balaam in the context of Moab in 1400 b.c. conform perfectly with extrabiblical information.

The task Balak assigned to Balaam was to utter curses against Israel in the name of Yahweh, Israel's God. This presupposes that Balaam's precise specialty lay in his use of the power-charged word which, with divine enablement, brought about its own fulfilment. Thus he differed from the Old Testament *nābî'* or *rō'eh*, a prophet who could only announce the will of God, not bring it about. At least on this occasion Balaam acted as a *bārû* or *maḫḫû*, a prophet who used various means to discern and interpret omens. He was also a manipulator, one who had the reputation of being able to persuade the gods to a course of action.[82] Since Yahweh was Israel's God, it was only logical, of course, that Balaam work through Yahweh to achieve Balak's desired ends. This was not to be, however, and the curses Balaam intended to pronounce became blessings on his lips, and he had to return to Pethor in disgrace. He apparently came back to Moab later and was instrumental in encouraging Israel to worship Baal at Peor, a cult center a few miles east of the Jordan (Num. 25; 31:8, 16; 2 Peter 2:15; Jude 11; Rev. 2:14). Because the Midianites participated in this seduction of Israel (Num. 25:6, 16–18), they suffered retribution and many of them perished along with Balaam (Num. 31:1–12). It is ironic that the very people among whom Moses had found refuge and from whom he had taken a wife should emerge as the instigators of Israel's first significant post-Sinai apostasy from Yahweh.

This crisis over, Moses now gave his attention to the conquest of Canaan. He himself would not participate in it, he knew, because of his intemperate smiting of the rock. But as covenant mediator he still had the responsibility of arranging for the acquisition and allocation of the land of promise. In anticipation of the decisions Moses was about to make, the leaders of the tribes of Reuben and Gad (and later Manasseh) requested of him that they be allowed to remain in Transjordan and take their allocation there. The basis of their plea was that

82. For Mesopotamian prophetism or divination in general see A. Leo Oppenheim, *Ancient Mesopotamia* (Chicago: University of Chicago Press, 1964), pp. 206–27. Balaam practiced a form of incantation which, by a combination of ritual word and act, could allegedly effect change in the course of divine events. See H. W. F. Saggs, *The Greatness That Was Babylon* (New York: New American Library, 1968), pp. 311–14; Frederick L. Moriarty, "Word as Power in the Ancient Near East," in *A Light unto My Path*, ed. Howard N. Bream, Ralph D. Heim, and Carey A. Moore (Philadelphia: Temple University Press, 1974), pp. 345–62. For attestation of Balaam as a diviner-curser see Jacob Hoftijzer, "The Prophet Balaam in a 6th-Century Aramaic Inscription," *BA* 39 (1976): 12–13.

the land was eminently suitable for cattle, and since they were cattle-men there was no need for them to seek inheritance elsewhere. After eliciting from them a pledge to assist the remaining tribes with their conquest of Canaan, Moses granted the request and set about distrib-uting their shares. To Reuben and Gad fell all the territory between the Arnon on the south and Jazer on the north, that is, all that had previously been ruled by Sihon of Heshbon. Since the cities allotted to Reuben and Gad were scattered amongst each other (Num. 32:34–38), the two tribes apparently began to intermingle and might well have lost their independent identities. Joshua later redistributed the territories to preclude this very eventuality (Josh. 13:8–33). The eastern territory of Manasseh, divided between the clans of Makir and Jair, was essentially identical to the old kingdom of Og. The Makirites took the southern part, that is, Gilead as far south as the allocation of Reuben and Gad. The Jairites received the region north of Gilead, defined more precisely as Og's kingdom of Argob. It presumably ex-tended as far north as Mount Hermon and was bordered on the south by the little kingdoms of Maacah and Geshur, just above the Yarmuk (Deut. 3:13–14). A third entity, Nobah, has no apparent connection with Manasseh, but took in Kenath and the surrounding villages (Num. 32:42). Kenath (Qanawat) was located about sixty miles due east of the Sea of Galilee, deep in the Hauran Desert.

At last the time came for Moses to die. Having provided for such matters as the plan of conquest, allocations for the western tribes, and the designation of cities of refuge, he recapitulated all these and many other instructions in his final address to Israel, an address which finds formal expression in the Book of Deuteronomy. Though denial of Deu-teronomy to Moses and ascription of the book instead to an anony-mous "deuteronomistic" historian of the seventh century are almost a cardinal tenet of critical scholarship, there is nothing in Deuteron-omy in terms of both form and content that requires this. The details and flavor of the book accord with what is known of Late Bronze Age Canaan, it is internally consistent with the rest of the Pentateuch, and it provides an eminently satisfying literary and theological conclusion to the Mosaic literature. The older generation of Israel has died, and the younger must now be confronted with a fresh, contemporary expression of the covenant. Deuteronomy is a covenant initiative to which Israel, on the eve of the adventure of conquest, can and must respond.[83] To document God's faithfulness to his covenant and the meaning of Israel in history, Moses also composed Genesis and the rest of the Torah at this time.

83. Peter C. Craigie, *The Book of Deuteronomy*, New International Commentary on the Old Testament (Grand Rapids: Eerdmans, 1976), pp. 30–32.

3 The Conquest and Occupation of Canaan

The Land as Promise Fulfilment

A central and indispensable element of the promise of Yahweh to the patriarchal fathers was eternal occupation of the land of Canaan. He had led Abraham there from Haran, had blessed him with covenant and seed, and had told him that though his descendants would toil in foreign bondage for four hundred years, they would someday return to Canaan. At long last Yahweh had appeared to Moses and selected him to lead his people, Israel, out of Egypt and into the land of promise. Israel Yahweh described as his son. But the son had become the slave of another overlord, a ruthless taskmaster who refused to acknowledge the prior claims of Yahweh over his own people. Therefore, in a mighty demonstration of power and love, Yahweh had unshackled his people, had defeated their slavemaster, and had brought them through the Reed Sea to the place of covenant at Sinai. There he asserted his own sovereignty and offered to his redeemed people the awesome privilege of being his slaves in the mission of reconciling humanity to himself. Israel's acceptance produced a covenant, a contract by which Yahweh and Israel bound themselves by mutual obligation and which offered to Israel a reaffirmation of all the ancient promises to the fathers. They had become a nation and like any other nation had a king, Yahweh himself, and a constitution, the book of the covenant (Exod. 20–23) and (later) Deuteronomy. All they lacked now was a land to give their nationhood objectivity and stability. Even this was theirs by promise. All that was needed was for vassal Israel to carry out their divine mandate to seize and occupy the land for Yahweh the king.

Thus Israel stood poised in the plains of Moab on the eve of conquest. Moses had died and the mantle of covenant mediatorship had fallen on the shoulders of Joshua. Encouraged by the promise of Yahweh to be with him as he had been with Moses, Joshua set about with confidence to plan the strategy that would result in the conquest and occupation of the land of promise.

The Ancient Near Eastern World

Before the biblical story is pursued further, however, it is important that some attention be paid to the larger world in which these momentous events were to transpire. This is necessary not only that we may be reminded that biblical history was part of a vastly larger historical horizon, but that we may be able to integrate the history of Israel with that of contemporaneous peoples and events. A problem we face here is that the traditional date of the conquest proper (ca. 1406–1399; see p. 147), like that of the exodus, has come under severe criticism in recent generations, a date of 1250 or later being generally preferred. Surely Joshua's narrative of the conquest must reflect in some way the ancient Near Eastern world of which it was a part. Conversely, and equally important, close attention to the milieu of which the Book of Joshua claims to be a part must yield an en-

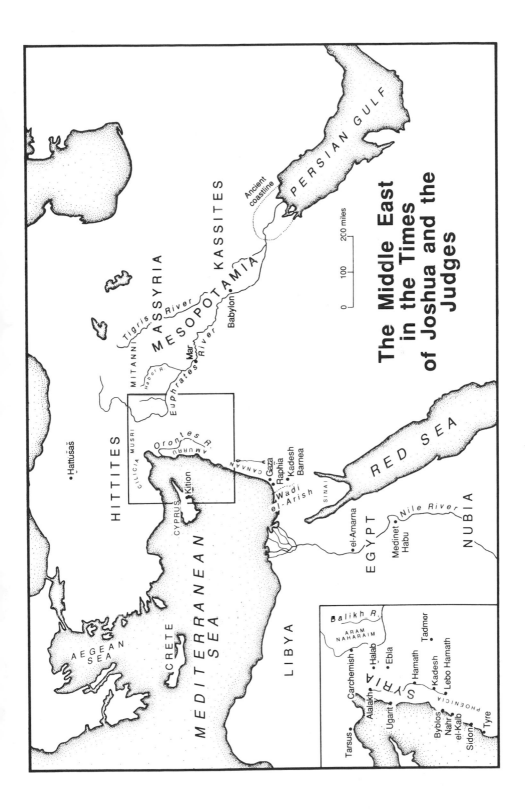

The Middle East
in the Times
of Joshua and the
Judges

PERSIAN GULF

Ancient coastline

ASSYRIA

KASSITES

MESOPOTAMIA

MITANNI

Tigris River

Habur River

Euphrates River

Mari

Babylon

0   100   200 miles

Hattušaš

HITTITES

CILICIA   MUSRI

Orontes R.

AMURRU

CANAAN

CYPRUS

Kition

Gaza
Raphia
Kadesh
Barnea

Wadi
el-Arish

SINAI

RED SEA

el-Amarna

Medinet
Habu

Nile River

EGYPT

NUBIA

MEDITERRANEAN
SEA

AEGEAN
SEA

CRETE

LIBYA

Balikh R.

ARAM
NAHARAIM

Carchemish

Halab

Ebla

Tadmor

Alalakh

Ugarit

SYRIA

Hamath

Kadesh

Lebo Hamath

PHOENICIA

Byblos
Nahr
el-Kalb

Sidon

Tyre

Tarsus

hanced comprehension of the special nuances of this part of Old Testament history.

Mesopotamia

Though Mesopotamia was of only marginal importance to Canaan in the Late Bronze Age, a few remarks may be helpful. Following the sacking of Babylon by the Hittites under Muršiliš I in 1595, the vacuum created in central Mesopotamia was quickly filled by an eastern mountain people, the Kassites, who held sway from then until about 1150 B.C.[1] Though the Kassites were not as barbaric as they are sometimes described, their rule is for the most part shrouded in comparative darkness. Of particular interest is some correspondence sent by the Kassite king Burnaburiaš II to Amenhotep III of Egypt. This letter, found in the archives of el-Amarna, protests the new alliance the Egyptians had forged with Assyria, Burnaburiaš's foe to the north.[2] He wrote another letter to Amenhotep IV in which he complained about the shoddy treatment of his messengers who had been traveling through Canaan, an ostensibly Egyptian province.[3] This letter, to be dated around 1370, reflects conditions at the end of the conquest period according to traditional biblical chronology, an era which the Old Testament itself describes as lawless and dangerous.

To the north of Babylon, Assyria was beginning to stir following a long dormancy caused by Hurrian political and cultural supremacy. Full revival came under Aššur-uballit (1365–1330), who began to suppress both the Hurrian kingdom of Mitanni to the west and the kingdom of Kassite Babylonia to the south. He wrote at least two letters requesting gold and other gifts from Amenhotep IV,[4] and eventually (and reluctantly) gave his daughter as wife to that Egyptian monarch. This no doubt was done to enlist Egyptian support in his Hurrian and Kassite struggles. There is no record of any involvement in Canaan by Aššur-uballit, however, nor would Assyria undertake any activity in that direction until the reign of Tiglath-pileser I (1115–1077), near the end of the period of the judges of Israel.

1. For an account of this obscure era of Babylonian history see C. J. Gadd, "Hammurabi and the End of His Dynasty," in *Cambridge Ancient History*, 3d ed., ed. I. E. S. Edwards et al. (Cambridge: Cambridge University Press, 1973), vol. 2, part 1, pp. 224–27; Margaret S. Drower, "Syria c. 1550–1500 B.C.," *CAH* 2.1, pp. 437–44; D. J. Wiseman, "Assyria and Babylonia c. 1200–1000 B.C.," in *CAH* 2.1, pp. 443–47.

2. Jørgen Alexander Knudtzon, *Die El-Amarna Tafeln*, 2 vols. (Aalen: Otto Zeller, 1964 reprint), #9.

3. Ibid., #8.

4. Ibid., #16; Albert Kirk Grayson, *Assyrian Royal Inscriptions* (Wiesbaden: Otto Harrassowitz, 1972), vol. 1, pp. 47–49, #10–11.

Mitanni

Mitanni, the kingdom of the Hurrian peoples, was situated as a buffer state between Assyria to the east and the Hittites to the west. Lying along the Balikh and Habor tributaries of the upper Euphrates, Mitanni reached its greatest peak of influence precisely in the Amarna age (ca. 1400–1350), that is, at the time of Israel's conquest.[5] Because of its indefensible location Mitanni was constantly overrun by first one major power and then another. It was seldom if ever any threat to Canaan.

The Hittites

Anatolia, now the central part of Turkey, was the home of the Hittites. These Indo-European peoples of uncertain origin, having taken control over the Ḫatti, the original population, had created a stable and highly cultured political state by about 1800 B.C.[6] After a period of decline the Middle Hittite Kingdom came into being and not only reaffirmed Hittite power in Anatolia, but began to undertake imperialistic adventures in all directions. Of most relevance to the history of Israel was the movement to the south and southeast by Tudḫaliyaš II, who, by 1440 or so, attacked and captured Ḫalab (Aleppo) from Mitanni and most of Syria from Amenhotep II of Egypt.[7] The gains were short-lived, however, for a series of Mitanni-Egyptian treaties on the one hand and internal unrest on the other forced Tudḫaliyaš and his immediate successors to relinquish their Syrian holdings.

This was redressed eventually by a Hittite king usually recognized as the founder of the Hittite Empire, Šuppiluliumaš (1380–1346).[8] It was he who raised the Hittites to a place of preeminence in the eastern Mediterranean world at precisely the time of the conquest and occupation of Canaan under Joshua. This was achieved by military means and by international treaties of both the parity and suzerain-vassal types. In about his first year Šuppiluliumaš launched a trial invasion of Syria, at that time under the nominal control of the Mitannian king Tušratta; but according to a letter written by Tušratta to Amenhotep III of Egypt, the Hittites were forced to withdraw in defeat.[9] The

5. J.-R. Kupper, "Northern Mesopotamia and Syria," in *CAH* 2.1, pp. 36–41; Drower, "Syria," in *CAH* 2.1, pp. 417–36; A. Goetze, "The Struggle for the Domination of Syria (1400–1300 B.C.)," in *CAH* 2.2, pp. 1–8.

6. O. R. Gurney, *The Hittites* (Baltimore: Penguin, 1964); Seton Lloyd, *Early Highland Peoples of Anatolia* (New York: McGraw-Hill, 1967).

7. O. R. Gurney, "Anatolia c. 1600–1380 B.C.," in *CAH* 2.1, p. 676.

8. Goetze, "Domination of Syria," in *CAH* 2.2, pp. 5–20.

9. Knudtzon, *El-Amarna*, #17.

Egyptians and Hittites meanwhile maintained proper but cool relations. Šuppiluliumaš, for example, wrote a congratulatory letter to
Amenhotep IV upon his accession to Egypt's throne,[10] and Amenhotep,
though related by marriage to Tušratta, did not interfere in Hittite-
Mitannian problems. Finally, not to be restrained any longer, the ambitious Hittite initiated a general invasion of Syria (ca. 1365) and took
everything between the Mediterranean and the Euphrates as far south
as Lebanon. This caused considerable alarm in Gubla (Byblos), as may
be seen in the frantic correspondence between Rib-Adda of Gubla and
Amenhotep IV.[11] In order not to antagonize Egypt, however, Šuppiluliumaš pressed no farther south. Since Amenhotep was engaged in
religious and philosophical introspection, the Hittites had nothing to
fear from him. The effect in Canaan was to create a vacuum of major
powers, a situation which would allow Israel free rein in achieving
occupation there.

The Syrian States

The Syrian states now found themselves torn between the Hittites
and Mitanni. Ḥalab, along with Alalakh and Tunip, was made a
Hittite vassal. Ugarit at first remained independent of both the Hittites
and Egypt, but later sided with Egypt. The state of Amurru, however,
took advantage of the stalemate of the major powers to expand its
influence from the middle Orontes to the Mediterranean. Its king 'Abdi-
Aširta was a great threat to Rib-Adda, and his son Aziru finally took
Gubla. Aziru then made a treaty with Niqmaddu of Ugarit in which
the two decided to cast their lot with the Hittites. This prompted a
Mitannian response which in turn provoked Hittite retaliation. Šuppiluliumaš made a treaty with Niqmaddu and then attacked the capital of Mitanni itself, Waššugani, but Tušratta the king had fled. Thus
Šuppiluliumaš brought Syria under firm Hittite control and might
have pressed on through Canaan and all the way to Egypt were it not
for the mounting Assyrian threat which diverted his attention to the
east until his death.[12]

Egypt

Also significant during the conquest period were, of course, the
Egyptians. It might seem strange that Egyptian history knows nothing

10. Ibid., #41.
11. Ibid., #68–96; Ronald F. Youngblood, "The Correspondence of Rib-Haddi, Prince
of Byblos," Ph.D. diss., Dropsie College, 1961.
12. For the reign of Šuppululiumaš and his involvement in Syria see Kenneth A.
Kitchen, *Šuppiluliuma and Amarna Pharaohs* (Liverpool: University of Liverpool, 1962).

of the exodus and conquest, but given the Egyptian penchant for recording only victories and not defeats, one should not be surprised at the omission. Amenhotep II (1450–1425), the pharaoh of the exodus, had either little interest in or little stomach for Palestinian conquest following his fifth year, the year of the exodus. His son Thutmose IV (1425–1417) apparently undertook only one northern campaign—to Aram Naharaim. This would have occurred while Israel was in the Sinai wilderness and so would have had no effect on the conquest. Amenhotep III (1417–1379) was ruling during Israel's invasion and occupation of Canaan, but his attention was directed not toward defending his interests in Canaan, but toward hunting and the arts. Whatever military activities he did undertake were against Nubia in the south. This obviously was providential for Israel, for, as has been seen, the Mitannians, Hittites, and (later) the Assyrians were for the most part at loggerheads, unable to fill in the vacuum that Egypt's disinterest in Canaan had produced. Only the Canaanites, themselves totally disorganized, stood in the way.

Egyptian fortunes did not change with the accession of Amenhotep IV (1379–1362).[13] This son of Amenhotep III and his Mitannian queen Tiy is one of the most intriguing characters of ancient Near Eastern history. His major contribution was not in the political, military, or even cultural world, but in his development of a quasi monotheism which worshiped Re-Harakhte, an all-encompassing deity represented by the Aton or disk of the sun. He centralized his new cult in a city built for the purpose, Akhetaton (el-Amarna), and changed his own name to Ikhnaton to signify his religious commitment. So consumed was Ikhnaton by his religious devotion that he lost virtually all interest in external affairs. Many of the Amarna Letters, found in his royal archives at Akhetaton, are from Canaanite princes who, recognizing his formal sovereignty over them, appeal to Ikhnaton to come to their aid and deliver them from all kinds of dangers. Such appeals, which had been sent to his father as well, alas, went unanswered because of the preoccupation of the pharaohs with their respective hobbies. One should note that the dates of Amenhotep III and Ikhnaton coincide with the traditional date of the conquest. The other side of the coin of Egyptian indifference to Canaanite affairs surely has to be the hand of Yahweh, who provided exactly the right circumstances in which his people could possess the land he had promised them.

13. For an engaging account of the history, culture, and contributions of Amenhotep IV (Ikhnaton) see John A. Wilson, *The Culture of Ancient Egypt* (Chicago: University of Chicago Press, 1951), pp. 213–31.

The 'apiru

Our sketch of the Near Eastern world prior to and during the conquest cannot be concluded without attention to events in Canaan itself. This involves primarily a consideration of the 'apiru or Ḫabiru, a people whose disruptive and terrifying presence is pervasive in the Canaanite Amarna Letters. There they appear as marauding mercenaries who at times pose a threat to all the Canaanite states and at other times are to be found on opposing sides of intercity warfare.

When the existence of the 'apiru was first discovered in the Amarna texts, many Bible scholars immediately concluded that at long last extrabiblical corroboration had been found for the Israelite conquest of Canaan.[14] This was based on (1) the coincidence of the dating of the letters and the traditional date of the conquest and (2) the remarkable linguistic similarity of 'apiru (or Ḫabiru) and 'ibrî ("Hebrew"). Before long, however, references to the 'apiru were being attested from throughout the ancient Near Eastern world as early as the Old Akkadian period (ca. 2360–2180 b.c.). In many of the texts the name appeared in the logographic form SA.GAZ, a form preferred in the Amarna Letters except for those from Abdi-Ḫepa, king of Jerusalem.[15] Etymologically SA.GAZ is connected to a Sumerian verb meaning "to murder"; a ᴸᵁSA.GAZ was a murderer. In Akkadian this appears as ḫabbātu, "robber" or perhaps "displaced person."[16] The syllabic form ḫabiru/ḫapiru/'apiru is widespread chronologically and geographically. The Akkadian etymology is unclear, however, though William Albright associated the term with epēru ("dust"; cf. Heb. 'āpār) and suggested that the 'apiru were caravaners or "dusty ones."[17] This suggestion has not met with widespread acceptance.

It is clear that none of the terms used to denote the 'apiru has any ethnic significance. The 'apiru were not a nationality but more likely a social class. They are generally looked down upon as wandering, rootless mercenaries willing to sell their services to the highest bidder. This is the picture that emerges clearly in the Amarna texts.[18]

Of particular concern to us is the question of the relationship of the

14. For the history of the 'apiru-Hebrew equation see Moshe Greenberg, *The Ḫab/piru* (New Haven: American Oriental Society, 1955), pp. 3–12.

15. To explain the exception, William L. Moran posits a Syrian origin for the scribe and perhaps his master as well ("The Syrian Scribe of the Jerusalem Amarna Letters," in *Unity and Diversity*, ed. Hans Goedicke and J. J. M. Roberts [Baltimore: Johns Hopkins University Press, 1975], p. 156).

16. *Assyrian Dictionary*, ed. Ignace J. Gelb et al. (Chicago: Oriental Institute, 1956), vol. Ḫ, pp. 13–14.

17. William F. Albright, "Abram the Hebrew," *BASOR* 163 (1961): 36–54.

18. Greenberg, *Ḫab/piru*, pp. 70–76.

'apiru to the Hebrews. It should be obvious that the terms and the peoples are not synonymous, since 'apiru appear in history earlier than any plausible date for Abraham and exist in numbers far beyond any conceivable population of Hebrews at least until the time of the conquest. Moreover, the character and habits of the 'apiru hardly square with the biblical picture of the Hebrews. Finally, the terms 'apiru and 'ibrî, though phonetically and linguistically alike, seem not to have a common etymology. As already suggested, the etymology of 'apiru is unknown,[19] but 'ibrî appears to go back to Abraham's ancestor Eber ('ēber). A Hebrew, then, was an Eberite. This seems almost certain in light of Genesis 10:21, which states that "Shem was the ancestor of all the sons of Eber." The Shemite genealogy of Genesis 11:10–26 begins with Shem and ends with Abraham, but near its midpoint focuses on Eber (vv. 14–17). It is as though the genealogist is saying that Abraham was a Shemite whose ancestry has specific roots in Eber, making Abraham an Eberite, that is, a Hebrew.[20]

Because of the similarity of 'apiru and 'ibrî, however, it is quite possible and even likely that the latter was sometimes confused with the former.[21] The patriarchal lifestyle might have led some observers to conclude that Abraham the Hebrew was actually Abraham the 'apiru. This might explain why in the Old Testament the Israelites seldom refer to themselves as Hebrews. It was an epithet found usually on the lips of foreigners and frequently in a pejorative sense. For example, when Potiphar's wife in frustration accused Joseph of making improper advances to her, she described him as a Hebrew (Gen. 39:14, 17). Pharaoh's daughter also spoke of Moses as a Hebrew (Exod. 2:6), and the Philistines referred to Israel in similar fashion (1 Sam. 4:6, 9).

Though outsiders may not have clearly distinguished between 'apiru and Hebrew, the Israelites were very much aware of the difference. This is seen, as already suggested, in their general reluctance to call themselves Hebrews, but it also seems to be confirmed by one or two passages where Israelites speak of Hebrews (more correctly, 'apiru) in describing people other than themselves. In 1 Samuel 13 Saul has the battle trumpet blown and says, "Let the Hebrews hear" (v. 3). That this is not a reference to Israelites is suggested by the subsequent differentiation between "the men of Israel" and "Hebrews" (vv. 6–7). The whole passage implies that Saul, at this early point in his career and in face of the Philistine threat, had engaged mercenary troops to fight alongside his own Israelite militia. These mercenaries could well have been 'apiru rather than Hebrews. The fickle nature of the 'apiru,

19. Ibid., pp. 90–91.
20. Ibid., pp. 92–93.
21. Ibid., pp. 93–94, n. 44.

a well-attested trait, appears to be reflected in a later Philistine encounter: "those Hebrews who had previously been with the Philistines . . . went over to the Israelites who were with Saul and Jonathan" (1 Sam. 14:21). Surely the Hebrews and Israelites here are not one and the same.[22]

The 'apiru and the Conquest

While the Israelites made a clear distinction between themselves and the 'apiru, that distinction was apparently quite blurred in the perception of the scribes who composed the Amarna correspondence. Since these letters refer to chaotic conditions in Canaan in the second quarter of the fourteenth century, conditions attributed largely to the onslaught of the 'apiru, and since the traditional date of the Israelite conquest and occupation corresponds generally to that period, one cannot help but suppose that the turmoil in Canaan must be attributed to both the 'apiru and the Israelites, even though the two are not separately identified in the Amarna texts. To the Canaanites, in other words, 'apiru were Hebrews and Hebrews were 'apiru.

This is so probable that many advocates of a late date for the exodus, as we saw previously (p. 72), maintain that the conquest under Joshua preceded the exodus under Moses.[23] In addition to requiring a radical reinterpretation of the biblical tradition which asserts the contemporaneity of the two, this thesis obviously necessitates rejection of the tradition of a twelve-tribe exodus, Sinai-covenant, and wilderness wandering in favor of one in which the exodus is associated with certain tribes and the early conquest with others. It would seem far more satisfying simply to abandon the late-exodus hypothesis and see in the Amarna documents an extrabiblical witness to an early conquest of Canaan by all twelve tribes.

This position is not without its problems, however, since the Book of Joshua does not appear to speak of 'apiru, nor can the behavior of the 'apiru as described in the Amarna texts always be squared with the biblical narratives of the Israelites. The lack of reference to the 'apiru is not a major difficulty since the greater part of the conquest narrative precedes the Amarna period by about twenty-five years and therefore precedes as well the earliest attested references to the 'apiru

22. This is argued forcefully by Norman K. Gottwald, *The Tribes of Yahweh* (Maryknoll, N.Y.: Orbis, 1979), pp. 417–25. For an excellent recent discussion of the evolution of the terms referring to the Hebrews, see Nadav Na'aman, "Ḥabiru and Hebrews: The Transfer of a Social Term to the Literary Sphere," *JNES* 45 (1986): 271–88.

23. E.g., T. J. Meek, *Hebrew Origins* (New York: Harper and Row, 1960), pp. 21–23.

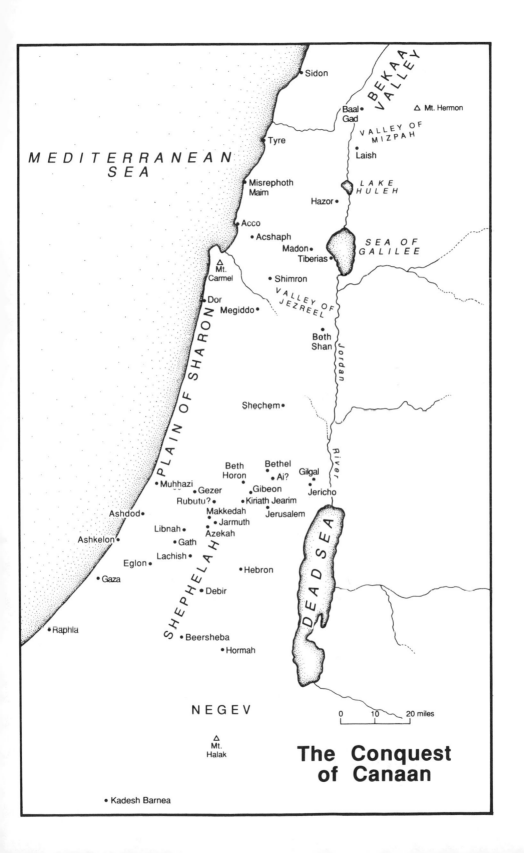

MEDITERRANEAN
SEA

• Sidon

BEKAA VALLEY

Baal •
Gad

△ Mt. Hermon

VALLEY OF MIZPAH

• Tyre

• Laish

Misrephoth
Maim

LAKE HULEH

Hazor •

Acco

• Acshaph

Madon •
Tiberias •

SEA OF
GALILEE

△ Mt.
Carmel

• Shimron

VALLEY OF JEZREEL

• Dor
Megiddo •

PLAIN OF SHARON

Beth
Shan •

Jordan

Shechem •

River

Beth
Horon •
Gezer •

Bethel
• Ai?
Gibeon •

Gilgal

Jericho

• Muhhazi

Rubutu? •

Kiriath Jearim •

Makkedah •
• Jarmuth
Azekah •

Jerusalem •

DEAD SEA

Ashdod •

Libnah •
• Gath

Ashkelon •

Lachish •

Eglon •

• Hebron

• Gaza

• Debir

• Raphia

SHEPHELAH

• Beersheba

• Hormah

NEGEV

0   10   20 miles

△
Mt.
Halak

The Conquest
of Canaan

• Kadesh Barnea

in Canaan.[24] Also, it is characteristic of biblical historiography to be extremely selective in its rehearsal of detail. If the 'apiru were perceived by the historian as having little relevance to the redemptive purposes of the conquest, they would be entirely passed over. Such major powers as the Kassites, Mitanni, and Egyptians were at least indirectly involved in Canaanite affairs in the early fourteenth century, yet none of these involvements is mentioned even once in Joshua. Nor will it do to argue that the reason for this omission is that the conquest actually occurred much later, in the thirteenth century, for the involvements of the major powers of that time—Assyrians and Egyptians—are also not mentioned. All that can be said is that the peculiar predilections of the historian dictated who would and who would not be included in his account. Besides, it may well be that with typical imprecision he lumps the 'apiru (as he does many other peoples) together with the Canaanites, Hittites, Amorites, or others.

As to the Amarna description of the 'apiru and its variance from the biblical view of the Israelites, all that need be said is that this comports perfectly with our argument that the 'apiru and Hebrews, though having much in common, were essentially altogether different peoples. The 'apiru appear to have been in Canaan prior to the Amarna age and to have frequently taken sides with opposing Canaanite kings. The Israelites entered Canaan en bloc at one time and were consistently hostile to the Canaanites. How the 'apiru and Israelites related to each other during and following the conquest cannot be known today, but it is likely that the 'apiru, in the wake of Israel's successful occupation of Canaan, moved on to other areas in their typical nomadic fashion or, as has been postulated above, remained (at least to some extent) to become assimilated by Israel or to serve her as mercenaries.

It is important to note that 'apiru activity is attested in the Amarna materials from two areas of the eastern Mediterranean littoral—Syria and Palestine. Since the conquest did not extend beyond Palestine, the Syrian letters are of no immediate relevance. As for the Palestinian texts of certain provenience, there are only sixteen which mention the 'apiru:[25]

24. Greenberg (*Hab/piru*, p. 74, n. 62) dates the Palestine letters to the early years of Amenhotep IV. Edward F. Campbell, Jr., dates the letters as a whole from the thirtieth year of Amenhotep III to the end of the reign of Ikhnaton ("The Amarna Letters and the Amarna Period," *BA* 23 [1960]: 10).

25. The texts are published in Knudtzon, *El-Amarna* (EA). William F. Albright identifies the author of AO 7096 as Shuwardata (in James B. Pritchard, *Ancient Near Eastern Texts Relating to the Old Testament*, 2d ed. [Princeton: Princeton University Press, 1955], p. 486, n. 13). There are, of course, many more texts which originate in Palestine and which do not mention the SA.GAZ/'apiru. The picture which emerges from them is no different. There are the same intercity squabbling, the same pettiness and servile

1. EA 243. Biridiya of Megiddo observes that "strong is the hostility of the SA.GAZ in the land."
2. EA 246. Biridiya complains that two sons of Lab'ayu of Shechem have bribed SA.GAZ to make war against him.
3. EA 254. Lab'ayu of Shechem notes that he was unaware that his sons had dealings with the SA.GAZ.
4. AO 7096. Shuwardata of the southern hill country says that despite the fact that all his friends but ÈR-Ḫeba deserted him, he has smitten the SA.GAZ man who arose in the land.
5. EA 271. Milkilu of Gezer pleads for help against the SA.GAZ, who appear to be his own servants.
6. EA 273. Ba'lat-UR.MAḪ^{MEŠ} of Ṣapuna, noting that "the land of the king" has deserted to the SA.GAZ, urges him to send help.
7. EA 274. Ba'lat-UR.MAḪ^{MEŠ} appeals for help lest Ṣapuna be lost.
8. EA 286. ÈR-Ḫeba of Jerusalem points out that all the land has been lost to the 'apiru. In addition, all the governors have defected.
9. EA 287. ÈR-Ḫeba says that Gezer, Ashkelon, and Lachish have supplied the enemy with food, oil, and other necessities. The "enemy" here is apparently Milkilu of Gezer and the sons of Lab'ayu of Shechem, who are collaborators with the 'apiru.
10. EA 288. ÈR-Ḫeba complains that the king is silent despite the deaths of Turbazu of Zilu, Zimrida of Lachish, and Yaptiḫ-Addu of Zilu, all at 'apiru hands.
11. EA 289. ÈR-Ḫeba indicates that Milkilu has taken Rubutu for himself, the people of Gath-Carmel have established an outpost at Beth Shan, and Lab'ayu has given Shechem to the 'apiru.
12. EA 290. ÈR-Ḫeba complains that Milkilu and Shuwardata have seized Rubutu, and a city near Jerusalem has fallen to the people of Qeila—thus the land of the king is now in the hands of the 'apiru.
13. EA 298. Yapaḫi of Gezer says that his brother has capitulated to the SA.GAZ at Muḫḫazi.
14. EA 299. Yapaḫi says that the SA.GAZ are strong against him.
15. EA 305. Shubandu of southern Palestine observes that the SA.GAZ are strong against him.
16. EA 318. Dagantakala of southern Palestine describes the great duress he suffers at the hands of the SA.GAZ/ḫabbāti.

The most important persons named in these texts are Lab'ayu of Shechem and Milkilu of Gezer. Lab'ayu's sons paid 'apiru mercenaries

acquiescence to the Egyptian kings, and the same chaotic and lawless environment brought on by real and anticipated invasion by ruthless outsiders. See the description in Campbell, "Amarna Letters," *BA* 23 (1960): 2–22.

to attack Megiddo, and they themselves became allies of the 'apiru in an attack on Jerusalem. Interestingly enough, Shechem is not listed as a city conquered by Joshua, but was the setting for the covenant renewal which took place near the end of Joshua's life. This would allow more than enough time for Lab'ayu and his sons to have capitulated fully to the 'apiru (Israelites), a process which began in the Amarna period (EA 287, 289).[26]

As for Megiddo, its king is mentioned as one of the thirty-one defeated by Joshua (Josh. 12:21), but there is no narrative explaining how this was accomplished. It is entirely possible that the king of Megiddo is describing an Israelite attack when he speaks of the sons of Lab'ayu having hired SA.GAZ (EA 246).[27]

Milkilu of Gezer appears in one instance (EA 271) to be under attack by the SA.GAZ and in another (EA 287) to be their ally. According to Joshua 10:33, Horam of Gezer lost his life and his army[28] in a foray against Israel when he came to assist Lachish. Horam most likely was a predecessor of Milkilu, who at first was hostile to the SA.GAZ and then joined them. Of great interest is Joshua 16:10, which points out that the Israelites did not drive the Canaanites out of Gezer, but the inhabitants became the slaves of the Ephraimites. This is perfectly in line with ÈR-Ḫeba's complaint that Milkilu has "given the land of the king to the 'apiru" (EA 287).

Ba'lat-UR.MAḪ[MEŠ] of Ṣapuna, a place otherwise unknown,[29] speaks of imminent danger from the SA.GAZ, as do Shubandu and Dagan-takala, likewise of unknown location. Yapaḫi[30] of Gezer says that his brother has capitulated to the SA.GAZ at Muḫḫazi (Tel Maḥoz,

26. Edward F. Campbell, Jr., and James F. Ross, "The Excavation of Shechem and the Biblical Tradition," *BA* 26 (1963): 9–11. Campbell and Ross speak of the fact that Shechem was acquired by Israel "without resort to force of arms" and then of the "peaceful symbiosis reflected in the Jacob narratives." The latter remark is strange because the story of Jacob and Shechem (Gen. 33:18–34:31) is anything but peaceful. By stark contrast the Amarna texts point beyond question to a peaceful assimilation of Shechem.

27. H. H. Rowley, *From Joseph to Joshua* (London: Oxford University Press, 1950), pp. 110–11.

28. Rowley (ibid., p. 100) is wrong when he asserts that there is inconsistency between Joshua 10:33 and 16:10 in that the former passage indicates that Gezer was annihilated and the latter says that it was under Israelite domination. Joshua 10:33 says that Horam, king of Gezer, was slain along with those who had joined him in battle against Joshua at Lachish. This does not by any means suggest that Gezer itself was destroyed.

29. Campbell, "Amarna Letters," *BA* 23 (1960): 20, identifies Ṣapuna with Zaphon of the lower Jordan valley, a view which has not been generally accepted.

30. Or Yapa'u according to Shlomo Izre'el, "Two Notes on the Gezer-Amarna Tablets," *Tel Aviv* 4 (1977): 163. Izre'el offers here a new study of EA 299.

west of Gezer).[31] Since this place is not mentioned in the conquest narrative, it is of little relevance for us.

The letters from Jerusalem are, however, of great importance. Their sender, ÈR-Ḥeba (Abdi-Ḥepa), describes a general defection to the 'apiru. He is particularly disturbed by the disloyalty of Gezer, Ashkelon, and Lachish. Under Milkilu, Gezer, as we saw, apparently surrendered to Joshua without a battle. Ashkelon does not appear in the Book of Joshua but is mentioned in Judges 1:18 as having been taken by the men of Judah as part of their allotment. Since Ashkelon is associated with Gezer in the Amarna correspondence, and Gezer was initially hostile to Israel before its accommodation to Joshua, it is not beyond question that Ashkelon like Gezer may after initial hostility have become an ally of Israel (EA 287).

Lachish appears in Joshua 10 as one of Jerusalem's confederates in the Amorite opposition to the Israelites. After Joshua slew the king of Lachish (v. 26), he took the city itself (vv. 31–32), even though the king of Gezer had come to its aid (v. 33).[32] There is no reason why Lachish could not then have become, with Gezer, a collaborator with the Israelites, as ÈR-Ḥeba suggests (EA 287). Zimrida of Lachish (EA 288) is clearly not to be identified with Japhia king of Lachish (Josh. 10:3). It might well be, however, that Zimrida succeeded Japhia after the latter was slain at Makkedah.

In another letter (EA 289) the king of Jerusalem says that Milkilu of Gezer has taken Rubutu (Rabbah, near modern Latrun).[33] Joshua says nothing of its capture, so perhaps Milkilu saved Israel that problem. The same letter describes a garrison which the king of Gath (Shuwardata?) had established at Beth Shan, far to the north. Gath remained untouched by Joshua (Josh. 11:22), and Manasseh was unable to drive the Canaanites out from Beth Shan (Josh. 17:16; Judg. 1:27).

The Amarna texts leave the impression that the SA.GAZ/'apiru fought primarily against cities and towns that were outside the area of the Israelite conquest as described in the biblical sources. Those letters which do mention sites also connected with the conquest are, as we have shown, in no way disharmonious with the biblical evidence. In fact, they complement it in a remarkable way. It is possible that the

31. Yohanan Aharoni, *The Land of the Bible* (Philadelphia: Westminster, 1979), p. 440.

32. It is true that the biblical account indicates that the population of Lachish was wiped out. This would not prevent the city from being repopulated, however, and becoming friendly with the 'apiru (Israel), as suggested in EA 287, only to fall once more out of favor, as seen in EA 288. Note that the text does *not* say that the structures of the city were destroyed. See Eugene H. Merrill, "Palestinian Archaeology and the Date of the Conquest: Do Tells Tell Tales?" *GTJ* 3 (1982): 114.

33. Aharoni, *Land of the Bible*, p. 174.

SA.GAZ/'apiru who operated outside central Palestine are to be distinguished from those inside, who may have been the Israelites. Yohanan Aharoni is amazed that only four of the towns which existed in the hill country during the Amarna period are mentioned in the Amarna documents. He attributes this to the complete dominance of the whole region by Shechem and Jerusalem.[34] Is it not more reasonable to assume that the reason for this silence is that all of interior Canaan was in Israelite hands by this time *except for* Shechem and Jerusalem, the picture given by the Bible itself?[35]

In conclusion, there is nothing in either the Amarna correspondence or the Old Testament to militate against an early-fourteenth-century date for the conquest. In fact, there is much to favor it. It should be apparent that the overall historical milieu of that period provides the best possible backdrop against which to view the conquest. All the great international powers were stymied with regard to their Canaanite interests, thus leaving a vacuum which Israel, by the providential hand of Yahweh, could fill.

The Strategy of Joshua

The Jericho Campaign

Joshua, Moses' successor as covenant mediator, had already distinguished himself as a wise and courageous military leader. As he stood now on the east bank of the Jordan in anticipation of the conquest of Canaan, he had clear military objectives in mind. He correctly perceived Canaan as consisting of two major areas with two predominant ethnic elements. To the south and in the hill country were cities controlled by the Amorites, while to the north, especially in the Jezreel plain, lay Canaanite concentrations. In line with tried and tested strategy he knew that the best chance for success lay in the principle of "divide and conquer." To achieve this it would be necessary to penetrate Canaan just north of the Dead Sea via the route to the interior which led past Jericho. At precisely this point, however, Joshua saw his greatest problem: Jericho was heavily fortified and defended for the very purpose of preventing enemy penetration into interior Ca-

34. Ibid., p. 175.

35. It is important to note that our reconstruction of the historical milieu of the conquest is not without its problems, not least of which is the lack of correspondence between the personal names in the Amarna texts and those in Joshua-Judges. When one recalls, however, that Joshua's conquest was largely over by the time the 'apiru upheaval was attested in the Amarna materials, one can easily understand why at least some of the names are different.

naan. Moreover, the river itself, now at its flood stage following the spring run-offs, posed an apparently insurmountable barrier to immediate progress.

Yahweh had commanded Joshua to undertake the conquest immediately, however (Josh. 1:2, 11), so Joshua sent scouts across the river to reconnoiter the land and especially to sound out the possible weaknesses in Jericho's defenses. They learned that word of Israel's intentions had long preceded them and that the people of Canaan were terrified because of Israel's victories in the Sinai and Transjordan. This created a climate extremely favorable to conquest, but the propitiousness of the moment would be lost if some way to traverse the Jordan were not found.

At just this moment Yahweh revealed that he, the divine Warrior, would fight for Israel now as he had in Egypt. As he had parted the waters of the Reed Sea as a sign of his cosmic and redemptive sovereignty, so now he would stop the flooding river. He, as the Great King, would initiate the conquest by conquering the river which, as it were, protected the land. Thereafter his people Israel would know that the battle was Yahweh's and that they could achieve triumph upon triumph by recognizing that they were a part of the host of the Almighty.[36]

Thus it was that as the ark of the covenant, the symbol of the presence of Yahweh of hosts, entered the river, the waters retreated submissively before him and Israel, allowing the people to cross on dry land. As a further sign of the redemptive nature of what he had done in bringing Israel across the river, Yahweh commanded Joshua to circumcise the males who had been born in the wilderness, thus exhibiting their identity as the covenant people, and to celebrate the Passover, the feast which had been established just prior to the exodus to commemorate Yahweh's redemption of his covenant people. Finally, he appeared in theophany to Joshua as he had to Moses, thereby confirming to Joshua his role as covenant mediator. The whole sequence—circumcision, Passover, and theophany—emphatically declared that the Israel of conquest was the Israel of exodus. The God who had saved his people out of Egypt would now save them in Canaan.

After the Israelites had erected memorial cairns of stone to celebrate their crossing of the Jordan, their men of war marched south from Gilgal (Khirbet el-Mafjar), their first encampment in Canaan, to Jericho (Tell es-Sultan), only two miles distant. The Old Testament city crowned an impressive mound which rose steeply from the adjacent wadi, alongside which also passed "the road going up to Beth Horon"

36. Frank M. Cross, *Canaanite Myth and Hebrew Epic* (Cambridge: Harvard University Press, 1973), pp. 103–5.

(Josh. 10:10), the major route into the interior. Relatively small even by Late Bronze Age standards (ca. ten acres), Jericho was easily defended and well-nigh impregnable. Joshua was eager to take the city not only because it guarded the route he wished to take, but because if he left it standing, it would continue to harbor a pocket of Canaanite resistance which would be a source of annoyance if not danger to Israel's rear flanks. Moreover, and for reasons not explicitly delineated, Jericho was singled out by Yahweh as a special object of his judgment. When a place or a people were thus designated, they were said to be "devoted" to Yahweh, that is, put under the ban. The technical Hebrew verb is *ḥāram* ("to devote to destruction"). Objects under the ban had to be annihilated (if living) or given to Yahweh for his own use. In no case could such an object be retained without the express permission of Yahweh.[37]

The first example of this policy was the destruction of the Canaanites and their cities near Hormah (Num. 21:3). In fact, the name *Hormah* reflects the underlying root *ḥērem*. The policy was similarly applied after the defeat of Sihon and the Amorites in the Transjordan (Deut. 3:6). Moses also exhorted Israel to put certain Canaanite cities under *ḥērem*, explaining that this meant that they could make no treaties with them nor intermarry with their citizens (Deut. 7:1–3). Rather, Israel must destroy their altars, sacred stones, Asherah poles, and images (v. 5). The reason was that Israel, though a people set apart by God, might under Canaanite influence resort to paganism (Deut. 20:17–18).

It is obvious that *ḥērem* was sometimes limited to annihilation of the people and did not apply to the cities themselves. This is certainly the import of Moses' statement that Yahweh would give Israel cities which they had not built and houses and cisterns with food and water which they had not provided (Deut. 6:10–11; 19:1). When at last the conquest was over, Joshua reminded his people that Yahweh had done as he had said—he had given them cities which they had not built and vineyards and olive groves which they had not planted (Josh. 24:13).

A careful study reveals that during the conquest only three Canaanite cities actually suffered the full extent of *ḥērem*, that is, were physically destroyed along with their populations. They are Jericho, Ai, and Hazor. Of the others it is said only that they were "taken" (*lākad*) by Israel and their citizens put to the sword. For now we can only speculate as to why Jericho was selected to be placed under total *ḥērem*. Perhaps as the first Canaanite city encountered west of the

37. Roland de Vaux, *Ancient Israel* (New York: McGraw-Hill, 1965), vol. 1, pp. 260–63.

Jordan its fate would serve as a warning to all the others regarding the holiness of Yahweh and his mighty work in behalf of his conquering people.

The village of Jericho was occupied perhaps as early as 7500 B.C.[38] Unfortunately the ravages of time and weather and both amateur and professional excavation have combined to nearly obliterate Jericho's usefulness archaeologically and historically. On the basis of some scarabs of Amenhotep III, the British archaeologist John Garstang dated level D at about 1400 B.C. and postulated that it was the city destroyed by Joshua.[39] Thus Garstang held to 1400 as the date of the conquest and a corresponding early date for the exodus. His conclusion was buttressed by his discovery of walls which, contrary to the normal results of battering, had fallen outward, down the slopes of the tell, rather than inward. This he associated with the biblical description which says that Jericho's walls fell down "under it" (*taḥtêhā*), that is, down the slopes of the city (Josh. 6:20).[40]

More recently, however, Kathleen Kenyon, another respected British archaeologist, spent several seasons at Jericho and concluded, among other things, that Garstang had misread the evidence and that the Amenhotep scarabs belonged to a later burial. His level D, then, had to be reassigned to about 1300.[41] If this reevaluation has caused problems for the early dates proposed for the exodus and conquest, it has hardly benefited the late dates, since conquest of Jericho in 1300 would place the exodus in 1340. Clearly, this fits no one's position. The best we can say, then, is that the Jericho evidence is inconclusive and at this point is of little or no value in establishing a chronological or historical framework within which to view the conquest.

The Central Campaign

After Jericho fell and was destroyed—an event which from beginning to end is described as a miracle of God—Joshua sent spies up the winding road from Jericho to the next Canaanite fortification at Ai. Since the town no longer existed (its very name means "ruin"), it was necessary for the historian to locate Ai as being "near Beth Aven to the east of Bethel" (Josh. 7:2). Though Ai is identified by many scholars

38. Kathleen Kenyon, *Archaeology in the Holy Land* (New York: Praeger, 1960), p. 42.

39. John Garstang and J. B. E. Garstang, *The Story of Jericho* (London: Marshall, Morgan and Scott, 1940), p. 120.

40. Ibid., p. 136.

41. Kathleen Kenyon, *Digging Up Jericho* (New York: Praeger, 1957), p. 260; idem, "Palestine in the Time of the Eighteenth Dynasty," in *CAH* 2.1, p. 545.

as the site known simply as et-Tell ("the mound")[42] less than three miles east of Bethel (Beitin), this view by no means enjoys consensus. In fact, there are many cogent arguments against it, as David Livingston and other scholars have shown.[43] It is ironic that the second of the three places which suffered *ḥērem* should, like Jericho, be of minimal value in dating the conquest. Indeed, the violent nature of *ḥērem* may be the very reason that neither Jericho nor Ai has yielded meaningful chronological clues.

After suffering initial defeat in his assault on Ai (Josh. 7:4–5), Joshua learned that the terms of *ḥērem* had been violated in the destruction of Jericho. A private citizen, Achan, had stolen booty which belonged to Yahweh only; Achan and his family were themselves destroyed as a result (Josh. 7:22–26). Only then could Joshua, with thirty thousand men, attack and destroy Ai by a clever strategy involving decoy and ambush. The troops of Bethel also joined in the fray but with the men of Ai were soundly defeated. Joshua then set about to slaughter men and women alike—twelve thousand in all—until there was no survivor. The city itself was set afire until nothing was left but a smoking ash heap, a ruin (*'ay*) in every sense of the word. Only the cattle and certain treasures from the city were spared and that at the express command of Yahweh (Josh. 8:27). Ai represents an example of *ḥērem* with very explicit qualifications.

Nothing more is said here of Israel's encounter with Bethel. The archaeological evidence is ambiguous though there does appear to be some sign of tribal settlement during the fourteenth century.[44] It may be assumed that the Bethelites were destroyed but that their city, like almost all the Canaanite cities, was spared to provide residence for Israel. While the Book of Judges indicates that the Ephraimites did in fact take Bethel, this appears to have occurred after Joshua's death.[45]

42. See especially Joseph A. Callaway, "The 1964 'Ai (Et-Tell) Excavations," *BASOR* 178 (1965): 13–40; "New Evidence on the Conquest of Ai," *JBL* 87 (1968): 312–20; "The 1968–69 'Ai (Et-Tell) Excavations," *BASOR* 198 (1970): 7–31.

43. David Livingston, "The Location of Biblical Bethel and Ai Reconsidered," *WTJ* 33 (1970): 20–44. Livingston opts for el-Bireh as the site of Bethel (p. 40) and locates Ai at the small tell nearby (p. 43).

44. Aharoni, *Land of the Bible*, p. 210. There are signs of fourteenth-century settlement at Beitin, but if, as Livingston suggests, Beitin is not Bethel, those signs are irrelevant to our discussion. John J. Bimson concludes that even if Beitin is Bethel and et-Tell is Ai (uncertainties at best), the date of the conquest remains unresolved, since et-Tell supports neither a fifteenth- nor a thirteenth-century date and Beitin was destroyed at the close of the Middle Bronze Age *and* in the thirteenth century (*Redating the Exodus and Conquest* [Sheffield: JSOT, 1978], p. 255).

45. Judges 1:22–26 is the only account of warfare against Bethel. A Bethelite allowed the Israelites into his city with the result that its population, except for the collaborator, was destroyed. The city itself, however, was spared. For the technical phrase, "they put the city to the sword" (lit., "they smote the city with the edge of the sword," v. 25), see Merrill, "Palestinian Archaeology," *GTJ* 3 (1982): 113–14.

Shechem and Covenant Renewal

Having cut the hill country in half by destroying Ai, Joshua turned north and made his way, apparently without opposition, to Shechem (Tell Balâṭah), about twenty-five miles north of Bethel.[46] There, at this place so hallowed by association with the patriarchs, Joshua led the people in a ceremony of covenant reaffirmation as Moses had commanded him to do (Josh. 8:30–35; Deut. 27:2–8). Years later on the eve of his death Joshua gathered Israel back to Shechem so that the next generation could similarly pledge its fidelity to Yahweh (23:1–24:28).[47] That Israel had access to the mountains Ebal and Gerizim, between which Shechem was located, implies either that Shechem was abandoned at the time or that it surrendered without a struggle.[48] Tradition criticism maintains, however, that Shechem fell, if at all, only after savage attacks by the tribes of Simeon and Levi. The basis for this view is the assumption that the story of the rape of Jacob's daughter Dinah by Shechem, son of Hamor (Gen. 34), is an aetiological account whose purpose is to explain how Israel happened to bring Shechem under control.[49]

The problems with this assumption are too numerous to consider here, but a few observations should be made. First, the story of Dinah indicates that though the Shechemites were indeed decimated by Jacob's sons, Jacob was so fearful of retaliation that he set out immediately for Bethel. The conquest narrative exactly reverses the direction. Israel was already at Bethel and set out for Shechem. Second, why would the tribes of Simeon and Levi be involved in the conquest of

46. This occurred at the very beginning of the conquest or about 1406 B.C. The second convocation at Shechem took place forty years later (see p. 138). Israel's ready access to Shechem implies either that its inhabitants welcomed Joshua or that there were no people there. The former seems to be the case, for the Canaanites of Shechem cooperated freely with the 'apiru of the Amarna texts (see p. 105). Though the assembly of Joshua 8 preceded the earliest Amarna letter by about thirty years, it is entirely possible that the cordiality of the Shechemites toward the 'apiru/Israelites was a matter of long-standing policy.

47. Most scholars, of course, see Joshua 8 and Joshua 24 as variant traditions of the same event. For a recent and thorough presentation of this position see J. Alberto Soggin, *Joshua: A Commentary* (Philadelphia: Westminster, 1972), pp. 220–44. What this view fails to appreciate is the need for every generation to affirm its commitment to covenant with Yahweh. It was most appropriate for the assembly to meet at the commencement of the conquest and for the next generation to do so on the eve of Joshua's death. See Marten H. Woudstra, *The Book of Joshua*, New International Commentary on the Old Testament (Grand Rapids: Eerdmans, 1981), pp. 148–49; Meredith G. Kline, *The Structure of Biblical Authority* (Grand Rapids: Eerdmans, 1972), pp. 54–56.

48. See note 46.

49. Robert G. Boling, *Joshua*, Anchor Bible (Garden City, N.Y.: Doubleday, 1982), pp. 251–54; Meek, *Hebrew Origins*, pp. 124–28.

Shechem, particularly since Simeon's allotment was in the Negev and Levi was, in Joshua's time, a religious tribe exempted from normal military service? Third, and most fatal to the aetiological interpretation, there is absolutely no sign of a struggle at or concerning Shechem in the conquest narrative. Why should Genesis 34 have been concocted to explain a battle which the Book of Joshua by its silence implies never happened? Appeal to the Amarna Letters which describe the perilous predicament of the king of Shechem at the hands of other Canaanite kings is to little avail, since it is beyond question that the events described therein took place between the times of the two assemblies at Shechem (i.e., between 1406 and ca. 1366).

The Southern Campaign

Once it was apparent that Joshua had severed northern Canaan from the south and had effectively installed Israel in the central hill country, the Canaanites and other populations throughout the length and breadth of the land decided to forgo their petty differences and forge a common front against Israel. The Hivites (Horites or Hurrians?) of Gibeon (el-Jîb),[50] just seven miles south of Bethel, were so terrified when they saw what had happened at Jericho and Ai that they decided on a diplomatic rather than military course of action. Disguising themselves as travelers from afar, a delegation from Gibeon went to Gilgal, by now Israel's home encampment, and persuaded Joshua to sign a nonaggression treaty with them. Since Moses' instructions had permitted such treaties with distant lands (Deut. 20:10–15), Joshua did not hesitate to make covenant. This required that the people serve Israel as slaves (Deut. 20:11; Josh. 9:15, 21, 27), a condition which though undesirable was infinitely better than death.[51] Of course, the Gibeonites were in reality subject to ḥērem along with the Canaanites and thus should have been destroyed (Deut. 20:16–17; Josh. 9:24). Nevertheless, unwitting though Joshua was, the treaty stood, and the Gibeonites with their fellow Hivites from Kephirah (Tell Kefireh), Beeroth (Nebi Samwil?), and Kiriath Jearim (Qiryat Ye'arim), all villages within five miles of Gibeon, were allowed to live.

50. H. A. Hoffner, "The Hittites and Hurrians," in *Peoples of Old Testament Times,* ed. D. J. Wiseman (Oxford: Clarendon, 1973), p. 225. For the excavation, history, and significance of the site see James B. Pritchard, *Gibeon, Where the Sun Stood Still* (Princeton: Princeton University Press, 1962), esp. pp. 24–34.

51. That this was a sovereign-vassal treaty is argued by F. Charles Fensham, "The Treaty Between Israel and the Gibeonites," *BA* 27 (1964): 96–100. Jehoshua M. Grintz, however, holds that a "protégé" type of treaty is in view here. The difference was in degree of servitude, the protégé having much more independence than did the vassal ("The Treaty of Joshua with the Gibeonites," *JAOS* 86 [1966]: 114–16, 124–26).

The Israel-Hivite treaty was soon put to the test, for Israel, as the superior partner, had responsibility to defend her new vassal against enemy threat. That threat came in the form of a coalition of Amorite kings who decided to punish Gibeon for her defection to Israel (Josh. 10:1–5). The leader of this *ad hoc* league was Adoni-Zedek[52] of Jerusalem, a Jebusite stronghold. Evidently the Jebusites were considered Amorites, for Adoni-Zedek is numbered among the Amorite kings (Josh. 10:5). How long Jerusalem had been under Amorite domination cannot be known, but presumably at least since the putative Amorite migration into Canaan in the Early Bronze IV period (ca. 2200). With perhaps only minor interludes it remained Jebusite until the time of David, who in 1004 B.C. brought it under his rule and made it his capital city. Confederate with Adoni-Zedek were Hoham of Hebron, Piram of Jarmuth (Khirbet Yarmuk, ca. eighteen miles west-southwest of Jerusalem), Japhia of Lachish (Tell ed-Duweir, ca. thirty miles southwest of Jerusalem), and Debir of Eglon (Tell el-Hesi, ca. thirty-five miles southwest of Jerusalem). These five cities, whose locations formed somewhat of a triangle occupying all of northern Judah, were apparently the most important Amorite enclaves at that time. Their defeat, therefore, would open the whole area to Israelite occupation.

When the five kings laid siege to Gibeon, word was dispatched to Joshua at Gilgal that the city was under attack and needed Israel's promised relief. After an all-night march Joshua arrived at Gibeon, about twenty miles to the west of Gilgal. After a fierce battle the Amorites retreated with Israel in hot pursuit. Crossing through the Beth Horon mountain pass west of Gibeon, the Amorites turned south, skirting the western edge of the Shephelah, and ended up at Azekah and Makkedah, nearly twenty miles from Gibeon. All along the way they suffered the wrath of Yahweh, the warrior God of Israel, who cast down great hailstones upon them.[53] The kings themselves escaped, however, and found refuge in a cave at Makkedah. When Joshua learned of their whereabouts, he sealed them up in the cave for the time being and then set out to finish off the Amorites who had survived the hail.

---

52. The fact that this name is unattested in the Amarna Letters as a king of Jerusalem is not surprising since Adoni-Zedek would have preceded the earliest letter by about thirty years. Thus, Rowley's observation that the personal names found in the two sources disagree is of no moment, at least in this instance (*From Joseph to Joshua*, pp. 41–42).

53. Critical scholarship denies the historicity of the miracle in this story, of course, though most interpreters do at least concede a historical kernel around which has been built this poetic account of holy war. See, for example, Trent C. Butler, *Joshua*, Word Biblical Commentary (Waco: Word, 1983), pp. 113, 115–17. John S. Holladay, Jr., argues that the reference to the sun and moon standing still pertains to an astrological appeal for "good signs" from the heavens so that Joshua can have confidence of victory ("The Day(s) the Moon Stood Still," *JBL* 87 [1968]: 170, 176).

His instruction to his soldiers at this point is most interesting: they must not allow the Amorites to reenter their cities, for he wanted to preserve the cities intact (Josh. 10:19). Once again, then, *ḥērem* does not include the physical structures but only the people. Therefore, one must not look for devastation of cities as evidence for the conquest and its date, for Joshua's policy, as has been stressed repeatedly, was to spare the cities for Israel's own use. Once the task of crushing the Amorite armies had been completed, Joshua returned to the cave, brought out the imprisoned kings, and summarily disposed of them.

There then follows the account of the capture of several Amorite cities and the slaughter of their inhabitants. Careful attention to details will yield the distinct impression that the cities themselves, with perhaps one exception, were spared material destruction whereas the populations in each case were decimated. The first city to suffer this fate was Makkedah (Khirbet el-Kheisun?).[54] The historian relates that Joshua "took" it (*lākad*), a verb which always refers to capture rather than demolition.[55] Where subsequent destruction is involved, there are statements to that effect. Another item to note is that Joshua "struck Makkedah with the edge of the sword." This metaphor, here literally translated, is appropriate only to the taking of life.[56] The leveling of walls[57] and buildings can hardly be described as being struck with the sword. It is best, then, to assume that the annihilation of Makkedah's citizenry is in view here, particularly since the writer goes on to say that this havoc wrought by the sword included the king and that he and all the inhabitants were totally destroyed (*heḥĕrim*). In summary, Joshua *took* Makkedah, *put its inhabitants* ("the city") and king *to the sword, totally destroying* them.

Joshua next moved to Libnah (possibly Tell eṣ-Ṣâfi, ca. eight miles southwest of Makkedah), which suffered the same calamity as Makkedah. This time Yahweh "gave" (*nātan*) the city and king to Israel, and Joshua put it and all its inhabitants to the sword, leaving no survivors. Lachish was attacked next. This important city about ten miles south of Libnah was also delivered over to Joshua, who did to it as he had done to Makkedah and Libnah. Even assistance from Horam king of Gezer, more than twenty miles north of Lachish, was

54. So *Oxford Bible Atlas*, ed. Herbert G. May, 3d ed. (New York: Oxford University Press, 1984), p. 134.

55. Merrill, "Palestinian Archaeology," *GTJ* 3 (1982): 113.

56. Francis Brown, S. R. Driver, and Charles A. Briggs, *A Hebrew and English Lexicon of the Old Testament* (Oxford: Clarendon, 1962), pp. 352–53.

57. In a most revealing study, Rivka Gonen points out that most of the Late Bronze cities were unfortified—there were no defensive walls to create a barrier to conquest. At the same time there was a rapid increase in the number of settlements in the fourteenth and early thirteenth centuries. This comports well with the population infusion attending the Israelite conquest ("Urban Canaan in the Late Bronze Period," *BASOR* 253 [1984]: 61–73).

not able to spare Lachish and its people. The next city, Eglon, lay only eight miles southwest of Lachish. With almost monotonous formula, the historian describes the fall of Eglon as he had that of the other cities. Hebron appears next and may be an exception to the policy of preserving the physical city. The difference lies in the fact that the summary statement implies that Joshua put both the city proper and its people under the ban. Again, however, "city" (or "it," v. 37) may mean the population (as it regularly does), and the following phrase may be explicative—"they totally destroyed the city, that is, everyone in it."[58] In that case even Hebron and the surrounding villages survived materially. That it was repopulated within five years (see Josh. 14:6–15)[59] would certainly support the idea that the walls and buildings stood and were reoccupied by Israelites. The last city in the list is Debir (Tell Beit Mirsim), fifteen miles southwest of Hebron. Its judgment was exactly the same as all the others.

The account of the so-called southern campaign is summarized in Joshua 10:40–43. The narrator states that "Joshua subdued the whole region, including the hill country, the Negev, the western foothills and the mountain slopes, together with all their kings. He left no survivors. He totally destroyed all who breathed, just as the LORD, the God of Israel, had commanded." Note that there is no mention of material devastation of cities and towns. The objective student will conclude that the reason such reference is omitted in the summary—the very place one would most expect it—is that the urban structures were left intact as Moses had prescribed.[60]

The Northern Campaign

With the southern strategy now successfully achieved, Joshua returned to Gilgal, Israel's home base in the early conquest years.[61] Be-

58. Wilhelm Gesenius, *Gesenius' Hebrew Grammar*, ed. E. Kautzsch and A. E. Cowley (Oxford: Clarendon, 1957), §154a.

59. The conquest against the Amorite league was certainly no earlier than 1405, and Caleb, according to his own testimony, was eighty-five when he took Hebron as his inheritance (Josh. 14:10, 13–14). Since he was forty years old two years after the exodus (v. 7), the date of his acquisition of Hebron must be around 1399.

60. Even Manfred Weippert, who sees the Israelite occupation of Canaan as a gradual penetration of tribes in a settlement pattern, not as a military operation, must acknowledge that the archaeological evidence is essentially silent (*The Settlement of the Israelite Tribes in Palestine*, trans. James Martin [Naperville, Ill.: Allenson, 1971], pp. 128–29). J. Maxwell Miller, who views the occupation as a violent overthrow, nonetheless must concede that "the available archaeological evidence simply does not square very well with the biblical account of the conquest regardless of what one proposes as a date" ("Archaeology and the Israelite Conquest of Canaan: Some Methodological Observations," *PEQ* 109 [1977]: 88). Of course, one would not expect the evidence to agree if a wrong interpretation is given to the conquest.

61. For Gilgal as an ideal logistic and strategic center see Abraham Malamat, "How Inferior Israelite Forces Conquered Fortified Canaanite Cities," *BAR* 8 (1982): 31.

fore long, however, he undertook the final phase of his plan, the invasion of the Canaanite lands in the Valley of Jezreel and in Galilee to the north. The Canaanites by now were well aware of all that had transpired in the central and southern parts of Palestine and so hastily created an alliance to withstand what they knew to be certain conflict with Israel.

The initiator and leader of the alliance was Jabin king of Hazor (Tell el-Qedaḥ), the largest city of the north and possibly of all Canaan. This metropolis, covering over 110 acres and housing perhaps as many as forty thousand people, was strategically located on a high mound about twelve miles north of the Sea of Galilee and less than five southwest of Lake Huleh (the waters of Merom).[62] It had traditionally been recognized as the leading city of the region (Josh. 11:10), so it was not difficult for Jabin to enlist the support of his neighbors. These included Jobab king of Madon (Qarn Hattin), about five miles west of Tiberias, and the kings of Shimron (Tell Semuniyeh) and Acshaph (Tell Keisan). Shimron lay on the northern edge of the Plain of Jezreel, about fifteen miles from the Mediterranean, and Acshaph was about six miles southeast of Acco. Hazor's immediate sphere of influence thus extended in a semicircle to her south and west with a radius of about forty miles. Other kings enlisted but not named ruled over territories in north Galilee, in the Jordan valley south of Kinnereth (the Sea of Galilee), in the lowland (the Plain of Jezreel), and in the heights of Dor, probably the southern slopes of the Carmel range along the Mediterranean. In addition Jabin solicited the support of Canaanite, Amorite, Hittite, Perizzite, Jebusite, and Hivite rulers on both sides of the Jordan and from Hermon in the north to the hill country of Ephraim. With a massive deployment of infantry and chariotry these combined forces awaited the coming of Israel near the waters of Merom, a natural battlefield.

With a lightninglike charge Joshua set upon the Canaanites and completely overwhelmed them. Those who could escaped and fled as far as Sidon, more than forty miles to the north; to Misrephoth Maim (Khirbet el-Musheirefeh), on the seacoast between Carmel and Tyre; and to the Valley of Mizpah (Marj-'Ayyun?),[63] just south of Mount Hermon. Joshua then attacked Hazor itself, took (*lākad*) the city, killed its king, and slaughtered its populace. Then, in what clearly was an exception to the policy he had followed up to this point, he set the city afire and leveled it to the ground. If convincing proof is yet needed that taking a city and putting it to the sword is not tantamount to

---

62. For the excavation and history of the site see Avraham Negev, ed., *Archaeological Encyclopedia of the Holy Land* (Englewood, N.J.: SBS, 1980), pp. 138–41.
63. Aharoni, *Land of the Bible*, p. 239.

material destruction, note the manner in which the historian describes what happened to the remaining cities. Israel, he says, took the cities in league with Hazor, struck them with the edge of the sword, totally destroying them, but *burned none of them except Hazor* (Josh. 11:12–13). To take and to subject a city to the sword, even to the extent of placing it under the ban, is not necessarily to reduce it to ashes. When such is the case, as here with Hazor, an explicit statement that the city itself was burned follows.

The Date of Joshua's Conquest

The reason we have emphasized, perhaps to the weariness of the reader, that most of the Canaanite cities were not materially destroyed by Joshua is that, of all the arguments used in support of any date suggested for the conquest, that of archaeological attestation of violent conflagration of Canaanite cities has been the most important.[64] Indeed, without the archaeological argument few grounds remain for the late date (thirteenth century). The massive thirteenth-century destruction documented by archaeological research is attributed by most scholars to the Israelite conquest. On the strength of this assumption the traditional date for the conquest (the early fourteenth century) has had to be rejected. As a corollary, the early date for the exodus (1446) has also had to be adjusted.

Besides resulting in a cavalier and uncritical rejection of the clear and consistent biblical witness, this assumption based on archaeology is just that, an assumption, and an ill-founded one at that. First, there are no extant documents from the thirteenth century to provide written testimony identifying either the inhabitants of the destroyed cities or their destroyers. It is presumptive, on the basis of nonliterary artifacts, to maintain that the destroyed cities of thirteenth-century Canaan were populated by Canaanites and demolished by Israelites. There is so little cultural difference between sites that are clearly Canaanite and those clearly Israelite that a Canaanite city cannot, on cultural grounds, be distinguished from an Israelite city.[65] The devastation of cities throughout Canaan (or Israel) in the thirteenth century, a trag-

---

64. Yigael Yadin, for example, argues that "archaeology broadly confirms that at the end of the Late Bronze Age, semi-nomadic Israelites destroyed a number of major Canaanite cities; then, gradually and slowly, they built their own sedentary settlements on the ruins" ("Is the Biblical Account of the Israelite Conquest of Canaan Historically Reliable?" *BAR* 8 [1982]: 23). It is amazing that Yadin misreads the biblical account of the conquest and fails to be open to the possibility that the Late Bronze destruction is to be attributed to the era of the judges rather than to that of the conquest.

65. Kenyon, *Archaeology*, p. 209.

edy whose reality and general time frame cannot be denied, can be as
easily explained as the overrunning of Israelite cities and towns by
their enemies in the days of the judges as it can be explained as the
overrunning of Canaanite cities and towns during the Israelite conquest. Furthermore, Old Testament chronology requires that the suffering of Israel during, for example, the time of Deborah (see p. 164)
fall squarely in the period alleged to be that of the conquest—the
thirteenth century.

The second and more telling reason for the rejection of a thirteenth-
century date for the conquest is, ironically, the archaeological attestation of massive ruin in that era. If the thesis being argued here—
that Joshua deliberately undertook and successfully pursued a policy
of preservation of urban structures—is correct, and the biblical record
consistently confirms it, it follows that evidence of destruction in the
early fourteenth century would be an embarrassing contradiction to
the biblical witness. Thus, the efforts of some conservative scholars to
interpret artifactual evidence to favor an early date must be given up
as fruitless.

As pointed out earlier, only three cities—Jericho, Ai, and Hazor—
were clearly placed under unqualified *ḥērem* and totally destroyed.
Jericho and Ai, for reasons already given, are of no help in establishing
chronology. This leaves only Hazor, about which, unfortunately, much
controversy swirls. In his initial publications of Hazor its excavator,
Yigael Yadin, argued unequivocally that Hazor underwent one of its
many conflagrations in about 1400, exactly the date suggested by the
traditional chronology.[66] Later, however, Yadin revised his estimate
downward by 150 years, thus allowing it to conform to the thirteenth-
century date accepted by most scholars. This revision in turn has not
gone unchallenged. John Bimson, for example, in a meticulously researched analysis of the archaeological data from Hazor and elsewhere, has shown that Yadin's adjustment was not only unnecessary
but completely unwarranted. The date Yadin originally proposed, that
is, 1400, is in fact correct. And so the one site which can be used in
our discussion—Hazor—undeniably supports an early date for the
conquest.[67]

The summary of all three phases of the conquest (Josh. 11:16–20)
confirms the interpretation of its nature and extent which we have
proposed all along. The narrator says that Joshua took all the land
from Mount Halak (Jebel Halaq), deep in the Negev, to Baal Gad, in
the Bekaa Valley west of Hermon. He captured and put to death all

66. Yigael Yadin, "Further Light on Biblical Hazor," *BA* 20 (1957): 44; "The Third
Season of Excavation at Hazor, 1957," *BA* 21 (1958): 30–47.
67. Bimson, *Redating*, pp. 185–200.

the kings of the area and totally destroyed the populations except for the Gibeonites, who had tricked Joshua into making covenant with them. Not one word is mentioned about material destruction, however, though one would expect it here if anywhere, since this passage recapitulates the general policy and procedure.

The Campaign Against the Anakim

As almost an addendum to the main account of the conquest the historian refers to a special campaign of Joshua to deal with the problem of the Anakim (Josh. 11:21–23). Israel had encountered this race of giants previously in the course of spying out the land of Canaan (Num. 13:21–33). The Old Testament traces their origin to a certain Anak (Num. 13:22), a descendant of Arba (Josh. 15:13), after whom the city of Kiriath Arba, later known as Hebron, was named (Josh. 14:15). In Joshua's time the Anakim consisted of three major clans—the sons of Ahiman, Sheshai, and Talmai (Num. 13:22; Josh. 15:14), most of whom lived in the hill country of Judah. The historian probably singles out this particular operation because it was the Anakim who had terrorized the Israelite scouts, except for Joshua and Caleb, and had indirectly been the cause of the long delay in Israel's conquest of the land. It was altogether fitting that Joshua himself return to the strongholds of the Anakim to demonstrate the superiority of Yahweh over even these giant foes.

It is difficult to date this expedition against the Anakim, though the phrase "at that time" (Josh. 11:21) would certainly appear to link this event with the previous accounts. Moreover, we are told that Caleb was granted the cities of Hebron and Debir as his inheritance and to secure them had to drive out the Anakim (Josh. 15:13–15). There is no doubt that Joshua's razzia against the Anakim was Caleb's as well—the two worked in concert with Joshua in command. This campaign obviously followed Caleb's request for his inheritance, a request which he made in his eighty-fifth year (ca. 1399 B.C.—see Josh. 14:7, 10). He specifically asked for the hill country of Hebron, to which Joshua gladly gave assent. How much time elapsed between assignment of Hebron to Caleb and the military operation which actually placed it in his hands cannot be known, though, as suggested already, "at that time" would suggest only a brief interlude.

The Anakim who survived were now confined to Gaza, Gath, and Ashdod, three of the five Philistine cities. Perhaps Goliath and the other gigantic "Philistines" were not true Philistines after all. They may well have been descendants of Anak who lived among the Philistines and for that reason were so identified.

Alternative Models of the Conquest and Occupation

Joshua 12–19 consists essentially of the tribal allocations. Once the initial conquest was completed, a task which took about seven years (ca. 1406–1399), it was necessary for the process of occupation to begin, for the abandoned cities would soon be repossessed by the people of the land were Israel to remain much longer outside them. One may assume that some such occupation had been in progress all this time, but it is clear that for the most part Israel remained concentrated in and about Gilgal. Indeed, until distribution of the conquered land was determined by lot and other means, no official or permanent residence could be taken up. Before the settlement patterns are described, however, it is well to consider briefly two alternative ways of viewing the conquest and settlement: the traditio-critical and sociological approaches. Since each of these approaches has produced a variety of models, only the best-known or most popular model of each will be analyzed here.

The Traditio-historical Model

The documentary and developmental hypotheses of Old Testament criticism which have dominated biblical scholarship for the past two hundred years have produced a particular approach to the question of Israel's origins and nature which challenges the straightforward account of the Old Testament narrative itself. The thesis of this book, however, is that the Old Testament record of Israel's history, including that of her origins, is to be accepted *prima facie* as reliable historiography unless there are compelling reasons, internal or external, to do otherwise. Among the internal problems which have been adduced as reasons to call the trustworthiness of the biblical witness into question are the presence of alleged contradictions, doublets (dual accounts of the same event), and the like. External considerations consist of extrabiblical archaeological and historical data which appear to contradict the biblical point of view. If one can demonstrate, however, that all the internal and external problems that have been adduced as reasons for rejecting the Old Testament's own witness are themselves capable of explanation and resolution within the traditional biblical framework, there is no longer any reason to doubt the Old Testament record. Though one can never hope to do this to everyone's satisfaction, since theological, philosophical, and various other assumptions underlie every discipline including historiography, one can nonetheless hope that the unbiased student will recognize that the biblical construction of Israel's history has as much claim to reliability as any other. Nowhere can this be better demonstrated than in the case of the conquest and settlement of Israel in Canaan.

No modern scholar has dominated the discussion of Israel's origins and development more than has Martin Noth. His analysis of the matter will therefore serve as representative of the mainstream traditio-historical school.[68] Virtually all proponents of this school agree that there was a twelve-tribe confederacy known as Israel by 1200 B.C. at the latest. This is based on the existence of admittedly early poetic compositions, such as the "Song of Deborah" (Judg. 5), which attest to the fact of confederacy. The fact then requires explanation. What compelling reasons could have created the unification of tribal units which obviously at one time existed independently? Here there is difference of opinion. Noth argues that one cannot know what produced the union, but that once it was formed it created a common religious faith.[69] John Bright, on the other hand, maintains that this is exactly the reverse of what would normally occur and that it must be the common faith which drew the tribes together.[70] Both agree, however, that the merging of the tribes brought about a commingling of both religious and historical traditions imparted to the league by the various tribes, with the result that each tradition became the common property of all Israel. This implies that the tribes did not in fact have a common origin certainly they were not descended from twelve sons of one father; rather, the Old Testament story of common origin simply reflects the final product of the merging of traditions.

The confederation is further explained on the basis of political and geographical exigencies. The Israelite tribes, it is held, were primarily if not totally non-Canaanite, and in the face of Canaanite and especially Philistine pressures were forced to align themselves together to preserve common interests and avoid destruction or assimilation. Moreover, many of the tribes may indeed have shared similar historical experiences or traditions. For example, they may have been nomadic, they may have experienced oppressive slavery, or they may have embraced similar pantheons of deities for whatever reason. These

68. Martin Noth, *Das System der zwölf Stämme Israels* (Darmstadt: Wissenschaftliche Buchgesellschaft, 1966); *History of Pentateuchal Traditions*, trans. Bernhard W. Anderson (Englewood Cliffs, N.J.: Prentice-Hall, 1972); *The History of Israel*, 2d ed. (New York: Harper and Row, 1960), esp. pp. 53–163. For a presentation and critique of the Noth hypothesis as well as alternative reconstructions see J. Liver, "The Israelite Tribes," in *World History of the Jewish People*, vol. 3, *Judges*, ed. Benjamin Mazar (Tel Aviv: Massada, 1971), pp. 193–208.

69. Noth, *History of Israel*, pp. 137–38.

70. John Bright, *A History of Israel*, 3d ed. (Philadelphia: Westminster, 1981), pp. 148–50, 164–65.

factors would all be conducive to amalgamation once together in the same land.

A rather typical reconstruction of how this process came about is as follows. Some tribes, perhaps all, were descended from Amorite immigrants to Canaan who arrived in the period 2200–2000 B.C. from the upper Euphrates-Balikh-Habor region. Some of them (Asher, Naphtali, Zebulun, Gad, Issachar) were successful in their attempts at settlement. Others, being less successful, scattered widely. Reuben was restricted to the east side of the Dead Sea and began to die out. Simeon and Levi tried to take Shechem but were repelled. Simeon, as a result, became greatly diminished in population and eventually was absorbed into Judah. Levi was either forced to go to Egypt or was dispersed throughout Canaan, never again to exist as a political entity. Joseph (Ephraim and Manasseh) went on to settle in Egypt. An alternative view is that these two tribes originated in the desert country east of Jericho and entered Canaan during the Amarna period, perhaps as the infamous 'apiru of the Amarna Letters. Judah resided from earliest times in the Negev, probably around Kadesh Barnea. Dan was at first restricted to a tiny area near the Plain of Sharon and later, under (Philistine?) pressure, was forced to relocate far in the north at Laish. Finally, Benjamin, originally in the east with the Joseph tribes, settled down in a small area in central Canaan (around Jericho).

The exodus, then, did not involve all the tribes by any means, but only Levi and the Joseph tribes at most or perhaps Levi alone. Strong and persistent biblical tradition links Moses to the tribe of Levi; since Moses was in Egypt, the tribe of Levi must also have been there. If the Joshua-Moses relationship has any historical basis, then Ephraim also must be an exodus tribe because Joshua came from Ephraim. And no one can deny the brotherhood of Ephraim and Manasseh, so Manasseh must also have settled in Egypt. This poses a very real problem for the many scholars who, while holding to a late date for the exodus, wish to identify the 'apiru with Ephraim and Manasseh: they need to push the activity of the Joseph tribes in Canaan more than a century before the date of the exodus. This means that Joshua preceded Moses chronologically and that if Joshua was a participant in an exodus, it could not have been that of Moses. Perhaps, then, the Joseph tribes had been in Egypt with Levi but left more than a century earlier under Joshua. Moses' later dominance in their relationship is not so much the reflection of historical fact as the result of the strength of the tradition which featured Moses as deliverer and lawgiver.

So, it is alleged, Moses led at least Levi to Sinai where he was introduced to Yahwism by the Midianite priest Jethro. Knowing already of the "gods of the fathers" (Elohim, El Shaddai, etc.) through his own tribal traditions, Moses made his greatest and most creative contribution by identifying the Midianite desert and mountain god Yahweh as both the God responsible for the exodus deliverance and the God of his ancestors, the God who had always been there but had not been known by this name. Moses therefore became a missionary for Yahweh, and when he and his tribe Levi encountered Judah at Kadesh Barnea, Judah converted to Yahwism. Judah then moved north into Canaan, assimilated Simeon, and became the very center of Yahwism. The J document, the alleged pentateuchal source which emphasizes the divine name *Yahweh* (*Jahve* in German), eventually was created in Judah and disseminated from there to all Israel, probably in the days of Solomon. When Moses arrived in the Transjordan, he came across Reuben and Gad. These tribes preferred to remain there, but they too embraced Yahwism and at the same time imparted to Moses traditions of their own which came to be accepted as normative for all Israel. Moses then died. According to the view that the Joseph tribes participated in the Mosaic exodus, they and Levi were led by Joshua across the Jordan in about 1250. He there joined both Judah and Benjamin to the south with the indigenous tribes of the north (Asher, Naphtali, Zebulun, Gad, Issachar) by settling his tribes, Ephraim and Manasseh, in the hill country between them. Thus the whole land from Dan to Beersheba came to be occupied by non-Canaanite tribes that eventually regarded themselves as having a common origin and history.[71]

The thesis then goes on to explain how the merging of traditions might have occurred. It is likely that the tribes had early on recognized (whether accurately or not) a common Aramean origin and common eponymous ancestors and deities. Moses introduced Yahwism to Levi, Joseph, Judah, Reuben, and Gad. Joshua then encouraged Yahwism among the indigenous tribes with the result that traditional tribal distinctives became submerged in the interests of a common pan-Israelite history and faith. The formal creation of this bond may be seen in the Shechem convocation of Joshua 24. The question as to whether the "conversion" produced the unity or the political unity the conversion yet remains, however.

Again turning to Noth and his construct of an amphictyonic league,[72] we observe that he and many tradition critics insist that the confederation was based on a common acceptance of several originally independent traditions:

71. For a variation of this scenario see Benjamin Mazar, "The Exodus and the Conquest," in *World History of the Jewish People*, vol. 3, pp. 79–93.

72. A definition of "amphictyonic" and a strong protest against the view that ancient Israel's tribal union was of such a nature may be found in N. P. Lemche, "The Greek 'Amphictyony'—Could It Be a Prototype for the Israelite Society in the Period of the Judges?" *JSOT* 4 (1977): 48–59.

1. The promises to the fathers. Some of the tribes understood their existence in and rights to the land of Canaan as the fulfilment of promises made by God to their ancestors.
2. A miraculous deliverance. Rescue from bondage was experienced by some of the tribes, though Noth is not sure which. Amazingly, he disassociates Moses from the original event.
3. A manifestation of God in covenant. Some tribe or tribes, again unidentified but probably including Levi at least, experienced something profoundly significant at Sinai, which they took to be a revelation of Yahweh.
4. A wilderness wandering. Since the theme of a wilderness sojourn is so dominant in the tradition, some of the tribes must have had such an experience.
5. A conquest or inheritance of the land. Since conquest, too, is a major motif, at least some of the tribes must have acquired their territories by force.

These five major traditions, distributed somehow among the twelve tribes, eventually were reshaped and refined and became the common stock of the entire confederation. Thus pentateuchal (or hexateuchal) history as it appears in the canonical Old Testament is a blending and editing of these and perhaps other originally independent strands. The redaction was so artfully done that one can scarcely see the seams where they were stitched together. The naive reader, it is suggested, fails to see that underlying what at first glance is a beautifully consistent rendering of the early history of Israel is a complex process of collecting, editing, and weaving together of materials whose essential historical value is highly suspect at best. We can know nothing of that history as it really happened. We can know only how the redactors perceived that history to be as they appropriated the traditions for their own theological, political, or apologetic purposes.[73]

The Sociological Model

If the traditio-historical model is an unsatisfying reconstruction, what may be said of recent attempts to view the conquest and settlement along certain sociological models, especially as a peasant re-

---

73. For a clear presentation of the philosophy and method underlying the alleged redaction see J. Maxwell Miller, *The Old Testament and the Historian* (Philadelphia: Fortress, 1976), esp. pp. 49–69.

volt?[74] This approach finds its fullest and clearest expression in the massive work of Norman Gottwald, *The Tribes of Yahweh*. It is Gottwald's thesis, based on the work of George Mendenhall,[75] Robertson Smith,[76] and Max Weber,[77] that the Israelite confederation came about as the result of an organized peasant revolt which challenged the Canaanite state. Though not denying the non-Canaanite origin and identity of the Israelite tribes, Gottwald minimizes that point and concentrates on the *de facto* existence of Israel in Canaan and her efforts to achieve a new social order there.[78]

The movement began, Gottwald says, with the Amarna age 'apiru, who provided a model for the peasants to emulate. Next followed the binding together of previously separate groups by cultic, sociopolitical, and military interests. These he calls Elohistic Israel. Finally emerged a coalition of the 'apiru, Elohists, and transhumant pastoralists from Canaan and Egypt, an association which called itself Israel and which now worshiped Yahweh.[79] In sum, Gottwald's hypothesis is not related at all to the notion of conquest but has to do with class struggles between peasants (Israel) and nobility (the Canaanites). The end results were tribal confederation and, in turn, a monarchy.

It is not possible nor necessary to challenge this model here and now. First of all, it has met with vigorous criticism by scholars of all stripes as reference to reviews of *The Tribes of Yahweh* will show.[80] Second, as J. Maxwell Miller points out, it is a "modern construct superimposed upon the biblical traditions"[81] and lacks even a hint of support in the biblical texts. It is, in effect, a hypothesis (peasant re-

74. An excellent review of recent sociological approaches to Israelite history and literature is that of Walter Brueggemann, "Trajectories in OT Literature and the Sociology of Ancient Israel," *JBL* 98 (1979): 161–85.

75. George E. Mendenhall, *The Tenth Generation: The Origins of the Biblical Tradition* (Baltimore: Johns Hopkins University Press, 1973).

76. W. Robertson Smith, *Lectures on the Religion of the Semites* (Edinburgh: Adam and Charles Black, 1889); *Kinship and Marriage in Early Arabia* (London: Adam and Charles Black, 1903).

77. Max Weber, *The Sociology of Religion*, trans. Ephraim Fischoff (Boston: Beacon, 1963).

78. Gottwald, *Tribes of Yahweh*, pp. 210–19.

79. Ibid., p. 497. This hypothesis presupposes a mass religious conversion for which there is no evidence. See Jacob Milgrom, "Religious Conversion and the Revolt Model for the Formation of Israel," *JBL* 101 (1982): 169, 175–76.

80. Marvin L. Chaney, *JBL* 103 (1984): 89–93; Walter R. Wifall, "The Tribes of Yahweh: A Synchronic Study with a Diachronic Title," *ZAW* 95 (1983): 197–209; Eugene H. Merrill, *Bib Sac* 138 (1981): 81–82; Frederic R. Brandfon, "Norman Gottwald on the Tribes of Yahweh," *JSOT* 21 (1981): 101–10.

81. J. Maxwell Miller, "The Israelite Occupation of Canaan," in *Israelite and Judaean History*, ed. John H. Hayes and J. Maxwell Miller (Philadelphia: Westminster, 1977), p. 279.

volt) built on a hypothesis (tradition criticism à la Noth and others), an approach which in most academic disciplines would subject its proponent to scorn and rejection as a scientific investigator.

To return to the biblical historian's account, we are impressed by the lack of any need to rescue his credibility or to explain away the means by which the conquest and occupation were reportedly accomplished. There is nothing improbable in the report that several hundred thousand people set up temporary encampment at Gilgal while their fighting men undertook military missions against cities and towns the length and breadth of Canaan. The region around Gilgal, Jericho, and the lower Jordan valley is well able to sustain a population of this size both in terms of its area and the availability of pasturage, cultivable fields, and water. There is nothing in the record to preclude a wide-ranging occupation of the region extending perhaps over a large part of the western slopes of the valley. That Joshua and Israel should be so eminently successful in their military exploits is not surprising either. The Canaanites and their allies had already been demoralized by news of Israel's past victories and impending invasion. Moreover, they were sorely unprepared and, in fact, were at each other's throats in constant internecine warfare right up until the conquest began. Also, Israel must have greatly outnumbered the enemy except possibly in the northern campaign against Hazor. Last, but certainly not least, Yahweh himself fought for Israel. This was holy war, and by divine intervention deeds were accomplished that otherwise could never have been done. To argue that the conquest as the Bible describes it was impossible because it required or presupposed the supernatural is to argue against that which is central to biblical faith: God could and did bare his mighty arm to enable his people to have victory against impossible odds. This can be challenged not on historical grounds but only theological.

The Tribal Allotments

The allotment of the conquered land to the tribes and their occupation of it are also not inconceivable. The process was, admittedly, very complex, and some of the reports appear to be conflicting. Nevertheless, that Joshua did cast lots, did supervise the efforts at settlement, and did live to see most of this objective realized does not tax the imagination. Indeed, all scholars agree that there was a time in Canaan when there were no Israelites, and that eventually the composition of the population was such that the whole land was called

Israel.[82] The traditio-critical view allows only about 200 years for this metamorphosis to take place, whereas the traditional view has 350 years at its disposal, a likelier length of time for the complex and difficult transition from Canaanite to Israelite implied by the Old Testament and required also by alternative hypotheses.

The Overall Distribution

Joshua's distribution of the land is introduced by a general description of the boundaries of the Transjordanian territories (Josh. 12:1–6) and a list of all the principal cities taken in Canaan proper (vv. 7–24). Reuben, Gad, and half the tribe of Manasseh had requested and received the former kingdoms of Sihon and Og, the Amorite rulers of Heshbon and Bashan respectively. This included everything from the Arnon River on the south to Mount Hermon on the north, and from the Sea of Kinnereth, the Jordan valley, and the Dead Sea on the west to the deserts and the kingdom of Ammon on the east. The inheritance of the remaining tribes consisted of the thirty-one cities listed and no doubt a great many others of lesser importance. The order of the list suggests the order of conquest, though a number of the cities are not mentioned in the conquest narratives.

Despite the apparent extensiveness of the conquest there were areas adjacent to those brought under control and even some pockets within them which had remained untaken (Josh. 13:1–7). This included all the Philistine territory from Wadi el-Arish on the south to Ekron on the north, that is, the Shephelah and coastal plain. The Philistines lived mainly in their five important towns, but other people such as the Geshurites[83] and Avvim lived among them, particularly in the southern desert areas (Josh. 13:1–4a). In the north of Canaan the unconquered sections stretched from Mearah (unknown), a Sidonian dependency, to Aphek on the border of the Amorites. This is probably Afqa, just southeast of Byblos in Phoenicia.[84] The "Amorites" then would not refer to those of Canaan, but to the kingdom of Amurru which controlled central Syria. This apparently was the northern boundary of the Promised Land.[85] The eastern boundary of the north-

---

82. For a moderately critical view which takes the biblical tradition seriously see Yohanan Aharoni, "The Settlement of Canaan," in *World History of the Jewish People*, ed. Benjamin Mazar, vol. 3, pp. 94–128.

83. These Geshurites, who lived in a yet unidentified location in the Negev, must not be confused with those of the kingdom of Geshur to the east of the Sea of Galilee. See Soggin, *Joshua*, p. 132.

84. Aharoni, *Land of the Bible*, p. 238.

85. M. Liverani, "The Amorites," in *Peoples of Old Testament Times*, ed. D. J. Wiseman, pp. 123–26.

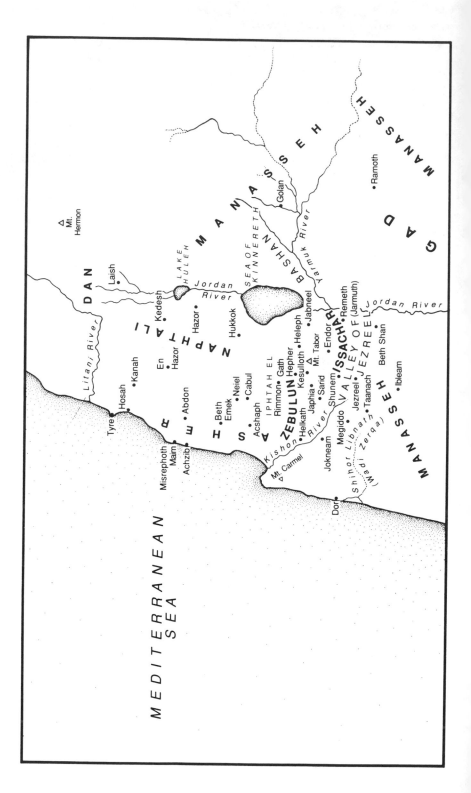

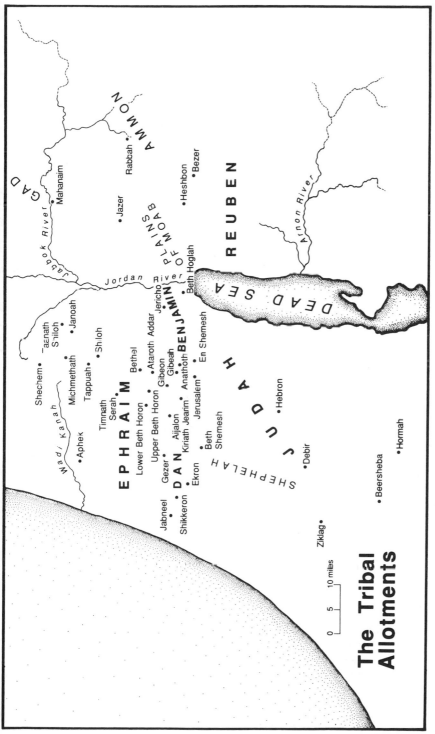

The Tribal
Allotments

0   5   10 miles

AMMON

GAD

Rabbah •

Mahanaim •

Jazer •

• Heshbon

• Bezer

REUBEN

PLAINS OF MOAB

Jabbok River

Jordan River

Arnon River

DEAD SEA

Beth Hoglah •

Jericho •

Ataroth Addar •

BENJAMIN

Anathoth •

Gibeah •

Gibeon •

• Bethel

• En Shemesh

Jerusalem •

Shechem •

Tirzath
Shiloh •

• Janoah

Tappuah •

• Shiloh

Michmethath •

EPHRAIM

Timnath
Serah •

Lower Beth Horon •

Upper Beth Horon •

• Aphek

Wadi Kanah

Jabneel •

Gezer •

Shikkeron •

DAN

Aijalon •

Kiriath Jearim •

Ekron •

Beth
Shemesh •

JUDAH

• Hebron

SHEPHELAH

• Debir

• Hormah

• Beersheba

Ziklag •

ern territories not yet subjugated extended from Baal Gad, just west of Mount Hermon, to Lebo Hamath (or "the entrance of Hamath") in the Bekaa just east of Gebal (Byblos). The southern boundary then would extend northeasterly from Misrephoth Maim, on the Mediterranean coast about eighteen miles south of Tyre, to Baal Gad.[86] The area enclosed in these borders would include the kingdoms of Tyre, Sidon, and perhaps part of Gebal. Geographically it embraced the Lebanon mountain range from the Orontes valley south to the hills of Galilee and everything from the Mediterranean to the Bekaa Valley. Subsequent events show that this northern region was seldom if ever under Israelite domination.

The Specific Distribution

The land that was in fact in Israelite hands was apportioned as follows. Reuben received the area east of the Dead Sea and between the Arnon River on the south and a line about fifteen miles north of the Dead Sea, somewhere just south of Jazer. Gad claimed everything north of Jazer and along the Jordan to the Sea of Kinnereth. Its eastern border ran from a few miles west of the Ammonite city of Rabbah northwesterly to Mahanaim on the Jabbok River and thence up the Jordan valley to Kinnereth. The eastern territory of Manasseh included the land between Ammon to the east and Gad to the west. Its southernmost point was at Mahanaim, and it stretched north beyond the Yarmuk. Gad thus occupied roughly the southern and western parts of the Transjordan area and Manasseh the northern and eastern parts. The allocations described in Joshua 13 appear to be at variance with those of Numbers 32. There is every reason to believe, however, that the two passages, rather than being contradictory, as many scholars would suggest,[87] reflect the original Mosaic distribution and changes under Joshua several years later. The earlier distribution interspersed Reuben and Gad, creating the potential for bitter strife later on.[88] Joshua, then, may have reassigned the territory of these tribes to preclude this very possibility.

Joshua and Eleazar the priest then turned to the task of determining the pattern of settlement in Canaan proper for the remaining tribes (Josh. 14:1–5). First came the leaders of Judah with their aged spokesman Caleb. Joshua was reminded of Moses' promise that Caleb would

86. Yohanan Aharoni and Michael Avi-Yonah, *Macmillan Bible Atlas* (New York: Macmillan, 1968), map 62, equate Misrephoth Maim with the Litani River, which is otherwise unmentioned in the Old Testament.

87. Butler, *Joshua*, pp. 157–63.

88. Eugene H. Merrill, "Numbers," in *The Bible Knowledge Commentary*, ed. John F. Walvoord and Roy B. Zuck (Wheaton, Ill.: Victor, 1985), vol. 1, p. 252.

someday receive a portion of the land on which he had walked as a spy. This, Caleb said, had taken place forty-five years previously when he was forty years old. The scouting party had gone out in the second year after the exodus (1445 B.C.), so Caleb's reminder to Joshua must be dated at about 1399 or seven years after the conquest began. When the spies returned, Caleb, with Joshua, had encouraged Israel to enter Canaan despite the Anakim who lived in the southern hills. Now Caleb pressed his claim against these same Anakim and was given Hebron and other Anakim cities. The conquest of Hebron must have followed this bequest (Josh. 11:21–22; 15:13–19; Judg. 1:9–15).

After displacing the Anakim from Hebron, Caleb also took Debir, fifteen miles southwest. This he achieved by offering his daughter as wife to any hero who could take the town, a feat accomplished by his own nephew Othniel. Apparently Othniel, later Israel's first judge, settled in Debir—an inference drawn from his wife's requesting a dowry of springs of water near the town. One is tempted to assume that this conquest of Hebron and Debir is the same as that described in Joshua 11:21–23, since both cities are mentioned there as well. The connection between the two cities evidently lies in their both being populated by Anakim, a people particularly odious to Caleb.

The rest of Judah's inheritance consisted of a large area bounded by a line on the south from the Dead Sea southwest to Kadesh Barnea and thence northwest to the mouth of the Wadi el-Arish. The eastern border was the Dead Sea and the western, at least theoretically, the Mediterranean. The northern frontier began just above the effluence of the Jordan into the Dead Sea and ran west through Beth Hoglah ('Ain Ḥajlah) to the waters of En Shemesh ('Ain el-Ḥod) and En Rogel, at the junction of the Kidron and Hinnom valleys at Jerusalem. Its course up the Hinnom implies that Jerusalem itself lay north of Judah in the territory of Benjamin. From Jerusalem Judah's boundary continued west to Kiriath Jearim (modern Tell el-Azhar) and Beth Shemesh (Tell er-Rumeileh). Finally it passed through Shikkeron (Tell el-Fûl), just north of Ekron, and to the Mediterranean near Jabneel (Yebna). The list of cities which follows the boundary delineation includes both those actually taken in the conquest and those which were Judah's by promise only. The reference to Jerusalem (Josh. 15:63) does not imply that that city was allotted to Judah, but only that Judah had made an unsuccessful attempt to evict the Jebusites permanently (cf. Judg. 1:8).

The inheritance of Ephraim (Josh. 16:5–10) was marked by borders commencing at Ataroth Addar (Kefr 'Aqab),[89] eight miles due north of Jerusalem. The south border then went west to Upper Beth Horon (Beit 'Ur el-Foqa) and presumably southwest to join the border of Judah

89. *Oxford Bible Atlas*, p. 123.

somewhere near Shikkeron. On the north the beginning point was Michmethath (Khirbet Makhneh el-Foqa), less than five miles south of Shechem. From Michmethath the boundary went east to Taanath Shiloh (Khirbet Ta'na el-Foqa) and Janoah (Khirbet Yanun), south toward Jericho, and east to the Jordan. The southern boundary then must have begun at the Jordan and headed west through Jericho to Ataroth Addar. Again from Michmethath the northern border went west to Tappuah (Sheikh Abu Zarad) to the Wadi Kanah and down its course to the Mediterranean, joining the sea at modern Tel Aviv. In addition Ephraim was assigned certain cities within Manasseh (Josh. 16:9). Other cities remained in Canaanite hands, notably Gezer; and a number of Canaanites lived amongst the Ephraimites as slaves.

The clans of Manasseh which did not remain in the Transjordan occupied the area just north of Ephraim all the way to the Jezreel Valley on the north. The southern border, then, was Ephraim's northern boundary. The town of Tappuah, which was geographically a part of the region of Tappuah, was allotted for some reason to Ephraim (Josh. 17:8). On the other hand, Manasseh took certain towns that geographically might have been more appropriate to Asher and Issachar, namely, Beth Shan (Tell el-Ḥuṣn or Beisan), Ibleam (Khirbet Bel'ameh), Dor (Khirbet el-Burj), Endor (Khirbet Ṣafṣâfeh), Taanach (Tell Ti'innik), and Megiddo (Tell el-Mutesellim). Because of Canaanite entrenchment in this northern region, however, Manasseh could not possess these cities at once, but only gradually subdued the Canaanites, putting them to slave labor. Both Ephraim and Manasseh felt the constraints of these Canaanite elements in the valleys and plains which adjoined their territories and so demanded of Joshua that he give them more land. To this Joshua replied that they should drive out the Canaanites who already lived among them in the wooded hills; then gradually they would be strong enough to remove the Canaanites from Jezreel as well (Josh. 17:14–18).

Seven tribes yet remained to whom the rest of the land had to be assigned. Joshua therefore gathered their leaders to Shiloh (Khirbet Seilun), the new cultic and political center,[90] and advised them to send out scouts through the regions yet to be allocated. These scouts returned with a report describing the land and advising how it could best be apportioned.

Following the report Joshua resumed the process of distribution. First, Benjamin received the small area between Judah and Ephraim, including the important cities of Jericho, Bethel, Gibeah, Gibeon, and

90. Though Shiloh "was largely uninhabited throughout the Late Bronze Age" (Boling, *Joshua*, p. 422), it was occupied at times and clearly could have served as the cult center of Israel in the fourteenth century onward.

Jerusalem. Simeon, perhaps decimated by the judgment of Yahweh at Peor, had insufficient population to warrant a separate district and so was in effect a clan within Judah. Some of their major towns were Beersheba, Hormah, and Ziklag, later famous as the Philistine fiefdom of David.

North of the Valley of Jezreel was the allotment of Zebulun. From Sarid (Tell Shadud), less than ten miles north of Megiddo across the Jezreel plain, Zebulun's southern border went west to Jokneam (Tell Qeimun). From Sarid east the border went toward Japhia (Yafa) and then north to Gath Hepher (Khirbet ez-Zurra') and Rimmon (Rummaneh). Just above Rimmon the boundary turned west through the Valley of Iphtah El (Wadi el-Malik).

The second tribe assigned to the Galilee region was Issachar. Its western border was on a line from Jezreel (Zer'in) north through Shunem (Sôlem) to Kesulloth (Chisloth-tabor). East from Jezreel the border ran toward Remeth (Jarmuth),[91] three miles from the Jordan and eight north of Beth Shan. From there it proceeded north along the Jordan and then west to Mount Tabor. Issachar, then, had a very small portion, much of which was Canaanite-controlled in early history.

Asher was on the Mediterranean coast north of Mount Carmel. From Helkath (Tell el-Qassis) on the Kishon its border went north to Acshaph and probably to Achzib (ez-Zîb). On the south the border began at the Mediterranean coast and touched Mount Carmel and Shihor Libnath (Wadi Zerqa).[92] It then turned northeast along the border of Zebulun and the Iphtah El Valley. From there it turned north to Beth Emek (Tell Mîmâs), passing through Neiel (Khirbet Ya'nîn) and Cabul (Kābûl), and then proceeded farther north to Ebron (Abdon?), Kanah (Qânā), and Hosah (Usu?) on the Mediterranean just four or five miles south of Tyre. The border then, of course, followed the Mediterranean coast south to Achzib.

There are many problems in attempting to reconstruct Asher's boundaries, chief of which is the tribe's apparent loss of Mount Carmel and the Mediterranean coast from there to Achzib. The first boundary given, from Helkath to Acshaph (and Achzib?), appears to be the western border while the eastern runs from the Iphtah El Valley to Tyre itself. It is, of course, very possible that a Canaanite population controlled Carmel and the coast to the north during this early period. A second problem is the apparent location of Dor within Asher when it had previously been assigned to Manasseh. The solution lies evidently in the fact that for unspecified reasons Manasseh possessed towns,

91. *Oxford Bible Atlas*, p. 138.
92. *Oxford Bible Atlas*, p. 49. Aharoni, *Land of the Bible*, p. 258, identifies Shihor Libnath with the Kishon, thus specifically placing the Carmel outside of Asher.

including Dor, that actually were within the borders of Asher (Josh. 17:11).[93]

The sixth allocation at Shiloh was for Naphtali. The southern border, beginning at Heleph (Khirbet 'Irbâdeh?), went eastward to Jabneel (Tell en-Na'am) and ended at the Jordan. Again from Heleph the border to the west and north passed through Hukkok (Yakuk) near the northwest curve of Kinnereth. Though the remainder of the western border and the northern boundaries are not specified, the summation of the extent of Naphtali's holdings—to Zebulun on the south, Asher on the west, and the Jordan on the east—implies that Naphtali stretched as far north as Tyre on its western frontier and as far east as the Jordan. This is supported by the list of its fortified cities: En Hazor (Hazzur), Kedesh (Tell Qades), and Hazor (Tell el-Qedah) all lay in north Galilee.

The final assignment—that of Dan—fell to the west of Benjamin and between Judah and Ephraim. But because of Dan's inability to occupy this western territory in the Shephelah and coastal plains, the tribe immigrated north and seized the little kingdom of Leshem (Laish) north of Lake Huleh. Judges 18 provides details of this move.

The final disposition of land was to Joshua himself (Josh. 19:49–50). Like Caleb, he had affirmed Yahweh's sovereignty over the land of promise and so now had his own inheritance therein. The city he requested and received was Timnath Serah (Khirbet Tibnah) in the western hill country of Ephraim.

The Cities of Refuge

Before Moses' death he had stipulated that six cities of refuge should be designated in Canaan, three east of the Jordan and three west (Num. 35:6–34; Deut. 4:41; 19:2). The purpose was to provide sanctuary for one guilty of homicide until there was opportunity to be fairly tried. A person guilty of murder would be executed, but someone who had killed another accidentally could remain in a city of refuge until the death of the high priest then in office. The cities set apart were Kedesh (Tell Qades) in Naphtali, just five miles from Lake Huleh; Shechem (Tell Balâtah) in Ephraim; Hebron in Judah; Bezer (Umm el-'Amad) in Reuben, five miles east of Heshbon; Ramoth (Tell Rāmîth) in Gad; and Golan (Sahm el-Jōlân) in Manasseh, about twenty miles due east of the Sea of Kinnereth. Thus from anywhere in the land a refugee would not be a great distance from a place of sanctuary.

93. Another possible solution is suggested in note 92: if Shihor Libnath be identified with the Kishon, Dor would lie outside of Asher.

The Cities of the Levites

The six cities of refuge were among forty-eight in all which had been assigned to the Levites (Num. 35:1–8) as their inheritance. As the tribe given to Yahweh in lieu of all the firstborn of Israel (Num. 3:41) and in service to him in matters of the cult, the Levites unlike the other tribes had no territorial allocation. They instead were granted towns with their outlying pasturelands where they could live among the people and minister to them. While prohibited from employment in secular occupations, they could raise limited crops and keep a few livestock. Exactly how they functioned within their towns is unclear, though presumably they supervised any religious activities that were permitted outside the central sanctuary. Then too, of course, they took their turn in the ministry of the tabernacle and temple according to the prescribed schedule.[94]

The Kohathites were assigned cities in Judah, Simeon, Benjamin, Ephraim, Dan, and western Manasseh. The priests (all of whom were descended from Aaron and thus were Kohathites) were limited to Judah, Simeon, and Benjamin. Thus the Levitical towns of these tribes, of which there were thirteen, were all inhabited by priests. The reason for this is unclear, especially in this early period; but when Jerusalem became both capital and cult center, the wisdom of having the priests living in proximity to Jerusalem is most obvious. Prominent among the priestly cities were Hebron, Debir, Beth Shemesh—all in Judah/Simeon—and Gibeon and Anathoth in Benjamin. Hebron and Debir had been granted to Caleb, a non-Levite, but now it is clear that his claim extended only to the environs of these towns and that the cities proper were inhabited by priests. Beth Shemesh was very briefly (and appropriately in view of its being a priestly community) the home of the ark of the covenant (1 Sam. 6), Gibeon was the location of the Mosaic tabernacle in Davidic times (2 Chron. 1:3), and Anathoth the home of the priest-prophet Jeremiah. Occupation of Gibeon by priests implies, of course, the eventual dispossession of the Hivites who lived there. The nonpriestly Kohathites lived in ten cities including Shechem, Gezer, and Beth Horon in Ephraim; Aijalon in Dan; and Taanach in western Manasseh.

The Gershonite clan of Levi was allotted thirteen cities in Issachar, Asher, Naphtali, and eastern Manasseh. Especially important among them were Golan, a city of refuge; Jarmuth; and Kedesh, another city of refuge. The Merarites settled in twelve cities of Reuben, Gad, and Zebulun including Bezer, a refuge city; Ramoth, another city of refuge;

94. Roland de Vaux, *Ancient Israel* (New York: McGraw-Hill, 1965), vol. 2, pp. 358–71.

and Heshbon. Again, the wise distribution of the Levitical cities guaranteed ready access for all Israelites who needed them.

The allocation having been determined, Joshua at last allowed the fighting men of Reuben, Gad, and eastern Manasseh to return to their Transjordanian homes. They had fully complied with Moses' insistence that they assist their tribal brothers in the Canaanite conquest in return for the privilege of settling east of the Jordan. On their way home, however, they erected an altar by the Jordan the purpose of which, they said, was to serve as a commemorative monument, a symbol of the perpetual unity of the eastern tribes with the west and of their common faith. Before this was clarified, however, Joshua was prepared to go to war over the matter, for he perceived the construction of the altar as the establishment of a rival shrine in competition with the central sanctuary at Shiloh. Joshua's concern reflects beyond question his understanding of Deuteronomy 12, which specifies that Israel's community worship must be centralized. Local altars for private sacrifice were indeed permitted; but for all Israel, the covenant people of Yahweh, one and only one place of corporate worship was appropriate. Joshua therefore sent a delegation to the leaders of the eastern tribes to ascertain the meaning of the altar. Satisfied that the intent was not to create an alternative religious center, Phinehas, the head of the interrogation party, returned to Shiloh and made his report, thus allaying Israel's fears.

The Second Covenant Renewal at Shechem

Many years after this episode, Joshua, aware that the time of his death was imminent, assembled the leadership of the tribes together at Shechem to admonish them to covenant fidelity and to lead them in a ceremony of covenant reaffirmation. In obedience to Moses' express command Joshua had held such a ceremony when Israel entered the land (Deut. 27:1–8; Josh. 8:30–35); now he did so again, no doubt to forestall the very kind of covenant defection which he had suspected in the altar by the Jordan erected by the eastern tribes. Moreover, he was now addressing a new generation of Israelites, a generation which had for the most part not participated personally in covenant renewal. Thus, after a period of more than thirty years, the community reaffirmed its commitment.[95]

95. The rationale for this dating rests on the fact that Joshua, who died at 110 years of age (Josh. 24:29), delivered this address at the very end of his life (Josh. 23:1–2, 14). Since he was undoubtedly about the age of (or a little younger than) Caleb, who was eighty-five years old in 1399 B.C. (Josh. 14:6–12), he would have died around 1375 at the earliest or at least thirty years after the covenant renewal of Joshua 8. See p. 147 for an argument that Joshua actually died in about 1366.

Joshua first rehearsed all of God's mighty works in Israel's behalf (Josh. 23). He had fought for them and had given them inheritance in the land. Though they even yet had not occupied their territories fully, he assured their ultimate success. However, this would depend in large measure on their obedience and firm adherence to the covenant requirements. Failure in this respect would invite the judgment of Yahweh, who would remove them from the land.

Then in Joshua 24 appears the account of covenant renewal. It was the custom in the ancient Near East for each generation of vassal people to hear and respond to the terms of the covenant which had first brought their forebears into relationship with their suzerain. Moses had initially received the revelation of the covenant from Yahweh at Sinai and had recorded both the covenant text itself (essentially Exod. 20–23) and the historical context in which it was offered (Exod. 19) and accepted (Exod. 24). Nearly forty years later he had reiterated the terms of the covenant on the plains of Moab, this time with embellishments and amendments appropriate to the new generation which was about to leave the wilderness and embark on conquest and sedentary life. Joshua had reaffirmed the covenant at the beginning of conquest (Josh. 8:30–35); and now, in the realization that a new generation had arisen and faced new conditions, he once again assembled the nation for covenant renewal.

The renewal ceremony followed standard procedure.[96] Joshua gathered the people before Yahweh (Josh. 24:1); he rehearsed God's past dealings with them, repeating, as it were, their sacred history up to the present moment (vv. 2–13); and he urged them to join him in rejecting all rival monarchs (i.e., other gods) and being loyal only to Yahweh (vv. 14–15). The people concurred with Joshua's interpretation of their history and pledged their total obedience (vv. 16–18). Joshua then reminded them that covenant obedience was difficult and that failure to carry it through would result in the wrath of a holy God (vv. 19–20). They in turn vowed to serve him and reject other gods (vv. 21–24). Next the covenant ceremony itself was performed, a rite which included the recording of the commitment and the erection of a commemorative stela which ever afterward would serve to witness to the promises they had made (vv. 25–28). It was most appropriate that the ceremony took place precisely at Shechem, for it

96. For Joshua 24 as a covenant text and record of a renewal ceremony see Delbert R. Hillers, *Covenant: The History of a Biblical Idea* (Baltimore: Johns Hopkins Press, 1969), pp. 58–66. Hillers correctly points out that this passage does not contain the actual text of a covenant, but a description of how the covenant was fulfilled (p. 61). There was no need for a lengthy covenant text here, since presumably Joshua was calling the attention of the people to essentially the covenant as articulated in Deuteronomy.

was there that Israel's father Abraham, called into the covenant by Yahweh, had himself erected an altar in celebration of the theophanic presence of God. The God of the fathers was the very God of Joshua and his generation.

Soon afterwards Joshua died and was buried in his city of Timnath Serah. And then, as though to suggest the end of an era—the patriarchal age through the fulfilment of the patriarchal promise of the land— the historian records that Joseph's bones, preserved faithfully for more than four centuries, were buried at Shechem. Just as the general region of Shechem (actually the town of Dothan) had marked the point of Joseph's descent to Egypt in preparation for the salvation of his people Israel, it now marked the point of his ascent in celebration of Yahweh's deliverance and the fulfilment of his promise. Last of all, Eleazar died and was likewise buried in Ephraim. Clearly Israel was about to cross a threshold and enter a new era of her historical experience.

4 The Era of the Judges: Covenant Violation, Anarchy, and Human Authority

The Literary-critical Problem in Judges

Most students of the Old Testament are aware of the perplexing historical and literary problems presented by the transition from the

Book of Joshua to the Book of Judges. At the heart of the difficulty are the references to the death of Joshua in Judges 1:1 and 2:8, which are followed respectively by accounts of conquest and apostasy. The usual approach of critical scholars at least is to posit opposing traditions which failed to achieve satisfying redaction.[1]

The most satisfying solution to this apparent conflation or overlapping of sources is to understand Judges 1:1–2:9 as a literary bridge connecting the end of the account of Joshua with the introduction to the narratives of the judges. Joshua 24:29 states that "Joshua son of Nun, the servant of the Lord, died at the age of a hundred and ten." In exactly the same words the author of Judges 2:8 records Joshua's death. To avoid beginning the book with Israel's apostasy and to show that this apostasy did not immediately follow Joshua's death, the historian starts out by recounting a campaign by Judah and Simeon against the Canaanites who still remained here and there in the southern hill country. It is important to note that the enemy is no longer the Amorites, as was the case in the initial conquest under Joshua, for the Amorites presumably had been driven out of Judah once and for all.[2] The Canaanite king named specifically is Adoni-Bezek, king of Bezek (Khirbet Bezqa), some three miles northeast of Gezer.[3] Having taken him prisoner, the Judahites brought the king into Jerusalem where he died.

At this point the careful reader might ask how it was possible for the Judahites to have access to Jerusalem since that city remained in

1. Otto Eissfeldt, *The Old Testament: An Introduction*, trans. Peter R. Ackroyd (New York: Harper and Row, 1965), pp. 253–55, 257–58; J. Alberto Soggin, *Introduction to the Old Testament*, trans. John Bowden (Philadelphia: Westminster, 1980), pp. 166–70. Typical of the skepticism regarding the historicity of the book is that of Sean Warner: "It seems generally accepted among historians that the data contained in the first part of the book are historically problematical, that the editorial framework of the second, main part of the book is definitely secondary and in fact bears little relationship to the stories contained in it, and that the third part of the book is also problematical, it being difficult, if not impossible, to decide on the authenticity of its data" ("The Dating of the Period of the Judges," *VT* 28 [1978]: 455–56). Given such unfounded assumptions, there is little wonder that Judges has posed a problem to critical scholarship.

2. The campaign in the hill country of Judah under Joshua had involved Amorites (Josh. 10:6) and, of course, was not limited to the tribes of Judah and Simeon. It therefore cannot be the one in view here. Moreover, Joshua is now dead (Judg. 1:1), Judah and Simeon have been allotted their joint territory (Josh. 15:1; 19:1), and there is an overall distancing of the event from anything known in the Book of Joshua. As Robert G. Boling says, Judges 1 "is a review of the performance of the generation that outlived Joshua" (*Judges*, Anchor Bible [Garden City, N.Y.: Doubleday, 1975], p. 66).

3. There are no grounds, textual or otherwise, to assume that Adoni-Bezek is a corruption of the name Adoni-Zedek (Josh. 10:1), an assumption made, for example, by George F. Moore, *A Critical and Exegetical Commentary on Judges* (New York: Scribner, 1895), p. 16.

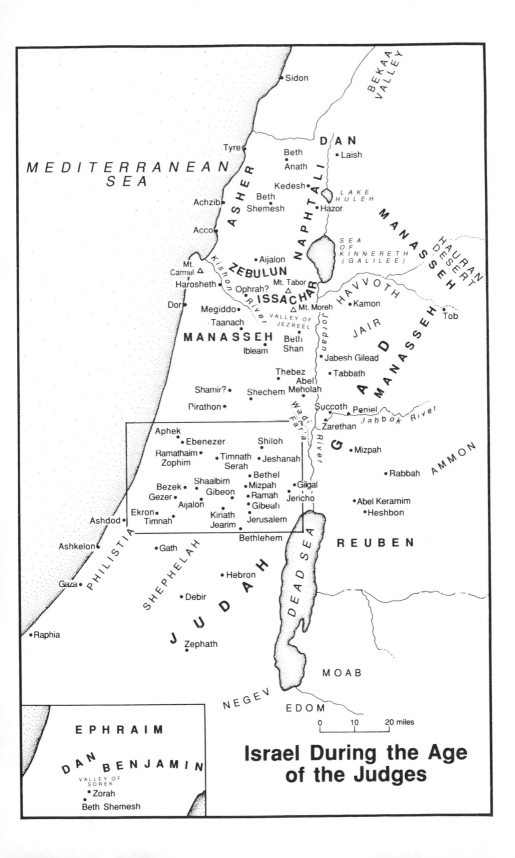

Israel During the Age of the Judges

MEDITERRANEAN SEA

BEKAA VALLEY

Sidon

Tyre

DAN

Beth Anath

Laish

Kedesh

ASHER

Beth Shemesh

Achzib

Hazor

LAKE HULEH

NAPHTALI

MANASSEH

Acco

HAURAN DESERT

Aijalon

ZEBULUN

SEA OF KINNERETH (GALILEE)

Mt. Carmel △

Harosheth

Ophrah?

Mt. Tabor △

ISSACHAR

Dor

Megiddo

Kishon River

Mt. Moreh △

HAVVOTH

Kamon

Taanach

VALLEY OF JEZREEL

Jordan River

JAIR

Tob

MANASSEH

Beth Shan

Ibleam

Jabesh Gilead

Tabbath

Thebez

Abel Meholah

Shamir?

Shechem

Wadi Fara

Succoth

Peniel

Jahbok River

Pirathon

Zarethan

G

Aphek

Ebenezer

Shiloh

Mizpah

Ramathaim Zophim

Timnath Serah

Jeshanah

Bethel

Rabbah

AMMON

Bezek

Shaalbim

Gibeon

Mizpah

Gilgal

Gezer

Ramah

Jericho

Ekron

Aijalon

Gibeah

Abel Keramim

Ashdod

Timnah

Kiriath Jearim

Jerusalem

Heshbon

Bethlehem

Ashkelon

Gath

REUBEN

DEAD SEA

Gaza

PHILISTIA

SHEPHELAH

Hebron

Raphia

Debir

JUDAH

Zephath

MOAB

NEGEV

EDOM

0   10   20 miles

EPHRAIM

DAN BENJAMIN

VALLEY OF SOREK

Zorah

Beth Shemesh

Jebusite hands down to the period of David. Anticipating the question, the historian goes on to relate how it happened that Jerusalem, temporarily at least, came to be in Israel's possession. To do this the author uses the literary device of a flashback to an earlier period when Joshua was still alive. Thus, in Judges 1:8 there is the narration of the fall of Jerusalem, an event not explicitly related in Joshua, though suggested no doubt by the death of the king of Jerusalem during Joshua's southern campaign (Josh. 10:22–27). At that time Jerusalem was captured by Judahites and burned, but its population was not destroyed. In fact, shortly thereafter the Jebusites regained control, and neither Judah (Josh. 15:63) nor Benjamin (Judg. 1:21) could dislodge them again.

The retrospective summation continues with the account of Judah's conquest of the hill country, Negev, and Shephelah, and focuses on the capture of Hebron. This probably refers to a particular expedition against Hebron in response to Caleb's desire for an inheritance (Josh. 11:21–23; 14:13–15; 15:13–19) rather than to the earlier defeat of the Amorite kings by Joshua and all Israel (Josh. 10:36–37).[4] Likewise, the capture of Debir (Judg. 1:11–15; cf. Josh. 10:38–39) fits the story of Caleb's campaign, but not that of the Israelite conquest of the south. It is especially appropriate that the historian repeat the story of Caleb and Othniel, since Othniel will presently be introduced as the first of the judges. Here we have, then, another literary and historical bridge between the books of Joshua and Judges.

The parenthetical throwback to the time of Joshua apparently ends with the recounting of the allocation of Hebron and Debir to Caleb. Now the author resumes the narrative of verses 1–7, which concerns the continuing conquest by Judah and Simeon. The author speaks first of all of the attachment of the Kenites[5] to Judah and their combined attacks on the Canaanite stronghold of Zephath, a place earlier known as Hormah (Judg. 1:17).[6] They then managed to seize the three Philistine cities of Gaza, Ashkelon, and Ekron. Finally, the historian relates that Judah and Simeon took all the southern hill country, including

4. It is again important to note that the enemies in the early campaign (Josh. 10) were Amorites, whereas in the conquest of Hebron involving Caleb the enemies are the Anakim (Josh. 11) and the Canaanites (Judg. 1). It seems evident that the Anakim are a Canaanite people, not Amorite, though they may have coexisted with the Amorites (Num. 13:22; Josh. 15:13–14).

5. The Old Testament identifies the Kenites as Midianites (Judg. 1:16) and relates that their ancestor, Hobab, Moses' brother-in-law, had accompanied Israel at least part of the way from Sinai to Canaan (Num. 10:29–32). For this connection see H. H. Rowley, *From Joseph to Joshua* (London: Oxford University Press, 1950), pp. 152–55.

6. It will be recalled that Israel destroyed certain Canaanite cities en route to Canaan and that these collectively were called Hormah (from *ḥērem,* "the ban") as a result (Num. 21:1–3). Zephath must have been a city rebuilt from these ruins. See Yohanan Aharoni, *The Land of the Bible* (Philadelphia: Westminster, 1979), p. 216.

Hebron, though they were unable to occupy the plains because of the Canaanite use of iron chariots there.[7]

In line with the pattern of conquest described in the Book of Joshua, the historian now turns his attention northward to the conquest of Bethel by the Joseph tribes (Judg. 1:22–26). By a stratagem of bribery and threat they were able to take the city. Bethel had suffered a severe loss of population when Joshua conquered Ai, but nothing other than a brief mention in Joshua 12:16 is said of the capture of the city itself at that time. The event in Judges, then, must refer to a later episode in which the tribe of Ephraim made an effort to occupy its allocated territories (cf. Josh. 16:1–2). Similarly, western Manasseh tried unsuccessfully to lay claim to its inheritance. In words highly reminiscent of the account in Joshua (Judg. 1:27–28; cf. Josh. 17:12) the narrator says that Manasseh could not repel the Canaanites from certain cities, primarily in the Plain of Jezreel (Beth Shan, Taanach, Ibleam, and Megiddo) and the coastal plain (Dor). These five towns were eventually inhabited by Manassehites, even though technically they belonged to Issachar and Asher (Josh. 17:11). The reason is that in each case they were geographically contiguous to Manasseh and cut off by Canaanite intervention from the tribes which had original claim to them.

North of the Plain of Jezreel the situation was the same. Zebulun could not evict the Canaanites of Kitron and Nahalol; Asher was frustrated at Acco, Sidon, Achzib, and many other places; and Naphtali was forced to coexist with the Canaanites at Beth Shemesh and Beth Anath. As for the Danites to the south, they faced stiff opposition from Amorites who apparently settled in the valleys after the conquest, particularly at Aijalon and Shaalbim (Selbit) in the Valley of Aijalon.[8] The Ephraimites came to Dan's aid, however, and kept the Amorites

7. Since the Iron Age of Palestine began around 1200 B.C., this use of iron by the Canaanites would seem to be a problem for the chronology consistently adopted in this volume, which would place the Judah-Simeon campaigns of Judges 1 at about 1350. However, the Hittites at least had mastered the production and use of iron by 1400, so there is no reason why Canaan could not have imported ironware by the fourteenth century. See Jacquetta Hawkes, *The First Great Civilizations* (New York: Knopf, 1973), p. 113; Leonard Cottrell, *The Anvil of Civilization* (New York: New American Library, 1957), p. 157; V. Gordon Childe, *New Light on the Most Ancient East* (New York: Norton, 1969), p. 157.

8. The movement of Dan to a northern location (Laish) must have occurred early in the period of the judges. It could not have taken place earlier than the effort at settlement described in Judges 1:34–36, however, since it was this Amorite pressure which initiated the relocation. It also clearly preceded the arrival of the Sea Peoples/Philistines in about 1200 B.C. As Roland de Vaux points out, this is the only text in which the Amorites are located in the plains, a fact that would seem to support the view that the conquest of the hill country under Joshua was already a *fait accompli* (*The Early History of Israel* [Philadelphia: Westminster, 1978], p. 133, n. 28).

west of a line from Scorpion Pass (the "ascent of Akrabbim") north-ward. This probably refers to the demarcation between the hill country proper and the Shephelah or western lowlands. If so, Amorites and early Philistines probably occupied the same area at least until the invasion of the second wave of Philistines, the Sea Peoples, in about 1200.

Perhaps in response to the understandable sense of frustration and failure which Joshua and Israel must have felt over their inability to conquer and occupy the land quickly, the angel of Yahweh appeared to Israel at Bokim (unknown) and told the people that their inability to take complete possession of the land was the result of their violation of Yahweh's covenant requirements. They had made covenant with some of the natives (the Gibeonites) and had failed to tear down the altars of others. As he had threatened to do in the event of such disobedience, Yahweh had left the Canaanites and their gods in the land as instruments of his discipline.

It appears that the narrator once more interrupts his account of postconquest occupation, this time to hark back to the second covenant renewal at Shechem. This follows from the wording of Judges 2:6 ("after Joshua had dismissed the Israelites . . . each to his own inheritance") and Joshua 24:28 ("then Joshua sent the people away, each to his own inheritance"). Judges 2:6–7 ("they went to take possession of the land") is a recapitulation of 1:1–2:5 (with the exception of 1:8–15), a summation of all the subsequent efforts at settlement. For following the ceremony at Shechem the people went their way to undertake the task of occupation as the vassal of the sovereign God. And they did so faithfully throughout the days of the generation of elders who outlived Joshua. Only then did they undertake the worship of Baal and plunge the nation into the abysmal apostasy and anarchy which are the hallmark of the Book of Judges.[9]

The Chronology of Judges

The Length of the Period

The beginning date

Before we pursue the topic of Israel's apostasy, however, it is necessary that a chronological and historical underpinning be established for the entire era of the judges. Our approach will be first to consider

9. The period of the judges was a time of almost no central authority and no sense of national or even religious cohesiveness, a point well made by Alan J. Hauser, "Unity and Diversity in Early Israel Before Samuel," *JETS* 22 (1979): 289–303.

the internal biblical evidence and then, summarily at least, that of the contemporary ancient Near Eastern world.

In determining the chronological structure of the period of the judges, our initial step will be the establishing of *termini a quo* and *ad quem*.[10] The latter rests on rather precise data to be carefully considered later, but the former requires reconstruction on more subjective grounds. First, it is clear that Joshua died at the age of 110, some years after the conquest began. The date of the conquest proper is about 1406–1399, since it began exactly forty years after the exodus of 1446 (Deut. 1:3) and ended seven years later. This is apparent from the testimony of Caleb, who said that he was forty at the time he and Joshua spied out the land and eighty-five at the completion of the conquest (Josh. 14:7–10). The spies had gone out two years after the exodus, so Caleb was forty in 1444 and eighty-five in 1399. One may assume that Joshua was about the same age. He was a capable warrior against the Amalekites as early as 1446 (Exod. 17:10) and yet is called "young" shortly thereafter (Exod. 33:11). While it may be risky to speculate, an age of thirty for Joshua at the time of the exodus is certainly not unreasonable. This would place his birth date at about 1476 and the date of his death at 1366. Othniel, the first judge, commenced his judgeship after that date.

The second consideration is even more telling. Both Joshua 24:31 and Judges 2:7 emphasize the point that Israel served Yahweh faithfully not only in the lifetime of Joshua, but throughout the time of the elders of Israel who outlived him. This cannot refer to elders contemporary with Joshua in the exodus and early wilderness period, since they presumably were included in the rebellious generation of Israel sentenced to die in the wilderness (Num. 14:26–35). Only a total disregard for the text will allow that any significant number of men over twenty years of age survived the wilderness. But even if a few did, there were elders appointed subsequent to the judgment at Kadesh Barnea, all of whom must have been under twenty at that time. Some, of course, would have been considerably younger. Even in the most conservative view an elder who was eligible to enter Canaan could not have been born earlier than 1464, twenty years before the Kadesh Barnea rebellion. If he lived to be as old as Joshua, he would have lived until 1354. If, however, he had been born just prior to the rebellion, he could have lived until about 1340. A date of 1340 is not at all unlikely for the beginning of Israel's worship of Baal. In fact, it might even be a little early, since Judges 2:10 indicates that the whole gen-

10. For a helpful survey of various approaches see J. H. John Peet, "The Chronology of the Judges—Some Thoughts," *Journal of Christian Reconstruction* 9 (1982–1983): 161–81.

eration of elders had died and another generation, one that knew nothing of Yahweh and his saving work, had taken their place. And, of course, Othniel, the first judge, did not exercise his office until eight years after the commencement of Yahweh's judgment (Judg. 3:8–9).

Against such late dates, however, is the introduction of Othniel himself. Following Caleb's acquisition of Hebron and Debir, Othniel, a nephew of Caleb, had taken Caleb's daughter Acsah as his wife. If this occurred in 1399 or shortly thereafter, then by 1340 Othniel would have been quite aged even if he was only a youth at the time of his marriage. This is entirely possible, though improbable, for it seems that Othniel died forty years after he delivered Israel (Judg. 3:11). Also, one may argue that elders of Joshua's own age may have been allowed to enter Canaan: Eleazar, son of Aaron, had done so and clearly was more than twenty at the time the older generation was precluded from entering Canaan (see Exod. 6:23, 25). It may be that the apostasy and subsequent era of the judges came after these elders had passed away.[11] On balance it seems that 1360–1350 is a reasonable date for the transition between Joshua and the judges.

The closing date

As indicated already, the dates for the end of the period of the judges can be more precisely defined. The argument, however, is extremely complex and at every point assumes the accuracy and integrity of the biblical text. In the first place, the datum of Judges 11:26 is of crucial importance. Jephthah the judge is there pointing out to the hostile king of Ammon that his claim that Israel is in illegal occupation of Ammonite territory is invalid: Israel has already been there for three hundred years, and, in fact, the land at the time of the Transjordanian conquest did not belong to Ammon anyway, but to the Amorites. If, Jephthah says, Ammon has any legitimate claim, why have the Ammonites waited for three hundred years to press that claim?

The point that must be addressed here is the fact that Jephthah communicated with the Ammonites three hundred years after the conquest of Sihon, an event which occurred in 1406, and eighteen years after the Ammonite oppression had begun (Judg. 10:8). That oppression, then, commenced in 1124 and ended only when Jephthah defeated Ammon in 1106, the very year of his communication to the king (Judg. 11:33). To be connected to these dates is the story of the judgeship of Samson. A careful reading of Judges 10:7–8 will show that the Ammonite oppression which began in 1124 coincided with the com-

---

11. Warner, in fact, is willing to date the commencement of the era of the judges as early as 1373 B.C. ("Period of the Judges," *VT* 28 [1978]: 463).

mencement of Philistine oppression.[12] The historian traces one course of events at a time, however, and so goes on first to write of the Ammonite danger and its conclusion (Judg. 10:8b–12:7) and then deals with the Philistine menace and its resolution (Judg. 13:1–16:31).

The Philistines harassed Israel for forty years (Judg. 13:1) or from 1124 until 1084. Samson was born early in that period and judged Israel "for twenty years in the days of the Philistines" (Judg. 15:20). That is, his years of leadership fell within the forty-year span of Philistine rule (Judg. 14:4), but apparently did not outlast it, for the Philistines seem to have been a threat for a short time after Samson pulled down the temple of Dagon (Samuel subdued them at Mizpah). Most likely Samson began his heroic deeds about midway through the oppression, when he was about twenty years old, and died after twenty years of judgeship just preceding the end of the oppression.

Proceeding from another angle, it is interesting to note that the judges' final blow against Philistine incursion occurred under Samuel at Mizpah (1 Sam. 7:11, 13) twenty years after the ark of the covenant had been taken by the Philistines (v. 2).[13] The end of the oppression, as noted above, was in 1084, so this date marks also the battle of Mizpah. The battle of Aphek, which resulted in the capture of the ark, would have taken place, then, in 1104 or at the midpoint of the forty-year Philistine period. It is tempting to speculate that the Philistine attack may have been in retaliation for Samson's early heroics against them. Be that as it may, the chronology proposed here fits all that is known of the life and career of Samuel as well as of Samson. The great prophet was surely very young at the time of the battle of Aphek, but "old" when Israel demanded a king and he anointed Saul (1 Sam. 8:1, 5; 10:1). Admittedly, "old" is an extremely subjective term, but it is the same word used to describe David when he was seventy (1 Kings 1:1, 15; cf. 2 Sam. 5:4). Saul was anointed in 1051 B.C., a date which will be defended in due course (p. 192), and so if Samuel were then seventy, he would have been born in 1121. This would make him seventeen years of age in 1104 when the ark was captured. We know Samuel lived at least twenty-five years after Saul's accession, for the judge-prophet anointed David as king when David was likely about twelve. David was born in 1041, so a date in the early 1020s for his anointing cannot be far off. Samuel lived until David fled from Saul into the wilderness of Paran (1 Sam. 25:1), probably in the late 1020s.

12. Moore, *Judges*, p. 277; Abraham Malamat, "The Period of the Judges," in *World History of the Jewish People*, vol. 3, *Judges*, ed. Benjamin Mazar (Tel Aviv: Massada, 1971), p. 157.

13. Ralph W. Klein, *1 Samuel*, Word Biblical Commentary (Waco: Word, 1983), pp. 65–66.

The prophet then was close to one hundred if he was born in 1121. Of course, if that seems overly aged (but compare Eli, who died at ninety-eight), one can reduce Samuel's birth date a few years. If, for example, he was born in 1116, he was only twelve when the ark was captured and about ninety-five when he died.

The Compression of Chronology

The purpose of this lengthy discussion of the chronology of the era of the judges is both to show the consistency of the biblical data themselves and to answer related questions concerning the total time between the exodus and Solomon. On the basis of the late dates which most scholars assign to the exodus and conquest (ca. 1275–1250) there are only 300 years at the most to accommodate the judges, Saul, David, and the first 4 years of Solomon, who began to build the temple in 966, the fourth year of his reign. One can hardly question David's 40 years, and Saul, by any view, must be granted at least 20. This leaves only about 235 years for all the events of the Book of Judges. The usual solution is to reject the figures of the book or to postulate considerable overlapping of the periods of oppression and deliverance. Some overlapping, we shall see, is necessary in any viable position.

Even the early date proposed for the exodus (1446) poses serious problems considering the fact that of the 480 years between the exodus and Solomon's fourth year (1 Kings 6:1), 4 are needed for Solomon, 40 for David, 40 for Saul, at least 45 for the conquest and occupation, and 40 for the wilderness wandering. This leaves only 311 years for the judges. But if we add up the figures in Judges which specify the lengths of the oppressions, judgeships, and intervening periods of rest, we arrive at a total of 407 years. This is clearly incompatible with even the early date proposed for the exodus as well as with 1 Kings 6:1 itself unless we allow that figures given in the Book of Judges overlap.

Another problem is presented by Acts 13:19–20, where Paul the apostle, in addressing the synagogue at Pisidian Antioch, indicates that a period of 450 years elapsed between the end of the conquest and the coming of Samuel the prophet (this is the interpretation of, e.g., the King James Version). While it may not be possible to know what Paul means by his reference to Samuel, it seems best to understand it as alluding to the commencement of Samuel's public ministry as a prophet. Now Samuel took over from Eli, who died upon hearing that the Philistines had captured the ark of the covenant at the battle of Aphek. This, as argued above, should be dated about 1104. Following Paul then requires a date of 1554 for the inception of Othniel's tenure, an obvious impossibility. In fact, the figure of 450 cannot fit any dating scheme that takes 1 Kings 6:1 seriously. This is why many scholars opt for an alternative reading of the text of Acts 13:19–20, a reading which suggests that the 450 years refers to the Egyptian sojourn (400 years), the wilderness wandering (40 years), and the conquest (7 years), the total of which approximates 450. Not least of the objections to this reading is the fact that it flatly contradicts Exodus 12:40, which emphatically declares that the sojourn lasted for 430 years and not 400.

A better solution is the view that Paul has added the figures given in the Book of Judges for the years of oppression, judgeships, and peace, which, as we have seen, total 407 years. The 40 years of Eli (1 Sam. 4:18), the judge who preceded Samuel, should also be included, thus yielding approximately 450 years.[14] While this method of chronological reconstruction may not be satisfying to the modern Western mind, Paul may well have used it. His was not a scientific calculation, but one which took account of the data of the books of Judges and Samuel and arranged them as was deemed appropriate. That he would incorporate his interpretation of these data in a public address implies that his audience understood and shared his peculiar (to us) way of computing chronology.

There is no reason, then, to reject the biblical data on the chronology of the judges, for, as has been seen, the figures are capable of resolution provided one takes the basic assumptions of Old Testament chronology in general seriously. It is only when scholars perceive a need on subjective critical grounds to reject or reinterpret the information of the canonical text that they find themselves with virtually insuperable problems which require more-creative (and perhaps even nihilistic) solutions.

The Ancient Near Eastern World

The Silence of the Old Testament

In turning to the history of the nation of Israel under the judges, one is surprised initially to discover not one reference to crucial developments involving the major nations of the day, not even to the activities of Egypt. The maelstrom of international politics and military campaigns seems to have bypassed Israel completely. It is as though the history of Israel had turned into a cul-de-sac totally removed from the turbulent course of world events.

14. See Eugene H. Merrill, "Paul's Use of 'About 450 Years' in Acts 13:20," *Bib Sac* 138 (1981): 246–57.

The reason for this silence in respect to global affairs is twofold. First, the silence is itself a statement loud and clear to the effect that the major powers were so preoccupied with other matters that they had no time or energy to devote to what was in fact a petty state isolated from the main routes of international intercourse.[15] Second, true to the spirit and method of biblical historiography, the historian simply has no interest in the larger world of that time. His is sacred history in the best sense of the term, and his interests coincide with the interests of Yahweh, the Lord of history, who wishes above all to tell the story of his own people as a redemptive factor in the world. Only when Babylonia, Assyria, or Egypt is important to the story of salvation will it take its place in the biblical narrative. Accordingly, until one comes to the record of the monarchy, a time when Israel became in its own right a significant kingdom, one looks in vain for a glimpse of the larger world.

Mesopotamia

To understand how Palestine was able to exist in a vacuum for three hundred years, however, it is necessary to speak at least briefly to the question of extrabiblical history. Geographically it is appropriate to begin with Mesopotamia. As was pointed out previously (p. 96), the Old Babylonian Empire had given way by 1595 B.C. to the Kassites, who continued to dominate central and lower Mesopotamia until about 1150. This was a period of relative regression and inactivity for the whole region, with the result that little or no threat existed toward the west from that quarter. To the north, however, the Assyrians had steadily become stronger and had begun the imperialistic policies for which they were ever afterward famous. It is Aššur-uballiṭ (1365–1330) who must receive much of the credit for Assyria's rise from earlier Hurrian domination. He was on Assyria's throne at the close of Joshua's conquest and the beginning of the era of the judges. His troubles with the Kassites to his south and the Mitannian Hurrians to the west, however, left him little time or appetite for adventures in Canaan.

Anti-Kassite activity occupied Assyria for about forty years until Adad-nirari I (1307–1275) launched a series of invasions of the kingdom of Ḫanigalbat, a Hittite vassal state located in the upper Habor and Balikh valleys.[16] This obviously antagonized the Hittites, who at

15. Abraham Malamat, "The Egyptian Decline in Canaan and the Sea Peoples," in *World History of the Jewish People*, vol. 3, p. 23.

16. J. M. Munn-Rankin, "Assyrian Military Power 1300–1200 B.C.," in *Cambridge Ancient History*, 3d ed., ed. I. E. S. Edwards et al. (Cambridge: Cambridge University Press, 1975), vol. 2, part 2, pp. 276–79.

first were unable or unwilling to take punitive measures because of their greater fear of Egypt. Eventually, however, Ḥattušiliš king of the Hittites made a treaty with Rameses II of Egypt (in 1284) and with his moral support retook Ḥanigalbat from Assyria.

Tukulti-Ninurta I (1244–1208), though achieving smashing success in his northern, eastern, and southern campaigns, failed miserably in the west when he tried to bring the Hittites to heel.[17] This so weakened Assyria that she eventually was unable to control even Kassite Babylonia any longer. In fact, Aššur-nirari III (1203–1198), grandson of Tukulti-Ninurta, became subservient to Adad-šuma-uṣur, king of Babylonia (now non-Kassite). This state of affairs persisted until the reign of Aššur-rēši-iši I (1133–1116), who defeated Babylonia, which was then being governed by the illustrious Nebuchadnezzar I (1124–1103).[18] This ushered in a period of temporary Assyrian resurgence sparked primarily by Tiglath-pileser I (1115–1077).[19] Before long he turned west and defeated Muṣri, Tadmor, and other Aramean territories and finally reached the Mediterranean where he demanded and received proper deference from Egypt, Phoenicia, and the Hittites (now in northern Syria). He made no attempt, however, to march south into Israel itself. Note that his reign ended some seven years after 1084, which we have proposed as the closing date of the era of the judges.

The Hittites

Our attention now shifts to the second giant power of the time, the Hittites. This kingdom, which had fallen dormant for some time, was raised to a place of preeminence under Šuppiluliumaš (1380–1346). By the time of Joshua's death Šuppiluliumaš had invaded Syria and laid claim to everything as far south as Gubla (Byblos).[20] He did not press south into Canaan, however, for he was uncertain of Egypt's strength. Besides, he was continually harassed on his eastern flanks by Mitanni and Assyria and so remained north of Canaan in order not to overextend himself.

Hittite control of Syria continued until the reign of Muwatalliš (1320–1294), who began to encounter the imperialism of Egypt (Dynasty 19).[21] In 1300, Rameses II of Egypt attacked the Hittites at Ka-

---

17. Ibid., pp. 284–94.

18. D. J. Wiseman, "Assyria and Babylonia c. 1200–1000 B.C.," in *CAH* 2.2, pp. 453–54.

19. Ibid., pp. 457–64.

20. Anthony J. Spalinger, "Egyptian-Hittite Relations at the Close of the Amarna Period and Some Notes on Hittite Military Strategy in North Syria," *BES* 1 (1979): 55.

21. A. Goetze, "The Hittites and Syria (1300–1200 B.C.)," in *CAH* 2.2, pp. 252–56.

desh on the Orontes but was defeated and thrown back. The Hittites could not follow up on this major blow at Egypt because of continuing threat from Assyria. In fact, Ḫattušiliš of the Hittites (1286–1265), as we have seen, was forced to sign a parity treaty with Rameses II in 1284 in which each nation pledged not to encroach on the territory of the other.[22]

After the death of Ḫattušiliš, the Hittites continued to weaken and certainly never made an effort to enter Israel. They did control most of Syria, however, until the empire came to a sudden and violent end at the hands of the Sea Peoples by 1200.[23] The Hittites thus were no factor at all in the period of the later judges.

Egypt

Egypt in the days of the judges of Israel was ruled by the latter eighteenth, the nineteenth, and the twentieth dynasties. The Amarna age (ca. 1379–1350), during which the conquest ended, has already been examined in part (pp. 99–108). It is clear from that discussion that though Canaan was technically an Egyptian province, the Egyptian kings took little or no interest in it despite the desperate appeals of their Canaanite vassals to do otherwise.

It was not, in fact, until the reign of Seti I (1318–1304) of Dynasty 19 that a well-attested expedition was undertaken to Canaan.[24] On a stela at Beth Shan he describes a campaign to Jezreel. He mentions that he took Raphia (Rapha) and Gaza, both along the southern Mediterranean coast, as well as Beth Shan, Acco, Tyre, and other cities farther north. At Beth Shan, he says, he encountered 'apiru, very likely a reference to Israelites in view of this late date.[25] One cannot help but note that Seti studiously avoided contact with any part of Canaan except the coastal plains and the Valley of Jezreel, both of which were

22. Ibid., pp. 258–59.
23. For the last desperate years of Hittite independence see Itamar Singer, "Western Anatolia in the Thirteenth Century B.C. According to the Hittite Sources," *AS* 33 (1983): 205–17, esp. 216–17.
24. R. O. Faulkner, "Egypt: From the Inception of the Nineteenth Dynasty to the Death of Ramesses III," in *CAH* 2.2, pp. 218–21. There is some possibility that Horemheb, a commander under Tutankhamon, may have conducted a campaign into some part of Canaan at the beginning of that king's reign (ca. 1360). See Cyril Aldred, "Egypt: The Amarna Period and the End of the Eighteenth Dynasty," in *CAH* 2.2, p. 72. If so, it little changed the course of events in interior Canaan.
25. Benjamin Mazar, "The Historical Development," in *World History of the Jewish People*, vol. 3, p. 15, describes these Semitic tribes as being "ethnically close to the Israelites." More likely, they actually were Israelites.

outside the area of Israelite occupation.[26] In his second campaign he pressed north to Kadesh and Amurru, and in his fourth he lost Kadesh and made a treaty with the Hittite Muwatalliš.[27] In every instance he avoided interior Canaan.

Not much more need be said of Rameses II (1304–1236).[28] Although disqualified as the pharaoh of the exodus, he remains nonetheless contemporary for almost seven decades with Israel's history during the very heart of the age of the judges. Yet never once is he mentioned in the Book of Judges, nor does he refer to Israel in all his extensive annals.[29] One can only conclude that there was an obvious mutual lack of interest.

The first major foreign campaign of Rameses was against the Hittites at Nahr el-Kalb in Lebanon in his fourth year. The next year (1300) he faced the Hittites at Kadesh on the Orontes and, as noted above, suffered a humiliating setback. This must have encouraged rebellion amongst the Canaanite vassals because for several years Rameses had to attend to these little states, but not once does he claim to have intervened in the Canaanite interior, the very area held by Israel. In 1284 he made a parity treaty with Ḫattušiliš, and in 1270 married that Hittite king's daughter, a fact he attributes to his own superiority over Ḫattušiliš. The only other contacts he documents in the north are minor engagements in Moab, Edom, and the Negev, none of which involves confrontation with Israel for obvious reasons—Israel made no claim on those areas.

Merneptah (1236–1223), however, not only made at least one campaign into Palestine (in his fifth year, 1231), but he mentions a defeat which he administered to Israel.[30] This foray also seems to have been limited to the Jezreel area.[31] We have already seen (p. 69) that this reference to Israel is proof against the late date for the exodus and

26. Yohanan Aharoni, "The Settlement of Canaan," in *World History of the Jewish People*, vol. 3, pp. 94–95.

27. The loss of Kadesh is implied by the fact that Rameses II had to make an effort to retake it in his fourth year. See Faulkner, "Nineteenth Dynasty," in *CAH* 2.2, p. 221. For the text of the treaty see James B. Pritchard, *Ancient Near Eastern Texts Relating to the Old Testament*, 2d ed. (Princeton: Princeton University Press, 1955), pp. 476–79.

28. Faulkner, "Nineteenth Dynasty," in *CAH* 2.2, pp. 225–32, Anthony J. Spalinger, "Traces of the Early Career of Rameses II," *JNES* 38 (1979): 271–86.

29. An exception might be the reference to the coastal people "Asar," which some scholars identify with the tribe of Asher. This would place that tribe in north Canaan at least as early as the beginning of the thirteenth century. See Mazar, "Historical Development," p. 19.

30. Faulkner, "Nineteenth Dynasty," in *CAH* 2.2, pp. 232–35.

31. Malamat, "Egyptian Decline," in *World History of the Jewish People*, vol. 3, p. 24. Malamat points out that Gezer at this time was under Egyptian control, a fact quite in line with the biblical statement that the Israelite conquest had left Gezer in Canaanite hands (Josh. 16:10).

conquest, for it is difficult to see how Israel could have been a major foe to Merneptah in Canaan if, as the evidence for a late date would require, the exodus occurred at the beginning of his reign.[32]

With Merneptah came the end of any meaningful involvement of Egypt in Syro-Palestine until the reign of Shoshenq (945–924) of Dynasty 22. Even Rameses III (1198–1166), who was able to defeat and repel both the Libyans and the Sea Peoples, undertook only one expedition into Palestine and that was limited to Edom.[33] Following his death the Syro-Palestinian provinces were all lost, and for the remainder of Dynasty 20 (till ca. 1085) Egypt played no role at all in Israelite affairs.[34]

The Syro-Canaanite States

Finally, the situation of Syria and Palestine during the period of the judges must receive at least brief attention.[35] At about the commencement of Othniel's .tenure the Hittites began to dominate all of Syria between the Mediterranean and the Euphrates and as far south as Lebanon. The alarm this caused to the Canaanite states may be seen, for example, in a letter written by Rib-Adda of Gubla (Byblos) to his Egyptian superior. Other kingdoms in Syria quickly chose sides between the Hittites and Mitanni. Ḥalab (Aleppo), Alalakh, and Tunip became vassals of the Hittites. Ugarit, with its characteristic independence of spirit, eventually chose to be loyal to Egypt. Amurru, however, saw the stalemate between the major powers as providing opportunity for it to expand its own influence. Its king 'Abdi-Aširta threatened Gubla, and his son and successor Aziru actually annexed

32. The determinative which is used to describe Israel as a "people" does not suggest a disorganized body, but rather one so pervasive as to occupy the entire interior of the hill country. This is the conclusion of the fine literary-structural study of the Merneptah stela by G. W. Ahlström and D. E. Edelman, "Merneptah's Israel," *JNES* 44 (1985): 59–61.

33. Faulkner, "Nineteenth Dynasty," in *CAH* 2.2, p. 244. Pierre Grandet, however, has recently proposed that Rameses constructed fortifications at Beth Shan, a theory which if correct still has no bearing on the involvement of Egypt in central Canaan ("Deux Etablissements de Ramses III en Nubie et en Palestine," *JEA* 69 [1983]: 109–14; so also Malamat, "Egyptian Decline," in *World History of the Jewish People*, vol. 3, p. 35).

34. James M. Weinstein tries to make a case for unparalleled Egyptian involvement in Canaan during the thirteenth and early twelfth centuries, but of all the places he lists as Egyptian fortifications, not one is in the hill country of interior Canaan where Israel was dominant ("The Egyptian Empire in Palestine: A Reassessment," *BASOR* 241 [1981]: 17–18).

35. A. Goetze, "The Struggle for the Domination of Syria (1400–1300 B.C.)," in *CAH* 2.2, pp. 8–16; for a view from the standpoint of Ugarit see Anson F. Rainey, "The Kingdom of Ugarit," *BA* 28 (1965): 107–12.

that important Phoenician city. He then made a treaty with Niqmaddu of Ugarit which served to draw both of them into the Hittite orbit. By then Šuppiluliumaš of the Hittites had brought Mitanni control of Syria to an end and created his own system of vassal states, which included Ugarit and Amurru.

With the penetration of Seti I of Egypt's Dynasty 19 into Syria, Amurru broke its treaty with the Hittites, but they retook it after the successful battle at Kadesh against Rameses II (1300).[36] Near the end of the Hittite Empire, Syrian states such as Ugarit began to assert their independence, but until the Hittites' violent overthrow by the Sea Peoples most of the Syrian states remained under Hittite control.

The Sea Peoples were a confederation of various ethnic and national groups who originated primarily in the Aegean area, although some may have come from as far west as Sicily and Italy.[37] They may have assisted Muwatalliš in his victory over Rameses at Kadesh. Some of their names are the Dardani, Masa, Pitassa, Arawanna, Karkisa, and Lukka. Their first penetration (ca. 1230) into Palestine was by land through Cilicia, and they apparently marched as far south as Egypt. Merneptah claims to have repulsed certain Sea Peoples who invaded Egypt by way of Libya.[38] It may well be that the six hundred Philistines struck down by Shamgar (Judg. 3:31) were Sea Peoples penetrating from the north.[39]

A second penetration, attested in the Ras Shamra texts and elsewhere, totally destroyed the Hittite capital Ḫattušaš (Boghazkeui) as well as Tarsus, Carchemish, Sidon, Kition,[40] and Ugarit itself. The Sea Peoples this time established a permanent settlement on the lower Mediterranean coast where they became known to Israel as the Philistines. These Philistines should not be identified with those associated with the patriarchs and the exodus, though they do represent a second wave of essentially the same stock as the earlier Philistines.[41]

Related to this overland invasion of Sea Peoples was one by sea which attempted to establish an Egyptian beachhead. Rameses III, in

---

36. Faulkner, "Nineteenth Dynasty," in *CAH* 2.2, pp. 220–21.

37. For the background of the following discussion see especially Trude Dothan, *The Philistines and Their Material Culture* (New Haven: Yale University Press, 1982), pp. 1–23.

38. Trude Dothan, "What We Know About the Philistines," *BAR* 8.4 (1982): 25.

39. See Benjamin Mazar, "The Philistines and Their Wars with Israel," in *World History of the Jewish People*, vol. 3, pp. 172, 324–25, n. 16.

40. Kition is on Cyprus, an island which has yielded abundant evidence of conquests by the Sea Peoples. See Vassos Karageorghis, "Exploring Philistine Origins on the Island of Cyprus," *BAR* 10 (1984): 16–28.

41. For a plausible hypothesis that the Philistines originated in Canaan, migrated to the Aegean, and then returned as part of the Sea Peoples, see T. D. Proffit, "Philistines: Aegeanized Semites," *NEASB* 12 (1978): 5–30.

wall reliefs at Medinet Habu, describes this invasion, which occurred in his eighth year (ca. 1190) and included the following elements: Peleset, Tjekker, Sheklesh, Sherden, Weshesh, and Denyen. These, he says, had conquered the Hittites and Amurru previously. The Peleset and Tjekker went on to settle in Canaan, the former as the biblical Philistines on the lower coast and the latter on the upper coast around Dor.[42] The Philistines proved to be inveterate foes of Israel from 1200 onward, and much of the books of Judges and 1 Samuel has to do with this problem.

As we conclude this overview of the history of Israel's neighbors in the period 1360–1085, it should be obvious that Israel remained almost completely untouched by international affairs. Only the advent of the Philistines posed a major problem, and this, of course, is abundantly attested in the biblical record. Otherwise the Old Testament is silent about the larger world with all its struggles precisely because they were almost irrelevant to Israel's history. We see here the providential and sovereign hand of God at work to incubate his people during this critical period of their development.

The Judges of Israel

The Cyclical Pattern of the Period

The retrospective section of Judges ends with the reference to Joshua's death in 2:6–9. Then, in 2:10 through 3:6, the author introduces the cyclical pattern which characterized Israel's history for more than three hundred years. After the passing of Joshua's generation the people began to forsake Yahweh for the gods of Canaan. This angered Yahweh so he sent enemies against Israel both to punish her and to cause her to return to him. When Israel repented, Yahweh raised up judges who would deliver the nation and provide a period of peaceful leadership. Again, however, Israel would lapse into apostasy, and the whole chain of events just described would be repeated. An important reason why Israel could not expel all her Canaanite enemies, in fact, was that they might remain in the land as instruments whereby Yahweh could discipline her. They also remained in order to provide a test of Israel's loyalty to Yahweh and to teach the new generation of Israelites the skills of warfare. The enemies allowed to remain—the Philistines, Canaanites, Sidonians, and Hivites—all lived either in the coastal plain or in the lower Bekaa Valley north of Galilee. In addition there

---

42. Malamat, "Egyptian Decline," in *World History of the Jewish People*, vol. 3, p. 34.

were various other peoples (Amorites, Hittites, and Jebusites) with whom Israel entered into marriage and syncretistic worship.

The Nature of Canaanite Idolatry

Canaanite religion was to pervade all levels of Israelite life and thought from the period of the judges on at least to the time of the Babylonian exile. Thanks mainly to the Canaanite epic and cultic texts from Ugarit (Ras Shamra) as well as the Old Testament it is possible to reconstruct at least the main lines of Canaanite religious thought and practice.[43]

Essentially, the religion of Canaan was based on the assumption that the forces of nature are expressions of divine presence and activity and that the only way one could survive and prosper was to identify the gods responsible for each phenomenon and by proper ritual encourage them to bring to bear their respective powers. This is the mythological approach to reality. Ritual involves human enactments, particularly by cultic personnel such as priests, of the activity of the gods as described in the myths.[44]

It is not possible to re-create the entire Canaanite myth in detail since the texts themselves are incomplete and lack in any case a harmonious, systematic point of view. But the general picture seems to be somewhat as follows. El is the head of the pantheon of gods. As his name implies, he is almost impersonal, a transcendent, powerful, benevolent father-figure with little or no interest in human affairs. He seems to be on the verge of senility at times and finds himself seduced and victimized over and over again by the younger gods. He sits in remote and lofty splendor on the mountain of the north, at the sources of the rivers, where he holds court and entertains the other gods. His wife is Asherah, the mother goddess, by whose fecundity the whole earth is vitalized. It is she who is referred to when the Bible speaks of

43. See Johannes C. de Moor, "The Semitic Pantheon of Ugarit," *UF* 2 (1970): 187–228; Cyrus H. Gordon, "Canaanite Mythology," in *Mythologies of the Ancient World*, ed. Samuel N. Kramer (Garden City, N.Y.: Doubleday, 1961), pp. 183–218; Arvid S. Kapelrud, *Baal in the Ras Shamra Texts* (Copenhagen: G. E. C. Gad, 1952); P. D. Miller, "Ugarit and the History of Religions," *JNSL* 9 (1981): 119–28; Julian Obermann, *Ugaritic Mythology* (New Haven: Yale University Press, 1948); Ulf Oldenburg, *The Conflict Between El and Ba'al in Canaanite Religion* (Leiden: E. J. Brill, 1969); Helmer Ringgren, *Religions of the Ancient Near East* (Philadelphia: Westminster, 1973), pp. 124–76.

44. For an important study of myth, especially as it relates to the Old Testament, see J. W. Rogerson, *Myth in Old Testament Interpretation*, BZAW 134 (Berlin: Walter de Gruyter, 1974). Myth in general is brilliantly elucidated in the works of Mircea Eliade, particularly his *Cosmos and History: The Myth of the Eternal Return* (New York: Harper, 1959).

"the Asherim" or "groves." The symbol of her presence and power was originally the evergreen tree or clumps thereof. Eventually even a wooden pole could represent Asherah and serve as a shrine where ritual was performed.

The most important deity, however, was Baal, the "master" of the land. According to many scholars Baal was an epithet of the god Hadad, son of Dagan (Dagon), who is frequently mentioned in the Mari texts and other sources from upper Mesopotamia.[45] These scholars propose that with the Amorite migration into Canaan after 2200 B.C. came also the Amorite pantheon and cult including, of course, Hadad. The introduction of the new gods to Canaan would lead either to rejection of the native gods or, more likely, to an assimilation of the new to the old. He who was Hadad at Mari became Baal at Ugarit. In support of this interpretation is the Baal myth itself, which shows Baal in contention with various other deities including El. The picture generally is that of a receding El and a gradually more prominent Baal.

Hadad was the Amorite storm god who manifested himself in rain, thunder, and lightning. Baal played this role in Canaan, and since Canaanite agriculture was totally dependent on rain, his importance is obvious. But Baal had to struggle to achieve recognition and prominence. Not only did he threaten El, who was regarded as the source of virility, but he encountered a host of other foes such as Yammu (the Sea), Naharu (the River), and even Motu (Death). These, all jealous for their own role in relation to the cycles of nature—sowing and reaping, moisture and drought, life and death—waged incessant war with Baal in the hope of preventing his construction of a palace, a sure sign of his sovereignty, and of bringing about his death.

Baal frustrated them all, however, one way or another. He took the wife of El as his own consort on occasion. He engaged both Yammu and Naharu in hand-to-hand combat and trounced them mercilessly, thus showing the superiority of rain to sea and river. Even when he was slain by Motu, he came back to life again thanks to his sister Anat and eventually vanquished Death himself. At long last he achieved supremacy and dominated both the pantheon and the cult.

The ritual involved a dramatization of the myth just described. It centered in sexual activity since the rainfall attributed to Baal was thought to represent his semen dropping to earth to fertilize and impregnate the earth with life just as he impregnated Asherah, the goddess of fertility, in the myth. Canaanite religion, then, was grossly sensual and even perverse because it required the services of both male and female cultic prostitutes as the principal actors in the drama.

---

45. For what follows see especially Oldenburg, *Conflict*, pp. 46–163.

Unlike the requirement in Israel, there was no one central sanctuary. Baal could be worshiped wherever there was a place especially visited by the numinous presence of the gods. These places were originally on hills (hence, "high place") but later could be found in valleys or even within the cities and towns. Each site would be marked by a pole (*'ăšērâ*), a pillar (*maṣṣēbâ*), or some other symbol of the cult. Since Baal was not omnipresent in the strict sense, each cult center would have its own local Baal. Thus there could be Baal-Peor, Baal-Berith, Baal-Zebub, and so on. This explains why the gods of Canaan are sometimes called Baalim ("the Baals") in the Old Testament. There was only one Baal theoretically, but he was lord of many places.

This greatly oversimplified and somewhat synthesized description of Canaanite myth and ritual is sufficient for now to introduce the nature of Israel's apostasy—it was turning from Yahweh, the real source of prosperity and fertility, to the figment of depraved imaginations which confused the result of divine blessing with its cause. It was in every way an egregious act of covenant rebellion and disloyalty best described as "whoring after other gods" (Judg. 2:17, KJV).

Othniel

The first outbreak of apostasy on a wide scale followed Joshua's death and resulted in the invasion of Israel by Cushan-Rishathaim of Aram Naharaim. The writer uses a formula which will often be repeated: Israel "forgot the LORD their God and served [i.e., worshiped] the Baals and the Asherahs" (Judg. 3:7). All this implies not just a casual interest in the myth but active participation in the ritual, precisely as had been the case when Israel worshiped the Baal of Peor (Num. 25). Cushan-Rishathaim cannot be further identified, but the latter part of his name, "Rishathaim," is no doubt more an epithet applied by his enemies than a name since it means "double wickedness." Aram Naharaim, literally "Aram of the two rivers," refers to a region of the upper Euphrates or northern Syria perhaps to be identified with the "Kushan-rôm" of the annals of Rameses II or the region "Nhr(y)n" of other Egyptian sources.[46] There is nothing in either part of the name to preclude a date of around 1340 since "Naharin" and "Nahrima," at least, appear in Egyptian and Akkadian texts as early as the fifteenth century.[47] It is true that attestation of the "Aram"

46. Merrill F. Unger, *Israel and the Aramaeans of Damascus* (Grand Rapids: Baker, 1980 reprint), pp. 40–41, 134–35.

47. Abraham Malamat, "The Aramaeans," in *Peoples of Old Testament Times*, ed. D. J. Wiseman (Oxford: Clarendon, 1973), p. 140.

element is denied by many scholars, but Merrill Unger has shown its existence in a text of Naram-Sin as early as 2300 B.C.[48]

As argued above (p. 148), Othniel's judgeship must be dated at about 1350, which places the invasion of Cushan-Rishathaim at 1358, eight years earlier. This is quite possible since at that time Aššur-uballiṭ, the powerful king of Assyria, was himself under incessant attack from an Aramean tribe known as the Sutu. The Hittite king Šuppiluliumaš found himself stymied by both Mitanni and Assyria, and though he had brought most of northern Syria under his sovereignty by 1360, his vassal states, including Naharema (Aram Naharaim), enjoyed a large measure of freedom and could well have undertaken foreign conquest independently or at the behest of the Hittite king himself.[49] Egypt at this time was, of course, helpless to interfere in any way.

What kind of damage Cushan-Rishathaim may have inflicted on Israel cannot be known, but one surely must assume that an eight-year occupation was not imposed without resistance. Othniel's expulsion of the Arameans must also have brought about a certain amount of destruction, evidence for which may be attested by a number of archaeological investigations.[50] Speculation beyond this is not advisable.

What is of more interest and importance is the nature and function of a judge. It is clear that these individuals were selected and empowered by Yahweh alone to meet certain emergencies and that their office was not hereditary. It is likewise apparent that the term *judge* does not suggest a juridical function, since that responsibility fell to the elders, but rather the office of a military leader and protector.[51] Parallels have been recently adduced from Ebla, where, coexistent with kings and elders, were judges (*di-ku*) who also appear to have had nonjuridical positions.[52] In Israel in the era between the great covenant mediators (Moses and Joshua) and the kings, the judges served as *ad hoc* governors and generals entrusted with the particular task of delivering the people from the enemies who harassed them repeatedly throughout these centuries.

48. Unger, *Israel and the Aramaeans*, p. 39.

49. Goetze, "Domination of Syria," in *CAH* 2.2, p. 16.

50. William F. Albright points out that Palestine in the fourteenth century was at a very low ebb in terms of population, a conclusion he maintains on the basis of the paucity of fortified towns in that period ("The Amarna Letters from Palestine," in *CAH* 2.2, p. 108). This evidence of few surviving urban centers could reflect destruction occasioned by the Arameans and other predators during the days of the early judges.

51. Malamat, "Period of the Judges," in *World History of the Jewish People*, vol. 3, p. 131.

52. Giovanni Pettinato, "Ebla and the Bible—Observations of the New Epigrapher's Analysis," *BAR* 6 (1980): 40.

Ehud

After Othniel drove out the Arameans, Israel had rest for forty years. Since the oppression of Cushan-Rishathaim seems to have affected all Israel, we may assume that no other oppression overlapped with it and that Othniel alone was judge for the ensuing years. The period of peace would have existed throughout the land. Given a date of 1358–1350 for the oppression, Othniel's judgeship would have come to an end in about 1310. Then Othniel died and the cycle resumed.

The oppression which came next appears to have affected a limited area centered around Jericho, "the City of Palms" (Judg. 3:13). The enemy was Eglon king of Moab, whose existence, though as yet undocumented outside the Bible, can scarcely be doubted. Together with Ammonite and Amalekite allies Eglon attacked Israel and exercised at least local hegemony for eighteen years. It is impossible to date this period precisely because some time must have elapsed between the death of Othniel and the Israelite resumption of covenant defection. A date in the first quarter of the thirteenth century (1300–1275) is not at all unreasonable.[53] In response to the cries of his people Yahweh raised up Ehud of Benjamin, who, under the pretense of offering tribute to Eglon,[54] assassinated him. Ehud then escaped into the hill country of Ephraim where he summoned the Israelite militias to follow him to the fords of the Jordan. When the Moabites tried to retreat to their homeland, they found their way blocked and were slain to the last man. The eighty years of rest which followed must refer to that east-central part of Israel over which Moab had exercised control. It was at least that long before that region again suffered at enemy hands.

Shamgar

The third judge, Shamgar, delivered Israel from Philistines sometime after the judgeship of Ehud. This event, presumably a single incident, may be associated with an early penetration of the Sea Peoples in about 1230.

Deborah

After Ehud's death, an event which cannot be dated but which need not have occurred until after the eighty years of rest, Israel turned to evil ways once more. This time the judgment of Yahweh was concentrated in the north, in and above the Jezreel Valley, and involved Jabin

53. Disputing Nelson Glueck, Sean Warner concedes that the Moabites, Edomites, and Ammonites occupied the Transjordan between 1400 and 1375 and were well in place by the time of Ehud ("Period of the Judges," *VT* 28 [1978]: 459).

54. Malamat, "Period of the Judges," in *World History of the Jewish People*, vol. 3, p. 155.

king of Hazor and his general Sisera of Harosheth (Tell el-'Amr), a town on the Kishon River east of Mount Carmel. For twenty long years the northern tribes suffered Canaanite oppression about which they could do nothing because of the Canaanite military superiority. The reference to iron chariots (Judg. 4:3) not only emphasizes this strategic advantage, but helps to date the account since iron did not come into common use in Canaan until around 1200. A date of 1240–1220 for this oppression is not out of keeping with the biblical data or extrabiblical information gleaned from archaeological research.[55]

The agent of salvation on this occasion was Deborah of Ephraim, who set up her place of administration between Ramah and Bethel. Since the area under attack was far to her north, she responded to the urgent appeals first by encouraging Barak of Kedesh in Naphtali, less than ten miles north of Hazor, to take matters into his own hands and to confront Jabin at Mount Tabor. Yahweh would lead Sisera to the river Kishon. Barak and his Naphtalite and Zebulunite troops could then descend from Tabor and overcome the enemy at the river. Barak refused to follow Deborah's advice, however, for he quite properly understood that she, the anointed judge of Israel, symbolized the presence and power of Yahweh.[56] Deborah therefore joined him at Tabor, and Barak, emboldened by her presence, struck the chariotry of Sisera, which apparently became immobilized by a rapid and unexpected rising of the Kishon (Judg. 5:21).[57]

Sisera himself escaped to Zaanannim, a town near Kedesh in Issachar,[58] and took refuge in the tent of Heber the Kenite. The Kenites were related to the Midianites as one can see from the fact that Moses' father-in-law is called both a Midianite and a Kenite (Exod. 18:1; Judg. 1:16). Their name reflects a Hebrew root meaning "smith," so their

55. Yigael Yadin suggests 1230 ("Excavations at Hazor, 1955–58," in *Biblical Archaeologist Reader*, ed. Edward F. Campbell, Jr., and David Noel Freedman [Garden City, N.Y.: Doubleday, 1964], vol. 2, p. 223). Scholars who insist on a late date for the conquest have difficulty here since they cannot explain the existence of Hazor at the end of the thirteenth century if that city was destroyed by Joshua. If, however, Hazor was destroyed by Joshua around 1400, it could easily have been rebuilt and then destroyed once more by Deborah in 1230. See Malamat, "Period of the Judges," in *World History of the Jewish People*, vol. 3, p. 135, who, however, contrary to Yadin, dates the fall of Hazor between 1150 and 1125.

56. For Deborah the prophetess as the agent of Yahweh himself in the call of Barak see James S. Ackerman, "Prophecy and Warfare in Early Israel: A Study of the Deborah/Barak Story," *BASOR* 220 (1975): 5–14.

57. Since the rising of the Kishon is not mentioned in Judges 4, the nonpoetic account, G. W. Ahlström argues that the reference to the river in chapter 5 is mythopoeic and has no historical value. As "proof" he then cites the part played by the Reed Sea in the exodus story ("Judges 5:20f. and History," *JNES* 36 [1977]: 287–88). This approach, which denies the possibility of poetry as historiography, is without basis.

58. See map 16 in Aharoni, *Land of the Bible*, p. 222.

dwelling in tents may indicate not so much a pastoral nomadism as the pursuit of an occupation that entailed travel from job to job.[59] Heber's move to the north and his affiliation with Jabin may, in fact, have to do with the development of the iron industry by the Philistines and Canaanites. In any case, Heber's wife Jael apparently allowed her sense of loyalty to her Israelite kin to prevail over that of Semitic hospitality, for she slew Sisera in her own tent.

The defeat of Sisera and subsequent end of Jabin's oppression (Judg. 4:24) were celebrated in the song of Deborah and Barak.[60] With special reference to the decisive encounter at the Kishon they rehearsed Yahweh's dealings from the Transjordanian conquest until the present hour (Judg. 5:1–5; cf. Deut. 33:2–3; Ps. 68:7–9; Hab. 3:3). In the days of Shamgar and Jael, which had just preceded, the roads were unsafe for travel because of brigands and outlaws of every kind. These chaotic conditions existed because Israel had adopted new gods and had therefore known divine judgment. Then Yahweh had raised up Deborah, who mustered an army from the tribes and achieved a mighty victory at Kishon and Zaanannim.

But the poem also betrays something of the provincial nature of the oppression and the lack of tribal unity. Deborah seems to have been judge of all Israel, but was unable to command a united front against the Canaanites in the north. She mentions the participation of only certain "Amalekite" Ephraimites, Benjamin, Makir, Zebulun, Issachar, and Naphtali. Reuben only considered participation, Gilead (i.e., Gad) did not do even that much, Dan "linger[ed] by the ships," which may be a proverbial way of describing cowardice, and Asher remained at home. Conspicuous by their absence from the list are Judah and Simeon. This does not mean, contrary to many tradition critics,[61] that Judah and Simeon were not yet part of the Israelite confederation, but only that distance and the beginnings of sectional rivalries were already starting to undermine the nation.[62] Judah by now may have

59. de Vaux, *Early History*, pp. 537–38.
60. For literary and traditio-historical analyses of this important poem see David Noel Freedman, "Early Israelite History in the Light of Early Israelite Poetry," in *Unity and Diversity*, ed. Hans Goedicke and J. J. M. Roberts (Baltimore: Johns Hopkins University Press, 1975), pp. 3–35; Richard D. Patterson, "The Song of Deborah," in *Tradition and Testament: Essays in Honor of Charles Lee Feinberg*, ed. John S. Feinberg and Paul D. Feinberg (Chicago: Moody, 1981), pp. 123–60.
61. For example, A. D. H. Mayes, "The Period of the Judges and the Rise of the Monarchy," in *Israelite and Judaean History*, ed. John H. Hayes and J. Maxwell Miller (Philadelphia: Westminster, 1977), p. 310; Freedman, "Early Israelite History," in *Unity and Diversity*, p. 15.
62. Aharoni, "Settlement of Canaan," in *World History of the Jewish People*, vol. 3, p. 109; see also Carol L. Meyers, "Of Seasons and Soldiers: A Topological Appraisal of the Premonarchic Tribes of Galilee," *BASOR* 252 (1983): 56–57.

sensed its isolation, and the eastern tribes without doubt were beginning to go their own way.

Gideon

After the triumph of Deborah the land had rest for forty years. This must be taken to include central Israel at least, for the next oppression is concentrated in that area. The forty years would be 1230–1190 if one accepts Yigael Yadin's date of 1230 for the destruction of Hazor. The Midianite conquest of seven years apparently took place in the decade 1190–1180 and was particularly violent, as the historian takes pains to point out. Cities and houses were so devastated as to necessitate the use of dens and caves for residence (Judg. 7:2). Field crops and livestock were also swept away and the land ravaged.

The extent of this carnage was severe, extending from the Jordan valley as far southwest as Gaza, but the narrative does not indicate that it was nationwide.[63] It is important to note this, for it is often objected that the Midianites could not have been populous or powerful enough to overrun all Israel. In addition to the fact that the record itself does not assert Midian overran the whole nation, there is no warrant to assume anything about Midian's size or strength since only the Old Testament supplies any information on the matter. The historian, in fact, stresses that the Midianites were accompanied by the Amalekites and other eastern hordes, that they were like "swarms of locusts" (Judg. 6:5) and impossible to count (cf. Judg. 8:10). Even allowing for hyperbole it is clear that the Midianites represented a formidable foe, especially in light of Israel's lack of tribal solidarity and the absence of strong political and military leadership.

With infinite patience Yahweh raised up a champion to deliver his people when they cried out to him (Judg. 6:7). This was Gideon, son of Joash the Abiezrite, who lived in the Manassehite town of Ophrah (perhaps modern 'Affuleh in the Jezreel plain).[64] That there could be an Israelite settlement in what was previously Canaanite-held territory attests to the thoroughness of Deborah's conquest of the Canaanites forty years earlier. As he had done with others, Yahweh manifested himself in the person of the angel of Yahweh. Initially Gideon resisted the call of Yahweh, arguing that he had abandoned his people to Midian and that he, Gideon, was in any event hardly qualified to lead the people since he came from such humble stock. His protests were silenced, however, when Yahweh miraculously caused fire to flare forth

---

63. Malamat, "Period of the Judges," in *World History of the Jewish People*, vol. 3, p. 143.

64. Aharoni, *Land of the Bible*, p. 263.

and consume the sacrifice which Gideon had prepared for him. That night Gideon dismantled the Baal altar and Asherah pole his father had erected, and built an altar to Yahweh in their place. This token of his commitment to Yahweh brought upon Gideon the wrath of his apostate community, and were it not for his father's intercession, he would have died at their hands. If Baal is indeed a god, Joash said, he should take up his own defense against Gideon's sacrilege!

At length the Midianites and their allies assembled in the Plain of Jezreel to confront Israel. Having won over his own clan of Abiezer, Gideon called them and the other Manassehite clans along with the tribes of Asher, Zebulun, and Naphtali and prepared them for the battle. This list of tribes confirms our thesis that the enemies of Israel at this time harassed only limited areas—in this case the Jezreel and Galilee regions—and that the judges also functioned over limited areas.

Gideon, having certified (by signs involving a fleece spread on a threshing floor) the presence of Yahweh with him, established his position at the spring of Harod. This lay just south of Mount Moreh, the campsite of the Midianite host. There Yahweh ordered Gideon to reduce the size of his army, so that when the battle was won, it would be clear to everyone that Yahweh, not Israel, was the victor. That night, using a strategem of surprising the enemy by blaring trumpets and smashing jars, Gideon achieved a triumph with only three hundred men. In total panic and disarray the Midianites set upon one another; only after inflicting tremendous casualties upon themselves did they take flight east to the deserts. Gideon followed in hot pursuit as far as Beth Shittah (location unknown) on the route to Zererah (Zarethan—modern Tell Umm Hamad),[65] which is on the Jabbok east of the Jordan. The approximate location of Beth Shittah can be determined from its association with Abel Meholah (Khirbet Tell el-Hilu), which is just west of the Jordan, across from Tabbath (Ras Abu Tabat), and northwest of Zarethan.[66]

To prevent the escape of the two Midianite chieftains, Oreb and Zeeb, across the Jordan, Gideon sent word to the Ephraimites to guard the fording places of the Jordan as far south as Beth Barah, possibly near the mouth of the Wadi Far'a, across the Jordan from the Jabbok. Thus Ephraim became involved because the Midianite routes of escape were within Ephraimite territory. The strategy was successful, and the Ephraimites presented to Gideon the heads of the two chieftains as evidence. They complained at the same time of having been omitted from the muster of Gideon's army, but Gideon pacified them by con-

---

65. So *Oxford Bible Atlas*, ed. Herbert G. May, 3d ed. (New York: Oxford University Press, 1984), p. 143.
66. Aharoni, *Land of the Bible*, p. 284, n. 222.

vincing them that theirs was the greater glory for having slain the Midianite leaders.

Gideon himself then crossed the Jordan in pursuit of two other Midianite leaders, Zebah and Zalmunna. He arrived first at Succoth (Tell Deir 'Alla) in the lower Jabbok valley less than five miles due east of the Jordan. He there asked sustenance for his famished troops, but the people of Succoth refused it on the grounds that Gideon had not yet defeated the enemy and so did not deserve support. They would recognize his leadership when he came back with the severed hands of the Midianite chieftains. The residents of Peniel (Tulul edh-Dhahab),[67] seven miles farther up the Jabbok, responded to Gideon in the same way. Gideon therefore threatened both towns with punishment when he returned from his pursuit.

What is remarkable about the narrative of the Transjordan foray is the very evident spirit of regionalism which had developed in Israel over the previous 150 years, a spirit which reflects a breaking down of any sense of brotherhood or tribal cohesion. The men of Succoth and Peniel were, after all, Israelites, specifically Gadites. Their resistance to Gideon illustrates the very concerns expressed by both Moses and Joshua in regard to the tribes that settled east of the Jordan (Num. 32:6–15, 20–27; Josh. 22:13–20). The river not only was a physical boundary, but had created a psychological and philosophical barrier. The seeds of Israelite disintegration were already beginning to germinate, and it would not be long before the Transjordan tribes would be lost to the confederation for all practical purposes.

Gideon overtook the Midianites at Karkor (Qarqar), deep in the Syro-Arabian desert, more than sixty miles east of the Dead Sea. Despite the overwhelming odds (fifteen thousand Midianites to his band of three hundred) Gideon prevailed, scattering the Midianites and capturing Zebah and Zalmunna. Triumphantly he returned to Peniel, broke down its citadel, and slew its inhabitants. He then executed the Midianite kings in retaliation for their years of terrorizing and slaughtering the people of Manasseh.

When at last Gideon reached his home at Ophrah, the people wished to make him king, the first recorded expression of such a sentiment. It had become clear that only central authority of a sustained nature could guarantee security and stability. Gideon, however, rejected the overture, for it violated the very essence of theocratic government— the divine election of nonhereditary leadership. He did allow a golden ephod to be made and placed in Ophrah, perhaps as a kind of palladium or "divinatory cloak,"[68] but this became in itself an object of

---

67. *Oxford Bible Atlas*, p. 137.
68. Boling, *Judges*, p. 161.

worship which was to undermine much of what Gideon had achieved on behalf of Yahweh.

The Abortive Kingship of Abimelech

The defeat of Midian ushered in a period of forty years of peace, extending from about 1180 to 1140. However, after Gideon's death Israel defected from Yahweh. The central part of the nation at least began to worship the pagan deity of Shechem, Baal-Berith. This without doubt was because Abimelech, Gideon's son by a Shechemite concubine, had attracted a following among the people of Shechem and was able to integrate the Canaanite cult there with his own monarchical ambitions.

Shechem had, of course, long been associated with the special presence of Yahweh. Abraham had built his first altar there, Jacob had there bought property and dug a well, Joseph was buried there, and Joshua had led the nation in covenant reaffirmation at Shechem. The central sanctuary had been established at Shiloh, however, and so it appears that Shechem had been taken over by anti-Yahwist elements who had seized upon its hoary sanctity as justification for the establishment of a Baal cult center.[69] The very name of Baal there, Baal-Berith ("Lord of Covenant"), probably harks back to the covenant traditions of the place beginning with Abraham and continuing through Joshua. In line with common practice, the covenant-making function of Yahweh was simply transferred to Baal so that he, not Yahweh, was viewed as the god who made Shechem a holy place.[70]

Abimelech capitalized on this antitheocratic development, and as the son of the popular hero Gideon and his Shechemite concubine soon attracted the people of Shechem to his political cause. The people, after all, had already requested that Gideon be their king. He had declined, but perhaps they would accept his son as their sovereign. The only obstacles were the other sons of Gideon, so Abimelech hired assassins who went with him to Ophrah to slaughter all of them. Then, at Shechem, Abimelech was made king.

One of Gideon's sons escaped the fratricide, however. Jotham predicted that Abimelech's reign would not last, and indeed within three years the people of Shechem turned against him. After a series of plots and conspiracies Abimelech found it necessary to attack and destroy

69. Ronald E. Clements, "Baal-Berith of Shechem," *JSS* 13 (1968): 31–32.

70. This interpretation runs counter to that of most scholars, who argue the reverse; that is, that the site was originally devoted to a Canaanite cult and was appropriated by Israel for Yahweh worship. See Martin Noth, *The History of Israel*, 2d ed. (New York: Harper and Row, 1960), pp. 98–99; G. Ernest Wright, "Deuteronomy," in *Interpreter's Bible*, ed. George A. Buttrick (New York: Abingdon, 1953), vol. 2, p. 326.

Shechem.[71] He then went on to Thebez (Tubas), about nine miles north of Shechem, but in attempting to burn its citadel was killed by a woman who dropped a millstone upon him from the roof. Thus, Israel's earliest experiment in monarchy was aborted.

The list of places in the story of Abimelech makes it clear that his reign was limited not only in years but in geographical extent. All of his activity was confined to the region of Manasseh; there is not the slightest hint that he attracted any interest at all outside his own tribe. Plainly, Israel as a whole was not ready for monarchy or at least not the kind that Abimelech could offer.

Minor Judges

The reign of Abimelech may have been the occasion for the judgeship of Tola, for he was from the tribe of Issachar, Manasseh's neighbor to the north. One can well imagine the turbulence created by the civil strife which attended Abimelech's ill-conceived adventures in Manasseh. Tola's judgeship, then, did not involve an outside enemy, but was designed to restore peace within Manasseh itself. He lived in Shamir (Samaria?)[72] and held office for twenty-three years. In line with our proposed date of 1180–1140 for the period of peace following the defeat of Midian, Gideon may have died in 1120, in which case Abimelech would have reigned from 1120 to 1117 and Tola judged from 1117 to 1094. Though one cannot hope for precision, as we have warned repeatedly, these dates are not at all incompatible with what little is known of this period.

Probably parallel to or a little later than the era of Tola was that of Jair in Gilead. This wealthy citizen of Kamon (Qamm), about twelve miles southeast of the Sea of Kinnereth, judged Israel (i.e., Gilead) for twenty-two years. If one assumes that he followed Tola in the sense of commencing his judgeship after Tola's had begun, a date of 1115–1093 is possible. If Jair followed the death of Tola, the date might be 1094–1072. In either case one can harmonize Jair's judgeship with that of Jephthah, for though Jephthah's dates are almost certainly around 1106–1100, his administration was apparently centered in Mizpah (Jal'ad),[73] at least forty miles south of Kamon. Jair was limited

71. Bernhard W. Anderson dates Shechem's destruction at 1100 b.c., not out of line with our own chronology which places the time of rest following the defeat of Midian at 1180–1140. Gideon appears to have died some years after the rest ended (Judg. 8:28, 32–33), perhaps as late as 1120 ("The Place of Shechem in the Bible," *BA* 20 [1957]: 16).

72. *Oxford Bible Atlas*, p. 140.

73. Yohanan Aharoni and Michael Avi-Yonah, *Macmillan Bible Atlas* (New York: Macmillan, 1968), p. 181; see also map 78. Martin Noth, however, places Mizpah at el-Mishrefe, two kilometers north of Jal'ad; see Malamat, "Period of the Judges," in *World History of the Jewish People*, vol. 3, p. 322, n. 78.

to the towns of Havvoth Jair, a district just south and east of the Sea of Kinnereth.

Following the Midianite threat and the short-lived monarchy of Abimelech, Israel again turned away from Yahweh and this time on a massive scale. They began to worship the Baals and Ashtoreths as usual, but added to them the gods of Aram, Sidon, Moab, Ammon, and Philistia. In response Yahweh gave them over "into the hands of the Philistines and the Ammonites, who that year shattered and crushed them" (Judg. 10:7–8). This statement can mean only that the Philistine and Ammonite oppressions came simultaneously (see pp. 148–49). The historian proceeds to narrate the Ammonite account first (Judg. 10:8b–12:7) and after that the Philistine (13:1–16:31). This fact is of great importance in reconstructing the chronology of this period.

Jephthah

The Ammonites, the exclusive referent in Judges 10:8b, oppressed the Transjordan Israelites for eighteen years. They even managed to cross the river to harass Judah, Benjamin, and Ephraim. Finally the Israelites assembled at Mizpah and began a frantic search for a leader capable of delivering them. Jephthah, the son of Gilead, had been forced into exile in Tob (et-Taiyibeh) deep in the Hauran wilderness, where he soon gathered about him a band of outlaws. Sometime after his exile the Ammonite oppression began. The Gileadite elders, well aware of his prowess and leadership qualities, summoned him to Mizpah and there made him their commander. Jephthah's first action was to attempt a diplomatic settlement with the Ammonites. Their grievance was that the eastern tribes of Israel had been illegally occupying their land for three hundred years. Jephthah sent a delegation to the Ammonite king and reminded him that Israel had not taken any Ammonite land at the time of the conquest. In fact, what Ammon was now claiming as its territory was at that time the kingdom of Sihon the Amorite. It was he whom Moses had dispossessed, not the Ammonites. Whether Ammon had had claim to the area before the Amorite occupation was neither here nor there.[74] Moreover, Jephthah asked, why was Ammon laying claim to these regions only now, three centuries after the conquest of Sihon (Judg. 11:26)?

As pointed out before (pp. 148–49), the figure of three hundred years is important in establishing the dates not only of the exodus and the

---

74. It does, indeed, appear to be true that the Ammonites held title to the area before Sihon's time (Num. 21:26). See Eugene H. Merrill, "Numbers," in *The Bible Knowledge Commentary*, ed. John F. Walvoord and Roy B. Zuck (Wheaton, Ill.: Victor, 1985), vol. 1, pp. 240–41.

conquest, but of the Philistine and Ammonite oppressions as well. The conquest of the Transjordan occurred in 1406, just forty years after the exodus, so Jephthah's communication with the Ammonites must be dated close to 1106. There is, in fact, no reason to take three hundred as anything other than an exact figure. It is certain that Jephthah's defeat of the Ammonites, which immediately followed their rejection of his negotiations, ended the Ammonite threat. Since it had lasted for eighteen years, it must have begun in 1124. At that time the lands on both sides of the Jordan were enjoying rest thanks to the effective removal of the Midianites by Gideon in the preceding decades. It is possible that the Ammonite claims were pressed following Gideon's death since they then would have had no cause for fear of Israel.

After the Ammonites rejected Jephthah's terms of peace, he attacked them on a front from Aroer (unknown), which was somewhere east of Rabbah (modern Amman), to Minnith (unknown), which was somewhere in Ammon east of the Jabbok, and on to Abel Keramim (Na'ûr?),[75] a few miles northwest of Heshbon. He then returned to Mizpah, where he fulfilled the vows he had made in seeking divine favor.

Evidence of continuing regional suspicions and latent hostility may be seen in the reaction of the Ephraimites to Jephthah's success. They had suffered at Ammonite hands and now crossed the Jordan to chide Jephthah because he had not invited them to share in Ammon's defeat. With little thought of consequences and in keeping with the anarchic spirit of the age, the Ephraimites threatened to burn Jephthah's house to the ground. Jephthah protested that he had in vain invited Ephraim to participate (Judg. 12:2). All the Ephraimites could reply was that the Gileadites were renegades from Ephraim and Manasseh and thus were disloyal to Israel.[76] All this, of course, reflects the problems stemming from the request of Reuben, Gad, and eastern Manasseh for Transjordanian inheritance. Further evidence of the developing alienation of the eastern and western tribes can be seen in the means Jephthah took to prevent Ephraimites from recrossing the Jordan after doing battle with the Gileadites. He posted his men near the fording places. Every survivor of the battle who attempted to cross to the west was commanded to pronounce "Shibboleth" (*šibbōlet*). If he said "Sibboleth" (*sibbōlet*), a phonetic peculiarity of the west, he was readily identified as an Ephraimite and put to death.[77] Here is graphic evi-

---

75. Aharoni, *Land of the Bible*, p. 429.

76. Aharoni, "Settlement of Canaan," in *World History of the Jewish People*, vol. 3, pp. 123–24. There is considerable evidence that Ephraim laid claim to much of Transjordan, as reference to the Transjordanian forest of Ephraim (2 Sam. 18:6; cf. 17:24) would suggest. See Malamat, "Period of the Judges," in *World History of the Jewish People*, vol. 3, p. 159.

77. See Ephraim A. Speiser, "The Shibboleth Incident," *BASOR* 85 (1942): 10–13;

dence that language distinctions had begun to mark the rapidly widening division of the nation.[78]

Jephthah lived on for six years after the Ammonite expulsion (1106–1100) and was followed by three local judges. Ibzan of Bethlehem (probably in Judah) served for seven years (ca. 1100–1093), Elon of Aijalon in Zebulun for ten years (ca. 1093–1083), and Abdon of Pirathon (Far'ata) in Ephraim for eight years (ca. 1083–1075). These may have been synchronous judgeships in whole or in part, but in any event they did not cover the areas oppressed by the Ammonites and the Philistines.

Samson

The Philistine oppression began in the same year as the Ammonite (1124) but is related in detail only after the account of Jephthah and the Ammonites has concluded (see p. 149). This view is not vitiated by the standard translations of Judges 13:1a—"again the Israelites did evil"—for the word translated "again" does not actually appear as such in the Hebrew text. Literally the original reads, "And the Israelites added to do evil," an idiom which can indeed but need not mean "to do again." The verb yāsap here certainly means "to continue to do," but only with the addition of the particle 'ôd would it mean "to do again" (cf. Judg. 11:14).[79] Thus Israel continued to do evil, just as the narrator stated in Judges 10:6 when he first introduced the Philistine oppression. Verse 13:1a serves as a literary link to the earlier passage and does not intend to suggest a Jephthah-Samson sequence.

The Philistine peril affected the Danites in particular though it had its impact on Ephraim, Benjamin, and Judah as well. For forty long years the Israelites groaned under the relentless and brutal pressure until at last Yahweh raised up Samson and then Samuel to relieve them from the Philistine yoke. The oppression began in 1124 and continued until 1084. Samson's judgeship coincided with the oppression (Judg. 15:20) but did not outlast it (1 Sam. 7:13–14). Since he was in office for twenty years (Judg. 16:31) he must have entered his ministry no later than the midpoint of the forty years or in 1104. He would have been no more than twenty years of age then because his birth followed the commencement of the Philistine judgment (Judg. 13:5). To sum up: the oppression lasted from 1124 to 1084, Samson was born

---

Eduard Y. Kutscher, *A History of the Hebrew Language* (Jerusalem: Magnes, 1982), pp. 14–15.

78. For other evidences of the rift see Malamat, "Period of the Judges," in *World History of the Jewish People*, vol. 3, pp. 160–61, who points out that Ephraim is always the principal instigator. See also Daniel I. Block, "The Role of Language in Ancient Israelite Perceptions of National Identity," *JBL* 103 (1984): 339, n. 75.

79. Boling, *Judges*, p. 85.

around 1123, he began his judgeship in 1104, and died in 1084 at the latest.

Born to godly Danite parents at Zorah (Ṣar'ah) in the Sorek Valley, Samson was from birth a Nazirite invested mightily by the Spirit of God.[80] That this need not imply personal spirituality is clear from the course of the young man's life. He serves as eloquent testimony to the nature of judgeship. It was not an office for which one was qualified by natural gifts, personal integrity, or inheritance, but only by the sovereign disposition of Yahweh. Samson's various affairs with the women of Philistia are sufficient to show that his success in Israel's behalf was due not to his own character but to his God, who came upon him and empowered him to be the savior of his people.

Samson fell in love with a Philistine maiden from Timnah (Tell Baṭash), a town on the Israelite-Philistine border. At his wedding feast he wagered thirty sets of clothes that his companions would not be able to solve a riddle. When tricked into revealing the answer, he went to the Philistine city of Ashkelon to slaughter thirty men that he might have their clothing to pay off his wager. This marked his first recorded attack on the Philistines. When Samson later returned to Timnah, he found that his wife had been given to another man. In a rage he tied together in pairs the tails of three hundred foxes, ignited them, and sent the animals running through the Philistine wheat fields, burning up the crops. When the Philistines retaliated by killing his wife and father-in-law, Samson slew a great number of Philistines in turn. This prompted them to set themselves for battle against Judah, a prospect which terrified Judah since, by their own admission, they were under Philistine domination (Judg. 15:11). They therefore delivered Samson over to the Philistines, but there at Ramath Lehi (site unknown) he slaughtered a thousand of the enemy.

The second woman of Samson's life was a prostitute at Gaza. While visiting her, Samson was discovered by certain Philistines who decided to lie in wait all night to seize him in the morning. At midnight, however, he got up, took hold of the city gate, and carried it all the way to Hebron forty miles away.

Finally, Samson fell to the charms of Delilah, who betrayed him by disclosing to the Philistines that his unshorn hair was the secret of his strength. Ironically, he was returned to Gaza and made to grind in a mill like a beast of burden. The city from which he in his strength had stolen the gate now in his weakness became his prison. In due course Samson was brought into the temple of Dagon, the principal Philistine god. His hair, the token of his Nazirite status and of the power of

---

80. For the nature and function of the Nazirite see Roland de Vaux, *Ancient Israel* (New York: McGraw-Hill, 1965), vol. 2, pp. 466–67.

Yahweh upon him, had regrown; and in one last mighty effort he pulled the temple of Dagon down upon himself and the Philistines, killing more of the enemy than he had slain during his lifetime.

Critical scholars refuse to view the Samson stories as history because of the superhuman exploits of the hero. They prefer instead to describe them as legends or sagas designed to enhance the reputation of Yahweh by attributing his victories over his enemies to one Spirit-filled man rather than to a whole army as, it is alleged, must actually have been the case.[81] The problem with this skepticism is that it misunderstands the nature of sagas as a literary genre[82] and, moreover, is based on an uncritical assumption that such single-handed exploits simply could not and therefore did not occur. But this kind of begging the question has no place in the assessment of history writing. If one concedes that there is nothing apart from the biblical account to contradict it and that biblical history is *sui generis,* that it is special and unique history, there is no good reason why the stories of Samson should be rejected out of hand. Historical uniformitarianism must not straitjacket and predetermine what happened in the past.

Samuel

The last five chapters of Judges form, with the Book of Ruth, what might be called a Bethlehem trilogy of stories whose setting is the era of the judges. Before these are examined, however, we will bring to a close our narrative of Philistine oppression and of the period of the judges as a whole. This requires attention to the first several chapters of 1 Samuel.

The Book of 1 Samuel begins with the story of Samuel's birth, in answer to Hannah's prayer, at Ramathaim Zophim (Rentis) in Ephraim, just five miles northwest of Timnath Serah, the burial place of Joshua, and about eighteen miles west of the tabernacle at Shiloh. Samuel was dedicated by his parents to be a Nazirite and to serve Yahweh at Shiloh. Though not a priest per se, Samuel was a Levite (1 Chron. 6:22–28), a descendant of Kohath, and so could minister at the tabernacle and at other local altars.

While Samuel was a lad at Shiloh, the high priest was Eli, a descendant of Ithamar as may be gathered from the fact that the priesthood later was taken from Eli's line and given to Zadok, a descendant

---

81. For a typical view see James L. Crenshaw, *Samson* (Atlanta: John Knox, 1978), pp. 19–26.

82. For an excellent discussion of saga, especially of the imprecision of the term as a translation of German *Sage,* see John J. Scullion, "*Märchen, Sage, Legende*: Towards a Clarification of Some Literary Terms Used by Old Testament Scholars," *VT* 34 (1984): 324–31.

of Eleazar (1 Kings 2:35; cf. Num. 3:4; 1 Chron. 6:8). Though one may not find evidence of apostasy in Eli himself, his sons in effect transformed the house of Yahweh at Shiloh into a Canaanite shrine with all the corruption and immorality associated with the Baal cult (1 Sam. 2:12–17, 22–25). It was in this environment that young Samuel was called by Yahweh and appointed to be both prophet and judge. It was also in and because of those circumstances that Yahweh had brought the Philistines to bear as an instrument of his chastisement.

The presence of the Philistines in the early years of Samuel must be related to the forty-year oppression mentioned in Judges 13:1. This is evident both from the fact that no chronology can allow Samuel to be a youth prior to 1124 (see pp. 149–50), the beginning of the only known Philistine oppression in the twelfth century, and from the clear statement that it was Samuel himself who finally ended the Philistine rule and enabled the Israelites to regain their former territories (1 Sam. 7:13–14). This accomplishment by Samuel must be dated at 1084 because the Philistine oppression lasted forty years, from 1124 to 1084. The ark of the covenant had remained at Kiriath Jearim for twenty years by the time Samuel overthrew the Philistines (1 Sam. 7:2). Since it had been there ever since Shiloh fell, except for seven months in Philistia (1 Sam. 6:1), Shiloh must have fallen around 1104.[83]

Let us look more closely at the events of 1104. The historian relates that the Philistines had assembled at Aphek, obviously with the intent of doing battle with the Israelites gathered at Ebenezer. The Aphek in view is Râs el-'Ain, about twenty-five miles west of Shiloh. Ebenezer ('Izbet Ṣarṭah?)[84] was only two miles to the southeast of Aphek.[85] When the battle was joined, Israel suffered a crushing defeat. Superstitiously they attributed their loss to the absence of the ark of the covenant from the battlefield. The presence of Yahweh as the Warrior of Israel leading his hosts in holy war was always symbolized by the ark. But holy war was war sanctioned by Yahweh—the mere presence of the ark did not certify the blessing of Yahweh. Nonetheless, the ark was fetched from Shiloh; and though it terrorized the Philistines, who also looked upon it as functioning automatically, they joined battle with

---

83. This date is about fifty years earlier than that usually assigned to the destruction of Shiloh; see, for example, John Bright, *A History of Israel*, 3d ed. (Philadelphia: Westminster, 1981), pp. 185–86. Note that the biblical account does not say that Shiloh was actually destroyed at the time the ark was lost to the Philistines. The destruction could have taken place fifty years after the city ceased to be Israel's cultic center. Psalm 78:60 speaks of Yahweh's abandonment of Shiloh, a matter attested in 1 Samuel 4:11, whereas Jeremiah refers to its destruction (7:12, 14; cf. 26:6, 9) as an aftermath of its rejection as the cult center. They may not be one and the same.

84. *Oxford Bible Atlas*, p. 127.

85. For an excellent graphic of the battle see Aharoni and Avi-Yonah, *Macmillan Bible Atlas*, map 83, p. 58.

Israel and achieved an overwhelming triumph. Eli's sons, Hophni and Phinehas, who had charge of the ark, were slain, and the ark itself taken as a trophy of war. When word of the disaster returned to Shiloh, Eli fell backward and died, and Phinehas's wife gave birth prematurely to a son whom she named Ichabod ("no glory"), an eloquent description of the loss of the ark.

The attack on Israel at Aphek could well have been a reaction to the early maraudings of Samson against the Philistines, which began at about this time (1104). Since Samson clearly was empowered miraculously by the God of Israel, what better way was there to address the problem than to attack the Israelite cult center at Shiloh? The Philistines soon learned, however, that Yahweh could not be contained within a box, nor were his powers diminished by virtue of exile to Philistia. As a virtual prisoner of war in the temple of Dagon at Ashdod, Yahweh lay in abject humility (or so the Philistines imagined) at the foot of the Philistine deity. But by the next morning Dagon had fallen prostrate before the ark. His attendants set him up again, but once more he crashed ignominiously to the floor, this time losing both his head and his arms. In unmistakable terms, the incomparability and invincibility of Yahweh were being asserted.

Dagon was not alone in his embarrassment for a plague of hemorrhoids broke out amongst the people of Ashdod. Seeing this as an act of Yahweh, they sent the ark on to a sister city, Gath. There too the plague erupted, and so the ark was removed to Ekron, where the same results came to pass. In utter frustration the lords of the Philistines decided to return the ark to Israel and make appropriate offerings to Yahweh in order to placate him and induce him to remove the plague. Led by Yahweh, the draft animals which pulled the cart containing the ark arrived at Beth Shemesh, where a certain Joshua took temporary charge of the ark. There the Levites offered to Yahweh a sacrifice of the animals. But some of the people of Beth Shemesh had looked into the ark, an act which violated its sanctity, and so they were struck dead. Terrified, the survivors requested the citizens of Kiriath Jearim (Deir el-ʿÂzar), some ten miles northeast, to take possession of the ark. Why the men of Beth Shemesh should have died for mishandling the ark while the Philistines could do so with relative impunity is quite clear—Yahweh's expectations of his own holy people are not incumbent on those who are not his. That is, the ark was holy only to the holy people.

For twenty years the ark remained at Kiriath Jearim in the house of Abinadab. Only after that time did Samuel enjoin the Israelites to do away with the pagan gods, serve Yahweh, and prepare to rid the land of the Philistines once and for all. Samuel's sudden assertion of leadership suggests that he was now mature and no other leaders were

available. Samson, then, must have died. He had died while destroying
the Dagon temple at Gaza at the end of twenty years of judging. This
must have been around 1084. Now, twenty years after the Philistine
capture of the ark in 1104, Samuel stepped into the leadership void as
judge and prophet in order finally to deal with the Philistine problem.
Gathering the people to Mizpah (Tell en-Naṣbeh), between Gibeon and
Bethel, Samuel offered sacrifices to Yahweh and encouraged Israel
against the Philistines, who were on their way to do battle. With the
aid of Yahweh Israel achieved a smashing victory and drove the Philistines back all the way to Beth Car. This place cannot be identified,
but since it is associated with Shen (Jeshanah or el-Burj),[86] just south
of Shiloh, it must have been in a northerly direction. In any event, this
encounter effectively ended the Philistine occupation of Israel (if not
the harassment); the oppression of forty years was finally over. The
reference to peace with the Amorites (1 Sam. 7:14) implies that Samuel's defeat of the Philistines also ushered in a period of peace with
the indigenous Amorite populations of the hill country.[87]

This exploit of Samuel marked him as a judge, the last in the long
succession of charismatic leaders which began with Othniel. But even
Samuel's jurisdiction was limited, for his circuit was from Bethel to
Gilgal to Mizpah, an area no farther than twenty miles at its greatest
extent. Nor was he constantly on the move, for he periodically returned
to Ramah (i.e., Ramathaim Zophim), where he made his permanent
home. Judgeship was giving way to monarchy; within thirty-five years
Samuel would preside at the coronation of Israel's first king.

The Bethlehem Trilogy

Before we examine the monarchy of Israel, however, some attention
must be paid to the so-called Bethlehem trilogy, three narratives whose
setting is the period of the judges. They are so designated because the
town of Bethlehem figures prominently in each of them. They share
many other themes and motifs as well.[88] We will subject these three
stories to rather detailed analysis because they well represent narrative in the service of history writing. They concern individuals in more
or less private settings whose identities and activities are nevertheless
inseparable from and crucial to a full understanding of the Davidic

86. The Masoretic text of 1 Samuel 7:12 has *haššēn*, but the preferred reading,
based on the Septuagint, is *hayšānâ*, Jeshanah.

87. P. Kyle McCarter, Jr., *I Samuel*, Anchor Bible (Garden City, N.Y.: Doubleday,
1980), p. 147.

88. See Eugene H. Merrill, "The Book of Ruth: Narration and Shared Themes,"
Bib Sac 142 (1985): 130–41.

monarchy which followed them. Accounts of actual events that transpired in the days of the judges, they are included in the sacred record for the purpose of tracing the roots of the Davidic dynasty and justifying its existence in opposition to Saul.

Micah and the Levite

The first of the narratives is the story of Micah and the Levite (Judg. 17–18).[89] It seems that a wealthy man of Ephraim named Micah had built a house of idols and installed his own son as priest of this pagan shrine. This, the narrator implies, was characteristic of those days when "Israel had no king" and "everyone did as he saw fit" (Judg. 17:6). When a Levite from Bethlehem passed through seeking employment, Micah persuaded him to serve as priest in place of his own non-Levitical son.

Meanwhile, the tribe of Dan, having found itself unable to occupy its inheritance, sent a scouting party north to look for other territory. On the way they came across the Levite and sought counsel from him concerning their venture. Satisfied, they went on to Laish (Tell el-Qadi) about twelve miles north of Lake Huleh, and found the inhabitants there to be peaceful and without protection. Their good report then encouraged the Danites to move en masse to Laish.

On their way north the six hundred Danite men charged with subduing Laish visited Micah and the Levite and persuaded the latter to join them and be priest of the new shrine which they would build at Laish. Once they arrived at Laish they destroyed the city and rebuilt it with the name Dan. Only at this point in the narrative is the name of the Levite revealed—he was none other than Jonathan son of Gershom, the grandson of Moses himself![90] This piece of information allows the historical setting of the story to be more precisely defined. Gershom, Moses' son, may have died before the conquest as part of the rebellious generation. Jonathan had to be twenty or under in 1444 to be qualified to enter the land. He therefore could have been as old as fifty-eight at the beginning of the conquest and yet is called "young" in Judges 17:7. While this is an imprecise term, it surely cannot apply to someone over fifty. Much more likely he was considerably younger.[91]

89. Frank Anthony Spina, "The Dan Story Historically Reconsidered," *JSOT* 4 (1977): 60–71.

90. The *nun suspensum* of the Masoretic text of Judges 18:30 reflects only apologetic considerations and cannot overthrow the strong manuscript evidence that reads "Moses" rather than "Manasseh." See Moore, *Judges*, pp. 401–2.

91. That Jonathan was considerably younger is suggested by evidence that Gershom was born to Moses and Zipporah after many years of marriage: he was circumcised by his mother as they were on their way to Egypt in anticipation of the exodus

Of importance also is the reference in Judges 18:1 to the effect that Dan's inheritance had not yet been occupied. In impatience the tribe decided to go its own way. It will be recalled that the allotment of tribal lands had been finished within seven years of the beginning of the conquest (i.e., by 1399—see p. 133). Dan's movement to Laish must have taken place not long after that.

Scholars generally understand Dan's migration to be the result of pressures from the populations indigenous to the land allotted to the tribe, a point suggested by Judges 1:34–36. One should note the comment made in Joshua 19:47 that the Danites took Laish (Leshem) after experiencing difficulty in occupying the cities of their inheritance. Judges 18:8–13 makes it clear that the taking of Laish preceded the occupation of the original allocation. The sequence, then, is that an element of Danites, impatient with their inability to seize their inheritance, moved north on their own to take Laish; then the remaining Danites occupied the cities mentioned in Joshua 19:40–46. These Danites were the stock from which Samson arose nearly three hundred years later.

The Levite and His Concubine

The second story of the trilogy is about a Levite of Ephraim who had taken as his concubine a maiden from Bethlehem (Judg. 19–21).[92] The Bethlehem-Ephraim connection is again stressed; it is obviously a deliberate motif of the narrator in both episodes. The Levite retrieved his concubine from Bethlehem (to which she had fled for some unknown reason) and returned to Ephraim via Gibeah (Tell el-Fûl) of Benjamin, where he was given shelter at the home of an old man. Unfortunately the concubine was set upon by the evil men of Gibeah, who brutalized her through the night and left her dead at the door of the Levite's host. The Levite thereupon related this experience to the

(Exod. 4:24–26). A birth date of 1450 is not unreasonable. In that event, he could have been among those who qualified to enter Canaan since he would have been younger than twenty in 1444. Furthermore, in 1399 he would be only about fifty, and his son Jonathan could easily be described as a young man. While the Hebrew *na'ar* ("young man") can, of course, refer to an attendant or minister, even so it is never used of an old man. See Aharoni, "Settlement of Canaan," in *World History of the Jewish People*, vol. 3, p. 308, n. 15.

92. The essential historicity of this story is defended by Malamat, "Period of the Judges," in *World History of the Jewish People*, vol. 3, p. 161, who places it between the judgeship of Jephthah and the Ammonite attack on Jabesh Gilead (1 Sam. 11). This late a date is impossible (see n. 95), though Malamat correctly draws attention to the connection between Benjamin and Jabesh Gilead.

elders of all Israel, who had assembled at Mizpah. They then went up to Bethel (Judg. 20:18),[93] where they sought divine instruction.[94]

Since the concubine was from Bethlehem, it was determined that the men of Judah should attack Benjamin first. After two days of setbacks, the Israelites retired to seek the favor and blessing of God through the high priest, Phinehas, grandson of Aaron.[95] On the third day Israel prevailed and Benjamin was nearly annihilated. Once more Israel assembled, this time to resolve the problem of Benjamin's near extinction. The solution was to obtain maidens from Shiloh and Jabesh Gilead to serve as wives for the six hundred Benjamite survivors and thus preserve the tribe of Benjamin among the twelve.

The reference to Jabesh Gilead is not without purpose in the historical scheme of things. The city was no doubt in a sense the ancestral home of Saul. It is obvious from the narrative under consideration that the wife of the Benjamite survivor who was the forebear of Saul came from either Shiloh or Jabesh Gilead. That the latter is more likely is suggested by Saul's interest in Jabesh Gilead. He had no sooner become king than Jabesh Gilead fell under Ammonite siege and would have been captured had Saul not intervened (1 Sam. 11:1–11).[96] Furthermore, after Saul's death and shameful exposure at Beth Shan, men of Jabesh Gilead retrieved his body and buried it in their town (1 Sam. 31:11–13), whence David later brought it for interment at Zela in Benjamin (2 Sam. 21:12–14).

The motivation for including this second narrative of the Bethlehem trilogy is evident. It reflects badly on Benjamin and by implication on

93. It has been suggested that *bêt-'ēl* here means "place of God" (i.e., Mizpah) rather than the city of that name. This suggestion obviates the need to explain the rise of Bethel as a cult center, which has no attestation for this period except in this narrative. Thus the references to Bethel (Judg. 20:18, 26; 21:2) should be understood not as a place name but as the "holy place," that is, Mizpah (see Boling, *Judges*, p. 285). Although Shiloh had early on been designated as the site of the tabernacle and ark (Josh. 18:1), it must have ceased to be so by the time of the Benjamite rebellion, a fact that is clear from both the presence of the ark at Mizpah (Judg. 20:18, 23, 26–28; 21:1–7) and the apparent disfavor into which Shiloh had fallen (Judg. 21:12, 19–23). That it later on resumed its place as the central sanctuary is made clear in the narrative of 1 Samuel 3–4.

94. For the nature and function of such gatherings see Hanoch Reviv, "The Pattern of the Pan-Tribal Assembly in the Old Testament," *JNSL* 8 (1980): 85–94.

95. Thus the events of this narrative, like those of the first, are to be placed early in the period of the judges. A grandson of Moses and a grandson of Aaron would be contemporaries about a generation after the conquest.

96. Saul's slaughter and dissection of his oxen is reminiscent of the Levite's treatment of his murdered concubine. This account clearly connects the commencement of Saul's reign with his roots in Jabesh Gilead and the historical event which was the occasion thereof.

the Saulide ancestry and dynasty. The pro-David sentiment is crystal clear.

The Story of Ruth: Patriarchal Links

The third story, that of Ruth,[97] appears to feature the Moabite maiden herself, but the blessing (Ruth 4:11–15) and genealogy (Ruth 4:17–22) at the end demonstrate that the main purpose of the novelle[98] is to trace the ancestry of David back to Judah and Bethlehem. As in the previous two stories there is a man who departed from Bethlehem in Judah (Ruth 1:1; cf. Judg. 17:7–8; 19:1–10), but whereas the other two sullied the reputation of the town by their subsequent behavior, Elimelech and his family enhanced it. In Ruth Bethlehem becomes a most suitable setting for the birthplace of King David. In the second story Saul's ancestors, the Benjamites, had humiliated and disgraced a Bethlehemite, much to their later sorrow to be sure; but Bethlehem not only survived, it went on to produce Saul's successor, the man after God's own heart. The place of Bethlehem in the stories is, then, of no little importance.

It is significant that the Book of Ruth does not trace David's ancestry back merely to the days of the judges. The genealogical section actually begins with Perez, son of Judah (Ruth 4:18); and the blessing of Boaz by the people of Bethlehem explicitly joins Bethlehem (and hence David) to Perez and Judah:

> May the LORD make the woman who is coming into your home like Rachel and Leah, who together built up the house of Israel. May you have standing in Ephrathah and be famous in Bethlehem. Through the

97. The ancient Jewish canonical tradition of considering Ruth to be a part of the Book of Judges rests on good historical and literary considerations. Its author places it squarely in the times "when the judges ruled" (Ruth 1:1), the setting also of the last two narratives of the Book of Judges. (While these other stories are early in that era, however, Ruth must be toward the end since its heroine is only three generations before David.) Moreover, the indictment which runs as a refrain throughout Judges— "in those days Israel had no king; everyone did as he saw fit" (Judg. 17:6; 18:1; 19:1; 21:25)—and which casts the entire age as one of moral anarchy and covenant defection, is surely echoed in the opening words of Ruth—"in the days when the judges ruled," that is, when there was no king.

98. Form critics since Hermann Gunkel have used this term, synonymous with "short story," to describe the Book of Ruth. For defense of the term see Edward F. Campbell, Jr., *Ruth*, Anchor Bible (Garden City, N.Y.: Doubleday, 1975), pp. 3–6, 21. Jack M. Sasson, however, prefers the classification "folktale" (*Ruth: A New Translation with a Philological Commentary and a Formalist-Folklorist Interpretation* [Baltimore: Johns Hopkins University Press, 1979], p. 215), as does Oswald Loretz ("The Theme of the Ruth Story," *CBQ* 22 [1960]: 391–99).

offspring the LORD gives you by this young woman, may your family be like that of Perez, whom Tamar bore to Judah. [Ruth 4:11b–12]

The obviously synonymous use of Ephrathah and Bethlehem in this passage is reminiscent of the first biblical juxtaposition of the two names, which occurs in connection with the death of Rachel and the birth of Benjamin (Gen. 35:16–19). Is it possible that this incident, in which Benjamin is the occasion of the death of Jacob's (Israel's) favorite wife at Bethlehem, anticipates in some way the Saul-David controversy, in which the Benjamite proves antagonistic to one who has Bethlehem associations? Be that as it may, there are other patriarchal antecedents to the Ruth-David narrative which have indubitable and most instructive bearing on our subject.

Judah and Tamar

A part of the community blessing to Boaz and Ruth was that their family might "be like that of Perez, whom Tamar bore to Judah" (Ruth 4:12). It will be recalled that Tamar, like Ruth, was a foreigner who had married into the covenant people (Gen. 38:6). When her husband Er (Judah's eldest son) died, the levirate custom was invoked and she married the second son Onan. This arrangement came to naught. The result, of course, was the incestuous relationship between Judah and Tamar which produced the birth of twins, Perez and Zerah (Gen. 38:24–30). The levirate custom is also featured in the story of Ruth (Ruth 4:5), but this time with favorable results—Boaz raised up seed in the name of Ruth's deceased husband.[99] The circumstances under which the respective relationships were initiated are also strikingly similar. Under the cover of a disguise Tamar seduced her father-in-law (Gen. 38:14–16). Ruth approached Boaz under the cover of night (Ruth 3:6–14). After it had become apparent that Tamar was pregnant, Judah haled her before the village tribunal in order to accuse her formally of prostitution and to seek her death. Instead, he himself was found out and became an object of shame and condemnation (Gen. 38:24–26). Similarly, Boaz and Ruth appeared before the elders to announce his redemption of her and their impending marriage. This

---

99. For instructive parallels (and differences) between the two situations see A. A. Anderson, "The Marriage of Ruth," *JSS* 23 (1978): 171–83. The complex question as to whether Ruth's was a levirate and/or a *gō'ēl*-type of marriage cannot be addressed here. See especially the monograph by Donald A. Leggett, *The Levirate and Goel Institutions in the Old Testament with Special Attention to the Book of Ruth* (Cherry Hill, N.J.: Mack, 1974). Leggett argues persuasively that Ruth's marriage was of the *gō'ēl* and levirate types (see esp. pp. 209–53). That the two need not always go together, however, is shown by Jack M. Sasson, "The Issue of Ge'ullah in Ruth," *JSOT* 5 (1978): 60–63.

time the couple was praised and blessed (Ruth 4:1–12). In each instance, moreover, the man was advanced in age and sired sons when the prospects for doing so would ordinarily be bleak. Most significant of all, of course, is the fact that both Tamar and Ruth bore sons in the Davidic/messianic line. This is the strongest link binding the two stories together.

The reason the Bible takes pains to trace David's ancestry back to Judah is to be found in Jacob's deathbed blessing on Judah:

> The scepter will not depart from Judah,
>   nor the ruler's staff from between his feet,
> until he comes to whom it belongs
>   and the obedience of the nations is his. [Gen. 49:10]

That this promise was actualized in David is clear from many passages, but never more unambiguously than in the story of Ruth, particularly the genealogy. Its first name is Perez, the illegitimate yet chosen son of Judah and Tamar who asserted his regal ambition by making a breach (*pereṣ*) for himself (Gen. 38:29). That is, contrary to all human expectation he seized the initiative to stand in the line of messianic promise.[100]

This theme of circumvention of the norm or the tradition is in fact a major feature of this brief genealogy. It is replicated in the circumstances of Boaz's inclusion since, as Matthew indicates, Boaz was the son of Salmon by Rahab, the Canaanite harlot (Matt. 1:5). Surely this was a bold and totally unpredictable turn of events. Judah had sired a son by a woman he took to be a Canaanite prostitute; his descendant Salmon did the same by a Canaanite harlot who had come to embrace Yahwistic faith. And even the choice of David was contrary to all convention since he was not the eldest son of Jesse but the youngest. Beyond the confines of the genealogy proper it is significant finally that David's own dynastic heir, Solomon, was born to Bathsheba, who had become a royal wife under most inauspicious circumstances. And he was not the eldest son of David, not the one who by every traditional criterion should have become heir apparent. Moreover, he was the son of a foreigner, a Hittite.

It is clear that a major purpose of the biblical narrator was to establish links between Judah and Tamar on the one hand and Boaz and Ruth on the other, links binding the royal promise given to Judah with the fulfilment in the Davidic dynasty. This was accomplished not only by demonstrating the affinities between the stories of Tamar and Ruth, but also by suggesting important contrasts.

---

100. The image is that of a violent interdiction of his brother. See John Skinner, *A Critical and Exegetical Commentary on Genesis* (New York: Scribner, 1910), pp. 455–56.

The patriarchs and the monarchy

The second function of the story of Ruth is to supply a genealogical link between the patriarchal and monarchical eras. The use of genealogies in the Old Testament has been carefully studied, and some very helpful form-critical results have been achieved.[101] Not least significant is the recognition that in the present case the patriarchs, represented by Perez, are directly related to the only true royal dynasty of Israel, represented by its head and messianic prototype David. Striking by its omission is any reference to Moses. One can conclude only that it was the author's intent to quickly bridge the gap between patriarchs and monarchy without commenting on what is otherwise the watershed of Israel's whole historical and theological experience, namely, the exodus and the Sinaitic covenant.

Although the complex topic of the biblical covenants lies outside our immediate purview, we must note at least the general recognition that the so-called Mosaic covenant differs both formally and functionally from other biblical covenants.[102] It is also conceded that there are important connections and correspondences between the Abrahamic and Davidic covenants. This is most apparent in Ruth itself. The narrator is writing, among other reasons, to clarify that the Davidic dynasty did not spring out of the conditional Mosaic covenant, but rather finds its historical and theological roots in the promises to the patriarchs. Israel as the servant people of Yahweh might rise and fall, be blessed or cursed, but the Davidic dynasty would remain intact forever because God had pledged to produce through Abraham a line of kings that would find its historical locus in Israel, but would have ramifications extending far beyond Israel. The kings (plural) promised to Abraham (Gen. 17:6, 16) became more specifically identified by Jacob as one (singular) to whom the royal scepter and staff would belong (Gen. 49:10). He, this one from Judah, would, moreover, exercise dominion over Moab and Edom (Num. 24:17–19). When Samuel was sent to Bethlehem to anoint a successor to Saul, he was told that Yahweh had provided for a king from among the sons of Jesse (1 Sam.

---

101. Robert R. Wilson, "The Old Testament Genealogies in Recent Research," *JBL* 94 (1975): 169–89; idem, *Genealogy and History in the Biblical World* (New Haven: Yale University Press, 1977); Marshall D. Johnson, *The Purpose of Biblical Genealogies* (Cambridge: Cambridge University Press, 1969).

102. The literature in this area is vast, but on this specific point one should consult especially Moshe Weinfeld, "The Covenant of Grant in the Old Testament and in the Ancient Near East," *JAOS* 90 (1970): 184–203; Delbert R. Hillers, *Covenant: The History of a Biblical Idea* (Baltimore: Johns Hopkins Press, 1969); and George E. Mendenhall, "Covenant Forms in Israelite Tradition," in *The Biblical Archaeologist Reader*, ed. Edward F. Campbell, Jr., and David Noel Freedman (Garden City, N.Y.: Doubleday, 1970), vol. 3, pp. 25–53.

16:1). David's anointing with oil, accompanied as it was by the descent of the Spirit of God upon him, confirmed not only that he was the proper selection from among Jesse's sons, but also that he was the long-awaited fulfilment of the patriarchal promise.

The juxtaposition of anointing and kingship is striking in many other Old Testament passages, not least of which is Psalm 2. Though this psalm is anonymous, there is every good reason to view it as a Davidic composition designed to attest to David's messianic kingship and his status as the son of God.[103] Psalm 110 likewise speaks of David's kingship as transcending a mere political office. This time, however, it is not his sonship that is stressed, but rather his priesthood.[104] Noteworthy here are the tie-in to Melchizedek, a contemporary of the patriarchs, and, once again, the complete bypassing of the whole Mosaic covenantal and cultic institution. David functions as both king and priest not by virtue of his Israelite citizenship, but because he stands in the direct continuum of Abrahamic promise and fulfilment.

The link to the patriarchs is clearly seen in the initiation of the Davidic covenant (1 Chron. 15–17). Having prepared facilities for the ark and having appointed cultic personnel to serve as its ministers, David, clothed in the priestly ephod, brought the ark to its new resting-place (1 Chron. 15:25–28). He then officiated at a sacrifice (1 Chron. 16:1–3), an act which under the Aaronic priesthood would have been entirely inappropriate for a Judahite.[105] Then, in celebration of the establishment of both ark and throne, David sang a thanksgiving hymn (1 Chron. 16:8–36) in which he made direct reference to the Abrahamic covenant (vv. 15–17), but studiously avoided any mention of the Mosaic. Even in the account of the revelation of the dynastic covenant to David and his prayerful response there is no explicit appeal to the Mosaic covenant, though the theme of Israel as God's people and David's nation does hold a prominent place (1 Chron. 17:7, 9, 22, 24).

Equally impressive is the patriarchal-Davidic association in the New Testament, where, of course, there is the extra dimension of the fulfilment of Davidic dynastic claims in Jesus Christ. Matthew commences his genealogy with the rubric, "A record of the genealogy of Jesus Christ the son of David, the son of Abraham" (1:1). What is emphasized

---

103. See Artur Weiser, *The Psalms: A Commentary* (Philadelphia: Westminster, 1962), pp. 110–14.

104. J. W. Bowker, "Psalm CX," *VT* 17 (1967): 36.

105. This very point is made by the author of Hebrews, who shows that Christ's priesthood is non-Aaronic (and hence unrelated to the Mosaic covenant) since he came from Judah, but it is superior to that of Aaron since it is after the order of Melchizedek (Heb. 7:11–17). For the Melchizedek-David priesthood see Aubrey Johnson, *Sacral Kingship in Ancient Israel* (Cardiff: University of Wales Press, 1955), pp. 27–46, which is a sound presentation except for its aetiological interpretation.

is the fact that the Messiah has his historical roots in Abraham and that he has come as a Davidic king in response to the promises to the patriarchs. That this was Israel's messianic expectation is clear from the acclaim of the multitudes when Jesus rode in triumph into Jerusalem: "Hosanna to the Son of David! Blessed is he who comes in the name of the Lord!" (Matt. 21:9). Jesus himself confirmed this when he pointed out to the Pharisees that by identifying the Messiah as the son of David, they were at the same time conceding Messiah's anteriority to and lordship over David, a matter patently clear from Psalm 110 (Matt. 22:41–46). This same psalm describes the messianic king as a priest according to the order of Melchizedek. The author of Hebrews makes much of this point, and though he nowhere mentions David in this connection, he speaks of Jesus Christ as such a priest precisely as the psalm does of David. David and Jesus Christ, as Melchizedekian priests, functioned outside the Mosaic priestly order and in an inherently more universal and comprehensive way since, as Hebrews 7:9–10 argues, even Levi in Abraham's loins payed tithe to Melchizedek. The continuum Melchizedek—David—Christ is thus uninterrupted by Mosaism in the priestly role just as that of Abraham—David—Christ is in the regal. A major purpose of Ruth is to establish this very continuity, at least between Abraham and David.

The role of the Moabite maiden

The third function of the Book of Ruth centers in Ruth herself, a most unlikely vehicle for divine transmission of messianic royalty and priesthood. In attempting to understand her role one must not overlook her nationality. She was a Moabite, the daughter of a nation descended from Moab, son of Lot by his older daughter (Gen. 19:37). Harold Fisch has recently pointed out that Lot had separated from Abraham, thus breaking family ties (Gen. 13:11); similarly, Judah parted from his brothers (Gen. 38:1), and Elimelech left Bethlehem and his clan to sojourn in Moab (Ruth 1:1).[106] In each case disaster followed: death left young women without husbands. In each case, moreover, the problem of perpetuating the family was solved through use of a father or father figure, though it was the woman who initiated the encounter, always in a furtive way. The most noteworthy link between the stories, however, is the ironic fact that a descendant of the wayward and schismatic Lot, the pure and noble Ruth, effected a reunification with the Abrahamic clan from which he had separated. She was, then, not only a vital link in the messianic chain from Abraham to David (and eventually to Christ), but also an instrument to

106. Harold Fisch, "Ruth and the Structure of Covenant History," *VT* 32 (1982): 429–32.

bridge the chasm between Judah and Moab, a type or paradigm of the reconciliation which God desires among nations, reconciliation which will fulfil the patriarchal blessing.

When we examine the genealogical list of Matthew 1, we are struck by the fact that only four women are mentioned there, one of them being Ruth.[107] Of these four, two (Tamar and Rahab) were Canaanites, one (Ruth) a Moabite, and one (Bathsheba) presumably a Hittite. Surely they exemplify the principle of the sovereign grace of God, who not only is able to use the foreign (and perhaps even the disreputable) to accomplish his eternal purposes, but even seems to delight in doing so. No one illustrates this better than gentle and loyal Ruth. In fulfilment of the prophetic blessing she became "like Rachel and Leah, who together built up the house of Israel" (Ruth 4:11).

107. We should also note that women played a significant role in the life of Jesus, particularly at the time of his passion and resurrection (see, e.g., Matt. 26:6–13; 27:55–56; 28:1–8).

5 Saul: Covenant Misunderstanding

The Demand for Kingship

The refrain of the Book of Judges, "in those days Israel had no king" (17:6; 18:1; 19:1; 21:25), was at last translated by the people of Israel into the demand that Samuel "appoint a king to lead us, such as all the other nations have" (1 Sam. 8:5). Though Samuel's reaction to this request was unqualifiedly negative (v. 6), its impropriety was not in

189

the desire for a king per se, but in the antitheocratic spirit in which it was made and in its prematurity.

Kingship, far from being antithetical to the purposes of God for Israel, was fundamental to his salvific design.[1] Man was created as the image of God in order to "rule over the fish of the sea and the birds of the air and over every living creature that moves on the ground" (Gen. 1:26–28). He was then placed in the Garden of Eden to exercise his sovereignty over it and all other things. Abraham and Sarah were told that they would produce kings (Gen. 17:6, 16), and the same covenant promise was reaffirmed to Jacob (Gen. 35:11). In his patriarchal blessing Jacob announced that "the scepter will not depart from Judah, / nor the ruler's staff from between his feet, / until he comes to whom it belongs / and the obedience of the nations is his" (Gen. 49:10). Finally, Deuteronomy 17:14–20 lays down regulations for a monarchy which will be brought about in Israel according to divine timing and in line with divine criteria. The king must be the man of Yahweh's choice (v. 15) and must govern the people according to the principles of Torah (vv. 18–20).

The alleged tension, then, between Samuel's negative attitude toward kingship in response to the people's demand (1 Sam. 8; 10:17–27) and his positive support of Saul at the time of his selection and anointing (1 Sam. 9:1–10:16) is without historical foundation.[2] Samuel's quarrel is not with kingship but, as has been suggested, with the character of kingship demanded by the people—"such as all the other nations have"—and with their refusal to wait for the man of God's own choosing.

The reason for the people's insistence is quite obvious. Samuel was now old, and his two sons whom he had appointed judges to succeed him were venal and corrupt. Moreover, external dangers were beginning to become apparent, particularly from the Arameans to the north

1. Walter C. Kaiser, Jr., *Toward an Old Testament Theology* (Grand Rapids: Zondervan, 1978), pp. 144–49; Claus Westermann, *Elements of Old Testament Theology* (Atlanta: John Knox, 1982), pp. 108–9; Shemaryahu Talmon, "The Biblical Idea of Statehood," in *The Bible World*, ed. Gary Rendsburg et al. (New York: Ktav, 1980), p. 239.

2. Most critics attribute the alleged tension to conflicting parallel narratives; see, for example, Siegfried Herrmann, *A History of Israel in Old Testament Times*, trans. John Bowden (Philadelphia: Fortress, 1975), pp. 131–37. For careful and convincing rebuttals of this whole thesis of conflicting traditions see J. Robert Vannoy, *Covenant Renewal at Gilgal* (Cherry Hill, N.J.: Mack, 1978), esp. pp. 197–239; and Lyle Eslinger, "Viewpoints and Point of View in 1 Samuel 8–12," *JSOT* 26 (1983): 61–76. A moderate position according to which the "deuteronomist" integrated and harmonized the early traditions to provide justification for the introduction of the monarchy is proposed by Dennis J. McCarthy, "The Inauguration of Monarchy in Israel: A Form-critical Study of 1 Sam. 8–12," *Interp.* 27 (1973): 401–22.

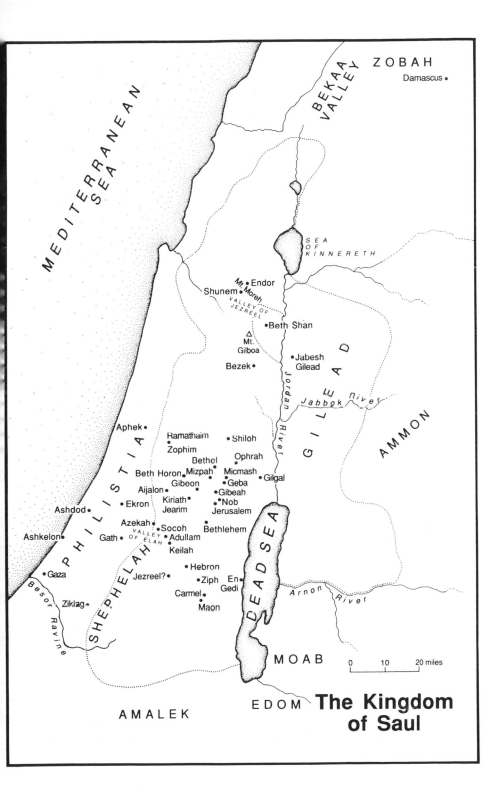

MEDITERRANEAN SEA

ZOBAH

BEKAA VALLEY

Damascus •

SEA OF KINNERETH

Mt. Moreh •Endor
Shunem •
VALLEY OF JEZREEL

•Beth Shan

△ Mt. Gilboa

•Jabesh Gilead

Bezek •

GILEAD

Jabbok River

AMMON

Aphek •

Ramathaim •Shiloh
Zophim

Bethel •Ophrah
Beth Horon •Mizpah •Micmash
Gibeon •Geba •Gilgal
Aijalon •Gibeah
•Ekron Kiriath •Nob
Jearim Jerusalem

Ashdod •

Azekah
Ashkelon • Gath • Socoh •Bethlehem
VALLEY OF ELAH •Adullam
Keilah

•Hebron
•Gaza Jezreel? • •Ziph En-Gedi
Carmel •
Ziklag • •Maon

Besor Ravine

PHILISTIA

SHEPHELAH

DEAD SEA

Jordan River

Arnon River

MOAB

AMALEK

EDOM

0   10   20 miles

The Kingdom of Saul

and the Ammonites to the east. Such times called for strong leadership, no longer merely on a local level, but nationwide, the kind of leadership which only a king could provide. Yahweh therefore acceded to the people; at the same time he assured Samuel that their demand for a king was a repudiation of the theocratic ideal and not of Samuel personally. Since they wanted a king like all the other nations and could not wait for the anointed of Yahweh, they would get their way, much to their future sorrow.[3] The king they demanded would create an authority structure entailing the forced enlistment of Israel's youth in royal service and the assessment of a heavy burden of taxes against which the people would someday cry out in vain protest (1 Sam. 8:11–18). Notwithstanding this warning, the people repeated their request, and so the machinery was put in motion to bring about the appointment of Saul as king.

The Chronology of the Eleventh Century

Before we consider the reign of Saul, however, it is important that the chronology of the eleventh century be outlined. Apart from the period of the judges, perhaps no era of Israel's history is more complex in this respect than the eleventh century.

Our starting point must be the reigns of Solomon and David, the dating of which rests on unassailable data. Edwin Thiele in his superb and definitive work has shown that the division of the kingdom occurred in 931 B.C. This coincided with the death of Solomon, who reigned for 40 years (1 Kings 11:42) and therefore must have succeeded David in 971. David in turn reigned for 40½ years (2 Sam. 2:11; 5:5), having come to power around 1011.[4]

The major problem concerns the length of the reign of Saul. It is evident that his death occurred in the year David began to reign at Hebron (2 Sam. 1:1; 2:1–4), that is, in 1011, but the year of Saul's accession is not so clear. The apostle Paul, in his address to the synagogue at Pisidian Antioch, stated that Saul reigned for forty years (Acts 13:21). This would date his tenure from 1051 to 1011. Most scholars reject this figure, however, usually on no better grounds than that another reign of forty years in addition to those of David and Solomon

3. On the permissive will of God, see J. Barton Payne, "Saul and the Changing Will of God," *Bib Sac* 129 (1972): 321–25.
4. Edwin R. Thiele, *The Mysterious Numbers of the Hebrew Kings* (Grand Rapids: Eerdmans, 1965), pp. 51–52. The conflict between assigning Solomon's coronation to the year 971 and his initiatory work on the temple, which we are told occurred in his fourth year, to 966 is more apparent than real. The matter is too complicated for the scope of this book. Suffice it to say, however, that there are various methods of reckoning regnal years, not all of which are based strictly on the year of accession.

seems suspect and no doubt stereotypical.[5] This, of course, is nothing more than begging the question. A careful examination of the biblical record leads to the conclusion that the figure of forty years is not a fabrication of Paul's nor a historically worthless tradition which he merely parroted, but is required by the text itself.

Unfortunately, at precisely the place that one might expect the usual formula summarizing a king's reign—1 Samuel 13:1—there is a textual corruption: "Saul was . . . years old when he became king, and he reigned over Israel two years." Besides the obvious lacuna involving his age, it is impossible to squeeze all the events of Saul's reign into two short years. Two solutions are commonly offered: (1) "Saul was thirty years old when he became king, and he reigned over Israel forty-two years"; and (2) "Saul was thirty years old when he became king. When he had reigned for two years. . . ." The former has in its favor that it follows the pattern of the usual formula (cf. 2 Sam. 5:4) and essentially agrees with Paul's round figure of forty years.

Against this reconstruction, however, is the fact that both "thirty" and "forty-two" must be supplied, the former from a few late manuscripts of the Septuagint and the latter by conjecture. The figure "thirty" would appear to be incorrect since Jonathan, Saul's son, was a leader of men at the very beginning of Saul's reign (1 Sam. 13:2–3) and could hardly have been the son of a thirty-year-old man. The "forty-two," it is usually argued, is necessary in order to account for Paul's datum and to explain the unusual plural rather than dual form of the figure "two" in the Hebrew text. Paul's information, however, could well be the result of the deductive process we are about to pursue, and the plural form of "two" is not without grammatical support elsewhere.[6] The best reading, then, would appear to be, "Saul was [forty] years old when he began to reign. When he had reigned for two years. . . ." The "forty" is a reasonable suggestion, given that Saul had an adult son at the time.[7]

In support of Paul's statement that Saul ruled for forty years is the fact that Ish-Bosheth, the son of Saul who succeeded him as king, was forty when he began to reign (2 Sam. 2:10) and yet was not born until

5. This is implied by J. Alberto Soggin, *A History of Ancient Israel* (Philadelphia: Westminster, 1984), p. 50.

6. Wilhelm Gesenius, *Gesenius' Hebrew Grammar*, ed. E. Kautzsch and A. E. Cowley (Oxford: Clarendon, 1957), §134e.

7. For further argument in support of this rendering see Eugene H. Merrill, "Paul's Use of 'About 450 Years' in Acts 13:20," *Bib Sac* 138 (1981): 256, n. 19. An interesting suggestion which involves no emendation is that of Robert Althann, who, on the basis of the Ugaritic preposition *b(n)*, renders the verse: "More than a year had Saul been reigning, / even two years had he been reigning over Israel. . . ." This supplies no information on Saul's age, but perhaps the passage was never intended to do so ("1 Sam. 13:1: A Poetic Couplet," *Biblica* 62 [1981]: 241–46).

after Saul ascended Israel's throne. This is clear from a comparison of the list of Saul's sons in the earliest years of his reign (1 Sam. 14:47–51) and the list of all his sons (1 Chron. 8:33; 9:39). The former names Jonathan, Ishvi, and Malki-Shua, and the latter Jonathan, Malki-Shua, Abinadab, and Esh-Baal. Esh-Baal is identical to Ish-Bosheth, and Abinadab is presumably another name for Ishvi (see 1 Chron. 10:2). When Saul was slain by the Philistines, his three sons Jonathan, Abinadab, and Malki-Shua died with him (1 Sam. 31:2). Since Ish-Bosheth survived, he obviously was not Abinadab[8] as some scholars maintain.[9]

Another factor of importance is the apparent interregnum between Saul and Ish-Bosheth during which time Abner maintained control (2 Sam. 2:8–11). For reasons not specified Ish-Bosheth did not immediately follow Saul, as is clear from the fact that he reigned only two years before he was assassinated. In the year of Ish-Bosheth's death David seized power over Saul's kingdom, and yet he had already been reigning in Hebron for more than seven years (2 Sam. 1:1; 2:4; 5:1–5). This means that Abner held the power in the north for about five years before he appointed Ish-Bosheth as king. Ish-Bosheth, forty years old at the time, was born, then, thirty-five years before Saul's death or around 1046. This further explains why his name does not appear in the list of Saul's children during the earliest part of his reign.

In any case, if Ish-Bosheth was thirty-five at the time of Saul's death and yet was not born until after the commencement of Saul's reign, Saul must have been king for more than thirty-five years, a figure entirely compatible with Paul's figure of forty. A date of 1051–1011 is therefore most likely.

In light of all this, a period of about thirty-three years had elapsed between the battle of Mizpah, when Samuel ended the Philistine oppression (see pp. 149, 178), and his encounter with the Israelite elders who demanded a king. The prophet was then old, as the narrative explicitly states (1 Sam. 8:1, 5), perhaps as old as seventy. It is no wonder that the people were concerned about a leadership crisis.

The Selection of Saul

Saul's Initial Encounter with Samuel

As many scholars have observed, the selection of Saul was more on the order of the charismatic appointment of the judges than on that

---

8. Eugene H. Merrill, "1 Samuel," in *The Bible Knowledge Commentary*, ed. John F. Walvoord and Roy B. Zuck (Wheaton, Ill.: Victor, 1985), vol. 1, p. 446.

9. E.g., Hans W. Hertzberg, *I & II Samuel* (Philadelphia: Westminster, 1964), p. 120.

of normal dynastic establishment and succession.[10] He was of no particularly celebrated lineage, having come from a small tribe, Benjamin, and being the son of Kish, who while "a man of standing" certainly had no claims to nobility.[11] Saul was, however, of impressive physical appearance (1 Sam. 9:1–2) and possessed a charming modesty, almost a self-abnegation.

The initial encounter with Samuel came in the course of Saul's searching for some lost asses, a search whose fruitlessness led him to seek illumination from the famous seer who made his home at Ramah in the land of Zuph (i.e., Ramathaim Zophim). Samuel's role as a seer (rō'eh) emphasizes the receptive aspect of the prophetic ministry. That is, a prophet was known as a seer when he came to understand the mind of Yahweh by dream or vision or some other similar means. When he proclaimed that message as a spokesman of Yahweh, particularly in a public way, he fulfilled the role of nābî' or prophet. It is clear in the case of Samuel as well as other prophets that one could be both a seer and a prophet at the same time, the difference being only one of function or emphasis. It is appropriate to digress somewhat at this point to address the matter of prophetism, since its beginnings are usually associated with Samuel.[12]

Early Israelite Prophetism

The phenomenon of prophetism was universal in the ancient Near Eastern world, for whenever people attempt to discern the purposes and intentions of the gods, there must inevitably be practitioners of the art of divination. Prophetic practice in Mesopotamia is abundantly attested in a vast corpus of divination texts which have come to light.[13] Similarly, a rather complete picture of the art of interpreting omens

10. Talmon, "Biblical Idea," in *Bible World*, pp. 244–45.

11. Bruce C. Birch, following Hugo Gressmann and other scholars, dismisses 1 Samuel 9·1–13 as a folktale with little or no historical basis and value ("The Development of the Tradition of the Anointing of Saul in 1 Sam. 9:1 10:16," *JBL* 90 [1971]: 58). Only if one a priori dismisses the historicity of the events to begin with, however, can the characteristics Birch adduces be used to prove that the pericope is strictly folklore. He fails to recognize that history can be related in the genre of folktale without sacrificing its historicity.

12. For Old Testament prophetism as an institution and office see the still authoritative work by Willis J. Beecher, *The Prophets and the Promise* (Grand Rapids: Baker, 1963 reprint), pp. 3–172. Popular, but helpful, is Hobart E. Freeman, *An Introduction to the Old Testament Prophets* (Chicago: Moody, 1968).

13. A. Leo Oppenheim, *Ancient Mesopotamia* (Chicago: University of Chicago Press, 1964), pp. 207–27.

has emerged from Mari, Alalakh, Ugarit, and Phoenicia.[14] While there are superficial similarities between what is known of pagan prophetism and that of ancient Israel, the divine origin and nonecstatic character of the latter make it unique in the ancient world. There was no manipulation of Yahweh, in contrast to the pagans' manipulation of their gods, but the prophet or seer of Israel was a passive, though totally self-conscious instrument who came to receive and proclaim divine revelation as the Spirit of Yahweh gave direction.

There was development of the prophetic office in Old Testament times, of course, as 1 Samuel 9:9 makes clear—"Formerly in Israel, if a man went to inquire of God, he would say, 'Come, let us go to the seer,' because the prophet of today used to be called a seer." Again, however, this is more a matter of changing emphasis than of anything else. Even Abraham was called a prophet (nābî'—Gen. 20:7), as were both Aaron (Exod. 7:1) and Moses (Deut. 34:10). Moses, in fact, was called the greatest of the prophets. But the major function of these early prophets lay elsewhere than in their preaching. They prophesied in support of whatever else they were or did, but were not prophets first and foremost.

The first major development was introduced by Samuel himself, who was the first full-time professional prophet, so to speak (1 Sam. 3:20). What that meant is succinctly stated: "The LORD continued to appear at Shiloh, and there he revealed himself to Samuel through his word. And Samuel's word came to all Israel" (1 Sam. 3:21–4:1a). In addition, Samuel established a company of prophets whom he trained in all those aspects of prophetism which could be imparted humanly. Obviously one could not be taught to be a vehicle of divine revelation, for that was a gift of God himself. Organized companies of prophets continued into the days of Elijah and Elisha (2 Kings 2:3). In the meantime individual seers and prophets appeared from time to time until the emergence of the great writing prophets of the ninth century. By then organized prophetism had gone into decline, and with the completion of the Old Testament canon Israelite prophetism of every kind disappeared.

The Anointing of Saul

To return to the narrative, when Saul and his servant arrived at Ramah, they learned that Samuel was going to officiate at a festival

14. Herbert B. Huffmon, "Prophecy in the Ancient Near East," in *Interpreter's Dictionary of the Bible*, Supplement, ed. Keith Crim et al. (Nashville: Abingdon, 1976), pp. 697–700; idem, "Prophecy in the Mari Letters," in *The Biblical Archaeologist Reader*, ed. Edward F. Campbell, Jr., and David Noel Freedman (Garden City, N.Y.: Doubleday, 1970), vol. 3, pp. 119–224; Virgil W. Rabe, "The Origins of Prophecy," *BASOR* 221 (1976): 125–28.

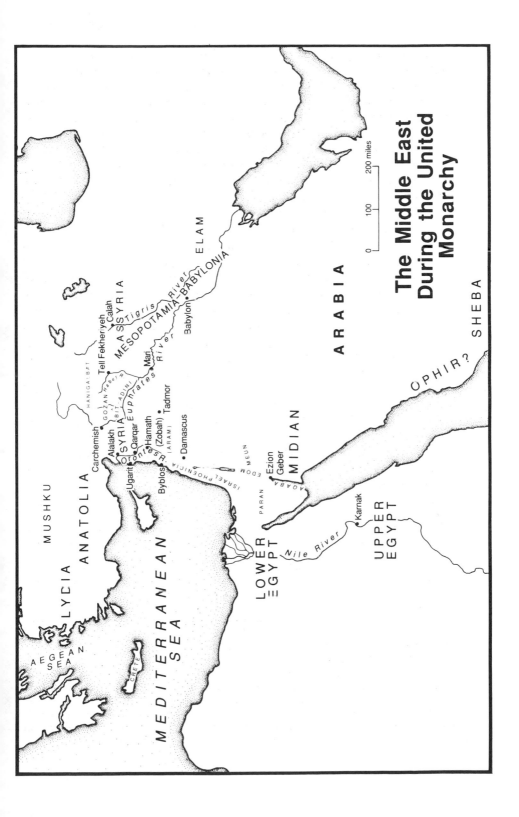

The Middle East
During the United
Monarchy

200 miles
0   100

MUSHKU

LYCIA

ANATOLIA

AEGEAN
SEA

CRETE

MEDITERRANEAN
SEA

Carchemish

Tell Fekheryeh

GOZAN

HANIGALBAT

ASSYRIA

Calah

Tigris River

Habor R.

BIT-ADINI

Alalakh

Ugarit

Byblos

Qarqar

Orontes R.

Hamath
(Zobah)
(ARAM)

SYRIA

Tadmor

Euphrates River

Mari

MESOPOTAMIA-BABYLONIA

Babylon

ELAM

Damascus

ISRAEL

PHOENICIA

EDOM

MEUN

PARAN

Ezion
Geber

MIDIAN

MOAB

AQABA

LOWER
EGYPT

Nile River

Karnak

UPPER
EGYPT

ARABIA

OPHIR?

SHEBA

at the nearby high place. They joined him in the procession, unaware that Yahweh had already revealed to Samuel that Saul would arrive on that day and that he would become the leader (*nāgîd*)[15] of Israel and would counter the renewed Philistine menace. When they reached the high place, Samuel entertained Saul with a lavish banquet. The next day Samuel revealed to Saul that he was the anointed prince of Israel. Confirmation would follow, Samuel said, in the form of three signs. First Saul would meet two men by Rachel's sepulcher at Zelzah (location unknown but probably between Jerusalem and Bethlehem), and they would assure him that the lost asses had been found.[16] Next he would encounter three men at the oak of Tabor (location unknown but certainly not the mountain in Jezreel). They would be on their way to worship at Bethel and would share two loaves of bread with him. Finally he would come to Gibeath-Elohim (Gibeon; i.e., el-Jîb),[17] location of a Philistine fortress, where he would join himself to a procession of prophets. Amazingly, he would participate in their playing and singing of music which he had never learned. This would be a sign of the blessing of God's Spirit, who had changed Saul from a lowly citizen to the anointed prince of his people. Later, Samuel said, Saul would find himself at Gilgal. As a test of his obedience he must wait there for Samuel to come and offer sacrifice.

When all three signs had come to pass, Samuel gathered Israel together at Mizpah for the public ceremony of coronation and investiture (1 Sam. 10:17–27). Unpretentious to the end, Saul hid himself from the assembly; only after a search for him did he reluctantly allow himself to be presented. There was first the formal introduction by Samuel (v. 24). Next followed the public acceptance and acclamation, "Long live the king!" Finally Saul accepted the protocols of office; that is, he and Israel heard Samuel explain the regulations of kingship,

15. Since David, Solomon, and other kings are also called *nāgîd*, and Saul in turn is called *melek* ("king") on occasion, one should not make too much of the fact that *nāgîd* is Saul's principal epithet. It means only "prominent one" or "chief one." See Francis Brown, S. R. Driver, and Charles A. Briggs, *A Hebrew and English Lexicon of the Old Testament* (Oxford: Clarendon, 1962), pp. 617–18. Albrecht Alt proposes that *nāgîd* was applied to Saul as the chosen one of Yahweh and that it was the nation that conferred upon him the title of *melek* ("The Formation of the Israelite State," in *Essays on Old Testament History and Religion* [Garden City, N.Y.: Doubleday, 1968], p. 254). See also the remarks by Roland de Vaux, *Ancient Israel* (New York: McGraw-Hill, 1965), vol. 1, pp. 70, 94. J. J. Glück resolves the *melek/nāgîd* tension by suggesting that *nāgîd* is equivalent to *nōqēd* ("shepherd") and thus a royal epithet rather than a synonym for king ("Nagid-Shepherd," *VT* 13 [1963]: 144–50).

16. For a proposed interpretation of the circuit, see Yohanan Aharoni and Michael Avi-Yonah, *Macmillan Bible Atlas* (New York: Macmillan, 1968), map 86.

17. So Aaron Demsky, "Geba, Gibeah, and Gibeon—An Historico-Geographic Riddle," *BASOR* 212 (1973): 27. Demsky argues that Gibeon was Saul's hometown and that Gibeah (Tell el-Fûl) was a city he later chose as his capital (p. 28).

which presumably reflected Moses' stipulations in Deuteronomy 17:14–20. Thus before Yahweh and the people a covenant had, in effect, been sworn binding Saul, the anointed shepherd of his people, to a proper course of action.

The First Challenge to Saul

The pomp of the occasion bore little resemblance to subsequent events, however. Though Saul was accompanied to his meager capital at Gibeah by a few retainers, others scoffed at him as an unlikely candidate for king. The humbleness of his origins and his obvious disdain for public display made this reaction understandable. Even after he was established at Gibeah, in a "palace" archaeological evidence shows to have been most unpretentious,[18] he displayed few of the trappings of royalty. In fact, when the first national crisis arose and appeal was made to Saul for help, the suppliants found him, the king, plowing in the field with his oxen. All this was in keeping with the transition between judgeship and monarchy, however, for in addition to having had no early political ambition himself, Saul was king over a people whose most urgent need was not the splendor of an elegant and impressive imperialism, but a tangible expression of solidarity and common national purpose. For too long the confederation had been splintering between east and west and between north and south, thus leaving it open to external aggression as well as internal disintegration. Saul, despite the primitive character of his kingship, represented at last a hope that Israel could survive.

That hope was put to a test almost immediately in the form of the siege of a Gileadite town, Jabesh Gilead, by Nahash the king of Ammon. Since the crushing defeat of Ammon by Jephthah more than fifty years earlier, the Ammonites had been waiting for opportunity for revenge. The drastic shift to monarchy in Israel, particularly in light of its unpromising first example, must have provided what seemed an opportune time to make the move. The selection of Jabesh Gilead also was carefully thought out. Besides being somewhat remote from Gibeah, and thus providing a stiff challenge to Israel's logistical capability, Jabesh Gilead most probably was the home of Saul's non-Benjamite ancestors (see p. 181).

18. Gibeah was excavated by William F. Albright, who, on the basis of the cultural remains of Saul's capital city, described him as a "rustic chieftain" (*From the Stone Age to Christianity* [Garden City, N.Y.: Doubleday, 1957], p. 292). So undistinguished is the site that Joseph Blenkinsopp has argued with some cogency that the capital of Saul for most of his reign was not Gibeah but Gibeon ("Did Saul Make Gibeon His Capital?" *VT* 24 [1974]: 1–7).

It is clear that Jabesh Gilead was both a militarily vulnerable and psychologically appropriate target for the Ammonites. They therefore laid siege to the city and threatened its total destruction unless the people agreed to make a covenant of submission and to allow their right eyes to be put out.[19] This barbaric demand, whose purpose was to show Nahash's superior might and Saul's total inability to provide protection, was followed by permission for messengers to go throughout Israel to seek help. So confident were the Ammonites, they challenged Israel in effect to do whatever they could to rescue Jabesh Gilead.[20]

The challenge did not go unanswered. As with the judges, the Spirit of God now came upon Saul; and he took a yoke of oxen, slaughtered them, and dispatched their remains throughout the nation. This bizarre behavior, reminiscent of the action of the Levite involving his dead concubine,[21] was to alert the nation to the gravity of the situation and to persuade them to come as one united body to the city's defense. In the greatest show of military strength since Joshua's day, three hundred thousand Israelites and thirty thousand men of Judah gathered at Bezek (Khirbet Ibziq), about fifteen miles west of Jabesh Gilead.

19. Frank M. Cross, on the basis of his study of the Qumran text 4Q Sam[a], points out that Reubenite and Gadite subjects of Nahash who had been similarly mutilated for their acts of treason against the Ammonite king had escaped Ammon and had found refuge in Jabesh Gilead. As those who rebelled in the first place were deserving of such punishment, no less were those who harbored them. So, as Cross shows, the Qumran fragment clarifies an otherwise obscure point in the received text of Samuel. See Cross, "Original Biblical Text Reconstructed from Newly Found Fragments," *Bible Review* 1 (1985): 26–33; idem, "The Ammonite Oppression of the Tribes of Gad and Reuben: Missing Verses from 1 Samuel 11 Found in 4Q Samuel," in *History, Historiography and Interpretation*, ed. Hayim Tadmor and Moshe Weinfeld (Jerusalem: Magnes, 1984), pp. 148–58; Terry L. Eves, "One Ammonite Invasion or Two? 1 Sam. 10:27–11:2 in the Light of 4Q Sam[a]," *WTJ* 44 (1982): 308–26.

20. On the basis of 2 Samuel 2:4b–7 Diana Edelman points out helpfully that Jabesh Gilead was not a constituent part of Israel but only a vassal state ("Saul's Rescue of Jabesh-Gilead [1 Sam. 11:1–11]: Sorting Story from History," *ZAW* 96 [1984]: 195–209). But she draws the erroneous conclusion that Saul's rescue of the city could not have been a test of his newly granted kingship (though 1 Sam. 11:12–14 clearly suggests that it was) since a vassal state could not exist and could not expect help if Saul had not already become monarch of a formidable Cisjordanian kingdom. Her error is in overlooking the possibility that Jabesh Gilead became a vassal state precisely because of Saul's defeat of the Ammonites and in failing to accept the historicity of Saul's ancestral connection to Jabesh Gilead, a connection which certainly would explain Saul's intense interest in the place and the confidence of the Jabesh Gilead population that he would intervene.

21. For a similar action at Mari, see *Archives royales de Mari*, ed. Charles-F. Jean (Paris: Geuthner, 1950), vol. 2, #48, cited by J. Maxwell Miller, "Saul's Rise to Power: Some Observations Concerning 1 Sam. 9:1–10:16; 10:26–11:15 and 13:2–14:4b," *CBQ* 36 (1974): 168.

The next day they attacked the Ammonite besiegers and completely routed them. This put to silence once and for all those who had ridiculed Saul's regal claims.

The Decline of Saul

Disobedience at Gilgal

In light of this incontrovertible evidence that Saul had been anointed by Yahweh, Samuel again summoned the people together, this time at Gilgal, in order that the nation, now united in its support of Saul, might enter into covenant with both Yahweh and the king.[22] As covenant mediator Samuel took the occasion first to verify his own credibility among the people (1 Sam. 12:1–5) and then to rehearse for them God's mighty acts in their behalf from the time of the exodus to the present hour (vv. 6–13). They had demanded a king, and Yahweh had graciously given them Saul. If now Saul and Israel would be true to the terms of the covenant, the protocols of Deuteronomy 17, all would go well. If not, they could expect the disfavor of Yahweh. Then, as a token of both his own authority and that of Yahweh, Samuel summoned thunder and rain from heaven. When it came, the people stood in awe for it was the wheat harvest, the very midst of the dry season. The God of Israel was sovereign over nature and history. The message was clear: Israel, even as a monarchy, must submit to him.

Encouraged by his defensive campaign against Ammon and by the spirit of solidarity and covenant favor he had experienced at Gilgal, Saul undertook the first of his offensive enterprises. The Philistines had indeed been removed from Israel by Samuel more than thirty years before, but they continued to harass Israel's borders and even to penetrate on occasion deep into the interior.[23] Saul saw the need to put a stop to these activities once and for all. His first assault on the Philistines was at the garrison of Geba (Jeba')[24] less than five miles from the capital (1 Sam. 13:3). Jonathan, Saul's son, was in command

22. For a detailed study of the Gilgal assembly as a covenant convocation see Vannoy, *Covenant Renewal at Gilgal*, esp. pp. 132–91.

23. Benjamin Mazar, "The Philistines and Their Wars with Israel," in *World History of the Jewish People*, vol. 3, *Judges*, ed. Benjamin Mazar (Tel Aviv: Massada, 1971), pp. 175–76.

24. Demsky, "Geba, Gibeah, and Gibeon," *BASOR* 212 (1973): 29–30, however, suggests that this Geba was named after the original Geba (i.e., Gibeah of Benjamin [Judg. 20], later known as Gibeah of Saul) and was also none other than Gibeon (el-Jîb). The "Geba of Benjamin" in most Hebrew manuscripts of 1 Samuel 13:16 is in this view the same as Gibeah of Benjamin.

of a thousand men at Gibeah while Saul had two thousand at Micmash (Mukhmâs) two miles beyond Geba. Jonathan struck the blow to rid Geba of the Philistines, but this provoked a strong Philistine response. With a vast host the Philistines arrived at Micmash, forcing the local inhabitants to evacuate, while the Israelite troops fled twelve miles east to Gilgal or even across the Jordan to Gilead.

While at Gilgal Saul recalled the words of Samuel two years before that a time would come when the king would have to wait seven days for the prophet to arrive at Gilgal.[25] Fearful of the imminent attack of the Philistines, Saul offered sacrifice to Yahweh and thus violated not only Samuel's precise instructions but the cultic prescriptions concerning proper ritual. When Samuel did arrive, he had to rebuke the king and inform him that his dynasty, which could in some sense have lasted forever (1 Sam. 13:13), would come to an untimely end. Instead, God would grant the rule to a man after his own heart.

Anger Toward Jonathan

After leaving Gilgal, Saul took refuge at Gibeah with only six hundred men. The Philistines were camped mainly at nearby Micmash but sent out raiding parties from there, some to Ophrah of Benjamin (eṭ-Ṭai-yibeh), just northeast of Bethel; some to Beth Horon, west of Micmash; and some to Zeboim, evidently northwest toward the Philistine border.[26] The freedom with which they moved in the very heartland of Israel testifies to Saul's perilous situation. This can be attributed partly, the historian hints (1 Sam. 13:19–22), to the lack of iron technology in Israel, a strategic advantage to the Philistines.[27]

25. Many scholars (e.g., P. Kyle McCarter, Jr., *I Samuel*, Anchor Bible [Garden City, N.Y.: Doubleday, 1980], p. 228) assume a hopelessly confused reconstruction of events at this point (1 Sam. 13:7b–8). They believe that the biblical historian (or redactor) is suggesting in 1 Samuel 10:8 that Saul appeared at Gilgal within a week of his election as king, when, in fact, he must have done so at least two years later (see 1 Sam. 13:1). As Carl F. Keil and Franz Delitzsch showed more than a century ago, there is no confusion at all once one recognizes the conditional nature of the Hebrew syntax of 1 Samuel 10:8. What the prophet is saying is that if Saul should ever go to Gilgal, Samuel would go there too. Whenever this might occur, Saul should wait at least seven days for Samuel to arrive. That Saul did not go to Gilgal until two years had passed is immaterial. See Keil and Delitzsch, *Biblical Commentary on the Books of Samuel* (Grand Rapids: Eerdmans, 1960 reprint), pp. 101–2.

26. Aharoni and Avi-Yonah, *Macmillan Bible Atlas*, map 171.

27. Though the word *iron* (Heb. *barzel*) does not appear in this passage, it is clear from other sources that the Philistines were dominant in metallurgy and exploited this dominance to the fullest. See Trude Dothan, *The Philistines and Their Material Culture* (New Haven: Yale University Press, 1982), p. 20; James D. Muhly, "How Iron Technology Changed the Ancient World and Gave the Philistines a Military Edge," *BAR* 8 (1982): 52–54.

Drawing somewhat closer to Micmash, Saul took up a defensive stance at Migron (Tell Miriam) between Micmash and Geba.[28] Jonathan, however, slipped away and with only his armor-bearer attacked a Philistine detachment near Micmash, killing about twenty men. This blow, together with an earthquake, caused such panic amongst the Philistines that Saul and his men were immediately aware that something unusual had happened. A quick check revealed that Jonathan and his armor-bearer were missing, so Saul called for Ahijah the high priest to fetch the ark,[29] presumably to ensure both divine protection and direction. But the Philistines were in such disarray they abandoned their position at Micmash and fled for their lives. As a result, the 'apiru mercenaries[30] who had been hired by the Philistines were encouraged to defect and take sides with Israel. They then joined both Israelite refugees who had been in hiding and the forces of Saul in pursuing the Philistines northwest to Beth Aven (i.e., Bethel) and from there at last to Aijalon, on the very border of Philistia.

Saul had put his army under an oath not to eat until God gave Israel victory, so his men were famished to the point of fainting (1 Sam. 14:24). When the Philistines fled, therefore, the Israelites slaughtered the animals which were left behind and ate them without properly draining the blood. This breach of the oath and of Mosaic ritual law so frightened Saul that he built an altar in order to offer appropriate sacrifice. Then he sought a word from Yahweh about continuing his pursuit of the Philistines, but no word was forthcoming. Saul took this to mean that someone had angered Yahweh by violating the oath. Casting the sacred lots, he discovered the guilty party to be his own son Jonathan, who, not knowing of the oath, had eaten some honey.

28. So *Oxford Bible Atlas*, ed. Herbert G. May, 3d ed. (New York: Oxford University Press, 1984), pp. 73, 135.

29. Thus the Masoretic text of 1 Samuel 14:18. It seems best, however, with the Septuagint and other witnesses, to read "ephod" for "ark," for the ark apparently remained at Kiriath Jearim all through the reign of Saul. Furthermore, the priestly technique described in the narrative suggests recourse to the ephod and not the ark (v. 19, cf. vv. 40–42; 23:9; 30:7) See Ralph W. Klein, *1 Samuel*, Word Biblical Commentary (Waco: Word, 1983), p. 132, n. 18. G. W. Ahlström, who supports the Masoretic text here, nonetheless points out that the ephod appears in the Samuel narratives throughout the period in which the ark is located by the tradition at Kiriath Jearim ("The Travels of the Ark: A Religio-Political Composition," *JNES* 43 [1984]: 145; so also Antony F. Campbell, "Yahweh and the Ark: A Case Study in Narrative," *JBL* 98 [1979]: 42–43, n. 32).

30. The older view that these are Hebrews is difficult to reconcile with their shifting allegiance here from the Philistines to the Israelites. It is better, with Norman K. Gottwald, to identify these folk as the 'apiru so well known from the Amarna correspondence (*The Tribes of Yahweh* [Maryknoll, N.Y.: Orbis, 1979], pp. 422–25; see also above, pp. 101–2).

Only the pleas of the people restrained Saul from killing Jonathan. Here we see the beginnings of Saul's irrationality and madness.

The Enemies of Saul

With the Philistine threat temporarily put aside, the narrator briefly gives his attention to a summation of all of Saul's military activities. He had, of course, dealt with the Ammonites at Jabesh Gilead and perhaps on other occasions. He also had to engage in campaigns against the Moabites, Edomites, and the Aramean kingdom of Zobah, none of which are elaborated in detail in the extant record. Nevertheless, in light of these episodes it is important that something be said of the world surrounding Saul in order that we might more fully appreciate the external tensions which contributed to his deterioration.

The Aramean states

Virtually nothing is known of eleventh-century Moab and Edom from either the Old Testament or extrabiblical sources, so it is fruitless to speculate about anything other than material civilization.[31] The picture is somewhat clearer for the Aramean states, however, thanks to rather abundant cuneiform materials primarily from Assyria. The earliest designation for Arameans was *Ahlamû*.[32] Not until around 1100 did the term *'armaya* (Arameans) appear, when it was used to describe seminomadic populations which by then occupied all of upper Syria and northwest Mesopotamia. Tiglath-pileser I (1115–1077) mentions them as enemies of Assyria whom he tried to control. But not only did they withstand Assyrian pressure, they soon began to occupy and control vast areas of central and lower Mesopotamia. By the time of Saul they dominated everything north of Damascus as far as the Euphrates and even beyond.[33]

31. John R. Bartlett, "The Moabites and Edomites," in *Peoples of Old Testament Times*, ed. D. J. Wiseman (Oxford: Clarendon, 1973), pp. 229–34; B. Oded, "Neighbors on the East," in *World History of the Jewish People*, vol. 4, part 1, *The Age of the Monarchies: Political History*, ed. Abraham Malamat (Jerusalem: Massada, 1979), pp. 252–61. Dennis Pardee has listed all the known extant inscriptions from Moab, Ammon, and Edom, of which there are only a few, and not one earlier than 850 B.C. (the Mesha inscription) ("Literary Sources for the History of Palestine and Syria II: Hebrew, Moabite, Ammonite, and Edomite Inscriptions," *AUSS* 17 [1979]: 65–69).

32. Albert Kirk Grayson, *Assyrian Royal Inscriptions* (Wiesbaden: Otto Harrassowitz, 1976), vol. 2, p. 13, # 1.

33. Merrill F. Unger, *Israel and the Aramaeans of Damascus* (Grand Rapids: Baker, 1980 reprint), pp. 38–44. Abraham Malamat, while denying that the Ahlamû are Arameans, agrees with Unger's assessment of Aramean dominance of Syria and upper Mesopotamia by the time of Saul ("The Aramaeans," in *Peoples of Old Testament Times*, ed. D. J. Wiseman, pp. 135–38; see also Yutaka Ikeda, "Assyrian Kings and the Mediterranean Sea: The Twelfth to Ninth Centuries B.C.," *Abr-Nahrain* 23 [1984–1985]: 29, n. 10).

A major Aramean kingdom of this period was Zobah, ruled by the Beth Rehob dynasty. This nation was located in the northern Bekaa Valley and effectively controlled all trade routes from Anatolia and Mesopotamia south to Egypt.[34] Assyrian weakness after the reign of Tiglath-pileser I and the continued decline of Egypt in her Third Intermediate Period made it possible for Zobah to move out in virtually all directions to expand her influence. This included Israel, and so is the occasion for Saul's need for defensive measures against Zobah. This Aramean kingdom continued to plague Israel well into the time of David and Solomon and even later.

The Philistines

It was Philistia, however, with which Saul was constantly involved throughout his reign. These non-Semitic survivors of the Sea Peoples had come to Canaan as a part of a massive migration of westerners to Anatolia, Egypt, Syria, and other eastern Mediterranean areas. They overran and destroyed the Hittite Empire including its Syrian city-states such as Ugarit. Unsuccessful in a similar attempt against Egypt, some of the Sea Peoples, particularly the Peleset and Tjekker, settled along the central and lower Mediterranean coast of Canaan. The former are the Philistines so familiar from the Bible (see p. 158).

Though there had been Philistines in Canaan as far back as patriarchal times (see p. 42), this group had either become Semitized or been absorbed by the new wave of invaders. The "new" Philistines established a beachhead in southwest Canaan by around 1200, settling especially in and about five major cities—Gaza (Ghazzeh), Ashkelon ('Askalon), and Ashdod (Esdûd) along the coast, and Ekron (Khirbet el-Muqanna') and Gath (possibly Tell eṣ-Ṣâfi) in the Shephelah.

It is customary to describe Philistine statecraft in terms of a pentapolis in which each city ruler (Heb. *seren*, "lord") apparently held equal power with the rest. No enterprise which involved the confederation as a whole could be pursued without a majority (and perhaps unanimous) vote. More than this cannot be known in the absence of Philistine texts.[35]

The paucity of our knowledge of the Philistine vocabulary limits any attempt to define precisely the language of the people, though most scholars believe it originated in the Aegean area, either in the

34. Benjamin Mazar, "The Aramaean Empire and Its Relations with Israel," in *Biblical Archaeologist Reader*, ed. Edward F. Campbell, Jr., and David Noel Freedman (Garden City, N.Y.: Doubleday, 1964), vol. 2, pp. 131–32.

35. Dothan, *Philistines*, pp. 18–19. See also Hanna E. Kassis, "Gath and the Structure of the 'Philistine' Society," *JBL* 84 (1965): 259–71. Kassis maintains that Philistine culture as described in the Old Testament had a large mixture of Canaanite elements, especially in Gath.

islands (e.g., Crete) or Asia Minor (Lydia). Until native texts are found, these philological questions too will remain unanswered.[36]

It is likewise impossible to know anything about the pre-Canaanite form of Philistine religion because all the known names of the deities are Semitic. It is likely that the Philistines assimilated the Canaanite gods into their own religious system, identifying their own traditional deities with the new ones they had encountered. Their principal god was Dagon, the grain deity, who is known in north Mesopotamian and Syrian sources as Dagan, father of Hadad or Baal. The half-human, half-fish representation suggested by 1 Samuel 5:4[37] may reflect the syncretism we have just suggested in that the Philistines, a seafaring people, likely would have retained the marine characteristics of their god while adapting him to their new agricultural lifestyle in Canaan. Thus Dagon was a grain deity superimposed upon an original god of fish or fishing. Other gods were Baal-Zebub and Ashtoreth, a goddess of the Canaanite pantheon who evidently was worshiped by the Philistines at Beth Shan at least (1 Sam. 31:8–13). Details of the cult are unclear though reference is made in the Old Testament to Philistine priests (1 Sam. 5:5; 6:2) and to the pagan practices of divining (1 Sam. 6:2) and of leaping on the threshold of a temple (1 Sam. 5:5).[38]

Israel's conflict with the Philistines is attested as early as Shamgar, Israel's third judge, who apparently resisted their earliest incursions around 1230 (see p. 163). It was Samson, however, who first undertook extensive measures to deal with the increasing encroachments of the Philistines which began around 1124. It could well have taken the Philistines sixty or seventy years from their permanent settlement in Canaan (ca. 1190) to achieve sufficient population and strength to undertake penetration into the Israelite highlands. For forty years they troubled Israel despite Samson's heroic exploits against them, until finally, in about 1084, they were forced to surrender the Israelite cities they had seized and to retire west of the Shephelah. From there, however, they persisted in their raids into Israel's interior, primarily into the plains and valleys where they could fully utilize their chariots. This unrelenting pressure contributed to Israel's demand for a king,

36. Kenneth A. Kitchen, "The Philistines," in *Peoples of Old Testament Times*, ed. D. J. Wiseman, pp. 67–68; Mazar, "The Philistines and Their Wars with Israel," in *World History of the Jewish People*, vol. 3, pp. 165–66.

37. The Hebrew says, "Only his Dagon [*dāgôn*] was left," a phrase which scholars since Julius Wellhausen have taken to mean, "Only his fishy part [*dāg*] was left." For various views on the matter see Lewis Spence, *Myths and Legends of Babylonia and Assyria* (London: Harrap, 1916), pp. 151–52; Ulf Oldenburg, *The Conflict Between El and Ba'al in Canaanite Religion* (Leiden: E. J. Brill, 1969), pp. 56–57; McCarter, *I Samuel*, pp. 119–20.

38. Dothan, *Philistines*, pp. 20–21; Kitchen, "The Philistines," in *Peoples of Old Testament Times*, ed. D. J. Wiseman, p. 68.

a demand which intensified when Samuel was old and unable to deliver them any longer.

This was the situation which faced Saul when he began his reign. Not only were the Philistines firmly installed in such areas as Beth Shan in the Plain of Jezreel, but they had managed to construct and occupy fortifications in the very midst of Israel's heartland, only a few miles, in fact, from Saul's capital of Gibeah (1 Sam. 10:5). As we have seen, he did manage to rid that area of them and force them to retreat to their coastal territory (1 Sam. 14:46), but there is no evidence that he ever succeeded in expelling them from the Jezreel. It was not until the days of David, after 1000 B.C., that the Philistines were contained within their original pentapolis of cities. Tribute to their tenacity even after that is the fact that, except for brief periods when they were forced to pay tribute to Israel, the Philistines did not lose their independence until the Assyrians destroyed Samaria in 722 and brought Judah under submission.

The Amalekites

Another enemy of Saul of an entirely different character and circumstance were the Amalekites. These desert nomads kept reappearing in Israel's history, almost always in an adversarial role. They had attacked Israel's rear flanks in a most shameful display of cowardice and treachery back in the Sinai wilderness (Exod. 17:8–16; Deut. 25:17–19). For this they were set apart by Yahweh for eventual judgment. They had then participated with the Canaanites in an attack on the Israelite forces which had made a premature attempt at invasion of Canaan from the south (Num. 14:45). Still later Eglon, king of Moab, had enlisted the Amalekites in his conquest of east-central Israel (Judg. 3:13). Evidently Amalekite contingents remained in the hill country of Ephraim even after Eglon was defeated, for Deborah speaks of them, this time favorably, as her allies against Jabin and Sisera (Judg. 5:14; cf. 12:15). By the early twelfth century, when the Midianites were raised up by Yahweh to discipline his people, they brought with them their Amalekite allies (Judg. 6:3, 33).

The picture that emerges, then, is that the Amalekites were inveterate enemies of Israel who joined themselves to whoever was in a position to do Israel harm. The roots of this animosity are unclear, though Amalek, the forefather of these tribes, is identified in Genesis 36:12 as a grandson of Esau. It may be that the wrath of Esau against Jacob over inheritance and birthright found expression historically in the anti-Israel activity of Amalek.

With the investiture of Israel's first king, the time had come, in the purposes of God, for the Amalekite problem to be settled once and for all (1 Sam. 15:1–3). Ironically, the destruction of the Amalekites would contribute to Saul's undoing as well. Samuel came to Saul and revealed the intentions of Yahweh to put the Amalekites to *ḥērem*; that is, to obliterate them and all their possessions from the face of the earth. Gathering his troops, Saul marched south to the desert haunts of the Amalekites and set upon them, destroying them to the very borders of Egypt.[39] He had first advised the Kenites among them to leave, however, for the Kenites, related to Moses himself by marriage (Judg. 1:16; 4:11), were innocent of the crimes for which Amalek was being punished. Saul failed to destroy all the Amalekites and their animals and, in fact, brought Agag the king and certain choice beasts back to Gilgal, where Samuel confronted Saul with his disobedience. Even Saul's plea that the animals had been brought back for sacrifice to Yahweh did not suffice to prevent his censure by the prophet, who informed him that he had been rejected as king in favor of a better man.

Theological Considerations

The Divine Intent for Human Kingship

The failure and disqualification of Saul as king of Israel pose no particular problem historically, for the record of kings and dynasties has traditionally been one of success and failure, of rise and fall. But Saul's tragic end has theological implications that go far beyond his role in history. Kingship was part and parcel of God's program to demonstrate and effect his sovereign rule over creation.[40] In fact, people throughout the ancient Near East thought of kingship as an institution designed to enable the gods in heaven to achieve their purposes on earth.[41] This is why the kings either were considered divine (as in Egypt) or at least understood themselves to be divinely called and authorized to bear rule. In some societies this amounted to a divine-human relationship described in terms of sonship: the human king was perceived to be the son of the gods, at least by adoption.[42]

This notion is clearly that of the Old Testament as well, though

39. Yohanan Aharoni, "The Negeb and the Southern Borders," in *World History of the Jewish People*, vol. 4, part 1, pp. 292–93.

40. The king as achiever and maintainer of order under God is a motif not only of Torah but of the Psalms and wisdom literature as well. See Helen Ann Kenik, "Code of Conduct for a King: Psalm 101," *JBL* 95 (1976): 402–3.

41. See especially Sidney Smith, "The Practice of Kingship in Early Semitic Kingdoms," in *Myth, Ritual, and Kingship*, ed. Samuel H. Hooke (Oxford: Clarendon, 1958), pp. 22–73; Henri Frankfort, *Kingship and the Gods* (Chicago: University of Chicago Press, 1948), pp. 343–44.

42. Ivan Engnell, *Studies in Divine Kingship in the Ancient Near East* (Uppsala: Almqvist and Wiksells, 1943), pp. 4–11, 80–81.

obviously divinity was never in any sense ascribed to the human king.[43] One should not assume, however, as many scholars do, that kingship in ancient Israel was patterned after that of the surrounding civilizations.[44] Rather, one must view ancient Near Eastern kingship as a reflection of God's original design which unfortunately became corrupted over the millennia in polytheistic societies, where, among other errors, powerful individuals used the notion of divinely authorized kingship as a justification of merciless despotism.

Kingship in Israel, as we have pointed out (p. 190), was expressly predicted and sanctioned by Moses and the patriarchs long before the institution itself came about. But until the Hebrew tribes underwent the metamorphosis from peoplehood to nationhood, a transition that occurred only after the exodus and Sinai experiences, they were not properly constituted to make kingship meaningful. In the providence of God it was only with the election of David, the "man after God's own heart," that the stage was set for human kingship in its pristine and finest form to come about. David, then, was not just a king, but in line with the regnal and saving purposes of God was in a unique sense the son of God. That is, he was adopted by God to represent God on the earth and to establish a human dynasty over which God's very Son (who was also the Son of David), Jesus Christ himself, would reign. Only David, therefore, could adequately serve as prototype of the messianic King. And just as the Messiah would be prophet and priest in addition to king, so David functioned in those capacities as well, and in a way which allowed him to operate outside the normal bounds of those offices.[45]

Saul's Covenant Misunderstanding: Violation of Priestly Prerogatives

Saul nonetheless remains an enigma, for not only had Yahweh permitted him to reign,[46] albeit as a concession to the people, but Yahweh

43. Edmond Jacob, *Theology of the Old Testament* (New York: Harper and Row, 1958), pp. 234–39; Frankfort, *Kingship and the Gods*, p. 339. In our opinion, Frankfort goes too far, however, in denying the central role of kingship in Israelite ideology (see his pp. 337–44).

44. So, for example, Engnell, *Studies in Divine Kingship*, pp. 174–77, the section in which he anticipated his later work on Old Testament kingship. This is the view of the so-called Myth and Ritual school, which flourished a generation ago and expressed its ideas in such publications as Hooke, ed., *Myth, Ritual, and Kingship*.

45. Dennis J. McCarthy, "Compact and Kingship: Stimuli for Hebrew Covenant Thinking," in *Studies in the Period of David and Solomon and Other Essays*, ed. Tomoo Ishida (Winona Lake, Ind.: Eisenbrauns, 1983), p. 82; Talmon, "The Biblical Idea of Statehood," in *The Bible World*, ed. Gary Rendsburg, pp. 247–48.

46. For the resolution of allegedly contradictory "deuteronomic" traditions as to whether Saul's reign had divine sanction, see A. D. H. Mayes, "The Rise of the Israelite Monarchy," *ZAW* 90 (1978): 9–10.

informed him that had he not failed in respect to cultic matters, Saul would have founded a dynasty that would rule over Israel forever (1 Sam. 13:13). This statement must be taken at face value, but since it is clear that the messianic kingship was reserved for David, we must conclude that the division of the kingdom was a foregone conclusion and that Saul's successors, had he been obedient, would have reigned over some kingdom, perhaps that of Israel in the north, while David's successors would reign, as they in fact did, over Judah in the south.[47] That both Saul's initial rejection and the final one occurred at Gilgal and in connection with the offering of sacrifice is not without significance in understanding his removal and the announcement of David's succession. On the first occasion Saul had failed to await Samuel's arrival at Gilgal and had, with his own hands, offered burnt offerings, a function totally and absolutely forbidden to a non-Levite unless granted a special dispensation by Yahweh. This is nowhere even hinted. On the second occasion Saul had presumed to violate *ḥērem* by sparing certain Amalekite animals, beasts which he intended to sacrifice to Yahweh. It is plausible that Saul also planned to offer these sacrifices personally. Samuel's indictment would favor this interpretation, for he reminded Saul that "to obey is better than sacrifice, and to heed is better than the fat of rams" (1 Sam. 15:22). Such disobedience, Samuel said, is rebellion, a sin as bad as divination or idolatry.

Saul's failure, then, lay in his appropriating to himself priestly prerogatives which may have been associated with pagan kingship but which, without specific divine sanction, were inappropriate to him or any king of Israel. The cultic role of kings was, indeed, well-nigh universal, so Saul, in emulating their behavior, might well be excused had he no contrary word from God in the law. But that word was clear—cultic affairs were reserved to the priests and Levites.

David, on the contrary, did function in cultic matters because, as messianic king, he transcended and was exempted from the restrictions of the law in this respect (see pp. 265–66). As the son of God he was a priest forever after the order of Melchizedek, if not after the order of Aaron. As the author of Hebrews is careful to show (Heb. 5:1–10; 6:13–7:28), the Melchizedekian priesthood was superior to that of Aaron, since Aaron and Levi submitted to Melchizedek while they were yet in the loins of Abraham their father. David, then, as a spiritual heir of Melchizedek (Ps. 110:4), could and did offer sacrifice

47. Since the royal messianic promise was specifically through Judah, as Genesis 49:10 clearly states, the saving purposes of God could have remained (as they actually did) within the confines of the southern kingdom until the eschatological day when the kingdoms of Israel and Judah would be reunited.

with impunity even though he was not of the tribe of Levi, just as Jesus Christ of Judah serves to this hour as the great High Priest in heaven, infinitely superior to the Aaronic priests.

Saul, though chosen to be king of Israel, was never designated as "son of God" nor granted priestly privileges by virtue of that relationship. Here, then, is where his disobedience and rejection lay—he arrogantly and consciously stepped beyond the bounds and entered an arena of kingship that was theologically as well as historically reserved for David and his dynasty alone.

The Rise of David

The Anointing of David

The decline of Saul is of course coincident with the appearance and rise of David. Though Samuel mourned the tragedy which had befallen Saul, he went, in response to the leading of God, to Bethlehem, where he found, among the sons of Jesse, the king whom God had provided (1 Sam. 16:1). Yahweh himself clearly indicated whom he had elected (1 Sam. 16:3). For when by process of elimination David finally appeared before Samuel, the old prophet knew that this lad was the divine choice, a fact confirmed by the visitation of the Spirit of God upon him.[48]

David at the Court of Saul

After the Spirit of Yahweh came upon David, a demonic spirit was allowed to trouble Saul until his dying day (1 Sam. 16:14). To counteract his fits of moodiness and rage, his servants sought a musician whose melodies might provide a soothing balm. Providentially, David was selected, a move which not only proved of benefit to Saul, but enabled David to become acquainted with life in the court and prepared him for the public role he must fill later on. Saul liked the lad very much and soon made him his armor-bearer as well as musician.

---

48. A word about chronology might be appropriate here at this moment of transition in Israel's history. David, who came to the throne of Judah in 1011 at the age of thirty (2 Sam. 5:4), was born in 1041, or some ten years after Saul began to reign. He certainly was a young lad at the time of his anointing, but not so young as to be unable to tend his father's flocks alone. An age of twelve would not be unreasonable. This gives a date in the early 1020s for the narrative of Saul's rejection and David's anointing, a date well in keeping with the age of Samuel, who then would have been about ninety.

For at least a brief time David remained with Saul, though when we next meet him he is back in Bethlehem.[49]

David and Goliath

A few years after Saul's disastrous Amalekite adventure, he found himself faced once more with the Philistine problem. Though the Philistines obviously hoped to regain a foothold in central Israel, they found themselves at best in a stalemate with Saul's forces at Ephes Dammim, a site which cannot be identified but which the narrator says lay between Socoh (Khirbet 'Abbâd) and Azekah (Tell Zakarî-yeh)[50] in the Valley of Elah, some twenty miles southwest of Jerusalem. Both sides had decided that the encounter would be resolved by duel rather than wholesale war, and so each was to select a champion who would represent his people.[51] The Philistines selected Goliath of Gath, a nine-foot giant who probably was descended from the Anakim, who had taken up residence in the Philistine cities after their expulsion from Hebron by Joshua (Josh. 11:21–22). Israel, however, could find nobody willing to stand up for them and Yahweh.

Finally David arrived upon the scene, having been at Bethlehem in order to assist his aged father, as was his periodic wont (1 Sam. 17:15). One need not conclude with many scholars that the present story and that of David's appointment as court musician represent variant and conflicting traditions just because Saul appears not to recognize David on this occasion.[52] It is impossible, first of all, to know how much time had elapsed since the two had last been together. It is well known that adolescents sometimes change rapidly and drastically in a year or two, so it is altogether possible that David, though still a youth here, had matured considerably since he had last served Saul. Furthermore, Saul's mental and emotional condition, always aberrational at best, would certainly have been aggravated in this hour of stress, perhaps to the point of his not recognizing even an old friend.

Though David was sent to the battlefront merely to carry provisions to his brothers, he became so offended at the cursing of the Philistine

49. The pericope of David's anointing (1 Sam. 16:1–13), often considered late and historically unreliable, is brilliantly analyzed by Martin Kessler, who sees it as an integral part of the narrative ("Narrative Technique in 1 Sam. 16:1–13," *CBQ* 32 [1970]: 552–53).

50. For identification of these sites see Yohanan Aharoni, *The Land of the Bible* (Philadelphia: Westminster, 1979), pp. 442, 431.

51. On the use of champions, see Roland de Vaux, *Ancient Israel* (New York: McGraw-Hill, 1965), vol. 1, p. 218.

52. So Otto Eissfeldt, *The Old Testament: An Introduction*, trans. Peter R. Ackroyd (New York: Harper and Row, 1965), p. 274.

that he volunteered to duel Goliath. He took slingshot in hand and slew the giant in the name and for the honor of Yahweh (1 Sam. 17:45–50). Thus David early on showed his holy zeal as the anointed of Yahweh, the warrior-king who joined his God in battle against all who would challenge his sovereignty.

David and Jonathan

This act of heroism so impressed Saul that he attached David permanently to his court and proceeded to fulfil his pledge to reward the hero who could avert the Philistine peril (1 Sam. 17:25). This included the exemption of David's family from taxation (the reason for Saul's inquiry concerning David's father in 1 Sam. 17:56), marriage to Saul's daughter, and riches, a boon not recorded but certainly to be expected as son-in-law of the king and commander of the army. Of greatest value to David, however, was the deep friendship he formed with Jonathan son of Saul. This was a remarkable relationship. Jonathan was considerably older than David, so much so that we ought to regard it as a father-son relationship rather than one of mere friends. This age disparity is clear from the fact that David, as we have seen, was born no earlier than 1041, while Jonathan was already a leader of men early in his father's reign, that is, by 1050. Jonathan must have been David's senior by thirty years. One can only speculate that Jonathan either had no sons of his own at the time he came to know David, or that he was so persuaded of David's election to kingship in place of Saul that he embraced David as Yahweh's anointed even before his actual rule came to pass.

In support of the latter is Jonathan's self-denial. He was the eldest son of Saul and surely would have followed his father in ordinary dynastic succession. This is without doubt the import of Saul's warning to Jonathan that as long as David was alive, Jonathan would have no hope of sitting on Israel's throne in continuation of the Saulide dynasty (1 Sam. 20:31). But Jonathan already knew what Saul tried in vain to deny—that David was the man after God's own heart.[53] He therefore disavowed any political ambition and joined himself to David in indissoluble bonds of friendship and loyalty. This makes clear the nature of the covenant which bound David and Jonathan together. First mentioned in 1 Samuel 18:1–3, it expressed more than mere

53. David Jobling argues that the selection of Jonathan as successor to Saul is already implicit in the battle account of 1 Samuel 14:1–46, which he sees as a pro-Jonathan narrative identifying Jonathan as the man after God's own heart ("Saul's Fall and Jonathan's Rise: Tradition and Redaction in 1 Sam. 14:1–46," *JBL* 95 [1976]: 371). This can be sustained only by overlooking the clear evidence of 1 Samuel 13:13 that Saul's entire dynasty (including Jonathan) was to be replaced by another.

friendship. It was a formal contract by which Jonathan not only articulated human love at its most profound level, but pledged himself to the lordship of David as the anointed of Yahweh.[54]

There are several indications that Jonathan deferred to Yahweh's selection of David. First, the covenant was not mutual; it was a pledge made by Jonathan to David and not vice versa (1 Sam. 18:1, 3b; 20:8, 16–17). Second, Jonathan symbolized his submission to the higher Davidic claims to the throne by clothing David in his own royal attire (1 Sam. 18:4). He later tacitly acknowledged that David would outlive him and would someday as king be in a position to show favor to his descendants (1 Sam. 20:14–15, 42). In fact, he said, David would indeed be king and Jonathan would be subservient to him (1 Sam. 23:17–18). Third, the covenant was made not only with David personally but with the Davidic dynasty (1 Sam. 20:16). Jonathan knew beyond any question that the election of David was more than an *ad hoc* choice. It was the inauguration by Yahweh himself of a line of kings which not only would replace the Saulide dynasty, but had redemptive ramifications only dimly understood at the time.

The Flight of David

The plot of Saul

Saul's promotion of David to rank and power was an astute political move, but it proved to be more than the fragile psyche of the troubled king could handle. With great courage tempered by circumspection and humility, David went to war, and so successful was he that it was not long before the bards of Israel began to sing of his exploits in almost legendary terms. Saul found himself eclipsed and so put in motion schemes whereby he might rid himself of his confidant-turned-rival.

First, under demonic influence Saul tried to spear David to the wall at least twice (1 Sam. 18:11; 19:10), but Yahweh delivered him. Frustrated, Saul released David from palace service and left him to military affairs only. Next he hit upon the plan of ridding himself of David by requiring David to pay the price (*mōhar*) of a hundred slain Philistines for the hand of his daughter Michal, this in lieu of what normally would have been an immense payment in silver and gold (1 Sam. 18:25). David rose to the occasion and then some, for he killed two hundred Philistines. When evidence of this was forthcoming, the marriage was arranged and Saul found that his foe, much to his dismay, had become his son-in-law.

54. See Tryggve N. D. Mettinger, *King and Messiah: The Civil and Sacral Legitimation of the Israelite Kings* (Lund: C. W. K. Gleerup, 1976), p. 39.

Saul now became more overt in his intentions and let it be known even to Jonathan that David must die. Jonathan, already very much aware of David's divine election, tried to communicate to his father the folly of spilling innocent blood (1 Sam. 19:4–5). This achieved a temporary reconciliation, but before long Saul again sought David's life, this time by sending assassins to murder him in his bed. Michal, when she learned of the plot, warned her husband, who escaped to Ramah to find refuge with the prophet Samuel (1 Sam. 19:18).

Staying there only briefly, David sought out Jonathan once more, and together they fashioned a plan whereby David might determine once and for all whether he had a future in the employment of Saul. This time Jonathan's intercession was totally without avail, for Saul was adamant in his determination to rid himself of David. He correctly perceived that Jonathan himself had come to recognize the legitimacy of David's royal appointment and that he had bound himself in loyalty to the man after God's own heart (1 Sam. 20:30–31). There was only one recourse now open to David—he must take up the life of a fugitive, exiled from family and home, if he hoped to survive and claim his throne.

David the outlaw

David went first to Nob,[55] a village on the Mount of Olives where Ahimelech the high priest presided over the tabernacle. Since Ahimelech (otherwise known as Ahijah; cf. 1 Sam. 14:3; 22:9) was the great-grandson of Eli, it is reasonable to assume that either his father Ahitub or he himself had removed the tabernacle from Shiloh and installed it at Nob. One can only speculate as to why this site was selected. The ark, of course, still remained at Kiriath Jearim in the custody of the family of Abinadab.

Having fled from Saul with only the clothes on his back, David and his companions were famished and requested rations from the priest. Ahimelech knew nothing of David's estrangement from Saul, so he provided the only nourishment available at the moment—the showbread of the tabernacle. Then, taking Goliath's sword, which had been retained behind the ephod, perhaps as a symbol of Yahweh's sovereignty over the Philistines, David made his way to Gath, the very home of Goliath.[56] This act of madness, supported by convincing theatrics

55. Nob is probably to be identified with el-'Isāwîyeh (Aharoni and Avi-Yonah, *Macmillan Bible Atlas*, p. 181). Denis Baly, however, identifies it with eṭ-Ṭor (*The Geography of the Bible* [New York: Harper, 1957], p. 162).

56. Mazar, "The Philistines and Their Wars with Israel," in *World History of the Jewish People*, vol. 3, p. 178, suggests that Gath may have become important as a Philistine political center because the Israelite wars prompted the Philistines to protect their eastern frontier with Benjamin.

on David's part, convinced Achish, lord of Gath, that David was indeed insane. The ecstatic prophets of the pagan world conducted themselves in precisely this way and, as holy men, were exempted from punishment such as David, the slayer of Goliath, had every right to expect in Gath.[57] In fact, David was hoping for sanctuary in Gath, but Achish, for whatever reason, was unwilling to go that far and so requested David to depart.

David then took up the life of an outlaw for perhaps the next ten years, constantly on the move and without visible means of support. He first found refuge in the cave of Adullam, a town in the Shephelah of Judah about fifteen miles southwest of Bethlehem. By then his family had heard of his plight, so they and many others gathered there to place themselves under his command. This clearly suggests that a consensus was emerging that David, having already been anointed as king, was about to lead a movement that would result in wholesale revolution and the deposition of Saul. Even the Philistines sensed this (1 Sam. 21:11); in fact, they may have spared David at Gath precisely because they felt they could use him for their own purposes in undermining Saul.

David, however, was concerned most immediately with survival, though it is clear that in the course of his exile he was careful to cultivate good relations with his own Judahite kin with the end in view of gaining their support when the time of his monarchy should arrive. As part of his strategy he made a trip to Mizpah in Moab (location unknown), where he requested and received permission to leave his family for protection. Since his great-grandmother Ruth came from Moab, his choice of that land is understandable. There may also have been the intent to curry the favor and potential alliance of Moab, for David knew full well that the time might come when he and Saul would head competing factions each of which would solicit support from neighboring kingdoms. Israel under Saul had already been at war with Moab (1 Sam. 14:47), so there is every reason to believe that the king of Moab would, like the Philistines, use the Saul-David rift to his own advantage. Any agreements along this line which David may have forged with both Philistia and Moab at this time did not last long, for early in his reign he reduced both nations to tributary states (2 Sam. 8:1–2).

The prophet Gad had joined David by now and advised him throughout the rest of his exile. Gad recommended that David leave Adullam and move to the forest of Hereth (location unknown). Meanwhile, Saul, enslaved by paranoia, accused his fellow Benjamites of disloyalty because they had failed to tell him of Jonathan's defection

---

57. Hertzberg, *I & II Samuel*, p. 183.

and apparent solidarity with David. To pacify Saul, Doeg, who had observed Ahimelech's favor toward David at Nob, related to the king all that had transpired there. Furious, Saul summoned the priests from Nob, accused them of treachery, and summarily slaughtered them all. He then placed Nob itself under *ḥērem*, wiping it from the face of the earth. Abiathar, a son of Ahimelech, managed to escape to David, however, and continued to serve him throughout the wilderness years. He later became high priest of Israel along with Zadok, a position he held until David's dying days when he conspired with Adonijah, David's son, to prevent Solomon from becoming king. This led to Abiathar's removal from office and exile to Anathoth when Solomon came to power.

David may have been in flight from Saul, but he remained acutely aware of the needs of his own tribal kinfolk. The Philistines, perhaps testing David's resolve, had undertaken a raid against Keilah (Khirbet Qîlā), a village of Judah just south of Adullam. Carefully seeking the mind of God through the ephod which Abiathar had brought from Nob (1 Sam. 23:6), David was assured of victory and so went to Keilah to deliver his countrymen. Saul heard that he was there and marched rapidly south to trap David and his men within the city. David learned of Saul's coming in time to escape, however; and he took to hiding in the Desert of Ziph just southeast of Hebron. He had determined that the people of Keilah, whom he had just saved from the Philistines, were not to be trusted to defend him from Saul. This reveals that David did not enjoy unanimous support even in Judah.

The Ziphites also proved to be treacherous for they wasted no time in informing Saul that David was hiding among them. Always a step ahead, David pressed south to the Desert of Maon. Saul eventually arrived there and narrowly missed apprehending David's band. Before he could proceed farther, however, he had to return to the north to deal with a Philistine incursion. David then traveled east to En Gedi (Tell ej-Jurn), on the very shores of the Dead Sea.

Relentlessly Saul, having dealt with the Philistine emergency, returned to his pursuit. He tracked David down at En Gedi but this time could have lost his own life, for David was in a position to rid himself of Saul once and for all had he chosen to do so. No doubt every human instinct told him to do that very deed to pave the way for acquisition of the promised monarchy. The divine instinct countervailed, however, for David knew that until Yahweh himself removed Saul, he remained the anointed of Yahweh. His personal character and conduct might seem to belie his divine appointment, but that was irrelevant to David. All he knew was that the God who had elected him would put him in power at precisely his own chosen time. Temporarily confounded and repentant at David's magnanimity, Saul returned home. David also left En Gedi and went into the Desert of Paran to Carmel (Kirmil), a mile or two from Maon (Khirbet Ma'în).

David had heard of a wealthy man, Nabal by name, who lived at Maon and owned extensive lands and flocks at Carmel. Again at the verge of starvation, David requested that Nabal replenish his men, not an unfair petition in light of David's having refrained from the typical outlaw's practice of appropriating property. Besides, by the admission of Nabal's own men, David had provided protection to Nabal's shepherds without remuneration (1 Sam. 25:15). Nabal nevertheless denied the request; were it not for the intercession of his wise and beautiful wife Abigail, he would soon have experienced the outrage of David. Abigail herself supplied the needed commodities. When Nabal heard how narrow his escape had been, he suffered a heart attack and died. So grateful was David to Abigail and so smitten by her sagacity and charm, he immediately arranged to take her as wife. He also married Ahinoam of Jezreel (Khirbet Terrama?),[58] a town just southwest of Hebron. His first wife Michal had in the meantime been taken from him by her father Saul and had been given to another husband, Paltiel. After David became king at Hebron, Ahinoam bore his first son, Amnon, and Abigail bore his second son, Kileab (2 Sam. 3:2–3).

Once again the Ziphites, who seemed to have an uncontrollable hatred of David, notified Saul that his enemy was among them, at Hakilah (unknown). When Saul arrived there, David and his nephew Abishai (see 1 Chron. 2:13–16) crept up to the king's campsite in the night and easily could have slain both Saul and Abner, the commander of his army. Again, however, David recognized the sanctity of Israelite kingship and left Saul's fate in the hand of Yahweh (1 Sam. 26:10). When Saul awoke and became aware that he had been spared only because of the mercy of Yahweh and David, he confessed once more his sin toward David and pledged never again to seek David's harm. But David knew that the protestations of a paranoid demoniac held little value and that Saul would only intensify his efforts to destroy him.

The Philistine Exile of David

It was obvious to David that it was only a matter of time before Saul caught up with him, so he resorted to a drastic measure—he sought asylum with Achish, lord of Gath. Clearly, certain factors must have been at work to create a climate of mutual trust between David and the Philistine. First of all, Achish and his cohorts could not have been anything but pleased over the irreparable rift that had developed

58. *Oxford Bible Atlas*, p. 132.

between Saul and David. Without David, Saul lacked military leadership sufficient to eliminate the Philistine threat; without Saul, David lacked a power base from which to operate. Second, David had conducted himself vis-à-vis the Philistines in such a way as to allay any fears that he might do them further harm. Only once in his years of exile, at Keilah, had he fought them, and that was a defensive measure. Third, David must have conveyed to Achish his willingness to submit to the Philistine in return for protection. It may even be that he pledged to make Judah a vassal state to Philistia after he seized power at Hebron. Subsequent events make this seem very likely.

In any event, Achish received David and his men gladly and even granted him a fiefdom at Ziklag (Tell esh-Shari'ah).[59] There David lived for more than a year (ca. 1012–1011), leaving only after Saul's death and his own accession to the throne of Judah. He spent his time primarily in undertaking razzias into the deserts against the Geshurites, Girzites, and Amalekites. With superb diplomatic skill (but less than admirable candor) he took the spoil of these raids back to Achish and said it came from Judah (1 Sam. 27:10)! It is no wonder that Achish came to see David as a renegade against his own people and a staunch ally of the Philistines. David was proving to be a most devoted vassal.

His masquerade soon came to haunt David, however, for he found himself caught up on the wrong side of the decisive battle of the long wars between Israel and the Philistines. The latter had gathered at Aphek to deal the fatal blow to Israel, and Achish had, of course, insisted that his vassal join him and the other lords in the *coup de grâce*. The other four were not convinced of David's loyalty, however; in fact, they were quite persuaded that in the heat of battle he would reassess his position and rejoin his former lord, Saul. Reluctantly Achish had to tell David of their decision against his participation. Though David masterfully registered a convincing protest, he returned with great relief to Ziklag.

In the meantime Israel had gathered at Gilboa (Jebel Fuqu'ah), a mountain some seven or eight miles south of Shunem (Sôlem). Terrified by the prospect of the Philistine host on its way for battle, Saul resorted to a medium at nearby Endor, on the north side of the mountain of Moreh. He tried to disguise himself since he had banned divination practices (1 Sam. 28:9), but when he prevailed upon the woman to conjure up a vision of Samuel, she recognized that he was the king. Nevertheless, she went on to describe the apparition, which Saul at once knew to be the prophet Samuel. Patiently Samuel explained once more that Saul by his disobedience had forfeited his right to rule and

59. Aharoni and Avi-Yonah, *Macmillan Bible Atlas*, p. 184.

that David would take his place. Furthermore, Samuel said, Saul and his sons would die the very next day as Israel fell in disastrous defeat to the Philistines.

The Death of Saul

By the next morning the Philistines arrived at Shunem from their staging area at Aphek. After a fierce battle Israel gave way and beat a hasty retreat. Saul and his sons were unable to escape, however; and when it was clear that the end was at hand, Saul committed suicide rather than die at the hands of the Philistines (1 Sam. 31:4). When the people of the area saw that all was lost, they abandoned their cities and towns to the Philistines. The next day the Philistines found the bodies of Saul and his sons. In a brutal act of revenge they decapitated Israel's king, displayed his armor in the temple of their goddess Ashtoreth, and fastened his body to the outer wall of Beth Shan. That night the men of Jabesh Gilead, twelve miles southeast of Beth Shan, stole across the Jordan River and retrieved the bodies of Saul and his sons from the wall. After burning the bodies in order to hide the effects of the horrible mutilation, they buried the bones in their city. Thus Saul returned to the home of his non-Benjamite ancestress.

After David had been dismissed from military service by the Philistine lords, he returned to Ziklag to find it in ruins and its population, including his family, taken captive by the Amalekites. Abiathar the priest consulted the Urim and Thummim and discerned that it was the will of God for David and his six hundred men to set out after the Amalekite enemy. After having been on the road for four days, two hundred of David's party were so exhausted they remained at the Besor Ravine (Wadi Ghazzeh), fifteen miles south of Ziklag. The others went on and found an Egyptian who had been abandoned by the pillagers and who was willing to show where the Amalekites had gone. David's men then overtook and decimated the Amalekites, and recovered their loved ones unharmed. After some of the spoils were divided amongst the four hundred who had fought and the two hundred who had remained behind, David sent the rest to the elders of Judah for further distribution. Significantly, the last city mentioned to which David's largess was sent was Hebron. His generosity, while sincere no doubt, also served the end of ingratiating him with the Judahites, who would soon anoint him as their king.

On David's third day back in Ziklag an Amalekite runner came from the Gilboa battlefield to report that Saul and his sons were dead. The messenger claimed that he himself had killed Saul as an act of mercy. As evidence he presented David with Saul's crown and bracelet (2 Sam. 1:1–10). The young man had, in fact, not been responsible for Saul's death, as the narrator has already made clear, but he must have been a witness. Viewing the whole situation as a means of gaining David's favor, he claimed that it was he who had destroyed David's only remaining obstacle to the throne of Israel. But David did not see it that way. He who had spared the life of God's anointed king on at least two occasions could hardly countenance the murder of Saul by someone else, most particularly a pagan Amalekite! He therefore ordered the lying messenger to be executed for a crime he had not committed. Then, in one of the most poignant expressions of grief and lament in all literature, David poured out his soul for Saul and Jonathan.

But the deed was done. The reign of Saul had come to an end, just as Samuel had predicted, and David stood at the crossroads. He could not simply go up to Gibeah and assert his sovereignty, for Saul had a surviving son, Ish-Bosheth, who no doubt would lay claim to succession. And yet the pressure for David to take command of his own people of Judah, a pressure which had been building for some time, had reached the bursting point with Saul's death. Judah was ready to acknowledge the kingship of David, and the clear leading of Yahweh indicated that the seat of authority should be Hebron. So David went to Hebron in 1011 B.C. and was formally crowned king of Judah (2 Sam. 2:4).

6 David: Covenant Kingship

The Lack of Nationhood Before David

The eighty-year period of the reigns of David and Solomon is in many respects the golden age of Israel's long history. Up to that point, even in the best years of Saul, Israel hardly warranted the name *kingdom* or even *state* because by and large there had not emerged any significant recognition of fundamental political unity. And this was not because there was a theocratic spirit in Israel, for that spirit had not in fact been translated into anything more than a theological ideal. The whole burden of the Book of Judges, as we saw, was the lament that there was no king in Israel; the people did not even view God as their king. Consequently, there was no political oneness.

This lack of statehood for the nearly 450 years between the issuance of the Sinaitic covenant and the installment of David at Hebron can be explained in many ways. First of all, for practical reasons it was not possible for the tribal units in nomadic transit to Canaan to exist

223

MEDITERRANEAN
SEA

ZOBAH

LEBANON

BEKAA
VALLEY

BETH
REHOB

ANTI-LEBANON

Sidon

Damascus

Tyre

Abel
Beth
Maacah

Dan

MAACAH

LAKE
HULEH

GESHUR

SEA
OF
KINNERETH

Helam

TOB

VALLEY OF JEZREEL

Lo
Debar

Rogelim

Mt.
Gilboa △

Beth
Shan

Jabesh
Gilead

Shechem

Forest of
Ephraim

Jordan River

Jabbok River

Mahanaim

Shiloh

Baal Hazor

Bethel

Gilgal

Rabbah

AMMON

Gezer

Baal Perazim?

Gibeah

Jerusalem

VALLEY OF
REPHAIM

Bethlehem

PHILISTIA

Gath

Adullam

Keilah

Hebron

Ziph

DEAD SEA

Ziklag

Arnon River

Beersheba

VALLEY
OF
SALT

Arad

MOAB

Zered River

NEGEV

EDOM

Border of Judah
and Israel

Conquered
Kingdoms

0   10   20 miles

AMALEK

The Kingdom
of David

Mizpah

Gezer

Gibeon

Ramah

Zela?

Kiriath Jearim

Nob

Jerusalem

in a normal national sense. There was certainly a cohesion in the covenant federation, a recognition of common ancestry and ethnicity and of common theological bases and objectives. There was even a constitution of sorts by which community and individual life could be regulated. But there was no land, and without land nationhood is just an ideal.[1]

During the transitional period of the conquest (the early fourteenth century) the tribal identity still prevailed. Yet there was also an ongoing recognition that Israel was the people of God, a covenant people whose commonalities far outweighed tribal differences. It was this attitude that enabled Joshua to galvanize the tribes with a spirit of cooperation and common interest to achieve the subjugation of the Canaanite populations and to bring about at least a tentative occupation of the land. There were, to be sure, signs of independence even this early, as the request for Transjordanian inheritance by Reuben, Gad, and Manasseh attests (Josh. 1:12–18). But this was addressed adroitly by Joshua with the result that the confederation remained intact until the day of his death.

To call Israel under Joshua a nation would, in spite of all that has been said, be a misnomer. Joshua himself was more a covenant mediator and military leader than politician. Real authority rested in the hands of the elders, who apparently seldom if ever acted outside very parochial limits. There was no capital city whence national policy could issue, unless one think of Gilgal or even Shiloh as such. The mode of operation seemed rather to be *ad hoc*. Any emergency which called for intertribal response was met by Joshua's personal appeal for cooperation, sometimes with not much support or success.

The period of the judges, from Joshua's death (ca. 1366) to the reign of Saul (1051), gave rise to a more or less effective occupation of territories, but this was accompanied almost inversely by a disintegration of solidarity. The judges themselves were not politicians as such and administered only local jurisdictions for the most part. But they were the only leaders on a national scale. There was not even a Moses or Joshua who could command unity of purpose and action. The office of elder survived, but in only extraordinary circumstances did the elders exercise any kind of decisive leadership. The age, as has been stressed repeatedly, was one marked by anarchy, an almost total breakdown of law and order on every level.

The principal reason for this chaotic condition was, of course, covenant infidelity. The people, from the leaders on down, had defected from Yahweh and had begun to embrace syncretism and outright pa-

---

1. On land ("space") as a fundamental necessity for nationhood see Walter Brueggemann, *The Land* (Philadelphia: Fortress, 1977), esp. pp. 28–44.

ganism. This, in fact, was the very reason for the discipline of Israel in the form of external enemies such as the Moabites and Midianites (Judg. 2:11–23). But there were other factors, more difficult to identify, which encouraged and accelerated the tendencies toward regional division and national decomposition.

Geography obviously played a part, particularly in the formative period.[2] The Jordan River, for example, formed a natural cleavage between eastern and western tribes. At certain times of the year it was almost impossible to ford the river, and certainly intercourse on a wide scale would be discouraged at any time. This no doubt was at least part of Joshua's concern about settlement east of the Jordan (Josh. 22:13–20). He knew full well that geographic borders lead easily to psychological and even spiritual borders. Further evidence of the east-west alienation may be seen in the attitude of the eastern leaders toward Gideon in his pursuit of the Midianites through their region (Judg. 8:4–9). Jephthah, an eastern judge, similarly raised the hackles of the Ephraimites to the west: they alleged that he had refused to invite them to participate in his subjugation of Ammon (Judg. 12:1–6). Interesting in this connection is that by Jephthah's time (ca. 1100) dialectical differences between the eastern and western tribes had begun to surface (Judg. 12:6).[3] And while they do not necessarily cause mutual suspicions and antagonism, the fact is that differences in dialect often serve to intensify them.

Ruptures in the sociopolitical body of Israel are also apparent elsewhere. One of the clearest instances relates to the story of Deborah. The Canaanites had begun to devastate the tribes north of the Plain of Jezreel. In response, Deborah solicited the support not only of the northern tribes most directly affected, but, as her song so poignantly recounts, she also looked to the remaining tribes as well (Judg. 5:12–18). The results were anything but encouraging. There was virtually no aid from the eastern tribes, none from south of Jerusalem, and only token assistance from elsewhere, including her own tribe of Ephraim. If not reflecting outright intertribal hostilities, this reaction at least revealed colossal indifference.

An even better insight into regional and tribal rivalries is gained by careful attention to the story of the Levite and his concubine (Judg. 19–21). This is of profound significance both because of its early date, which indicates that rupture was not late in manifesting itself, and

2. The connection between geography and history is self-evident. For Syria-Palestine see the still important discussion by George Adam Smith, *The Historical Geography of the Holy Land* (London: Hodder and Stoughton, 1900), pp. 43–59.

3. On this interesting development see Eduard Y. Kutscher, *A History of the Hebrew Language* (Jerusalem: Magnes, 1982), pp. 14–15.

because of its disclosure of the schismatic tendency which would ultimately express itself in complete division between Israel and Judah.

It has already been proposed that one of the purposes of this narrative was to draw attention to a Gibeah-Bethlehem antagonism (see p. 181). Gibeah, the capital of Saul, obviously represents the Saulide monarchy as Bethlehem represents that of David. The fact that the Levite was from Ephraim ties that tribe (and all of the northern kingdom) to the controversy as well. The Judahite concubine was ravished at Gibeah and left dead outside the door of the house where the Levite had spent the night. Not only did the incident violate every expectation of ancient hospitality, but it revealed the total absence of authority in Gibeah and Benjamin. To compound the gravity of the situation the Benjamite elders refused to punish the wrongdoers and, in fact, went as far as to take up arms in defense of the criminals. Then, at the express command of Yahweh, the other tribes in unison went to war with Benjamin, nearly annihilating it. And what is more, even with all the Benjamite women dead and the survival of the tribe in jeopardy, the Israelites refused to provide wives to the few men still alive. Instead, wives were secured from Shiloh and Jabesh Gilead in the unorthodox manner already described.

It is a fact, of course, that this terrible incident occurred and that it was recorded to illustrate the lawlessness of the era of the judges. However, this particular episode, out of many others which no doubt could have served equally well as illustrations, was also included for the purpose of explaining the mutual antagonism of the Saulide and Davidic families and the political fragmentation of the kingdom even in David's time. The Benjamin-Judah hostility is everywhere apparent in the early years of David's reign. Indeed it lasted until, ironically, Benjamin was absorbed by Judah and became part of the southern kingdom.

The rise of the monarchy under Saul did little to heal the ever-widening breach between Judah and the northern tribes. In fact, during his reign an already serious cleavage was exacerbated. For example, the historian makes the point that when Saul issued a call to arms to deliver Jabesh Gilead from Ammon, three hundred thousand men came from Israel and thirty thousand from Judah (1 Sam. 11:8). When he undertook his campaign against Amalek, he is said to have summoned "two hundred thousand foot soldiers [obviously from Israel] and ten thousand men from Judah" (1 Sam. 15:4).[4] This is revealing since the ratio would suggest that Judah supplied very few

4. From this reference Ralph W. Klein concludes, rightly, that it is "doubtful whether Judah was ever (fully) incorporated into Saul's kingdom" (*1 Samuel*, Word Biblical Commentary [Waco: Word, 1983], p. 149).

men comparatively, a fact that is particularly striking in that Amalek lived along the south border of Judah. Is Judah showing signs of an anti-Saul posture? Moreover, we are told that after David had slain Goliath, "the men of Israel and Judah" pursued the Philistines (1 Sam. 17:52), and when David became attached to Saul's court, "all Israel and Judah" loved him (1 Sam. 18:16). It is clear that Israel and Judah were perceived as two entities following their own separate interests.

David at Hebron

Early Diplomacy

That David's reign should commence at Hebron ought not to cause surprise, then. He was a Judahite, he had paved the way for his kingship by his exile in Judah and his beneficence to Judah during that time, and he clearly recognized that Judah was *de facto* a political if not an ethnic organism in its own right. Besides, the opportunity for him to assert a broader sovereignty over all Israel had not yet come, for Saul had left a surviving son who, by dynastic principle at least, would succeed him. In addition, Saul's cousin Abner, who was by now the most powerful figure in Israel, was strongly opposed to David as, indeed, was the northern kingdom as a whole. David's intent appeared to be to locate at Hebron where he would await further divine direction in regard to his leadership over all Israel.

What followed in the seven years at Hebron is a masterpiece of diplomatic skill. David, knowing full well that he was perceived as the enemy of Saul by both Israel and Judah, had already, upon learning of Saul's death, composed a song extolling the king. In this so-called lament of the bow (2 Sam. 1:19–27)[5] he described Saul as Israel's "glory" and as "the mighty." He it was, David sang, who had clothed Israel in fine, expensive garments, and so Israel ought to weep for him. This gesture, sincere to be sure, was also designed to demonstrate that David regarded Saul with favor. Whatever hostility may have existed was one-sided and beyond David's control.

David next sought to gain the favor of the people of Jabesh Gilead by commending them for their brave and devoted attendance to the body of Saul, which they had retrieved from Beth Shan and buried in

5. Support for its Davidic authorship and a fine analysis of its form and content appear in Masao Sekine, "Lyric Literature in the Davidic-Solomonic Period in the Light of the History of Israelite Literature," in *Studies in the Period of David and Solomon and Other Essays*, ed. Tomoo Ishida (Winona Lake, Ind.: Eisenbrauns, 1983), pp. 2–4. See also David Noel Freedman, *Pottery, Poetry, and Prophecy* (Winona Lake, Ind.: Eisenbrauns, 1980), pp. 263–74.

their own city (2 Sam. 2:4b–7). Success in this overture would give David a foothold in the northern Transjordan, a foothold that might result in a large-scale popularity in that distant but important region. Years later David retrieved the bones of Saul and Jonathan from Jabesh Gilead so that he might bury them in the tomb of their fathers in Zela (Khirbet Salah)[6] of Benjamin (2 Sam. 21:12–14).

David and Abner

The major obstacle to expanded control by David lay in the person of Saul's cousin Abner. From Saul's early reign he had served as chief military officer (1 Sam. 14:50). It was he who brought David to Saul after the duel with Goliath (1 Sam. 17:55–57) and who, with David, sat at the side of the king at table (1 Sam. 20:25). He had been the butt of David's taunt after David had come across him and Saul asleep in the Desert of Ziph (1 Sam. 26:5, 14–15). Now, with all these memories in mind, Abner was in a strong bargaining position. If unable to seize the throne of Israel for himself, he could at least make David pay dearly for it.

For five long years David patiently remained content with his little kingdom of Judah alone. To the north, Israel was caught up in the throes of seemingly irresolvable turmoil. Saul was dead and had left only a weakling of a son to fill his shoes. Originally named Ish-Baal ("man of Baal"), this youngest son became known as Ish-Bosheth ("man of shame"),[7] perhaps a testimony to both the syncretistic tendencies of Saul and the disappointing son whom he had sired. He apparently had not even participated in the conflict at Gilboa in which his father and brothers had lost their lives, and now he proved unable to sit upon Israel's throne. Finally, Abner, perhaps after defeating the Philistines and evicting them from the land, took Ish-Bosheth and appointed him as figurehead king at Mahanaim (Tell edh-Dhahab el-Gharbi)[8] in the land of Gilead. From there he reigned for a brief two years, the end of his tenure coinciding with David's move to Jerusalem from Hebron in 1004 B.C.

That Abner was the real power who pulled the strings of the puppet prince is clear from unfolding events. First, Abner and his men went

---

6. So *Oxford Bible Atlas*, ed. Herbert G. May, 3d ed. (New York: Oxford University Press, 1984), p. 143.

7. P. Kyle McCarter, Jr., *II Samuel*, Anchor Bible (Garden City, N.Y.: Doubleday, 1984), p. 86, suggests that the *'iš* in the Masoretic text of Samuel is preferable to the *'eš* in 1 Chronicles 8:33 and 9:39. The root in each case must have been *'iš* ("man"). The Qumran scrolls clearly support this position.

8. Avraham Negev, ed., *Archaeological Encyclopedia of the Holy Land* (Englewood, N.J.: SBS, 1980), pp. 191–92.

to Gibeon where they entered into negotiations with Joab, David's representative, presumably over the questions of unification and kingship (2 Sam. 2:12–13). When talks broke down, the suggestion was made by Abner that their differences be resolved by a contest of physical strength: each side would choose twelve men to engage in hand-to-hand combat, the outcome of which would decide the issue of sovereignty. David's men were victorious, and Abner's took to flight with their enemy in hot pursuit. Joab's younger brother Asahel unfortunately chose to tackle Abner, the seasoned warrior, who in self-defense killed the young man. Joab and another brother, Abishai, continued their pursuit, but at last Abner found refuge among his Benjamite brethren and was safe. His question to Joab at that moment is most interesting—"How long before you order your men to stop pursuing their brothers?" (2 Sam. 2:26). Is there not perhaps an overture of peace here? Is not Abner reaching out for reconciliation, knowing that the trend is inevitable and that David will at last prevail?

The historian proceeds to answer these questions by emphasizing that during the seven-year period in which David reigned from Hebron he had continued to grow stronger while the Saulide dynasty had grown weaker (2 Sam. 3:1). Evidence of David's increasing power is the multiplication of wives and children, a practice common to ancient Near Eastern kings, though obviously not sanctioned by biblical law. In addition to the sons of Abigail and Ahinoam, David sired Absalom by Maacah, Adonijah by Haggith, Shephatiah by Abital, and Ithream by Eglah. Of special interest is Maacah, for she is identified as the daughter of Talmai, king of Geshur. This suggests that some of David's marriages had political overtones and were contracted in order to cement international relationships.[9] The Geshur mentioned here is most probably the kingdom east of the Sea of Kinnereth.[10] An alliance with this principality would provide a buffer between Israel and the rising Aramean states to the north.

Commensurate with David's developing influence was Abner's realization that he had best make accommodation with David if he was to have any future at all. He had made every effort to seize control of the throne of Saul—as his appropriation of Saul's concubine attests—and yet had failed. He therefore began to explore means whereby he could use his influence to deliver Israel to David and thus secure at least as high a position as he had enjoyed under Saul. His very involvement with Rizpah, Saul's concubine, provided the occasion. Re-

9. Jon D. Levenson and Baruch Halpern, "The Political Import of David's Marriages," *JBL* 99 (1980): 507–18.

10. Yohanan Aharoni, *The Land of the Bible* (Philadelphia: Westminster, 1979), p. 38. After slaying Amnon, Absalom would flee to Geshur, the homeland of his mother (2 Sam. 13:37–38).

buked by Ish-Bosheth, and quite properly, for this bold and transparent grab for power, Abner turned against him and self-righteously denied any personal ambition. In revenge Abner would now undertake steps to bring all Israel under David's kingship, a pledge he immediately set out to accomplish (2 Sam. 3:6–11).

Abner first of all sent a delegation to David to offer his proposal for unification—a covenant which would guarantee peaceful transfer of power from the Saulide to the Davidic dynasty. What Abner's demands were can only be guessed, but surely he would expect nothing less than to be supreme commander of Israel's armies. David enthusiastically accepted the arrangement, but demanded as a sign of Abner's good faith that his first wife Michal, the daughter of Saul, be restored to him. This would symbolize the unification of the two royal families.

After Michal was returned to David, Abner persuaded the Israelite elders, particularly those from Benjamin, of the wisdom of placing themselves under David. His appeal, however, was not theological but purely pragmatic—David would be able to deliver Israel from their enemies. This lack of appreciation of David as the messianic king, the elected representative of Yahweh on earth, was a serious defect in Israel's political viewpoint. To Abner at least, David was a king like that of every other nation.

True to his word, Abner returned to David at Hebron with the solid backing of the elders of Israel. The two then decided to make a formal compact and arrange a ceremony of coronation at which all the nation could pledge its fealty to their new king. Before the festivities could be arranged, however, Abner was intercepted by Joab, who ruthlessly murdered him, ostensibly as an act of revenge for the death of his own brother Asahel. More likely, Joab saw the covenant with Abner as a threat to his own position as military leader.

King of All Israel

David now was faced with a problem with the potential of undermining all the effort which had gone into plans for reunification of the kingdom. Clearly the elders of Israel would interpret the assassination of Abner as a plot of David to remove the last obstacle to a seizure of power.[11] To forestall this perception David proclaimed a public mourning and buried Abner at Hebron with full state honor. So sincere was

---

11. James C. Vanderkam attempts to show that the murders of Abner and Ish-Bosheth were a plot hatched by David himself ("Davidic Complicity in the Deaths of Abner and Eshbaal: A Historical and Redactional Study," *JBL* 99 [1980]: 521–39). This thesis rests on the unproven allegation that the original form of the narrative indicted David and was later redacted heavily in a pro-David direction so that his complicity is now difficult to detect.

David's lament that all Israel and Judah accepted it at face value and exonerated him of any personal complicity (2 Sam. 3:36–39).

The feeling soon spread throughout Israel that desperate measures must now be taken lest the fragile agreement hammered out between David and Abner be aborted. Two assassins therefore went to Mahanaim and killed Ish-Bosheth while he took his afternoon siesta.[12] With his head as evidence they ran to David at Hebron and triumphantly announced that the way at last was cleared for David to sit on Saul's throne. Fearful lest he be implicated in this cowardly deed, David executed the murderers and hung their bodies publicly in Hebron; he then buried Ish-Bosheth's head in Abner's grave. Thus he hoped to make it clear that divine election and not overzealous personal ambition had brought him at last to the throne of Saul and all Israel.

With the removal of every possible contender to succeed Saul, the elders of Israel implemented the terms of the treaty which Abner had initiated with David on their behalf. They went as far as to go to Hebron, clearly an expression of submission and good intention, and there acknowledged David's right to rule because of his ancestral kinship with them, his proven record as a leader, and his divine election. The coronation followed in a covenant ceremony whose purpose was to enable king and people to make a commitment to each other and to Yahweh, the true sovereign.

Chronicles and Theological History

At this point the Book of 1 Chronicles begins its parallel account of Israel's history. The purpose of this document of unknown authorship was to record the history of Israel from the viewpoint of the Davidic dynasty.[13] This is not to say that the northern kingdom is overlooked or even regarded in an unusually negative way, but only that Judah, the messianic, Davidic tribe, is emphasized. Sometimes this involves the omission of narratives which are embarrassing to David and his

12. The murderers are identified as Benjamites from Beeroth, a Benjamite enclave in Philistine territory. Since the Beerothites had apparently had to flee from their tribal homeland at some time in the past (2 Sam. 4:2b–3), it may be that Saul had persecuted the Beerothites (cf. 2 Sam. 21:1–2) and that the killing of Ish-Bosheth was as much an act of revenge as anything else. On the other hand, Hans W. Hertzberg conjectures that the expulsion of the Beerothites followed the murder of Ish-Bosheth (*I & II Samuel* [Philadelphia: Westminster, 1964], pp. 263–64).

13. An excellent interpretation of the form and function of the chronicler's work can be found in Brevard S. Childs, *Introduction to the Old Testament as Scripture* (Philadelphia: Fortress, 1979), pp. 639–55. For an assessment of Chronicles as a work of history, see Sara Japhet, "The Historical Reliability of Chronicles," *JSOT* 33 (1985): 83–107.

dynasty—his affair with Bathsheba being the most infamous example—but these omissions do not necessarily imply that the chronicler was a fanatically loyal Davidite who wrote or rewrote history in such a way as to conform to the party line. Enough embarrassing incidents are included to put that suggestion to rest. Rather, what we have in 1 Chronicles is a history which avoids repetition of certain facts already well known through 2 Samuel, but which retells or amplifies on those events in David's life and career which are essential to the chronicler's own peculiar purposes. He is above all interested in stressing the cultic aspects of David's reign; that is, in showing that the messianic king also functions as the anointed priest of Yahweh. The chronicler, then, is more the theologian than the recorder of prosaic events. He is more interested in the meaning of David's reign than in any political or military processes which brought it about and enabled it to function.[14]

The chronicler's intent is clear from the very beginning in that he does not refer to David's youth or even the anointing by Samuel, facts which he takes for granted. He begins with the story of the Israelite entourage to Hebron to install David as king. There is not a word about the seven-year interlude between the death of Saul and David's accession to the throne. Seeing the accession as a *fait accompli*, the historian emphasizes only that it was Yahweh who had put Saul to death and had turned the kingdom over to David (1 Chron. 10:14).

On the other hand, the chronicler is careful to point out that already in the years of David's exile there were those in Israel as well as Judah who recognized his election. This is explicitly stated in 1 Chronicles 12:1–2: kinsmen of Saul were among those who joined David while he was living in Ziklag. Others came from Gad in Transjordan, and still others were non-Saulide Benjamites (1 Chron. 12:16–17). The latter David viewed with some suspicion initially, but when they pledged their loyalty to him against Saul, he gladly welcomed them. Moreover, when David went with the Philistines to fight Saul at Gilboa, he was joined by Israelite defectors from Manasseh (1 Chron. 12:19–22). Clearly, then, seeds of reunification between Israel and Judah had already been planted before Abner undertook formal negotiations to bring it to pass.

Further evidence of the chronicler's desire to show that David's kingship was embraced enthusiastically by the whole nation is his embellishment of 2 Samuel's very brief account of the delegation to

14. James D. Newsome, Jr., points out that the prophetic element also is strong in Chronicles, serving to connect cult and monarchy in such a way as to promote post-exilic reinstitution of temple worship and restoration of the house of David ("Toward a New Understanding of the Chronicler and His Purposes," *JBL* 94 [1975]: 216).

Hebron. Whereas 2 Samuel says only that all the tribes came to the king at Hebron (5:1–3), the chronicler lists each tribe by name and the total number of men it sent (1 Chron. 12:23–40). Included were three thousand Benjamites, even though they had remained loyal to Saul until the last moment. To emphasize the universal support given to David, the narrator says that the most distant tribes were not remiss in coming, and that they, with the others, came laden with all kinds of provisions. For three days the coronation ceremony was accompanied by festivity and joy. Without question, David's rule over all Israel was perceived as a healing, a melding of disparate and hostile elements into the mighty people of God. The long-delayed establishment of the chosen nation under the chosen king had finally come to pass. Unfortunately, however, subsequent history was to reveal that the pomp and pageantry of this glorious occasion was only a patina spread thinly over a political structure which could not rid itself of intertribal factionalism and division.

Jerusalem the Capital

Facing up to reality guided David to relocate the capital shortly after his coronation. Hebron had served well as long as David ruled over only Judah, but now for many reasons it could not suffice. First, it was far to the south and almost totally inaccessible to the Galilean and Transjordanian districts. Second, it was a city so important in the history of Judah that it almost epitomized that tribe. It would be unreasonable to expect the Israelites to develop any affection for or loyalty to a city so closely associated with the alienation of the past. Third, Hebron was a Levitical city; though not a fatal liability for a national capital, this fact may have tended to erode its neutrality in religious affairs.

On the other hand, David realized he could not locate the capital at some northern site such as Shechem or Shiloh because that would be interpreted by his Judahite kin as a betrayal of them. Certainly he could not take over Saul's capital at Gibeah, for Gibeah represented everything abhorrent to Judah. David's task was clear—he must find a central site which, at the same time, would be relatively neutral. By far the best choice was Jerusalem, the largest, most impressive, and most strategically situated city in the whole central region.[15]

15. G. W. Ahlström offers the interesting but biblically indefensible suggestion that David was a Jebusite for whom Jerusalem, therefore, was not at all a neutral site. This supposedly explains the ease with which he occupied the city and the enlistment of the Jebusite priest(!) Zadok to his cause ("Was David a Jebusite Subject?" *ZAW* 92

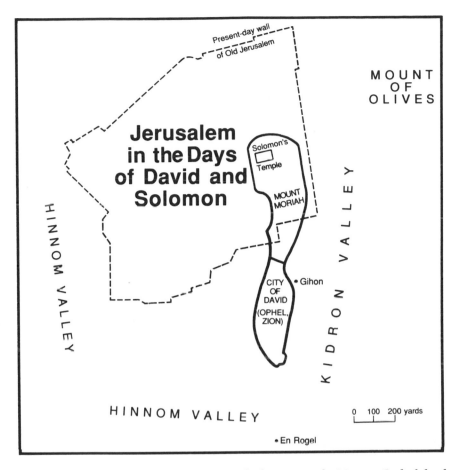

For at least two thousand years before David, Mount Ophel had been crowned with a settlement bearing many names, chief of which was Jerusalem or some related form.[16] The city was there in Abraham's day, as is attested now by the Ebla texts and, no doubt, by the reference to Salem, the city of the priest-king Melchizedek (Gen. 14:18).[17] The Amarna Letters know of Jerusalem as a principal Ca-

[1980]: 285–87). George E. Mendenhall does not go that far, but he does suggest that David took over Jerusalem and other Canaanite cities so that they could provide the sophisticated urban infrastructure necessary for him to lead Israel from its rural, peasant manner of life to the style requisite to a monarchical state worthy of the name. By doing this, however, David led the people to a paganization of their theocratic ideal ("The Monarchy," *Interp.* 29 [1975]: 161–66).

16. Jan Jozef Simons, *Jerusalem in the Old Testament* (Leiden: E. J. Brill, 1952).

17. Gordon J. Wenham, "The Religion of the Patriarchs," in *Essays on the Patriarchal Narratives*, ed. A. R. Millard and D. J. Wiseman (Winona Lake, Ind.: Eisenbrauns, 1983), p. 195.

naanite city of that period,[18] and, of course, Joshua and the Israelites did battle with Adoni-Zedek of Jerusalem in the course of the southern campaign (Josh. 10). If the city itself was not taken by Joshua at that time, it certainly was taken after his death (Judg. 1:8), though the Jebusite population was allowed to remain in it and, in fact, quickly retook it (Judg. 1:21). The city thereafter remained impervious to Israelite domination until David's conquest, when he made it his capital.

Jerusalem's long history of independence as an island in an Israelite sea can be attributed in no little way to her defensibility. This, with the previously cited advantages, must have made the city all the more attractive to David. But it also posed a real problem. How could he take the city without a long and costly siege?

As was characteristic of all the great walled cities of Canaan, Jerusalem had a vertical water shaft connecting with a tunnel leading to an underground water supply outside the walls.[19] As necessary as these systems were for the survival of a city under siege, they also constituted a major weakness in that they provided access into the city for anyone who could find the entrance. Somehow Joab found the outside mouth of the tunnel and led an attack through it into the city. Though he had become discredited because of his murder of Abner, he was rewarded now for his heroism in opening Jerusalem to David's conquest. Israel took possession of the little hill of Ophel, which became known as Zion or the City of David. By building (or rebuilding) terracelike fortifications to the east (i.e., the Millo), David both expanded the size of the city and enhanced its defensibility.[20]

The Establishment of David's Power

At this point in 2 Samuel the narrator departs from a strict chronological structure and addresses the Davidic history topically.[21] This

18. Charles F. Pfeiffer, *Tell El Amarna and the Bible* (Grand Rapids: Baker, 1963), pp. 50–51; Roland de Vaux, *The Early History of Israel* (Philadelphia: Westminster, 1978), pp. 103–4.

19. Kathleen Kenyon, *Jerusalem* (New York: McGraw-Hill, 1967), pp. 19–31. For the nature and course of the system see Arie Issar, "The Evolution of the Ancient Water Supply System in the Region of Jerusalem," *IEJ* 26 (1976): 131–33.

20. Kenyon, *Jerusalem*, pp. 49–51.

21. What follows is a radical departure from traditional approaches to the history of the Davidic period, a departure which nonetheless seems best able to accommodate both the biblical and extrabiblical documentary evidence. It is here proposed that the historian was not so much concerned with chronological sequence as with compressing David's major accomplishments into almost a collage of events. Ancient analogies to this historiographical procedure can be found in Mesopotamian records. See Hayim Tadmor, "The Inscriptions of Nabunaid: Historical Arrangement," *AS* 16 (Chicago: University of Chicago Press, 1965), pp. 351–63; Mordechai Cogan, "Tendentious Chro-

is most apparent initially from the fact that the Philistine attacks on David are mentioned after the notations concerning his building enterprises and the enlarging of his family. That the chronicler follows the same arrangement means nothing more than that he used 2 Samuel as a model in this particular situation.

The Philistine Problem

The clue to the chronological priority of the Philistine episodes lies in the reference to their seeking David after they had heard of his being anointed king of Israel (2 Sam. 5:17). This clearly happened immediately after the coronation ceremony at Hebron and before David besieged and captured Jerusalem. The Philistine objective appears to have been to nip the Israel-Judah reunification in the bud. For ten years or more it had appeared to the Philistines that David was leading an anti-Israel movement that promised nothing but benefit to the Philistines. Saul had been their inveterate foe since he had become king; though they had launched attack after attack upon him, they had failed to secure a foothold in the interior of the country. In fact, Saul had repelled them, forcing them to subsist within the narrow confines of their coastal plain. But with David's exile the situation changed. The Philistines began to look upon David, who had once been Israel's champion and Philistia's nemesis, as a potential ally in their struggle with Israel. David, it is true, had not taken offensive action against Saul, but he obviously was a divisive factor politically and was draining off much of the energy and resources of Saul which otherwise would have gone into the Philistine conflict. It is likely, indeed, that the Philistines were able to secure as much control of the Jezreel region as they did precisely because Saul was occupied with David in the south.

In any case, David did nothing to discourage Philistine hopes. Indeed, he gave them every sign that he wished to move closer to them and further from Saul. This finally found expression in the covenant David made with Achish of Gath in which he placed himself in vassalage to the Philistines (1 Sam. 27:5-7).[22] This guaranteed him both an inalienable territorial grant (Ziklag) and security against Saul. It

nology in the Book of Chronicles," *Zion* 45 (1980): 165–72 (Hebrew); idem, "Omens and Ideology in the Babylon Inscription of Esarhaddon," in *History, Historiography and Interpretation*, ed. Hayim Tadmor and Moshe Weinfeld (Jerusalem: Magnes, 1984), pp. 85–87; idem, "The Chronicler's Use of Chronology as Illuminated by Neo-Assyrian Royal Inscriptions," in *Empirical Models for Biblical Criticism*, ed. Jeffrey H. Tigay (Philadelphia: University of Pennsylvania Press, 1985), pp. 205–7; G. Frame, "Another Babylonian Eponym," *RA* 76 (1982): 157, 159.

22. P. Kyle McCarter, Jr., *I Samuel*, Anchor Bible (Garden City, N.Y.: Doubleday, 1980), pp. 414–15.

also obligated him to fight Philistia's battles, a requirement that nearly brought him to warfare with his own people.

It seems almost certain that when Saul died, David returned to Judah as much a continuing vassal of Achish as the potential king of Judah. It was evident to the Philistines that he enjoyed great popularity in Judah and equally evident that Israel still regarded David as an enemy. It would be to the advantage of the Philistines in every way for Israel and Judah to remain divided and for David to head a state which was under at least nominal Philistine control. David, of course, would also be willing to maintain the fiction of Philistine alliance since he had his hands full with Israel and the problem of royal succession there. One can well imagine that he made every effort to keep the reunification negotiations with Abner strictly secret.

Whether this hypothesis of Philistine-Davidic relationship is correct in every detail or not, the record suggests that the Philistines left David in peace until the day they learned of his establishment as king of all Israel. Only then, and too late, did they realize that his friendship had been merely a ploy to achieve his ultimate objective—unification of Israel. They therefore launched a preemptive strike against David at Rephaim (el-Buqei'a), a valley just southwest of Jerusalem. This battle is described in 2 Samuel 23, where the narrator relates that David took up his position at the cave of Adullam while the Philistines were entrenched in Bethlehem, fifteen miles up the valley toward the northeast.[23] On this occasion three of David's heroes risked their lives by stealing to Bethlehem to get water for their king from the well by the gate. How the Philistines happened to be at Bethlehem and how they were dislodged is not specified. We are told, however, that David did achieve victory over them at Baal Perazim (perhaps Sheikh Bedr).[24]

Undaunted, the Philistines struck again in the Valley of Rephaim, but once more they were defeated. This time David followed up by evicting the Philistines not only from the area south and southwest of Jerusalem, but from the north and west as well. Thus he succeeded in isolating Jerusalem from Philistine encroachment, a fact that facilitated his taking of the city from the Jebusites shortly thereafter.

The Building of the Tabernacle

Though it is impossible to be chronologically precise, it seems almost certain that virtually nothing is known of David's very first years

23. This supports the contention that the Philistine attack came before David's siege of Jerusalem, for why would he be at Adullam at all if he had begun to live in Jerusalem? Second Samuel 5:17 says that the Philistines "went up . . . to search for him," their objective being Hebron, but David had left there and had gone to the "stronghold," that is, the cave at Adullam (cf. 2 Sam. 23:13–14).

24. Proposed with hesitation in *Oxford Bible Atlas*, p. 123.

in Jerusalem. The extensive narratives which follow that of the taking of the city are predicated upon the brief account of his construction activity in Jerusalem, a project which was undertaken by Phoenician architects and builders at the behest of Hiram, king of Tyre. Hiram (or Ahiram) was the son of Abibaal and reigned in Tyre from about 980 to 947.[25] Thus he was contemporary with both David (1011–971) and Solomon (971–931), though only in David's last decade. This suggests that David's building projects must have been toward the end of his reign and not the beginning.[26] These late projects would include the tabernacle he erected on Mount Zion, for the chronicler clearly indicates that it was prepared only after David had constructed buildings for himself (1 Chron. 15:1). The ark of the covenant must, then, have been returned to Jerusalem late in David's lifetime, since the tabernacle was built for the express purpose of housing it. Then, too, David's desire to build a temple must have been broached at the very end of his life, because it presupposes the existence of the tabernacle.

This thesis flies in the face of the usual understanding of David's

25. Frank M. Cross, "An Interpretation of the Nora Stone," *BASOR* 208 (1972): 17, n. 11. These dates are at variance with those of other scholars. But since they are always raised or lowered along with those of David, the ten-year overlap is constant and the argument developed here is thus unaffected. See William F. Albright, *Archaeology and the Religion of Israel* (Garden City, N.Y.: Doubleday, 1969), p. 128 (969–936); John Bright, *A History of Israel*, 3d ed. (Philadelphia: Westminster, 1981), p. 204 (969–936); H. Jacob Katzenstein, *The History of Tyre* (Jerusalem: Schocken Institute for Jewish Research, 1973), p. 82 (ca. 970 + 34 years); Benjamin Mazar, "The Era of David and Solomon," in *World History of the Jewish People*, vol. 4, part 1, *The Age of the Monarchies: Political History*, ed. Abraham Malamat (Jerusalem: Massada, 1979), p. 90.

26. This conclusion is so contrary to the traditional interpretation that all kinds of ways around it have been suggested. Bright (*History*, p. 204), acknowledging that David's and Hiram's reigns overlapped by only a few years, suggests that the treaty of 2 Samuel 5:11–12 may have been between David and Abibaal, Hiram's father. J. Alberto Soggin concedes that there is a limited overlapping, and that there is no evidence that the treaty was made with either Abibaal or another Hiram. His solution is that "the sources are very confused over the chronology" (*A History of Ancient Israel* [Philadelphia: Westminster, 1984], p. 56). But since all scholars agree that only David's last decade is contemporary with Hiram, why cannot the treaty and the subsequent construction projects be dated then (ca. 980)? One must also bear in mind that if Hiram was in contact with David early in David's reign from Jerusalem (ca. 1004–1000) and Hiram reigned for thirty-three years, he could not possibly have lived long into Solomon's period (971–931), for at the latest he would have died around 970. The temple of Solomon, built by Hiram's craftsmen, was begun in 966, however (1 Kings 6:1), and Hiram was still reigning in Solomon's twentieth year (ca. 951; 1 Kings 9:10–14). At the earliest Hiram began his tenure in 984 according to this line of reasoning. The year 980, then, seems to be a sensible conjecture. Herbert Donner dismisses the problem of David and Hiram by arguing that the reference in 2 Samuel 5:11 is an unhistorical reflection of a relationship which actually existed only between Hiram and Solomon ("Israel und Tyrus in Zeitalter Davids und Salomos," *JNSL* 10 [1982]: 43–52).

reign; it also raises certain problems which must be satisfactorily addressed if it is to enjoy credibility. First, the mere fact that both Samuel and Chronicles *seem* to suggest that the ark was brought into Jerusalem immediately after the city was made Israel's capital need not make it so. One can easily demonstrate that Israelite historiography was not always concerned with strict chronological order.[27] A more serious objection is that it seems unlikely that David would wait for at least twenty-five years to make Jerusalem the cultic center as well as the seat of government. Where did Israel gather during all those years for community worship?

The center of the cult prior to the move to Jerusalem

Unfortunately, little can be known about the cult not only in David's early years, but even after the younger days of the prophet Samuel. The central sanctuary at Shiloh had deteriorated morally and spiritually, as is clear from the early Samuel stories, until the ark was captured by the Philistines in about 1104 and Shiloh presumably abandoned shortly thereafter (see p. 176). The ark, of course, remained at Kiriath Jearim after it returned from Philistia; and it was from there that David finally brought it into Jerusalem. On the other hand, the tabernacle, at least for a time, was located at Nob, where a descendant of Eli, Ahimelech, was high priest. This is a reasonable assumption in light of the explicit reference to the holy bread given to David (1 Sam. 21:4) and the designation of Nob as "the town of the priests" (1 Sam. 22:19).

Samuel had in the meantime become disassociated from the tabernacle and offered sacrifice at various shrines and high places.[28] Does this imply that the tabernacle did not exist in his lifetime following the debacle at Shiloh? In light of David's encounter with Ahimelech at Nob, the answer without doubt is no. The reason for Samuel's lack of connection with a central sanctuary must be seen in its appropriation by Saul. After Yahweh rejected Saul, Samuel did as well; and it follows that he rejected everything associated with Saul, including the tabernacle (1 Sam. 15:34–35).

27. Cogan, "Chronicler's Use of Chronology," in *Empirical Models*, ed. Jeffrey H. Tigay, pp. 197–209. Hayim Tadmor has shown that it was customary for Assyrian royal inscriptions to record that temple building or restoration was undertaken in a king's first year when in fact it might have been several years later ("History and Ideology in the Assyrian Royal Inscriptions," in *Assyrian Royal Inscriptions: New Horizons in Literary, Ideological, and Historical Analysis*, ed F. M. Fales [Roma: Istituto per L'Oriente, 1981], pp. 21–23).

28. Samuel was particularly associated with Mizpah (1 Sam. 7:5; 10:17), Gilgal (1 Sam. 10:8; 11:14), and Ramah (1 Sam. 8:4; 15:34; 16:13), though there is no evidence of cultic activity at Ramah.

One could wish for explicit information about the cult during Saul's monarchy, but very little can be found. It stands to reason, however, that there was a central place of worship and that it was located somewhere in or near the political center, Gibeah. One possibility is Mizpah, just five miles north of the capital. That Samuel offered sacrifice there (1 Sam. 7:9) does not in itself imply the presence of a tabernacle, but he also inquired of Yahweh on behalf of Israel there, particularly in the selection of a king (1 Sam. 10:17–24). In those days the will of God was determined by using the ephod of the priest, an article almost always inextricably bound up with the tabernacle. The very method by which Saul was chosen—a binary yes-or-no technique—suggests the casting of the priestly sacred lots.[29]

Another possibility, and perhaps the most likely one, is that the cult was centered at Gilgal. This would be logical since Gilgal was its location in the time of the conquest (Josh. 5:10; 9:6–15). Moreover, in both the account of Saul's hasty and unlawful offering of sacrifice when his forces were hard pressed by the Philistines (1 Sam. 13:8–10) and the account of Saul's plan to offer up the best of the Amalekite livestock (1 Sam. 15:10–15), the site selected was Gilgal, which in the former case was the site Samuel had chosen for sacrifices to Yahweh (1 Sam. 10:8). Saul, then, was correct in going to Gilgal to meet Yahweh, but grievously in error in arrogating to himself the priestly ministry.

Whether the tabernacle was at Mizpah or Gilgal before Saul's rejection, it clearly was not afterward. Rather, it seems to have been in the vicinity of Jerusalem, probably at Nob, at least as early as the time of David's slaying of Goliath (ca. 1027). This is suggested by the fact that David took Goliath's head *and perhaps his sword* to Jerusalem (1 Sam. 17:54). Later David retrieved Goliath's sword from Nob (1 Sam. 21:9), a village just across the Kidron from Jerusalem, and thus part of greater Jerusalem itself. For unknown reasons, then, Saul had either authorized or at least permitted the tabernacle to be set up at Nob. This was very near Mount Zion, where David later placed his own sanctuary.

The tabernacle remained at Nob until Saul, enraged that the priests had entertained David there, destroyed the town and evidently moved the tabernacle to another site (1 Sam. 22:11–19). This may have been Gibeon, just three or four miles northwest of Gibeah, for when the tabernacle next appears in the record (during David's reign), it is there

---

29. The language of the passage—"Saul . . . was chosen"—is reminiscent of the description of the process by which guilty Achan "was taken" (Josh. 7:16–19), a process which clearly was linked to divine selection (Josh. 7:14) and to the presence of Yahweh (Josh. 7:23). That the ephod was involved in both instances is confirmed by 1 Samuel 14:40–42, where, by the same process, Jonathan is singled out for his violation of the ban of his father. See Klein, *1 Samuel*, pp. 96–97, 140.

(1 Chron. 16:39; 21:29). And later, Solomon went to Gibeon to worship Yahweh at the tabernacle of Moses located at the great high place (1 Kings 3:4–5; 2 Chron. 1:3–6). Why he went there rather than to the tabernacle of David on Mount Zion is not altogether clear and for now is not relevant. It does suggest, however, that David's shrine, even though it contained the ark, was considered so innovative and problematic that even his son Solomon persisted in visiting the cult center at Gibeon. This, incidentally, supports our thesis that the ark was not introduced to Jerusalem until the latter years of David's reign.

The reason for the delay

The matter of moving the ark to Jerusalem from Kiriath Jearim was, of course, contingent on its having a proper home once it arrived there. This is implied in 2 Samuel 6:17 and explicitly stated in 2 Chronicles 1:4). The question arises, Why did David wait so long to build the tabernacle and thus to make Jerusalem the religious center of the nation?

First of all, it is clear that David's rise to power, as dramatic as it appears, was not without difficulty and required a long period of transition. It was one thing for him to receive popular acclaim as a political and military figure. It was something quite different to tamper with religious tradition and unify both cult and crown in himself and in Jerusalem. Throughout Israel's history until David the lines of demarcation between civil and religious leadership had been carefully drawn. Even Moses had his Aaron, and Joshua and all the judges stayed strictly within the limits of nonclerical responsibility. Saul had tried on more than one occasion to usurp priestly prerogatives, but he paid dearly. And there is not the slightest hint that he ever tried to establish the ark and tabernacle at Gibeah, his own capital. In light of this tradition, then, how could even David hope to establish Jerusalem as the central sanctuary without long preparation for it?

From a more practical standpoint, the record indicates that David more than had his hands full with the need to create and perfect a governmental structure on the one hand and the need to defend the nation against foreign threats on the other. He could have met these needs only gradually. As the author of Samuel says, David "became more and more powerful, because the Lord God Almighty was with him" (2 Sam. 5:10). He had already encountered the Philistines before taking Jerusalem, but that was not the end of his problems with that perpetually troublesome people. On at least one other occasion, impossible to date but certainly before the building of his tabernacle, David defeated the Philistines (2 Sam. 8:1). This same campaign or perhaps others are referred to among the exploits of David's mighty men (2 Sam. 23:9–12). Other enemies had to be subdued as well: Moab,

Zobah, Damascus, Ammon, Amalek, and Edom. With greater or lesser success David either incorporated these kingdoms into his empire directly or made them client states. In any event, a significant amount of time was required and it was not until these kingdoms were actually subdued that David turned wholeheartedly to religious pursuits (2 Sam. 7:1; 1 Chron. 17:1).

An Introduction to a Davidic Chronology

At this point it will be worth our while to attempt to reconstruct a chronology of the major events of David's life.[30] There is no question about the date of his conquest of Jerusalem (ca. 1004) or of his death (971). The dates of other events are not so clear, but some tentative suggestions can be made. First of all, though Solomon's age at his accession to the throne cannot be ascertained, he was obviously quite young. In his prayer at Gibeon he calls himself "a little child"; even allowing for hyperbole, this must preclude an age much over twenty (1 Kings 3:7).[31] Moreover, when David was making plans for construction of the temple, he had referred to his son as "young and inexperienced" (1 Chron. 22:5; 29:1). If Solomon was no more than twenty when he acceded to the throne, he could hardly have been more than eighteen when David discussed the temple construction with him (1 Chron. 22:6–16; cf. 23:1). Solomon would then have been born no earlier than 991, thirteen years after David had taken Jerusalem.[32]

Solomon's birth followed David's adulterous relationship with Bathsheba by a year or two. That in turn occurred at the time Joab was leading Israel's armies into battle with the Ammonites at Rabbah. A date for this campaign of around 993 is quite reasonable. This is the last recorded military adventure of David prior to his flight from Absalom, and there is good reason to believe it is the last chronologically as well. With the exception of 2 Samuel 8, which is a catalogue of foreign conquests and not part of the narrative in the strict sense, the

30. What follows is a brief overview of the whole problem of Davidic chronology and its resolution. This matter is discussed in fuller detail in Eugene H. Merrill, "The 'Accession Year' and Davidic Chronology," *JANES* 19 (1987), forthcoming.

31. The phrase *na'ar qāṭōn* is otherwise used to describe the lad who gathered Jonathan's arrows (1 Sam. 20:35), the skin of Naaman following his miraculous cure (2 Kings 5:14), the child of the eschatological kingdom who will lead the wild beasts (Isa. 11:6), the Edomite prince Hadad (1 Kings 11:17), and the youths who taunted Elisha (2 Kings 2:23). Without exception children or adolescents are in view. See Francis Brown, S. R. Driver, and Charles A. Briggs, *A Hebrew and English Lexicon of the Old Testament* (Oxford: Clarendon, 1962), pp. 654–55.

32. This is predicated on the dates of Solomon's reign (971–931), which are almost universally accepted.

Table 5   **The Life of David**

The birth of David	1041
The anointing of David by Samuel	ca. 1029
David's exile from Saul	ca. 1020–1011
The anointing of David as king over Judah	1011
The anointing of David as king over Israel and the conquest of Jerusalem	1004
The great famine	ca. 996–993
The Ammonite wars	ca. 993–990
The adultery with Bathsheba	ca. 992
The birth of Solomon	ca. 991
The rape of Tamar	ca. 987
The death of Amnon	ca. 985
The exile of Absalom	ca. 985–982
The building of David's palace	ca. 979
The building of the tabernacle and the moving of the ark	ca. 977
The rebellion of Absalom and exile of David	ca. 976
The census	ca. 975
The coregency of Solomon	ca. 973–971
The coronation of Solomon and death of David	971

other military accounts seem to be in the order in which the respective campaigns occurred.

The series of campaigns against the Ammonites was provoked by the shameful treatment of David's ambassadors by the Ammonite king Hanun (2 Sam. 10:1–5). This must have taken place before David became very powerful, for Hanun, with his advisers, seems unaware of David's ability to retaliate. In addition Hanun was the son of Nahash, the Ammonite king who had besieged Jabesh Gilead in the earliest years of Saul (1 Sam. 11:1–5). That Nahash had just died necessitates either an extremely long reign for Nahash or succession by Hanun early in David's reign.

Realizing that David was more of a threat than originally supposed, the Ammonites hired mercenaries from Beth Rehob, Zobah, Maacah, and Tob, and with them tried to stave off Israel's assault on Rabbah, the Ammonite capital. Joab and Abishai, David's generals, won the day, however; though they did not take the city, they forced the Arameans and Ammonites to retreat (2 Sam. 10:6–14 = 1 Chron. 19:6–15). This only inspired the Arameans to regroup and augment their forces for a return engagement. This time Hadadezer of Zobah joined Israel in battle at Helam ('Alma) in the desert east of the Sea of Kinnereth, but again he was defeated (2 Sam. 10:15–19 = 1 Chron. 19:16–19). This ended Aramean assistance to the Ammonites.

The siege of Rabbah then followed at the turn of the new year, as did David's affair with Bathsheba (2 Sam. 11:1). Thus the Aramean conflict and the first attack on Rabbah must have taken place between 1004 and 993, more likely toward the end of that period.

Another avenue to be explored concerns the rebellion of Absalom and related events. Absalom, son of David's wife Maacah, was born in Hebron and thus was old enough to lead a movement against his father soon after the birth of Solomon.[33] How long after is not clear, but we do know that David participated in the completion of the Ammonite campaign after Solomon was born and before the rape of Tamar occurred. A likely date for Amnon's rape of Tamar is 987. Two years later Absalom killed Amnon (2 Sam. 13:23). Absalom then went into exile for three years (985–982; 2 Sam. 13:38); when he finally returned to Jerusalem, he remained alienated from his father for two years (982–980; 2 Sam. 14:28). Then he spent four more years[34] winning the confidence of the people (980–976) until at last he made the open break with David (2 Sam. 15:7, 13).

We earlier argued (see p. 239) that since the Davidic tabernacle, built to accommodate the ark, was not constructed until various other projects, including David's own palace, were completed, the story of the procession of the ark into Jerusalem must reflect a period late in his reign. All this was predicated on the fact that Hiram of Tyre, who actually built the palace, did not begin his reign until 980 and so could not have undertaken construction projects before then. It should also be noted that there is not one reference specifically placing either the ark or tabernacle in Jerusalem until the time of Absalom's rebellion. Then, in the story of David's exile to the Transjordan occasioned by that rebellion, the narrator points out that the Levites with Zadok were bearing the ark of the covenant (2 Sam. 15:24). David asked them to return the ark to Jerusalem (implying that it had been there), expressing the fervent hope that he might see both it and the *dwelling-place* of Yahweh once more (2 Sam. 15:25). This presupposes the presence of the tabernacle in Jerusalem. In light of our argument regarding the date of Absalom's rebellion, the moving of the ark to the new tabernacle must be dated around 977, which fits remarkably well with the date of Hiram's accession (980).

It is important at this point to recognize that the dates under con-

33. If born early in David's reign from Hebron (say, 1008), Absalom would have been about seventeen years old at the time of Solomon's birth (991).

34. The Masoretic text here has "forty" instead of "four." Though it is the more difficult reading, the Hebrew here should be rejected in favor of the reading in the Septuagint, the Syriac, the Vulgate, and Josephus. See McCarter, *II Samuel*, p. 355.

sideration cannot be considered fixed and inflexible since both Hiram's chronology and that of Absalom are debated. However, and this is most important, no scholar is willing to date Hiram earlier than 980 nor can Absalom's rebellion be earlier by any reasonable reading of the evidence. In fact, the firm and mature leadership which Absalom exhibited in nearly every respect would point to an age of thirty or thirty-five. Dating the rebellion around 976, then, seems sensible.[35] A date of 980 for Hiram's accession would permit him time to build David's palace and give David adequate opportunity after that to construct a tabernacle and bring the ark into it.

This novel way of redating the transfer of the ark has a number of advantages. It first of all explains why the record prior to Absalom's rebellion is so strangely silent regarding Jerusalem as a central sanctuary. Second, it comports well with the notion that religious tradition is not easily broken and that David therefore could not have taken steps immediately to unify cult and government in one place. Michal's reaction (2 Sam. 6:16–20), in fact, may not be so much a matter of pettiness, as is usually alleged, as a representative reaction to the novelty of David's undertaking.[36] He had earlier attempted to bring the ark to Jerusalem only to be frustrated by the irreverence of Uzzah. Then, after a three-month delay, David finally succeeded; dressed as a priest and functioning in that capacity, he led the procession himself. This must have caused a great deal of consternation not only to Michal, but to the population as a whole. Perhaps this is why he distributed food to all the people in the crowd and also took pains to point out to Michal that he, not her father Saul, was the true anointed one. It is also possible that dissatisfaction with David's action reached such proportions that Absalom used it as a means of effecting his own revolution.

Third, the viewpoint defended here fits much better the history of the cult, especially as outlined by the chronicler. He begins his account of the ark, as does the author of 2 Samuel, by describing the abortive attempt to bring it to Jerusalem. The attempt failed not only because of Uzzah, but fundamentally because the religious personnel involved did not subscribe to proper protocol in the handling of the ark—they put it on a cart rather than carrying it on poles. On the second attempt to move the ark David took care to call together the priests and Levites and to instruct them as to proper procedure (1 Chron. 15:11–15). To be noted here is that Zadok and Abiathar are both named, the former for the first time in a narrative context (v. 11). Since shortly after this incident Zadok began to serve as co–high priest with Ahimelech the

35. If Absalom had been born about 1008, as proposed above, he would in fact have been in his early thirties in 976.

36. David F. Payne, *I & II Samuel* (Philadelphia: Westminster, 1982), p. 185.

son of Abiathar (2 Sam. 8:17; 1 Chron. 18:16), it is likely that he was much younger than Abiathar, too young perhaps to have been a priest in 1004 (the date usually assigned to the transfer of the ark), especially since he continued as priest well into the time of Solomon (1 Kings 2:35; 4:4).

Of greater interest still is the appointment of Heman, Asaph, Ethan, and other Levitical musicians and religious personnel, all within the context of the removal of the ark to Jerusalem (1 Chron. 15:19). Some of these officials remained in charge of the ark (1 Chron. 16:4–6), while others, including Zadok, were appointed by David to attend to the tabernacle of Moses, which still remained at Gibeon (1 Chron. 16:39–42). This responsibility continued at the respective tabernacles until Solomon's temple was finished in about 959 (1 Chron. 6:31 32). It is difficult to assume that their tenure began as early as 1004 and continued to 959. If, however, the tabernacle ministry commenced around 977, this problem is greatly alleviated.

Both Samuel and Chronicles indicate that the relocation of the ark to Jerusalem was followed immediately by David's desire to build a more permanent structure in which to worship Yahweh. That 2 Samuel 7:1 also indicates that David's desire came after Yahweh had given him rest from his surrounding enemies has caused problems for many interpreters. But this is precisely the point! David was occupied by military affairs throughout his early years; not until after the subjugation of Rabbah did he move the ark and make any plans for a temple. The chronicler makes it most evident that the desire for a temple came upon the heels of the relocation of the ark to Jerusalem. After describing the arrangements David had made for the care of the ark and the new tabernacle at Jerusalem and the Mosaic tabernacle at Gibeon (1 Chron. 16:37–42), the chronicler goes on to relate that David returned to his palace and, having contemplated its permanence in contrast to the temporality of the tabernacle, conceived the plan for a temple (1 Chron. 17:1).

Yahweh rejected David's overture; but after an indeterminate period of time during which Absalom's rebellion and the ill-advised census occurred, he allowed David to draw up the temple plans, appoint the temple personnel, and collect the materials necessary for construction. The rebellion probably ended in 975, just four years before David's death. The census likely followed: David may well have wanted to ascertain the degree of loyalty and strength he could count on in the event of similar uprisings or external attacks.

In any event, the end of the plague which Yahweh sent because of the census coincided with a renewed desire on David's part to build a temple (1 Chron. 21:14–22:1). He had offered sacrifice on the threshing floor of Araunah the Jebusite, which was just north of Jerusalem.

When Yahweh answered him there, David took it as a sign that that should be the site of Yahweh's dwelling-place. He therefore began to gather all the materials needed for construction and shared with his young son Solomon all that God would do. Because David was a warrior and preoccupied with the things of war, the work of temple building must be left to Solomon, a man of peace. To guarantee Israel's recognition of this arrangement David appointed his son as his coregent (1 Chron. 23:1). Together they then appointed the priests and Levites who would serve in the temple as singers, gatekeepers, and treasurers.

The formal announcement was made to all the nation. David told Israel's leaders that he had been chosen by Yahweh to reign, but because he was a warrior he could not build the temple. That privilege was reserved to his son Solomon. He then charged Solomon to be faithful in carrying out the will of God and to build the temple precisely according to the plans which Yahweh had revealed (1 Chron. 28:9–12). Finally he turned again to the leaders and urged them to give of their resources so the work could go forward, a request they willingly obeyed. He led them next in a prayer of praise and commitment and on the following day in a mighty sacrifice (1 Chron. 29:20–22a). Two years later the people gathered for the formal coronation of Solomon, this time as sole ruler in the place of his father (1 Chron. 29:22b–23).[37]

To summarize the last years of David's reign: David brought the ark into Jerusalem around 977, Absalom rebelled in 976, the census was undertaken in the next year, Solomon was made coregent around 973, and David died in 971. Thus the tabernacle of David was in use only for six years of David's administration and eleven years of Solomon's (1 Kings 6:1, 37–38). Worship at the Mosaic tabernacle at Gibeon presumably also came to an end at the same time (ca. 959).

37. See 1 Kings 1:32–40 for a description of the anointing of Solomon. The narrative of 1 Kings 1 indicates that the plot of Adonijah to preempt Solomon's succession (vv. 5–10) climaxed just before Solomon's coronation. This was about two years after Solomon's appointment as coregent (1 Chron. 23:1). There are various supports for our construal of events, which includes both a period of coregency and a clear linkage between 1 Chronicles 29:22b and 1 Kings 1:32–40: (1) when Solomon was anointed, he was acknowledged as king "a second time" (1 Chron. 29:22b); (2) Solomon's anointing is mentioned only in 1 Chronicles 29:22b and 1 Kings 1:39, a reference which occurs right after the account of Adonijah's rebellion; and (3) both reports of the coronation mention Zadok. Not previously mentioned in connection with any act of anointing, Zadok is himself anointed on the occasion of his anointing Solomon (1 Chron. 29:22b). And in fact, 1 Kings goes on to report that Zadok was appointed chief priest by Solomon after David's death (2:35). For the problems incurred if one fails to recognize a time interval between 1 Chronicles 29:22a and b see H. G. M. Williamson, *1 and 2 Chronicles*, New Century Bible Commentary (Grand Rapids: Eerdmans, 1982), pp. 186–87.

7 David: The Years of Struggle

Egypt and Israelite Independence

An important reason for the rapid rise of David and his Israelite kingdom was the lack of interference from the major powers, particularly Egypt. The kingdom on the Nile was at this time at a nadir known as the Third Intermediate Period (ca. 1100–650).[1] With only a few exceptions the kings throughout this long era were impotent in terms of foreign adventurism and influence. The records of Psusennes I (1039–991) of Dynasty 21, who was contemporary with both Saul and David, attest no specific military campaigns into Palestine, though they do speak of his domestic and cultural accomplishments.[2] Therefore, neither Saul nor David had anything to fear from Egypt, but of course neither did the Philistines. The successor of Psusennes, Amenemope (993–978), was even less active internationally and did not match Psusennes' cultural achievements. He may, however, have been the king who provided a haven for Hadad, prince of Edom, whom David drove into exile (1 Kings 11:14–22). David's conquest of Edom cannot be dated precisely, but, as shall be argued presently (p. 260), it must have occurred before 980 and thus within the period of Amenemope.[3] The Queen Tahpenes whose sister married Hadad (1 Kings 11:19) must have been the wife of Amenemope or, more likely, Siamun, though her name is not otherwise attested.[4]

Siamun (978–959), an active builder, was more interested in diplomacy than in military exploits. It was probably he who gave his daughter in marriage to Solomon sometime after Solomon's third year (967—1 Kings 2:39; 3:1) and presented her the city of Gezer as a dowry (1 Kings 9:16).[5] At some point early in his reign he had wrested Gezer

1. For a detailed discussion see Kenneth A. Kitchen, *The Third Intermediate Period in Egypt (1100–650 B.C.)* (Warminster: Aris and Phillips, 1973).

2. Donald B. Redford, "Studies in Relations Between Palestine and Egypt During the First Millennium B.C. II. The Twenty-second Dynasty," *JAOS* 93 (1973): 4.

3. The chronology of this period in Egypt is extremely complicated since the sources are contradictory and incomplete. In any event, it matters little to our case whether the pharaoh in question is Amenemope or Siamun. See J. Černý, "Egypt: From the Death of Ramesses III to the End of the Twenty-first Dynasty," in *Cambridge Ancient History*, 3d ed., ed. I. E. S. Edwards et al. (Cambridge: Cambridge University Press, 1975), vol. 2, part 2, pp. 644–49.

4. Pierre Montet, *Egypt and the Bible* (Philadelphia: Fortress, 1968), pp. 38–39.

5. Ronald J. Williams, "The Egyptians," in *Peoples of Old Testament Times*, ed. D. J. Wiseman (Oxford: Clarendon, 1973), pp. 94–95. On the chronological difficulties which make identification of the pharaoh in question uncertain, see Redford, "Studies in Relations," *JAOS* 93 (1973): 5. For the possibility that the pharaoh in view was Psusennes II see Abraham Malamat, "The Kingdom of David and Solomon in Its Contact with Egypt and Aram Naharaim," in *Biblical Archaeologist Reader*, ed. Edward F. Campbell, Jr., and David Noel Freedman (Garden City, N.Y.: Doubleday, 1964), vol. 2, p. 93.

from the Philistines and slain its Canaanite inhabitants. It may well be that David collaborated in the Egyptian conquest of Gezer (1 Chron. 20:4). If so, this action would have come after 978, the first year of Siamun, and about the time the ark was brought into Jerusalem. This thesis gains a great deal of credibility in that by helping the Egyptians conquer Gezer, David would have prevented the Philistines from interfering with the moving of the ark to Jerusalem. It also explains how a relatively weak Egyptian king could have penetrated so deeply into Canaan without Israelite opposition.

Apart from this one incident, nothing is known of Egyptian involvement in Palestine during the entire period of the united monarchy. This apparent indifference not only permitted the Philistines to maintain their independence, but it allowed David and Solomon to create a mighty political power in Israel that eventually became a match for any of its international competitors.

The Ammonite Wars

The Historical Source: The Succession Narrative

The first major conflict involving Israel following David's occupation of Jerusalem was with the Ammonites and their allies the Arameans. This is introduced at the beginning of a long section of 2 Samuel known as the succession narrative (2 Sam. 9–20; 1 Kings 1–2), so called because its major theme appears to be David's preparation for his succession by his dynastic heir. Virtually all scholars agree that this is one of the finest examples of history writing from the ancient Near Eastern world.[6] It is at the same time a masterpiece

6. See especially J. P. Fokkelman, *Narrative Art and Poetry in the Books of Samuel*, vol. 1, *King David* (Assen: Van Gorcum, 1981), and the literature cited therein. The prevalent view of the nature and extent of the succession narrative originated with Leonhard Rost, *Die Überlieferung von der Thronnachfolge Davids*, BWANT 3.6 (Stuttgart: W. Kohlhammer, 1926). Other important treatments are R. A. Carlson, *David, the Chosen King* (Uppsala: Almquist & Wiksells, 1964); David M. Gunn, *The Story of King David: Genre and Interpretation*, JSOT supplement 6 (Sheffield: University of Sheffield, 1978); Roger N. Whybray, *The Succession Narrative: A Study of II Samuel 9–20 and I Kings 1 and 2*, Studies in Biblical Theology, 2d series, vol. 9 (Naperville, Ill.: Alec R. Allenson, 1968); Ernst Würthwein, *Die Erzählung von der Thronfolge Davids*, Theologische Studiën (B)15 (Zurich: Theologischer Verlag, 1974). Not all scholars agree on the boundaries and interpretation of this corpus; indeed, some doubt that such an independent unit ever existed. See the helpful caution of Peter R. Ackroyd, "The Succession Narrative (so-called)," *Interp.* 35 (1981): 383–96. Such debates do not, however, affect the historical and narrative value of the material as it presently stands. For a positive evaluation of the narrative as history writing see Moshe Weinfeld, "Literary Creativity," in *World History of the Jewish People*, vol. 5, *The Age of the Monarchies: Culture and Society*, ed. Abraham Malamat (Jerusalem: Massada, 1979), pp. 41–43.

of biography and storytelling what with its ingenious interweaving of plots and subplots, its brilliant character sketches, and its attention to artistic touches such as climax and denouement.[7]

The center point of the whole narrative is, of course, the birth of Solomon and the intrigue which made it possible for him, though not the heir apparent, to succeed his father on Israel's throne.[8] His birth came to pass because David, who should have been leading his armies in battle with the Ammonites, stayed home and fell into an adulterous relationship with Bathsheba. Though their first child died, the union of David and Bathsheba later produced Solomon. Thus the detailed account of the Ammonite campaign in 2 Samuel 10 is related to the main plot of the succession narrative and, of course, to Israel's history.[9]

Chronological Considerations

David and Mephibosheth

The chronological setting of the Ammonite struggle, which is recounted in 2 Samuel 10, has already been treated briefly (pp. 244–45). It has been argued that it must have taken place quite soon after David's acquisition of Jerusalem (1004) because Hanun, son of Nahash, had just come to power in Ammon. Another chronological clue is to be found in 2 Samuel 9, which most scholars consider to be an integral part of the succession narrative. This chapter, which immediately precedes the account of the war, concerns David's inquiry as to whether there were any survivors of the house of Saul to whom he might show favor for Jonathan's sake. One might be cynical about such a search

7. For an interesting study of some of the genre varieties within the larger corpus, see George W. Coats, "Parable, Fable, and Anecdote: Storytelling in the Succession Narrative," *Interp.* 35 (1981): 368–82. Coats pays special attention to Nathan's parable (2 Sam. 12:1–4), which he prefers to call a fable, and the anecdote told by the wise woman of Tekoa (2 Sam. 14:5–7). David M. Gunn asserts that the very existence of such genres implies an oral basis for the whole composition and hence a lack of historical reliability ("Traditional Composition in the 'Succession Narrative,' " *VT* 26 [1976]: 214–19). For a convincing response to this, though one still essentially skeptical of the details, see John Van Seters, "Problems in the Literary Analysis of the Court History of David," *JSOT* 1 (1976): 22–29.

8. Whybray, *Succession Narrative*, pp. 19–21; J. Alberto Soggin, *A History of Ancient Israel* (Philadelphia: Westminster, 1984), p. 43; Tomoo Ishida, "Solomon's Succession to the Throne of David—A Political Analysis," in *Studies in the Period of David and Solomon and Other Essays* (Winona Lake, Ind.: Eisenbrauns, 1983), pp. 175–76; P. Kyle McCarter, Jr., "Plots, True or False: The Succession Narratives as Court Apologetic," *Interp.* 35 (1981): 355–67. For contrary viewpoints see Ishida, "Solomon's Succession," p. 175, n. 2.

9. Hans W. Hertzberg, *I & II Samuel* (Philadelphia: Westminster, 1964), p. 303. The linkage of the Ammonite hostilities to the succession narrative as a whole is well established by John I. Lawlor, "Theology and Art in the Narrative of the Ammonite War (2 Samuel 10–12)," *GTJ* 3 (1982): 193–205.

since it clearly was in David's best interests to cultivate rapport with the supporters of Saul, who still remained in great number. But whatever David's intents may have been, a servant of Saul, Ziba, informed David that Jonathan's son Mephibosheth was still alive and residing at Lo Debar (Umm ed-Dabar?), about ten miles southeast of the Sea of Kinnereth.[10] David sent for him, put him on public pension, and instructed Ziba and his family to attend to his every need.[11]

This story, besides laying the foundation for David's subsequent acceptance by the Benjamites, helps to establish certain chronological bounds. We are told in an earlier, almost parenthetical text that Mephibosheth was five years old when Jonathan died at Gilboa. At that time Mephibosheth's nurse picked him up and fled, but she dropped him, injuring both of his legs and leaving him a cripple (2 Sam. 4:4). The point here, of course, is that Mephibosheth was five years old in 1011 and so was born in 1016. In 1004, the year David took Jerusalem, Mephibosheth was only twelve. Yet he had a young son at the time he was brought under David's care (2 Sam. 9:12). It is precarious to build a case on such subjective data, but given the propensity to early marriage in ancient Israel, it is reasonable to suppose that Mephibosheth was approximately twenty years old at the time and that the date of his return was about 996.

The great famine

The middle 990s seems also to be the setting for the story of the three-year famine recorded in 2 Samuel 21:1–14. The reason that episode appears where it does, out of chronological order, is that the story of the famine comports well with a similar theme in chapter 24. All that separates the two are summaries of the Philistine wars (21:15–22), the Davidic song of praise (22:1–51), David's farewell address (23:1–7), and the list of his heroes (23:8–39). The historian's plan, again, is topical and not chronological.

There are several reasons for suggesting that the account of 2 Samuel 21:1–14 fits between the arrival of Mephibosheth at Jerusalem and the commencement of the Ammonite wars. First, the famine has come because of Saul's slaughter of Gibeonites (an event otherwise not mentioned), a breach of the covenant Joshua had made with that city centuries before (Josh. 9:15–20). It seems unlikely that retribution for that would have been delayed until David's last years. Moreover, the

10. Yohanan Aharoni and Michael Avi-Yonah, *Macmillan Bible Atlas* (New York: Macmillan, 1968), p. 180.

11. Policies similar to this provision for the offspring of Saul by David's royal prerogatives and largess are attested to in Ugaritic texts; see Anson F. Rainey, "The System of Land Grants at Ugarit in Its Wider Near Eastern Setting," Fourth World Conference on Jewish Studies (Jerusalem, 1967), p. 190.

price that the Gibeonites exacted of David that the famine might end was the death of seven of Saul's sons or grandsons. These included two sons of Rizpah, Saul's concubine, and five sons of his daughter Merab.[12] These seven were hanged by the Gibeonites at the beginning of the barley harvest; Rizpah maintained vigil over the corpses day and night until it rained and the drought was broken. Unless we are willing to postulate an aged woman tenderly guarding the bodies of her middle-aged sons, an interpretation required by dating the incident in the last years of David's life, we must accept an earlier date.

This earlier date is supported also by David's reaction to Rizpah's devotion to the dead bodies of her sons—he sent to Jabesh Gilead for the remains of Saul and Jonathan so that he might give them honorable burial in Benjamin. One can hardly conceive of his waiting nearly forty years after their death to give them honorable burial, particularly again in light of his desire to curry the loyalty of Benjamin and the other northern tribes. In fact, his removal of the bones from Jabesh Gilead must have followed by only a very few years his message of commendation to the people of Jabesh Gilead for having buried Saul, a message he sent at the very beginning of his reign at Hebron (2 Sam. 2:4–7).

Yet the drought could not have been earlier than the establishment of Jerusalem as capital and the subsequent attachment of Mephibosheth to David's court. This is evident from the fact that Mephibosheth was spared by David from being hanged by the Gibeonites, a circumstance that presupposes Mephibosheth's presence with David.

The best view seems to be that the three-year famine occurred around the years 996–993. Mephibosheth, we have suggested earlier, was by then old enough to be father to a young son. Moreover, the Ammonite wars, as we shall soon show, had to have commenced by 993 but not much earlier. It is possible that the Ammonites had little fear of David precisely because Israel had passed through a devastating drought which left the nation weak and impoverished, though, obviously, this can be only speculation. One thing is clear, however, if our reconstruction be correct. David's delivery of the seven male descendants of Saul to the Gibeonites could do nothing but undermine the bridges of reconciliation he was attempting to build with Benjamin. The least he could do, then, was return the bodies of Saul and Jonathan to Benjamin in the hope that this might soothe the ruffled feelings of the northern tribes.

12. The Masoretic text here reads "Michal" for "Merab" (2 Sam. 21:8), perhaps, as S. R. Driver suggests, a *lapsus calami* (cf. 1 Sam. 18:19) (*Notes on the Hebrew Text and the Topography of the Books of Samuel*, 2d ed. [Winona Lake, Ind.: Alpha, 1984 reprint], p. 352).

The Cause of the Conflict

At about this time Nahash, king of Ammon, died and was succeeded by his son Hanun. Unfortunately neither of these individuals is yet attested from extrabiblical sources, so nothing can be known beyond the accounts of Samuel and Chronicles. In fact, the whole early history of Ammon must be reconstructed from the Old Testament alone except for incidental artifactual remains.[13] The Ammonites had been among the oppressors of Israel (1124–1106) before the judgeship of Jephthah (1106–1100), and at that time laid claim to lands south of the Jabbok River which Israel had occupied for three hundred years. They evidently had indeed lived just east of the Jordan from earliest times until they had been forced farther east by the Amorites. In any case, Jephthah defeated them and forced them once more to remain in the eastern deserts. A subsequent attempt to lay claim to the west occurred under Nahash in Saul's early years (ca. 1050—1 Sam. 11). Again the Ammonites were defeated, but there is no record of their being driven east. Apparently they remained south of the Jabbok, having established their capital at Rabbah (modern Amman, Jordan). It was there at any rate that they were concentrated by the time of David.

It seems that when David ascended the throne of Saul, he had been congratulated by Nahash (2 Sam. 10:2). This would not be surprising given the animosity between Nahash and Saul. Perhaps Nahash hoped for a friendly Israel now that David, Saul's apparent enemy, was in power. However that may be, when Hanun succeeded Nahash, David sent a goodwill mission to Rabbah to tender his congratulations. His motives were misinterpreted, however, and David's official party was shamefully abused and sent home. Such breach of protocol could not be tolerated, so David sent Joab and the army to Rabbah to avenge the indignity.

The Allies of the Ammonites

The Arameans

It was most evident to Hanun that he had committed a serious blunder and that he must get help if he were to avoid annihilation. He

---

13. For a general overview see George M. Landes, "The Material Civilization of the Ammonites," in *Biblical Archaeologist Reader*, vol. 2, pp. 69–88. For the few extant Ammonite texts, none of which is as early as Israel's united monarchy, see Dennis Pardee, "Literary Sources for the History of Palestine and Syria II: Hebrew, Moabite, Ammonite, and Edomite Inscriptions," *AUSS* 17 (1979): 66–69. See also B. Oded, "Neighbors on the East," in *World History of the Jewish People*, vol. 4, part 1, pp. 258–62.

therefore engaged the services of the Arameans of Beth Rehob and Zobah as well as those of the little kingdoms of Maacah and Tob.[14]

Beth Rehob was the name of both a city and a state, the former no longer being identifiable. The kingdom lay in the great Bekaa Valley between the Lebanon and Anti-Lebanon mountain ranges, extending from Dan in the south to the kingdom of Zobah in the north.[15] The crushing of the Hittites by the Sea Peoples by 1200, coupled with the rapid decline of the Ramesside twentieth dynasty of Egypt, had left all of Syria and upper Mesopotamia in the hands of the Assyrians. Because of the need to deal with the newly installed post-Kassite Babylonian dynasty as well as the Elamites, the Assyrians were unable to move west to deal with the political vacuum in Syria until the rise of the illustrious Tiglath-pileser I (1115–1077). He marched upon Syria as much to put down increasing Aramean political and military power as anything else.[16] By 1100 the Arameans had begun to infiltrate lower Mesopotamia in a major way, and not long after an Aramean king actually sat on the throne of Babylon. This ruler, Adad-apla-iddina (1067–1046), was only the first of many Arameans who would occupy Mesopotamian royal palaces.[17] In fact, the great Chaldean Empire of Nebuchadnezzar, five hundred years later, found its roots in Syria.

Tiglath could not effectively handle the Aramean city-states because he had to withdraw in the face of increasing Babylonian hostility back in his homeland. Though other Assyrian rulers such as Aššur-bel-kala (1074–1057) made sporadic raids into Syria, the city-states there were for the most part free to develop as they wished until the rise of Israel under David.[18]

Zobah appears to have been the leading Aramean kingdom of the south. Saul had already fought against its kings (1 Sam. 14:47), but it was not until David's reign that Zobah, under Hadadezer son of Rehob, reached its zenith. Its territory extended from Beth Rehob north as far as Hamath, northeast of the Anti-Lebanon range to Tadmor, and south as far as Damascus.[19] Hadadezer, then, was a significant figure in his own right. It is probably he to whom Shalmaneser III (858–824) re-

14. For a succinct account of Israel's dealings with its northern neighbors in the period of David see Benjamin Mazar, "The Aramaean Empire and Its Relations with Israel," in *Biblical Archaeologist Reader*, vol. 2, pp. 131–33.

15. Merrill F. Unger, *Israel and the Aramaeans of Damascus* (Grand Rapids: Baker, 1980 reprint), p. 42.

16. Albert Kirk Grayson, *Assyrian Royal Inscriptions* (Wiesbaden: Otto Harrassowitz, 1976), vol. 2, #4, pp. 89–97.

17. D. J. Wiseman, "Assyria and Babylonia c. 1200–1000 B.C.," in *CAH* 2.2, pp. 466–67.

18. Yutaka Ikeda, "Assyrian Kings and the Mediterranean Sea: The Twelfth to Ninth Centuries B.C.,"*Abr-Nahrain* 23 (1984–85): 23.

19. Unger, *Israel and the Aramaeans*, p. 43.

ferred as the king of "Arumu" who had seized Assyrian territory from the Assyrian king Aššur-rabi II (1013–973).[20] This would tie in well with the biblical note that Hadadezer had to recall some of his troops from "beyond the River" (i.e., the Euphrates) to deal with David (2 Sam. 10:16).

Maacah and Tob were at this time small states tributary to Zobah (2 Sam. 10:6, 19). The former was east of Lake Huleh and the latter east and southeast of the Sea of Kinnereth. Otherwise virtually nothing is known of them.[21] Damascus, though mentioned in the résumé of 2 Samuel 8, was not an important kingdom this early, though, of course, it had been a major city long before David. It did become the center of Aramean power and influence toward the end of Solomon's reign.

Moab and Edom

Moab, whose oppression of Israel had led to the judgeship of Ehud early in the thirteenth century (Judg. 3:12–30), apparently either displaced or lived among the east Israelite tribes of Reuben and Gad from that time forward. Moabite territory fluctuated considerably, but generally was east of the Jordan, north of the Zered River, and south of the Arnon.[22] It is impossible to know anything about the strength and stability of Moab in the years before David, but the fact that Gideon avoided the area south of the Jabbok immediately east of the Jordan when he pursued the Midianite princes might imply a recognition of Moabite territorial claims. Early in David's exile from Saul (ca. 1020) he had sent his family to find sanctuary with the king of Moab at Mizpah, a site which unfortunately can no longer be identified (1 Sam. 22:3–4). Otherwise the Moabite kingdom of this period remains shrouded in mystery.[23]

Not much more is known of Edom.[24] This kingdom, located in the relatively isolated region of the high plateaus east and south of the Dead Sea, had been ruled by a dynasty of kings going back to Esau himself and even earlier. Moses had bypassed it, and its territories were exempted from Israelite conquest and occupation. The only reference to Edom between the Mosaic period and that of David is the

20. J. D. Hawkins, "The Neo-Hittite States in Syria and Anatolia," in *CAH* 3.1, pp. 391–92.

21. Unger, *Israel and the Aramaeans*, p. 45.

22. Yohanan Aharoni, *The Land of the Bible* (Philadelphia: Westminster, 1979), p. 295; Oded, "Neighbors on the East," in *World History of the Jewish People*, vol. 4, part 1, p. 256.

23. A. H. Van Zyl, *The Moabites* (Leiden: E. J. Brill, 1960).

24. John R. Bartlett, "The Moabites and Edomites," in *Peoples of Old Testament Times*, ed. D. J. Wiseman, pp. 229–58.

terse note of 1 Samuel 14:47 which says that Saul fought Edom. He may have enjoyed some measure of success because his hired assassin, Doeg, was an Edomite. Whether this implies that Edom itself was an Israelite vassal state under Saul cannot be determined.

The Defeat of the Ammonites

To return now to David's Ammonite wars, we find Joab besieging the city of Rabbah (2 Sam. 10:6–14). The Ammonite troops guarded its gates while their Aramean allies, some thirty-three thousand in number, assembled in the nearby fields. This, in effect, enclosed Joab, so he divided his army into two corps—his best men he led against the Arameans and the others he placed under his brother Abishai to attack the Ammonites. The strategy succeeded; the Arameans fled to the north, and the Ammonites retreated to the safety of the city walls. Joab therefore gave up the siege and returned to Jerusalem.

In a second encounter Hadadezer, having recalled his trans-Euphratean troops, sent them under his general Shobach to engage Israel at Helam ('Alma), forty miles east of the Sea of Kinnereth. David achieved an overwhelming victory, slaughtering the Aramean army including the commander. The result was the capitulation not only of Hadadezer, but of all his vassal states as well. David thus had begun to carve out an empire, though that appears not to have been his original purpose.

Both a summary and amplification of David's Aramean conquest appear in 2 Samuel 8. There the historian relates that the forty thousand slain (2 Sam. 10:18) consisted actually of twenty thousand men of Zobah and twenty-two thousand from Damascus.[25] He further records that David placed Damascus under tribute and took gold shields from Hadadezer's officers and bronze from cities which had been subject to Hadadezer. These metals, the chronicler adds, Solomon used in the manufacture of articles for the temple (1 Chron. 18:7–8).

The submission of Hadadezer led to the voluntary surrender of Tou, king of Hamath, to David's suzerainty. An enemy of Hadadezer, Tou now capitulated to David perhaps in order to enjoy his protection. Tou's sincerity was symbolized by the lavish gifts of gold, silver, and bronze which he sent by the hand of his own son Joram. These too David kept apart for the eventual service of Yahweh.

Virtually all of Aram now lay under Israel's hegemony, but the Am-

25. For the problem of the harmonization of the figures in 2 Samuel 8 and 10 and 1 Chronicles 18 see Eugene H. Merrill, "2 Samuel," in *The Bible Knowledge Commentary*, ed. John F. Walvoord and Roy B. Zuck (Wheaton, Ill.: Victor, 1985), vol. 1, pp. 465, 467; Gleason L. Archer, Jr., *Encyclopedia of Bible Difficulties* (Grand Rapids: Zondervan, 1982), p. 184.

monite problem still was not resolved. Again, therefore, attack was made on Rabbah, but this time David remained at home. While taking his ease in Jerusalem, the king spied Bathsheba, his neighbor's wife, who was bathing in full view of the palace rooftop. Filled with lust, he ordered her brought to him and adultery ensued. When it was learned that she was pregnant, David brought Bathsheba's husband Uriah back from the battlefront at Rabbah so that he might appear to be the father of the child. When the plot to have Uriah return to the embrace of his wife failed, David sealed his doom by having Uriah placed in the front line where the fighting was fiercest. After the child was born, the prophet Nathan informed David that the sword would never depart from his house. The child then died as evidence of the divine judgment, but Yahweh, in his grace, later allowed Solomon to be born of Bathsheba and thus prepared the way for dynastic succession.

Meanwhile Joab had defeated the Ammonite troops in the field and had once more placed Rabbah under siege (2 Sam. 12:26–31). Undoubtedly the Moabites also were brought under tribute at this time since the army of Israel likely had to traverse territory under nominal Moabite control in order to gain access to Rabbah from Jerusalem. In light of his kinship with Moab, David's harsh treatment of the Moabites (2 Sam. 8.2, 12) is difficult to understand unless, as seems likely, Moab had joined forces with Ammon or otherwise interfered with David's military objectives. The fall of Rabbah resulted in similar treatment of the Ammonites at David's hands. He made them slaves and perhaps even subjected them to barbarous reprisal (2 Sam. 12:31).

The Defeat of Edom

David's campaigns against Edom must also have been undertaken in these earlier years before the birth of Solomon. It was likely, in fact, that Edom had become allied with Moab and Ammon in an effort to withstand David's penetration of the Transjordan, for though that action was directed specifically against Ammon, it threatened Moab and Edom as well. The time can best be determined from the narrative of 1 Kings 11:14–22, which describes the flight of the Edomite prince Hadad to Egypt. In the résumé of David's wars in 2 Samuel 8, the historian points out that David had smitten eighteen thousand Edomites in the Valley of Salt (Wadi el-Milḥ), which was in the Negev near Beersheba and Arad. This may imply that Edom had launched an offensive strike against Israel from the south, since the valley was Israelite territory. The chronicler adds the detail that the Israelite victory actually was achieved under Abishai, who went on to establish garrisons in Edom and reduce Edom to vassalship (1 Chron. 18:12–13).

The account of 1 Kings is not at variance with all this but seems, rather, to be complementary and to relate subsequent events. After Edom had been reduced, it appears that David and Joab went there to bury the slaughtered and to put down remaining opposition. Some of the royal family of Edom, including Hadad, escaped and made their way to Egypt, where they found cordial hospitality. Later Hadad returned to Edom and proved to be a major cause of Solomon's decline. For now it is important to note that the author of Kings describes Hadad as "still only a boy" at the time of his exile. Then, having reached adulthood, married, and fathered a son, Hadad returned to Edom shortly after David's death (1 Kings 11:20–22). This period of Hadad's life must be dated around 969. A likely year for his flight to Egypt while "still only a boy" is 993, the date proposed for the Ammonite wars. Thus, the Edomite campaign may have been the finale to the Ammonite-Aramean wars described in 2 Samuel 10 and summarized in 2 Samuel 8.

The scenario can be reconstructed as follows: When Joab was dispatched to Rabbah to complete the siege of that city (2 Sam. 12:26–28), Abishai his brother went simultaneously to the Valley of Salt to put down an Edomite invasion (1 Chron. 18:12–13). After both objectives were accomplished, David, who had personally gone to Rabbah to oversee its collapse, went on with Joab to Edom to complete the work of conquest begun by Abishai. Edom then became a tributary state to Israel, but not before the Edomite royal family could escape to Egypt.

The Beginning of David's Domestic Troubles

It was after all this foreign conquest, according to 2 Samuel, that David's family became beset with the troubles, including rape and murder, which nearly cost David his crown and jeopardized the succession of Solomon. These troubles also followed the birth of Solomon to David and Bathsheba, whose earlier adultery was the specific reason for the turmoil (2 Sam. 12:10–14). It has already been suggested that Solomon must have been about twenty when he began his sole regency, so his birth took place around 991. Afterwards David's domestic troubles began. One implication of all this is that whereas the first half of David's reign was characterized by blessing and success, the latter half was marked by heartache and defeat.

The Rape of Tamar

The first recorded evidence of the sword which never would depart from David's house (2 Sam. 12:10) was Amnon's rape of his half-sister Tamar. Born to Ahinoam the Jezreelitess, Amnon was David's eldest son (2 Sam. 3:2). Since he was born in Hebron, he was very likely a young man of about twenty when he assaulted the virgin sister of Absalom. She was apparently born in Jerusalem (1 Chron. 3:4–9) and thus was several years younger than Amnon. After the lustful deed was done, Amnon's infatuation for the girl turned to hatred, and he refused to take her as wife, as the law required in such circumstances. Heartbroken, Tamar sought solace and refuge with her older brother Absalom.

The Revenge of Absalom

Absalom was filled with rage and a desire for revenge, but he realized that the situation must be handled with unusual diplomacy. It would do no good, he no doubt reasoned, to take the matter to David, for David had already compromised his own integrity in his adultery with Bathsheba and murder of Uriah and would therefore do nothing. Besides, Amnon was heir apparent to Israel's throne and would by virtue of this position enjoy immunity from prosecution and punishment. Absalom therefore let the matter brew until he could devise an appropriate occasion for revenge. One must also believe that his own designs on Israel's throne took root at this time. The death of Amnon would not only avenge the rape of Tamar, but would better the chances for Absalom to succeed to the throne.

In the meantime, David learned of Amnon's crime, and though he was angry seemed paralyzed in effecting the proper response. Perhaps he too realized that it might be perceived as hypocritical if he were to punish his son for a sin so similar to his own. In any case, Absalom plotted and planned for two full years until at last he concocted a scheme which involved inviting David to a sheepshearing festival at Baal Hazor (Tell 'Aṣûr), which lay between Bethel and Shiloh. When David declined, Absalom pressed him to send the crown prince Amnon in his stead. After Amnon had become quite drunk at the festivities, Absalom's assassins murdered him; and Absalom fled to his grandfather, Talmai king of Geshur, with whom he found sanctuary for three years.

A case has already been made for a date around 987 for the rape of Tamar, 985 for Amnon's assassination, and 985–982 for Absalom's exile in Geshur (p. 245). When Absalom returned to Jerusalem, an achievement engineered by Joab, he remained for two more years (982–980) physically estranged from his father. By this time the handsome young prince had fathered four children, including a daughter named Tamar, and had begun to make a favorable impression on the people of Israel. At long last Joab brought David and Absalom face to face, and the two were reconciled, at least by every appearance. The spirit of rebellion was smoldering in Absalom's heart, however, and within four years would burst out in open flames of revolution.

Jerusalem as Cult Center

It is almost certain that it was in this period (980–976) that David undertook his vast building programs (2 Sam. 5:9–12) including, finally, preparations for the construction of a temple. It is obvious that he had some kind of a palace and other public edifices by this time, but his occupation with empire building and, more recently, the troubles within his own family had prevented the kind of impressive infrastructure requisite to a monarch of his stature. His reconciliation with Absalom gave him the long-awaited opportunity to make Jerusalem the political and religious center it ought to be.

David therefore engaged Hiram, who had just come to power in the Phoenician city-state of Tyre, to provide materials and expertise for the construction of various massive projects.[26] Once the city had appropriate symbols of its political significance, David undertook measures to make Jerusalem the center of the cult as well. This involved the building of a temporary sanctuary, a tabernacle, and removal of the ark of the covenant from Kiriath Jearim,[27] where it had been housed for 130 years, to this new dwelling-place of Yahweh.[28]

Such a step could not be taken lightly. First of all, there was no clear precedent for the merging of Israel's religious and political bases in one place and under one head, at least not in post-Mosaic history. Saul, David's predecessor, had made Gibeah his capital, but the tabernacle throughout his reign had never been located there. It is true, of course, that Saul appears to have functioned in the cultic pattern of ancient Near Eastern kings, but he did so with disastrous results. Under Saul Israel was not yet ready to view the king as a religious as well as political head. Would it be any more prepared to do so under David?

Second, the Mosaic tabernacle was situated at Gibeon, and there the people, including David, presumably had gathered for community worship all through the years of his reign (1 Chron. 16:39; 21:29; 1 Kings 3:1–4). Could David now simply remove it from Gibeon and place it in Jerusalem without specific revelation from God? It had most likely been

26. For the extent of David's building activity, see Yohanan Aharoni, "The Building Activities of David and Solomon," *IEJ* 24 (1974): 13–16.

27. Baalah of Judah (2 Sam. 6:2) was either identical to or near by Kiriath Jearim (Aharoni, *Land of the Bible*, pp. 350–51). Joseph Blenkinsopp suggests that Kiriath Jearim may refer to "a fairly large area" of which Baalah was a part ("Kiriath-jearim and the Ark," *JBL* 88 [1969]: 146–47).

28. As Antony F. Campbell shows, the major purpose of the narratives about the ark (1 Sam. 4–6; 2 Sam. 6) is to legitimate "the Davidic dynasty and the election and Zion theology" as well as to demonstrate the rejection of the old tribalism in favor of the Davidic monarchy ("Yahweh and the Ark: A Case Study in Narrative," *JBL* 98 [1979]: 42–43).

put there in the first place by Saul, and since Gibeon was in Benjamin, Saul's tribal territory, arbitrary removal of the tabernacle from Gibeon would be viewed by Benjamin and the north with extremely jaundiced eye. The most David could do—and what he actually did—was leave the Mosaic sanctuary at Gibeon and build another on Mount Zion.

The third consideration had to do with the relocation of the ark itself.[29] The ark represented the very presence of Yahweh among his people. Without specific authorization from Yahweh (and in this case there is no clear biblical record of one) it would be deemed presumptuous to say the least for David to undertake its removal. The suspicion of presumption can hardly have been ameliorated by the tragic death of Uzzah, who helped supervise the initial journey of the ark from Kiriath Jearim (2 Sam. 6:6–8).

Fourth, but by no means of least importance, was the lack of recent religious tradition associated with Jerusalem. From patriarchal times until David captured it, in fact, it had been a pagan Canaanite center untouched, except intermittently, by the sanctifying presence of the people of Yahweh. Undoubtedly, then, it was the city's patriarchal associations that constituted David's justification of Jerusalem as the only fitting location for the ark and tabernacle. In fact, it may have been his awareness of the Abrahamic connection with Jerusalem which led him to select it as his capital to begin with. This awareness certainly gave him sufficient boldness to make of Zion the permanent dwelling-place of his God on earth, notwithstanding all the problems which attended this decision otherwise.[30]

Melchizedek, Jerusalem, and the Royal Priesthood

The historical incident in view is Abraham's encounter with Melchizedek as described in Genesis 14 and later interpreted theologically

---

29. Many scholars of the so-called Myth and Ritual school deny the historicity of the narratives about the ark (1 Sam. 4–6; 2 Sam. 6), preferring to see them as part of a complex of myths celebrating Yahweh's triumphs over chaos and other foes. For a brief discussion supporting such notions see Aage Bentzen, "The Cultic Use of the Story of the Ark in Samuel," *JBL* 67 (1948): 37–53. Perhaps the historicity of the narratives cannot be proved, but the existence of arklike objects in ancient Semitic cultuses contemporary with Mosaic Israel would certainly undermine much of the argument that the accounts are mythical; see William F. Albright, *From the Stone Age to Christianity* (Garden City, N.Y.: Doubleday, 1957), p. 266.

30. David himself articulates his awareness of Yahweh's choice of Zion as the site of both palace and temple (Ps. 78:68; 87:2; 132). For parallels see Giorgio Buccellati, "Enthronement of the King and the Capital City in Texts from Ancient Mesopotamia and Syria," in *Studies Presented to A. Leo Oppenheim,* ed. Robert M. Adams (Chicago: University of Chicago Press, 1964), pp. 54–61; Baruch Halpern, *The Constitution of the Monarchy in Israel* (Chico, Calif.: Scholars Press, 1981), pp. 17–23; Shemaryahu Talmon, "The Biblical Idea of Statehood," in *The Bible World,* ed. Gary Rendsburg et al. (New York: Ktav, 1980), p. 239.

by David himself in Psalm 110. On his return from defeating the eastern kings north of Damascus, Abraham had met the mysterious Melchizedek, king of Salem and priest of El Elyon, "God Most High" (Gen. 14:18). Having taken spoil from the conquered kings, Abraham paid a tithe of it to Melchizedek after the priest had blessed him in the name of El Elyon.

Psalm 76:2 equates Salem with Zion; that is, Salem is none other than Jerusalem. With this a significant Jewish and Christian tradition agrees.[31] The identity of Melchizedek is much more problematic, however.[32] Some scholars dismiss the historicity of the account entirely and suggest that the tale is an etiology designed to legitimize Jerusalem as a Hebrew sacred place.[33] Others view it as recording an encounter by the early fathers of Israel with a Canaanite priest who thus introduced El worship to the Hebrews.[34] Certain conservative writers have seen Melchizedek as a Christophany; that is, as a preincarnate manifestation of Jesus Christ. This is based on such factors as the meaning of Melchizedek's name ("king of righteousness"), his association with Salem (he was "king of Salem" or "king of peace"), and the explicit comparisons of Melchizedek to Jesus, particularly in the Epistle to the Hebrews (7:3, 15–17, etc.).[35]

The best interpretation, however, is that Melchizedek is a type of Christ.[36] He foreshadowed the life and ministry of Christ in a variety of ways, but chiefly in that he was both a king and a priest just as Jesus Christ also, as Messiah, came to fill both roles. Moreover, he typified the life and ministry of David as well, a fact which may have surprised David but which he nonetheless came to accept. In Psalm 110 David expressly refers to the messianic King to come as "my Lord" (v. 1), but he goes on to identify himself as a priest after the order of

31. See, for example, Artur Weiser, *The Psalms: A Commentary* (Philadelphia: Westminster, 1962), pp. 524–26. This is by no means a consensus, however. John G. Gammie contends that Salem cannot be Jerusalem and that the Melchizedek tradition must find its roots elsewhere, specifically at Shechem, from where it migrated to Shiloh, Nob, and finally Jerusalem ("Loci of the Melchizedek Tradition," *JBL* 90 [1971]: 385–96). This goes against the clear equation in Psalm 76:2 and other passages, however.

32. For various views see Leopold Sabourin, *The Psalms: Their Origin and Meaning* (Staten Island, N.Y.: Alba House, 1974), pp. 360–62.

33. Gerhard von Rad, *Genesis: A Commentary*, trans. John H. Marks (London: SCM; Philadelphia: Westminster, 1961), pp. 173–76.

34. Georg Fohrer, *History of Israelite Religion*, trans. David E. Green (Nashville: Abingdon, 1972), pp. 104–5.

35. Cited and convincingly rejected by James A. Borland, *Christ in the Old Testament* (Chicago: Moody, 1978), pp. 164–74.

36. Patrick Fairbairn, *The Typology of Scripture* (Grand Rapids: Baker, 1975 reprint), vol. 1, pp. 302–5.

Melchizedek through whom the Lord will judge the nations (vv. 4–6). Not only the Messiah but David himself is such a priest.[37]

The notion of royal priesthood was not at all strange in the ancient Near Eastern world.[38] Kings regularly took a leading role in the cult and were sometimes the chief priests in their sacerdotal systems. Nor was royal priesthood totally foreign to Israel's experience and ideology.[39] In patriarchal times the fathers had been both civil and religious leaders of their families and clans, offering sacrifice and performing other cultic functions as they wished. It was, in fact, not until the creation of the Aaronic priesthood that a clear historical basis can be seen for the demarcation between royal and priestly authority residing in different persons. This understanding prevailed throughout Old Testament times, and even the disciples of Jesus could not understand how he could be both King and Priest, Sovereign and Savior. The Qumran sect of Judaism in fact anticipated two messiahs—a priestly descendant of Aaron and a royal descendant of David.[40] It was the author of Hebrews who first clearly articulated the dual role of Jesus as King and Priest. Jesus could be a priest in spite of his non-Aaronic ancestry precisely because he was of a superior order, that of Melchizedek (Heb. 7:4–25).

David as Priest

Being of the order of Melchizedek was also the basis of David's role as royal priest and of his selection of Jerusalem as the site of the ark and tabernacle. He understood that just as Melchizedek had been king of Salem, so he, as successor to Melchizedek, must reign from Jerusalem. And just as Melchizedek was priest of God Most High, so he, as successor to Melchizedek in an order that was superior to that of Aaron, could exercise the holy privilege of priesthood before Yahweh.[41]

Thus on theological grounds David could establish Jerusalem as cult

37. Leslie C. Allen, *Psalms 101–50*, Word Biblical Commentary (Waco: Word, 1983), pp. 78–87.

38. Sidney Smith, "The Practice of Kingship in Early Semitic Kingdoms," in *Myth, Ritual, and Kingship*, ed. Samuel H. Hooke (Oxford: Clarendon, 1958), pp. 22–73.

39. Roland de Vaux, *Ancient Israel* (New York: McGraw-Hill, 1965), vol. 1, pp. 113–14.

40. Helmer Ringgren, *The Faith of Qumran* (Philadelphia: Fortress, 1963), p. 182.

41. Walther Zimmerli, *Old Testament Theology in Outline*, trans. David E. Green (Atlanta: John Knox, 1978), pp. 88–93; Walther Eichrodt, *Theology of the Old Testament* (Philadelphia: Westminster, 1961), vol. 1, pp. 446–47; Dennis J. McCarthy, "Compact and Kingship: Stimuli for Hebrew Covenant Thinking," in *Studies in the Period of David and Solomon and Other Essays*, ed. Tomoo Ishida (Winona Lake, Ind.: Eisenbrauns, 1983), pp. 82–85.

center as well as political capital, but he faced a serious practical problem. Were the people prepared for this radical theological adjustment? Would they tolerate the shattering of tradition which hitherto had denied to the king any special role in the nation's religious life?

There is little wonder that David resumed the procession with unusual caution; but then, with proper procedure and great rejoicing, the ark made its way at last to Mount Zion. David led the procession, clothed in the priestly linen ephod, and sacrificing and dancing before Yahweh. When the ark was safely ensconced in the tabernacle, David and the Levites offered up burnt offerings and fellowship offerings before Yahweh, thus attesting to the covenant union which existed between Yahweh and Israel. Neither the chronicler nor the author of Samuel mentions a priest in the whole course of sacrificing. Clearly David saw himself as a priest and was accepted by the people and the Levites as such. His sacerdotal role is seen also in his appointing of the religious personnel to attend to the tabernacle (1 Chron. 16:4–6). These were led by the Levite Asaph at Jerusalem and by Zadok the priest at the Mosaic tabernacle at Gibeon (1 Chron. 16:37–39).[42] That no mention is made of a priest at Jerusalem may imply that David himself fulfilled that responsibility at least initially (or that Abiathar did so).

---

42. That the earliest reference to Zadok represents him as occupying a priestly ministry at Gibeon rather than Jerusalem is an embarrassment to the commonly held hypothesis that Zadok descended from a Canaanite line of priests, originating possibly with Melchizedek, who functioned at the Jerusalem shrine. According to this view, David brought Zadok into the Yahwistic priesthood and eventually promoted him over Abiathar (Zimmerli, *Old Testament Theology in Outline*, p. 94). Fully aware of the difficulties of this position and of the equally difficult problems concerning Zadok's genealogy, Frank M. Cross suggests that Zadok was an Aaronic priest in Hebron before David's kingship at Jerusalem (*Canaanite Myth and Hebrew Epic* [Cambridge: Harvard University Press, 1973], pp. 209–15). This is entirely possible but cannot be proved. Walter Brueggemann views the two priesthoods as the expression of tensions between a narrow Mosaic tradition of concrete liberation (Abiatharite priesthood) and a creation and messianism tradition involving a universal and royal order (Zadokite priesthood). The latter, he says, prevailed eventually under David but was nearly aborted under Solomon. Brueggemann offers no convincing evidence, however ("Trajectories in OT Literature and the Sociology of Ancient Israel," *JBL* 98 [1979]: 170–71). Assuming that the Eleazar of 1 Chronicles 24:3 was Zadok's father and identifying him with Eleazar the priest of Kiriath Jearim (1 Sam. 7:1), J. Dus (cited by P. R. Davies, "The History of the Ark in the Books of Samuel," *JNSL* 5 [1976]: 17) proposes that Zadok came from Kiriath Jearim. This cannot be sustained, however, for Eleazar was appointed at Kiriath Jearim more than a century before Zadok came on the scene. Saul Olyan proposes that Zadok was an aide to Jehoiada (1 Chron. 12:27–28), the father of Solomon's general Benaiah, and so came from Kabzeel, deep in the Negev ("Zadok's Origins and the Tribal Politics of David," *JBL* 101 [1982]: 185). Jehoiada was indeed a *nāgîd* ("leader") of Aaron (1 Chron. 12:27) and a priest (1 Chron. 27:5), but one cannot therefore deduce that Zadok had Aaronic connections nor even that this is the same Zadok as Zadok the priest.

Not long after David had completed the Zion tabernacle and placed the ark within it, he began to contemplate the stark difference between his own massive and beautifully appointed palace and the tentlike structure which represented the residence of Yahweh, the almighty God. It was hardly fitting, he said, for him, a mere man, to live in such luxury while Yahweh lived like a nomad. And so David undertook plans to build a temple.

The Rebellion of Absalom

The Occasion

Before these plans could proceed further, however, Absalom, according to the reconstruction proposed so far, instigated his rebellion and forced David not only to delay planning the temple, but to flee Jerusalem altogether. This must have happened around 976, six years after Absalom's return from Geshur. Absalom had in the meantime gradually gained a following, particularly in Judah. When the moment seemed propitious, he begged leave of his father to go to Hebron, his birthplace, to offer sacrifice in fulfilment of a vow he had sworn in Geshur. When he arrived at Hebron, he at last made public what he and his fellow conspirators had been planning for years—ironically, he claimed kingship at Hebron as David had first done thirty-five years earlier (2 Sam. 15:7–12).

By the time David learned of the plot, it was too late to do anything but escape the capital. Absalom had gained a following all over Israel—including Jerusalem—and had managed to recruit even David's chief adviser, Ahithophel. The reasons for the decline of David's popularity and the rise of Absalom's are not clear, though Absalom may well have been close to the truth when he suggested to all the citizens who sought an audience with the king that the king was preoccupied and unable to see them and redress their complaints. If only he, Absalom said, could be made a judge, he would see to it that justice was done. This assessment of things, together with some astute politicking, the ancient equivalent of handshaking, soon won over the hearts of the people. If our suggestion that these years were busy with construction and with the establishment of Jerusalem as cult center is correct, it is likely that David neglected other affairs of state. Moreover, his arrogation of religious authority along with political may have contributed to his lack of support, for it is quite clear that this action alienated him from certain elements of the nation, particularly the Benjamites. The reaction of Michal, Saul's daughter, may have been fairly typical (2 Sam. 6:20).

David's Exile

Eager to spare his city from violence, David left voluntarily with his closest friends and followers. Notable among the latter were his mercenary troops, who, of course, were committed to him personally rather than to the nation. David fully intended to return, for he left some of his concubines to manage the palace in his absence and told Zadok the priest that he would come back someday in the mercy of Yahweh (2 Sam. 15:25).

It is worth pointing out at this juncture that David, as he crossed the Kidron on the way to the Transjordan, was joined by Zadok and the Levites bearing the ark of the covenant. This implies, obviously, that the ark and tabernacle were by then located in Jerusalem. That this is the first reference placing them in Jerusalem supports the thesis that Jerusalem did not become the central sanctuary until at least midway through David's reign. It will be recalled that Zadok had been assigned to oversee the shrine at Gibeon when the ark first arrived at Zion. Evidently, sometime between then and the rebellion of Absalom, Zadok had left Gibeon and become attached to the Davidic tabernacle. David now urged him to take the ark back to Jerusalem because Yahweh would someday allow the king to return to see it and the habitation of Yahweh there.

When he reached the Mount of Olives, David learned that his trusted counselor Ahithophel had defected to Absalom. Just then Hushai, a dear friend of the king, came on the scene, and David hit upon a plan to frustrate Ahithophel's usefulness to Absalom—Hushai would return to Jerusalem, gain the confidence of Absalom, and offer Absalom advice contrary to Ahithophel's. He would also serve as an undercover agent to gain intelligence from Absalom and pass it on to David through the sons of Abiathar and Zadok.

Next David encountered Ziba, the servant of Mephibosheth. Ziba promptly informed David that Mephibosheth had remained in Jerusalem because he was convinced that the overthrow of David would result in the reestablishment of the Saulide dynasty over Israel with him at its head (2 Sam. 16:1–4). This information, though apparently untrue and slanderous, suggests that there must have been a significant residue of pro-Saul sentiment. It might even be that these elements saw the David-Absalom rupture as a golden opportunity to divide Israel from Judah once more and set up a descendant of Saul on Israel's throne. Most striking is the fact that all of David's efforts to unify the kingdom had proved only superficially successful at best.

The Benjamites' latent hostility toward David found overt expression almost before he was out of sight of the capital. At Bahurim (perhaps Ras el-Temim),[43] the southern flank of the Mount of Olives, Shimei, a relative of Saul himself, began to curse and mock David, reminding him that he had, in effect, usurped the throne of Saul and that Absalom had now come as the agent of Yahweh to turn the tables. With remarkable restraint David allowed the cursing to continue for, said he, it was of God. And if God had sent Shimei to curse David, he could also in his own time turn the curse into a blessing.

Back in Jerusalem Absalom had taken steps to seize the reins of government. This was symbolized, among other ways no doubt, by his public appropriation of his father's concubines, an act which in the ancient Near East generally indicated transfer of power from one king to another.[44] He also began to formulate a plan to pursue his father and remove him forever as a threat. This plan was largely the creation of Ahithophel, who advised Absalom to undertake pursuit immediately while David was still weak and confused. Just as Absalom was about to do so, Hushai, who had convinced Absalom that he was loyal to the new regime, offered counteradvice. He persuaded Absalom that it would be foolhardy for only twelve thousand troops to attack the seasoned warrior David. The prince ought rather to wait until he had amassed an army large enough to destroy David in the field or to drag him out of any fortress.

This counsel seemed good to Absalom, and so he postponed his chase. Hushai then sent Jonathan and Ahimaaz, the sons of Abiathar and Zadok respectively, to David's encampment near the Jordan with the advice to cross the river immediately and seek refuge on the other side. Ahithophel, his counsel rejected, returned to his house and hanged himself.

David made his way east to Mahanaim (Tell edh-Dhahab el-Gharbi)[45] on the upper Jabbok. This had been the seat of government under Ish-Bosheth, but perhaps because of David's kind treatment of Mephibosheth, Saul's grandson, he found a welcome there. Transjordanian friends came to his aid including, surprisingly enough, Shobi, son of Nahash, king of Ammon (2 Sam. 17:27). He was evidently a brother of Hanun, who had treated David's messengers so shamefully. By showing friendliness to David, Shobi probably wished to try to undo the evil of his brother. Of course, Ammon by then was a tributary state to Israel, so he may have felt he had no choice.[46] Makir of Lo Debar also came with supplies. Since Mephibosheth had lived with this good man before David took him in, Makir's generosity is understandable.

---

43. Tentatively so identified in Aharoni and Avi-Yonah, *Macmillan Bible Atlas*, p. 176.
44. de Vaux, *Ancient Israel*, vol. 1, p. 116.
45. Aharoni and Avi-Yonah, *Macmillan Bible Atlas*, p. 181.
46. John Bright, *A History of Israel*, 3d ed. (Philadelphia: Westminster, 1981), pp. 203, 209.

The third benefactor, Barzillai of Rogelim (Bersinya),[47] a village twelve miles southeast of Lo Debar, is otherwise unknown, but his favor toward the king later led to his being invited to return with David to Jerusalem.

The Death of Absalom

Meanwhile Absalom had crossed the Jordan with his army led by Amasa, David's own nephew. David divided his troops into three companies under the command of Joab, Abishai, and his Gittite mercenary Ittai. Then, remaining in Mahanaim at the behest of the people, he sent his army forth with the solemn request that they do Absalom no personal harm. The two hosts met in the forest of Ephraim where Israel under Absalom suffered a staggering defeat and retreated west in total disarray. Absalom became caught in the low-lying branches of an oak and while suspended there was cruelly murdered by Joab (2 Sam. 18:4–15).

Despite Joab's protest, Ahimaaz ran to inform David of the death of his son, but when he arrived before the king, he did not have the heart to tell him what had happened. A Cushite messenger instead relayed the gruesome news, and David, as Joab had anticipated, broke out in bitter lamentation. The grief of David undermined the morale of his victorious troops. They had risked their necks for their king only to have him mourn for the one who had fomented the rebellion in the first place.

This was the final straw as far as Joab was concerned. David had punished the young man who claimed to be the assassin of his enemy Saul (2 Sam. 1:15); he had held a state funeral and had lamented publicly for Abner, whom Joab himself had slain (2 Sam. 3:31–39); he had executed the murderers of Ish-Bosheth, the chief obstacle to his reigning over Israel (2 Sam. 4:12); and now, once again, he wept for all the world to see when Joab had done him the favor of ridding him of his rebellious son and competitor (2 Sam. 18:33). The cynic might with some justification discern a degree of political motivation in some of David's propensity to grieve over his enemies, but that can hardly be the case here. David sincerely wished that he had died in place of his son, for was it not David's own adulterous and murderous acts which had brought the sword upon Absalom?

Joab did not see the situation this way, however. He chided David for his insensitivity toward him and the others who had done what they thought to be in David's best interests. "You love those who hate you and hate those who love you," he said (2 Sam. 19:6). Furthermore,

47. So, with hesitation, Aharoni and Avi-Yonah, *Macmillan Bible Atlas*, p. 182.

Joab went on, if David did not assuage the wounded feelings of his people, he would end up the loser anyway.

David's Efforts at Reconciliation

Overtures to Judah

Joab's rebuke forced David to consider how he might go about regaining the loyalty of Israel and, most ironically, of his own tribe Judah.[48] The people of the northern tribes had already realized that David must be restored to power since Absalom was now dead. Judah, however, was expressing no such sentiment, a fact of which David was most aware. He therefore sent a message asking the elders of Judah why they were reluctant to have him back, especially since Israel had already indicated a willingness to do so. Then, having shamed them by his appeal to their common kinship, he made the astute move of appointing Absalom's erstwhile commander, Amasa, as his own commander in place of the insolent and now discredited Joab. This suited the people well, so they sent a delegation to Gilgal to meet the king and reaffirm their allegiance to him (2 Sam. 19:15).[49]

The Winning of Benjamin

When it was clear to all that Judah had rallied around David once more, Shimei and Ziba, leaders of Benjamin, led an entourage from their tribe to seek reconciliation with David. Though Abishai was eager to kill Shimei then and there for his previous cursings of the king, David saw in Shimei's coming an opportunity to heal Judah's breach with Benjamin and the rest of Israel, so he let him live.

Mephibosheth now made his appearance. Ziba had earlier accused him of treachery toward David, so when David was making his way toward Jerusalem, Mephibosheth was quick to explain to the king that he had been misrepresented. He had intended to join David in exile but was prevented from doing so by his physical handicap. Once more David demonstrated his diplomatic genius by not only restoring Me-

---

48. For a fascinating interpretation of the intrigue involved in David's return see Hayim Tadmor, "Traditional Institutions and the Monarchy: Social and Political Tensions in the Time of David and Solomon," in *Studies in the Period of David and Solomon*, ed. Tomoo Ishida, pp. 247–50.

49. Though Gilgal was a logical meeting place since it was near the ford of the Jordan, one should not overlook the fact that the monarchy of David is here being (re)affirmed in the very place that Saul had first entered into royal covenant with the nation (1 Sam. 11:14–15).

phibosheth to his household, but by forgiving the lying servant Ziba as well. This could not help gaining the favor of Benjamin.

So successful were David's efforts at reconciliation, in fact, that Judah and the other tribes began to quarrel as to who was the most loyal and who had greatest claim on the king. Judah argued that David was their own because of blood ties, but Israel protested that they comprised ten tribes whereas Judah was only one, and, besides, they had taken the initiative to restore David to his throne. So while David had effected harmony between himself and the people, he had done so at the price of a deep and eventually fatal division between north and south.

Additional Troubles

The Rebellion of Sheba

Capitalizing on the intertribal hatred, a Benjamite by the name of Sheba organized a new schismatic movement which quickly gained the following of a great number of the fickle Israelites. What happened, in effect, was an abortive precursor of the split of the kingdom that Jeroboam would bring about forty years later. David, after he had installed himself once more in Jerusalem, ordered Amasa to call up the militia of Judah and give chase to Sheba lest he do more damage than had been done by Absalom. When Amasa proved slow in gathering his troops, David sent Abishai and Joab out with the standing army. They all rendezvoused at Gibeon, where Joab, pretending to embrace Amasa, slew him instead and took command himself (2 Sam. 20:9–10).

Joab pursued Sheba to Abel Beth Maacah (Abil el-Qamḥ), far to the north near Dan. When it appeared that Joab would demolish the city in his attempt to capture Sheba, a wise woman who lived there arranged for Sheba to be killed and for his head to be thrown over the wall as evidence. Thus the revolution ended, but it held portents of much worse things to come.

The Ill-advised Census

After the revolutions of both Absalom and Sheba it would have been reasonable for David to reassess his military situation against the possibility of similar uprisings or other emergencies. This may in part explain the census of 2 Samuel 24 (= 1 Chron. 21), a census which the historian says was motivated by Yahweh because of his anger against Israel. The specific cause of this anger is unknown, but David did not hesitate to yield to the desires he already harbored to ascertain his strength and rely upon it as the situation might require.

Though Joab protested the census, he was assigned the task of taking the head count. Proceeding in a counterclockwise direction, Joab began in Transjordan, circled north to Dan, west to Sidon and Tyre, and eventually south to Beersheba. The total came to eight hundred thousand men from Israel and five hundred thousand from Judah, excluding the tribes of Levi and Benjamin.[50] Only after the tally was made did David realize the sin in what he had done—he had put his confidence in the flesh rather than in Yahweh. It was too late, however, for Yahweh was going to punish his people in one of three ways: three years of famine, three months of flight from the enemy, or three days of plague. Unable to make the decision, David left himself to God's mercy. The result was a plague which took seventy thousand lives from all over Israel.

When the judgment of Yahweh was about to strike Jerusalem itself, he stayed the sword of the angel at the threshing floor of Araunah, a Jebusite citizen of Jerusalem. Having seen the angel, David fell prostrate before Yahweh in repentance. He then rose, negotiated with Araunah for the purchase of the threshing floor, and erected there an altar on which he sacrificed burnt offerings and fellowship offerings before Yahweh. At last the plague ceased.

David's Plan for a Temple

David's Motives

Most significant in the whole narrative of the census and its aftermath is the realization of David that the threshing floor of Araunah must be the site of the temple of Yahweh which he had longed to build (1 Chron. 21:28–22:1). Having come to that understanding, he began the process of gathering building materials and laborers to undertake at least the preparation for the temple which his son Solomon would see to completion.

David's desire to build a temple was first articulated after Hiram of Tyre had built a palace for David and the ark had been brought into Jerusalem. For various reasons, including perhaps the revolt of Absalom, the work could not be undertaken at once. Now, some four or five years after the wish was first articulated, the time seemed pro-

---

50. For the problem of these and other large numbers, see J. W. Wenham, "Large Numbers in the Old Testament," *Tyn Bull* 18 (1967): 19–53, esp. 33–34.

pitious, particularly since the threshing floor of Araunah had been purchased and designated for that purpose.

The reason for David's proposal to build a temple is clear—he lived in an imposing palace of cedar while Yahweh resided in a mere tent (2 Sam. 7:1–2; 1 Chron. 17:1). It is important to understand that in the ancient Near East a king's sovereignty was not fully established or recognized until he had constructed an appropriate dwelling-place.[51] If this was true of human kings, how much more so was it true of the gods, who, after all, were the true kings under whom the rulers of earth served! Indeed, etymological studies indicate that the Hebrew word for "temple" connotes a palace. The Sumerians called their temples E.GAL ("great house"), which came into Hebrew (*hêkāl*) by way of Akkadian (*ekallu*). The temple of even Yahweh, then, was regarded not so much as merely a religious structure as the palace in which he, the Sovereign of heaven and earth, lived among his people.[52]

Furthermore, though it may have seemed suitable for Yahweh to live in a tent in the days of Israel's nomadic existence, the nation had for four hundred years been settled in the land. Why, then, should Yahweh's residence still give the appearance of transience? Yahweh, like his people, had come to Canaan to stay and thus should abide in a palace of sufficient stability and grandeur as to suggest both his permanence there and his sovereignty over all other powers, real and imaginary.

Yahweh's Response: The Davidic Covenant

Clearly, these were David's concerns, and they formed the basis for his implicit request to begin such a project. The answer from Yahweh was stunning—"the LORD himself will establish a house for you" (2 Sam. 7:11). He had been satisfied, he said, to live in a tent from the exodus to the present hour. And in any case, even if Yahweh were someday to live in a temple, such an edifice would not be built by David, but by his son who would succeed him as king. Then, in one of the most remarkable and significant theological statements of the Bible, Yahweh revealed that David, far from building a house for Yahweh, would himself be established as a house, that is, a dynasty, which would have no end (2 Sam. 7:11–13). The ancient promises to the patriarchs concerning an everlasting kingship were at last being fulfilled in David and his descendants.

Yahweh points out that he had taken David from the sheepfold to

51. A. Leo Oppenheim, *Ancient Mesopotamia* (Chicago: University of Chicago Press, 1964), pp. 95–98.

52. de Vaux, *Ancient Israel*, vol. 2, pp. 282–83.

make him the shepherd of his people. Confirmation of this divine election could be seen in both David's successes in the past and the promises concerning the future. David's name (i.e., reputation) would be great, his people would dwell forever in the land, and his son would build a temple for Yahweh. This son—Solomon, the continuing dynastic succession, and the messianic Son of David—will rule forever.[53]

This promise, generally described as the Davidic covenant, is technically in the form of a royal grant by which a sovereign graciously bestowed a blessing, usually in the form of land or a fiefdom, upon a vassal. This may have been in return for some act performed by the vassal in behalf of his lord, or it may have been simply a beneficence deriving from the sheer love and kindness of the king.[54] The latter clearly is the case here, for the promise of eternal kingship through David had been articulated long before the birth of David himself. From the beginning it was the purpose of God to channel his sovereignty over his own people (and, indeed, over all the earth) through a line of kings that would eventuate in the divine Son of God himself. That line, David now came to understand, would begin with him.

The Uniqueness of the Davidic Kingship

Thus David, who had already assumed a priestly role apart from and superior to that of the Aaronic order, assumed the role of the vice-regent of God, the human king who, by virtue of his adoption by God, became God's son in a unique and dramatic way. The kings of the ancient Near East had long seen themselves as either divine or invested with divine authority, but David now, and all his descendants forever after, came clearly to understand that the true and only God of the universe had graciously bestowed his own sovereignty on them so that they might represent him now and prepare for the eschatological day when the last of their line, the second David, will rule alone forever.[55]

It is impossible here to pursue the theological or even historical implications of Davidic kingship in any complete way, but brief attention should be given to a few of the so-called royal psalms which

53. Walter C. Kaiser, Jr., *Toward an Old Testament Theology* (Grand Rapids: Zondervan, 1978), pp. 149–64; Talmon, "Biblical Idea," in *The Bible World*, pp. 247–48.

54. Moshe Weinfeld, "The Covenant of Grant in the Old Testament and in the Ancient Near East," *JAOS* 90 (1970): 184–203, esp. 185–86. E. Theodore Mullen, Jr., points out that among the Hittites such grants required a divine witness. Mullen suggests that though this is missing in 2 Samuel 7 and 1 Chronicles 17, it may be found in Psalm 89:37 (v. 38 in the Hebrew text), a royal oracle whose purpose, he says, is to interpret the oracle of Nathan ("The Divine Witness and the Davidic Royal Grant: Ps. 89:37–38," *JBL* 102 [1983]: 207–18).

55. Kaiser, *Toward an Old Testament Theology*, pp. 152, 161–62.

deal with that motif. In Psalm 2 David describes himself as Yahweh's "anointed one" (v. 2) who has been begotten as his son (v. 7) and who will reign over the nations of the earth (vv. 8–9). This description is hardly suitable for a mere earthly king, but only for one who, like David, has been specially chosen by Yahweh.[56] Similarly, in Psalm 18 David speaks of reigning over people who would not know him personally (v. 43) and of being the recipient of Yahweh's *hesed* ("kindness") forever (v. 50). Psalm 45 celebrates the marriage of the king and asserts that God has anointed him so that he stands above others (v. 7). In Psalm 72 Solomon speaks of the universal and eternal reign of the king (vv. 8–11); the name of the king will endure forever and in him all nations will be blessed (v. 17). David in Psalm 101 stands like Yahweh himself in the role of moral and spiritual judge. He claims prerogatives that otherwise are reserved to God alone (vv. 5–8).

It is in Psalm 110 that the two offices of David—king and priest—are juxtaposed.[57] His adoption by Yahweh is clearly expressed in verses 1–2, and he is promised victory over all his enemies by virtue of that relationship. Then he is described as a priest forever after the order of Melchizedek (v. 4). Finally, David (i.e., Christ) will, in the eschaton, judge among the nations and raise up his head in ultimate triumph (vv. 5–7).

David's response to God's unconditional promises to him and Israel in this royal grant is most important. He is first amazed that Yahweh would select him from among all people, treating him as though he were the most exalted among them (1 Chron. 17:17). He furthermore is stunned that the grant made to him is everlasting, that it pertains to his descendants after him (2 Sam. 7:19). All this, he says, has been done by the only God, who has graciously chosen and redeemed his people Israel as his everlasting possession. Finally, he prays that God might remember him and his house forever, a prayer he is confident God will answer (1 Chron. 17:27). The same sentiment is voiced in David's so-called last words (2 Sam. 23:1–7) where he asks:

> Is not my house right with God?
> Has he not made with me an everlasting covenant,
> arranged and secured in every part? [v. 5]

Beyond any question David knew that God had sovereignly chosen him as an instrument through whom he would bring both temporal and eternal blessing to the world.

---

56. Peter C. Craigie, *Psalms 1–50*, Word Biblical Commentary (Waco: Word, 1983), pp. 65–69.

57. Samuel Terrien, *The Elusive Presence* (New York: Harper and Row, 1978), pp. 295–96.

Preparation for the Temple

David's desire to build a temple for Yahweh resulted, then, in a totally unexpected benefit. He might not be able to fulfil the longings of his heart, but God instead would build for him a house through which his own sovereignty would find eternal and universal expression. Furthermore, while David would not himself construct the temple, he could at least make preparation for it. The author of 2 Samuel barely hints at this preparation, but the chronicler, who is particularly interested in cultic matters, goes into some detail.

The chronicler makes it clear, first of all, that the actual undertaking of the preparations followed the acquisition of the threshing floor of Araunah, an event which in turn must have occurred shortly after the rebellions of Absalom and Sheba. This would require a date very late in David's reign, but early enough to accommodate the recruitment of personnel, the assembling of materials, and the brief coregency with Solomon. A likely date is 973.

David began by choosing stonecutters from among the aliens living in the land and ordered them to prepare building blocks ready-cut according to specification (1 Chron. 22:2). This was possible because the Spirit of God had already revealed to him all the plans and specifications for the temple to the smallest detail (1 Chron. 28:12). He then made provision for iron, bronze, and cedar along with the stone.

Next, David charged his son Solomon with the task of completing what he could only begin (1 Chron. 22:6–13). He had wished to build the temple, he said, but God had denied him that privilege since he was a man of war. Instead God had promised him a son whose very name, Solomon (Šĕlōmōh), would speak of peace (šālôm). He would be the very son of God, as Yahweh had promised in the royal grant, and would sit on the eternal throne of David (1 Chron. 22:10). So now, David went on, the time of succession being at hand, Solomon must commit himself not only to building the temple, but to the covenant as well.

David commanded the leadership of Israel to cooperate with Solomon in every way (1 Chron. 22:17). God had given them rest on every hand, so it was now time to build the temple and move the ark into it as a sign of the residence of God among them. He then cemented this request to honor and obey Solomon by making him his coregent, thus legitimizing Solomon's authority (1 Chron. 23:1).[58]

This done, David reminded the officials of Israel of their obligations

---

58. That this is appointment to coregency is clear from the fact that David later referred to Solomon as God's chosen (1 Chron. 29:1) and that Solomon was made king "a second time" (v. 22). See Leon J. Wood, *Israel's United Monarchy* (Grand Rapids: Baker, 1979), pp. 276–77; E. Ball, "The Co-Regency of David and Solomon (1 Kings 1)" *VT* 27 (1977): 268–79.

with regard to the covenant and the temple (1 Chron. 28:1–8). He had wished to build the temple, he reiterated, but could not because he was a man of blood. However, he continued, God had chosen him to be king forever, a choice made as early as the tribal blessing of Jacob himself. Then, out of all of David's sons, Yahweh had elected Solomon to succeed him. Solomon's divine appointment, therefore, was as legitimate as his own.

In the presence of the assembled officials David proceeded to charge Solomon with his awesome responsibility of kingship (1 Chron. 28:20–21). He must not fail to be obedient and loyal to Yahweh. This included even the most minor details of temple construction. Having received by direct revelation specific instructions about the construction and appointments of the temple, David had made careful notes which he shared with Solomon (1 Chron. 28:11). The building might be undertaken by human hands, even those of Phoenician pagans, but it must conform to the design of heaven. The earthly structure was, after all, an antitype of that which existed in the mind of God, and its every detail was designed to communicate something of the nature and purposes of God. Not even the king, then, could use his imagination or creativity in such a holy project.[59]

Turning to the matter of cost, David pointed out that he had all along been accumulating precious metals and stones in the public treasury (1 Chron. 29:1–5). These objects, no doubt military spoils and tribute, were laid aside specifically for the service of Yahweh. Now David added to them his own personal resources and challenged the leaders to do likewise. The response was overwhelming—together the leaders gave over 190 tons of gold, 375 tons of silver, 675 tons of bronze, and 3,750 tons of iron in addition to precious stones (1 Chron. 29:6–9)!

Finally, David ended the assembly with a prayer of praise and supplication (1 Chron. 29:10–19). He extolled God as the one who bestows all blessing, including wealth, and the one upon whom humans depend for their very existence. He then entreated Yahweh to keep the new king and the people forever loyal and obedient to the covenant requirements. When the prayer was over, the people again expressed their commitment by bowing before both Yahweh and his anointed one, the king.

The Solomonic Succession

About two years later Solomon was brought before the people for the public coronation (see p. 248). Solomon had already been desig-

---

59. Tryggve N. D. Mettinger goes as far as to say that the temple was "heaven on earth." Though his parallels from ancient Near Eastern mythology may be questionable, his point that the temple was a terrestrial localizing of a celestial divine abode is well taken ("YHWH SABAOTH—The Heavenly King on the Cherubim Throne," in *Studies in the Period of David and Solomon*, ed. Tomoo Ishida, pp. 119–23).

nated as successor by David, but it was necessary now for this appointment to be solemnized and ratified. A similar procedure had been followed in the cases of both Saul and David. They first were chosen privately and then presented to the people for the formal ceremony of installation. The chronicler therefore points out that Solomon was acknowledged as king a second time and was anointed now before Yahweh (1 Chron. 29:22b). Pledges of submission were later tendered by all the public officials, including David's sons (1 Chron. 29:23–24).

The impression communicated by the chronicler is that the transition of power from David to Solomon was tranquil and unopposed. Such, however, was not the case, as the author of the early parts of 1 Kings makes clear. The chronicler, as usual, was interested in basic results, not in the circumstances or actions by which they were brought to pass. This is particularly true in the political area, for he was concerned primarily with matters of temple and cult.

First Kings 1–2 is connected by most scholars to the succession narrative of 2 Samuel 9–20 because the succession narrative is incomplete without it.[60] The initial setting of 1 Kings 1–2 is the last days of David, specifically the time between David's appointment of Solomon as coregent and successor (1 Chron. 23:1) and Solomon's formal coronation (1 Chron. 29:22b–24). David was now old and infirm and perhaps somewhat out of touch with everyday affairs of state. He had already disclosed his plans for building the temple and had begun to assemble workers and materials for the project. And he had let it be known that his son Solomon would both succeed him to the throne and actually oversee the construction of the temple.

Word of the official selection of Solomon did not sit well with everybody, particularly his brother Adonijah, who thought he had prior claim. Solomon, after all, was not the eldest son and so by custom could not expect to succeed his father. The eldest son, Amnon, had of course been assassinated by his brother Absalom. And Absalom, next in line apparently (Kileab, the second oldest, has disappeared from the scene), had died in an unsuccessful rebellion. Adonijah was the fourth son of David but the eldest survivor. Solomon, to the contrary, was about fifteen years younger than Adonijah; in addition, he was the product of a union that at best was scandalous. Nonetheless, Solomon was loved by Yahweh from his birth (2 Sam. 12:24), and it was clear to David from that time forward that Solomon would be king in his place (1 Chron. 22:9–10).

When it became obvious to Adonijah and his followers that David

60. Ishida, "Solomon's Succession," pp. 186–87.

was about to make the selection of Solomon official by public coronation, he undertook preemptive measures. He gathered a personal military contingent, evidently without causing any alarm to David, and then surreptitiously enlisted both Joab and Abiathar as co-conspirators. These, together with his remaining brothers and other officials, he assembled at En Rogel (Bir Ayyub) near the junction of the Kidron and Hinnom valleys. There the rebel throng acclaimed Adonijah king (1 Kings 1:9, 11, 18).

The prophet Nathan meanwhile learned of the plot and through Bathsheba informed David of all that had transpired. Nathan then entered the king's chambers and confirmed what Bathsheba had said. He went on to point out to David that hesitation to act would mean that David's plans for the orderly succession of Solomon would be to no avail, for Adonijah would usurp the throne. David therefore called Zadok the priest and others of his loyal men and ordered them to take immediate steps to arrange a ceremony of coronation for Solomon at Gihon, which was in the Kidron Valley just north of En Rogel.

In accordance with David's command, Zadok, Nathan, and others escorted Solomon, who was riding upon David's own royal mule, to Gihon, where Zadok formally anointed Solomon as king. The people, though assembled hastily and perhaps not in great number, acknowledged with joy and solemn commitment the sovereignty of Solomon and pledged to serve him (1 Kings 1:39–40; 1 Chron. 29:22). The sounds of acclamation and festivity reached the ears of Adonijah and his conclave, who were still celebrating their own political triumph not far away. Just then a messenger arrived to tell them that their plot had failed, for Solomon had been crowned with the sanction of both David and the general population. Adonijah's fellow schemers therefore fled in panic while he himself rushed to the great altar on Mount Zion to find sanctuary from the punitive wrath of Solomon. Solomon graciously pardoned him, however, and invited him to share in the celebration of royal succession. Accordingly, the chronicler states, "All the officers and mighty men, as well as all of King David's sons, pledged their submission to King Solomon" (1 Chron. 29:24).

Sometime very shortly after Solomon's coronation, his father David died at the age of seventy, having reigned for a total of forty years—seven at Hebron and thirty-three at Jerusalem. The chronicler notes that he had enjoyed long life, wealth, and honor and that the details of his reign might be found in the records of Samuel, Nathan, and Gad. The records of Samuel have, of course, survived in the canonical books of Samuel. The works of Nathan and Gad are mentioned only in the books of the chronicler, having evidently served as the major sources of information not found in Samuel.

The Davidic Bureaucracy

The Military

A state as large and important as Israel had become under David required an elaborate political and religious superstructure.[61] Indeed, as early as his days of flight from Saul, David had begun to attract persons around him who eventually became the nucleus of his government. For obvious reasons this core group of six hundred (1 Sam. 27:2) was essentially military in character at the beginning. In the course of his exile he was also joined by Abiathar, the son of Ahimelech the priest; Abiathar was to serve for many years as David's personal chaplain.

Little is known of the seven years at Hebron except that Joab served as military commander, at least unofficially. After he later led the way into Jerusalem, he was confirmed in that position and maintained it, albeit very tenuously at times, until the accession of Solomon, when he opted to follow Adonijah rather than Solomon. Abiathar also presumably continued to function as priest, though how and with what kind of cultic apparatus is not clear. David's own family grew in those years partly, at least, by virtue of political marriages which he contracted with the daughters of foreign kings and chieftains. He was thus establishing at least modest international relations even during his reign at Hebron.

The six hundred men of David must have become a much greater force after he became king over Judah, but there is no specific information to that effect. The fact that Abner felt the need to negotiate with David rather than go to war with him indicates that David posed a formidable military challenge to Israel. One must remember, of course, that Israel's armies had been decimated by the Philistines at Gilboa. Once installed as king over all Israel, however, David was able to defeat these same Philistines at least twice at Rephaim.

The unification of Judah and Israel brought with it not only a great deal more responsibility for David, but the need to create structures adequate to enable the nation to recover from the traumas of external military threat and internal intertribal conflict. Once a modicum of unity had been achieved, David was able to centralize government in Jerusalem without sacrificing local tribal distinctions and interests. At best, however, this was a loose federation, for up till the last years of his life David had to struggle with the tendency toward fragmentation, especially between Judah and the north. Yet the success of his

61. For a helpful overview see S. Yeivin, "Administration," in *World History of the Jewish People*, vol. 5, pp. 147–71.

early wars with the Ammonites, Arameans, and others attests to his ability to organize the nation, at least on a temporary basis.

The heart of David's army, however, continued to consist of those who had served him in the desert in the early years. These troops were led by thirty chiefs over whom were "three mighty men" and Joab (2 Sam. 23:8–39). While he was at Ziklag, David had been joined by certain kinsmen of Saul himself as well as a number of Gadites and Manassehites (1 Chron. 12:1–22). These were greatly augmented by thousands from the remaining tribes who went to Hebron in armed militias to make David king of all Israel. Most of these, however, were not regular troops but reserves called up as the need required.

During ordinary times twenty-four thousand men were on duty each month (1 Chron. 27:1–15). While each tribe had its own top military official (vv. 16–22), there is nothing to indicate that those officials had anything to do with the monthly assignments. Rather, the officers in charge of each month and the twenty-four thousand men under their command apparently were not assigned by tribal divisions.

The Civilian

In addition to the military component there were, of course, civilian officials attending to the various departments of the central government. These included a recorder (or chronicler), a scribe (or secretary), counselors, and other officers whose duties are not specified; among the last-mentioned category were David's own sons (1 Chron. 18:17). Lesser administrators were in charge of the central and outlying storehouses, the field workers, the vineyards and the wine industry, the olive and sycamore-fig trees, the olive-oil industry, the herds, the camels, the donkeys, and the flocks (1 Chron. 27:25–31). This implies both royal ownership of these commodities and businesses and strong regulatory control of the private sector.

The Religious

The religious structure of Israel under David was also highly organized. One can only speculate, however, as to the nature of the cult and the composition of the cultic personnel prior to the arrival of the ark in Jerusalem. Abiathar, a descendant of Eli, was the chief priest in the pre-Hebron and Hebron years, but how he functioned is unclear. He did have the priestly ephod with him by which he could ascertain the will of God in certain matters, but state sacrifice and other religious exercises must have been conducted at various high places, particularly that at Gibeon where the Mosaic tabernacle was erected.

Once David had built his own tabernacle and installed the ark at

Zion, he introduced, along with the plans for the temple, a highly refined religious hierarchy that would minister there (1 Chron. 23–26). David himself presumably continued to take his place as royal priest. Both Abiathar and Zadok served as Aaronic priests on the occasion of the transfer of the ark to Jerusalem (1 Chron. 15:11). Zadok later served in that capacity at the Mosaic tabernacle at Gibeon (1 Chron. 16:39–40). This must have been for only a few years, however, for at the time of Absalom's rebellion Zadok was in charge of the ark, which, of course, was at Jerusalem. Some time later Abiathar apparently stepped aside from an active role, and his son Ahimelech became priest (2 Sam. 8:17; 1 Chron. 18:16). For some unknown reason Ahimelech disappears from view, and at the time of Solomon's succession Abiathar once more appears as priest, this time opposed to David.[62] This mistake on Abiathar's part cost him the priesthood, for Solomon, once he had become king, deposed him and replaced him with Zadok alone. Thus the priesthood of Eli came to an end and the Zadokite began in a formal manner.

The Levites had participated with the priests in the relocation of the ark. Not until then is there any sign of organization and assignment of responsibility to the various Levitical families. In fact, the failure to bring up the ark the first time is attributed to a lack of proper Levitical procedure (1 Chron. 15:13). David therefore commanded certain Levites to attend to the proper care and maintenance of the ark (1 Chron. 16:4–6).[63] What that meant in terms of everyday worship at Zion is not entirely clear, since the great bronze altar of Moses was still at Gibeon. One must suppose that an altar was built at Zion as well (we do know, of course, that David erected an altar after purchasing the threshing floor of Araunah), since ministering before the ark required sacrifice (1 Chron. 16:1–2).

With the plans for the temple and the more elaborate cultus it would entail came a further delineation of Levitical responsibility. David took a count of the Levites and tallied up thirty-eight thousand who were thirty years old or more. Of these, twenty-four thousand were assigned to be temple ministers, six thousand to be officials and

---

62. P. Kyle McCarter, Jr., *II Samuel*, Anchor Bible (Garden City, N.Y.: Doubleday, 1984), pp. 253–54, suggests, with many scholars, that 2 Samuel 8:17 is corrupt and should read "Abiathar son of Ahimelech." This is unlikely since elsewhere Zadok and Ahimelech are listed as copriests (1 Chron. 24:3, 31) and Ahimelech is identified as a son of Abiathar (1 Chron. 24:6). For a strong argument in support of our view that Abiathar was replaced for a time by his son and then reappeared see Carl F. Keil and Franz Delitzsch, *Biblical Commentary on the Books of Samuel* (Grand Rapids: Eerdmans, 1960 reprint), pp. 355–67.

63. For the function of priests, Levites, and other temple personnel in the Davidic period see de Vaux, *Ancient Israel*, vol. 2, pp. 372–86.

judges, four thousand to be gatekeepers, and four thousand musicians. All of these in turn were further divided by their respective Levitical clans—Gershon, Kohath, and Merari. The priests were organized into twenty-four divisions determined by the casting of lots; each division took its turn in the service of the temple. Since the Levites served the priests, they were divided similarly (1 Chron. 24:31).

By the time of David's death, then, a carefully devised political and religious apparatus was in place. The old tribal distinctions still existed, but with David there had come at last a sense of national unity in both secular and spiritual affairs. Israel was now a full-fledged nation among the nations of the world. All the constituent elements associated with nationhood—army, political bureaucracy, and central cult—were well established. It was up to Solomon now to build on that foundation and to make God's people a kingdom of priests through whom God would bless the world.

8 Solomon: From Pinnacle to Peril

Problems of Transition

By the time of David's death he had created and was able to pass on a monarchy that allowed Israel to take a leading place among the nations of the contemporary world. He had united the tribes without obliterating their separate identities and loyalties; he had secured Israel's borders against her traditional enemies; he had entered into relationships with newly emerging states such as the Aramean kingdoms, usually in a role of superiority to them; and he had established Jerusalem as both the political and religious center of the nation. This last contribution is the most significant of all, for it symbolized the merging of the patriarchal and Sinaitic covenant traditions with the notion of divinely appointed human monarchy. David had come to understand that he, as the adopted son of Yahweh, not only ruled over but also represented his people. He was able to persuade the nation of this truth and thus to prepare it for its historical and eschatological role as the servant nation to whom the peoples of the earth must look for salvation.

The Concept of Dynastic Succession

As was noted previously (pp. 279–80), the transfer from David to Solomon did not proceed without a hitch or two. The very idea of dynasty was itself distasteful to some of the Israelites. Moreover, those who did accept a Davidic dynasty maintained, in line with the norms prevailing elsewhere, that the throne should not go to Solomon, but to Adonijah, the eldest surviving son. This view of kingship was so keenly felt that even though David had made it known well in advance of his death that Solomon should be his regal heir, an attempt was made by Adonijah and his supporters to preempt his brother's coronation. While the plot failed, it did have the result of alerting Solomon to the dangers, actual and potential, which confronted his new administration.

The reasons for the support of Adonijah by individuals who had been among David's staunchest and most loyal friends are not altogether clear. They must go beyond the tradition of the eldest son as dynastic heir, however, for surely David's expressed wishes in the matter outweighed that consideration. Nor can the answer lie only in a dislike of Solomon, for there is nothing in the record to that effect. In fact, the tenor of the account of the conspiracy is that it was not directed against Solomon at all but against David. Solomon just happened to be the person who stood between Adonijah and the throne.

The Disloyalty of Joab

The best solution appears to be the personal vainglory and ambition of the conspirators. Adonijah felt victimized because David had bypassed him in favor of Solomon, so he decided to take matters into his own hands. This required collaborators, men who shared his ambition and acted out of a similar sense of frustration. That one of these was Joab is not at all surprising. Joab was, of course, a nephew of David, the son of his sister Zeruiah (1 Chron. 2:16). He had distinguished himself by faithful service to David since the pre-Hebron years and had eventually become Israel's chief military officer. But Joab seemed baffled over and over again by what he perceived to be a vacillating or at least ambiguous attitude on David's part concerning diplomatic and military policy. Where Joab would advise and pursue a vigorous and violent course of action against David's enemies—including Abner and Absalom—David invariably "turned the other cheek" and sought more peaceful means of dealing with them. Without doubt Joab viewed this as a sign of weakness in David, a weakness he may have seen in young Solomon as well.

An even stronger motivation was Joab's awareness of his own diminishing role in David's plans. Joab's responsibility for the death of Absalom and insensitivity to David's grief had led to his being replaced, much to his chagrin, by his cousin Amasa of all people, a man who had just served in the same capacity under Absalom! Joab did manage to regain his position by murdering Amasa, but relations with David must have been extremely strained from that time on. It was most likely that in the transfer of power to Solomon, Joab would be demoted once more. And so he decided to side with Adonijah in the hope that Adonijah would prevail and make him commander in the new regime.

The Disloyalty of Abiathar

The second major ally of Adonijah was the priest Abiathar. Abiathar, like Joab, had stayed with David through thick and thin since the time he had fled the sanctuary at Nob to join David in the wilderness. He even enjoyed the privilege of ministering at the sacred ark in the Davidic tabernacle while his copriest Zadok officiated at Gibeon. What, then, convinced Abiathar to abandon David and Solomon and participate in the pro-Adonijah movement? The answer, we submit, is similar to the reason for the disloyalty of Joab—and, indeed, that of Adonijah himself. Abiathar feared loss of influence and perhaps even replacement as chief priest.

Abiathar was a direct descendant of Eli, a priest of the Aaronic line of Ithamar (1 Chron. 24:1–6),[1] which was to end because of the sins of

1. For defense of this genealogy see Eugene H. Merrill, "1 Chronicles," in *The Bible Knowledge Commentary*, ed. John F. Walvoord and Roy B. Zuck (Wheaton, Ill.: Victor, 1985), vol. 1, p. 613; Carl F. Keil and Franz Delitzsch, *Biblical Commentary on the Books of Samuel* (Grand Rapids: Eerdmans, 1960 reprint), pp. 39–40. Even Frank M. Cross admits that "the Chronicler traces Zadok to the Aaronid Eleazar, Abiathar to the Aaronid Ithamar" (*Canaanite Myth and Hebrew Epic* [Cambridge: Harvard University Press, 1973], p. 196).

Eli's sons (1 Sam. 2:30–36; cf. 1 Kings 2:27). Surely Abiathar was aware of that judgment and must have constantly guarded against the possibility of its being fulfilled in his lifetime. As long as he enjoyed David's favor he had little to fear. But that favor had come under a cloud somewhat in more recent years. Abiathar, to be sure, had remained chief priest even after the ark came to Jerusalem, but he found himself more and more threatened by the young priest Zadok. Zadok, in fact, first appears in the record in connection with the removal of the ark from the house of Obed-Edom (1 Chron. 15:11). Before long he was copriest with Abiathar, serving first at Gibeon and then with the ark on Mount Zion (2 Sam. 15:24), until at last his name preceded that of Abiathar when they were mentioned together (2 Sam. 20:25).

Most alarming to Abiathar, however, was the fact that Zadok traced his lineage back to Eleazar, son of Aaron, and therefore represented the priestly branch which someday would replace the branch of which he himself was a part. It is no wonder, then, that Abiathar thought it prudent to join the pro-Adonijah movement, which seemed to offer such promise. It seemed entirely logical to him that a change in kingship to Solomon would also usher in a sweeping change in priesthood—Zadok would be in and he would be out.

Zadok's background as priest is shrouded in mystery though 1 Chronicles 16:39 may offer some hint—"David left Zadok the priest and his fellow priests before the tabernacle of the LORD at the high place in Gibeon." Does this imply that Zadok had served there previously?[2] If so, it is more than likely that he was descended from a family of priests installed there by Saul after the atrocity at Nob. If this view is correct, Saul, by turning to the descendants of Eleazar rather than those of Ithamar, had played a role in bringing about the fulfilment of Samuel's prophecy about a new priestly succession. This would have made Zadok's employment by David all the more odious to Abiathar, for he, Abiathar, had shown his loyalty to David from the beginning by his having left Saul. For Zadok now to gain the priestly ascendancy would have been more than Abiathar could tolerate.

The Failure of the Opposition to Solomon

Even with such influential support Adonijah was unable to have his way. Zadok, Benaiah, Nathan, and other confidants of David were more than capable of undercutting Adonijah's ambitious scheme; and they did, of course, see to it that David secured Solomon on his throne

---

2. Roland de Vaux argues that this is the intended meaning of the chronicler (*Ancient Israel* [New York: McGraw-Hill, 1965], vol. 2, pp. 373–74).

before it was too late. But even then the apparent acquiescence by Adonijah and his cohorts soon gave way to other signs of disloyalty and dissatisfaction. David had warned Solomon about such contingencies, especially with reference to Joab, and in fact had advised Solomon to do what he himself had never mustered the resolve to do—punish Joab in kind for the bloody assassinations he had engineered in the past (1 Kings 2:5–6). It seems, however, that Solomon was genuinely interested in forgiveness and reconciliation. A bloody purge at the very beginning of his reign would belie David's characterization of his son as a man of peace and undermine the high level of popular morale which was everywhere evident.

No sooner had David died than the undercurrents of opposition to Solomon began to surface. First, Adonijah requested permission of Bathsheba, now the queen mother, to take David's concubine Abishag as his own. Solomon clearly understood the intent of the request: "You might as well request the kingdom for him—after all, he is my older brother"(1 Kings 2:22). Adonijah was seeking once more to further his political interests, and not so subtly at that, for transfer of the royal harem would imply transfer of the royal authority as well. Solomon, convinced now of Adonijah's hopeless intransigence, ordered Benaiah to execute him.

Solomon was also persuaded of the continuing disaffection of Abiathar and therefore confined him to virtual house arrest in his home village of Anathoth.[3] At last the priestly line fell exclusively to the descendants of Eleazar. Joab, when he heard of Solomon's drastic and decisive measures, fled for his life to the great altar on Zion. After repeated requests to leave the sanctuary, all unsuccessful, Joab, so often the instigator of murderous brutality, fell by the hand of Benaiah. Thus the vengeance called for by the deaths of Abner and Amasa took effect. Benaiah then took Joab's place as head of the military command.

Though by these means Solomon overcame the threat from Adonijah, his appetite for revenge seemed whetted for more. He first summoned Shimei, the kinsman of Saul who had derisively mocked David on his way into exile (2 Sam. 16:5 8). Solomon placed him under

3. Nob, probably to be identified with el-'Isāwîyeh, was less than two miles from Anathoth, without doubt Râs el-Kharrûbeh. Both lay less than three miles northeast of Jerusalem (Yohanan Aharoni and Michael Avi-Yonah, *Macmillan Bible Atlas* [New York: Macmillan, 1968], map 154). It is likely that following the collapse of Shiloh as the cult center the priests in the line of Ithamar (and of Eli) resided at Anathoth, but made Nob the site of the tabernacle. See Tryggve N. D. Mettinger, "YHWH SABAOTH—The Heavenly King on the Cherubim Throne," in *Studies in the Period of David and Solomon and Other Essays*, ed. Tomoo Ishida (Winona Lake, Ind.: Eisenbrauns, 1983), p. 129.

house arrest as well, warning him that if he left Jerusalem he would die. Three years later Shimei left the city to catch two runaway slaves, and Solomon had him put to death. In light of such acts of retribution it is no wonder that the author of Kings says, "The kingdom was now firmly established in Solomon's hands" (1 Kings 2:46).

The Conclave at Gibeon

The chronology of the reign of Solomon does not pose nearly the difficulty as does that of David. With the exception of the nonnarrative passages, which appear as usual to be inserted topically, the order found in both 1 Kings and 2 Chronicles reflects the general flow of events. It does seem, however, that Solomon's alliance with Siamun of Egypt (1 Kings 3:1) did not come to pass until after he had begun negotiations with the Tyrians to help on the temple. This in turn presupposes Solomon's having sought and been granted wisdom, for Hiram takes note of that fact (1 Kings 5:7).

The chronicler, then, is correct in beginning his account of the reign of Solomon with Solomon's appearance before Yahweh at Gibeon. Why Solomon went there to assemble the people rather than to Mount Zion is not clear. It may well be, as the chronicler suggests (2 Chron. 1:1–6), that Solomon's interest on this occasion was in sacrificing and not in the ark. After all, the great bronze altar at Gibeon was the Mosaic original; the one at Zion enjoyed no such hoary tradition.[4]

In any case, Solomon's decision to hold the conclave at Gibeon was not displeasing to Yahweh, for Yahweh appeared to him there and granted him the desire of his heart—that he might have wisdom to lead his people. In addition, Yahweh promised him riches and honor without compare.

The prayer of Solomon on this occasion is particularly significant, for it reveals clearly his perception of his role as covenant heir in the Davidic dynastic succession. He saw himself as the fulfilment of the divine promise to David (1 Kings 3:6) and as the occupant of David's throne by virtue of Yahweh's election and sovereign choice. These thoughts were to be more fully elaborated in Solomon's prayer dedicating the temple.[5]

---

4. In addition, as Jacob M. Myers observes, Zadok was still associated with Gibeon and may well have urged Solomon to seek Yahweh there (*II Chronicles*, Anchor Bible [Garden City, N.Y.: Doubleday, 1965], p. 6).

5. Roddy L. Braun points out that the chronicler begins the entire account of Solomon with his being chosen to construct the temple (1 Chron. 22, 28–29), as though that were Solomon's primary if not sole objective ("Solomon, the Chosen Temple Builder: The Significance of 1 Chronicles 22, 28, and 29 for the Theology of Chronicles," *JBL* 95 [1976]: 581–90).

International Relations

Israel and Tyre

Very shortly after this theophanic visitation Solomon received messengers from Hiram, king of Tyre, who tendered his congratulations to Solomon upon his accession to Israel's throne. This he did, 1 Kings 5:1 says, because he had always been on friendly terms with David. Having come to power in the great seaport of Tyre by 980,[6] Hiram was contemporaneous with David for nearly ten years. He had undertaken building programs for David, so now Solomon capitalized on both his friendship and his expertise by inviting him to cooperate with him in the construction of the temple and other public projects which he had in mind.

Hiram was delighted with the proposal and suggested that he send the timber by sea to Joppa where Solomon could pick it up for transshipment to Jerusalem. He would also send skilled craftsmen to help with the intricacies of construction. These artisans would be placed under the supervision of Huram-Abi, a half-Israelite who was proficient in every kind of art and craft (2 Chron. 2:13–14; cf. 1 Kings 7:13–14).[7] In return Solomon would provide Hiram with grains and other foodstuffs in huge amounts. When all these arrangements had been agreed upon, they were ratified by a formal contract (1 Kings 5:12).[8]

Israel and Egypt

Sometime between the accession of Solomon and the commencement of temple construction in his fourth year he had made a treaty with the pharaoh of Egypt, a treaty which may have been prompted by the one which Solomon had just consummated with Hiram. The pharaoh at this time was Siamun of Dynasty 21, who reigned from 978 to 959. Though primarily concerned with domestic affairs, Siamun

6. See p. 239. Michael B. Rowton, though lowering the dates of both Solomon and Hiram by nine years, shows that there is remarkable agreement between biblical and Phoenician sources on the date of the temple ("The Date of the Founding of Solomon's Temple," *BASOR* 119 [1950]: 20–22).

7. For identification of Huram-Abi see H. Jacob Katzenstein, *The History of Tyre* (Jerusalem: Schocken Institute for Jewish Research, 1973), p. 100. The author of Kings calls him the son of a widow of Naphtali, while the chronicler says he was a Danite. His mother was likely a Danite by birth and Naphtalite by residence or vice versa. See Eugene H. Merrill, "2 Chronicles," in *Bible Knowledge Commentary*, vol. 1, p. 621.

8. That this contract involved more than a business transaction is clear from the use of the technical term *šālôm* ("peaceful relations"). See John Gray, *I & II Kings* (Philadelphia: Westminster, 1970), p. 154.

did take some interest in Palestine, as is attested by a relief depicting him in a victory pose over a group of prisoners who can be identified as Philistines by virtue of a double axe of a type used in the Aegean and west Anatolian regions.[9] These may have been subdued when, as 1 Kings 9:16 tells us, Pharaoh attacked and captured Gezer, setting it on fire and killing its Canaanite inhabitants. The date of this anti-Philistine campaign is unclear. We earlier suggested (p. 251) that if David collaborated in this action, a date soon after 978 is probable. If, on the other hand, David did not participate, the destruction of Gezer likely occurred in the last few years of his reign, when he was distracted by other problems such as the devastating plague brought on by his ill-advised census.[10]

In any case, Siamun soon realized that Solomon was to be ruler of a kingdom which would rival or even exceed his own in power and influence. He therefore decided it was to his best advantage to cultivate amicable relations with the young monarch, even to the extent of recognizing him as an equal.[11] That this is the case is clear from his willingness to provide his own daughter as a wife for Solomon, a concession almost without parallel in Egyptian history since it was a candid admission to the world of Egypt's weakness and conciliation. Normally Egyptian kings took foreign princesses but did not give up their own daughters to foreign kings.[12]

The reason for this arrangement, as has been suggested, may well have been that Siamun, fearing that the Israel-Tyre treaty might turn Solomon against Egypt, felt the need for a counterbalance. There is also the possibility that Siamun wished to deal with the irritating presence of the Philistines on his northeastern border by using Solomon as a neutralizing agent against them. Most likely of all, however,

9. Pierre Montet, *Egypt and the Bible* (Philadelphia: Fortress, 1968), pp. 36–39. For objections to this interpretation of the so-called Tanis relief see Alberto R. Green, "Solomon and Siamun: A Synchronism Between Dynastic Israel and the Twenty-first Dynasty of Egypt," *JBL* 97 (1978): 363–64. Green still considers Siamun to be Solomon's father-in-law, however.

10. Abraham Malamat concedes that the conquest of Gezer may have preceded Solomon's sole regency ("A Political Look at the Kingdom of David and Solomon and Its Relations with Egypt," in *Studies in the Period of David and Solomon*, ed. Tomoo Ishida, p. 198).

11. The prestige of Solomon was so great that Egyptian administrative practice began to be modeled after that of Israel. See Alberto R. Green, "Israelite Influence at Shishak's Court?" *BASOR* 233 (1979): 59–62.

12. Alan R. Schulman, "Diplomatic Marriage in the Egyptian New Kingdom," *JNES* 38 (1979): 190–91. H. Darrell Lance suggests that Gezer belonged to Egypt at the beginning of Solomon's reign and that an unsuccessful attack on Israel by Siamun led to the city's becoming a property of Solomon. The "giving" of the city as a dowry was, then, a gift over which Siamun had no control ("Gezer in the Land and in History," *BA* 30 [1967]: 34–47).

is that Siamun viewed with apprehension the increasing militance and imperialism of the Assyrians far to the north and east. An alliance with Solomon would create a buffer between Egypt and Assyria extending all the way to the Euphrates River.

Concerns about Assyria would have been well founded, for Tiglath-pileser I had, one hundred years earlier, established an intimidating presence in Syria and Phoenicia and had even wrung concessions from Egypt.[13] It is true that Assyria had then entered a period of decline, primarily because of difficulties with the Arameans, but it was clear to all astute observers of the international scene that Assyria would eventually pose a major threat to the entire eastern Mediterranean world. This would not actually materialize until long after Siamun and Solomon, but the possibility persuaded Egypt and Israel to make common cause at least as long as Solomon was powerful.

As part of the marriage transaction Pharaoh ceded to Solomon the city of Gezer as dowry for his daughter. Gezer lay on the route between the seaport of Joppa and Jerusalem. Since the building materials Solomon secured from Hiram passed along that route with no apparent interruption, one may conclude that Gezer was under Solomon's control by the time construction of the temple actually began. Two chronological considerations may now be adduced to enable us to date the treaty between Siamun and Solomon and the marriage it entailed. The temple was begun in 966, Solomon's fourth year; this event must have followed Solomon's acquisition of Gezer. We also know that the death of Shimei took place in 967, the third year of Solomon's reign (1 Kings 2:39). That act and others like it testified to Solomon's firm control of the kingdom (1 Kings 2:46) and probably led to Siamun's recognition of Solomon's power.

The Building Projects of Solomon

The Temple

Construction and design

Once Solomon had firm control, he turned his attention to massive construction projects, beginning with the building of the temple itself. David had, of course, purchased the threshing floor of Araunah, the divinely chosen site, and had already cleared the area so the work could begin. He had also prepared building materials, particularly

13. D. J. Wiseman, "Assyria and Babylonia c. 1200–1000 B.C.," in *Cambridge Ancient History*, 3d ed., ed. I. E. S. Edwards et al. (Cambridge: Cambridge University Press, 1975), vol. 2, part 2, p. 461.

ready-cut stone blocks and precious metals, and had entered into preliminary negotiations with the Phoenicians for timber. All Solomon
had to do now was to bring the materials and builders together and
undertake the actual construction.

Word was sent to Hiram that all was ready, so Hiram began to
deliver timber as he had promised. In return, Solomon sent foodstuffs
and other goods as payment. He also conscripted thirty thousand lum-
bermen to go in monthly shifts of ten thousand to assist Hiram's workers in the Lebanon mountains. Seventy thousand carriers were pressed
into service along with eighty thousand stonecutters. All of these laborers were supervised by thirty-three hundred foremen who in turn
answered to Adoniram, the officer in charge of forced labor (1 Kings
5:13–18).[14]

Unfortunately, even though a great deal of information is given in
the sources concerning the specifications and appearance of the temple, it is impossible to reproduce it in precise detail.[15] Its basic pattern
is identical both to the Mosaic tabernacle and to ancient Near Eastern
temples in general,[16] but beyond that its unique features must for the
most part remain the subject of architectural and artistic imagination
based on the rather sparse and at points unintelligible descriptions in
the text. It is clear, nonetheless, that the temple was a breathtakingly
beautiful and imposing monument to the awesome majesty and glory
of God. Seven years in the making, it must have been without compare
amongst the creations of human skill in the ancient Near Eastern
world.

The appearance of the Lord

When the building was completed and its furnishings, manufactured under the supervision of Huram-Abi, had been installed, Solomon set about to bring the ark of the covenant from its place in the
Davidic tabernacle on Mount Zion to its new resting-place on Mount
Moriah (1 Kings 8:1–11).[17] With proper protocol and reverence the
elders, priests, and king joined in procession with the ark, offering

14. For the system of corvée or forced labor in Israel see J. Alberto Soggin, "Compulsory Labor Under David and Solomon," in *Studies in the Period of David and Solomon*, ed. Tomoo Ishida, pp. 259–67.

15. For efforts at reproducing the temple see Carol L. Meyers, "The Elusive Temple," *BA* 45 (1982): 33–41; Mina C. Klein and H. Arthur Klein, *Temple Beyond Time*
(New York: Van Nostrand Reinhold, 1970), pp. 35–49.

16. William F. Albright, *Archaeology and the Religion of Israel* (Garden City, N.Y.:
Doubleday, 1969), pp. 138–50.

17. Richard E. Friedman has argued cogently that the very tabernacle itself was
removed and placed within the temple ("The Tabernacle in the Temple," *BA* 43 [1980]:
241–48).

sacrifices without number along the way. Once the ark was placed in the Holy of Holies behind the veil and the priests withdrew, the whole building was filled with the cloud of Yahweh's presence. This signaled that Yahweh approved of all that David and Solomon had done in erecting the temple as the visible symbol of his residence among his people.

Solomon responded to this evidence of God's localized presence by equating the thick darkness of the cloud with divine possession of the temple. He then, as royal and priestly mediator, turned to the people to bless them as David had done when the ark was brought to the Zion tabernacle. The blessing consisted of the recognition that the promise to David that his son would build the temple had been fulfilled. Solomon clearly perceived and articulated the dynastic aspect of the covenant which Yahweh had made with his father (1 Kings 8:20). Now he, Solomon, sat on the throne of David and in the office of king had provided a place where the ark, the symbol of God's redemptive work in behalf of Israel, might find repose. Thus he linked the Mosaic covenant, in which a servant people had been elected and delivered, with the Davidic, in which a messianic king had been called to establish a line that would someday reign over all the earth.[18]

The prayer of Solomon and dedication of the temple

The connection of covenants only hinted at in the blessing by Solomon is more fully presented in his dedicatory prayer which follows. In this remarkable theological treatise Solomon first celebrates the uniqueness and incomparability of Yahweh, the God who has kept covenant with David and now with his son (1 Kings 8:22–26). The king then acknowledges the insufficiency of even this magnificent temple to house the Sovereign of heaven and earth. Yet, he says, God has condescended to localize himself in the temple in a special way and insists that his people look to him there. If they sin and consequently suffer defeat, drought, pestilence, or even captivity, they must in repentance look to Yahweh in the temple that he might forgive and restore them. This Yahweh will do, Solomon prays, because they are his people whom he redeemed from Egypt as his own special inheritance (vv. 27–53).

Following the prayer Solomon stood again to bless the assembly. He reminded them that the dedication of the temple was a sign of the fulfilment of the promises Yahweh had given through Moses. That is, the Davidic kingship and Solomonic succession were not inimical to the covenant purposes of God for Israel; they were, in fact, the logical and theological extension of those purposes (vv. 54–61).

18. Gray, *I & II Kings*, p. 213.

Finally, as royal priest Solomon led in the offering of an immense sacrifice to Yahweh.[19] He then proclaimed a nationwide festival lasting for fourteen days. On the following day the people returned to their homes, rejoicing in the blessing of God upon their king and their nation (vv. 62–66).

The Royal Palace

Upon the completion of the temple Solomon undertook the construction of his own magnificent palace, a project which required thirteen years. It seems quite clear that the two were undertaken in sequence and not simultaneously, for even though 1 Kings 3:1 speaks of Solomon's "building his palace and the temple of the LORD," the historian elsewhere indicates that it took seven years to build the temple (1 Kings 6:38) and thirteen to build the palace (1 Kings 7:1) and that the entire period of construction was twenty years (1 Kings 9:10). The temple, then, was completed by 959 B.C., and the palace not until 946.

The royal residence was even larger than the temple, consisting apparently of a major central building, the Palace of the Forest of Lebanon, and either wings or semidetached structures such as the Hall of Justice and Solomon's own private quarters. It is not possible to determine how these various edifices were oriented to each other or to the temple, but the whole complex must have been extremely impressive.[20] Israel's kingship without doubt began to compare favorably with those of the great nations of the world, if public buildings are any kind of a barometer.

All the while Siamun's daughter had resided in temporary facilities on Mount Zion. Now that the temple and his own palace had been finished, Solomon built a palace for this, his favorite wife, a building which resembled the Hall of Justice and his own quarters. The reasons for her transfer from Zion are not without interest—protective walls had not previously been built around the new section of the city where the temple was located (1 Kings 3:1; cf. 9:24); and, on a more negative note, her continued residence in the palace of David was an affront to its holiness (2 Chron. 8:11). The chronicler thus records Solomon's

19. Solomon's actual function in sacrifice is not as clear as was David's when he led the procession bringing the ark to Jerusalem (2 Sam. 6), but it is obvious, nonetheless, that he is carrying out some cultic duties. See Dennis J. McCarthy, "Compact and Kingship: Stimuli for Hebrew Covenant Thinking," in *Studies in the Period of David and Solomon*, ed. Tomoo Ishida, pp. 81–82.

20. David Ussishkin identifies at least six separate structures, some of which were joined together into complexes ("King Solomon's Palaces," *BA* 36 [1973]: 78–105).

sensitivity to the problem of a pagan wife in the midst of the covenant people.[21]

Other Projects

Though none of Solomon's other construction projects can be dated with precision, it is appropriate to mention them here as tribute both to his industry and domestic prosperity and to his far-flung political and commercial dominion. First of all, he strengthened and enlarged Jerusalem itself by building a circumferential wall which enclosed the original Jebusite town of Ophel (i.e., Mount Zion or the City of David) and the area of the temple and public buildings just to the north of Ophel. The area enclosed was, on the average, one thousand yards from north to south and two hundred from east to west. By the standards of that part of the ancient world this was a significant city.[22] As part of the defensive structure or as a leveling project Solomon also worked on the Millo (1 Kings 9:15, 24; 11:27). This word, which literally means "filling," probably refers to terracelike structures built on the precipitous hillsides.[23] This would of course facilitate the construction of both defensive walls and buildings of various kinds.

Outside the capital Solomon authorized the reconstruction and fortification of other cities, particularly Hazor, Megiddo, and Gezer (1 Kings 9:15).[24] These three sites, all of which were strategically located on commercial routes, provided storage facilities and military headquarters from which Solomon could exercise effective control. Excavation at all three places has yielded abundant evidence of common design and purpose in Solomonic times. Beth Horon (Beit 'Ur et-Taḥtā), just northwest of Gibeon, and Baalath (Qatra), just southwest of Gezer, were also refortified, mainly, no doubt, against the Philistines or any others who might attempt to penetrate interior Israel from the

21. H. G. M. Williamson, *1 and 2 Chronicles*, New Century Bible Commentary (Grand Rapids: Eerdmans, 1982), p. 231.

22. Kathleen Kenyon, *Jerusalem* (New York: McGraw-Hill, 1967), pp. 56–58.

23. Ibid., pp. 50–51. For a contrary view—that the terraces ought to be identified with the "fields of the Kidron Valley" (*šadmôt qidrôn*—2 Kings 23:4) and not the Millo—see Lawrence E. Stager, "The Archaeology of the East Slope of Jerusalem and the Terraces of the Kidron," *JNES* 41 (1982): 111–21.

24. See, respectively, Yigael Yadin, "Excavations at Hazor (1955–1958)," in *The Biblical Archaeologist Reader*, ed. Edward F. Campbell, Jr., and David Noel Freedman (Garden City, N.Y.: Doubleday, 1964), vol. 2, p. 199; Yadin, "New Light on Solomon's Megiddo," in *The Biblical Archaeologist Reader*, vol. 2, pp. 240–43; Yohanan Aharoni, "The Stratification of Israelite Megiddo," *JNES* 31 (1972): 302–11; William G. Dever, "Gezer Revisited," *BA* 47 (1984): 206–18.

coastal plain (1 Kings 9:17–18). Tamar ('Ain Ḥuṣb), in the Arabah twenty-five miles south of the Dead Sea, guarded the southern frontier.[25]

Outposts outside the homeland also received attention. The author of Kings speaks in general terms of locations "in Lebanon and throughout all the territory [Solomon] ruled" (1 Kings 9:19); but the chronicler specifies that Solomon rebuilt the villages which had been given to him by Hiram, captured and rebuilt Hamath Zobah (Ḥamā) on the Orontes, and even restored and fortified the important desert oasis of Tadmor (or Palmyra), 140 miles northeast of Damascus (2 Chron. 8:2–6). Solomon thus created a chain of defensive positions that protected not only Jerusalem and Israel proper, but the principal routes to and through his larger empire.

Cracks in the Solomonic Empire

Solomon's control of these widely scattered cities presupposes in turn control of the nations and regions in which they were located.[26] This is not surprising since in the Ammonite wars David had reduced much of Syria and the Transjordanian kingdoms to vassalage or even outright provincial status. There is nothing to indicate that any of this changed when David's fortunes took a turn for the worse in his later years; certainly the empire passed intact to Solomon. Furthermore, the alliances David had made with friendly states such as Tyre were not only continued by Solomon but became stronger. In addition, of course, he forged new relationships such as the important one with Egypt.

The Beginnings of Decline

In Solomon's last years, however, the empire began to disintegrate all around him; even the old Israel-Judah schism began to rear its ugly head. The reason is clearly stated in the record—"The LORD became angry with Solomon because his heart had turned away from the LORD" (1 Kings 11:9). Specifically this involved at least the toleration of idolatrous worship, if not the promotion of a syncretistic cult by the king himself. The many wives he had taken, probably in the course of establishing international treaties and other alliances, demanded that he make provision for their native pantheons, so Solo-

25. For archaeological evidence of Solomonic fortification in the Negev see Rudolph Cohen, "The Iron Age Fortresses in the Central Negev," *BASOR* 236 (1979): 77–78.

26. John Bright, *A History of Israel*, 3d ed. (Philadelphia: Westminster, 1981), p. 214.

mon built high places and other cult installations to pacify them. The judgment of Yahweh was the loss of the empire, a judgment which Solomon saw with his own eyes. For the sake of David, however, not all would be lost. Israel, indeed, would fall to Jeroboam, one of Solomon's chief officials, but Judah and Jerusalem would remain the realm of the house of David forever.

The Independence of Edom

The first crack in Solomon's imperial structure appeared east of the Dead Sea in the province of Edom. This proud kingdom had been brought under David's domination sometime in the first half of his reign, probably in connection with the Ammonite wars (see pp. 259–60). In the course of that conquest Joab had implemented a policy of genocide which destroyed a major part of the male population. One of the escapees was young Hadad, a prince of the royal family. Traveling through the desert by way of Midian and Paran, Hadad and his protectors eventually reached Egypt where they found sanctuary, probably under Pharaoh Amenemope (993–978).[27] Hadad likely did not reach a marriageable age until the reign of Siamun (978–959), and so it was probably Siamun's sister-in-law whom Hadad wed (1 Kings 11·19). If this is correct, one cannot help noting the irony of Siamun's having given his daughter to Solomon and his sister-in-law to Solomon's mortal enemy.

Hadad's return to Edom must be dated early in Solomon's reign because, as the historian is careful to point out, it was news of David's and Joab's deaths which encouraged him to return (1 Kings 11:21). He presumably bided his time there for about the next thirty years, for it was after Solomon was old that Hadad, like Solomon's other adversaries, first asserted his independence. To what extent the Edomites regained their sovereignty is not clear,[28] for the next time they are mentioned (about seventy-five years later) they appear to be under at least the loose control of Jehoshaphat, king of Judah (1 Kings 22:47).

Rezon of Damascus

The second source of external difficulty for Solomon was Rezon of Damascus.[29] After David had defeated Hadadezer king of Zobah, Re-

27. Green, "Solomon and Siamun," *JBL* 97 (1978): 363, n. 49.

28. It may be, as B. Oded suggests, that Hadad regained firm control of Edom but not in the region of the Gulf of Aqaba ("Neighbors on the East," in *World History of the Jewish People*, vol. 4, part 1, *The Age of the Monarchies: Political History*, ed. Abraham Malamat [Jerusalem: Massada, 1979], p. 254).

29. For the suggestion that Rezon is identical to Hezion, founder of the Damascene dynasty, see Merrill F. Unger, *Israel and the Aramaeans of Damascus* (Grand Rapids: Baker, 1980 reprint), p. 57.

zon, the erstwhile vassal of Hadadezer, was able to break from his overlord and establish his own seat of power in Damascus.[30] Although Damascus was at least theoretically a province of Israel under Solomon until the end of his life, it is clear that Rezon was a constant irritation through all those years. At last either he or his successor Tabrimmon removed Damascus from Israelite domination. This probably happened shortly after Solomon's death and the division of the kingdom.

The Rebellion of Jeroboam

The third recorded instrument of Yahweh's punishment of Solomon was the person of Jeroboam ben Nebat, one of his most trusted and important officials. The historian recounts that in the process of the building of the Millo at Jerusalem Solomon came across young Jeroboam, who impressed the king so much by his industry that he was promoted to overseer of all the corvée laborers in the district of Ephraim (1 Kings 11:27–28). Yahweh had also taken note of Jeroboam. Thus it happened that after Solomon had begun his apostate ways, the prophet Ahijah of Shiloh one day called Jeroboam aside and informed him that ten tribes of Israel would free themselves of Davidic rule and that he had been chosen by Yahweh to lead them. Word of this soon leaked out to Solomon, so Jeroboam, though apparently innocent of any personal political ambition, had to flee for his life to Egypt. The king of Egypt at this time was Shoshenq (945–924) of Dynasty 22, an able ruler who would raid and devastate both Judah and Israel five years after Solomon died. Jeroboam remained with Shoshenq until the death of Solomon and then returned to become the first king of the northern kingdom of Israel.

Solomonic Statecraft

Four Spheres of Political Influence

The homeland

The question arises, Is the term *empire* applicable to Israelite hegemony in the tenth century?[31] If by "empire" one means sheer territorial expanse, it is not. If, however, one has in view a domination

---

30. Ibid., p. 54.

31. For terms describing the various phases of the Israelite state and their sociopolitical ramifications, see Malamat, "A Political Look," in *Studies in the Period of David and Solomon*, ed. Tomoo Ishida, pp. 192–97.

over foreign lands and peoples which falls short of physical incorporation into the dominant state, then the situation under David and Solomon certainly qualifies.[32] A more fruitful line of inquiry, however, might be to consider the various spheres over which David and Solomon exercised political influence. The first was the homeland itself. Israel under David had made the transition from a rather loose confederation of nearly autonomous tribes to a clearly definable national entity with a strong central government and a unified diplomatic and military presence among the nations of the world. But Israel under both David and Solomon was geographically coextensive with the older tribal territories; that is, she occupied only that area which had been assigned to the tribes in conquest times. Historically and eschatologically the Old Testament knows of an Israel expanded beyond the tribal borders, but this never appears to have been the case in the period of the united monarchy.

The provinces

Israel under Solomon did not, then, formally incorporate under her jurisdiction lands which lay outside her traditional borders. Solomon did, however, inherit from David a complex of provinces consisting primarily of kingdoms and states immediately contiguous to Israel. These included Damascus, Ammon, Moab, Edom, and several smaller principalities. As provinces these areas were not considered integral parts of the homeland, but they nonetheless lost their independence and were ruled directly by Solomon through Israelite governors or other subordinates. They were subject to taxation and conscription and were expected to defend Israel against all hostilities. In return they could expect the protection and benefits of the central government.[33]

Vassal states

The third sphere of political influence, and that which makes the term *empire* applicable to the Israel of Solomon, was the more distant and less rigid collection of vassal states. These client nations—including Zobah, Hamath, Arabia, and possibly Philistia—were brought under Israelite control by military or diplomatic means, but were allowed to retain a certain measure of autonomy, including native rulers and internal fiscal policy. They were obligated, however, to recognize the suzerainty of the Israelite king, to provide tribute of goods and services

32. For the problems in defining "empire" see Carol L. Meyers, "The Israelite Empire: In Defense of King Solomon," *Michigan Quarterly Review* 22 (1983): 415–16.

33. Albrecht Alt, *Essays on Old Testament History and Religion* (Garden City, N.Y.: Doubleday, 1968), pp. 284–97.

to the king on stated occasions, and to maintain loyalty to the central government under all circumstances, especially in times of war. Solomon, as Great King, was responsible to defend these areas of his empire and otherwise to render such assistance as they might require.[34]

Allied states

Finally, Solomon's imperial policy included a network of parity treaties with neighboring or even distant powers with whom he was on friendly terms. These treaties, as the name implied, recognized the equality of the contracting parties and usually contained provision for mutual defense, trade, safe passage, extradition, and the like. The best-known example is the relationship between Solomon and Hiram of Tyre.[35] Neither ruler was subordinate to the other, and the provisions of their treaty were clearly to the advantage of both. Tyre provided men and materials for the massive construction projects of Solomon, while Israel compensated with shipments of food. Later Solomon ceded twenty cities in Galilee to Hiram; though Hiram was dissatisfied with them, he made payment of 120 talents of gold (1 Kings 9:10–14). The Phoenicians also—no doubt as an ongoing expression of their treaty obligation—provided sailors for Israel's merchant marine (1 Kings 9:26–28).[36]

Solomon also made such a pact with Egypt early in his reign. This agreement was ratified by the marriage of Solomon to Siamun's daughter and her dowry, the Canaanite city of Gezer. What Solomon gave in return is unknown, though it may have been nothing more than a guarantee to protect Egypt's northeastern frontier. The document also contained clauses relating to trade, for Solomon purchased chariots in Egypt, which he in turn exported to the Hittite and Aramean kings to the north. It must not have included provision for extradition, however, since Jeroboam fled to Egypt and remained there in safety until after Solomon's death (1 Kings 11:40). Of course, it is entirely possible that by that time relations between Egypt and Israel had been broken off anyway. Certainly they were broken off in the latter years of Shoshenq, as his invasion of Judah and Israel attests.

34. Details on Solomon as the Great King exercising authority over a system of vassal states are, admittedly, sparse in the biblical record, but such a relationship may be assumed on the basis of similar structures in the ancient Near East. See George E. Mendenhall, "Covenant Forms in Israelite Tradition," in *The Biblical Archaeologist Reader*, ed. Edward F. Campbell, Jr., and David Noel Freedman (Garden City, N.Y.: Doubleday, 1970), vol. 3, pp. 28–32.

35. Dennis J. McCarthy, *Old Testament Covenant* (Atlanta: John Knox, 1972), p. 43.

36. Jack M. Sasson, "Canaanite Maritime Involvement in the Second Millennium B.C.," *JAOS* 86 (1966): 126–37.

Internal Administration

There is very little information as to how the process of imperial administration functioned day by day, but the record does speak to the matter of organization and bureaucracy in Israel proper.[37] Almost coincident with his accession Solomon had taken firm steps to solidify his position by making key administrative appointments. These included the replacement of Abiathar the priest with Zadok and the selection of Benaiah as commander of the army. Among the other chief officials were the secretaries, the recorder, the supervisor of the district officers, the king's personal adviser, the head of the palace staff, and the director of forced labor.

The district officers just referred to were in effect governors of jurisdictions which were more or less synonymous with the tribal areas. Aware of the strength of tradition, Solomon dared not abandon tribal distinctions altogether. And yet he knew that perpetuation of these distinctions would impede any genuine spirit of unity and preclude the establishment of Israel as a nation in the truest sense of that term. Solomon's dilemma, then, was how to go about restructuring Israel's body politic so as to foster homogeneity and centralized control without offending the hoary and cherished tribal ideals.

The answer lay in dividing the nation into twelve administrative districts in keeping with the twelve tribes and, coincidentally, in keeping with the twelve months of the year.[38] Each of these districts was under a governor (1 Kings 4:7–19) who reported to the supervisor of the district officials. Each district had the responsibility to provide rations to the central government for an entire month every year. As the need arose, manpower for both civil and military service was conscripted from the districts presumably on the basis of their populations and without regard to the monthly rotations. For example, when Solomon recruited the 180,000 men needed for his enormous building projects, he called them from all over the realm without respect to tribal affiliation (1 Kings 5:13–15).

A distinction was made, however, between the Israelites who were conscripted for temporary service and non-Israelites who were, in effect, reduced to slave labor on a permanent basis (1 Kings 9:15–22). These non-Israelites were remnants of the indigenous populations of Canaan. Being without covenantal status, they enjoyed no rights as

37. S. Yeivin, "Administration," in *World History of the Jewish People*, vol. 5, pp. 147–71.

38. John Bright, "The Organization and Administration of the Israelite Empire," in *Magnalia Dei, the Mighty Acts of God: Essays on the Bible and Archaeology in Memory of G. Ernest Wright*, ed. Frank M. Cross et al. (Garden City, N.Y.: Doubleday, 1976), pp. 193–208; de Vaux, *Ancient Israel*, vol. 1, pp. 133–36.

free persons and so were prime candidates for all sorts of menial labor as the king required. The Israelites, on the other hand, served permanently only in the military—probably in the standing or professional army—and as supervisors over the work gangs engaged in various civil projects.[39]

The Administrative Districts

It has been pointed out that the twelve districts corresponded roughly to the twelve tribal areas, but exactly to what extent is a matter of debate since it is not possible to determine the boundaries with certainty. The historian does provide some information, however; so an effort should be made at least to get a general idea of the borders and of their implications for the history of Israel.[40]

The first of the districts is described as "in the hill country of Ephraim" and may be regarded as roughly identical to the tribe of Ephraim. The second was west of Judah and Benjamin, in the region of the original inheritance of Dan. The third district, "the land of Hepher," lay along the Mediterranean coast between Joppa to the south and the Wadi Shihor on the north. It thus fell in what had been western Ephraim and Manasseh in theory, but was actually under Canaanite control until the time of David or Solomon. The fourth district embraced the coastal plain north of Hepher up to and including Mount Carmel. This region had been part of Manasseh and Zebulun, but, like Hepher, had for the most part remained in Canaanite hands. The fifth district followed an irregular shape from Megiddo in the northwest to Beth Shan in the east and Jokmeam in the southeast. This was essentially the same as western Manasseh, except that the coastal areas of that tribe were not included. The sixth district, centered in Ramoth Gilead, was a vast area in the Transjordan which occupied nearly everything between the Jabbok and Yarmuk rivers from ten miles east of the Jordan into the vast eastern deserts. It was roughly comparable to the old tribal region of eastern Manasseh. The seventh district was also in the Transjordan; running the whole length of the Jordan valley between the Sea of Kinnereth and the Dead Sea, it lay west of the district just described and the kingdom of Ammon. The eighth was far to the north and consisted of the original area of Naphtali and the territory seized by Dan. The ninth district lay just to the west and included all of Asher and the part of Zebulun not taken in by the fourth district. It was from this ninth district that Solomon ceded certain

---

39. Soggin, "Compulsory Labor Under David and Solomon," in *Studies in the Period of David and Solomon*, ed. Tomoo Ishida, p. 266.

40. See the helpful chart of de Vaux, *Ancient Israel*, vol. 1, p. 134.

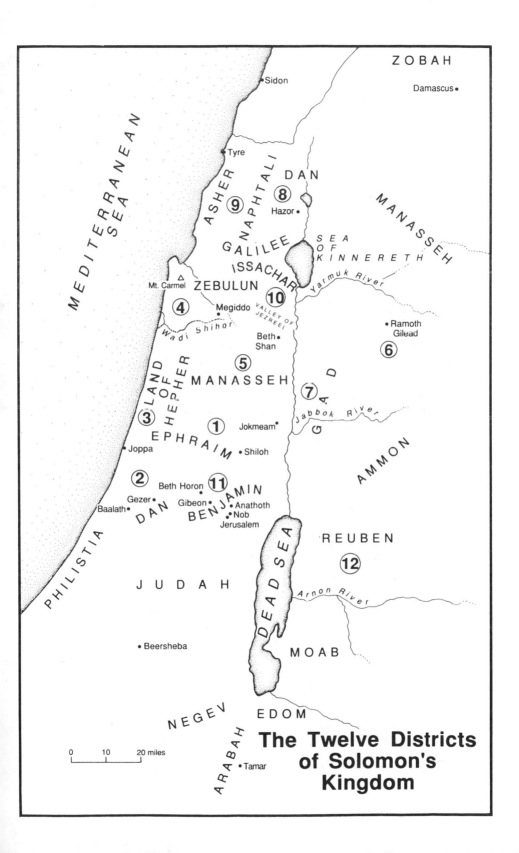

The Twelve Districts of Solomon's Kingdom

cities to Hiram (1 Kings 9:11) with the result that the entire coastal region north of Carmel became Phoenician territory.[41] The tenth district was virtually the same as tribal Issachar, lying in the eastern Valley of Jezreel and north of Beth Shan. The eleventh was coextensive with Benjamin but did not include Jerusalem. The twelfth was in the Transjordan south of Gilead and Ammon and north of the Arnon River, the border with Moab. It therefore was basically the same as Reuben.

One can see, then, that the original tribal boundaries were generally preserved in the redistricting, though there were new districts created in areas which hitherto had been under Canaanite or other foreign control. Several other features of Solomon's districts are worthy of mention. First, no attempt was made to include Philistia in the overall plan, though surely Solomon had the military capability of conquering and incorporating Philistia as a constituent part of Israel itself. And he would have had ample theological grounds for doing so, because Philistia lay within the boundaries of the land promised to the patriarchs and Moses. It may well be that for practical reasons Solomon thought it wiser to coexist with a compliant Philistia than to expend his energies and resources in keeping these recalcitrant and ambitious people under control by force.[42]

Second, one cannot help but note the disappearance of Dan and Zebulun as independent entities. At present there appears to be no way to account for this except that, in the former case, Solomon may have deliberately eliminated Dan or incorporated it into Naphtali in order to neutralize the tendency toward paganism which had characterized that tribe since the early days of the judges.

The third arresting fact is the removal of coastal Asher from Israel to Phoenicia.[43] The only hint of a rationale for this is an apparent need on Solomon's part for cash, for it seems that after twenty years of building he lacked the wherewithal to pay Hiram for the timber and gold the Tyrian king had provided. The gold alone amounted to 120 talents. Hiram was displeased with the transaction once he looked the newly acquired cities over carefully, but it seems that he kept them nonetheless (at least for a short time; see p. 309).

Most remarkable of all is the omission of Judah and Jerusalem from

41. For the perplexing problem of the Israel-Phoenicia border in general and the transfer of the cities in particular see B. Oded, "Neighbors on the West," in *World History of the Jewish People*, vol. 4, part 1, pp. 234–35.

42. Oded, "Neighbors on the West," p. 239, argues, however, that Philistia was at least a tributary state under Solomon.

43. Herbert Donner, "The Interdependence of Internal Affairs and Foreign Policy During the Davidic-Solomonic Period (with Special Regard to the Phoenician Coast)," in *Studies in the Period of David and Solomon*, ed. Tomoo Ishida, pp. 207–8.

the districting.[44] This implies that Jerusalem and the surrounding area were considered a federal district exempt from the obligations which attached to the remainder of the nation. That a line of demarcation existed between Israel and Judah even in Solomon's time is clear from the comments of the historian that "the people of Judah and Israel were as numerous as the sand on the seashore" (1 Kings 4:20) and that "Judah and Israel, from Dan to Beersheba, lived in safety, each man under his own vine and fig tree" (1 Kings 4:25). Exemption from taxation, forced labor, and other burdens can be understood given Solomon's Judahite ancestry, but it also may have been the single most important contributing factor in the division of the kingdom following his death.[45] When Rehoboam, Solomon's successor, rebuffed the overtures of the people of Israel regarding their onerous burden of taxation and labor, they rallied behind the cry,

> What share do we have in David,
>   what part in Jesse's son?
> To your tents, O Israel!
>   Look after your own house, O David! [1 Kings 12:16]

It is obvious that theirs is a complaint concerning not only heavy burdens per se but discriminatory burdens. The very silence of the people of Judah regarding this oppression says clearly that they were not its victims.

The Fiscal Policy

The matter of taxation leads us now to a consideration of the fiscal base upon which the Solomonic empire rested.[46] We are told that the central government was supported both by forced labor and by revenues elicited from the citizens themselves. Nothing is said, however, of tax rates or of what percentage of the total imperial income came directly from Israelite sources. Though the burden may have seemed

44. Roland de Vaux, *Ancient Israel*, vol. 1, p. 136, suggests that Judah is probably referred to in 1 Kings 4:19b ("the district"; cf. RSV: "And there was one officer in the land of Judah"). There is no basis, however, for his suggestion that the districts of Judah under Solomon may be ascertained from the divisions of Joshua 15:21–62, a passage he dates to postschism times.

45. Simon J. De Vries suggests that there was a separate, unrecorded system of taxation and conscription for Judah—otherwise there would be an account of the unrest which inevitably would have resulted (*1 Kings*, Word Biblical Commentary [Waco: Word, 1985], pp. 71–72). But this is precisely the point! Discriminatory treatment was in fact a major issue in the eventual division of the kingdom. See J. Alberto Soggin, *A History of Ancient Israel* (Philadelphia: Westminster, 1984), pp. 82–83.

46. de Vaux, *Ancient Israel*, vol. 1, pp. 140–41.

excessive to the people, as taxes always do, the vast wealth of Solomon's Israel cannot be accounted for solely on the basis of domestic taxation.

The answer lies, of course, in Solomon's exaction of tribute from the provinces and vassal states and in the celebrated shrewdness of his international trade. One must not forget also that he had at his disposal almost unlimited slave labor from the Canaanite remnants that still lived in various enclaves throughout the land. The employment of these unfortunate people left the Israelites themselves free to pursue crafts and trades and to engage in merchandising. Thus a whole new phenomenon arose in Israel—an affluent middle class that had the time and means to undertake creative new ways of developing culture and commerce.[47]

Something of the leisurely lifestyle made possible by Solomon's economic policies is captured by the historian, who writes of Judah and Israel that "they ate, they drank and they were happy" (1 Kings 4:20). And then, as though to explain how this state of affairs came about, he goes on to speak of Solomon's rule of all the lands from the Euphrates to Egypt, a rule which required these client states to pay tribute to him all the days of his life. Specifically, and by way of example, the needs of the palace alone consisted of 185 bushels of flour, 375 bushels of meal, 10 head of stall-fed cattle, 20 head of pasture-fed cattle, 100 sheep and goats, and miscellaneous wild game *every day*. Some of this was supplied from within Israel itself, of course, but much if not most of it came as part of the foreign tribute.

Solomon's personal requirements, as enormous as they might appear, were a pittance compared to the income which flowed into the state coffers. Every year, the historian says, Israel took in 666 talents of gold apart from that acquired by trade and commerce (1 Kings 10:14–15). This staggering amount must have come from tribute and taxation alone. It is no wonder that Solomon could lavish such splendor on Jerusalem and elsewhere in his realm, nor is it any surprise that visitors from throughout the eastern world came to see his opulence and magnificence with their own eyes.

International Trade

International trade was the other major source of Israel's material prosperity. This must surely have been undertaken with nations under Israel's political control, but the record attests most especially the commercial ties between Israel and those peoples with whom she enjoyed relationships of peaceful parity. The remarkable thing about

47. Hanoch Reviv, "The Structure of Society," in *World History of the Jewish People*, vol. 5, pp. 138–43.

Solomon's role is that he served more as international broker than anything else. Capitalizing on Israel's strategic location at the overland and maritime crossroads of the eastern Mediterranean world, he established a clearinghouse in Israel through which international merchandise passed. As it entered and left Israel's borders, it was assessed customs taxes which, of course, accrued to Israel's treasury. Furthermore, Solomon was able to corner the market on many commodities, so that he could sell at exorbitant profit.

Some inkling of this process may be seen in the treaty between Hiram of Tyre and Solomon which stipulated that Hiram would provide timber for Solomon's building projects in return for wheat and olive oil. This appears to have been a straightforward transaction with no special advantage to either party. Israel had no significant stands of timber, and Tyre, pressed between the sea and the mountains, was heavily dependent on agricultural imports.[48] Later, however, after the construction was completed, the treaty had to be renegotiated, for it seems that Solomon was unable to supply sufficient wheat and oil to pay for the building materials he had imported from Hiram. Why, in light of Solomon's immense wealth, this was so is unclear, unless that wealth was accumulated after the renegotiation of the treaty under consideration. In fact, the chronicler appears to support this hypothesis. He says that after the twenty years of construction Solomon "rebuilt the villages that Hiram had given him, and settled Israelites in them" (2 Chron. 8:2). This can mean only that Solomon, shortly after he ceded these towns to Hiram, was able to repurchase them because of a sudden turn in his fortunes.

In any case Hiram cannot have remained upset with Solomon over the business of the villages, for we learn that he provided sailors to man Israel's merchant marine (1 Kings 9:26–28).[49] Operating out of Ezion Geber, the Edomite port on the Gulf of Aqaba, this fleet traversed great distances in quest of gold, sandalwood, precious stones, ivory, apes, and baboons (1 Kings 10:11–12, 22). Destinations included Ophir (probably in lower Arabia[50] or east-central Africa) and Tarshish (possibly Sardinia[51] or even Spain). It is not impossible that trade took Solomon's fleet as far east as India.

Land commerce was particularly centered on horses and chariots.[52] Solomon himself had fourteen hundred chariots and twelve thousand

48. Oded, "Neighbors on the West," in *World History of the Jewish People*, vol. 4, part 1, p. 233.

49. The Phoenicians were, of course, celebrated maritimers. See Oded, "Neighbors on the West," pp. 228–30.

50. Aharoni and Avi-Yonah, *Macmillan Bible Atlas*, map 15.

51. Ibid.

52. Yutaka Ikeda, "Solomon's Trade in Horses and Chariots in Its International Setting," in *Studies in the Period of David and Solomon*, ed. Tomoo Ishida, pp. 215–38.

horses at his chariot cities and Jerusalem. But he no doubt dealt in far greater numbers, because he served as the conduit for the buying and selling of these highly prized goods. The Hyksos and Hurrians had introduced chariotry to the Near Eastern world, and its popularity had been enhanced by the Canaanites and Philistines.[53] Not until David did Israel enjoy the use of this sophisticated military equipment; under Solomon, ironically, Israel came to control its availability to a considerable extent. The reason is that Egypt produced both the best horses and chariots (1 Kings 10:28–29).[54] Each horse brought a price of 150 shekels of silver, and each chariot sold for 600 shekels. These would be traded between Egypt on the one hand and the Hittite and Aramean city-states of northern Syria on the other. From all these transactions one can be sure that Solomon skimmed off a hefty profit.

Another source of income lay outside the normal channels of tribute and trade. This consisted of the gifts brought voluntarily by wealthy potentates who visited Solomon from all over the known world. The most celebrated of these was the queen of Sheba (later known as Saba'), a kingdom located on the southwest corner of the Arabian peninsula more than twelve hundred miles from Jerusalem.[55] Obviously fabulously wealthy herself, this noble woman, having heard of Solomon's wisdom and association with Yahweh, came laden down with all manner of rare and precious goods, including spices, gems, and 120 talents of gold. Solomon responded in kind though to what extent is not specified. Clearly, such visits made a major contribution not only to Solomon's treasury, but also to his stature among the rulers of the earth. One can say without fear of contradiction that Israel under Solomon had reached the very pinnacle of international power and prestige. With Assyria and Egypt Israel could rightly claim to be one of the three great powers of the tenth century.

Spiritual and Moral Apostasy

Israel's political, military, and economic prowess was, however, only a veneer covering the rottenness of social, cultural, and spiritual institutions in Solomon's latter years. The records univocally attest to

53. Ibid., pp. 216–18.

54. The Masoretic text here reads *mimmiṣrāyim* ("from Egypt"), but many scholars suggest the emendation *mimmuṣri* ("from Muṣri") on the basis of various ancient Near Eastern references to a place called Muṣri (Gray, *I & II Kings*, pp. 268–69). There is no textual support for this, however, and Ikeda ("Solomon's Trade," pp. 215, 227–29) has argued not only that the very existence of a Muṣri apart from Egypt is in doubt, but that Egypt indeed became a center of horse breeding in pre-Solomonic times.

55. Gus Van Beek, "Frankincense and Myrrh," in *The Biblical Archaeologist Reader*, vol. 2, p. 125.

the essential righteousness and morality of both king and kingdom at the beginning, but they are equally in agreement that the picture had radically changed forty years later.

Solomon had, of course, inherited from his father both the awesome responsibility of government and the even more awesome privilege of spiritual leadership. The former he discharged reasonably well—or at least effectively—as we have seen. In the latter, on the other hand, he proved to be a failure. This is all the more tragic because in his youth Solomon had taken every precaution, it seems, to guard against this very eventuality. He had begun his reign with a holy convocation at Gibeon and there had had an encounter with the living God (1 Kings 3:4–5). When asked what he desired above all else, he prayed for wisdom that he might lead his people in a godly way. He had then undertaken the building of the temple and brought this God-ordained task to a glorious completion. After more than twenty years God appeared to Solomon a second time and reaffirmed his covenant promises (1 Kings 9:1–9). He told Solomon of his satisfaction with the temple and of his intention to place his name there forever. On the other hand, he said, his continued blessing upon the royal house and the temple itself was conditional: If Solomon proved loyal and obedient, they would go on forever without interruption; if he proved unfaithful, both kingship and temple, along with the whole nation, would be placed in abeyance until Yahweh in his sovereign grace brought restoration. Subsequent history reveals that this is precisely what came to pass. Solomon and his descendants violated the letter and spirit of the covenant relationship, so Israel and Judah suffered the consequences of defeat and deportation.

Solomon's (and Israel's) spiritual deterioration did not occur overnight, of course, nor can one divide his reign into a righteous period and an evil period. Rather, one should view its course as a gradual divergence from the holy standard to which he committed himself (ideally at least) at the beginning of his rule. It seems that the young king, though blessed with the noblest intentions, found himself caught up in the vortex of historical circumstances which he was powerless to control. The Book of Ecclesiastes describes most succinctly what that struggle entailed.

The author of Kings drops hints that Solomon made certain compromises early on that set the tone for his future behavior and attitudes.[56] He married the daughter of the pharaoh; though this was a marriage of convenience for political ends, it violated the code of con-

---

56. For the chronicler's omission of these negative assessments of Solomon and the theological reasons for doing so, see Raymond B. Dillard, "The Chronicler's Solomon," *WTJ* 43 (1981): 290–92; Roddy L. Braun, "Solomonic Apologetic in Chronicles," *JBL* 92 (1973): 503–16.

duct expected of the elect, royal son of Yahweh (Deut. 17:14–17). Moreover, though he loved Yahweh and walked according to his statutes, Solomon worshiped at the high places, which, other than the one at Gibeon, were taboo. The historian makes crystal clear the connection between Solomon's illicit marriages and illicit worship. He points out that Solomon loved many foreign women besides Pharaoh's daughter, and that they encouraged him in his apostasy and syncretism (1 Kings 11:3).

This forbidden polygamy was not late in its inception. There is evidence, for example, that Solomon had already married a pagan wife, Naamah the Ammonite, before he married Pharaoh's daughter. In fact, we know that he married Naamah even before he became king, for she was the mother of his son Rehoboam, who was forty-one years old when he succeeded Solomon's forty-year reign (1 Kings 14:21). In addition Solomon took wives from Moab, Edom, Sidon, and the Hittites, though such behavior had been forbidden to Israel (Exod. 23:31–33; 34:12–16). Gradually they turned his heart away from Yahweh until at last he worshiped Ashtoreth, Molech, and Chemosh along with Yahweh. He even provided high places where he and his wives could participate in the pagan cults associated with these deities. It was this blend of physical and spiritual polygamy which brought upon Solomon and the kingdom the judgment of Yahweh, a judgment which found particular historical expression in the dissolution of Israel into two irremediably separate parts.

Solomon and the Nature of Wisdom

All of this moral and spiritual apostasy came to pass in spite of the fact that Solomon was blessed with the wisdom of God and, indeed, was known throughout the ancient world as the wisest of all mortals (1 Kings 4:31). How could a man so gifted of God be so insensitive to the great issues of the heart and spirit? The answer lies in the nature of biblical wisdom.

It is impossible here to get into the complex subject of wisdom, but at least a brief statement should be made.[57] One should recognize, first of all, that in Israel and the ancient Near East, wisdom was not synonymous with knowledge or education or science, but had to do with the ability to live life in a skillful way, an ability possessed only by the individual who knew and feared God. This is why the Old Testa-

57. For a helpful overview see James L. Crenshaw, *Old Testament Wisdom: An Introduction* (Atlanta: John Knox, 1981).

ment emphasizes the dichotomy between the wise person and the fool (i.e., between the righteous person and the sinner).[58]

This does not mean, however, that one could be wise without attention to facts and phenomena. Evidence of Solomon's wisdom, for example, included his composing three thousand proverbs and over one thousand songs which dealt with such mundane matters as trees, animals, birds, and fish (1 Kings 4:32–33). What is meant by wisdom here is not only some understanding of the botany and zoology involved, but the astuteness to recognize that these organisms, like all creation, are the work of God and that in their characteristics and habits the purposes of God for life in general can be discerned.[59]

In addition to employing similes and metaphors drawn directly from the world of nature,[60] the Old Testament wisdom literature was also insightful in terms of human character and personality. Even without the benefits of modern psychology and psychiatry it understood the basic human drives and emotions and could therefore offer counsel based on the moral and ethical nature of God himself. While the wisdom texts themselves afford ample illustrations, the best example is to be found in the narrative concerning the two prostitutes who claimed the same baby and brought the matter to Solomon for adjudication (1 Kings 3:16–28). In a marvelous display of Old Testament wisdom in its truest sense the king ordered the baby to be cut in two and shared between them. The true mother, giving in to genuine maternal instincts, surrendered her claim in order that the child might live. The wisdom in Solomon's decision came not from a textbook or even long experience, but from a fundamental understanding of the character of God and of those who are created in his image.

To return now to the matter of Solomon's defection in the face of his preeminent wisdom, we must simply make the point that it is possible to be wise in the biblical sense of the term and yet to fail to live out the implications of that wisdom. Solomon's sin in multiplying wives and in turning after other gods does not vitiate the fact of his wisdom, but it certainly undercuts any claim on his part that he ordered his own life and that of his kingdom according to its principles.

Finally, after forty years in which he saw Israel rise to heights she had never known before and would never know again, Solomon died. In the mercy of the Lord he died before he was forced to see with his own eyes the fruit of his misguided and disastrous policies: the rupture of the kingdom into two irreconcilable parts.

58. Ibid., pp. 24, 31.
59. Ibid., pp. 50–52.
60. Delbert R. Hillers, "The Effective Simile in Biblical Literature," *JAOS* 103 (1983): 181–85.

9 The Divided Monarchy

The Roots of National Division

The death of Solomon paved the way for one of the most decisive and traumatic events in Israel's long history—the formal and permanent di-

315

vision of the kingdom between the ten tribes of the north, henceforth known as Israel or Ephraim, and the tribe of Judah in the south. Though shattering in the extreme to the national psyche, this cleavage should have come as no surprise to thoughtful people, for the political and theological roots of the schism reached deep into Israel's past.

We have already taken note of events and attitudes symptomatic of the sickness in the body of the covenant people. This was exacerbated by other factors, some of which were beyond human control. For example, the very allotment of tribal territories under Joshua contained within it the seeds of alienation—natural boundaries that, of necessity, separated the people. There was the Jordan, of course, which sealed off the eastern tribes from the west; the result was mutual suspicion and even military skirmishes between the two sides from time to time. Similarly, the so-called Galilean tribes were isolated from Manasseh and Ephraim by the Valley of Jezreel. In this case the wedge between the two was not so much geographical as it was practical. The Canaanites, who could not be driven out of the Jezreel and other broad valleys and plains, occupied the space between northern and central Israel from the time of the conquest to the reign of David. Evidences of the Galilean isolation found expression as late as New Testament times.[1]

Of most significance now, however, was the early and continually intensifying sense of bifurcation between Judah and the other tribes. Again geography seems to have played a role, at least in providing the kind of setting in which tribal independence could be nurtured. To the north Judah was psychologically and physically cut off from central Israel by the deep and broad Valley of Sorek. To the west were a foreign people, the Philistines; to the south the hostile Negev deserts with their equally hostile nomadic populations; and to the east the obviously real barrier of the Dead Sea. Judah, then, of all the tribes was the most isolated and therefore most subject to a sense of not belonging.

This is very ironic, for it was Judah that from the beginning was promised in the patriarchal covenants a place of political and theological centrality. When Jacob gave his final blessing to his sons, he affirmed that "the scepter will not depart from Judah" (Gen. 49:10), an incontestable indication that the locus of historical and messianic kingship would be found in that tribe. The genealogy of David in the Book of Ruth and in 1 Chronicles 2:3–17 unambiguously establishes the connection between patriarchal promise and historical fulfilment and demonstrates once and for all Judah's theological primacy amongst the tribes despite its geographical handicap.[2]

1. Denis Baly, *The Geography of the Bible* (New York: Harper, 1957), p. 190.
2. Eugene H. Merrill, "The Book of Ruth: Narration and Shared Themes," *Bib Sac* 142 (1985): 130–41.

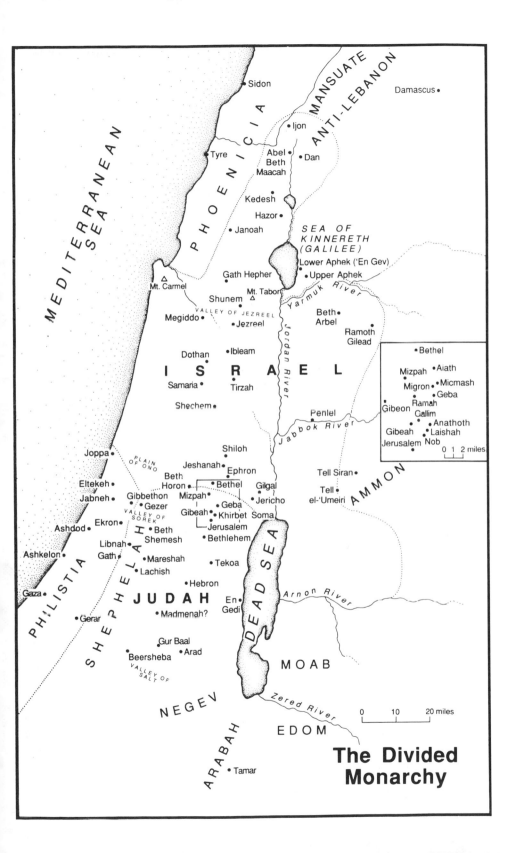

MEDITERRANEAN SEA

P H O E N I C I A

MANSUATE

ANTI-LEBANON

• Damascus

• Sidon

• Ijon

• Tyre

Abel
Beth
Maacah

• Dan

• Kedesh

• Hazor

• Janoah

SEA OF
KINNERETH
(GALILEE)

△ Mt. Carmel

• Gath Hepher

Lower Aphek ('En Gev)

• Upper Aphek

Shunem △ Mt. Tabor

VALLEY OF JEZREEL

Yarmuk River

Jordan River

• Megiddo

• Jezreel

Beth
Arbel

Ramoth
Gilead

• Dothan

• Ibleam

I S R A E L

• Samaria

• Tirzah

Shechem •

Penuel

Jabbok River

Shiloh

Jeshanah

Ephron

Beth
Horon •

• Bethel

Joppa •

PLAIN
OF ONO

Tell Siran

Mizpah

Gibeah •

Gilgal

Jericho

Tell
el-'Umeiri

A M M O N

• Eltekeh

Gibbethon

Gezer

Geba

Jabneh •

VALLEY OF
SOREK

Khirbet
Soma

Ashdod •

Ekron •

Jerusalem

Beth
Shemesh

Ashkelon •

Libnah
Gath

• Bethlehem

DEAD SEA

Gaza •

• Mareshah

• Lachish

• Tekoa

PHILISTIA

SHEPHELAH

J U D A H

• Hebron

En
Gedi

Arnon River

• Gerar

• Madmenah?

Gur Baal

• Beersheba

• Arad

VALLEY
OF
SALT

M O A B

N E G E V

Zered River

A R A B A H

E D O M

• Tamar

inset map:

• Bethel

Mizpah

• Aiath

Migron

• Micmash

• Geba

Ramah

Gibeon

Gallim

Gibeah

• Anathoth

• Laishah

Jerusalem Nob

0 1 2 miles

0 10 20 miles

**The Divided
Monarchy**

During the long period of the judges, however, there emerged a perceptible tension between the principle of Judah's royal destiny on the one hand and the tribe's actual alienation from the north on the other. One of the purposes of the so-called Bethlehem trilogy of narratives (see pp. 178–88), especially the story of Ruth, is to establish Bethlehem (and hence Judah) as the birthplace of the true dynasty. Another purpose is to reveal, in almost parable form, the roots of the rivalry between the Saulide kingship, which was centered in Gibeah of Benjamin, and that of David, which, of course, originated in Bethlehem. This is particularly evident in the story of the Levite who brought his Bethlehemite concubine to Gibeah, where she was savagely raped and murdered by the Benjamites. Far from showing remorse and bringing appropriate punishment to bear on the offenders, the tribe went to war with Judah and the other tribes until Benjamin was virtually annihilated. In fact, the tribe would have died out and there would consequently have been no Saul or Saulide kingship had not women from Jabesh Gilead and Shiloh been forced to marry the Benjamite survivors. Clearly the intent of the story is to show the injustice done to Judah and the evil propensities of Benjamin.

By the close of the era of the judges the Judah-Israel polarization was a *fait accompli*. The author of Samuel speaks of Saul's army as consisting of men of Israel and men of Judah (1 Sam. 11:8; 15:4; 17:52); he also makes much of the Philistine perception of Judah (i.e., David's forces) as an entity to be distinguished from Israel. Part of this perception no doubt reflected the Philistine desire to drive a wedge between the two segments of Israel, but part of it must have come from a generally prevailing recognition that such a division did, in fact, already exist.

Any lingering doubt would have been put to rest when David acceded to the wishes of his countrymen and became king at Hebron over what was, in effect, the independent kingdom of Judah. Only by the most creative and winsome kind of diplomacy was David able to extend his rule over the north; and, at that, it took more than seven years. But the apparent unity which he thus achieved was nothing more than a façade, for Absalom instigated his rebellion by fanning the flames of the smoldering Judah-Israel antagonism. Moreover, when David did return from exile, he had to palliate the bitter hatreds and jealousies of the respective national elements before he could claim their loyalty once again. Indeed, he even had to nip in the bud another revolution, this one led by a member of the Saulide faction.

Though nothing specific is said to the effect that the Judah-Israel conflict continued under Solomon, a loud and clear statement is nonetheless made by the exemption of Judah from Solomon's burdensome corvée and taxation. How and why the wise Solomon could have committed such an egregious blunder must remain a mystery, but he could hardly have thought of a more disastrous and divisive maneuver if he had tried. The miracle is that the open rebellion of the northern kingdom occurred only after Solomon's death and not before. It was only the sheer force of Solomon's personality and diplomatic skill which kept the seething cauldron of Israel's discontent from boiling over in his lifetime.

There was also a theological aspect to the rupture of the kingdom.[3] In fact, one could argue that the intertribal rivalries and Solomon's intemperate policies were only an expression of the underlying factor. Solomon had violated the letter and spirit of the covenant between Yahweh and David, a covenant under which he, as dynastic heir, had obligations. Specifically, his disobedience was manifested in his ill-advised marriages and in his toleration of pagan gods, but these defections may not have been the most serious of his sins. The narrator points out that Yahweh "became angry with Solomon because his heart had turned away from the LORD, the God of Israel, who had appeared to him twice" (1 Kings 11:9). Solomon had gone after other gods, the very quintessence of covenant infidelity. For that reason more than any other, the kingdom, except for Judah and Jerusalem, would be taken from Solomon and his descendants and delivered over to Jeroboam (1 Kings 11:11–13).

The Immediate Occasion of National Division

The Succession of Rehoboam

Jeroboam ben Nebat, the supervisor of civilian labor in the district of Ephraim, had already been told by the prophet Ahijah that he would become ruler of ten tribes of Israel (1 Kings 11:31). One tribe, Judah, would remain in the hands of the Davidic dynasty because of Yahweh's unconditional commitment to David.[4] God had chosen Jerusalem as

---

3. This is the major point of the so-called deuteronomistic view of the books of Kings, which holds that the primary concern of these histories is to assess the reign of each king on the basis of its conformity (or lack thereof) to the covenant of Yahweh. See John Van Seters, *In Search of History* (New Haven: Yale University Press, 1983), pp. 311–14, 359–61.

4. As it turned out, Benjamin affiliated with Judah, and the two together were counted as one tribe known as Judah (see 1 Kings 12:21; 2 Chron. 11:1, 10; 15:2, 9; Ezra 4:1). It is significant that Benjamin joined Judah in welcoming David back from Transjordanian exile (2 Sam. 19:16–17). Thus the defection of Benjamin to the Davidic family may have occurred even in pre-Solomonic times. For the problem of ten tribes left to the north and only one to the south see Carl F. Keil, *The Books of the Kings* (Grand Rapids: Eerdmans, 1950), pp. 179–81; Z. Kallai, "Judah and Israel—A Study in Israelite Historiography," *IEJ* 28 (1978): 256–57.

his dwelling-place on earth, and David and his descendants would forever serve there as a lamp shining forth to the world the radiance of God's presence and his saving purposes. Nothing could ever extinguish that. The seed of David might be disciplined for its disloyalty to Yahweh, but not forever. In his own inscrutable plan Yahweh would accomplish his eternal purposes through his chosen servant David (1 Kings 11:34–39).

Table 6 **The Kings of the Divided Monarchy**

Israel		Judah	
Jeroboam	931–910	Rehoboam	931–913
Nadab	910–909	Abijah	913–911
Baasha	909–886	Asa	911–870
Elah	886–885		
Zimri	885		
Omri	885–874		
Ahab	874–853	Jehoshaphat	873–848
Ahaziah	853–852		
Joram	852–841	Jehoram	848–841
Jehu	841–814	Ahaziah	841
		Athaliah	841–835
Jehoahaz	814–798	Joash	835–796
Jehoash	798–782	Amaziah	796–767
Jeroboam II	793–753	Uzziah	792–740
Zechariah	753		
Shallum	752		
Menahem	752–742	Jotham	750–731
Pekahiah	742–740		
Pekah	752–732	Ahaz	735–715
Hoshea	732–722	Hezekiah	729–686
		Manasseh	696–642
		Amon	642–640
		Josiah	640–609
		Jehoahaz	609
		Jehoiakim	608–598
		Jehoiachin	598–597
		Zedekiah	597–586

Solomon was succeeded by his son Rehoboam, who reigned for seventeen years, from 931 to 913.[5] He was apparently Solomon's first

5. For the dates of the divided monarchy see Edwin R. Thiele, *The Mysterious Numbers of the Hebrew Kings* (Grand Rapids: Eerdmans, 1965). For a helpful assessment of the difficulties involved in reconstructing a chronology based on the biblical data see Hayim Tadmor, "The Chronology of the First Temple Period," in *World History of the Jewish People*, vol. 4, part 1, *The Age of the Monarchies: Political History*, ed. Abraham Malamat (Jerusalem: Massada, 1979), pp. 44–60; Alberto R. Green, "Regnal Formulas in the Hebrew and Greek Texts of the Books of Kings," *JNES* 42 (1983): 167–80; J. Maxwell Miller, "Another Look at the Chronology of the Early Divided Monarchy," *JBL* 86 (1967): 276–88.

son, the product of a marriage of diplomacy with Naamah of Ammon (1 Kings 14:21). Since Rehoboam was forty-one when he became king and Solomon had reigned for forty years, it is likely that Solomon had taken Naamah as wife during the brief period of his coregency with David. The marriage, in fact, could well have been undertaken to lend credence to Solomon's designation as heir apparent.

Like his father, Rehoboam was polygamous. He married a grand-daughter of David (thus his own cousin), Mahalath (2 Chron. 11:18), and Maacah, daughter of Absalom.[6] Altogether he accumulated eighteen wives and sixty concubines, some of whom he may have inherited from Solomon. The general characterization of Rehoboam is that "he did evil because he had not set his heart on seeking the LORD" (2 Chron. 12:14).

The remarkable thing about the succession of Rehoboam to the throne of Solomon is that it occurred not at Jerusalem but Shechem (1 Kings 12:1; 2 Chron. 10:1). Regardless of whether this is to be understood as a coronation by the northern tribes separate from an earlier coronation at Jerusalem by Judah,[7] the fact remains that the nation was so divided that Rehoboam felt it necessary to go to the old center of covenant renewal in order to win over the northern tribes. Shechem was the place where Joshua had called the nation together to reaffirm its commitment to Yahweh. Perhaps Rehoboam felt that it was appropriate and necessary to gather there again in order to mend the fabric of an unraveling monarchy.

The Rebellion of Israel

The tenuousness of the whole situation is apparent in the fact that the coronation became a negotiating session in which the spokesmen of Israel, led by Jeroboam, set forth conditions which Rehoboam had to meet if he expected their support (1 Kings 12:3–4). Solomon, they said, had dealt with them harshly and unfairly. Rehoboam must redress this situation and promise to do better. Rehoboam then sought the counsel of the old advisers[8] of his father, and they urged him to

6. There are several indications that this Absalom is not the son of David: (a) the daughter of David's son Absalom was named Tamar (2 Sam. 14:27); (b) 1 Kings 15:2, 10, has Abishalom rather than Absalom; (c) Maacah's father is elsewhere called "Uriel of Gibeah" (2 Chron. 13:2). See Eugene H. Merrill, "2 Chronicles," in *The Bible Knowledge Commentary*, ed. John F. Walvoord and Roy B. Zuck (Wheaton, Ill.: Victor, 1985), vol. 1, p. 629.

7. So Jacob M. Myers, *II Chronicles*, Anchor Bible (Garden City, N.Y.: Doubleday, 1965), p. 65.

8. Abraham Malamat has proposed that the elders (*zĕqēnîm*) and young men (*yĕlādîm*) do not represent different age groups so much as a bicameral political system composed of delegates of the people and the princes ("Kingship and Council in Israel and Sumer: A Parallel," *JNES* 22 [1963]: 247–53).

meet Israel's demands. His young peers, however, suggested that he pay no heed and, in fact, that he whip the rebels into line by continuing and even intensifying his father's oppressive policies. Unfortunately, Rehoboam disregarded the sagacity of the elders and threatened the people with an even heavier yoke. Thus the stage was set for Yahweh to bring about the judgment he had promised if David's house proved disloyal to the covenant.

With one voice the Israelite delegation articulated what had long been developing but had hitherto been unexpressed, a declaration of independence:

> What share do we have in David,
>   what part in Jesse's son?
> To your tents, O Israel!
>   Look after your own house, O David! [1 Kings 12:16]

This marked a final, irreversible break. In a last desperate move at reconciliation Rehoboam sent his chief public-works administrator, Adoram, to plead with Israel's leaders, but to no avail—they stoned him to death and Rehoboam had to make an ignominious retreat to Jerusalem.

The Accession of Jeroboam

Meanwhile the people of Israel by acclamation placed Jeroboam as king over their newly formed monarchy.[9] He at once displayed his considerable administrative abilities by establishing his capital at the central and hallowed city of Shechem and by taking advantage of the close relationship which he while in exile had developed with Egypt's powerful King Shoshenq.[10]

The final break between Israel and Judah had come, of course, as the judgment of God, a point repeatedly made by the historians. It was therefore useless for Rehoboam or anyone else to try to repair it. But try Rehoboam did. Returning to Judah he raised a vast army with the intention of retaking Israel by force, but Shemaiah, a prophet of

9. Following the announcement of his selection as king over the northern kingdom Jeroboam had fled from Solomon and had found refuge with Shishak (or Shoshenq), founder of Egypt's twenty-second dynasty (1 Kings 11:40). See Pierre Montet, *Egypt and the Bible* (Philadelphia: Fortress, 1968), p. 40.

10. J. P. J. Olivier, on the grounds that Jeroboam was ruler over a national rather than a territorial state, tries to argue that there was no capital in the north until Omri built Samaria ("In Search of a Capital for the Northern Kingdom." *JNSL* 11 [1983]: 117–32). This argument is based on social-anthropology theories which appear to have little support from the biblical texts.

Yahweh, dissuaded him with the word that what had taken place was of God and so must be accepted perforce (1 Kings 12:21–24; 2 Chron. 11:1–4).

The Reign of Rehoboam

For the first three years of his reign Rehoboam accommodated himself as best he could to the undeniable and unalterable fact that he presided now over a kingdom that was only a shadow of its former self. Judah was still the people of God, and he was heir to the glorious Davidic dynasty with all its covenant claims and privileges, but from a practical standpoint Judah's position in the community of nations bore no resemblance to the glory of Israel in the heyday of Solomon. Rehoboam therefore had to take steps to reconcile the theocratic ideal of Judah as the chosen people and the day-to-day realities of political and military life.

One of the first measures Rehoboam undertook was the fortification of his tiny kingdom against outside interference, especially from Israel. This involved the incorporation of Benjamin into his territory, an important achievement whose means are not disclosed,[11] and the building of citadels in a perimeter surrounding the kingdom (2 Chron. 11:5–12).[12] He then appointed his son Abijah (Abijam) as vice-regent[13] and placed his other sons throughout the land as commanders of the fortified cities (2 Chron. 11:22–23).

The most significant event of these early years, however, was not planned or executed by Rehoboam at all. The priests and Levites of the northern tribes deserted their homes after Jeroboam established his illegitimate cult there. Their taking up residence in Judah encouraged others from the north either to follow them to Judah or at least to be sympathetic to the Davidic royal family (2 Chron. 11:13–17). In response Jeroboam developed his own rival shrines at Dan and Bethel.

Before long Rehoboam forsook Yahweh and the covenant, and in his fifth year Judah suffered the consequences—an invasion by Shoshenq of Egypt. This celebrated founder of Egypt's Dynasty 22 was the first pharaoh in many years to recapture the greatness of ancient

11. See note 4.
12. For the distribution of these cities see Yohanan Aharoni and Michael Avi-Yonah, *Macmillan Bible Atlas* (New York: Macmillan, 1968), map 119.
13. There is no evidence of coregency here, however, as S. Yeivin has shown ("The Divided Kingdom: Rehoboam-Ahaz/Jeroboam-Pekah," in *World History of the Jewish People*, vol. 4, part 1, p. 130).

Egypt.[14] In the course of his twenty-one-year reign (945–924)[15] he reunited Upper and Lower Egypt, reestablished foreign-trade alliances with Byblos and other Phoenician and Aramean states, and waited patiently for events in Israel to work to his advantage. He had already provided sanctuary to Jeroboam, Solomon's enemy and Israel's king-to-be, an act prompted not so much by mercy as by political ambition.

When Solomon died in 931 B.C., Shoshenq did not delay long before he made his move. Using as an excuse a border incident with some Semitic tribesmen,[16] Shoshenq moved north to Judah. Having taken the fortified cities and having come to the very walls of Jerusalem itself by the spring of 926/925, Shoshenq with his Egyptian and mercenary hordes moved north into Israel. This must have surprised Jeroboam to the extreme, for the king of Israel had every reason to feel safe from Egypt. But in a move characteristic of the traditional fickleness of the Egyptians, Shoshenq made a grab for Israel once he saw how easily Judah had yielded.[17]

Why Shoshenq made no attempt to follow up on this campaign is unclear. He apparently was satisfied for the time being with the plunder he had taken from Judah and Israel, particularly the rich treasures of gold from the temple. In any case his death soon after precluded any further measures by him. His son Osorkon I (924–889) also refrained from further conquest, at least for a time, being more interested in lavishing wealth on the temple of Atum. The enormous amount of gold and silver which he employed[18] may well have come primarily from the Jerusalem temple.

The sin which had occasioned this devastation of the land and spoliation of the temple was serious indeed. The author of 1 Kings indicates that Rehoboam and his compatriots reached a new low in idolatrous behavior. They set up high places, sacred stones (*maṣṣēbôt*), and Asherah poles and even engaged in ritual prostitution featuring

14. I. E. S. Edwards, "Egypt: From the Twenty-second to the Twenty-fourth Dynasty," in *Cambridge Ancient History*, 3d ed., ed. John Boardman et al. (Cambridge: Cambridge University Press, 1982), vol. 3, part 1, pp. 539–49.

15. The dates for Dynasty 22 of Egypt rest on virtually unassailable data. See Kenneth A. Kitchen, "Late-Egyptian Chronology and the Hebrew Monarchy," *JANES* 5 (1973): 231–33.

16. Edwards, "Egypt," in *CAH* 3.1, p. 546.

17. Yeivin, in fact, interprets Shoshenq's record of this expedition (an inscription found on the wall of the great temple at Karnak) as indicating that Israel, not Judah, was his original objective. Yeivin suggests that Shoshenq was attempting to open up trade routes to Byblos and Mesopotamia and to discipline Jeroboam for not having paid an expected tribute ("Divided Kingdom," in *World History of the Jewish People*, vol. 4, part 1, pp. 133–34).

18. According to James H. Breasted no less than 560,000 pounds (*A History of Egypt* [New York: Bantam, 1967], p. 444).

sodomites.[19] Given the syncretism introduced by Solomon because of his pagan wives, including Naamah the mother of Rehoboam, one is not surprised at this turn of events.

The last twelve years of Rehoboam's reign seem to be viewed more favorably by the narrators. Because "Rehoboam humbled himself, the LORD's anger turned from him, and he was not totally destroyed" (2 Chron. 12:12). But they were also years of conflict with Jeroboam. The record indicates that Judah and Israel fought continually (1 Kings 14:30). Unfortunately there is no hint as to who, if either one, had the advantage. In one sense, of course, everyone lost, for the spectacle of brother fighting brother brought disrepute not only on the sons of Jacob, but on their God as well.

The Reign of Jeroboam

If the religious situation was bad in Judah, it was even worse in Jeroboam's Israel.[20] The newly installed king, who had been given promise of an unending dynasty if he proved true to the Lord (1 Kings 11:38),[21] wasted no time at all in establishing his reign as the very paradigm of evil against which all subsequent kings of Israel were measured (1 Kings 13:34; 15:30; cf. 16:2–3, 19, etc.). His dynasty, if indeed it can be called that, lasted for only two generations, twenty-four years. And this was to set the pattern in Israel. Judah, in spite of its times of apostasy, remained always under Davidic kingship. Israel, however, suffered the turbulence of one royal family ever giving way to another; the nation was to know five different dynasties in her short lifetime of 210 years.

Jeroboam, as we have seen already, rebuilt Shechem and made it his capital. Peniel (Tulul edh-Dhahab),[22] east of the Jordan on the Jab-

19. For these pseudoreligious appurtenances and practices see Helmer Ringgren, *Religions of the Ancient Near East* (Philadelphia: Westminster, 1973), pp. 158–69.

20. Robert L. Cohn has provided an excellent literary analysis of the chiastic structure of the Jeroboam narrative (1 Kings 11:26–14:20). This study illustrates once again the point that the historical sections of the Bible, while true to fact, could be and often were couched in literary forms which run counter to modern style and even deviate from such modern conventions as chronological order, though there is no evidence of the latter in this particular case ("Literary Technique in the Jeroboam Narrative," *ZAW* 97 [1985]: 23–35).

21. This promise is analogous to the promise given to Saul (see 1 Sam. 13:13). Since in both cases the king failed to meet Yahweh's conditions and consequently there was no unending dynasty, it is fruitless to speculate about these promises vis-à-vis the Davidic covenant. See Cohn, "Literary Technique," *ZAW* 97 (1985): 27.

22. Yohanan Aharoni, *The Land of the Bible* (Philadelphia: Westminster, 1979), p. 440.

bok River, was also rebuilt, possibly as a Transjordanian provincial center (1 Kings 12:25). The association of Shechem and Peniel with Jacob without doubt influenced Jeroboam in his selection of those sites.[23]

Whatever sacred traditions may have motivated Jeroboam in his choice of Shechem and Peniel were of little consequence in his next step, however, that of the establishment of Bethel and Dan as cult centers. It was clear to Jeroboam that no amount of political partitioning of the nation could forestall the tendency of the Israelites to attend the great religious festivals at Jerusalem, where they would imbibe the spirit of national as well as religious unity. What was needed, therefore, was places in his own northern kingdom where the Israelites might gather for sacrifice and worship.

Such a move was, of course, squarely in contradiction to the Mosaic requirement that community worship be centralized (Deut. 12:1–14). Practical exigencies, however, outweighed theological requirements in the mind of Jeroboam. He must at any cost prevent a reunification of Israel with Judah, for reunification would mean the immediate cessation of his regal privileges. Besides, he might have reasoned, since Israel was independent of Judah, Jerusalem was no longer the cultic center for Israel, the presence of the ark and temple there notwithstanding.

Why Jeroboam located his shrines at Bethel and Dan rather than at Shechem is somewhat problematic. In Judah, after all, political and religious life were combined at Jerusalem. Why should they not be combined in Israel as well? Shechem, to be sure, would not have been an inappropriate choice as a spiritual center, for no site in all Israel enjoyed such a venerable tradition. Abraham, Jacob, and Joseph were all closely associated with the place, and Joshua had called the people to covenant recommitment with Yahweh at Shechem. But one must suppose that Jeroboam, always the pragmatist, sought for a place that enjoyed both the benefits of strong tradition *and* a suitable location. Bethel was eminently qualified.[24] Jacob had met Yahweh there—on at least two occasions—and one could thus make a compelling argument that Bethel was the birthplace of Israel's faith. Besides—and this was of crucial importance to Jeroboam—Bethel lay just north of the border and on the principal highway between north and south. The people of Israel could easily gather there from all over the southern and central part of the nation. In addition, they would have to pass through Bethel

23. Baruch Halpern, "Levitic Participation in the Reform Cult of Jeroboam I," *JBL* 95 (1976): 31–32.
24. Ibid., p. 32.

if they insisted on making their way to Jerusalem. This would, of course, be seriously discouraged.

The selection of Dan, on the other hand, is much more difficult to explain. It was, indeed, on the northern border of Israel just as Bethel was on the southern border. And it was reasonably accessible to the people of the Jezreel region and all points north. However, it was identified in everyone's mind with open idolatry of a type that exceeded even Jeroboam's tolerance. It will be recalled that when the Danites slaughtered the people of Laish and occupied their territory, they brought with them Jonathan, grandson of Moses, as their priest and set up the silver images which they had stolen from Micah (Judg. 18:30–31). They had then made at Dan, their city, a center of worship that could hardly be defined as Yahwistic; it would be more accurate to call it unmitigated paganism. How could Jeroboam expect the people of Israel to undertake pilgrimage to a place of such heathen associations?

The answer lies, perhaps, in the nature of the cult which Jeroboam introduced. He set up golden calves at the two shrines, describing them as the gods who had brought Israel up out of Egypt. He then appointed non-Levitical priests and, at Bethel at least, designated the fifteenth day of the eighth month as a day of special festivity. Scholarship is divided as to the full signification of Jeroboam's cultic innovations, but one thing is clear—he was identifying Bethel and Dan with the exodus.[25] The two calves, whether idols themselves or merely pedestals upon which the invisible Yahweh was presumed to stand,[26] are reminiscent of the golden calf which Aaron made while Moses was absent on Mount Sinai. The words of presentation are exactly the same in both instances: "These are your gods, O Israel, who brought you up out of Egypt" (Exod. 32:4; cf. 1 Kings 12:28). Both stories also point out that the creation and recognition of the new gods were followed by a time of festival. Further, Aaron had functioned as priest and, in Moses' absence, as covenant mediator; now Jeroboam, in addition to his royal office, installed himself as head of the cult, as can be seen clearly in his appearance at the Bethel altar to offer sacrifices. That is, he evidently viewed himself as a second Aaron who had the right to establish and oversee a religious system apart from that at Jerusalem. He arrogated to himself the prerogative of the Davidic monarchy, namely, the right of the king as the elect and adopted son of

25. Ibid., pp. 39–40.

26. William F. Albright, *Yahweh and the Gods of Canaan* (Garden City, N.Y.: Doubleday, 1969), pp. 197–98. John N. Oswalt argues rather persuasively that the calves were indeed idols; as pedestals for the invisible Yahweh they would not have evoked such intense prophetic abhorrence of what both Aaron and Jeroboam did ("The Golden Calves and the Egyptian Concept of Deity," *EQ* 45 [1973]: 13–20).

God to act not only as the political leader of the people, but as the priestly mediator as well.[27] Jeroboam perceived himself to be Israel's equivalent of the messianic dynast of Judah, a kingly priest after the order of Melchizedek.

This interpretation of Jeroboam's perception of his role explains his boldness in assuming the priesthood and making priestly appointments outside the Aaronic line. It also explains his daring to locate worship centers at Bethel and Dan, for just as David, as Melchizedekian priest, had moved tabernacle and ark to Jerusalem, a place up till then of no significance in Israelite tradition, why could Jeroboam not arbitrarily create his own cult at Bethel and Dan, especially since the former, at least, did enjoy the benefit of long and holy tradition?

How Jeroboam could feature golden calves in his cult, especially in light of the fate of that calf which Aaron had made, is rather baffling. (That idol had been ground to powder, mixed with water, and drunk by the Israelite apostates who had worshiped it.) I suggest that the motivation behind Jeroboam's action may have been an intense animosity against the Levites.[28] It was the Levites who had taken sword in hand to slay the worshipers of Aaron's golden calf. Jeroboam now bypassed the Levites by appointing his own priests and, in a supreme irony, manufactured his own golden calves as a symbol of his disdain for the Levitical priesthood. Had not Moses' own grandson, Jonathan, anticipated Jeroboam by serving as the first priest of the competing shrine at Dan? Besides according a measure of legitimacy to Dan, this story revealed that even within Moses' family there was room for diversity in religious practice. How could Jeroboam be faulted for his golden calves when Moses' own grandson had officiated over a cult at Dan which worshiped idols having no connection at all with the exodus?

Admittedly, much of the preceding line of argument is quite speculative. One cannot, in the final analysis, know what motives or considerations prompted Jeroboam. That he viewed himself as royal priest of a new and, to him, legitimate religious system is quite clear. How he connected this to the past, especially to the incident of the golden calf following the exodus, is debatable. But all will agree that Jeroboam's action was viewed by Yahweh as sinful and, in fact, as the very epitome of apostasy.

Yahweh's displeasure is obvious in that he sent a prophet from Judah to inveigh against Jeroboam and his newly formed religious sys-

27. John Gray, *I & II Kings* (Philadelphia: Westminster, 1970), pp. 315–18.
28. Frank M. Cross argues, with many other scholars, that Jeroboam's attack on the Aaronic priesthood is only an interpretation by the deuteronomist (the redactor of Kings) and that Jeroboam in fact appointed an Aaronic priesthood at Bethel (*Canaanite Myth and Hebrew Epic* [Cambridge: Harvard University Press, 1973], pp. 198–200). This can be supported only by totally disregarding the biblical narrative.

tem (1 Kings 13). When he arrived at Bethel, this unnamed man of God cried out against the altar there, for it symbolized the very heart of the apostasy. The time would come, he said, when a scion of David, Josiah by name, would destroy the altar, having offered on it the corpses of its wicked priests. Then the prophet turned to Jeroboam; when that pseudopriest reached out his hand to apprehend the man of God, it withered and became impotent. Even though Yahweh graciously restored the king's hand, it was evident that he and his deviant religion were under irrevocable divine judgment.

In due course Abijah, the heir apparent, became fatally ill; despite his mother's frantic appeals to the prophet Ahijah, the young prince died (1 Kings 14:17). The reason, Ahijah pointed out, was clear. Jeroboam, though blessed with most of David's kingdom, had not measured up to the standards of David. He had blatantly violated the covenant of Yahweh by making other gods and rejecting the God of Israel. Yahweh, therefore, would terminate Jeroboam's dynasty quickly and would eventually remove Israel itself beyond the river Euphrates because of its sin in following Jeroboam (1 Kings 14:6–16).

Details are extremely sketchy concerning the last years of Jeroboam's reign. He had evidently relocated the capital to Tirzah (Tell el-Fâr'ah), about eight miles northeast of Shechem, for it was to Tirzah that his wife returned after her interview with the prophet Ahijah. Why the move was made cannot be known for sure, though it may be that the invasion of Shoshenq against Judah and Israel in 926/925 had resulted in the destruction of Shechem or at least precipitated Jeroboam's move from Shechem to safer quarters.[29] What is known otherwise is that Jeroboam found himself at war continually with Rehoboam and, after Rehoboam's death, with his son Abijah, who ruled for but three years. Unfortunately, we do not have a shred of concrete information concerning the reason for this unremitting conflict. The most plausible theory is that the Davidic kings yearned to restore Israel to Judah and thus to recover the full Davidic kingdom.

The Pressure of Surrounding Nations

From extrabiblical sources one can glean a certain amount of information that sheds at least indirect light on life in Israel and Judah from 931 to 910 B.C. In Egypt, as we saw, Osorkon I succeeded his illustrious father Shoshenq and reigned from 924 to 889, well beyond

29. J. Alberto Soggin, *A History of Ancient Israel* (Philadelphia: Westminster, 1984), p. 198.

the time of either Rehoboam or Jeroboam.[30] Though there is no record of his direct involvement in Palestinian affairs until 897 (see p. 334), he did take measures to reaffirm Egyptian relations with Byblos.[31] While having obvious commercial value to both parties, such a step also guaranteed Egypt a foothold to the north of Israel and a friendly ally between herself and the increasingly powerful and expansionist Arameans.

We earlier noted (pp. 299–300) the establishment of an Aramean dynasty at Damascus by Hezion (Rezon) during the reign of David, perhaps as early as 990 B.C. Though the chronology is most uncertain, it seems that Hezion lived at least until the death of Solomon and was then followed by his son Tabrimmon and grandson Ben-Hadad (ca. 900–841).[32] This succession is documented by the biblical historian (1 Kings 15:18) and apparently confirmed by the so-called Ben-Hadad stela, which reads in part, "Bir-hadad, son of Ṭab-Rammân, son of Ḥadyân, king of Aram."[33]

Of Hezion's exploits nothing is known except that he had broken from Hadadezer, king of Zobah, and had relocated in Damascus (1 Kings 11:23–24). From that strategic center he harassed Solomon and presumably Jeroboam and Rehoboam as well. This he could do with relative impunity because of the incessant struggle between Israel and Judah. Other factors in the rise of Damascus were the relative

30. Edwards, "Egypt," in *CAH* 3.1, pp. 549–52.

31. H. Jacob Katzenstein, *The History of Tyre* (Jerusalem: Schocken Institute for Jewish Research, 1973), p. 121.

32. These dates are rough approximations deduced from the data cited by Merrill F. Unger, *Israel and the Aramaeans of Damascus* (Grand Rapids: Baker, 1980 reprint), pp. 56–61. The early date for Ben-Hadad (which necessitates an extremely long reign of almost sixty years) is based on the fact that King Baasha of Israel in about his thirteenth year (896 B.C.) suffered defeat at the hands of Ben-Hadad (1 Kings 15:20). To avoid the problem of such a long reign some scholars argue for a Ben-Hadad I and a Ben-Hadad II prior to Hazael. See William H. Shea, "The Kings of the Melqart Stela," *Maarav* 1.2 (1978–1979): 159–60. As Shea points out himself, however, to posit successive Ben-Hadads goes contrary to the ordinary dynastic pattern in Syria-Palestine (p. 171). Frank M. Cross complicates matters still further with three successive Ben-Hadads between 885 and 841 ("The Stele Dedicated to Melcarth by Ben-Hadad of Damascus," *BASOR* 205 [1972]: 42).

33. Unger, *Israel and the Aramaeans*, p. 56. This reading of the Ben-Hadad stela (otherwise known as the Melqart stela) is by no means universally accepted. For a helpful discussion of alternatives see J. Andrew Dearman and J. Maxwell Miller, "The Melqart Stele and the Ben Hadads of Damascus: Two Studies," *PEQ* 115 (1983): 95–101. Dearman contends that there was no ruler named Ben-Hadad between 865 and 806 (thus he denies the historicity of 1 Kings 20 and 22:1–38), while Miller identifies the Ben-Hadad of the stela as the son of Hazael (after 806), thus also loosing the Ahab stories from their historical moorings. See also Shea, "The Kings of the Melqart Stela," p. 170; B. Oded, "Neighbors on the East," in *World History of the Jewish People*, vol. 4, part 1, p. 267.

weakness of the other Aramean states and the continued impotence of Assyria, at least until the reign of Adad-nirari II (911–891); moreover, the Sealands people of lower Mesopotamia were no threat this early.

Abijah of Judah

The situation in Judah following the death of Rehoboam steadily deteriorated, for his son and successor Abijah (913–911) did not walk in the ways of David. Yet, the narrator says, "God gave him a lamp in Jerusalem by raising up a son to succeed him" (1 Kings 15:4), a favor done for David's sake. Once more, then, the unconditional covenant blessing of Yahweh, based on his promise to David, guaranteed the stability of David's kingdom despite its ruler.

Evidence of Yahweh's ongoing grace is seen in Abijah's success against every effort of Jeroboam to defeat him. The chronicler particularly emphasizes this fact.[34] After his accession Abijah found himself facing seemingly insuperable odds as Jeroboam confronted him on Mount Zemaraim (Ras eṭ-Ṭahuneh), only a mile or two from Bethel.[35] Abijah had marched north with the purpose of winning Israel back to the Davidic kingdom (2 Chron. 13:4–12). Reminding the Israelites that Yahweh had made the covenant of kingship with David only, he claimed that their nation under Jeroboam was illegitimate. Jeroboam, Abijah said, had taken advantage of the naive Rehoboam to carve out his own rival dominion. Though one may quarrel with Abijah's objectivity on this point, his continuing argument, that Jeroboam's idolatrous cult was antithetical to the will of God in every respect, can hardly be gainsaid. Since the true faith was only in Judah and in Judah's observance of the requirements of Yahweh, Israel ought, Abijah said, to return to David without further ado.

Jeroboam ignored this appeal and surrounded Abijah's army front and rear. To validate Abijah's theological stand, Yahweh himself took up arms as the divine Warrior and delivered his people from calamity.

---

34. For various reasons—the lack of a parallel in 1 Kings, the enormous numbers of soldiers, evidence of theologizing by the chronicler—many scholars dismiss the record of the battle of Zemaraim as unhistorical. See the arguments of Ralph W. Klein, "Abijah's Campaign Against the North (2 Chron. 13)—What Were the Chronicler's Sources?" *ZAW* 95 (1983): 210–17. To deny historicity to an event simply or primarily because it is not recounted in both synoptic accounts is, however, to beg the question and to overlook the chronicler's access to other sources. John Bright concludes that "the incident is certainly historical" (*A History of Israel*, 3d ed. [Philadelphia: Westminster, 1981], p. 234).

35. For a reconstruction of the strategy see Aharoni and Avi-Yonah, *Macmillan Bible Atlas*, map 121.

Abijah followed through and captured the Israelite cities of Bethel, Jeshanah (el-Burj?), and Ephron (eṭ-Ṭaiyibeh), thus undermining Jeroboam both religiously and politically. Jeroboam never recovered from this blow. Abijah, however, grew in power, as the size of his harem attests (2 Chron. 13:21).

Asa of Judah

Chronological Considerations

Jeroboam survived Abijah by a year or two and so was briefly contemporaneous with Asa, the next ruler in the line of David. The author of Kings identifies Asa as the son of Maacah (1 Kings 15:10), but since he is clearly the son of Abijah, the actual intent is that Maacah was his grandmother. The reason for pointing out this relationship is that Maacah had authorized the erection of an Asherah pole in Jerusalem, and Asa, among his other reforms, cut it down and destroyed it. It may be assumed that Asa was very young when he came to power because his father had reigned only three years and, therefore, was probably quite young himself when he died. One also should note that Asa reigned for forty-one years (911–870), a not unparalleled and yet an unusually long period of time. Even so, his death may have been somewhat premature, for the historian takes pains to point out that Asa was diseased in his feet in the last years of his life (1 Kings 15:23). Whether he actually died of this malady cannot be determined, but it apparently incapacitated him enough that he appointed his son Jehoshaphat as his coregent for the last three years of his reign.[36]

The chronological structure of the reign of Asa is somewhat complicated and justifies rather detailed discussion. The chronicler begins by stating that with the succession of Asa came ten years of peace (911–901). It was evidently within that period (or just after it) that Asa undertook his great religious reformation, culminating in his deposition of his grandmother and destruction of her Asherah pole. If our thesis that he came to power as a minor is correct, the reformation was probably not begun immediately. It may have taken ten years for Asa to achieve the maturity and independence to make it possible.

During this time Asa also built up Judah's defensive posture by refortifying the outposts which Rehoboam had built and perhaps adding to them. Through all these years, the chronicler stresses, Judah

---

36. Thiele, *Mysterious Numbers*, p. 70. For the pattern of coregency as a hallmark of Israelite and Judean monarchy see Thiele, "Coregencies and Overlapping Reigns Among the Hebrew Kings," *JBL* 93 (1974): 174–200.

was at peace (2 Chron. 14:6). Finally, the period of reformation was climaxed by a great assembly at Jerusalem to which not only Judah, but the faithful of Ephraim, Manasseh, and Simeon were invited (2 Chron. 15:8–15). This assembly was held in Asa's fifteenth year (ca. 896).

Eventually Asa found himself embroiled in war. The narrator indicates that this took place in Asa's thirty-fifth year (2 Chron. 15:19), and with this datum the chronology becomes most difficult to resolve. The problem is that while Asa's thirty-fifth year would be 876, the very next verse (2 Chron. 16:1) indicates that Asa went to war in his thirty-sixth year, presumably 875, with Baasha of Israel, who died in 886—eleven years earlier! The war in Asa's thirty-fifth year was probably that against Zerah the Cushite, a battle that is generally dated shortly after 900.[37]

Various ingenious means have been suggested to solve this dilemma. Some scholars simply emend "thirty-fifth" and "thirty-sixth" to "fifteenth" and "sixteenth" respectively, but there is no textual evidence whatsoever for this.[38] Others drastically shift the years of Baasha downward to make him contemporary with Asa's last years.[39] This not only totally disregards the biblical witness, but forces an adjustment of the dates for virtually every other king of Israel and Judah as well. Besides, it disturbs the date of the campaign against Zerah to an intolerable degree.

The best solution appears to be that of Edwin Thiele, who proposes that "thirty-fifth" and "thirty-sixth" refer not to the years of Asa's reign per se, but to the years that had transpired from the fixed *terminus a quo* of the division of the kingdom.[40] Since this is dated at 931, the thirty-fifth year would be 897 and the thirty-sixth 896. Though this is an unusual way of pinpointing events in a king's reign, there is nothing inherently impossible or improbable about it. Besides, if the years of

---

37. Edwards, "Egypt," in *CAH* 3.1, p. 552, dates it at 897. This dovetails nicely with our date for the great assembly (896), to which were brought spoils (2 Chron. 15:11), presumably from the Cushite foe. See also Yeivin, "Divided Kingdom," in *World History of the Jewish People*, vol. 4, part 1, p. 136; Kenneth A. Kitchen, *The Third Intermediate Period in Egypt (1100–650 B.C.)* (Warminster: Aris and Phillips, 1973), p. 309.

38. This solution is cited but not accepted by Edward L. Curtis, *A Critical and Exegetical Commentary on the Books of Chronicles* (Edinburgh: T. & T. Clark, 1910), p. 387. Raymond B. Dillard assumes that the chronicler is working with a different textual tradition and that the modern reader must live with the possibility that that tradition was in error or at least at variance with Samuel/Kings ("The Reign of Asa [2 Chronicles 14–16]: An Example of the Chronicler's Theological Method," *JETS* 23 [1980]: 217).

39. William F. Albright, *The Biblical Period from Abraham to Ezra* (New York: Harper, 1963), pp. 116–17.

40. Thiele, *Mysterious Numbers*, p. 60.

Rehoboam (17) and Abijah (3) are added to the 15 of Asa which preceded his first war (cf. 2 Chron. 15:10 and 19), they total 35, exactly as the narrator suggests.

If the conflict between Asa and Baasha occurred in the thirty-sixth year (2 Chron. 16:1), the war in the thirty-fifth year (15:19) must, as we have proposed, be that in which Asa encountered Zerah at Mareshah, since the record is silent about any other. The date of this battle would have been the fifteenth year of Asa's reign—897. Virtually nothing is known of Zerah from extrabiblical texts; the description in the Old Testament seems to indicate that he was a Nubian or Arabian mercenary who was serving under Osorkon I.[41]

The Wars of Asa

In this, his initial military adventure, Asa recognized the need of divine favor and so called upon Yahweh. The chronicler says that Yahweh not only helped, but he himself "struck down the Cushites" (2 Chron. 14:12), a phrase recalling the old tradition of holy war. Zerah suffered tremendous losses from Mareshah (Tell Sandaḥannah),[42] near Lachish, all the way to Gerar, more than twenty miles southwest. Gerar apparently was in Egyptian hands at this time, for 2 Chronicles 14:12–15 pictures the destruction and plunder of enemy territory.

The campaign of Asa against Baasha in the very next year is of far greater interest and importance not only because it involved the divided house of Israel, but because it included the Arameans as well. The author of Kings says that there was war between Asa and Baasha all their days (1 Kings 15:16), by which he undoubtedly means a spirit of hostility, but eventually this spilled over into outright aggression.

The provocation came from Baasha (909–886), who, in what must have been his thirteenth year, built a fortification at Ramah (er-Râm) near the border between Israel and Judah. The purpose of the structure was to prevent Israelites from going to Judah. This was in effect what Jeroboam had hoped to accomplish when he chose Bethel as a cult center. During Baasha's rule increasing numbers of Israelites had come to see the moral and spiritual bankruptcy of the north and were opting to travel south, whether only to participate in the Jerusalem festivals or to emigrate permanently.

Baasha's goal, then, was to stem this traffic. Asa, for whatever reason, saw this move as a threat to his own security, so he took steps to

41. T. C. Mitchell, "Israel and Judah Until the Revolt of Jehu (931–841 B.C.)," in *CAH* 3.1, pp. 462–63; Kitchen, *Third Intermediate Period*, p. 309.

42. Aharoni, *Land of the Bible*, p. 439; Aharoni and Avi-Yonah, *Macmillan Bible Atlas*, map 122.

enlist the support of Ben-Hadad, king of Damascus. Ben-Hadad had at some point made a treaty with Israel; Asa now prevailed upon him to break it and to honor the commitment that their predecessors had made (2 Chron. 16:3). As added inducement Asa offered Ben-Hadad silver and gold from the temple and the royal treasuries.

Thus persuaded, Ben-Hadad marched south against Israel's northern territories and in rapid succession took the cities of Ijon (Tell ed-Dibbîn), Dan, Abel Beth Maacah, and much of Naphtali including the Kinnereth region just west of the Sea of Kinnereth or Galilee.[43] This forced Baasha to leave his project at Ramah and retreat to his capital at Tirzah, perhaps in expectation of a further advance by Ben-Hadad even to Tirzah. Asa then dismantled the unfinished work of Ramah and with the building stones constructed his own wall of defense at Geba (Jeba') and Mizpah (Tell en-Naṣbeh), the former to the east and the latter to the west of Ramah.

The fact that Ben-Hadad made treaties with both Judah and Israel is indicative of the rising stature and influence of Damascus amongst the smaller states of Syria and Palestine. It also is a tribute to the diplomatic skills of Ben-Hadad, who knew how to play off one side against the other to his own ultimate advantage. Not only had he been rewarded handsomely by the payment of silver and gold from Jerusalem, but he had taken under his hegemony virtually all of the north Galilee region, thus giving him access to the Mediterranean coast and beyond. Damascus already enjoyed the benefits of its location astride the King's Highway and other major routes south and east of the Anti-Lebanons. Now it controlled the principal highways from Egypt via the coastal plain and on to Mesopotamia.[44]

The Reemergence of Assyria

The rise of Damascus was made possible in part by the absence of outside interference from major powers such as Assyria.[45] But this freedom which the eastern Mediterranean world had enjoyed since the

43. For the route see Aharoni and Avi-Yonah, *Macmillan Bible Atlas*, map 124.
44. Unger, *Israel and the Aramaeans*, p. 62.
45. Parallel Assyrian and Aramaic inscriptions on a mid-ninth-century statue recently discovered at Tell Fekheriyeh in the region of Gozan indicate that the Arameans were having tremendous cultural if not political influence upon their Assyrian neighbors. It may be this very ascendance of the Arameans that prompted Assyrian westward expansionism beginning especially under Aššur-naṣirpal II. For the significance of the statue see A. R. Millard, "Assyrians and Aramaeans," *Iraq* 45 (1983): 106; Ran Zadok, "Remarks on the Inscription of Hdys'y from Tell Fakhariya," *Tel Aviv* 9 (1982): 117–29.

days of Tiglath-pileser I, more than a century earlier, was coming to an end. Perceptive observers of the world scene could already discern by 900 the stirrings of the Assyrian giant. Though it would be almost fifty years before they fell beneath its heel, the little kingdoms of the west could hear it coming.

Table 7   **The Neo-Assyrian Kings**

Adad-nirari II	911–891
Tukulti-Ninurta II	890–884
Aššur-naṣirpal II	883–859
Shalmaneser III	858–824
Shamshi-Adad V	823–811
Adad-nirari III	810–783
Shalmaneser IV	782–773
Aššur-dan III	772–755
Aššur-nirari V	754–745
Tiglath-pileser III	745–727
Shalmaneser V	727–722
Sargon II	722–705
Sennacherib	705–681
Esarhaddon	681–669
Ashurbanipal	668–627
Ashur-eṭil-ilāni	627–623
Sin-šum-lišir	623
Sin-šar-iškun	623–612
Aššur-uballiṭ II	612–609

In his fourth campaign Adad-nirari II (911–891)[46] made his first westward penetration, an assault on the region of Ḫanigalbat on the upper Euphrates. Here he made contact with the Aramean Aḫlamû and Suḫu tribes, whom he managed to isolate and defeat.[47] In a series of successive strikes (ca. 901–896) he finally conquered all of Ḫanigalbat and incorporated it into the Assyrian sphere of influence. Other Aramean tribes in the upper Habor area fell by 900. Thus when Ben-Hadad began to rule (ca. 900), all of upper Mesopotamia was firmly under Assyrian domination. Ben-Hadad, as well as Asa, Baasha, and other rulers, were certainly well aware of these momentous events to the north and understood clearly what they portended for their own little kingdoms. There is little wonder that one step, at least, that was taken was the forging of international treaties among the various states of Syria and Palestine, treaties like those attested in the Old Testament

46. Albert Kirk Grayson, "Assyria: Ashur-dan II to Ashur-Nirari V (934–745 B.C.)," in *CAH* 3.1, p. 250.

47. See Albert Kirk Grayson, *Assyrian Royal Inscriptions* (Wiesbaden: Otto Harrassowitz, 1976), vol. 2, pp. 86–87, #2, 11. 30–41.

between Asa and Ben-Hadad on the one hand and Baasha and Ben-Hadad on the other.

The successor to Adad-nirari, Tukulti-Ninurta II (890–884), continued the policies of his predecessor with the clear intent of creating an Assyrian empire. Of interest to students of Israel's history is his conquest of lands in the west all the way to Mushku in west-central Anatolia, a campaign which took place in 885.[48] His career was cut short, however, so the task of imperialism was left to Aššur-naṣirpal II (883–859).[49] He initiated a program of annual western campaigns which became notorious for their cruelty. By around 875 he had brought all the northern Aramean states as far as Bît-Adini under Assyrian control. Even so, Israel, Judah, and Damascus were given a reprieve for twenty-five more years until, at last, even they were drawn into the maelstrom of international upheaval occasioned by the inexorable westward and southward sweep of the Assyrian war machine under Shalmaneser III.

Nadab of Israel

Soon after Asa began to rule over Judah, Jeroboam died and his son Nadab sat upon the throne of Israel (1 Kings 14:20). His reign of but two years (910–909) was distinguished only by his evil imitation of the pattern of his father. Then the predictive word of the prophet Ahijah was fulfilled: Nadab was cut off violently, thus ending the dynasty of Jeroboam after just two generations (1 Kings 14:14). To ensure that the house of Jeroboam would never rise again, Baasha, Nadab's assassin, went on to exterminate the entire royal family. This all happened, the theologian-historian says, "because of the sins Jeroboam had committed and had caused Israel to commit" (1 Kings 15:30). Similar characterizations of the reigns of the rest of the kings of Israel will become a wearisome litany.[50]

The Dynasty of Baasha of Israel

The Reign of Baasha

The agent of Yahweh's holy wrath was Baasha ben Ahijah of Issachar, an Israelite officer. It seems that Nadab was laying siege to Gib-

---

48. Grayson, "Assyria," in *CAH* 3.1, p. 252; *Assyrian Royal Inscriptions*, vol. 2, p. 104, #1, 11. 33–45.

49. Grayson, "Assyria," in *CAH* 3.1, pp. 253–59; Yutaka Ikeda, "Assyrian Kings and the Mediterranean Sea: The Twelfth to Ninth Centuries B.C.," *Abr-Nahrain* 23 (1984–1985): 23–26.

50. This is only one of the prevailing themes found in 1 and 2 Kings which reflect prophetic condemnation of Israel's history of covenant violation. See Ziony Zevit, "Deuteronomistic Historiography in 1 Kings 12–2 Kings 17 and the Reinvestiture of the Israelian Cult," *JSOT* 32 (1985): 57–73.

bethon (Tell el-Melât), a Philistine fortress just west of Gezer, hoping perhaps to establish a foothold along Judah's northwestern flank and, at the same time, to eliminate a bothersome Philistine presence so close to the important storage city of Gezer. In the course of the siege Baasha turned on his king, slew him, and returned to Tirzah to claim the royal throne.

Baasha, founder of Israel's second dynasty, reigned for twenty-four years (909–886), all of them contemporary with Asa of Judah. The dynasty may have changed, but the nature of government did not, for Baasha, like Nadab, walked in the way of Jeroboam. Before long a prophet, Jehu ben Hanani, pronounced on Baasha the very judgment Ahijah had pronounced on Jeroboam: the king's house would be utterly annihilated, even though God in his mercy had allowed him to come to power in the first place (1 Kings 16:1–4). Yahweh's offers of a perpetual kingship were genuine but conditional. If Jeroboam or Baasha or anyone else whom God might choose would be obedient to the covenant will of God in whatever form it might be revealed, that king had assurance that his line would never end in Israel. If, however, he became disloyal and defected—and the kings of Israel did so without exception—he could count on the swift and awful judgment of God. The messianic monarchy was reserved to David and his Judean descendants, to be sure, but this did not preclude an everlasting royal house from ruling over Israel as well.

Apart from his struggles with Asa, which occupied the latter part of his reign (ca. 896–886), little is known of Baasha. He had made a treaty with Ben-Hadad of Damascus, a pact which Ben-Hadad broke in favor of Asa; and, of course, Baasha lost considerable territory in the north to his erstwhile ally. At least it can be said of Baasha that he apparently died a natural death, an experience, as we shall see, that became something of a rarity among the kings of Israel.

The Reign of Elah

Baasha, like Jeroboam, founded a dynasty of only two generations, himself and his son Elah. And like Nadab Elah also reigned for only two years (886–885). Amazingly, the comparison continues, for Elah, like Nadab, was the victim of assassination at the hands of a trusted lieutenant and confidant. In a drunken spree at the home of his majordomo, Arza, Elah was attacked by Zimri, the commander of a chariotry corps; and he died then and there (1 Kings 16:8–14). Zimri, in an act of poetic justice, proceeded to exterminate the entire family of Baasha, exactly as Baasha had dealt with the kin of Jeroboam. But Zimri was an interloper without divine sanction of any kind. He therefore originated no dynasty and, in fact, survived for only seven days.

The partying at the house of Arza had evidently taken place while Israel's army, under its commander Omri, was once again laying siege to Gibbethon. When word of the coup reached the camp, the troops there at once acclaimed their general, Omri, to be king, thus setting him in clear opposition to Zimri (1 Kings 16:16). Omri and his followers then made their way to Tirzah. When it became apparent to Zimri that he had no support and, in fact, was about to be taken by Omri, he set fire to the palace and died in the flames.[51] The way to kingship, as a result, appeared to lie open before Omri.

Omri of Israel

But an easy accession was not to be, for Tibni ben Ginath had somehow gained a following, thus precipitating another crisis of leadership. Who he was and whence he came we do not know, but in any event his efforts to provide an alternative to Omri quickly foundered, he himself was slain, and Omri stood alone and unopposed (1 Kings 16:21–22). For the first six of his twelve years (885–874) Omri retained the capital at Tirzah, but around 880 he bought an imposing hill from Shemer and renamed it Samaria. He then built extensive fortifications around its summit and placed within them a new palace and other government buildings.

The site had been occupied on and off since earliest times, but not until Omri made it Israel's seat of government did Samaria become a significant city.[52] This is most surprising in light of its advantageous position. Located high on its hilltop, the site had a commanding view of the valley below, which surrounded it on all sides. It was thus safe from sneak attack and was easily defended. Samaria remained Israel's capital until it fell to the Assyrians in 722; after that it was a provincial seat under both the Assyrians and Persians. Herod the Great rebuilt it and named it Sebaste after Augustus Caesar, his patron (*Sebastos* is the Greek word for "Augustus"). The modern name of the adjacent village—Sebastiyeh—reflects this Herodian rechristening.

The move of the capital from Tirzah to Samaria, twelve miles west, did not meet with universal approval. For years thereafter, in fact, a rebel community made its headquarters in Tirzah and as late as the mid-eighth century continued to vie with Samaria for political dom-

---

51. For archaeological evidence of the fire and of Omri's preliminary rebuilding at Tirzah, see D. N. Pienaar, "The Role of Fortified Cities in the Northern Kingdom During the Reign of the Omride Dynasty," *JNSL* 9 (1981): 151–52.

52. G. Ernest Wright, "Samaria," in *The Biblical Archaeologist Reader*, ed. Edward F. Campbell, Jr., and David Noel Freedman (Garden City, N.Y.: Doubleday, 1964), vol. 2, pp. 248–57.

ination. Why Omri made such a move in the face of clear resistance to it is difficult to ascertain. It may be that he saw himself and his new dynasty as the agent of change from the now discredited rule of Jeroboam and his successors. A clear signal of that change would have been a renunciation of Tirzah, Jeroboam's capital, in favor of a brand new city which was uncontaminated by the past.[53]

Though the biblical historians offer little information on the subject, Omri was in fact one of the most influential of Israel's early kings. So highly regarded was he by even the great powers of the world that his name became synonymous with the name of his kingdom. For example, in Assyrian texts written more than one hundred years after his death Israel is called *Bīt Ḫumrî* ("house of Omri").[54] Israelite kings who followed him were sometimes called sons of Omri even though they were of different dynasties.

The reason for Omri's prestige is not certain, though the relatively prosperous and powerful reign of his son Ahab suggests that Omri had laid a firm foundation. He must have followed a sound fiscal policy and by means of astute diplomacy managed both to forestall enemy attack and to forge commercial and political alliances which worked greatly to his advantage. An important example is his relationship with Ethbaal, king of Tyre and Sidon (887–856), which eventually led to the marriage of his son Ahab to the Tyrian princess Jezebel.[55] This marriage, of course, would prove to be disastrous to Israel's (and Judah's) spiritual well-being. Otherwise, the relationship between Omri and Ethbaal had obvious advantages for both parties. Tyre no doubt had felt threatened by the growing power of Damascus to the east and welcomed a friendly intervening ally.[56] As for Israel, since Davidic times a link with Tyre had meant access to the larger world of trade and commerce. That link had apparently been broken or at least become very tenuous in post-Solomonic Israel, so Omri, eager to restore the benefits that increased commerce could bring, gladly welcomed renewed contact with Tyre. At the same time, however, closer Israelite-Phoenician ties must have been viewed with suspicion in Damascus. It is not surprising, then, that the next time we hear of Ben-Hadad he is at war with Israel under Ahab.[57]

53. For other suggestions see Herbert Donner, "The Separate States of Israel and Judah," in *Israelite and Judaean History*, ed. John H. Hayes and J. Maxwell Miller (Philadelphia: Westminster, 1977), pp. 402–3.

54. Mitchell, "Israel and Judah," in *CAH* 3.1, p. 467.

55. Katzenstein, *History of Tyre*, p. 144.

56. B. Oded, "Neighbors on the West," in *World History of the Jewish People*, vol. 4, part 1, p. 234.

57. For the many reasons behind the hostilities see Unger, *Israel and the Aramaeans*, p. 66.

Jehoshaphat of Judah

Coregency with Asa

Before we consider the conflict between Ahab and Ben-Hadad, however, it is necessary to review briefly the transfer of power from Asa of Judah to his son Jehoshaphat. The best chronological reconstruction necessitates a date of 870 for the death of Asa and 873 for the accession of Jehoshaphat. This obviously involves a three-year coregency, which is at least suggested by the chronicler's report that Asa was afflicted by a foot disease in his thirty-ninth year (2 Chron. 16:12). This would have been the year 873, the very year that Jehoshaphat began his tenure. Asa's incapacity, then, introduced a coregency system which would frequently be employed thereafter by the kings of both Judah and Israel.[58]

The assessment of Asa's reign in the historical sources is mixed. Both accounts agree that he was essentially a godly ruler, one who walked in the ways of David. He had removed idolatry from the land, except for some high places, and had sought to restore the pure worship of Yahweh. This reform was undertaken at the behest of the prophet Azariah (2 Chron. 15:1–8). Yahweh, Azariah said, would be with Judah as he had been with their ancestors in the days of the judges. But his favor depended on their seeking after God. Upon completion of the reform Asa convened a great assembly at Jerusalem to offer a vast sacrifice to Yahweh and reaffirm their covenant with him (2 Chron. 15:9–15).

On the other hand, Asa had made a treaty obtaining Ben-Hadad's support against Baasha, an overture for which the prophet Hanani severely condemned him (2 Chron. 16:1–9). Rather than trusting Yahweh for deliverance, Asa had turned to human resources and even emptied the sacred treasury to buy an answer to his problem. To compound his sin, Asa imprisoned the man of God who had brought the word of rebuke and, in his frustration, lashed out with oppressive measures against his very own people. Even after his foot ailment came upon him, he looked to his physicians rather than to Yahweh, whose purpose in bringing the affliction was to turn Asa back to himself.

There is a significant difference between the nature of Asa's disobedience and that of his Israelite contemporaries, however. Their sin was one of total defection from the covenant standards of Yahweh, a repudiation of his lordship. Asa despite his lapses had a heart for God. His sin did not consist in failure to submit to divine sovereignty but in reliance on human wisdom and resources at important junctures

---

58. Thiele, *Mysterious Numbers*, p. 70.

in his life. God, who knows the heart, can read the motivations and impulses which remain unintelligible to mere humans.

The Accomplishments of Jehoshaphat

Jehoshaphat, son of Asa, came to Judah's throne when he was thirty-five years of age and he reigned for twenty-five years (873–848), including the three years of coregency with his father. By this time Ahab was ruling from Samaria, having succeeded Omri in 874. Thus Jehoshaphat commenced his sole regency in Ahab's fourth year (1 Kings 22:41); since Ahab ruled for twenty-two years (until 853), the two were contemporaries for most of their respective reigns.

The verdict of history is kind toward Jehoshaphat—he walked with Yahweh, especially in his early years, and removed all vestiges of idolatry except for the high places (1 Kings 22:43; 2 Chron. 17:3–6). It is quite apparent that in the beginning he did not trust Ahab, for the first projects he undertook were the refortification and manning of the garrisons along his border with Israel (2 Chron. 17:1–2). This suspicion did not last long, however, and eventually Jehoshaphat made common cause with Ahab, even marrying into the Israelite royal family. This alliance with Ahab would one day elicit a stern prophetic rebuke: "Should you help the wicked and love those who hate the LORD?" (2 Chron. 19:2).

As a fruit of divine blessing as well as sage fiscal programs Jehoshaphat brought Judah to a prosperity and strength unknown since Solomon. This evoked such esteem among his neighbors that some of them, specifically the Philistines and Arabs, submitted to his domination voluntarily and provided him with their tribute (2 Chron. 17:10–11). Their reasons were not totally devoid of self-interest, for they were motivated to a large extent by the need for Judean protection against an increasingly visible Assyrian war machine. They turned quite naturally to Jehoshaphat because he had accumulated vast provisions in storage depots throughout Judah and raised an army of enormous proportions.

An even greater source of Jehoshaphat's strength, a strength of the heart and spirit, was the missionary activities he inaugurated throughout Judah in his third year (2 Chron. 17:7–9). Various leaders—priestly and secular alike—made their way through the length and breadth of the nation, teaching Torah as they went. Later, evidently after Jehoshaphat's alliance with Ahab, some of these evangelists penetrated even the hill country of Ephraim with their plea for reconciliation to Yahweh (2 Chron. 19:4).

Jehoshaphat also introduced sweeping changes in the nation's judiciary (2 Chron. 19:5–11). He placed judges in all the fortress cities of Judah and in Jerusalem itself created a kind of supreme court made up of religious and nonreligious personnel. It was their responsibility to hear cases referred to them from the lower courts. Over all of them were Amariah, the chief priest, and Zebadiah, the leading official of Judah. All of these appointees the king charged to judge fairly, as before Yahweh, for it was he to whom they were ultimately responsible and his holy standards to which all human behavior must conform.

The historical record is nearly silent concerning specific events following 868, Jehoshaphat's third year (see 2 Chron. 17:7). The story picks up at 853, when Ahab persuaded Jehoshaphat to lend a hand in retaking Ramoth Gilead from the Arameans (1 Kings 22:1–4). The ensuing conflict proved disastrous for both kings. Ahab died in the fray, leaving his son Ahaziah to succeed him. And the ill-advised collaboration by Judah not only earned the rebuke of Jehu the seer that Jehoshaphat loved those who hated Yahweh, but plunged the nation of Judah into a series of wars and other tragedies.

Inspired perhaps by the defeat and death of Ahab at the hand of the Arameans, the little Transjordanian states of Moab, Ammon, and Meun[59] launched an attack on Jehoshaphat (2 Chron. 20:1). By the time he learned of it the enemy forces had already crossed the Dead Sea and were bivouacked at Hazazon Tamar (i.e., En Gedi).[60] Alarmed, Jehoshaphat proclaimed a nationwide fast and assembled the people at Jerusalem for prayer. In his petition Jehoshaphat reminded God of his ancient promises and pointed out the irony that the peoples whom Yahweh had spared from Israel's sword under Moses were now coming to devour Judah (2 Chron. 20:10–12).

Yahweh then answered through a Levite, Jahaziel, who assured the king and people of God's presence. All they needed to do was stand by and observe the deliverance Yahweh would give them. The next day Judah's army headed for the Desert of Tekoa to confront the foe. The appeal to Yahweh, the outpouring of praise, the direct intervention of Yahweh—all attest to the fact that this was holy war and that the battle was Yahweh's.[61] In confusion the enemy hosts turned upon one another until no one was left alive. Jehoshaphat and Judah then re-

59. The *mēhāʿammônîm* ("of the Ammonites") in the Masoretic text should be read (with the Septuagint) *mēhammēʿûnîm* ("of the Meunites"). The Meunites were an Arabian tribe living in Edom and elsewhere east and south of the Dead Sea (cf. 1 Chron. 4:41; 2 Chron. 26:7). See Merrill, "2 Chronicles," in *Bible Knowledge Commentary*, vol. 1, p. 634; H. G. M. Williamson, *1 and 2 Chronicles*, New Century Bible Commentary (Grand Rapids: Eerdmans, 1982), pp. 293–94.

60. Most scholars identify Hazazon Tamar as Tamar ('Ain Ḥuṣb) in the Arabah south of the Dead Sea. See Aharoni, *Land of the Bible*, p. 140. One ought not deny the equation of Hazazon Tamar with En Gedi, however, since the narrative says the enemy had come "from the other side of the Sea" (i.e., the Dead Sea). See the route suggested by Aharoni and Avi-Yonah, *Macmillan Bible Atlas*, map 133.

61. Frank M. Cross, *Canaanite Myth and Hebrew Epic* (Cambridge: Harvard University Press, 1973), pp. 105–6.

turned in triumph to Jerusalem, singing the praises of Yahweh and bearing the rich spoils of war.

As we already noted, Ahab of Israel was succeeded by his son Ahaziah, who ruled for only two years (853–852). One would think that Jehoshaphat might have learned the folly of alignment with the wicked house of Ahab, but evidently he had not because he also made a covenant with Ahaziah (2 Chron. 20:35–36). It is true that this agreement was for commercial rather than military purposes, but it nonetheless was evil in the sight of Yahweh. A prophet once again came to Jehoshaphat and this time announced that the great convoy of ships which he had built at Ezion Geber in cooperation with Ahaziah would be destroyed, and so they were.

The presence of Judean ships at Ezion Geber, the Edomite port city on the Gulf of Aqaba, implies that Judah continued to dominate Edom. The author of Kings, in fact, points out that in Jehoshaphat's latter years Edom had no king but was under the administration of a deputy, an appointee, no doubt, of Jehoshaphat himself (1 Kings 22:47). This arrangement did not outlast Jehoshaphat, however, for the next time Edom appears in the record, during the reign of Joram, Ahab's second son, she is once again under her own king (2 Kings 3:9).

Edom's independence must have been achieved without a struggle, or so the record suggests, for when Joram of Israel prevailed upon Jehoshaphat to assist him in bringing his rebellious province of Moab to heel, he also enlisted the help of the king of Edom. It may well be that the disaster to Jehoshaphat's ships at Ezion Geber had resulted in his relinquishing control of Edom.[62] Even so, the Edomite independence was of very brief duration, for in the time of Jehoram, son of Jehoshaphat, it had to be regained all over again (2 Kings 8:20).

Be that as it may, the most significant aspect of the Moabite rebellion is the fact that Jehoshaphat, for the third time, made a compromising alliance with the dynasty of Ahab. His penchant for involvement with his ungodly colleagues from the north is beyond explanation, for he neither needed the relationship nor ever gained anything from it but sorrow.

Ahab of Israel

The Evil of Ahab

The impetus for Jehoshaphat's various entanglements came from the northern kingdom, beginning with Ahab. Having succeeded Omri

62. John R. Bartlett, in fact, suggests that the destruction of the ships was not the result of natural disaster but of Edomite (or even Israelite) hostility ("The Moabites and Edomites," in *Peoples of Old Testament Times*, ed. D. J. Wiseman [Oxford: Clarendon, 1973], p. 236).

in 874, Ahab for the next twenty-two years presided over a kingdom that enjoyed a certain measure of prosperity and international influence—thanks to the energetic policies of his father—but that was also shot through with moral and spiritual decadence. As though the internal apostasy from Yahweh were not enough, Ahab married Jezebel, daughter of the Sidonian king Ethbaal, and brought her Baal and Asherah worship into Samaria. For the first time, then, the cult of Yahweh was officially replaced by paganism and not allowed to coexist with it.[63]

The Ministry of Elijah

Rather than write his people off, however, Yahweh raised up one of the most fascinating and mysterious persons of all biblical history—Elijah the prophet—to confront them with their sin and with his judgment. Appearing suddenly one day to Ahab, the prophet announced that Israel must experience a few years of drought because of her defection from Yahweh and attachment to the Baals (1 Kings 17:1). Three years later (1 Kings 18:1) Elijah reappeared to confront the prophets of Baal and Asherah at Mount Carmel, the site of a major Baal shrine. The result of their contest was the total discrediting of the pagan prophets and their gods. After these prophets had been slain, Elijah announced to Ahab that the drought was at an end. Baal, the alleged god of thunder, rain, and fertility, had been forced to retire in utter shame from before the face of Yahweh, the only true God, who had shown himself to be the source of life and blessing.[64]

Even this miraculous demonstration of Yahweh's power did not bring Ahab to faith, however, and he and Jezebel forced Elijah to retreat to Horeb (Sinai). There the prophet met Yahweh face to face at the very site where Moses had met him six hundred years before. The meaning clearly is that the God of covenant promise was still there to meet his people and to bless them as they met the conditions of faith and obedience. The God of Carmel was the God of Horeb. And he was also the sovereign God of Israel and the nations. Evidence of his supremacy over all was his commission to Elijah—he must return

63. For the nature of the Phoenician cult see Donald Harden, *The Phoenicians* (New York: Praeger, 1962), pp. 82–114.

64. For this story as anti-Canaanite polemic see Leah Bronner, *The Stories of Elijah and Elisha* (Leiden: E. J. Brill, 1968); George E. Saint-Laurent, "Light from Ras Shamra on Elijah's Ordeal upon Mount Carmel," in *Scripture in Context*, ed. Carl D. Evans et al. (Pittsburgh: Pickwick, 1980), pp. 123–39. Frank E. Eakin, Jr., points out that the victory of Elijah declared the distinctives of Yahweh and prevented the absorption of Yahwism into Baalism ("Yahwism and Baalism Before the Exile," *JBL* 84 [1965]: 413).

the way he came and anoint Elisha as his prophetic successor, Jehu as king of Israel, and Hazael as king of Damascus (1 Kings 19:15–16).

The chronology of the stories of Elijah is extremely difficult to reconstruct,[65] but the reference to Jehu and Hazael would suggest that they were persons already known to Elijah. Jehu, however, did not become king until 841, twelve years after Ahab's death, and he reigned for twenty-eight years. It would seem, then, that Elijah's commission came late in Ahab's life. We know also that it came at least four years before the king's death. The basis for this assertion is that the commission was given before Ben-Hadad's siege of Samaria, which in turn was four years before Ahab was slain in the Ramoth Gilead campaign of 853 (1 Kings 20:1, 26; 22:1). A date of 857 for Elijah's trek to Horeb would appear to be reasonable. Since that journey was after the three-year drought, Elijah must have first encountered Ahab in about 860, fourteen years after he had commenced his reign. This would be ample time for the apostate conditions described in the narrative to have taken firm root.

The Invasions of Ben-Hadad

The reason for Ben-Hadad's attack on Samaria is not given, but it might well have been in response to the growing friendship between Israel and Sidon as evidenced, for instance, by Ahab's marriage to Jezebel. Ben-Hadad would surely have viewed this alliance as an impediment to his own access to the sea and to the trade routes up and down the coast.[66] Moreover, if the chronology we have proposed is correct, Shalmaneser III of Assyria would by this time have begun his campaigns west into Aram and Palestine, thus forcing Ben-Hadad into some sort of defensive posture. The biblical historian indicates that Ben-Hadad was accompanied by thirty-two other kings, an indication that he had already forged alliances to deal with the impending Assyrian menace. It may be, of course, that he had solicited Ahab's co-

65. The chronology of the stories was of little interest to the historian; he was more concerned with thematic association and development. See Robert L. Cohn, "The Literary Logic of 1 Kings 17–19," *JBL* 101 (1982): 333–50.

66. Unger also suggests that Ben-Hadad, taking advantage of Israel's weakness following the famine, was trying to avert an Israel-Assyria alliance (*Israel and the Aramaeans*, p. 66). From the language of 1 Kings 20:3–4 Burke O. Long concludes that Ahab was a vassal of Ben-Hadad and that Ben-Hadad was merely exacting the tribute expected in such a relationship. When the demand became excessive, Ahab went to war and gained his independence. In the second encounter (vv. 26–34) the two protagonists are viewed as equals ("Historical Narrative and the Fictionalizing Imagination," *VT* 35 [1985]: 407–12). Though there is nothing else in the record to suggest such a relationship, it is not impossible.

operation, and when that overture failed had determined to bring Israel into his coalition by force.

However that may be, Ben-Hadad came, laid siege to Samaria, and demanded payment of an exorbitant ransom (1 Kings 20:3). Ahab, presumably with no options, agreed to the harsh terms, but Ben-Hadad then proceeded to increase his demands, asking for a free hand with all Ahab possessed. Ahab refused, of course, and then, encouraged by a word from a man of God, marched out of the city with his troops, encountered the enemy while Ben-Hadad and the other kings were engaged in a bout of drunkenness, and administered a sound defeat to the Aramean hosts.

The very next year Ben-Hadad returned, but this time Ahab intercepted him at Aphek, probably to be located in the plain just east of the Sea of Kinnereth.[67] The Arameans were confident of achieving victory there, for they attributed their defeat in the previous year to the fact that Yahweh was a god of the hills (1 Kings 20:28). Now, in the flatlands, they reasoned they would do better, for Yahweh was out of his element. This parochial view of the God of the universe proved to be a colossal and fatal misunderstanding, for God gave Israel complete victory. Indeed, were it not for Ahab's poorly conceived desire to make covenant with Ben-Hadad, the Aramean king would himself have died.

Under the terms of the treaty Ben-Hadad returned the cities his predecessors had taken from Israel and guaranteed Ahab free commercial access to Damascus (1 Kings 20:34). The cities returned were likely those which Ben-Hadad had taken from Baasha forty years before (1 Kings 15:20) as well as others lost to Hezion and Tabrimmon even earlier. Without doubt both kings viewed the treaty as having other benefits as well, particularly the creation of a common front against Shalmaneser.

The Death of Ahab

The alliance so hastily conceived was extremely fragile, however, and within three years—after its usefulness was over—it was broken. This time Ahab determined to recover Ramoth Gilead (Tell Rāmîth) from Damascus. This important city had been a district capital under Solomon, but it apparently had fallen to Damascus some years before Ahab's time, probably during the conflict between Baasha and Ben-Hadad. Ahab may have taken interest in Ramoth Gilead because of its strategic location along a major route from Assyria. Then again, it

---

67. Aharoni, *Land of the Bible*, p. 381, n. 45, associates it with 'En Gev, a "lower Aphek" lying below and a few miles northwest of Fiq, "Upper Aphek."

might well be that Ahab, fresh from the successful encounter with Shalmaneser at Qarqar (see below), found the spirit of imperialism coursing through his veins and decided to reannex the Transjordan as the first step in restoring something of Israel's glory.

The whole matter was academic in any case, for Ahab died in the effort. His body was brought home to Samaria, where it suffered the humiliation of dogs licking up the blood (1 Kings 22:38), just as Elijah had predicted (1 Kings 21:19). So the wicked and yet intriguing reign of Ahab was over. But the evil house of Omri was not yet finished, for Ahab's son Ahaziah stepped in to take his place.

The Threat of Assyria

At this point it will be helpful to examine the international scene in an effort to understand the frenetic machinations of Ben-Hadad, Ahab, Jehoshaphat, and the other rulers of the little states of the Mediterranean littoral. It is clear that the eyes of the world, including Aram and Palestine, were riveted on one nation—mighty Assyria. The revived empire had begun a sustained westward movement under Adad-nirari II (911–891). This was intensified under Tukulti-Ninurta II (890–884) and, by the time of Ahab and Jehoshaphat, had achieved extremely threatening dimensions under Aššur-naṣirpal II (883–859).[68] By about 875 he had pressed west as far as Bît-Adini on the upper Euphrates, bringing all the Aramean states of that region under Assyrian control. It was his successor, Shalmaneser III (858–824), who first made it clear, however, that Assyria's objective was to extend her hegemony over the entire western world.[69]

Within three years Shalmaneser had taken Bît-Adini and then moved west across the Euphrates to conquer the important city of Carchemish.[70] This campaign occurred in 857, one year before Ben-Hadad and Ahab made their treaty at Aphek, so the real reason for that pact now becomes clear—these two strange bedfellows forgot their differences in the interest of self-preservation. By 853[71] Shalmaneser pushed as far south as Qarqar (Khirbet Qerqur) on the Orontes River, not

68. Grayson, "Assyria," in *CAH* 3.1, pp. 253–59.

69. For the Assyrian imperial policy of this period—one largely motivated by economic and commercial interests—see Hayim Tadmor, "Assyria and the West: The Ninth Century and Its Aftermath," in *Unity and Diversity*, ed. Hans Goedicke and J. J. M. Roberts (Baltimore: Johns Hopkins University Press, 1975), pp. 38–40.

70. Grayson, "Assyria," in *CAH* 3.1, p. 260.

71. William H. Shea argues that the battle of Qarqar occurred in 854, a date that actually allows more time for the subsequent falling out between Aram and Israel ("A Note on the Date of the Battle of Qarqar," *JCS* 29 [1977]: 242).

much more than a hundred miles from Damascus. There, according to his own annals, he engaged a great coalition of kings led by Ben-Hadad and including Ahab.[72] In true Assyrian fashion he claims to have achieved a smashing victory, but the truth is surely something less than that. The very fact that he pressed no farther and, in fact, retreated to Calah, his capital, indicates that at best the affair was a stalemate. Moreover, Ben-Hadad and Ahab, following Qarqar, felt so free of Assyrian pressure that they broke their treaty and renewed hostilities.

While he was back east, Shalmaneser incorporated Babylon into his sphere of influence following a civil war there (850). He eventually returned to the west, besieging Damascus in 841, which then was governed by Hazael.[73] Israel, under her new king Jehu, staved off a similar fate only by paying Shalmaneser a heavy tribute.[74] At last, however, Shalmaneser left off his harassment of the western world, allowing Israel and Judah some breathing space for almost a hundred years.

Ahab's Successors

Ahaziah of Israel

The twelve-year period between the death of Ahab and the accession of Jehu was occupied by the reigns of two of Ahab's sons, Ahaziah (853–852) and Joram (852–841). Ahaziah, like his father, continued the worship of Baal and other pagan gods and also, like his father, was rebuked by the prophet Elijah for doing so. The confrontation between the two occurred after Ahaziah had injured himself in a fall and had sent messengers to the Philistine god Baal-Zebub to inquire concerning the prospects of recovery (2 Kings 1:1–2). Elijah intercepted these

72. For the text see James B. Pritchard, *Ancient Near Eastern Texts Relating to the Old Testament*, 2d ed. (Princeton: Princeton University Press, 1955), pp. 278–79.

73. J. A. Brinkman, "Additional Texts from the Reigns of Shalmaneser III and Shamshi-Adad V," *JNES* 32 (1973): 43–44.

74. This is recorded on the famous Black Obelisk. For a photograph and translation see D. Winton Thomas, ed., *Documents from Old Testament Times* (London: Thomas Nelson, 1958), pp. 54–55. P. Kyle McCarter, Jr., argues, however, that the *ia-ú-a* (or *ia-a-ú*) on the stela should be identified with Joram, not Jehu. Reading Yaw as a hypocorism for Joram solves two problems: (a) the king in view is called the "son of Omri," an improbable designation for Jehu in that he wiped out the family of Omri and founded his own dynasty; and (b) it is unlikely that a king would pay tribute in his first year (" 'Yaw, Son of 'Omri': A Philological Note on Israelite Chronology," *BASOR* 216 [1974]: 5–7). For a response see Edwin R. Thiele, "An Additional Chronological Note on 'Yaw, Son of 'Omri,' " *BASOR* 222 (1976): 25–28.

messengers and sternly announced to them the displeasure of Yahweh at their king's wicked recourse to pagan deities. The man of God then delivered the somber word that Ahaziah would not recover.

We have already spoken of Jehoshaphat's joint attempt with Ahaziah to establish a maritime industry (p. 344). When this venture came to ruin, it seems that Edom took advantage of the situation and became temporarily free of Judah's domination. Apparently Edom's neighbor to the north, the kingdom of Moab, likewise broke away at the same time, though not from Judah but Israel, under which it had served as vassal since the time of Omri at least.[75] More precisely, the break occurred after Ahaziah's fatal accident and perhaps even after the succession of his brother Joram. The Moabites had found a new and effective leader, Mesha by name, and amid the turmoil brought about by Ahab's death and Ahaziah's injury had renounced Israel's sovereignty.[76] Joram therefore took immediate measures to whip Mesha back into line (2 Kings 3:4–9a).

Joram of Israel

This second son of Ahab was evil but, the narrator says, not as evil as his father and mother, for he put away their bold and open Baal worship in favor of the quasi-Yahwistic cult of Jeroboam. This must have appeared to be a positive step, but it hardly qualifies Joram as a reformer. Jehoshaphat, predictably, joined his northern cohort's effort to recover Moab.[77] As in his collaboration with Ahab against the Arameans, however, Jehoshaphat insisted that a genuine man of God be consulted regarding the outcome of their enterprise. That prophet

75. Gary Rendsburg argues that Moab had broken from Israel during the turbulent times of the Jeroboam schism and had remained free until the reign of Omri ("A Reconstruction of Moabite-Israelite History," *JANES* 13 [1981]: 67).

76. Extrabiblical documentation is found in the so-called Mesha inscription, the text of which appears in Pritchard, *Ancient Near Eastern Texts*, pp. 320–21. For an excellent integration of the data contained therein and in the Old Testament, see Oded, "Neighbors on the East," in *World History of the Jewish People*, vol. 4, part 1, pp. 256–57; Bayla Bonder, "Mesha's Rebellion Against Israel," *JANES* 3 (1970–71): 82–88. Rendsburg, "Reconstruction," p. 68, says that the revolt took place in the last days of Ahab, but this is a misreading of the Mesha text.

77. James D. Shenkel argues that the Judean king here is Ahaziah and not Jehoshaphat. He builds his case on evidence from the Septuagint, especially Lucian's revision of it, whose chronologies he regards as superior to those of the Masoretic text (*Chronology and Recensional Development in the Greek Text of Kings* [Cambridge: Harvard University Press, 1968], pp. 92–108). If he is correct, this whole period of biblical history must be rewritten. Thiele, "Coregencies," *JBL* 93 (1974): 184–88, has shown, however, that Shenkel reaches his conclusion by "adjusting" the text of the very Greek versions he uses for proof.

was Elisha ben Shaphat, the disciple of Elijah; he revealed that Yahweh would intervene and grant an overwhelming success.[78]

Thus heartened, Joram, Jehoshaphat, and the king of Edom traveled south around the Dead Sea and then north through Edom to Moab.[79] When they reached the Zered River, the border between Edom and Moab, they found the stream overflowing. The Moabites had in the meantime marched south to meet the invaders. In the early daylight the water, as it reflected the rays of the sun, looked red—like blood. Assuming that their enemies must have had a falling out and slaughtered each other, the Moabites attacked, only to discover, too late, the terrible mistake they had made. In desperation they sacrificed the crown prince of Moab, the son of Mesha (2 Kings 3:27). Appalled by the horror of this human sacrifice, Israel and Judah retreated, leaving Moab untaken.

A second significant event in the reign of Joram was the visit of Naaman (2 Kings 5). This heroic commander of Ben-Hadad's armies had contracted a dreadful skin disease. Having learned from his wife's Israelite maidservant of Elisha's miracle-working power, Naaman decided to go to Samaria for relief. His ready access to Israel's capital city implies that the rupture between Israel and Damascus which had resulted in Ahab's death must have been healed, though Joram's reaction to Ben-Hadad's letter in behalf of Naaman certainly reveals that no love was lost between the two.

The tenuous nature of the reconciliation between Israel and Damascus is all the more apparent in the fact that after Naaman was healed and returned to Damascus as a believer in Yahweh, hostilities erupted once more (2 Kings 6:8). Evidently initiated by Ben-Hadad, this war turned sour for the Arameans, for their every move was known ahead of time by Israel. Eventually it was discovered that Elisha the prophet was the source of this intelligence (God revealed to him the Aramean strategy). So Ben-Hadad decided to go to Dothan, where Elisha was living, and remove this informer once and for all. But Yahweh protected his servant by blinding the enemy and leading them to Samaria. Elisha advised Joram to spare them, however, and allow

78. The appearance of Elisha here (2 Kings 3:11) could conceivably be interpreted as an indication that Elijah had already ascended to heaven. Yet Elijah wrote a letter to Jehoram of Judah (2 Chron. 21:12–15), who reigned after Jehoshaphat. Green, "Regnal Formulas," *JNES* 42 (1983): 176, suggests that it was Elisha who wrote the letter, but Green's own suggestion (p. 173) of a coregency between Jehoshaphat and Jehoram would clearly resolve the tension (cf. 2 Kings 1:17).

79. For the itinerary see Aharoni and Avi-Yonah, *Macmillan Bible Atlas*, map 132. J. Liver theorizes that the kings undertook this circuitous route rather than one north of the Dead Sea because of the strong fortifications which, as the Mesha inscription attests, Mesha had built north of Moab ("The Wars of Mesha, King of Moab," *PEQ* 99 [1966]: 27).

them to return to their homes. Never again did the Arameans send small companies of troops against Israel.[80]

The Arameans did return shortly, however, with a vast host and laid siege to Samaria. So effective was the siege that the citizens of the city were reduced to cannibalism. When it seemed as though they would be starved into submission, some beggars outside the walls discovered that the Arameans had fled in panic. Yahweh had caused them to believe that the Hittites and Egyptians were coming to bring the Israelites relief. The flight of the Arameans was so sudden they left their camp intact, thus providing the Samaritans with the food they so desperately needed.

The dates of Naaman's visit and Ben-Hadad's two invasions are a little unclear, though the following narrative offers some clues (2 Kings 8:1–6). In this story Elisha warns the Shunammite woman whose son he had earlier restored to life (2 Kings 4:8–37) that she should leave the land because a seven-year famine is imminent. She does so and at the end of the seven years returns to find her house and lands taken by someone else. She therefore appeals to the king, who, upon learning of her identity from Elisha's servant Gehazi, restores her property to her. The point of historical interest here is the reference to Gehazi. At the end of the story of Naaman, Gehazi is struck with a skin disease and forced to leave the service of Elisha. The story of Naaman must, then, follow the famine. Moreover, if the famine took place entirely in Joram's reign (852–841), it must have lasted until at least 845. The healing of Naaman and Ben-Hadad's two invasions of Israel took place, therefore, near the end of Joram's tenure.[81]

The Anointing of Hazael of Damascus

Then, at the very end of Joram's tenure, Elisha proceeded to implement the two as yet unfulfilled parts of the commission which his

80. This must be the meaning of 2 Kings 6:23, for some time thereafter Aram returned with a great army (6:24). See T. R. Hobbs, *2 Kings*, Word Biblical Commentary (Waco: Word, 1985), p. 78.

81. Green, "Regnal Formulas," *JNES* 42 (1983): 178, suggests that the siege of Samaria (2 Kings 6:24–7:20) took place between 845 and 841. This is a reasonable date, for it is late enough for the seven-year famine and the siege of Dothan (2 Kings 6:8–23) to have preceded. Green also suggests (p. 177) that the initial contact of Elisha with the Shunammite woman (2 Kings 4:8) occurred ten years prior to the end of the seven-year famine—her child was born at least a year after that contact, he was at least two years old when he died, and the famine lasted another seven years. In addition, Green concludes that the first contact of Elisha and the Shunammite must have taken place in the reign of Jehoshaphat since Jehoram reigned less than ten years. The appearance of Jehoshaphat in the Moabite campaign (2 Kings 3) is therefore historically accurate.

master Elijah had been given at Horeb: the anointing of Jehu to be king of Israel and of Hazael to be king of Damascus. Elisha first went to Damascus (2 Kings 8:7–15). Whether or not Ben-Hadad and Joram had again been reconciled by this time is irrelevant. Whatever the case, Ben-Hadad, hoping for divine healing from an illness which had befallen him, welcomed the prophet with open arms. When Ben-Hadad's servant Hazael inquired as to whether the king would recover, however, Elisha made a most enigmatic reply: "Go and say to him, 'You will certainly recover'; but the LORD has revealed to me that he will in fact die" (v. 10). Elisha then announced that Hazael would be king—a great tragedy for Judah, for he would wage cruel and incessant war against God's people. Encouraged by this word Hazael went to Ben-Hadad's bedchamber and smothered the king in his sleep. In this way Hazael ushered in a new and bloody era of Aramean history.

Jehoram of Judah

Before we describe the anointing of Jehu, it is necessary to pick up the history of Judah contemporaneous with Joram. Jehoshaphat had outlived both Ahab and his son Ahaziah and had survived into the fifth year of Ahab's second son Joram. He died in 848 and was followed by his son Jehoram, who reigned for only eight years (848–841).

One of the results of Jehoshaphat's wicked alliances with the dynasty of Omri now comes to the fore. Jehoram, the historian says, was evil like Ahab and the kings of Israel, for his wife was Athaliah, the daughter of Ahab. At some time or other Jehoshaphat had apparently arranged such a marriage for the sake of a compromising league with the enemies of Yahweh. But as sinful as Jehoram was, Yahweh did not destroy Judah, for he remained faithful to his promise to David never to allow the lamp of witness to be extinguished (2 Chron. 21:5–7).

From the very beginning of his reign Jehoram exhibited the bloodiness which would characterize his whole administration. Fearing a possible coup by his powerful brothers, he had them slain (2 Chron. 21:4). But he also began to suffer reverses. First, Edom revolted and set up its own king. This principality had experienced an ever-fluctuating relationship with Judah for many years.[82] In Jehoshaphat's latter years Edom had gained its independence briefly (cf. 1 Kings 22:47 and 2 Kings 3:9). But by the beginning of Jehoram's reign she had been brought back under control. Now once more she rebelled. Though Jehoram dispatched a sizable force to put down the insurrec-

---

82. For a good analysis of the alternating periods of Edomite independence and subservience to Judah see Green, "Regnal Formulas," *JNES* 42 (1983): 176–77.

tion, he was unable to do so and Edom remained thereafter free of Judean suzerainty (2 Kings 8:20–22).

Libnah (Tell eṣ-Ṣâfi?),[83] an important city in the Shephelah, also rebelled, possibly at the instigation of the nearby Philistines who, with the Arabs who lived near the Cushites, launched an attack on Jerusalem itself. The royal palace was despoiled, and the king's entire family, except for his youngest son Ahaziah, were put to the sword (2 Chron. 21:16–17).[84] All this happened, the historian relates, because Jehoram built high places and led Judah astray. Moreover, it had all been predicted by the prophet Elijah in a letter to Jehoram (2 Chron. 21:12–15), the only writing which has survived from that illustrious man of God.

Jehoram died an excruciating death brought on by a disease of the bowels[85] and was succeeded by Ahaziah, who in turn reigned for only one year (841). As the son of Athaliah and nephew of Joram, king of Israel, his behavior, predictably, was anything but godly. But that family connection would mean even more than spiritual deficiency; it would be the cause of his untimely death.

The Anointing of Jehu

We return now to the fulfilment of the commission Elijah received at Horeb, specifically, to the replacement of the Omride dynasty by a new one founded by Jehu. Hazael, who had come to the throne of Damascus by assassination, commenced his lengthy reign (841–801) by resisting an attack on Ramoth Gilead by Joram and Ahaziah (2 Kings 8:28–29). Joram no doubt hoped to regain this strategic outpost in the confusion which attended Hazael's coup against Ben-Hadad. In any case, matters turned out poorly for the king of Israel, for he was wounded in the fray and had to retire to Jezreel, his northern administrative center, to recuperate. Ahaziah, his young nephew, also left the battlefield to pay his ailing uncle a visit.

Meanwhile, Jehu ben Nimshi (he was actually the son of Jehosha-

---

83. This identification is somewhat debated. See Avraham Negev, ed., *Archaeological Encyclopedia of the Holy Land* (Englewood, N.J.: SBS, 1980), p. 188; Yeivin, "Divided Kingdom," in *World History of the Jewish People*, vol. 4, part 1, p. 150.

84. The fact that there is no evidence either in the narrative or from archaeology that the city was destroyed leads most scholars to interpret the campaign in question as an attack upon outlying towns which fell short of Jerusalem because a ransom was paid in the form of the royal family and the king's treasury. See, for example, Myers, *II Chronicles*, p. 122.

85. Green, "Regnal Formulas," *JNES* 42 (1983): 176, n. 31, proposes that this was an intussusception caused by intestinal hypermotility associated with ulcerative colitis.

phat, the son of Nimshi), a commander in Israel's army, received a young prophet from Elisha who informed him that he was the choice of Yahweh to be the king of Israel. The young prophet then anointed him with oil. When Jehu told his fellow officers what had transpired, they accepted it as from Yahweh and acclaimed Jehu as king. At once Jehu conceived a plot to advance his cause, and having sworn his friends to secrecy, he rode to Jezreel to carry it out. When he arrived, he was met by both Joram and Ahaziah, who soon learned the reason for the visit. Too late they tried to make an escape, but Jehu killed Joram in the field of Naboth, as Elijah had predicted (2 Kings 9:25–26; cf. 1 Kings 21:19, 29). Ahaziah managed to flee to Samaria but was soon apprehended and brought to Jehu, who was then apparently near Ibleam, ten miles south of Jezreel. Again Ahaziah broke away, but this time he was mortally wounded and died at Megiddo.[86]

In such summary fashion did Jehu destroy the kings of both Israel and Judah and find himself in full control. The dynasty of Omri had come to an end, the related line entrenched in Judah had been partially purged, and a new opportunity for God's people had come.

86. This scenario concerning Ahaziah is a reconstruction based on 2 Kings 9:27 and 2 Chronicles 22:7–9. For further detail see Merrill, "2 Chronicles," in *Bible Knowledge Commentary*, vol. 1, p. 636.

10 The Dynasty of Jehu and Contemporary Judah

The Reign of Jehu of Israel

The date 841 B.C. is one of the most significant in Old Testament history for it marks the end of the reigns of Joram of Israel and both

Jehoram and Ahaziah of Judah as well as the commencement of the reign of Jehu, the founder of the longest-lasting dynasty that the northern kingdom was to know (841–753).[1] Moreover, 841 was the year when, from a human viewpoint, the Davidic messianic line was suspended by its slenderest thread, for in the aftermath of Jehu's slaughter of Ahaziah, Athaliah, Ahaziah's mother and Ahab's daughter, undertook a systematic purge of all the Judean royal family. Providentially, an infant son of Ahaziah survived, and the Davidic dynasty therefore continued. Finally, 841 was a date of international significance for in that year Shalmaneser III made one of his most successful and far-reaching campaigns into the west.[2] He besieged Hazael of Damascus and would no doubt have conquered Israel had not Jehu, in his very first year, paid an enormous tribute to the Assyrians.

As we noted in the preceding chapter, Jehu had been raised up by Yahweh and charged with the task of removing the wicked house of Omri from Israel's throne forever. He accomplished this not only by slaying its last king, Joram, but also by removing the queen mother Jezebel from the scene (2 Kings 9:21–37). It was she, as much as anyone, who had been responsible for Israel's wholesale adoption of Baalism. For this Elijah had foretold that she would die a gruesome death (1 Kings 21:23), and Jehu was only too happy to fulfil the prophecy.

Jehu next turned to the matter of Ahab's surviving offspring. Once he had made sure of the loyalty of the leaders of Samaria, he ordered them to exterminate the royal family and send their heads to him at Jezreel as proof. When this was done, he used the act to convince the people of Jezreel that he now enjoyed the support of the citizens of Samaria and that, indeed, they had repudiated the family of Ahab. He followed this up by slaughtering the family and friends of Ahab who lived in Jezreel (2 Kings 10:11). Thus the two governmental centers of Israel were in Jehu's hands.

Two more tasks awaited him, however, and to accomplish them Jehu journeyed to Samaria. Along the way he encountered some of the kinfolk of Ahaziah of Judah; he slew them as he had the king himself a little earlier. Then, having reached Samaria, he purged out the remnant of Ahab's family until there was not one left of royal blood. But this was not his only motive in coming to Samaria. Jehu knew full well that Israel's defection from Yahweh must be traced to her religious leaders, so he convened the prophets and priests of Baal under

---

1. Edwin R. Thiele, *The Mysterious Numbers of the Hebrew Kings* (Grand Rapids: Eerdmans, 1965), pp. 50–52.

2. Albert Kirk Grayson, "Assyria: Ashur-dan II to Ashur-Nirari V (934–745 B.C.)," in *Cambridge Ancient History*, 3d ed., ed. John Boardman et al. (Cambridge: Cambridge University Press, 1982), vol. 3, part 1, pp. 262–63.

the pretense of offering worship to Baal and reinforcing their positions as Baal officiants. Then, having gathered them all into the great temple of Baal, he guarded the doors and windows, sent a band of armed men into the temple, and slaughtered every last one. Finally Jehu commanded that the temple itself be emptied of its pagan paraphernalia and converted into a public latrine (2 Kings 10:27),[3] thus showing his utter contempt for the cult of Baal and all it represented.

It might seem that Jehu's harsh and thorough work of eradicating both the family of Omri and the public worship of Baal would pave the way for a return to pure Yahwism. Unfortunately, this did not come to pass, for Jehu, while a bitter foe of classic Baalism, was not a Yahwist. Rather, he was a syncretist in the mold of Jeroboam and practiced the cult of the golden calves at Dan and Bethel. For this the word of judgment came to him from Yahweh: he had been faithful in executing the will of God vis-à-vis Ahab and his house and for that would know the blessing of a long dynasty, but his line would not endure forever (2 Kings 10:30–31). And even in his own lifetime he began to see the inroads of divine punishment, particularly in the diminishing of his nation at the hands of foreign kings.

Athaliah of Judah

Young King Ahaziah of Judah had been under the baneful influence of his mother Athaliah, and his principal advisers had been members of Israel's royal court. Whatever they proposed, he did, including joining Joram in his ill-fated campaign against Hazael at Ramoth Gilead (2 Chron. 22:5). Following the untimely deaths of Ahaziah and many members of his family in Jehu's bloody purge, there was no one powerful enough to take Ahaziah's place in Judah, and so, by default, his mother stepped in.

Daughter of Israel's royal house that she was, Athaliah saw the death of her son not as a tragedy but as a means of bringing Judah under Israelite control, an achievement which she no doubt hoped would eventually result in the restoration of the line of Omri to Samaria as well. She therefore followed up Ahaziah's death by undertaking the murder of her own sons and grandsons left in Jerusalem! Providentially Jehoram's daughter Jehosheba[4] stole away her little nephew Joash, the infant son of Ahaziah. For the six years of Athaliah's

---

3. See T. R. Hobbs, *2 Kings*, Word Biblical Commentary (Waco: Word, 1985), p. 130.

4. Jehosheba was a daughter of Jehoram (2 Kings 11:2) but perhaps by a wife other than Athaliah. The chronicler points out that Jehosheba was the wife of the high priest Jehoiada (2 Chron. 22:11).

usurpation (841–835) the boy was hidden in the temple and reared under the tutelage of Jehosheba and the high priest Jehoiada, her husband.[5]

Finally the time was propitious for Jehoiada to make his move and set Joash in his rightful place as Davidic king. Jehoiada gained the support of the military officers, who in turn won over the Levites and the heads of the clans to the proposed plan. This involved stationing soldiers in strategic places to guard the temple. Except for priests and Levites anyone who attempted to enter the temple must die. Then at last Joash was brought out from his hiding place and positioned near the great altar in front of the temple. Jehoiada, with a copy of the Mosaic royal protocol in his hand, placed the Davidic crown on the young lad's head. The assembled throng no longer could contain its joy and excitement and cried, "Long live the king" (2 Kings 11:12).[6] Athaliah, who seems to have been oblivious to all this planning and scheming, heard the acclamation and rushed to the temple to see what it might mean. In a moment she understood, but her shout of "Treason! Treason!" fell on deaf ears. In panic she fled to the Horse Gate, but Jehoiada's men caught her there and put her to the sword. The high priest then led the people in a covenant reaffirmation pledging that they and their new king would be God's faithful people (2 Kings 11:17). As evidence of their pledge they demolished the temple of Baal, smashed down the pagan idols and altars, and killed the priest of Baal. Then, on a more positive note, Jehoiada restored the worship at the temple precisely as prescribed in Mosaic law. Finally, he led the young king out of the temple and sat him upon the throne of his father David to symbolize the continuity of the promise of God that David would never lack offspring in the messianic line.

The Role of Other Nations

The Inroads of Assyria

The interregnum under Athaliah coincided with the first six years of Jehu's reign in the north, a period about which very little is said in the biblical record. The Assyrian annals, however, are helpful in filling

5. The illegitimacy of Athaliah's reign may be seen in the fact that the historian breaks his pattern by providing no direct chronological reference for her tenure. The figure of six years is arrived at by deduction only. See Walter R. Wifall, "The Chronology of the Divided Monarchy of Israel," ZAW 80 (1968): 328–29; Thiele, Mysterious Numbers, p. 71.

6. The language of the text reflects the coronation ritual; see John Gray, I & II Kings (Philadelphia: Westminster, 1970), pp. 573–75.

the lacuna. After the battle of Qarqar, in which a coalition of western kings including Ahab resisted Assyrian imperialism, Shalmaneser III retired to his homeland to deal with problems there for the next four years. He returned west in 849, 848, 845, and 841, each time except for the last encountering stiff opposition. In 841, however, he managed to defeat Hazael, king of Damascus, and brought Jehu of Israel under tribute as well, as is attested on the famous Black Obelisk.[7] That this was Jehu's very first year may be coincidental, but it is entirely possible that the instability almost certainly engendered by Jehu's violent overthrow of Israel's government played a part.[8] In any event, Shalmaneser's near reduction of Damascus and his overlordship of Israel left him free to deal with other matters, so that after 838 he occupied himself with north Syria and with Media and Armenia to the east and north.

As a consequence of Shalmaneser's withdrawal, Israel became vulnerable to Hazael's depredations. Acting as the instrument of Yahweh he marched against the Transjordan and wrested from Israel everything as far south as the Arnon (2 Kings 10:32–33). The political reason for this is most apparent. Jehu, rather than siding with Hazael in his valorous resistance to Assyria, had meekly submitted and counted himself as an Assyrian vassal. Hazael's invasion of Israel was, therefore, as much a measure against Assyria as it was against Israel. A reasonable date for Hazael's attacks would appear to be 837–836: they could not have taken place while Shalmaneser was still present in the west (he left after an unsuccessful campaign against Damascus in 838); on the other hand, Hazael's obvious desire for quick vengeance would have prompted him to act soon after Shalmaneser's departure.[9]

The Weakness of Egypt

Egypt during all this time was certainly well aware of the turmoil in Israel and Judah; while no doubt eager to capitalize on it, the pharaohs were, however, unable to do so because of the rise of Assyrian imperialism. Egypt was no match for Shalmaneser, so her king Osor-

7. For the text see James B. Pritchard, *Ancient Near Eastern Texts Relating to the Old Testament*, 2d ed. (Princeton: Princeton University Press, 1955), p. 280.

8. Michael C. Astour offers the intriguing suggestion that Jehu's pogroms were motivated by a desire to appease Assyria by destroying anti-Assyrian elements in both Israel and Judah ("841 B.C.: The First Assyrian Invasion of Israel," *JAOS* 91 [1971]: 388–89).

9. Herbert Donner, "The Separate States of Israel and Judah," in *Israelite and Judaean History*, ed. John H. Hayes and J. Maxwell Miller (Philadelphia: Westminster, 1977), p. 413.

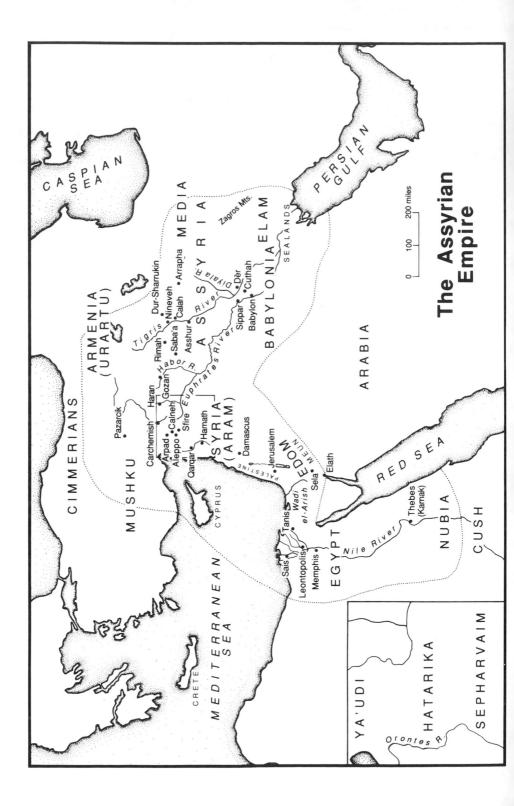

The Assyrian Empire

0   100   200 miles

kon II (874–850) attempted to establish alliances with the Aramean and Palestinian states in hopes of preventing Assyrian advance in Egypt's direction.[10] That his effort was more than merely on paper is clear from the fact that Egyptian troops were among those who encountered Shalmaneser at Qarqar in 853.[11]

With Osorkon's succession by Takeloth II (850–825) Egypt's position weakened further, for Thebes now began to exert itself against the north in an effort to achieve independence for Upper Egypt. Hence neither Jehu nor Joash could look to the kingdom of the Nile for any kind of support against the other or any common foe such as Hazael or Shalmaneser.

Joash of Judah

The Years of Righteousness

The events of the illicit reign of Athaliah are undocumented though one may assume that Judah during these six years (841–835) enjoyed immunity from the crises that her neighbor to the north, Israel, was experiencing at the hands of Hazael. Hazael in fact most likely viewed the daughter of Ahab as his ally or at least as a fellow antagonist to Jehu, whose annihilation of her family could hardly have endeared him to her.

Finally, however, Joash, the Davidic offspring, sat on Judah's throne, commencing a reign of forty years (835–796). Since he was only seven years old when he became king, he was under the sponsorship of Jehoiada the high priest, whose guidance went as far as the selection of wives for the young ruler (2 Chron. 24:3). The years of apostasy under Athaliah had taken their toll in Judah's religious life. Particularly grievous was the fact that the temple had fallen into disrepair and its services were neglected. Young Joash, early in his reign, decided to rectify the situation and to repair and restore the house of Yahweh (2 Kings 12:4–5). He therefore charged the priests and Levites to set about to collect the offerings required of all Israelites for maintaining the temple worship.

Though some funds began to accumulate as a result of this appeal, work on the temple was delayed for some reason or another, and as late as Joash's twenty-third year (ca. 814)[12] nothing had been accom-

---

10. Kenneth A. Kitchen, *The Third Intermediate Period in Egypt (1100–650 B.C.)*. (Warminster: Aris and Phillips, 1973), p. 324.

11. Ibid., p. 325.

12. For the coincidence of Joash's twenty-third year and Jehu's last in 814 see Thiele, *Mysterious Numbers*, p. 74. For the argument that 835 was Joash's accession year and 814 his twenty-third year see pp. 71–72.

plished. Joash therefore ordered Jehoiada to provide a chest beside the great altar into which the priests could place the offerings of the people.[13] He then issued a kingdomwide proclamation instructing the people to bring their gifts to the temple. With gladness the people came, filling the chest over and over. Joash then hired workers to begin the work of restoration and subsidized its cost with the funds the people had contributed. So reliable and honest were the money handlers that they were not required to give an accounting. The money raised to pay the laborers was used by the supervisors for that purpose only. Not even the furnishings of the temple were paid for out of these designated funds. At last, when the repair was done and the workers paid, the vessels of the house of Yahweh were crafted from the silver and gold which were left over from the people's generosity.

The Years of Apostasy

Evidently very shortly after the temple repairs were completed, Jehoiada the priest died (2 Chron. 24:15). With him died the spiritual stability which had inspired Joash almost from his birth, for now the king began to turn away from Yahweh and to tolerate the worship of Asherah, the goddess of his grandmother Athaliah. To compound his sin, Joash authorized the murder of Zechariah the prophet, who was the son of his own godly mentor Jehoiada and who had been sent by Yahweh to rebuke the king and urge him to turn from his wicked ways.

This invited in turn a divine reprisal in the form of an Aramean invasion of Judah which threatened the very city of Jerusalem itself (2 Chron. 24:23–25). Many of Judah's leaders were slain, and Joash himself was wounded. And then, most tragic of all, Joash became the victim of assassins from within his own ranks who killed him as he lay in his bed recovering from his injuries in battle. All this came about, the historian notes, because Judah and Joash had forsaken Yahweh (2 Chron. 24:24).

The Foreign Situation

Hazael of Damascus

The Aramean invasion which set the stage for Joash's death cannot be the same as the campaign under Hazael which is described in 2 Kings 12:17–18, for Hazael died by 801 and Joash lived on until 796. Besides, the two accounts share virtually nothing except the common

13. This practice of a shared custody of temple funds has been illuminated by an Assyrian text cited by Victor Hurowitz, "Another Fiscal Practice in the Ancient Near East: 2 Kings 12:5–17 and a Letter to Esarhaddon (*LAS* 277)," *JNES* 45 (1986): 289–94.

foe.[14] For example, only 2 Kings records the detail that Jerusalem would have fallen had not Joash bought off the Aramean king by emptying the temple treasury.

As we have already noted (p. 361) Hazael had taken advantage of the absence of Shalmaneser III of Assyria by applying relentless pressure on Israel, his inveterate enemy to the south. This resulted in the loss of a great amount of Israelite territory, especially in the Transjordan. After the death of Jehu of Israel, matters only got worse, for Jehu's son Jehoahaz (814–798) was constantly the victim of Hazael's harassment. Indeed, as the author of Kings indicates, the Aramean hostilities outlasted Hazael himself and were pursued by his son Ben-Hadad II (2 Kings 13:3, 22–25). Were it not for the intervention of the Assyrian king Adad-nirari III into Syro-Palestinian affairs, the Arameans might well have brought both Israel and Judah completely to their knees.

The return of Assyria

Hazael's immunity from Assyrian interference had lasted not only for the remainder of the reign of Shalmaneser III but throughout that of his son and successor Shamshi-Adad V (823–811).[15] Shamshi-Adad came to power amidst serious rebellion and by virtue of the support of the king of the Sealands, Marduk-zakir-šumi I. Except for Damascus the Assyrian client states to the west remained subservient and well administered, so there was no pressing need for the Assyrian king to be involved there. In fact, such involvement became a moot point because from 818 until his death Shamshi-Adad was totally occupied by war with his erstwhile allies in Babylonia. It is easy to see why Hazael was free from 837 to 805 to pursue virtually any policy he wished toward his neighbors.

At about the time of the accession of the next king of Assyria, Adad-nirari III (810–783), Babylon was subjugated, but this did not lead at once to Assyrian interest in the west. Adad-nirari was only a boy when he succeeded his father, and so he ruled under the patronage of his mother Sammuramat.[16] Together they rebuilt the city of Calah and made it their capital. Then, after retaking Gozan in 808, Adad-nirari pushed west and in 805 undertook a campaign against Damascus and

14. Most scholars incorrectly see 2 Kings 12:17–18 and 2 Chronicles 24:23–25 as varying accounts of the same event; see, for example, Jacob M. Myers, *II Chronicles*, Anchor Bible (Garden City, N.Y.: Doubleday, 1965), pp. 138–39.

15. Grayson, "Assyria," in *CAH* 3.1, pp. 269–71.

16. William W. Hallo and William K. Simpson, *The Ancient Near East* (New York: Harcourt Brace Jovanovich, 1971), p. 129. Grayson, "Assyria," in *CAH* 3.1, pp. 271–72, disagrees, arguing that the notion of a coregency is based upon a misinterpretation of the relevant text.

Palestine. Succeeding campaigns until 796[17] brought most of Syria under control, but all this territory, including Damascus and the south, was soon lost because of threats to Assyria from other quarters. It was not until 743, under Tiglath-pileser III, that Assyria would return to resume her imperialism over the west.

Jehoahaz of Israel

Hazael's invasion of Judah, attested to only in 2 Kings, appears to have taken place after Joash's twenty-third year (i.e., after 814).[18] This was the year when the temple treasuries began to be replenished and repairs on the temple began in earnest. The tribute Joash paid to Hazael to save Jerusalem surely came from these riches. Moreover, the twenty-third year of Joash was also the year of the death of Jehu and accession of his son Jehoahaz to the throne of Israel (2 Kings 13:1). The author of Kings is careful to note that it was then that the raids of Hazael against Israel resumed in a new, more intensive way (13:3).[19] One is tempted to assume that the death of Jehu in 814 prompted Hazael to launch an attack against Israel and at the same time against Gath and Jerusalem. Shamshi-Adad of Assyria was totally occupied by his struggle with Babylon at precisely this time, and so of course could do nothing to impede Hazael's conquests even if he desired to do so.

Jehoahaz of Israel was an evil king who nonetheless called upon Yahweh in his day of distress at Hazael's hand, and Yahweh answered by sending a "deliverer" who freed Israel from Aramean domination (2 Kings 13:5). This is thought by most scholars to be none other than Adad-nirari III, who, as we saw, launched an effective campaign to the west in 805, which resulted in the subjugation of Hazael and thus the

17. On the basis of the Rimah stela, which mentions Jehoash of Samaria (798–782), most scholars place Adad-nirari's last campaign, against Mansuate, in 796. William H. Shea, however, argues that the Rimah stela, like the Saba'a stela, refers to an earlier campaign (805) in the same area. This obviously requires a dating of Jehoash at least that early as well ("Adad-Nirari III and Jehoash of Israel," *JCS* 30 [1978]: 101–13). Shea overlooks the stereotypical way in which royal inscriptions are composed and makes insufficient allowance for the possibility that identical places were encountered and subdued in campaigns almost ten years apart. See also Hayim Tadmor, "The Historical Inscriptions of Adad-Nirari III," *Iraq* 35 (1973): 141–50.

18. S. Yeivin dates Hazael's invasion in 813 ("The Divided Kingdom: Rehoboam-Ahaz/Jeroboam-Pekah," in *World History of the Jewish People*, vol. 4, part 1, *The Age of the Monarchies: Political History*, ed. Abraham Malamat (Jerusalem: Massada, 1979), p. 152.

19. The reduction of Israelite territory may be reflected in ostraca from Samaria which record the payment of taxes in kind from only a few cities close to the capital (Yeivin, "Divided Kingdom," p. 153).

deliverance of Israel.[20] Meanwhile, Israel had been reduced to such a miserable state that the historian says the army numbered only fifty horsemen, ten chariots, and ten thousand infantry!

The second campaign of Damascus against Jerusalem, that which resulted in the wounding and eventual death of Joash, could not, as we have said, have been led by Hazael, for he died by 801[21] but Joash lived on until 796.[22] The unnamed Aramean king on that occasion must have been the son of Hazael, Ben-Hadad II, who continued his father's policies of intervention in Israelite and Judean affairs. It is he into whose hand Yahweh delivered Israel continually in the days of Jehoahaz (2 Kings 13:3), but Jehoash, son of Jehoahaz, was able to retrieve the Israelite cities Ben-Hadad had taken (13:25). And Jeroboam II eventually recovered from Ben-Hadad the vast Aramean territories which had belonged to Israel in the years of Solomon's glory (2 Kings 14:25–27).

The International Scene

Assyria

Before moving on into the eighth century and the reigns of Jehoash of Israel and Amaziah of Judah, it is necessary once more to look briefly at the larger world which increasingly and inevitably played a major role in shaping the history of the divided kingdom. We begin with Assyria, which was at the time and would continue for almost two hundred years to be the major power of the Near Eastern world.

The withdrawal of Adad-nirari III from the west after 796 left that region generally free of Assyrian interference for more than fifty years. He was succeeded by his son Shalmaneser IV, who reigned for only ten years (782–773).[23] Shalmaneser found himself on the defensive against the kingdom of Urartu most of the time and was unable to retain control of parts of the empire itself, to say nothing of more

---

20. For documentation, the "Nimrud slab," see Pritchard, *Ancient Near Eastern Texts*, pp. 281–82. Here Hazael is identified as *Mari'* ("lord"), as though that were his name rather than his title. See Merrill F. Unger, *Israel and the Aramaeans of Damascus* (Grand Rapids: Baker, 1980 reprint), p. 83. Adad-nirari also defeated Damascus and its king Ben-Hadad in 796, so he might also at that time have been serving as the "deliverer" of Israel, which by then was under the rule of Jehoash (Hayim Tadmor, "Assyria and the West: The Ninth Century and Its Aftermath," in *Unity and Diversity*, ed. Hans Goedicke and J. J. M. Roberts [Baltimore: Johns Hopkins University Press, 1975], p. 40).
21. Unger, *Israel and the Aramaeans*, p. 82.
22. Thiele, *Mysterious Numbers*, pp. 72–73.
23. Grayson, "Assyria," in *CAH* 3.1, pp. 276–77.

distant lands like Aram. His brother Aššur-dan III (772–755) fared little better, though his annals do attest an attack on Damascus in his first year and several against Hatarika (Hadrach) subsequently.[24] Assyria's military impotence is clearly suggested by Aššur-dan's failure to campaign in at least four years—an omission which is almost unique—and by his inability to put down revolts, particularly at Gozan.

A third son of Adad-nirari became king next. The brief reign of Aššur-nirari V (754–745) saw only one significant campaign, that against Arpad in 754. His assassination in Calah brought the end of Assyrian weakness, for his death was followed (if not occasioned) by one of Assyria's most celebrated monarchs, Tiglath-pileser III.

Egypt

To the south of Palestine, in Egypt, the political situation was very complex because of the synchronous and competing Dynasties 22 and 23.[25] Takeloth II of Dynasty 22 (850–825) witnessed the increasing struggle of Thebes to split away, a break which appeared inevitable. Before it could materialize, however, Takeloth died and was succeeded by his son Shoshenq III, who usurped the throne from the heir apparent, his older brother Osorkon. Initially Shoshenq appeared to be reuniting north and south successfully, but then, for reasons not now clear, a rival king appeared at Leontopolis. This was Pedubast, founder of Dynasty 23, who reigned for twenty-five years over the western Delta (818–793).

Though Shoshenq III sat as pharaoh at Tanis for over fifty years (825–773), his kingdom was only a minor sheikdom compared to that of his predecessors. To make matters worse, various chieftains in the Delta began to assert their independence against both Shoshenq and Pedubast. Upper Egypt in the meantime professed allegiance to Pedubast, but this was offset by the rise of the princes of the northern Delta and an emerging Nubian presence in the far south. By 737 Piankhy of Nubia claimed rulership of Thebes and founded Dynasty 25 there. Ten years later Tefnakht I (727–720) founded Dynasty 24, the so-called Saite line of kings in the northern Delta. These two new royal houses paralleled each other as well as Dynasties 22 and 23 during their last years. The former ended under Osorkon IV in about 715 and the latter under Shoshenq VI at the same time.[26]

24. Ibid., p. 277.

25. Kitchen, *Third Intermediate Period*, pp. 326–33. For slightly different dates and a detailed discussion of the Egyptian chronology for this period see Klaus Baer, "The Libyan and Nubian Kings of Egypt: Notes on the Chronology of Dynasties XXII to XXVI," *JNES* 32 (1973): 6–15.

26. Kitchen, *Third Intermediate Period*, pp. 362–77.

What is clear in this otherwise chaotic picture is that Egypt was hopelessly fragmented and nearly powerless for the greater part of the eighth century. Israel and Judah had nothing to fear from that quarter; and yet, ironically, both looked to Egypt eventually for help against the encroachments of Assyria.

Damascus

Once more Damascus was free to molest her weaker southern neighbors, a situation which she quickly used to her advantage. But this time things would prove to be much different. Both Israel and Judah now found themselves with strong, imaginative rulers who not only resisted Aramean intrusion, but took decisive measures to extend their territory at the expense of their enemies, who for too long had taken advantage of them.

Jehoash of Israel

The third in the line of Jehu of Israel was Jehoahaz's son Jehoash, who reigned from 798 to 782 B.C. Like his father and grandfather he did not turn from the sins of Jeroboam, "which he had caused Israel to commit." But God was nevertheless gracious to Jehoash and enabled him to prevail not only against the Arameans on several occasions, but also against Amaziah of Judah. The fact that he went to console the dying prophet Elisha and seek counsel from him (2 Kings 13:14–19) also mitigates somewhat the stark assessment of Jehoash as just another Israelite king in the tradition of all his predecessors.

The visit of Jehoash to Elisha must have occurred very early in his reign, perhaps about 796. This is suggested by the fact that Ben-Hadad II had just come to power in Damascus in succession to Hazael, who died in 801. Hazael had been a constant nemesis to Jehu and his son Jehoahaz; now that he was dead the time must have seemed propitious for Israel to exact revenge and attempt to regain lost territories. This, then, is surely what motivated Jehoash to seek out the aged prophet. He wished to know if the Arameans under Ben-Hadad would be susceptible to Israelite conquest. When he received a favorable response, he moved against Ben-Hadad and, as Elisha had predicted, achieved three notable victories, all of which resulted in the recovery of lost territories. If he had had more faith in Yahweh, he would, of course, have destroyed his Aramean foe completely.

The cities of Israel which Jehoash recovered are not specified except that they were the ones which Ben-Hadad had captured from Jehoahaz, father of Jehoash (2 Kings 13:25). This is a most helpful datum

for it implies that Ben-Hadad, who began to reign in 801, had continued his father's aggressive actions against Israel. Though Yahweh had
raised up a "deliverer," the Assyrian king Adad-nirari, in the years
between 805 and 796, now that he was forced to deal with urgent
matters in his homeland, Israel again stood defenseless. Without question, then, Ben-Hadad took the Assyrian departure as a cue to appropriate more Israelite territories. It is no wonder that Jehoash looked
to the man of God for advice.

Amaziah of Judah

Another indication that the campaigns of Jehoash against Damascus occurred in the early years of his reign is that it seems that after
Amaziah became king of Judah, Jehoash had little time for the Arameans. Judah now became Israel's major concern. Amaziah, the son
of Joash, came to the Davidic throne in 796 and reigned until 767,
thus outliving Jehoash by fifteen years. On balance he is rated favorably in the sources though he did not follow Yahweh wholeheartedly.

Having established himself in firm control, a difficult matter considering the fact that his father was the victim of assassination, Amaziah set out to punish his father's murderers. This done, he proceeded
to reorganize and rebuild Judah's military machine, a move designed
both to protect Judah from an obviously more militant and powerful
Israel and to enable Judah to recover lands that had been lost to her
in the preceding half century.

That relations with Israel had not yet deteriorated to the point of
open warfare may be seen in Amaziah's employment of a hundred
thousand Israelite mercenaries. Yet, as the chronicler suggests, this
was unwise because Israel had been rejected by Yahweh and could
therefore be of no help to his people. Judah must trust in the Lord and
not in the arm of flesh. Ironically, Amaziah's subsequent refusal to
retain the Israelites brought about the very hostilities with Israel which
he had anticipated all along (2 Chron. 25:5–13).

The immediate objective Amaziah had in mind in raising his vast
army was the recovery of Edom as a Judean province. No mention
has been made of Edom since the record of Jehoram's reign, fifty years
earlier, when it rebelled against Judah and became an independent
nation under its own king.[27] It may, indeed, have remained so from

27. Evidently the revolt against Judah in the time of Jehoram (2 Kings 8:20–22)
permitted Edom to be independent from that time until Amaziah's reconquest. See
B. Oded, "Neighbors on the East," in *World History of the Jewish People*, vol. 4, part 1,
p. 255.

that time till the reign of Amaziah, so that Amaziah's move was not so much a reaction to a recent Edomite secession as it was an attempt to recover Judah's ancient glory.

In any event, the hosts of Judah encountered the defensive forces of Edom in the Valley of Salt (Wadi el-Milḥ), between Beersheba and Arad, and administered to them a crushing defeat. With indescribable and unwarranted brutality Amaziah slew ten thousand of the Edomites in battle and cast ten thousand others from the top of a cliff to their deaths on the rocks below. He went on to Sela, the capital city of Edom, and brought it once again under Judean domination (2 Kings 14:7; 2 Chron. 25:11–12).

His triumphant encounter with the Edomites might have brought Amaziah a certain amount of prestige, but it did nothing to enhance his role as spiritual leader of his people, for among the spoils of war were Edomite idols which he set up and worshiped in Jerusalem. Even the outcries of a man of God were not sufficient to bring him to his senses, so that anonymous prophet predicted a tragic and violent end for the king (2 Chron. 25:14–16).

Meanwhile, the Israelite mercenaries whom Amaziah had released from service had returned to their homeland in a rage, looting, pillaging, and killing as they went. The special objects of their fury were, according to the chronicler, "Judean towns from Samaria to Beth Horon" (2 Chron. 25:13). This surprising information must be construed to mean that Judean colonies existed here and there throughout the northern kingdom.[28] Perhaps these were the towns in Israel which Asa had captured; they may also have been the towns to which Jehoshaphat had sent priests and Levites as teachers (see 2 Chron. 15:8; 17:2; 19:4).

Amaziah obviously believed that this massacre was tolerated if not encouraged by Jehoash, for he immediately challenged the king of Israel to a confrontation (2 Chron. 25:17; cf. v. 21).[29] His own recent overwhelming conquest of Edom must have given Amaziah the confidence he needed to turn upon his more powerful northern neighbor. Jehoash, too, was confident, for by this time he had subdued Ben-Hadad of Damascus and had recovered the cities which had been lost

28. Some scholars assume an error here. H. G. M. Williamson, for example, suggests reading Migron for Samaria (*1 and 2 Chronicles*, New Century Bible Commentary [Grand Rapids: Eerdmans, 1982], p. 330). Yeivin, "Divided Kingdom," in *World History of the Jewish People*, vol. 4, part 1, p. 159, proposes that "from Samaria" refers to the point of origin of the attackers; that is, the troops from Samaria raided Judean towns.

29. Yeivin, "Divided Kingdom," in *World History of the Jewish People*, vol. 4, part 1, p. 160, maintains that this was a friendly overture designed to bring about commercial ties, but the use of the same idiom ("to look one another in the face") in 2 Kings 14:11 and 2 Chronicles 25:21 clearly rules this out.

by his father. The stage was set for a showdown between the two, a contest that might even result in the reunification of the two kingdoms under one or the other.

Jehoash's response to the gauntlet thrown down by Amaziah was in the form of a parable in which he compared himself to a mighty cedar of Lebanon and the king of Judah to a mere thistle (2 Chron. 25:18–19). This thistle arrogantly demanded that the cedar provide its daughter as wife for the thistle's son, but a great beast came and trampled the thistle into the earth. Jehoash then warned Amaziah that his victory over little Edom should not give him false hope that he could vanquish mighty Israel.

This warning did Amaziah no good, however, for he led his army into battle at Beth Shemesh. The chronicler underscores the fact that Amaziah's stubborn persistence was of Yahweh, for Yahweh intended to use Jehoash to punish Amaziah for his idolatry (2 Chron. 25:20). Not only was Judah routed in disgrace, but Amaziah was taken prisoner and forced to return with Jehoash to Jerusalem. There he witnessed the destruction of the wall of his city and the robbing of the sacred treasures of the temple of Yahweh.

Amaziah himself narrowly escaped with his life. Why Jehoash spared him at all is a mystery, for he evidently took him back to Samaria as a prisoner (2 Kings 14:13–14). The answer may lie in the date of these events. Both the author of Kings and the chronicler stress that Amaziah outlived Jehoash by fifteen years (2 Kings 14:17; 2 Chron. 25:25). This may be their oblique way of suggesting that Amaziah's release from Israelite control is to be tied in with the death of his captor; if that is so, the battle of Beth Shemesh probably occurred in 783 or 782.[30]

The last fifteen years of Amaziah were not made any easier by the departure of Jehoash from the scene, for the next king of Israel, Jeroboam II, was even more powerful and threatening. Besides, a conspiracy was afoot in Judah to remove Amaziah from the throne. In 767 the plotters struck, and Amaziah was forced to flee Jerusalem. He made his way to Lachish, but was overtaken there and put to death. That this was not a move against the dynasty of David is clear from the fact that Amaziah was replaced by his own son Azariah (= Uzziah), who had been coreigning with him for over twenty years. The most

---

30. Another possibility for consideration is that the appointment of Uzziah to succeed Amaziah was necessary because of the latter's capture by Jehoash. In that case the battle of Beth Shemesh would have taken place around 792, the year of Uzziah's promotion. Thiele suggests that the "fifteen years" by which Amaziah outlived Jehoash refers to the period between Amaziah's release upon Jehoash's death (782) and his own death in 767 (*Mysterious Numbers*, pp. 86–87). Uzziah would then have served as king alone for the ten years of Amaziah's captivity.

likely theory is that the foul deed of murder had, ironically, been motivated by the desire to restore a pure worship of Yahweh to the kingdom (see 2 Chron. 25:27).[31]

Jeroboam II of Israel

The Chronology of the Period

The deaths and successions of both Jehoash and Amaziah raise some complicated chronological problems that must be at least briefly addressed. Jehoash died in 782, at which time his son Jeroboam II began to reign. Jeroboam in turn died in 753, but the author of Kings speaks of a total reign of forty-one years (2 Kings 14:23). The best solution to the problem of the excess twelve years is to posit a twelve-year coregency between Jeroboam and Jehoash so that the forty-one years actually commence in 793.[32] There is, to be sure, no explicit statement in the record in support of this hypothesis; but we have already been introduced to coregency in Judah at least, and such a system was rather commonly practiced in the ancient Near Eastern world at that time. Moreover, the reigns of both Jehoahaz and Jehoash of Israel were marked by dangers from within and without which no doubt impressed upon them the tenuousness of their situations and the need to secure the succession of the dynasty. Other factors such as illness may also, of course, have necessitated coregency.

If a twelve-year overlapping between Jehoash and Jeroboam is problematic, what must be said of the twenty-five years shared by Amaziah of Judah and his son Uzziah? Scholars are virtually united in accepting a date of 740 for the death of Uzziah, so the fifty-two years mentioned by both Kings and Chronicles requires an accession date of 792, only four years after Amaziah's coronation. Since Amaziah died in 767, Uzziah coreigned with him for twenty-five years. While this would ordinarily seem improbable, it is certainly not impossible and, in fact, is the best way to accommodate all the evidence.[33] Amaziah was twenty-five years old when he began to rule in 796 (2 Kings 14:2). In 792, the year in which Uzziah's coregency began, Amaziah would have been twenty-nine or thirty. Uzziah was sixteen at that time,[34] so Amaziah was about fourteen when his son was born. This

31. Myers, *II Chronicles*, p. 146.
32. Edwin R. Thiele, "Coregencies and Overlapping Reigns Among the Hebrew Kings," *JBL* 93 (1974): 192–93.
33. Ibid., p. 193.
34. This is the meaning of 2 Kings 14:21. See Thiele, *Mysterious Numbers*, pp. 83–84. For most of his reign, then, Amaziah was coregent with his son.

is admittedly a young age to father a son, but in the context of the marriage customs of the ancient world was certainly not unheard of.[35]

Thus the chronological data regarding the reigns of both Jeroboam II and Uzziah can be resolved by postulating long coregencies with their fathers. The political and military exigencies of the first half of the eighth century make such a postulate eminently reasonable. It should also be noted that Jeroboam and Uzziah were contemporaries for most of their reigns, the former ruling from 793 to 753 and the latter from 792 to 740.

The Glory of Israel

The account of Jeroboam's reign is sparse indeed in the historical texts, but, as we shall see, the prophets of the period have much to say about the conditions which existed during his rule. The judgment is that he was evil in the same way as was his namesake, Jeroboam ben Nebat. What he lacked in godliness, however, he made up for in sheer political leadership. Following in the footsteps of his father Jehoash, whom he presumably aided in his military campaigns, Jeroboam was able not only to recover the territories of Israel proper which had fallen over the years to Damascus, but to bring all of south Aram and the Transjordan back under Israelite hegemony (2 Kings 14:25–28). Not since the days of Solomon had Israel dominated such a vast area.

But all this came to pass not because of Jeroboam's piety; to the contrary, it was despite his wickedness. For, as Jonah the prophet proclaimed, the reason for Israel's deliverance was that Yahweh had mercy on his people and remembered his pledge not to destroy them from under heaven (2 Kings 14:25–27). The day of Israel's judgment would surely come, but this was not the time. This, rather, was a time of reprieve and even favor. Perhaps the recovery of the kingdom would move the nation to a recovery of covenant obedience.

Jeroboam's exploits were possible first of all because of Assyria's inability to intervene. The mighty empire was at such a nadir that it was totally immobilized as far as foreign affairs were concerned. As for Ben-Hadad II of Damascus, he had suffered a crushing blow at the hands of Zakir of Hamath in about 773.[36] Indeed, he may have died in that battle. Having previously lost a number of cities to Jehoash of Israel, he left Damascus in a greatly weakened condition at his death.

35. Roland de Vaux, *Ancient Israel* (New York: McGraw-Hill, 1965), vol. 1, p. 29.

36. For a discussion of the suggested dates see Unger, *Israel and the Aramaeans*, pp. 85–89. A translation of and commentary on the Zakir stela may be found in D. Winton Thomas, ed., *Documents from Old Testament Times* (London: Thomas Nelson, 1958), pp. 242–50.

Either in the interval between the death of Jehoash (782) and that of Ben-Hadad II (ca. 773) or shortly thereafter Jeroboam undertook his work of empire restoration. This eventually included even Damascus itself, though the conquest of Damascus is not attested in extrabiblical texts and is usually discounted by critical scholars.[37] Most probably Damascus fell to Jeroboam during the reign of Ben-Hadad's successor, whose very name, unfortunately, has been lost to history. The next known ruler was Rezin, who came to power in Damascus in about 750 and, as her last king, expired with his city in 732.[38] One intriguing possibility is that we know of no king of Damascus between 773 and 750 precisely because there was no native ruler.[39] Jeroboam's conquest of the area north to Hamath may have been so decisive that Damascus did not even enjoy the privilege of tributary status, but rather was incorporated directly under Jeroboam's sovereignty. One cannot help noticing that the reappearance of an Aramean king in the person of Rezin (ca. 750) coincides nicely with the date of the deaths of Jeroboam and his son Zechariah (both in 753), the last members of the powerful dynasty of Jehu.

Uzziah of Judah

Judah, too, was experiencing unparalleled prosperity and renascence during this period under her resourceful and godly king Uzziah. During the coregency with his father Amaziah he must have learned a great deal about affairs of state. Both the author of Kings and the chronicler make much of the fact that Uzziah was a popular appointee and not one of his father. A normal dynastic succession upon the death of a king would not be described in such words as we find here: "the people of Judah took Uzziah . . . and made him king." It is clear that his appointment was an action undertaken while Amaziah was still alive and reigning. It was, in other words, a coregency forced upon the king.[40]

37. Oded, "Neighbors on the East," in *World History of the Jewish People*, vol. 4, part 1, p. 268, leaves open this possibility, however, citing the 'En Gev excavations and the treaty of Sfire as evidence.

38. Unger, *Israel and the Aramaeans*, p. 95.

39. T. C. Mitchell refers to a certain Hadianu (= Hezion) of the period who is attested to only in an unpublished inscription of Shalmaneser IV ("Israel and Judah from Jehu Until the Period of Assyrian Domination [841–c. 750 B.C.]," in *CAH* 3.1, p. 510). This is the so-called Pazarcik stela. The identification of Hadianu as a king of Damascus is, however, uncertain.

40. Yeivin ("Divided Kingdom," in *World History of the Jewish People*, vol. 4, part 1, p. 161) goes as far as to suggest that Amaziah was actually deposed in favor of Uzziah; but there is no reason to think that the matter was carried this far, for Amaziah's regnal years are counted to 767 while Uzziah's coregency commenced in 792.

Support for the theory of a coregency may be found in two other statements. First, both historical sources emphasize what otherwise appears to be a matter of only marginal interest—Uzziah rebuilt Elath and restored it to Judah after his father's death (2 Kings 14:22; 2 Chron. 26:2). The clear impression is that this action by Uzziah was contingent upon his father's death though it was something he as coregent had contemplated sometime earlier. Otherwise, the note that it occurred after Amaziah died is so self-evident as to be meaningless.

Even more significant is the chronicler's statement that Zechariah instructed young Uzziah in the fear of God (2 Chron. 26:5). In the absence of any other identification one is forced to conclude that this Zechariah is none other than the son of Jehoiada mentioned in connection with the idolatry of Joash. It will be recalled that this redoubtable prophet rebuked the king for having allowed idols to be worshiped in Jerusalem; for his troubles Zechariah was executed (2 Chron. 24:17–22). This led to a series of events which culminated in Joash's death in 796. The martyrdom of Zechariah took place only a year earlier. Thus, for Uzziah to have been instructed by Zechariah necessitates his having been of teachable age by 797 at the latest, which comports well with the theory of a coregency commencing in 792 when Uzziah was sixteen. For in that case he would have been eleven years old in 797, well able to seek after God in the days of Zechariah.

The reign of Uzziah, summarized only briefly in 2 Kings, is described in rather glowing terms by the chronicler. Uzziah's interest in military matters is emphasized: he reorganized and enlarged Judah's army until it consisted of more than three hundred thousand well-trained men. These he provided with the most up-to-date hardware including both siege engines which permitted the scaling of enemy walls and platforms from which his men could lob missiles into enemy cities.

Having thus mobilized, Uzziah launched attacks on Judah's ancient enemies the Philistines, breaking down the walls of Gath, Jabneh (Yebna), and Ashdod and then rebuilding towns near Ashdod and elsewhere as his own defensive positions (2 Chron. 26:6). He next turned upon the Arabs of the region of Gur Baal (Tell Ghurr), between Beersheba and Arad,[41] and brought them to heel. The Meunites, who lived in the Arabah in the vicinity of the Dead Sea, also capitulated. Finally, Uzziah prevailed over the Ammonites and made their nation a client state of Judah.[42] This apparently was by no means a permanent state of affairs, for Jotham, Uzziah's son, had to repeat the subjugation of

41. *Oxford Bible Atlas*, ed. Herbert G. May, 3d ed. (New York: Oxford University Press, 1984), pp. 69, 130.
42. Oded, "Neighbors on the East," in *World History of the Jewish People*, vol. 4, part 1, p. 262.

Ammon at least once (2 Chron. 27:5). The result of all this foreign involvement was a greatly strengthened nation under a king whose reputation became celebrated far and wide.

But Uzziah was not only a destroyer—he was a famous builder as well. He constructed defensive facilities in and around Jerusalem which must have been impressive enough. His most significant achievement, however, was his placement of settlements in the deserts and the Shephelah, a feat of engineering and agricultural technology that would provide a model for later generations including the Nabateans and even the Israelis of the twentieth century.[43] The chronicler's remark that Uzziah "loved the soil" (2 Chron. 26:10) is indicative of the motives which impelled him to such creative and far-reaching projects.

Tragically, however, the very successes of Uzziah in military and domestic affairs contributed to his demise, for, as the historian relates, "his pride led to his downfall" (2 Chron. 26:16). With reckless disregard for Mosaic prescription (Num. 16:40) he arrogated to himself the Aaronic priestly privilege of offering incense to Yahweh in the temple. He was thereupon confronted by Azariah the priest and ordered to leave the sacred precincts. When he arrogantly refused to do so, he was afflicted by a skin disease at the hand of Yahweh and thus, contaminated and rendered ceremonially unclean, was forced to withdraw. Nor would he ever know Yahweh's grace in healing. For the rest of his days, he lived isolated from the community, having handed the reins of government over to his son Jotham. Even in death he was ostracized, for rather than being interred in the tombs of the kings he was buried in an adjoining field, a silent memorial ever after to his disregard for the holy things of God.

It is important to point out here that Uzziah's sin was not in his offering incense per se but in his doing so in the very temple itself and on the altar of incense. This was a privilege reserved to the priests of the Aaronic line. As the Davidic heir—the priest after the order of Melchizedek—he did, indeed, enjoy priestly prerogatives as had David and Solomon before him. But his role as messianic priest was not to be confused with the specific function of the Aaronic priest. While the regulations governing the messianic priest are not spelled out in the Old Testament, they clearly precluded the offering of incense in the house of the Lord.[44]

43. Eugene H. Merrill, "Agriculture in the Negev: An Exercise in Possibilitism," *NEASB* 9 (1977): 25–35; Lawrence E. Stager, "Farming in the Judean Desert During the Iron Age," *BASOR* 221 (1976): 145–58; Yohanan Aharoni, "The Negeb and the Southern Borders," in *World History of the Jewish People*, vol. 4, part 1, p. 296.

44. As de Vaux points out, the kings could and did function as priests on special occasions, but this privilege did not extend to actions which are "properly sacerdotal" (*Ancient Israel*, vol. 1, p. 114).

The Ministry of the Prophets

Our discussion has almost reached the end of the one-hundred-year period which began with Jehu and was climaxed by the violent death of his fourth successor in Israel, Zechariah, and the pathetic end of Uzziah, ruler of the rival southern kingdom, just thirteen years later. But the whole story has not yet been told, for through the writings of contemporary prophets who knew these kings and were citizens of their kingdoms it is possible to learn more of the social, economic, political, and religious forces which combined to shape the history of the dual monarchy.

Prophetic Organization

We have already seen that the prophets and seers of ancient Israel played a significant part in the life of the nation. Samuel particularly is notable for his ministry of mediation between Yahweh and the people in his early years and then for his role as God-ordained kingmaker. His greatest legacy perhaps was the school of prophets which he apparently founded and whose members such as Nathan and Gad appeared over and over again to announce the word of God to the kings under whom they served.

Though it is difficult to know to what extent the prophets were formally organized under Samuel and subsequently, it is clear that they frequently appeared in groups or bands and participated in some kind of communal life. There were, however, great numbers of them who seemed to operate alone, to come and go as they were led by the Spirit of God. Were they members of a prophetic guild, or did they repudiate prophetic associations as something akin to pagan institutions? How were they related to the cult and the priesthood? Were they constituent elements of the established religious hierarchy, or did they see themselves as its adversaries? Were they ever attached to the palace? If so, were they merely hirelings who proclaimed a word only to please the king? If not, how were they viewed by the king?

The Office of Prophet

These and many other important questions have been addressed in various full-fledged treatments of the office of the prophet.[45] For our

45. See, for example, Willis J. Beecher, *The Prophets and the Promise* (Grand Rapids: Baker, 1963 reprint); Joseph Blenkinsopp, *A History of Prophecy in Israel* (Philadelphia: Westminster, 1983); C. Hassell Bullock, *An Introduction to the Old Testament Prophetic Books* (Chicago: Moody, 1986).

purposes, however, it is necessary only to recognize that the true prophets of God were raised up by him to serve as a kind of third order along with priest and king. Their role was as much of divine origination and importance as were those of priest and king; it was not, however, "official" in the same sense as were the others. Indeed, rather than standing within the circles of established religion and politics, the prophets stood outside as correctors or advisers.[46] Even so they were not viewed as opponents to the temple and state, but as spokesmen of God who were called to speak words of blessing, encouragement, advice, rebuke, or judgment to people, priest, and king as the need required. Nowhere in the Old Testament do the prophets look with disapproval or disdain upon the priestly and royal institutions as such.[47] Rather, they distinguished between these God-ordained offices and the individuals who held them. There were righteous and evil priests and kings, and they were addressed as such by the prophets. There were likewise righteous and evil prophets, and they also were dealt with accordingly in full recognition that the office itself, no matter who claimed it, was a holy thing.

Every society of the ancient world had its prophets, of course, but those of Israel were unique in many ways.[48] First of all, they were all conscious of the call of God and, if they were truly servants of Yahweh, conformed to strict criteria which could attest their credibility and genuineness to the satisfaction of all. They performed their ministry in the name of Yahweh only, and any predictive word they uttered came to pass (or would come to pass) within the time frame and historical context suggested in the oracle itself.

True prophets, moreover, were instruments of God and did not, as did the pagan diviners and practitioners of magic, seek to manipulate their God to their own plans and purposes. The prophets of Yahweh could not know his mind except as Yahweh took the initiative to reveal himself in dream or vision or some other way. Nor could they avert the purposes of God by apotropaic incantations or other such mechanical means. They could, however, earnestly pray or urge others to do so, and in response it might be that God would change his announced intentions. But such a response was never based on any ability or winsome quality in the prophet. Rather, it proceeded from the merciful and gracious heart of God and was given for no other reason than to bring glory to himself and good to his people.

46. G. Ernest Wright and Reginald H. Fuller, *The Book of the Acts of God* (Garden City, N.Y.: Doubleday, 1960), pp. 149–51.

47. Walther Eichrodt, *Theology of the Old Testament* (Philadelphia: Westminster, 1961), vol. 1, pp. 364–69.

48. Walther Zimmerli, *Old Testament Theology in Outline*, trans. David E. Green (Atlanta: John Knox, 1978), pp. 99–107.

Finally, the true prophet, whether associated with a prophetic guild or not, was responsible to God alone for his ministry. This again is radically different from the professionals of the surrounding cultures, who merchandised their services to the highest bidder and always managed somehow to hear a word from the gods to the liking of their employer. Israel's seers, then, did more than solve the mysteries of the phenomena of heaven and earth. They reached beyond the mere interpretation of signs and portents and dealt with issues of morality, righteousness, and the kingdom of God. This is why the oracles of the prophets were not only predictive, but, more characteristically, were fundamentally proclamatory. The prophets did indeed speak to the themes of the near and distant future, but they never lost contact with the present world in which they lived. As the need required, they spoke to the contemporary world whether with a word of encouragement and comfort or with a word of bitter condemnation. Only in Israel was this kind of prophetism known, for only in Israel was the prophet an objective, disinterested mouthpiece of the one and only God.

History of Prophetism

The prophetic movement as such began with Samuel and produced several outstanding individuals whose names have already surfaced in our historical review, men of God such as Samuel himself, Nathan, Gad, Ahijah, Jehu ben Hanani, and Zechariah. In addition there were a host of others who grace the pages of the record in anonymity. Many of these were associated with the school of the prophets established by Samuel. Whether that school remained intact as a cohesive, institutional body after Samuel's passing is not at all clear. In any case it served as the model for a similar movement under Elijah and Elisha, particularly the latter, in whose days it bore the name "sons of the prophets" (2 Kings 2:3, 5, 7; 4:1, 38; 5:22, KJV).[49]

This fellowship was apparently begun with Elijah's anointing of Elisha in about 855 B.C. Elisha by that act became the disciple of the Tishbite, learning from him and preparing to succeed him as master. At some point other young prophets became attached to Elijah and Elisha. By the time Elijah was translated bodily to heaven, the group had become centered in Bethel and Jericho. It is clear that the men lived together in somewhat of a monastic or communal lifestyle. This is evident from the fact that at Jericho their numbers began to increase

49. James G. Williams correctly understands the phrase to suggest the leadership role of a major figure (e.g., Samuel, Elijah, or Elisha) who headed a fraternity of prophets ("The Prophetic 'Father': A Brief Explanation of the Term 'Sons of the Prophets,' " *JBL* 85 [1966]: 344–48).

to the extent that they were crowded for living space. Elisha therefore encouraged them to build suitable quarters, which they did (2 Kings 6:1–2).

Before Elijah's translation he was regarded by the community as its master. The transfer of his prophetic mantle to Elisha communicated unmistakably that he was now the head, and the young prophets immediately recognized him as such. The very term used by them to describe their mentors—"father"—suggests an almost reverential respect and also, no doubt, helps to explain the phrase "sons of the prophets" as well. Though this phrase and the very existence of the community itself are not attested elsewhere (even immediately after the lifetime of Elisha),[50] the prophet Amos twenty-five years after Elisha's death disclaimed any connection with formal prophetism by pointing out to King Jeroboam II that he had not been a prophet by training nor was he "a prophet's son" (Amos 7:14). This was not, of course, a denunciation of the prophetic order, but simply an admission that he had not been affiliated with it.

A distinction is frequently made between the writing or canonical prophets and others, such as Elijah and Elisha, who left no extant written messages (except for Elijah's brief letter in 2 Chron. 21:12–15). It is then sometimes concluded, on the basis of their preserved compositions, that the canonical prophets were somehow of a higher order or more theologically significant.[51] This, of course, is without basis, for two of the greatest prophets of all—Moses and Samuel—are not numbered among the canonical prophets and yet created literary works almost without compare for both literary craftsmanship and theological maturity.

The difference lies in the fact that God, in his sovereign pleasure, chose to preserve the writings of the prophets after Elijah and, for reasons known only to him, not those of Nathan, Gad, or any of the other earlier prophets. Moreover, it is obvious that not everything the prophets wrote came to be considered as canonical. Why the selecting process which determined canonical prophecy should begin with Obadiah and end with Malachi cannot be known and would, in any event, be irrelevant in this study. All one can know in view of the supernatural character of the Old Testament Scriptures is that the Spirit of God controlled the selection as much as he did the composition of the texts themselves.

---

50. J. R. Porter, in fact, sees the "sons of the prophets" as an *ad hoc* fellowship which arose as an anti-Omride element, especially under Elisha, and was limited to the period of the Omride dynasty (בְּנֵי־הַנְּבִיאִים, *JTS* 32 [1981]: 423–29). There is no evidence, however, that the movement had such a limited scope.

51. W. O. E. Oesterley and Theodore H. Robinson, *Hebrew Religion: Its Origin and Development*, 2d ed. (New York: Macmillan, 1937), pp. 222–23.

The Earliest Writing Prophets

Obadiah

The first four canonical prophets—Obadiah, Joel, Amos, and Jonah—wrote during the period under consideration (ca. 840–740). The best critical analysis of the little Book of Obadiah suggests that its setting is the mid-to-late ninth century, thus making it (along with Joel) the earliest production of the writing prophets.[52] Unfortunately, nothing is known of the author, nor does he mention specific persons or events that could lead to secure dates. The message concerns Edom, which, in great arrogancy and self-sufficiency, had failed to render help to Judah when Jerusalem was being pillaged. Though several historical events might qualify, one thinks of the reign of Jehoram of Judah when Philistines and Arabs attacked Jerusalem, sacked the palace, and carried off the royal family except for Ahaziah, Jehoram's youngest son (2 Chron. 21:16–17). The reason this is a plausible setting for Obadiah is that Jehoram had previously invaded Edom in an effort to put down a rebellion against Judah. Jehoram's effort miserably failed, so in all likelihood the boastful pride of Edom described by the prophet issued from that successful struggle for independence (2 Kings 8:20–21). Then, when Jerusalem itself came under enemy attack, Edom would obviously have refused to offer assistance and might even have participated in Judah's humiliation. The sin in all this, Obadiah says, is that Judah was Edom's brother and therefore was deserving of Edom's support. The tragic result of Edom's pride would be destruction in the day of Yahweh and submission to his people.

Joel

The prophecy of Joel speaks of a time of severe plague and famine (1:2–20) followed by an anticipated invasion of Judah by an innumerable and terrifying northern army (2:1–10). God would have mercy upon his people, however, and divert the enemy host, bringing it to ruin (2:12–20). Then the famine would also end, and the land would be restored to plenty and prosperity (2:21–27).

Both military conquest and famine were, of course, rather regular sources of disaster for Israel and Judah, but their juxtaposition as described by Joel could not have been common. One such sequence can be found in the years of Elisha's ministry. It will be recalled that the prophet had interceded before King Joram in behalf of a woman who had fled to Philistia to escape the ravages of a seven-year famine. When she returned, she found that her house and properties had been

52. Gleason L. Archer, Jr., *A Survey of Old Testament Introduction* (Chicago: Moody, 1964), p. 288.

appropriated by others, and so she had turned to Elisha for help. The king then demanded that everything be restored to her (2 Kings 8:1–6). For reasons advanced previously (p. 352), it seems clear that the famine occurred near the beginning of Joram's reign, that is, from about 852 to 845.

It will also be recalled that Shalmaneser III had fought a coalition of Aramean and Palestinian kings to a stalemate at Qarqar in 853. The Assyrian was then forced to retire to Assyria for several years to attend to pressing matters there. In 841, however, he managed to besiege Hazael of Damascus and exacted heavy tribute from Jehu in his very first year as king of Israel. There is no reason whatsoever that Shalmaneser could not have continued on past Samaria all the way to Jerusalem. Jehoram was then on the throne of David. Given the problems which confronted him, such as the Edomite rebellion, he would hardly have been able to offer serious resistance to the vastly superior Assyrian armies.

Why did Shalmaneser not follow up on what could have been an assured success? To anyone attuned to the fact that history is in the final analysis the outworking of divine purpose the answer is clear. The Lord God of Judah graciously interposed, turned the mighty northern army about, and brought an end to the calamitous plagues (see 2 Chron. 21:7). In our view, Joel describes precisely these events and writes of them at some point between the beginning of the famine (ca. 852) and the Assyrian invasion (841). Joel therefore would have been a contemporary of both Obadiah and Elisha, and all three would have carried on significant ministries during the reign of Jehoram of Judah.[53]

Amos

Amos of Tekoa, the bold and independent prophet to the court of Jeroboam II, ministered, as he himself attests, in the days of Uzziah and Jeroboam (Amos 1:1). Since no other kings are mentioned, one must assume that Amos intended to say that his public ministry fell entirely within the period when only those two kings were ruling, that is, between 767 and 753. More precisely, he says that the divine message came to him "two years before the earthquake" (1:1), but that event cannot be dated dogmatically.[54]

53. For alternative views and especially arguments for a postexilic date see Leslie C. Allen, *The Books of Joel, Obadiah, Jonah, and Micah* (Grand Rapids: Eerdmans, 1976), pp. 19–25. The early date we are advocating is ably defended by A. F. Kirkpatrick, *The Doctrine of the Prophets* (London: Macmillan, 1892), pp. 57–72.

54. Hans Walter Wolff, however, draws attention to evidence from stratum VI at Hazor for a great earthquake in 760 B.C. This date falls exactly at the midpoint of the contemporaneous solo reigns of Jeroboam and Uzziah (*Joel and Amos* [Philadelphia: Fortress, 1977], p. 124).

The prophecy of Amos is replete with historical allusions, especially in the oracles concerning the nations (chs. 1–2). He refers, first, to the ravages of Damascus against Gilead which occurred under Hazael in the days of Jehu (1:3–5). These heinous deeds, the prophet says, would result in the destruction of Damascus itself and the deportation of its people. This came to pass in 732 when Tiglath-pileser III of Assyria captured Damascus, thus ending its importance for the rest of Old Testament times.

The Philistines are judged because of their collaboration with Edom against God's people in Judah (1:6–8). This information appears to fill in the historical record to some extent, for, as we saw in connection with the prophecy of Obadiah, Edom had rebelled against Judah successfully and the Philistines had then conquered Jerusalem and taken the royal family prisoner. The account in 2 Chronicles 21 leaves the matter at that, but Amos indicates that the prisoners taken by the Philistines had in turn been delivered over to the Edomites. One can be certain that they fared none too well there. For this reprehensible betrayal the prophet says the Philistine cities would suffer the wrath of Yahweh. Under Sargon II of Assyria this wrath fell in 712.[55]

Amos proceeds to indicate that Tyre, like the Philistines, had delivered Israelite prisoners to the Edomites (1:9–10). This was a direct violation of the covenant between Israel and Tyre which had been in effect since the days of David and Hiram. Unfortunately it is not possible to tie Amos's reference to Tyre to the account of Kings or Chronicles, but that does not mean that Amos is unhistorical at this point. He merely included a historical fact which for some reason or another was not recorded by either of the other two sources. Like Damascus and Philistia, Tyre would be destroyed for her sin against Israel. The Assyrian records abound in references to that empire's part in bringing this judgment to pass.

Edom is the next subject of the prophet's message of woe (1:11–12). Here is a general statement concerning the unremitting hostility which Edom had exhibited against Israel and Judah from the days of the wilderness journeys of the tribes to the present hour. Echoing the stern warning of Obadiah, Amos predicted the day when Edom would be reduced to ashes, a calamity which befell her under both Esarhaddon and Ashurbanipal of Assyria.[56]

Next was Ammon, still another nation which shared a common origin with Israel (1:13–15). The specific occasion for the prophet's

---

55. William W. Hallo and William K. Simpson, *The Ancient Near East* (New York: Harcourt Brace Jovanovich, 1971), p. 140.

56. John R. Bartlett, "The Moabites and Edomites," in *Peoples of Old Testament Times*, ed. D. J. Wiseman (Oxford: Clarendon, 1973), pp. 240–42.

ominous word against Ammon was her treatment of Gilead in the course of Ammonite territorial expansion. This area, lying just to the west of Ammon, had been claimed by Ammon at least as early as Jephthah in the late twelfth century. There may have been many unrecorded attempts over the subsequent centuries to appropriate it by force, so the particular occasion cited by the prophet cannot be determined. Perhaps it was in connection with the Ammonite, Moabite, and Meunite collusion against Jehoshaphat late in his reign; this alliance, while a failure, could well have reflected Ammonite efforts to encroach on Judean soil.[57] In any case, the pronouncement of the prophet was the same—Ammon would go down in inglorious defeat. The conquest of Ammon by Sennacherib in 701 could be the judgment in view,[58] as could that by Nebuchadnezzar in 582.[59]

Finally, Amos turns to the last of the neighboring nations, Moab, and levels his accusations and promises of judgment. The reason for the divine wrath this time, ironically, is Moab's desecration of the bones of the king of Edom, which were burned into lime. The prophetic referent is not immediately identifiable, nor is the significance of the deed. Amos cannot have in mind the effort by Joram of Israel and the kings of Judah and Edom to bring the rebellious ruler of Moab, Mesha, back under Israelite control (2 Kings 3). When Mesha on that occasion saw that his cause was hopeless and his very life was in jeopardy, he offered his own son to the god Chemosh as a burnt offering. This, the historian says, brought upon Israel great fury, and the battle was broken off. Amos, however, refers to the burning of the bones of the king of Edom, an act that likely took place closer to his own time.[60] It is possible that God's wrath upon Moab as articulated by Amos was not only because God was outraged by the disrespect for the dead, but also because the deed may have been a factor that prevented Israel from achieving its goal of subjugating Moab.[61] For this Moab would be punished, said the prophet, as indeed came to pass during several Assyrian campaigns.

Amos's main concern, however, was with his own people Judah and, even more, with the northern kingdom, Israel. He spoke of Judah's violation of the covenant and of the judgment which inexorably would

57. Oded, "Neighbors on the East," in World History of the Jewish People, vol. 4, part 1, p. 262, identifies the occasion as an Ammonite exploitation of Aramean pressure on Israel and Judah at the time of Ben-Hadad I and Hazael.

58. A. T. Olmstead, History of Assyria (Chicago: University of Chicago Press, 1975 reprint), p. 300.

59. John Bright, A History of Israel, 3d ed. (Philadelphia: Westminster, 1981), p. 352.

60. Wolff, Joel and Amos, pp. 150–51.

61. Thomas E. McComiskey, "Amos," in Expositor's Bible Commentary, vol. 7, Daniel–Minor Prophets, ed. Frank E. Gaebelein (Grand Rapids: Zondervan, 1985), p. 291.

follow. More specifically, he described the moral and spiritual conditions which characterized Ephraim or Israel in the days of Jeroboam II. The wealthy class, which had increased in both numbers and prosperity under Jeroboam's vigorous leadership, began to oppress the poor in every way imaginable. They sold the needy into slavery (2:6), they coveted ever more of the meager possessions of the helpless (2:7), and, with incredible hypocrisy, in the very act of worshiping Yahweh they lay on garments they had taken in pledge and consumed wine they had taken as fines. All this and more they did despite the fact that Yahweh had redeemed them from Egyptian vassalage to make them his own privileged servant-people. The result would be the destruction of Bethel, the place of syncretistic worship, and the tearing down of the luxurious dwelling-places of the rich and noble (3:13–15).

Portents of this judgment had already come in the form of famine, drought, and plagues of insects, to say nothing of Israel's incessant and debilitating wars (ch. 4). Unless Israel should reject her idolatrous ways and seek after Yahweh in true repentance, she faced inevitable desolation in the day of Yahweh. The Assyrians had already conquered Calneh (Kullâni)[62] in north Syria, perhaps in one of Shalmaneser III's early campaigns, and had followed this up by the taking of Hamath as well.[63] Even Philistia had by now suffered at the hands of foreign predators (6:2). How much longer, then, could the pampered citizens of Samaria expect to escape a similar fate? While lounging on their beds of ivory and gorging themselves on delicate foods and wines, they had become calloused to the poor and suffering of the land, and for this they would pay a bitter price.

In the midst of Amos's prophetic mission to Samaria he was interdicted by the priest of Bethel, Amaziah, who commanded him to cease his preaching and return to Judah (7:10–13). In response to the charge that he was prophesying for money as pagan prophets were prone to do, Amos denied any prophetic professionalism whatsoever. He had left a profitable business, he said, to take up the commission which Yahweh had given him. Now, as the true spokesman of God, he announced the judgment of Yahweh upon Amaziah, his family, and the whole land of Israel. They would be taken captive to a foreign land and there would languish in mourning and in hungering for the word of God.

A remnant would be saved, however, and in the day of Yahweh he would raise up the fallen tent of David and make it mighty as it was in days of old (9:11). In that day, Amos said, Yahweh would bring his

62. Martin Noth, *The Old Testament World* (Philadelphia: Fortress, 1966), p. 261.
63. J. D. Hawkins, "The Neo-Hittite States in Syria and Anatolia," in *CAH* 3.1, pp. 390–94.

redeemed back into the land, a land which would be indescribably fertile and productive. This time they would become so firmly rooted in his truth that they would never again be plucked up and carried away.

Jonah

Amos was not alone in his prophetic witness to Jeroboam II. Jonah ben Amittai of Gath Hepher (Khirbet ez-Zurra‘, five miles northwest of Mount Tabor),[64] the only prophet from Galilee, also delivered the word of Yahweh to this king of Israel, but his was a word of encouragement. Jeroboam, he said, would recover Damascus and Hamath and thus restore the kingdom of Israel to a measure of its former greatness (2 Kings 14:25). We have already proposed (p. 375) that this successful operation occurred no earlier than 773, so the prophecy of the event by Jonah must have been at least a few years prior to that date. The reference to Jonah in 2 Kings 14 should be sufficient evidence that he was a historical figure and not, as many scholars allege, the antihero of a parable.[65] Of course, his historicity is brought into question not because of the account of his prophecy to Jeroboam, but because of the account of his exploits as Israel's foreign missionary to Nineveh.

It is not possible here to enter into the full debate of the controversial issue of the literary genre and hence the historicity of the Book of Jonah. It is sufficient for us to realize that Jesus himself indirectly affirmed its historicity by comparing the historical fact of his own death, burial, and resurrection to the experience of Jonah in the belly of the great fish (Matt. 12:40).[66] The kind of redactionism that maintains that Jesus knew that Jonah was legendary and was comparing himself to a fictitious account or that Jesus never made the comparison himself—it was put in his mouth by the apologists of early Christianity—calls into question not only the story of Jonah but that of Jesus also. If one regards Jonah as anything other than historical narrative for whatever reason, it becomes difficult if not impossible to regard anything in the Old Testament as historical.

On a more positive note, the facts of the Book of Jonah fit precisely

64. Yohanan Aharoni, *The Land of the Bible* (Philadelphia: Westminster, 1979), p. 257.

65. Allen, *Joel, Obadiah, Jonah, and Micah*, pp. 175–81. George M. Landes, on linguistic grounds, dates the book to the sixth century ("Linguistic Criteria and the Date of the Book of Jonah," *Eretz-Israel* 16 [1982]: 162–63). But even if his conclusions are correct, all that they would prove is that the book in its present form comes from that period. For a rejoinder to Allen's view that Jonah is a parable, see D. J. Wiseman, "Jonah's Nineveh," *Tyn Bull* 30 (1979): 32–34.

66. Eugene H. Merrill, "The Sign of Jonah," *JETS* 23 (1980): 23–30.

the period in which the prophet is located by the writer of Kings. We have already seen that Jonah's prediction to Jeroboam antedated 773 by a few years. The setting of his own writings is surely later, for the book ends with Jonah in abject despair and defeat. It is most unlikely that he recovered from that condition to return to Israel and enjoy any kind of credibility among his own people.

We have emphasized several times already that Assyria, following the reign of Adad-nirari III (810–783), was in a dismal state of affairs. Internal upheavals and pressure from powerful enemies such as Urartu and the Aramean states kept her in a defensive holding position until mighty Tiglath-pileser III came to power in 745. This is precisely the period in which Israel under Jeroboam II and Judah under Uzziah regained territories which had been forfeited earlier and a great measure of their international prestige. It is also the period in which Jonah was occupied in his prophetic ministry.

Given these chronological limits, the most likely time for the mission of Jonah to Nineveh was in the reign of Aššur-dan III (772–755). Though no royal inscriptions whatsoever have survived from his years in power, the Assyrian eponym list and other indirect witnesses attest to his tenure as a period of unparalleled turmoil.[67] Asshur, Arrapḫa, Gozan, and many other rival states and dependencies revolted. In addition, plague and famine struck repeatedly until the empire was left impoverished and in total disorder.

This would have been an ideal time for Jonah to deliver his message of judgment and of the universal redemptive program of the God of Israel. Assyria's own pantheon and cult had failed miserably. Surely now, if ever, the king and people were prepared to hear a word from the only living God. Moreover, Assyria had already begun to function as the rod of chastening in his hand. With the passing of a few more years that role would be clarified and affirmed. How appropriate that that instrument of God's wrath should also first have had an opportunity to be the object of his grace. And the king and his people did repent, albeit superficially and without lasting results.[68] Because they did, they became a firstfruits of Gentile faith and salvation. Jesus, in fact, pointed out that the judgment of the Pharisees would be greater

67. Thiele, *Mysterious Numbers*, pp. 211–12. For the absence of royal inscriptions see W. Schramm, *Einleitung in die assyrischen Königsinschriften* (Leiden: E. J. Brill, 1973), vol. 2, p. 123.

68. Wiseman, "Jonah's Nineveh," *Tyn Bull* 30 (1979): 51, cites a letter from an unnamed king, possibly Aššur-dan III, to Mannu-ki-Aššur, governor of Gozan, which says: "Decree of the king. You and all the people, your land, your meadows will mourn and pray for three days before the god Adad and repent. You will perform the purification rites so that there may be rest (*qulū*, silence)." This is strikingly similar to the repentance described by Jonah.

than that of Nineveh. The people of Nineveh had repented at the preaching of Jonah (once again Jesus attested to Jonah's historicity), but the Pharisees refused to repent at the preaching of one who was greater than Jonah (Luke 11:32).

11 The Rod of Yahweh: Assyria and Divine Wrath

Factors Leading to Israel's Fall

At the midpoint of the eighth century a series of events commenced which, within thirty years, would bring about the collapse of Damascus, the conquest of Samaria and end of the nation of Israel, and the near capitulation of Judah. The impetus for this was the renascence of the mighty Assyrian Empire under Tiglath-pileser III and his indefatigable war machine. For more than 130 years Assyria terrorized not only Judah but the entire Near Eastern world until Nabopolassar and his illustrious son Nebuchadnezzar finally eliminated that menace forever.

The task of this chapter is to trace the complex factors which brought about Israel's demise and contemporary Judah's arrival at the brink of disaster. These are fundamentally theological in nature, of course, as are all of the events of biblical history. Historians and prophets alike make it clear that Israel and Judah had sowed the wind and therefore reaped the whirlwind. They had deviated from the straight course of covenant responsibility and so suffered the curses stipulated in the covenant documents.

Of course, there were more mundane reasons as well. There were tyranny and ineptness in government, irresponsible fiscal policy, unwise international relationships and alignments, class struggles, crime and violence, and a host of other ills that sickened the national and social life of the twin kingdoms. It is a wonder that either nation lasted as long as it did. One must conclude with the prophets that it was possible only because of the patient mercy of a loving God who remembered his covenant promises, though his people had forgotten theirs.

The End of the Dynasty of Jehu

Intimations of the violent course of Israel's last thirty years may be seen in the bloody end of the dynasty of Jehu. Because of his obedience in removing the family of Omri and its Baalism from the land, Jehu, it will be recalled, had been promised a long and prosperous rule (2 Kings 10:30). His descendants would occupy Israel's throne for four more generations, a record for longevity in the checkered history of the northern kingdom. Finally, after nearly ninety years, the last of Jehu's royal house, Zechariah, was murdered after only six months in power (753).[1] The perpetrator was Shallum ben Jabesh, but he was hardly able to savor the fruits of his violent act, for he in turn was assassinated within a month (2 Kings 15:8–15).

The leader of the anti-Shallum conspiracy was Menahem ben Gadi of Tirzah. The repetitious references to Samaria and Tirzah in the

---

1. Unless otherwise indicated, the dates in this chapter for the kings of Israel and Judah are those of Edwin R. Thiele, *The Mysterious Numbers of the Hebrew Kings* (Grand Rapids: Eerdmans, 1965), p. 81.

account (2 Kings 15:13–16) are of more than passing interest. What was involved was more than an ordinary grab for power; indeed, it was an attempt to reassert the domination of the old political base located at Tirzah.[2] One will recall that Jeroboam I, after residing briefly at Shechem, had established Israel's capital at Tirzah, where it remained until Omri purchased the hill of Shemer and built the new capital Samaria there in about 880 B.C. (see pp. 329, 339). One can be sure that that move from Tirzah was not universally popular and that a residue of resentment and even partisanship remained at Tirzah. Menahem must have represented that anti-Samaria faction though, in the interest of gaining popular support, he maintained the seat of government at Samaria.

Menahem reigned for ten years (752–742), a contemporary of Uzziah's last decade. He, like virtually all of his predecessors, is described as an evil king who did not depart from the ways of Jeroboam son of Nebat. Specifics of his evil reign are lacking until the invasion of the Assyrian king Tiglath-pileser, at which time Menahem paid the Assyrian a heavy tribute (2 Kings 15:19–20).

Assyria and Tiglath-pileser III

Following the virtual absence of Assyrian political and military influence in the decades after the death of Adad-nirari III (783), the void was finally occupied by a usurper, Tiglath-pileser III (also named Pulu or, in the Old Testament, Pul),[3] who reigned from 745 to 727.[4] He at once set out to accomplish three major objectives: restore order in Babylonia, regain control of Syria, and defend the northern borders against Urartu. The turmoil in Babylonia was of long standing but had been exacerbated by the arrival of Aramean immigrants, who, with the native stock, created a formidable political entity known as Kaldu (= Chaldeans).[5] Eventually this would give rise to the Neo-Babylonian Empire. Tiglath's solution to the Babylonian problem was

2. John Bright describes Tirzah as "the quondam capital" (*A History of Israel*, 3d ed. [Philadelphia: Westminster, 1981], p. 271), but, with other scholars, fails to elaborate on what clearly is an unusual interest in Tirzah on the part of the biblical historian.

3. A. T. Olmstead, *History of Assyria* (Chicago: University of Chicago Press, 1975 reprint), p. 181; Bright, *History*, p. 270.

4. For further details of Tiglath-pileser's reign see J. D. Hawkins, "The Neo-Hittite States in Syria and Anatolia," in *Cambridge Ancient History*, 3d ed., ed. John Boardman et al. (Cambridge: Cambridge University Press, 1982), vol. 3, part 1, pp. 409–15.

5. This development is thoroughly documented in J. A. Brinkman, *A Political History of Post-Kassite Babylonia, 1158–722 B.C.*, Analecta Orientalia 43 (Rome: Pontifical Institute, 1968).

to install a native ruler there, Nabonassar. The Urartian situation was brought under control by a series of campaigns which reduced Urartu to provincial status.

Tiglath's greatest interest lay in the west, however, so after the situation was stabilized elsewhere, he turned in that direction. In his first campaign to Syria in 743, he overcame Arpad (Tell Erfad), just north of Aleppo, and so terrorized the remaining small states of Syria and Palestine that many of them capitulated without a struggle while others offered only token resistance.[6] Menahem of Israel was among the former.[7] Both the annals of Tiglath-pileser and the Old Testament records attest to Menahem's eagerness to pay tribute to Tiglath-pileser in order to maintain his position in Samaria.[8] Though the Old Testament does not say so, Tiglath may also have made contact with Uzziah (= Azariah) of Judah. The Assyrian text on the basis of which such a connection has been hypothesized is, however, quite ambiguous, so one should not make too much of it.[9]

A second series of campaigns commenced in 734 and continued through 732. This resulted in the capture of Gaza and a frantic appeal by King Ahaz of Judah for Tiglath to make alliance with him against Pekah of Israel and Rezin of Damascus (2 Kings 16:5–7; Isa. 7:1–2).

6. For the improved situation that resulted in the Transjordanian lands under Assyria see B. Oded, "Neighbors on the East," in *World History of the Jewish People*, vol. 4, part 1, *The Age of the Monarchies: Political History*, ed. Abraham Malamat (Jerusalem: Massada, 1979), pp. 270–72.

7. William W. Hallo, "From Qarqar to Carchemish: Assyria and Israel in the Light of New Discoveries," in *The Biblical Archaeologist Reader*, ed. Edward F. Campbell, Jr., and David Noel Freedman (Garden City, N.Y.: Doubleday, 1964), vol. 2, pp. 169–70. Louis D. Levine, however, places in the year 738, four years after Menahem's death according to the biblical chronology, the campaign which persuaded Menahem to pay tribute ("Menahem and Tiglath-pileser: A New Synchronism," *BASOR* 206 [1972]: 40–42). While, Levine points out, this "firm synchronism" between Menahem and Tiglath-pileser must be taken into account (p. 42), his argument on the basis of the Iranian stela that Menahem's tribute was paid after 742 remains unproven. For an excellent rejoinder see H. Jacob Katzenstein, *The History of Tyre* (Jerusalem: Schocken Institute for Jewish Research, 1973), p. 205. William H. Shea, "Menahem and Tiglath-pileser III," *JNES* 37 (1978): 43–49, also faults Levine's line of argument, but dates the tribute to 740, still too late in our opinion. Mordechai Cogan also accepts 740, at least for the tribute of Tubail of Tyre ("Tyre and Tiglath-pileser III," *JCS* 25 [1973]: 96–99).

8. For the Assyrian text see James B. Pritchard, *Ancient Near Eastern Texts Relating to the Old Testament*, 2d ed. (Princeton: Princeton University Press, 1955), p. 283a.

9. Hallo, "From Qarqar to Carchemish," in *Biblical Archaeologist Reader*, vol. 2, p. 170, interprets "Az-ri-a-u of the Ia-ú-da-a-a" as a reference to Azariah, differing with such scholars as Siegfried Herrmann, who identifies the ruler in question as the king of the northwest Syrian state of Ya'udi (*A History of Israel in Old Testament Times*, trans. John Bowden [Philadelphia: Fortress, 1975], p. 246). In favor of Herrmann's position is the absence of any biblical reference to an Assyrian incursion as far south as Judah in Azariah's reign.

Tiglath complied and by 732 forced Damascus to surrender. Israel also would certainly have suffered the same fate had Pekah not been assassinated and replaced by a pro-Assyrian puppet, Hoshea.[10] Ahaz, meanwhile, had sold himself and his people to the pagan Assyrian overlord at a bitter price.

The final years of Tiglath-pileser were occupied with Babylonia once again. In fact, his need to deal with this chronic problem forced him to break off his western campaigns, giving Israel and Judah a few years' reprieve. Even after Babylonia, now under the tenacious and resilient leadership of Marduk-apla-iddina (Merodach-Baladan in the Old Testament),[11] was finally forced to submit, Tiglath-pileser never returned to the west.

Upon his death in 727 Tiglath was succeeded by his son Shalmaneser V, who reigned for only five years (727–722).[12] For two years he was occupied with the Babylonian rebellions that had consumed his father's last years. Then, in 725, he moved west to regain control of Phoenicia and Philistia. There followed a three-year siege of Samaria which resulted, in 722, in the city's collapse and deportation of its people. A siege of Tyre continued in the meantime and was completed by Assyria's next king, Sargon II. Sargon also claims to have taken Samaria,[13] but most scholars are agreed that he was merely taking credit for an achievement that should indeed be attributed to Shalmaneser.[14]

Menahem of Israel

To return now to Menahem of Israel, his voluntary submission to Tiglath-pileser may well have had something to do with a conspiracy against him; indeed, only two years after succeeding his father Menahem, Pekahiah was assassinated by Pekah and a Gileadite clique (2 Kings 15:25).[15] Whether Menahem became pro-Assyrian to ward off this threat in his declining years or whether the conspiracy came about

10. For the Assyrian text, the "Nimrud tablet," see D. Winton Thomas, ed., *Documents from Old Testament Times* (London: Thomas Nelson, 1958), p. 55.

11. For a full account of his life and career see J. A. Brinkman, "Merodach-Baladan II," in *Studies Presented to A. Leo Oppenheim*, ed. Robert M. Adams (Chicago: University of Chicago Press, 1964), pp. 6–53.

12. Hawkins, "Neo-Hittite States," in *CAH* 3.1, pp. 415–16.

13. This claim is made in the annals for the first year of his reign. See Pritchard, *Ancient Near Eastern Texts*, p. 284b.

14. The impartial Babylonian Chronicle unequivocally attributes Samaria's fall to Shalmaneser V. See Hayim Tadmor, "The Campaigns of Sargon II of Assur: A Chronological-Historical Study," *JCS* 12 (1958): 22–40, 77–100.

15. H. J. Cook, "Pekah," *VT* 14 (1964): 128.

because of his pro-Assyrian sentiments may never be known. What is known is that Menahem paid Tiglath-pileser "a thousand talents of silver to gain his support and strengthen his own hold on the kingdom" (2 Kings 15:19).

This strategem, though evil for a nation which claimed to trust in the covenant-keeping God, might have worked had Menahem lived and Tiglath-pileser not had to return to the north. But ifs are not the stuff of history. Menahem died after exacting the tribute money from Israel in a most painful manner and was succeeded by Pekahiah (742–740). And Tiglath-pileser, satisfied with Menahem's submission, had undertaken a reorganization of the northern Syrian states and Phoenicia,[16] leaving Israel to its own internal affairs.

The Last Days of Israel

The Rebellion of Pekah

The rebellion which apparently had begun in Menahem's lifetime came into the foreground now that Pekahiah ruled. He had hardly begun to enjoy his kingly prerogatives when he was attacked by Pekah ben Remaliah, an army officer who collaborated with a Gileadite element that was strongly anti-Assyrian (2 Kings 15:23–25). With Pekahiah out of the way Pekah proclaimed himself king and immediately broke the treaty with Assyria which Menahem had made. He no doubt felt safe in doing so because Tiglath-pileser was still detained elsewhere with matters of imperial responsibility. It is difficult to say whether Pekah acted as he did out of pure patriotic zeal or with a view to creating some kind of Syro-Palestinian confederation which could supplant Assyria and over which he could exercise leadership.

The Return of Tiglath-pileser

Whatever Pekah's objective, he was doomed to disappointment for within six years (by 734) Tiglath-pileser returned to the west and quickly began to annex vast areas of Syria and Palestine, especially in Galilee and the Transjordan.[17] The conquered cities included Ijon (Tell ed-Dibbîn), Abel Beth Maacah (Abil el-Qamḥ), Janoah (Yānûḥ), Kedesh (Tell Qades), and Hazor (Tell el-Qedaḥ),[18] all in the old tribal

16. See especially Katzenstein, *History of Tyre*, pp. 204–5. For a most illuminating discussion of Assyrian imperial structure in the west see I. Eph' al, "Assyrian Dominion in Palestine," in *World History of the Jewish People*, vol. 4, part 1, pp. 282–88.

17. B. Oded, "Observations on Methods of Assyrian Rule in Transjordania After the Palestinian Campaign of Tiglath-Pileser III," *JNES* 29 (1970): 177–86.

18. All these identifications are by Yohanan Aharoni, *The Land of the Bible* (Philadelphia: Westminster, 1979), pp. 429–43.

areas of Asher and Naphtali. Gilead may have been singled out because of its strong anti-Assyrian sentiment. For the first time the biblical historian speaks of an Assyrian custom that would have a profound
impact on all subsequent Israelite history—Tiglath-pileser took captives to Assyria.

In the meantime Hoshea ben Elah, seeing the handwriting on the
wall, disposed of Pekah and, with Assyrian approval if not explicit
direction, became Israel's last king. His reign (732–722) marks the last
decade of Israel's history in Old Testament times.

Chronology of the Reign of Pekah

Before the events of that decade are traced out, however, it is necessary to address the complicated question of the chronology of the
whole period, and particularly the data regarding Pekah.[19] Essentially,
the problem revolves around the statement that Pekah began to reign
over Israel in the fifty-second year of Uzziah, that is, in 740, and that
he reigned for twenty years (2 Kings 15:27). If this *terminus a quo* is
correct, he died in 720, which is obviously impossible because it post-
dates the end of the kingdom and leaves no room at all for the reign
of Hoshea.

Another possibility is that, with a twenty-year reign and succession
by Hoshea in 732 as givens, Pekah actually began to rule in 752. The
major objection to this view is that there is no evidence of a coregency
of Pekah with either Menahem or Pekahiah. The figure *twenty* is therefore rejected as a scribal error.[20] But before this interpretation is abandoned, one ought to consider the peculiar circumstances of Pekah's
accession. In a strict sense there was indeed no coregency between
Pekah and Menahem. Pekah was not of noble blood, so Menahem
would hardly have honored him in this way. But Pekah could have
been recognized as founder of a rival dynasty by some segments of the
population, particularly in and around Samaria itself.[21]

The rationale for this hypothesis lies in the fact that if Pekah reigned
for twenty years and was assassinated in 732, he began his rule in the

19. This problem occupies an entire chapter of Thiele's *Mysterious Numbers*
(pp. 118–40), an indication of its complexity. While the present discussion is indebted
to Thiele's work, there are differences at several points.

20. Rejection of the figure *twenty* is clearly implied by T. R. Hobbs, *2 Kings*, Word
Biblical Commentary (Waco: Word, 1985), p. 201. For proposed emendations see Cook,
"Pekah," *VT* 14 (1964): 121–22.

21. Thus the term "partisan dating," which is used by many scholars to describe
the practice of including within a king's tenure those years in which he was supported
by at least a significant minority. John Gray, for example, sees the *terminus a quo* for
Pekah as the moment he first arose against Menahem in an anti-Assyrian effort
(*I & II Kings* [Philadelphia: Westminster, 1970], pp. 64–65).

very year in which Menahem assassinated Shallum and began to reign (752). Menahem, we recall, was from Tirzah and evidently represented an anti-Samaria faction which had maintained itself there since the days of Omri. Pekah, then, would have been the champion of the pro-Samaria party; though he had to bide his time patiently for twelve years as commander of Israel's armies,[22] he enjoyed the endorsement of powerful persons in Samaria, many of whom even recognized him as king.[23] At last, with Menahem and Tiglath-pileser removed from the picture, Pekah felt free to act. He killed Pekahiah, declared Israel's independence of Assyria, and remained alone in power for the next eight years. One cannot prove this hypothesis, of course, but it is a reasonable explanation of all the known facts.

Hoshea of Israel

We have already seen that Hoshea, Israel's last king, came to power as an Assyrian puppet. His options were extremely limited, for in the very year of his accession, 732, Damascus was reduced to ashes and it was clear that Tiglath-pileser had Samaria next in mind. Hoshea was not a reliable puppet as it turned out, for when Tiglath-pileser had to return east to put down the Babylonian rebellions, Hoshea declared himself free of Assyrian suzerainty. He had little time to enjoy this independence, though, because Shalmaneser V resumed the imperialistic policies of his father. Shalmaneser came to Israel in 725 to demand Hoshea's loyalty. When this was not forthcoming, he laid Samaria under siege. Though the city held out valiantly for three years, it surrendered in 722.

The Role of Egypt

One reason for Hoshea's turn of heart and rejection of Assyrian hegemony was the increasingly visible rise of Egypt.[24] By the time of

22. Support for this premonarchic role of Pekah may now be found in a seal discussed by Pierre Bordreuil, "A Note on the Seal of Pekah the Armor-Bearer, Future King of Israel," *BA* 49 (1986): 54–55. See also Cook, "Pekah," *VT* 14 (1964): 124–26.

23. Cook, "Pekah," *VT* 14 (1964): 127, points out that Assyrian inscriptions (Pritchard, *Ancient Near Eastern Inscriptions*, pp. 283–84) call Menahem "Menahem of Samaria" whereas Pekah is known as the ruler of Bit Humria, the normal Assyrian designation of Israel. This clearly suggests a divided Israel; "Menahem of Samaria" might indicate only a formal recognition as king there. William H. Shea, in discussing a set of ostraca from Samaria, notes that years nine and ten refer to Menahem and year fifteen refers to Pekah. Shea concludes that Pekah's reign did in fact cover a full twenty years which were partly contemporary with and partly subsequent to Menahem ("The Date and Significance of the Samaria Ostraca," *IEJ* 27 [1977]: 21–23).

24. Kenneth A. Kitchen, *The Third Intermediate Period in Egypt (1100–650 B.C.)* (Warminster: Aris and Phillips, 1973), pp. 362–68.

Shalmaneser's succession Tefnakht I (727–720) of the royal house at Sais had founded Dynasty 24 of Egypt in the northern Delta. The princes of Dynasties 22 and 23 soon recognized his sovereignty; and so, greatly confident, Tefnakht tried to unify all Egypt by marching south to bring the Nubian dynasty of Piankhy (737–716) under his sway. This so-called Dynasty 25 proved to be more than capable of meeting Tefnakht's challenge, and in a decisive battle at Memphis Piankhy won not only the day but the lordship of all Egypt.

Piankhy returned south without having established any kind of administrative structure in the Delta. This permitted not only Tefnakht to reassert himself, but the other princes of the Delta as well. One of these, Osorkon IV (730–715) of Dynasty 22, is probably the "So king of Egypt" to whom Hoshea appealed for assistance (2 Kings 17:4).[25] Unfortunately that appeal was in vain, and Shalmaneser undertook his ultimately successful siege without interference.

The Impact of Samaria's Fall

Theological Implications

The fall of Samaria dealt a shattering blow not only to Israel's political life, but to her understanding of the nature of the covenant. Was 722 to mark the end of the northern kingdom? Had the promises as well as the patience of God at last been exhausted? These questions must have been on the lips not only of the Israelite survivors, but of the people of Judah as well. Even though the Davidic throne was situated in Jerusalem, could Judah hope for any better fate?

These questions were addressed primarily by the prophets. But in a manner almost unique to him the author of 2 Kings also deals with the theological meaning of Israel's demise. The fall of Samaria and deportation of its population, he says, took place because the Israelites had sinned against Yahweh (17:7). God's people had become disloyal to their Suzerain who had brought them redemptively out of Egyptian servitude. They had expressed disloyalty by worshiping other gods (17:15–17). And they did all this despite his persistent reminders to them through his spokesmen, the prophets, that what they were doing constituted high treason. The inevitable result was the judgment of God, a judgment which took the form of exile from the land of promise.

Judah, the author of 2 Kings goes on to say, was no better (17:19). They imitated Israel's apostasy and so could expect a similar fate. That apostasy was epitomized in Israel's very first king, Jeroboam,

25. Ibid., p. 374.

who became to all subsequent generations a model for iniquitous behavior. It is little wonder that the only remedy for 210 years of covenant infidelity was to be uprooted from the land of the covenant and delivered over to the very nations for whom Israel was responsible as the servant of Yahweh. The irony is inescapable.

Deportation

In line with common Assyrian policy, the inhabitants of Samaria and its vicinity were deported wholesale to various places throughout the Assyrian Empire, and captives from other nations were in turn settled in Samaria.[26] The purpose obviously was to stamp out feelings of nationalism and thus inhibit tendencies toward rebellion and independence. But the policy of deportation and resettlement was also to have a most profound impact upon Judaism and the early church. For the curious admixture of peoples which resulted became known as Samaritans, who were at once despised as a mongrel race by Judaism and tenderly regarded by the merciful Messiah.

The biblical narrator mentions only three destinations of the uprooted Israelites—Halah, Gozan, and "the towns of the Medes"—though surely their dispersion was more widespread than that.[27] Halah cannot be identified beyond doubt,[28] but Gozan is none other than the well-known and important city Tell Halaf[29] on the Habor River, approximately sixty miles southeast of Haran. How ironic that some of the Diaspora should end up so close to the adopted city of their father Abraham! It is almost as though they must resume the covenant quest all over again. The "towns of the Medes" were just east of the central and northern Zagros mountain range between present-day Iraq and Iran.

An earlier deportation had occurred under Tiglath-pileser, but it was limited largely to the two-and-a-half tribes of the Transjordan. The chronicler, in his rather summary recapitulation of the tribal genealogies, points out that Tiglath-pileser took the eastern tribes into captivity (1 Chron. 5:26). This is not an anachronism or a false attri-

26. Eph'al, "Assyrian Dominion in Palestine," in *World History of the Jewish People,* vol. 4, part 1, p. 283.

27. Various Hebrew names have been found at Calah; see William F. Albright, "An Ostracon from Calah and the North-Israelite Diaspora," *BASOR* 149 (1958): 33–36; I. Eph'al, "Israel: Fall and Exile," in *World History of the Jewish People,* vol. 4, part 1, pp. 190–91.

28. Eph'al, however, equates it with Halahhu, a city and district northeast of Nineveh ("Israel: Fall and Exile," in *World History of the Jewish People,* vol. 4, part 1, pp. 189–90).

29. Martin Noth, *The Old Testament World* (Philadelphia: Fortress, 1966), p. 261.

bution of Shalmaneser's conquest to Tiglath-pileser as some scholars allege,[30] but an amplification of 2 Kings 15:29, which briefly summarizes the campaign of 734–732: "He [Tiglath-pileser] took Gilead and Galilee . . . and deported the people to Assyria." Their destination was virtually the same as that of the main body of Israelites ten years later except that the chronicler adds the name *Hara*, perhaps a corruption of *'ārê (māday),* "cities (of the Medes)" (cf. 2 Kings 17:6; 18:11).[31]

The Origin of the Samaritans

The peoples brought to Samaria, on the other hand, originated in such places as Babylon, Cuthah (Tell Ibrahim, twenty miles northeast of Babylon), Avva (Tell Kefr 'Aya, on the Orontes River in north Syria),[32] Hamath (Ḥamā), and Sepharvaim (near Hamath in upper Syria).[33] Such a conglomeration of peoples obviously introduced a hodgepodge of languages, customs, and religious practices.[34] Despite their new surroundings the deportees naturally began to install their native cults in Samaria until Yahweh interposed his judgment: he sent lions to kill some of the people. When the Assyrian king (presumably Sargon II) heard of the disaster which had befallen his new colony, he sent an Israelite priest back to head the cult at Bethel and instruct the people in proper worship (2 Kings 17:27–28).[35] The result was a highly syncretistic system, for while each national group paid lip service to Yahwism, they also continued to serve their own gods in the vacated high places. This situation, the historian says, continued down to his own day, at least as late as 560 B.C. And that it persisted even later is clear from the testimony of such postexilic writers as Ezra and Nehemiah. In spite of missionary activities undertaken periodically by

30. This is intimated by H. G. M. Williamson, *1 and 2 Chronicles*, New Century Bible Commentary (Grand Rapids: Eerdmans, 1982), p. 67.

31. Edward L. Curtis, *A Critical and Exegetical Commentary on the Books of Chronicles* (Edinburgh: T. & T. Clark, 1910), p. 126.

32. *Oxford Bible Atlas*, ed. Herbert G. May, 3d ed. (New York: Oxford University Press, 1984), p. 123.

33. Yohanan Aharoni and Michael Avi-Yonah, *Macmillan Bible Atlas* (New York: Macmillan, 1968), map 150.

34. For the Assyrian practice of imposing foreign cults on newly acquired provinces such as Israel see Morton Cogan, *Imperialism and Religion: Assyria, Judah and Israel in the Eighth and Seventh Centuries B.C.E.* (Missoula, Mont.: Scholars Press, 1974), pp. 105–10. No such imposition was made on vassal states, however; so Judah, by virtue of tribute payments and other expressions of allegiance, was left totally autonomous in religious affairs. See Carl D. Evans, "Judah's Foreign Policy from Hezekiah to Josiah," in *Scripture in Context*, ed. Carl D. Evans et al. (Pittsburgh: Pickwick, 1980), p. 158.

35. For an exact parallel in an Assyrian text see Shalom Paul, "Sargon's Administrative Diction in II Kings 17:27," *JBL* 88 (1969): 73–74.

the Yahwists of Judah, only gradually did the Samaritan cult evolve into its monotheistic form as seen, for example, in the New Testament.

Judah and the Fall of Samaria

The Chronological Problem

The story of Samaria's fall and Israel's national demise is not complete, of course, without reference to the history of neighboring Judah. The year 740 marks the death of Uzziah of Judah and, as Isaiah the prophet notes, the starting point of his own ministry (Isa. 6:1). We pointed out previously (p. 377) that Uzziah had sinned by arrogating to himself Aaronic priestly privileges and had paid for his pride by being afflicted with a loathsome skin disease and quarantined to private quarters. This immobilized him so effectively in his last years that he was forced to hand the reins of government over to his young son Jotham (2 Chron. 26:21). When precisely did this occur?

The historian suggests that Jotham commenced his reign in the second year of Pekah and continued on the throne for sixteen years (2 Kings 15:32–33). On the other hand, Ahaz, his son, came to power twelve years prior to the accession of Hoshea of Israel (2 Kings 17:1), which would be 744.[36] The problem that emerges from these data is this: If Ahaz began to reign in 744 and his father Jotham reigned for sixteen years before him, Jotham must have become king in 760. To further complicate matters, for Jotham to have begun his reign in Pekah's second year requires Pekah to have undertaken his in 762. Yet traditional scholarship will date the beginning of Pekah's rule no earlier than 740, after the sixteen years of Jotham!

We have already proposed, however, that Pekah was actually recognized as king by some elements in Israel as early as 752. We now wish to postulate that the "sixteen years" of Jotham consists of two elements: (1) a period of what we might call a dominant regency and (2) a coregency with Ahaz. The former embraced the period from 750 to 740, the date of Uzziah's death. This would appear to have been an ordinary coregency since Uzziah lived on until 740 as titular head of state. The chronicler, however, is insistent that full authority was turned over to Jotham at the time of his father's incapacity, so in the truest sense he was sole ruler (2 Chron. 26:21).[37] It is therefore quite correct

36. Thiele, *Mysterious Numbers*, p. 129.
37. The term "dominant regency" is coined here to describe the unusual situation in which a son (here Jotham) coreigns with his father (here Uzziah/Azariah), but is actually in a superior position at least functionally. This is clearly the intent of 2 Chronicles 26:21.

to say that Jotham's reign began in Pekah's second year, but only if we grant that Pekah commenced his sovereignty in 752 as is required by other data.

Further support for these chronological boundaries for Jotham may be found in the fact that Rezin of Damascus, who ruled from about 750 to 732,[38] began, with Pekah, to harass Judah in the time of Jotham's kingship (2 Kings 15:37). This continued into the reign of Ahaz, Jotham's son (2 Kings 16:5). Since Rezin died in 732 (as did Pekah), Ahaz must have commenced his reign prior to that date. In fact, the author of Kings says that Ahaz began to reign in the seventeenth year of Pekah, which would be 735 (2 Kings 16:1). Like his father he reigned for sixteen years (v. 2), so one would expect the dates 735–719. However, as we have already pointed out, Hoshea of Israel began his reign in 732, which we are told in 2 Kings 17:1 was the twelfth year of Ahaz. This suggests that Ahaz actually began to reign in 744, not 735.

The resolution appears to be in the postulation of a coregency between Jotham and Ahaz from 744 to 735 after which Ahaz achieved dominance for sixteen years. The "sixteen years," in other words, refers only to his independent kingship, while "the twelfth year of Ahaz," which is tied to Hoshea's accession, refers to the twelfth year since the beginning of Ahaz's coregency. Yet, on the basis of other data, we know that Ahaz had to live until at least 715 because he was then succeeded by his son Hezekiah. This date for Hezekiah is virtually certain since his fourteenth year witnessed Sennacherib's invasion of Judah (2 Kings 18:13), a campaign which all scholars date to 701. The reference, then, to Hezekiah's coming to Judah's throne in the third year of Hoshea (ca. 729—2 Kings 18:1) must surely pertain to yet another coregency, this a long one of fourteen years between Ahaz and Hezekiah.

But if Ahaz lived until 715 and commenced his rule in 735, in what sense could he have reigned for sixteen years? The answer lies, we submit, in a four-year coregency between Jotham and Ahaz (735–731) which for some reason or another is not included in the total regnal years of either. In other words, they were truly coequal during this period.[39]

Let us summarize our reconstruction: Jotham became coruler in 750 while his father Uzziah was still alive. Having reigned as a functional superior for eleven years until Uzziah's death in 740, Jotham then became head ruler in the strict sense until 735. Meanwhile Jotham had appointed Ahaz as his vice-regent in 744 despite the fact

38. Merrill F. Unger, *Israel and the Aramaeans of Damascus* (Grand Rapids: Baker, 1980 reprint), p. 95.

39. Cook, "Pekah," *VT* 14 (1964): 121, suggests that 2 Kings 15:30 "retains a tradition that Jotham lived for four years after his official reign had ended."

that Uzziah was still alive. Then, in 735, the two became coequals until 731, neither claiming dominance. At that time Ahaz inaugurated his sole regency of sixteen years, which continued until 715. Hezekiah became assistant to his father in 729, served with him until 715, ruled alone until 696, and then coreigned with Manasseh until 686.

The ages at which these monarchs came to power are supplied in the record and are relevant to our discussion. Jotham, we read, was twenty-five when he took over from Uzziah in 750 (2 Kings 15:33). Ahaz was twenty when he began his sole regency (2 Kings 16:2). Our reasoning here is that if he had been twenty in 744, when he was appointed vice-regent, he would have been born in 764; yet Jotham was born in 775 and would thus have been just eleven years old when his son was born, a manifest impossibility. Obviously Ahaz was twenty in 735, when Jotham was forty, and died at age forty in 715. Hezekiah was twenty-five when he began his tenure. As in the case of Ahaz, this must refer to his age at the beginning of his sole regency in 715, for if he had been twenty-five in 729, he would have been only one year younger than his father Ahaz! If, on the other hand, he was twenty-five in 715, he was born in 740 when Ahaz was fifteen. This may still appear problematic, but it is possible and indeed there are parallels.[40] Moreover, it is much more reasonable than any alternative.

In conclusion to this lengthy excursus it must be stressed that what appear to be irreconcilable data to some scholars are capable of harmonious integration.[41] Postulating coregencies and young ages for kings at the birth of their sons is not at all out of keeping with what is known of the ancient Near Eastern world.[42] Moreover, the only data we have are those of the text; to reject them in favor of a skepticism which offers no alternative but the assumption of textual error is to beg the

40. Thiele, *Mysterious Numbers*, p. 128.

41. Thiele is so reluctant to assume twelve-year coregencies (according to his reconstruction) between Jotham and Ahaz on the one hand and Ahaz and Hezekiah on the other that he assumes an error on the part of the biblical editor, namely, that the editor wrongly placed the commencement of the reigns of Pekah and Jotham in 740–739 rather than twelve years before (*Mysterious Numbers*, pp. 138–40). No scholar has done more to unravel the complexities of the chronology of the monarchies of Israel by retaining the figures of the Masoretic text. It is strange, indeed, that he seems unable to do so here merely because of the unusual case of Jotham's having made Ahaz his vice-regent while he himself was coregent with his father Uzziah. Proper attention to 2 Chronicles 26:21 would, we feel, alleviate that tension. Admittedly, it is difficult to understand why the chroniclers would at times date events in terms of the years of a sole regency and at other times in terms of a coregency. A difficulty in modern understanding ought not, however, to disqualify the ancient biblical historians as faithful interpreters and recorders of their own times.

42. On this matter see the persuasive documentation offered by Nadav Na'aman, "Historical and Chronological Notes on the Kingdoms of Israel and Judah in the Eighth Century B.C.," *VT* 36 (1986): 83–91.

question in such a way as to set aside the scholarly method. Unless one can show *from the Old Testament record itself* that the reconstruction suggested here is impossible or unlikely, it should commend itself to the objective and unbiased student as at least worthy of consideration.

Jotham of Judah

In returning to the historical narratives, we begin with the reign of Jotham, king of Judah, who, as we have seen, reigned in his father's stead from 750 to 740, when Uzziah died, and then on to 731 (2 Chron. 27:1–9). He is characterized as a good king who did what was right before Yahweh. The people, however, continued their pagan ways, sacrificing and burning incense on the high places. Like Uzziah, Jotham engaged in monumental defensive programs in and around Jerusalem and throughout the hinterlands as well, a necessary work considering the troublous times in which he lived. At some point, perhaps following the earlier series of campaigns of Tiglath-pileser (743–738) when Menahem of Israel was forced to pay tribute, Jotham launched an attack against Ammon, reducing it to tributary status for about three years. It seems likely that this was made possible by Tiglath's forced retirement to Assyria after 738. If so, the Ammonite subjugation lasted until 735, the year that Ahaz, a partisan of the Assyrians, began his equal coregency with Jotham. There is undoubtedly a connection between Ahaz's accession even as coregent and the fact that whereas the Ammonites do not appear in the early tribute lists of Tiglath-pileser, we now find them paying tribute alongside Ahaz.[43]

Far more important to Judah's foreign policy, however, was the ominous threat which developed in Jotham's last years from the Damascus-Samaria alliance led by Rezin and Pekah respectively. Beginning in about 735, this was designed as a punitive action against Judah, now equally under Ahaz and Jotham, for her unwillingness to join the coalition which they had formed, along with other states such as Philistia and Edom, to confront and neutralize the second grand offensive of Tiglath-pileser (734–732). Ahaz not only refused to cooperate but, as Isaiah makes most clear, gladly collaborated with the Assyrians in order to be spared what he must have perceived to be certain destruction otherwise (Isa. 7).

Ahaz of Judah

The biblical narrative suggests, as does our proposed chronological scheme, that the Rezin-Pekah adventure against Judah was directed

---

43. Hallo, "From Qarqar to Carchemish," in *Biblical Archaeologist Reader*, vol. 2, p. 171.

not so much at Jotham, though he was still technically in command, as against his vigorous and bold son Ahaz, who was not yet twenty-five years old. Unlike his father and grandfather, this young monarch was evil and apostate, and so, as the chronicler points out in his theological interpretation of events, Yahweh handed him over to Rezin, the king of Aram (2 Chron. 28:5), who defeated him and took many Judean prisoners. Likewise, he fell prey to Pekah of Israel, suffering heavy casualties including his own son and several of his principal officials. Pekah, like Rezin, took many prisoners and much plunder back to his capital.

These two punitive campaigns, not mentioned at all by the author of Kings, must have been undertaken in 735 or not much later because both Rezin and Pekah were dead by 732. As we have already suggested, these campaigns probably were in retaliation for Ahaz's clear leanings toward Assyria and refusal to participate in an anti-Assyrian alliance which was being created throughout Syro-Palestine. The need for such a protective league was most apparent to these western states, for Tiglath-pileser was already initiating his second series of campaigns designed to reestablish Assyrian hegemony along the Mediterranean. He had previously brought Menahem of Israel under tribute and in the same year had also forced Rezin into submission.

Rezin, as suggested previously (p. 375), most likely reestablished the Aramean dynasty at Damascus after the death of Jeroboam II of Israel in 753. Jeroboam apparently had incorporated Damascus into his sphere of influence in his heyday of power (ca. 773), thus introducing a twenty-year interregnum in Damascus until Rezin's rise to power. The renewal of Damascene independence was surely linked to the chaotic conditions in Samaria which attended the violent overthrow of the dynasty of Jehu and the establishment of that of Menahem. Menahem's tribute to Tiglath-pileser may, in fact, have been designed as much to garner Assyrian support against Rezin as to strengthen his own upstart regime in Samaria.

With the withdrawal of Tiglath-pileser in 738, Rezin and Pekah of Israel were able to take steps to create a Syro-Palestinian confederation in preparation for an anticipated second conquest by the Assyrians. Damascus by now had become the power base and natural leader in all of Syria and so was able to recruit states to the north to the cause.[44] Before long Tyre, Sidon, and other Phoenician centers joined in and even Philistia and Edom complied, perhaps reluctantly. Only Judah was left—Ahaz, whatever his faults, was astute enough to see that total domination of the eastern Mediterranean world by Assyria

44. Eph'al, "Israel: Fall and Exile," in *World History of the Jewish People*, vol. 4, part 1, pp. 184–85.

was only a matter of time. He decided to throw in his lot with the eventual winner rather than with those who shortsightedly believed they could prevail.

The invasions of Rezin and Pekah (ca. 735) were soon followed up by a concerted effort to lay Jerusalem under siege and force it once and for all into compliance. Ahaz, encouraged by Isaiah, stubbornly refused to submit. Instead the king sent a frantic appeal to Tiglath-pileser for help. Meanwhile, the Edomites and Philistines took advantage of the situation by launching razzias into Judean territory and capturing certain Judean outposts (2 Chron. 28:16–18). Rezin, realizing perhaps the folly of further siege, left Jerusalem and headed south to the strategic port city of Elath, which he seized and delivered over to Edom (2 Kings 16:5–6). Judah thus lost access to the southern sea.

When Tiglath-pileser saw the turn of events which had come to pass, he moved west in 734, attacked and defeated Ashkelon, Gaza, and Gezer, and lifted the siege of Jerusalem. He next addressed the recalcitrant Rezin of Damascus and in 732 took him and his city with such finality that Damascus never again became a significant factor in Old Testament times. Finally he turned on Israel, stripped it of its northern and eastern territories, and placed his own appointee, Hoshea, on Israel's throne.[45]

Ahaz had paid a staggering price for survival, not only in monetary terms but most especially in the moral and spiritual compromises which his bargaining had required. As the chronicler notes, in the final analysis Tiglath-pileser gave Ahaz trouble and not help (2 Chron. 28:21). Ahaz had had to loot the temple to pay the heavy protection fees that Tiglath demanded, and as an act of thanksgiving Ahaz offered sacrifices to the gods of Assyria, whom he credited for his salvation. He also installed their shrines throughout the land. There is little wonder that Isaiah the prophet chastised Ahaz in the bitterest terms and predicted the day when Judah also would come to know the awful Assyrian scourge (Isa. 7:17).

That scourge did not come at once, however, for Ahaz maintained his servility to Assyria for the rest of his days. Moreover, Tiglath-pileser found himself up to his neck with rebellion in the homeland, especially from the Babylonians. He could not have returned to the west even if he wanted to, and by the time the pressures eased he was dead.

45. Hallo, "From Qarqar to Carchemish," in *Biblical Archaeologist Reader*, vol. 2, pp. 173–74. For the Assyrian texts see Pritchard, *Ancient Near Eastern Texts*, pp. 283–84. On the basis of a recently noted synchronism between Assyria and Israel Na'aman proposes that Hoshea deposed Pekah after Tiglath's withdrawal from the west in 732. The *coup d'état* and Hoshea's succession should therefore be dated in 731, thus relieving the problem of a nine-year reign of Hoshea ending in 722 ("Historical and Chronological Notes," *VT* 36 [1986]: 71–74).

Sargon II of Assyria

Tiglath-pileser's successor, Shalmaneser V (727–722), who eventually took Samaria in his last year, assiduously avoided any kind of hostility toward Judah, presumably because Ahaz's treaty with Assyria was still considered in full force. The same is true of Sargon, successor to Shalmaneser, at least until the death of Ahaz in 715. In not one inscription does Sargon record a campaign against Judah in those years—though his records are replete with actions taken against Judah's neighbors—nor does the Old Testament speak of any.[46] This eloquently testifies to the undying loyalty of Ahaz to his Assyrian masters, a loyalty made possible by an equally undying hostility toward and disobedience of the Lord God of the covenant.

Sargon, who probably was not the son of Tiglath-pileser, as some claim, but a usurper, reigned over the vast Assyrian Empire from 722 to 705. One of Assyria's most militant rulers, he claims to have undertaken significant campaigns in every one of his seventeen years. In the annals of his first year he takes credit for Samaria's fall. In actual fact the biblical assertion that Shalmaneser V was responsible is correct; as several scholars have shown, Sargon claimed this major conquest for his own reign so that the record of his first year would not be blank.[47]

Sargon's accession prompted numerous uprisings throughout the empire. In 720 he began to address these problems by engaging an alliance of Elamites and Babylonians at Dēr (Bedrai), eighty miles northeast of Babylon.[48] He was probably defeated, though each side claims victory. The leader of the Babylonian forces was none other than Marduk-apla-iddina (Merodach-Baladan in the Bible).[49]

Sargon then immediately moved west to subdue a large Syro-Palestinian coalition led by Hamath.[50] He retook Damascus and even Samaria,[51] now considered an Assyrian province, and demanded a reaffirmation of Judah's loyalty by the payment of a heavy tribute. He then moved through Ekron and Gaza to the very borders of Egypt,

46. Hawkins, "Neo-Hittite States," in *CAH* 3.1, pp. 416–17.
47. William W. Hallo and William K. Simpson, *The Ancient Near East* (New York: Harcourt Brace Jovanovich, 1971), p. 138.
48. Albert Kirk Grayson, *Assyrian and Babylonian Chronicles* (Locust Valley, N.Y.: J. J. Augustin, 1975), pp. 73–74, Chronicle 1.1. 33–37.
49. Brinkman, "Merodach-Baladan II," in *Studies Presented to A. Leo Oppenheim*, ed. Robert M. Adams, p. 13.
50. Pritchard, *Ancient Near Eastern Texts*, p. 285.
51. Samaria was thus taken twice. See Eph'al, "Israel: Fall and Exile," in *World History of the Jewish People*, vol. 4, part 1, p. 187.

where he forced the leader of Lower Egypt, Sib'e, to capitulate.[52] Finally, he turned back north to Tyre and completed the siege of that stronghold which Shalmaneser had undertaken five years before in 725.[53]

In a second western campaign in 717–716 Sargon overran Carchemish and again moved south all the way to Egypt, where he won a decisive battle near the Wadi el-Arish.[54] There is no word of engagement with Judah, and so one may conclude that Ahaz, who was now in his next-to-last year, remained docile and loyal.[55]

Hezekiah of Judah

The situation changed radically after 715, however, for then Hezekiah, son of Ahaz, asserted his loyalty to Yahweh alone and severed the ties with Assyria (2 Kings 18:7). It was not possible for Sargon to avenge this insubordination at once, but in 712 he (or his envoy) returned west to put down widespread insurrections which Hezekiah himself may have inspired.[56] After whipping his client states, possibly including Judah, back into line, Sargon returned to Assyria to deal once more with the intractable Marduk apla-iddina of the Sealands dynasty of Babylonia.[57] In addition Sargon found it necessary to protect his northwestern flanks from Mushku in Asia Minor until he came to terms of peace with its King Mita in 709.[58] Finally, Sargon suffered an invasion by the Cimmerians of the north in 706. It is possible that he died in the following year as a result of these hostilities.[59]

52. Kitchen, *The Third Intermediate Period*, p. 373, reads the Egyptian name as Re'e, not Sib'e, and identifies him as the army commander under Osorkon IV (n. 743). Moshe Elat suggests that Assyria's intense interest in Egypt from the time of Tiglath-pileser onward was fundamentally economic. Her conquests of Syro-Palestine were to keep trade routes to Egypt open ("The Economic Relations of the Neo-Assyrian Empire with Egypt," *JAOS* 98 [1978]: 20–34).

53. Katzenstein, *History of Tyre*, pp. 229–30.

54. Kitchen, *Third Intermediate Period*, pp. 375–76; Pritchard, *Ancient Near Eastern Texts*, p. 286c.

55. Evans says, in fact, that "there remains no evidence . . . that Judah ever suffered military action by Sargon II" ("Judah's Foreign Policy," in *Scripture in Context*, p. 161).

56. Pritchard, *Ancient Near Eastern Texts*, pp. 286–87. For an excellent overview of the entire campaign see Gerald L. Mattingly, "An Archaeological Analysis of Sargon's 712 Campaign Against Ashdod," *NEASB* 17 (1981): 47–64.

57. This was in the twelfth year of Merodach-Baladan or 710 B.C. See Grayson, *Assyrian and Babylonian Chronicles*, p. 75, Chronicle 1.2. 1–5; Brinkman, "Merodach-Baladan II," in *Studies Presented to A. Leo Oppenheim*, ed. Robert M. Adams, pp. 18–19.

58. Hawkins, "Neo-Hittite States," in *CAH* 3.1, p. 421.

59. Olmstead, *History of Assyria*, p. 267.

The Years of Coregency

To return to the beginning of Hezekiah's reign, we observe that he became coregent with Ahaz in the third year of Hoshea of Israel (2 Kings 18:1)—729 B.C. He was then only eleven years of age,[60] and so he probably had little or no positive impact on the apostate pattern of Judah's life under his father. But the apostasy without question made a profound impact on the young prince himself: by the time he became king in his twenty-fifth year he was so heartsick and frustrated by the long years of spiritual bankruptcy over which he had had no control that he immediately led the nation in a great reformation movement which pervaded every aspect of Judean life.

Hezekiah's Reformation

Integrally connected with the religious declension of the nation under Ahaz was Judah's dependency on Assyria. It was, in fact, the overtures to Tiglath-pileser that had resulted in Ahaz's wholesale abandonment of Yahweh and the covenant and his embracing of the religious system of pagan Assyria. It is not surprising, then, that following Hezekiah's reformation political relationships with Assyria, now under Sargon II, were severed.

A close reading of the available sources indicates that the spiritual renewal preceded but probably had no immediate connection with the formal breaking off of ties with Assyria.[61] The chronicler states pointedly that in the first month of his first year[62] Hezekiah reopened the temple and reestablished its services (2 Chron. 29:3). This required a thorough work of repair since the holy precincts had not only become ritually impure because of the sacrilege of Ahaz, but had simply deteriorated physically in the absence of proper maintenance. Hezekiah therefore gathered the priests and Levites and charged them to consecrate themselves once more for religious service and, with him, to enter into covenant renewal before Yahweh.

60. The "twenty-five years" in 2 Kings 18:2 obviously refers to Hezekiah's age in 715 B.C. when he began his sole regency.

61. Evans points out that there was no hint of anti-Assyrian rebellion in the reform ("Judah's Foreign Policy," in *Scripture in Context*, p. 162).

62. Mordechai Cogan quite reasonably describes this as a "pseudo-date" marking Hezekiah's interest in temple affairs but not necessarily the undertaking of reform ("The Chronicler's Use of Chronology as Illuminated by Neo-Assyrian Royal Inscriptions," in *Empirical Models for Biblical Criticism*, ed. Jeffrey H. Tigay [Philadelphia: University of Pennsylvania Press, 1985], pp. 202–3). For the reasons why the chronicler covers Hezekiah's reformation much more thoroughly than does the abbreviated account in 2 Kings see Jonathan Rosenbaum, "Hezekiah's Reform and the Deuteronomistic Tradition," *HTR* 72 (1979): 23–43.

For sixteen days the work of purification went on. When at last it was finished, the king called a solemn assembly and commanded the priests to offer up burnt offerings and sin offerings on behalf of all the people. Then, as the ritual of sacrifice was being carried out, the temple choirs and orchestras broke out in tumultuous expressions of worship and praise. The service was concluded by the presentation of thank offerings which attested to the sincerity and complete dedication of those who brought them.

When the month of the Passover arrived in Hezekiah's first year, he attempted to restore it as a national observance—it apparently had not been properly celebrated for many years—but he found it physically impossible to do so because of a shortage of qualified priests (2 Chron. 30:1–9). Moreover, there had not been sufficient time for him to publicize his intentions and for the people to come from the length and breadth of the two kingdoms. He therefore postponed the festival to the second month and sent out couriers from Dan to Beersheba to invite the people to come.[63] The message that was sent was more than a mere invitation; it was an appeal to Israel as well as Judah to return to the God of their fathers and to renew their covenant commitment to him. They might be only a remnant, he said, but God would bless the remnant and restore his favor to them.

So calloused had the people of Israel become, however, that many of them chose not to travel to Jerusalem to celebrate the Passover with their Judean kin. Nevertheless, a great throng assembled on the fourteenth day of the second month to participate in the festival which commemorated their election and redemption as the people of God. Some of them were ceremonially unclean, probably because of the long period of laxity in spiritual matters, but Hezekiah interceded for them before the Lord that he might not look upon their ritually unclean hands but into their devoted hearts (2 Chron. 30:18–19).

For not just the prescribed time of seven days but for fourteen the festival went on, so filled with joy were all the people. Not since the days of Solomon, the chronicler notes, had there been anything like it. And God in heaven heard their outpourings of thanksgiving and praise and was pleased.

The reverse side of the restoration of Yahweh worship was the removal and destruction of every vestige and symbol of pagan cult. This included not only the high places and altars in both the south and north, but even the bronze serpent which Moses had made long ago

63. The very fact that Hezekiah could send messengers throughout Israel with the expectation of a major favorable response shows, as Hanoch Reviv points out, that Assyria under Sargon had very little control of that region ("The History of Judah from Hezekiah to Josiah," in *World History of the Jewish People*, vol. 4, part 1, pp. 194–95).

in the Sinai desert (2 Kings 18:3–4; 2 Chron. 31:1). An index to the thoroughness of Israelite apostasy is the fact that they worshiped the very object which at one time had been a symbol of the healing grace of their God.

The formal affirmation of covenant renewal that was dramatized by the Passover celebration was followed by a total reorganization of the religious personnel and their responsibilities.[64] Hezekiah divided the priests and Levites as the Mosaic law prescribed, and he commanded the people to join him in giving a tithe to meet the needs of those who served the temple. To this command the people responded generously and after four months had accumulated vast amounts of produce and other goods at the temple. There was so much, in fact, that storage facilities had to be erected to accommodate it all. Certain men were then appointed to be in charge of these goods and to see that they were allotted and distributed fairly to all the clergy and their families, whether they lived in Jerusalem or distant villages. Thus Hezekiah faithfully discharged his royal and priestly responsibilities before the Lord. "And so," as the chronicler so laconically observes, "he prospered" (2 Chron. 31:21). It is easy to see why.

Rebellion Against Assyria

Sometime early in his reign, probably just after the religious reformation just described, Hezekiah rebelled against Sargon of Assyria and refused any longer to pay the crushing tribute the Assyrian had exacted from Ahaz. He followed this act of defiance by launching attack upon such Assyrian puppet states as Philistia, ridding the land of these detested foes who had been able to locate some of their settlements in Judah itself (2 Chron. 28:18).[65]

Strangely, neither Kings nor Chronicles provides an account of Sargon's reaction to this bold initiative taken by Hezekiah. The prophet Isaiah does, however, and we will look to him briefly for information. We have already mentioned Sargon's campaign of 717–716 in which he quelled a rebellion at Carchemish in north Syria (p. 409). He had then subjugated Shilkanni (= Osorkon IV) of Egypt at the Wadi el-Arish. At this time (715) Ahaz of Judah, a loyal Assyrian client, died,

64. The centralization of the cult naturally resulted in a major political and administrative reorganization as well. Such internal reorganization may be evidenced by more than a thousand jar handles bearing the royal stamp (lmlk) which have been discovered at Lachish and a variety of other sites. Evans believes that these royal storage jars were produced for the collection and distribution of religious offerings ("Judah's Foreign Policy," in Scripture in Context, p. 163).

65. B. Oded, "Neighbors on the West," in World History of the Jewish People, vol. 4, part 1, p. 244.

and his place was taken by his fiercely anti-Assyrian son Hezekiah. Why Sargon did not know of this change in administration or, if he knew of it, did not immediately take steps to bring Hezekiah into line must remain a mystery. Instead, he returned to Dur-Sharrukin (Khorsabad), his capital.[66]

The person of faith will, of course, see in Sargon's neglect of Hezekiah a classic case of providential timing. With the Assyrian back in his homeland, Hezekiah had a golden opportunity to bring about the reformation and even to send messengers throughout the Assyrian province of Samaria to encourage Israelite participation in the Passover. This respite lasted only until 712, however, at which time Sargon returned to put down a Philistine rebellion at Ashdod,[67] to enter relations with Shabako, the Nubian successor to Osorkon, and to punish Hezekiah for his refractory ways. Isaiah records this Assyrian campaign (20:1), but neither he nor other biblical or extrabiblical sources reveal the outcome where Hezekiah is concerned. One can only surmise that Sargon's malevolent objectives remained unfulfilled, though at least one Assyrian text refers to Judah as a tribute state, thus implying that Hezekiah was, temporarily at least, subject to Sargon.[68] For the remainder of Sargon's reign (712–705) Judah enjoyed immunity from further Assyrian interference, but with the accession of Sennacherib all that changed, and by 701 the Assyrians were once more wreaking havoc in the west.

Sennacherib and the Siege of Jerusalem

Sennacherib reigned from 705 to 681. Though he was the son of Sargon, he initiated some major changes in Assyrian policy including the removal of the capital from Dur-Sharrukin to Nineveh.[69] He had barely come to power when he was faced with a rebellion in Babylonia

66. Hallo and Simpson, *Ancient Near East*, p. 140.

67. Eph'al, "Assyrian Dominion in Palestine," in *World History of the Jewish People*, vol. 4, part 1, p. 277.

68. For the tribute list which included Judah see Cogan, *Imperialism and Religion*, p. 118. Cogan dates it at 712 B.C. On the basis of this and other evidence A. R. Jenkins goes as far as to link the siege of Jerusalem in Hezekiah's fourteenth year to Sargon and not Sennacherib ("Hezekiah's Fourteenth Year," *VT* 26 [1976]: 284–98), thus allaying the problem of the two-campaign hypothesis (see n. 74). Besides the fact that this would require an accession date for Hezekiah of 727 (so Jenkins) rather than 729 as already established, it goes against the unequivocal biblical witness connecting the fourteenth year of Hezekiah with Sennacherib (esp. 2 Kings 18:13).

69. Olmstead, *History of Assyria*, pp. 283–336. For the relevant Assyrian texts of Sennacherib see Daniel D. Luckenbill, *The Annals of Sennacherib* (Chicago: University of Chicago Press, 1927).

led by the perennial foe of Assyria, Marduk-apla-iddina.[70] This leader of the Aramean Sealands dynasty had just returned from exile imposed upon him by Sargon, but with characteristic tenacity gained support for Babylonian independence from such widely scattered sources as Elam to the east and the Aramean states to the west. Even Hezekiah might have joined the effort. Marduk-apla-iddina at least sent ambassadors to Jerusalem to solicit Hezekiah's aid; we do not know, however, whether it ever materialized (Isa. 39).

In any case, Sennacherib prevailed, took the city of Babylon, and reasserted Assyrian authority. He also undertook a systematic subjugation of the entire Sealands area. Amazingly, Marduk-apla-iddina rebounded, however, and instigated yet another rebellion in 700. Again, and for the last time, he was put down; and Aššur-nādin-šumi, a son of Sennacherib, was installed as regent in Babylon.[71]

Meanwhile, with Egyptian encouragement Hezekiah also rebelled (2 Kings 18:13, 21), so in 701 Sennacherib marched west, engaged Egypt and Judah at Eltekeh (Tell esh-Shallaf), west of Gezer, and threatened Jerusalem with punishment.[72] Hezekiah was forced to purchase his deliverance by an exorbitant tribute which nearly emptied the palace and temple treasuries of their contents.[73] Unsatisfied, Sennacherib again surrounded the city and would certainly have starved it into submission had not Yahweh intervened and destroyed the Assyrian army, forcing Sennacherib to return to Nineveh empty-handed.[74]

---

70. H. W. F. Saggs, "The Assyrians," in *Peoples of Old Testament Times*, ed. D. J. Wiseman (Oxford: Clarendon, 1973), p. 163; Louis D. Levine, "Sennacherib's Southern Front: 704–689 B.C.," *JCS* 34 (1982): 29–34. For the text see Luckenbill, *Sennacherib*, 1.1–64.

71. Olmstead, *History of Assyria*, pp. 289–90; Levine, "Sennacherib's Southern Front," *JCS* 34 (1982): 41; Brinkman, "Merodach-Baladan II," in *Studies Presented to A. Leo Oppenheim*, pp. 26–27.

72. For the text see Luckenbill, *Sennacherib*, 2.37–3.49.

73. It is interesting to note, as A. R. Millard has pointed out, that the tribute was *not* delivered immediately, but was later sent to Nineveh. This would suggest that Hezekiah merely made a promise of payment, an arrangement which was unsatisfactory to Sennacherib and brought a second siege, but which Hezekiah nonetheless honored even after the Assyrians were forced to retire ("Sennacherib's Attack on Hezekiah," *Tyn Bull* 36 [1985]: 71).

74. The thesis that Sennacherib undertook two campaigns against Jerusalem separated by fifteen years, advanced most notably by John Bright (*History of Israel*, p. 300), cannot be accepted. The premise upon which the argument rests is that Tirhakah of Nubia (2 Kings 19:9), who led an Egyptian army into Palestine at the time of Sennacherib's siege of Jerusalem, was only fourteen to eighteen years old in 701. This would obviously disqualify him from being a military commander, so it is alleged that he conducted another campaign fifteen years later, in 686. The idea that Tirhakah was a teen-ager in 701 rests, however, on a misinterpretation of both the chronology of Dynasty 25 and stelae 4 and 5 from Kawa. As Kitchen shows, Tirhakah was twenty or twenty-one in 701 and thus well able to be at least "titular head of the expedition."

The Involvement of Egypt

Before we examine the details of this crisis, it is necessary to look briefly at the political situation in Egypt, since the biblical sources, particularly Isaiah, make much of Egyptian involvement in Judah's affairs at this time.[75] We have already described the confusing situation in Egypt in the last third of the eighth century. Two dynasties, 22 and 23, had ruled over very limited realms in the Delta region, while Dynasty 24 was rising to power at Sais in the north and Dynasty 25 was doing so in the far south. By 737 Piankhy, the Nubian king of Dynasty 25, had won control over all of southern Egypt; then, pressing north, by a crucial battle at Memphis he brought Lower Egypt also under his sovereignty.

But when Piankhy returned to the south, Tefnakht of Dynasty 24 claimed headship over Lower Egypt. Osorkon IV of Dynasty 22 (King So of the Bible) was apparently his vassal. After Piankhy died, Shabako, the next king of Dynasty 25, moved north to unify Egypt against the threatened invasion of his country by Sargon. He managed to effect the unification he desired, but only by extraditing a Philistine prince to Sargon was he spared what surely would have been a devastating

The fact that he is called "the Cushite king" in 2 Kings 19:9 may be only a proleptic anticipation of his kingship, which in fact commenced in 690 (*Third Intermediate Period*, pp. 157–61). There is, moreover, no reference in Sennacherib's annals to a Jerusalem campaign after 701, nor does the Old Testament know of a second campaign, though Bright and other scholars claim to have discovered one by isolating 2 Kings 18:14–16 from its context (thus seeing it as the record of the 701 campaign), leaving 2 Kings 18:17–19:37 and Isaiah 36–37 as the record of the putative second campaign.

Danna Fewell has demonstrated that the passage from Kings on which the two-campaign hypothesis is based is a "cohesive unit" with a clearly perceptible concentric framework. While no conclusions are drawn about the number of campaigns, Fewell's analysis of the text can lead to no other conclusion than that the historian is speaking of one major episode ("Sennacherib's Defeat: Words at War in 2 Kings 18:13–19:37," *JSOT* 34 [1986]: 79–90). See also Anson F. Rainey, "Taharqa and Syntax," *Tel Aviv* 3 (1976): 40.

Recently, however, William H. Shea has compared some newly published texts from Assyria (K 6205 + BM 82-3-23, 131), Palestine (the Adon Papyrus), and Egypt (a temple inscription from Karnak), and has concluded that they point decisively to a second campaign of Sennacherib, one he dates at 688/687 ("Sennacherib's Second Palestine Campaign," *JBL* 104 [1985]: 401–18). Shea bases much of his argument on Hayim Tawil's study of the Assyrian texts which speak of Sennacherib's construction of irrigation projects at Muṣur (Mount Muṣri near Nineveh) in 694. Tawil equates Akkadian Muṣri with the Hebrew māṣôr of 2 Kings 19:24 (= Isa. 37:25) and points out that the Assyrian messengers cannot in 701 be boasting of an event which occurred in 694. Tawil does, however, suggest that the Hebrew word designating Muṣri may have been put into the speech by a later editor ("The Historicity of 2 Kings 19:24 [= Isaiah 37:25]: The Problem of Ye'ōrê Māṣôr," *JNES* 41 [1982]: 195–206).

75. For the following see especially Kitchen, *Third Intermediate Period*, pp. 356–87.

blow to Egypt. He ruled, then, almost by Assyrian permission until his death in 702.

Shebitku, a son of Piankhy, followed Shabako; and in the spirit of general rebellion following Sargon's death in 705, Shebitku with his armed forces moved north in 701 to join the Palestinian states, including Judah, in an effort to withstand the new king of Assyria, Sennacherib.[76] By the time Shebitku arrived, Hezekiah may already have promised his tribute to Sennacherib. Whatever the case, the Assyrian broke off further hostilities against Jerusalem when he learned that Shebitku was on the way. Sennacherib then confronted the forces of Egypt and Judah at Eltekeh.[77] Victorious, he divided his army, leaving part to provide defense against the Egyptians and sending the others to Jerusalem, apparently to punish Hezekiah for his collaboration with the rebels.

By then a second large contingent of troops from Egypt, led by the crown prince Tirhakah, was on its way. Sennacherib was soon apprised of this, but communicated to Hezekiah that he should take no comfort from it since the Assyrians had completely destroyed all their previous enemies (2 Kings 19:9–13). Egypt did indeed prove to be a "splintered reed" (2 Kings 18:21): Shebitku and Tirhakah retreated without doing the Assyrians further harm. But Hezekiah found that he did not need Egypt anyway, for the hosts of Yahweh soon disposed of Sennacherib's mighty machine.

The Death of Sennacherib

After Sennacherib returned to Assyria, he found his hands full with first the Sealands dynasty and then the Elamites.[78] He attempted a naval invasion of Elam but was repulsed, and the Elamites in turn attacked Babylon. Aššur-nādin-šumi, the son of Sennacherib who was governor there, was taken prisoner. Three years later, in 692, a major battle between the Elamites and Assyrians took place in the Diyala Valley, an encounter which ended in a stalemate. Babylon, which now was under the native rule of Mušēzib-Marduk, was attacked and sacked by Sennacherib in 689.[79] It remained without a king for the remaining

76. Nadav Na'aman, "Sennacherib's 'Letter to God' on His Campaign to Judah," *BASOR* 214 (1974): 33–34.

77. It is possible, of course, that the exacting of tribute and ravaging of Judah's outlying towns may have followed and not preceded the victory of Sennacherib at Eltekeh. See Eph'al, "Assyrian Dominion in Palestine," in *World History of the Jewish People*, vol. 4, part 1, pp. 278–79.

78. Olmstead, *History of Assyria*, pp. 283–86; Levine, "Sennacherib's Southern Front," *JCS* 34 (1982): 41.

79. J. A. Brinkman, "Sennacherib's Babylonian Problem: An Interpretation," *JCS* 25 (1973): 94–95.

eight years of Sennacherib's life, which ended with Sennacherib the victim of a plot engineered by two of his sons.[80] This left another son, Esarhaddon, to fill his father's shoes and keep the lid on a situation that was threatening to explode.[81]

Hezekiah's Last Years

With this background in view it may be somewhat easier to reconstruct the somewhat confusing record of the last part of the reign of Hezekiah as found in 2 Kings, 2 Chronicles, and Isaiah. The confusion comes about because the account is not always in chronological order, especially in Isaiah, and because the sacred historians, as is frequently the case, prefer to order their discussion along thematic, topical, or theological lines and not as a modern historiographer might do.[82] Nevertheless, the main threads are quite apparent, and the events on the whole can be properly related to one another. What follows is somewhat repetitious of our previous discussion, but the emphasis now is on the biblical viewpoint.

Hezekiah's sickness

The story begins with the sickness of Hezekiah, an episode recorded by all three sources (2 Kings 20:1–19; 2 Chron. 32:24–26; Isa. 38–39) This must have taken place even before Sennacherib's invasion, since that event is anticipated. The role of Merodach-Baladan is helpful here in that he sent messengers to Hezekiah, ostensibly to congratulate him on his recovery from illness, but actually to seek his support in the independence efforts of the Sealands kingdom. That rebellion commenced in 703, so it is almost certain that Hezekiah's illness was later.[83] In addition, the prayer of Hezekiah for recovery resulted in an extension of his life by fifteen years. He died in 686 (after a reign of

80. Grayson, *Assyrian and Babylonian Chronicles*, p. 81, Chronicle 1.3. 34–38. Simo Parpola has shown that the assassin was Sennacherib's son Arad-Ninlil, a name easily equated with the biblical Adrammelech ("The Murderer of Sennacherib," in *Death in Mesopotamia*, ed. Bendt Alster, *Rencontre assyriologique internationale* 26 [Copenhagen: Akademisk Forlag, 1980], pp. 171–82).

81. See the so-called Prism B in Pritchard, *Ancient Near Eastern Texts*, pp. 289–90.

82. Evans, "Judah's Foreign Policy," in *Scripture in Context*, p. 164.

83. Reviv dates the envoys at 703–702 ("The History of Judah from Hezekiah to Josiah," in *World History of the Jewish People*, vol. 4, part 1, p. 196). Partly because Merodach-Baladan is called king in Isaiah 39:1, John H. Walton suggests 703, the last year in which he is known by that title ("New Observations on the Date of Isaiah," *JETS* 28 [1985]: 129; see also Julian Reade, "Mesopotamian Guidelines for Biblical Chronology," *Syro-Mesopotamian Studies* 4.1 [1981]: 2; Brinkman, "Merodach-Baladan II," in *Studies Presented to A. Leo Oppenheim*, p. 33). The legation could not have been quite that early, however, because it followed Hezekiah's illness of about 702.

twenty-nine years which began in 715), so the prayer must have been offered in 701. The illness itself can therefore be dated in 702 or 701.

Sennacherib's campaign

Very shortly after Hezekiah's recovery and the departure of Merodach-Baladan's envoys, Sennacherib came to the west and pressed toward Jerusalem, a campaign recorded in Kings and Isaiah. The reason he did so must remain somewhat a matter for speculation, though most scholars assume that Hezekiah had participated in the rather wholesale struggle for liberation which was under way throughout Syro-Palestine. If our view that Merodach-Baladan had been to Jerusalem first and that Hezekiah had agreed to some kind of mutual defensive pact is correct, Sennacherib's attack on Jerusalem could have had a very specific objective—to punish Hezekiah for his disloyalty and to break up his affiliation with the Sealands dynasty.

That something like this occurred is implicit in Hezekiah's message to Sennacherib, who, having already laid waste much of Judah, was personally leading his troops against the Egyptians, Philistines, and others near Eltekeh. In abject contrition Hezekiah confesses, "I have done wrong. Withdraw from me, and I will pay you whatever you demand of me" (2 Kings 18:14). Clearly Hezekiah is admitting some kind of offense against Sennacherib, refusal to pay tribute being most likely. He then promises and later sends an enormous tribute, going as far as to strip off the gold from the temple doors and doorposts. One might observe, incidentally, that the representatives of Merodach-Baladan had been shown the vast treasures of the palace, a privilege which obviously they could not have enjoyed had they visited Hezekiah after Sennacherib's plunder.[84]

Apparently satisfied, and also under mounting pressure on the battlefield, Sennacherib withdrew from Jerusalem and engaged the coalition of rebels first at Lachish and then at Libnah (2 Kings 18:17; 19:8). He defeated them, devastated a great number of Judean towns and cities, and then made his way back to Jerusalem.[85] In preparation for a long siege Hezekiah blocked up the water supplies outside the city to prevent the Assyrians from using them. He then reinforced the walls and laid in store large quantities of weapons (2 Chron. 32:1–5).

84. Evans, "Judah's Foreign Policy," in *Scripture in Context*, p. 163.

85. The course of this campaign can now be much better understood thanks to the joining of two textual fragments (Na'aman, "Sennacherib's 'Letter to God,'" *BASOR* 214 [1974]: 25–39), which has proved to be a breakthrough in harmonizing the Assyrian and biblical accounts; see Nadav Na'aman, "Sennacherib's Campaign to Judah and the Date of the *LMLK* Stamps," *VT* 29 (1979): 69–70. The destruction of Lachish in 701 has also been made virtually certain in the careful analysis of David Ussishkin, "The Destruction of Lachish by Sennacherib and the Dating of the Royal Judean Storage Jars," *Tel Aviv* 4 (1977): 52–53.

As Sennacherib directed his major thrust at Lachish, he sent three of his officials, a *tartānu*, a *rab-sārîs*, and a *rab-šāqēh*[86] to negotiate terms of surrender with Hezekiah. In order to avoid a costly and time-consuming reduction of the city by military means, they tried to intimidate its citizens to surrender by reminding them of the awesome power of the Assyrian war machine, a power which had no respect for gods or men. Even the hosts of Egypt which were rumored to be on the way under the command of Tirhakah would be of no avail. The Assyrian officials then called out so that the people of the city could hear and understand. Capitulate, they said, and Sennacherib would not punish Jerusalem. Rather, he would reward the inhabitants of the city and guarantee them peace and prosperity such as they had never known before.

These tempting overtures might have achieved their desired ends had not Isaiah prevailed upon Hezekiah and the people to trust God for salvation. He, the prophet assured them, would intervene and bring about an Assyrian retreat (2 Kings 19:6–7). Meanwhile, the *rab-šāqēh*, returning to Sennacherib to make his report, found the king no longer at Lachish but Libnah. Sennacherib had by then heard of the movement north of a large contingent of Nubian troops under the command of Tirhakah. Sennacherib may have attributed Hezekiah's intransigence to his hope for Nubian support, for the Assyrian immediately sent another set of messengers to Jerusalem with a letter advising Hezekiah to surrender. How could Tirhakah be of any help, the letter read, when the kings of Assyria had time and again demonstrated their awesome might against the nations that opposed them?

When Hezekiah received the letter, he spread it out before the Lord and in urgent prayer asked Yahweh to reveal himself in mighty power against the blasphemous king of Assyria. Indeed, Hezekiah said, Sennacherib had run roughshod over the gods and kings of many nations, but those gods were not really gods at all nor were those nations the people of Yahweh. Now in saving grace the God of Judah could demonstrate once and for all that he is God alone.

No sooner had the prayer been made than there came a message from Isaiah assuring Hezekiah that God would answer. The God of Israel had known all of Assyria's successes long before they had come to pass; in fact, it was he who had ordained and permitted them. Assyria's boasting and failure to recognize that she was only the instrument of Yahweh would result in her own tragic downfall. As for Judah, she would escape the Assyrian war machine, for Yahweh would

---

86. For these three terms, meaning "commander in chief," "chief eunuch," and "chief butler" respectively, see Gray, *I & II Kings*, p. 678. For *rab-šāqēh* see Richard A. Henshaw, "Late Neo-Assyrian Officialdom," *JAOS* 100 (1980): 290, 299.

interpose dramatically and with his own strong arm would preserve the City of David.

That very night the angel of Yahweh struck down 185,000 men of the Assyrian army.[87] Totally demoralized and devastated, Sennacherib abandoned his quest and retreated, with the remnant of his once mighty armies, to Nineveh. The annals of Sennacherib record in boasting terms his success in shutting up Hezekiah in Jerusalem "like a caged bird,"[88] but, in keeping with the normal practice of propagandistic accounts, he fails to utter a word about the outcome of his tragic adventure.

The last fifteen years

The biblical historians are virtually silent about the remaining fifteen years of Hezekiah's long reign. The chronicler does point out, however, that they were years of unusual material prosperity (2 Chron. 32:27–29). His treasuries again were filled with riches, and new granaries had to be built to accommodate the bountiful harvests. Hezekiah also dug a tunnel to provide Jerusalem with access to water supplies outside the city walls—a miracle of engineering that still elicits amazement.[89] Other such enterprises were undertaken throughout his realm.[90] He died in 686, leaving the reins of government in the evil hands of his son and coregent Manasseh.

The Viewpoint of the Prophets

Before our recounting of this most crucial period of Israel's history can be brought to an end, it is necessary to review it through the eyes of the prophets who participated in its major events and helped shape its outcome. We have already referred repeatedly to Isaiah, that is, to historical data in his book which supplement Kings and Chronicles. But Isaiah's prosaic presentation of historical fact is only a small part

87. Skeptics will, of course, dismiss this account as "narrative theology," to use the phrase of Ronald E. Clements, *Isaiah and the Deliverance of Jerusalem*, JSOT supplement 13 (Sheffield: University of Sheffield, 1980), p. 21. For this episode as an example of divine intervention see Millard, "Sennacherib's Attack on Hezekiah," *Tyn Bull* 36 (1985): 75–77.

88. Luckenbill, *Sennacherib*, 3.18–23.

89. Kathleen Kenyon, *Jerusalem* (New York: McGraw-Hill, 1967), pp. 69–71. For the text of an inscription found in the tunnel and its historical significance see Victor Sasson, "The Siloam Tunnel Inscription," *PEQ* 114 (1982): 111–17.

90. The explosive growth of Jerusalem and vicinity following 700 B.C., which M. Broshi attributes to mass migration from Israel, is convincingly documented by archaeological evidence ("The Expansion of Jerusalem in the Reigns of Hezekiah and Manasseh," *IEJ* 24 [1974]: 21–26).

of his significance. Of even more importance are his interpretation of the facts and his role as a spokesman for God regarding Israel's political as well as religious affairs. True to the prophetic office in its best sense, Isaiah was both an active participant in his society and a mouthpiece through which both contemporary and eschatological truth were mediated. Isaiah was not alone, however, for Hosea and Micah were his contemporaries, and they too had their own unique contribution to make. As the earliest of the three, Hosea and his message will occupy us first.

Hosea

Hosea ben Beeri, a prophet whose ministry was concentrated mainly in the northern kingdom, exercised his office over many years. He himself says that he prophesied in the days of Uzziah, Jotham, Ahaz, and Hezekiah of Judah and of Jeroboam II of Israel (Hos. 1:1). This rather routine, formulaic introduction is not without historical interest in itself, because it implies a shift of residence, or of interest at least, from Israel to Judah. This is seen in the fact that the reign of Jeroboam II, the only king of Israel listed, ended in 753 while the coregency of Hezekiah did not begin until 729 and his independent rule not until 715. One can explain Hosea's omission of reference to such later kings of Israel as Menahem, Pekah, and Hoshea only on the grounds of his having departed from Samaria in Jeroboam's last years or having changed his focus.[91] The latter is, of course, much more reasonable.[92] Unfortunately, there are few if any clues in his writings about his place of residence at any given time.

In the very beginning of the book Yahweh commands Hosea to marry an adulterous wife. Shortly after he had done so—and there is no reason to assume that the marriage is only a parable or a figurative experience[93]—a son was born whose name, Jezreel, signified that the dynasty of Jehu was about to come to an end. This actually came to pass with the murder of Zechariah by Shallum in 753. Since Zechariah is not mentioned by Hosea, the prediction must have been uttered

---

91. Francis I. Andersen and David Noel Freedman offer the plausible suggestion that Hosea viewed Jeroboam as the last legitimate king of Israel both because he was the last (except for Zechariah) of the line of Jehu and because his death ushered in unparalleled political catastrophe (*Hosea*, Anchor Bible [Garden City, N.Y.: Doubleday, 1980], pp. 147–48).

92. As E. B. Pusey says, Hosea "marks his prophecy by the names of the kings of Judah, because the kingdom of Judah was the kingdom of the theocracy" (*The Minor Prophets* [Grand Rapids: Baker, 1967 reprint], vol. 1, p. 19).

93. For the various views see C. Hassell Bullock, *An Introduction to the Old Testament Prophetic Books* (Chicago: Moody, 1986), pp. 88–92.

while Jeroboam was still living. And since the structure of the whole composition is such that the "marriage metaphor" is clearly its earliest part, a date a little earlier than 753 seems most suitable as a *terminus a quo* for Hosea's public ministry.

Yahweh's command to marry adulterous Gomer was for the purpose of symbolizing the adulterous character of Israel, whom Yahweh, through his covenant at Sinai, had "married." Surely, then, Gomer, who is an illustration of covenant infidelity, was untainted when the prophet married her; only afterward did she become a prostitute, hiring herself out to every lover who could pay her fees. So, the prophet says, had Israel done, and for her iniquitous behavior ought to be put away by divorce. The great love and covenant commitment of Yahweh would not hear of this, however, no more than Hosea could reject Gomer. Though the nation had alienated herself from her divine lover by going after the Baals, he would yet bring her back to himself, having forgiven and cured her forever of her waywardness.

The references to the lovers of Israel (e.g., Hos. 2:5, 7) are a poignant way of describing the incredible apostasy which Hosea witnessed all around him in Jeroboam's Israel. Like his namesake he had tolerated the shrines at Dan and Bethel to the total neglect of Mosaic Yahwism. This produced every kind of crime and violence. There was a universal insensitivity to the will and wishes of the holy God. Instead of worshiping him the people resorted to the high places and groves where they practiced their rituals of literal and metaphorical whoredom. So pervasive and deep-rooted had the defection become that the prophet came to understand the hopelessness of further intercession. Ephraim was firmly joined to her idols; to some extent Judah remained free of such entanglement, however, and so Hosea prayed that Judah might remain aloof from Gilgal and Beth Aven (4:15).[94]

With this word Hosea may have actually begun to reside in Judah, for soon thereafter he seems to view Israel almost as from a distance. For example, referring to "king Jareb" (KJV) of Assyria—probably a cipher for Tiglath-pileser III[95]—the prophet says that Ephraim "turned to Assyria" (5:13). This very likely is his way of describing the submission of Hoshea to the Assyrian monarch in 732. Furthermore, the references to Judah become more prominent even though Ephraim still dominates Hosea's interests.

True to his prophetic calling, Hosea continues to appeal for Israel's

94. Most scholars see the reference to Judah here as an editorial interpolation of a later Judean redactor; see, for example, Hans Walter Wolff, *Hosea* (Philadelphia: Fortress, 1974), p. 89. James L. Mays, however, shows that this is not the case at all: the prophet is warning Judah not to fall into the same trap as her northern neighbor (*Hosea* [Philadelphia: Westminster, 1969], p. 77).

95. Wolff, *Hosea*, pp. 104, 115.

repentance. Realistically, however, he seems to sense its impossibility. God's people do not have any desire to return to him. Instead they look to Assyria and even Egypt, a strategy which can bring only destruction. The appeal to Egypt which Hosea cites (7:11) could very well be that of Israel's last king, Hoshea (2 Kings 17:4), who turned to Osorkon IV in the turbulent times of transition from Tiglath-pileser III to Shalmaneser V (ca. 727—this corresponds with the reference to the continuance of the prophet's ministry as late as the reign of Hezekiah). But Hoshea would be cut off, the prophet says, just as "Shalman devastated Beth Arbel" (Hos. 10:14–15).[96] Shalman is, of course, none other than Shalmaneser V (727–722), the Assyrian king who eventually took Samaria captive.

The historical predicament of Israel is hopeless, Hosea contends, but history is not the end of the matter. The day will come when God will bring back his people, now cured forever of their idolatry; and the bonds of covenant love, which once joined him and them in bonds of marriage as it were, will once more make the twain one.

Isaiah

The mightiest and best-loved, perhaps, of all the prophets of the Old Testament, Isaiah ben Amoz, was a younger contemporary of Hosea. According to his own specific information he became publicly involved in prophetic ministry in 740, the year that King Uzziah died, for it was in that year that the seraph touched his lips with the coal from off the altar, and the Lord, high and lifted up, commissioned him to go to his people with the message of salvation and judgment (Isa. 6).

It is impossible and out of keeping with the purpose of this book to enter into the full spectrum of Isaianic theology. Rather, we will examine his writings as background materials against which the history of Israel during the course of his ministry might be better understood. Frequently, of course, Isaiah speaks to that history in his addresses to his contemporaries concerning their own times, and even his eschatological oracles issue more often than not from a historical setting in which the prophet himself is deeply involved.

Though Isaiah sometimes provides chronological data or references to historical events by which his messages may be dated, this is not usually the case. It is therefore impossible to reconstruct with precision the historical pattern of his materials. The general flow of his narrative appears to be in chronological order, but there are many passages that are linked by topical or theological rather than chron-

---

96. Aharoni, *Land of the Bible*, p. 431, identifies Beth Arbel as Irbid or Arbela, a town in Gilead southeast of the Sea of Kinnereth.

ological concerns. A case in point is his call itself, for though it is clearly the earliest historical event in his book, it appears in chapter 6 rather than at the beginning.

There are two major historical narratives in the Book of Isaiah: chapters 7–8 and chapters 36–39. The former is set in the reign of Ahaz and the latter in that of Hezekiah. Both have been alluded to in our review of the reigns of those kings, but now it is important that the special nuances of Isaiah be given careful consideration. The chronicler, in fact, implies that one of the major sources for the reign of Hezekiah—a source upon which he may have depended primarily— was the work of Isaiah (2 Chron. 32:32). In addition to the two longer passages mentioned, incidental historical references occur throughout the book. These also help to complete the picture of the times and so will find a place in our discussion.

The long and brilliant career of the prince of prophets embraced parts or all of the reigns of Uzziah, Jotham, Ahaz, and Hezekiah (ca. 740–681). It is striking that he makes no reference to any king of Israel in the introduction to his book since he does so later on. The reason must be that as a prophet called to address Judah alone there was no need for him to refer to the rulers of the northern kingdom in his introduction.[97] Moreover, after Samaria's fall in 722 there was no state or king of Israel remaining in the land, so Isaiah would in any case have given Judah his undivided attention through most of the years of his ministry. And indeed, careful analysis of his writings reveals that the *Sitz im Leben* of virtually all of his writing is later than 722. The exception is the narrative of chapter 7, where Ahaz's fatal alliance with Assyria against Rezin of Damascus and Pekah of Israel is recounted.

In the very first message of the book, a *rîb*- or disputation-text,[98] Isaiah speaks of Jerusalem, "the Daughter of Zion," as being cut off from the ruined cities of Judah like a city under siege (1:2–9).[99] Clearly,

97. Edward J. Young, *The Book of Isaiah* (Grand Rapids: Eerdmans, 1965), vol. 1, pp. 28–29.

98. For this important prophetic literary genre see Berend Gemser, "The Rîb- or Controversy Pattern in Hebrew Mentality," *VT* supplement 3 (Leiden: E. J. Brill, 1955), pp. 120–37; Herbert B. Huffmon, "The Covenant Lawsuit in the Prophets," *JBL* 78 (1959): 285–95; James Limburg, "The Root ריב and the Prophetic Lawsuit Speeches," *JBL* 88 (1969): 291–304; Kirsten Nielsen, *Yahweh as Prosecutor and Judge: An Investigation of the Prophetic Lawsuit (Rib-Pattern)*, JSOT supplement 9 (Sheffield: University of Sheffield, 1978).

99. Peter Machinist takes note of the phraseology here and in other passages in Isaiah that have reference to the Assyrians and compares it to Assyrian royal inscriptions current at the time ("Assyria and Its Image in the First Isaiah," *JAOS* 103 [1983]: 724–29). It is clear that Isaiah was witness to what he records and that he was familiar also with the Assyrian language and literature.

Israel had already fallen and Jerusalem itself was in great danger. One immediately thinks of the campaign of Sennacherib in 701 when, as 2 Kings 18:13 says, the Assyrian came up against the fortified cities of Judah and took them. The next oracle, however, describes a much earlier period, perhaps that of Jotham, for the statement is made that children would rule over Judah (3:4—Ahaz?) and that Yahweh would enter into judgment against the wicked rulers of his people (3:13–15).[100] The women of Jerusalem resemble those of Samaria all arrayed in materialistic finery and pridefully prancing about in indifference to the Lord. This, too, is in keeping with that dark period between Uzziah and Hezekiah. Nor is there any internal evidence for dating chapters 4 and 5 otherwise.

Chapter 6, of course, relates the call of the prophet in 740, "the year that King Uzziah died" (6:1). The setting of Isaiah 7:1–10:4 is several years later, the time of the Rezin-Pekah alliance against Judah. This pact was created between states which for centuries had been hostile to each other but which, in the face of a far greater threat—the invasion of Tiglath-pileser III in 734—had momentarily forgotten their differences. Though Jotham was still technically king of Judah until his death in 731, it is clear that the real power lay in the hands of his young son Ahaz. Ahaz had cast his lot with Assyria, much to the consternation of Damascus and Israel, and so became the object of their wrath.

The narrative of Isaiah refers, apparently, to the cooperative effort by Rezin and Pekah to capture Jerusalem and not the independent actions each had taken just a short while previously (see 2 Chron. 28:5–8). Ahaz had, then, already suffered at the hands of his northern neighbors and was understandably terror-stricken at the thought of a campaign against him that most likely would result in the loss of his capital and possibly his life.[101]

Graciously Yahweh sent Isaiah to assure Ahaz that he would be spared further judgment at the hands of Rezin and Pekah. Their days were numbered, the prophet said, and their efforts to remove Ahaz and replace him with the son of Tabeel would come to nought. The prophet then advised Ahaz to seek a confirming sign from Yahweh that all this would come to pass, but Ahaz, having already determined to seek help from Assyria, refused to do so. Isaiah then predicted that a

100. Thomas K. Cheyne, *The Prophecies of Isaiah* (New York: Thomas Whittaker, 1886), vol. 1, p. 22; Franz Delitzsch, *Biblical Commentary on the Prophecies of Isaiah* (Grand Rapids: Eerdmans, 1954 reprint), vol. 1, p. 139.

101. Most scholars view the events of 2 Chronicles 28:5–8 and Isaiah 7:1–2 as identical, but a careful reading suggests that Rezin and Pekah first led separate attacks on Ahaz and then carried out a joint attack shortly thereafter. For a convincing presentation of this interpretation see Young, *Book of Isaiah*, vol. 1, pp. 267–69.

woman would bear a son whose name would be Immanuel. He would be the sign of God's favor despite Ahaz's unbelief. In the providence of God that Child, in the messianic sense, was Jesus of Nazareth. But the specific sign to Ahaz and his court was a child, otherwise unidentified, who would be born of a young woman known to the king.[102] Before that child came of age to know the difference between good and evil, both Rezin and Pekah would lose their thrones and Ahaz himself would begin to experience the depredations of the Assyrian conqueror. Damascus fell in 732, and Rezin, its king, was executed. Almost simultaneously Pekah was assassinated and succeeded by the Assyrian favorite, Hoshea. Thus the fulfilment of the prophetic word came within two years of its utterance. Seven years later Shalmaneser V came. He eventually took Samaria and, in the process, no doubt threatened Ahaz with further harm were he to prove disloyal. It was not until the reign of Hezekiah, some ten years later, however, that Assyria began its series of assaults upon Judah which nearly brought her to the ruin experienced by her sister kingdom to the north. It is this series which Isaiah is prophesying. The Assyrian maraudings, he says, will result in occupation of Judah's land, a great reduction of her population, and ruination of her agricultural industry.

From the same general period comes the warning of Isaiah 9:8–21, which speaks of the terrorizing of Samaria by the enemies of Rezin, that is, by the Assyrians and their allies. This will be followed, Isaiah says, by a similar judgment on Judah in which, ironically, Israel participates. This whole complex of events should be tied in to the capitulation of Israel to Tiglath-pileser in 743–742 and the subsequent invasion of Judah by first Rezin and then Pekah in the following decade.

The setting of the oracles of Isaiah 10:5–19 is much later than the preceding for they concern the judgment of the Assyrians whom Yahweh will have sent against Judah as his disciplining rod. In their hubris, the prophet says, the Assyrians fail to understand that their strength lies in the omnipotent power of the God of Israel. Rather, they recite a litany of their exploits over their vanquished foes, including Damascus and Samaria, as though they themselves are ultimately responsible (Isa. 10:8–11; cf. 2 Kings 18:34–35; 19:12–13). Such boasting can be found, of course, in the communication of the *rab-šāqēh* to

102. For this and other views of this important messianic passage see Herbert M. Wolf, "A Solution to the Immanuel Prophecy in Isaiah 7:14–8:22," *JBL* 91 (1972): 449–56; Walter C. Kaiser, Jr., *Toward an Old Testament Theology* (Grand Rapids: Zondervan, 1978), pp. 207–20. Kaiser suggests that the promised child was Hezekiah, son of Ahaz, but we have already argued (p. 404) that Hezekiah was born in 740. Only by conjecturing textual errors all through the accounts (something Kaiser does not do) can we allow this identification to stand. For one such effort, however, see John McHugh, "The Date of Hezekiah's Birth," *VT* 14 (1964): 446–53.

Hezekiah in the course of Sennacherib's siege of Jerusalem in 701. The imminence of the Assyrian threat is presented by the prophet in most graphic terms (Isa. 10:28–32). The Assyrians, he says, have already entered Aiath (Khirbet Ḥaiyân),[103] less than ten miles north of Jerusalem, and have passed through Migron (Tell Miriam),[104] even closer to the capital. They have laid in supplies at Micmash (Mukhmâs),[105] adjacent to Migron, and have made plans to encamp at Geba (Jeba'),[106] just to the south, in preparation for the siege of Jerusalem. The result is total terror at Ramah, Gibeah, Gallim (Khirbet Ka'kûl),[107] Laishah (el-'Isāwîyeh?),[108] and Anathoth (Râs el-Kharrûbeh),[109] all northern suburbs of the capital. Apparently an Assyrian advance is also under way from the south as well, for the prophet announces that the population of Madmenah,[110] between Beersheba and Hebron, has evacuated. The citizens of Gebim (unknown) and Nob,[111] on the Mount of Olives, are also preparing for inevitable devastation at Assyrian hands.

This oracle of Isaiah is extremely helpful in reconstructing the strategy involved in Sennacherib's two operations against Jerusalem in 701, particularly the earlier one, which resulted in Hezekiah's promise to pay tribute. At the time Sennacherib himself was in Lachish, having already attacked the fortified cities of Judah (2 Kings 18:13–14). These must certainly include the very cities listed by the prophet Isaiah. That Sennacherib was waging battle against Lachish may suggest that it too was a Judean fortress guarding access to Jerusalem from the southwest.[112] When Sennacherib's spokesmen returned after having demanded that Jerusalem surrender, a demand that was denied, they found Sennacherib no longer at Lachish but at Libnah, ten miles farther north. Thus it seems that the Assyrians, having taken towns north,

103. Aharoni, *Land of the Bible*, p. 430.

104. *Oxford Bible Atlas*, p. 135.

105. Aharoni, *Land of the Bible*, p. 439.

106. Ibid., p. 435.

107. *Oxford Bible Atlas*, p. 129.

108. Ibid., p. 134. Aharoni and Avi-Yonah, however, identify el-'Isāwîyeh with Nob (*Macmillan Bible Atlas*, p. 181).

109. Aharoni, *Land of the Bible*, p. 430. For a good map of Sennacherib's itinerary, see Aharoni and Avi-Yonah, *Macmillan Bible Atlas*, map 154.

110. Or Madmannah—see Aharoni, *Land of the Bible*, p. 346. Most scholars identify Madmenah with a northern point (perhaps Khirbet Soma), however, in which case the entire list of towns suggests a march from the north only. See Otto Kaiser, *Isaiah 1–12* (Philadelphia: Westminster, 1972), p. 152.

111. See p. 215, n. 55; p. 289, n. 3.

112. On the basis of the so-called *lmlk* stamps (see n. 64), Nadav Na'aman identifies the fortified cities with the list of fifteen towns found in 2 Chronicles 11:6–10, a passage he dates to the period of Hezekiah. He assumes that Hezekiah refortified outposts that were established as early as the time of Rehoboam ("Hezekiah's Fortified Cities and the LMLK Stamps," *BASOR* 261 [1986]: 10–11).

south, and east of Jerusalem, were bent on capturing the major defensive posts to the west as well, thereby leaving Jerusalem alone and defenseless. When this was achieved, Jerusalem was put under siege, and were it not for divine intervention would certainly have fallen.

A fuller account of Sennacherib's campaign of 701 is found in Isaiah 36–37. Here, however, the prophet dismisses the first phase—the devastation of the countryside and demand for tribute—with only one verse (36:1) and concentrates on the supernatural deliverance of Jerusalem from the Assyrian siege. The purpose clearly is to emphasize the intervention of Yahweh in behalf of his people in response to the prayerful intercession of both Isaiah and King Hezekiah. We have here, then, a classic example of "sacred history," of a historiography which accurately reports the facts to be sure, but which is fundamentally concerned with the theological meaning of those facts.

The real issue as Isaiah presents it is not the struggle between Assyria and Judah, but that between conflicting ideologies or theologies. The question at stake is, Who is God? The essence of the *rab-šāqēh*'s address is that Assyria is invincible because her gods are invincible (36:13–20). It is useless for Hezekiah to rely upon Yahweh, for he, like the gods of Hamath, Arpad, and Sepharvaim, will be swept away before the Assyrian might. The letter that Sennacherib sent as a follow-up contained exactly the same message: Yahweh will no more be able to save Judah than the gods of other nations have been able to save them (37:10–13).

Hezekiah correctly perceived the Assyrian threat as a theological issue, not a political or military one, for he turned to Yahweh and extolled him as the sole sovereign over all the kingdoms of the earth. Yahweh's claim to absolute sovereignty rested on his work as Creator of heaven and earth, a power possessed by him alone. By contrast the gods of the other nations could be destroyed by the Assyrians, for they were not gods at all, but only creations of their foolish worshipers.

Isaiah's message in response to Hezekiah's prayer regarding Sennacherib picks up the same refrain. The Assyrian, Isaiah said, had mocked and blasphemed the God of Judah (37:21–35). But it was the God of Judah who had raised up Assyria in the first place and had permitted her to be his instrument of judgment against his disobedient children. Assyria's gods had nothing to do with either Assyria's success or Judah's crisis. Furthermore, Yahweh would demonstrate for all to see that he who raised Assyria up could also bring her down. And that night he did so by annihilating Sennacherib's army. Another exhibition of the sovereignty of Yahweh over all competing religious systems occurred, ironically, in the very temple of the Assyrian gods in whom Sennacherib boasted (37:38). Sennacherib was slain in Nineveh while he was in the very act of worshiping his god Nisroch. The god who had failed him at Jerusalem was, twenty years later, exposed once and for all as a figment of Assyrian imagination: he could not even deliver his devotee who sought him in earnest worship.

We have examined the principal passages from the Book of Isaiah which serve as historical documents. This is not to say, of course, that the rest of the work of the prophet, even the strictly eschatological sections, is without value as a witness to the history of Israel. To the contrary, the rest of his book is extremely important as a gauge of the temper of the times in which the prophet lived. But the value of these other sections as history is limited by the fact that the prophet lived for such a long time (ca. 765–680). Thus any light he might shed on sociological, political, economic, or religious matters cannot be readily tied in with specific historical events. And the problem is exacerbated by our inability to date most of the oracles except on extremely subjective grounds. This uncertainty precludes the responsible historiographer from using them. Where the prophet was consciously engaged in the chronicling of events on the other hand, he provided information not only concerning the historical situation, but concerning its theological meaning as well.

Micah

Finally, the brief product of the prophet Micah must bring this chapter to a close. Unfortunately, he provides even less historical documentation than does his older and more illustrious contemporary Isaiah.[113] Like Isaiah he was a prophet of Jerusalem, but unlike him he divided his message evenly between the two kingdoms. The general impression of moral and spiritual decline in Israel and Judah which characterizes Isaiah's work is to be found in Micah as well, but he does not set his messages of judgment and hope in a matrix of historical narrative as Isaiah occasionally does. Thus, Micah must be used with caution as a witness to the sequence of events in his own day.

Micah's earliest oracles clearly antedate 722, for he prophesies the fall of Samaria as an expression of the wrath of Yahweh upon Israel's royal house (1:6–7). Jerusalem also came under the prophetic word of judgment because its king, no doubt Ahaz, had led Judah into equally grievous sin. The word of judgment must not be advertised in Philistia, however, for the Philistine foes had already raided Judah and must not have this opportunity to gloat over her impending defeat at the hands of Assyria.

---

113. An excellent, though brief, introduction to the historical setting of Micah may be found in Leslie C. Allen, *The Books of Joel, Obadiah, Jonah, and Micah* (Grand Rapids: Eerdmans, 1976), pp. 239–53.

The remainder of Micah's message cannot be dated precisely. Israel and Judah will eventually fall, but so will their Assyrian nemesis, Micah says (5:5–6). In the fullness of days, however, the people of the Lord will be restored and under their messianic king will enjoy forever the fruits of the eternal covenant made with the patriarchal fathers (7:7–20). And so Micah, like Isaiah, closes his message with a note of hope, a note that must have seemed to be in stark contrast to the doleful prospects that attended Judah at the beginning of the seventh century.

12 Fading Hope: The Disintegration of Judah

The Legacy of Hezekiah

The passing of good King Hezekiah in 686 and of Isaiah not long afterward ushered in a period of decline in every area of Judah's national life from which she would not recover, except briefly in the brilliant reign of Josiah. The seeds of this deterioration, which lasted for exactly one hundred years (686–586), are not easy to trace, but surely Hezekiah himself must bear some responsibility, even though history's assessment of him is on the whole most favorable.

431

Pride and Its Aftermath

A specific character flaw in Hezekiah is revealed in the account of his entertainment of the ambassadors from Merodach-Baladan of the Sealands dynasty. The chronicler refers to the incident briefly: Hezekiah's healing by Yahweh made the king's heart proud, an improper response to the kindness, so Yahweh used the ambassadors to test what was in his heart (2 Chron. 32:25, 31). The author of Kings and the prophet Isaiah point out that Hezekiah laid bare the treasuries of the kingdom for the Chaldeans to inspect (2 Kings 20:12–15; Isa. 39:1–4). These visitors had come to solicit the support of Hezekiah, an anti-Assyrian, to the cause of Merodach-Baladan, who for years had attempted to create a sovereign Chaldean state independent of Assyria. Hezekiah's opening of the public treasury can mean only that he favored the proposed Chaldean affiliation and that he wished to impress the delegation with the wealth and power of his kingdom. This, the chronicler says, was an act of pride which brought the wrath of Yahweh on Judah and Jerusalem.

Hezekiah repented, to be sure, but Isaiah informed him that the time would come when the political descendants of these same Chaldeans would return to Jerusalem. They would despoil all the treasures of Judah and carry her sons and daughters off to the royal court of Babylon (Isa. 39:5–7).

The Superficiality of the Reformation

By itself this sin of the king could not have precipitated the prophetic word of judgment. It was, after all, but a single public act, though an extremely serious one in that it was committed by none other than the king. Even more serious, however, were the general populace's private perpetrations of every kind of covenant violation imaginable. A cursory review of Isaiah's writing will reveal an undercurrent of immoral and apostate conditions pervasive throughout the kingdom despite the reformation in which Hezekiah had led the people in the early days of his reign. The worship had become hypocritical (1:10–15), the powerful exploited the weak and defenseless (1:21–23), and the upper classes flaunted the luxury which they had gained by oppressing the masses (3:16–24). Yahweh had brought his people out of Egyptian bondage and had planted them in the beautiful vineyard of the land of promise. But when he expected choice grapes of them, they produced worthless fruit (5:1–7). Consumed by a spirit of rapacity and gluttony, they amassed vast estates and drank from morning till night, with total disregard for the blessing of Yahweh (5:8–12). Even the leaders, including prophets and priests, had turned away from covenant truth and had prostituted their offices for their own gain.

The noble character of Hezekiah stands out in bold relief against his wicked generation. He was not a paradigm of the national life but stood in stark contrast to it. Whatever benefits had accrued from the religious reformation must have been superficial and of short duration, for the prophetic verdict on the age is unanimous—guilty of high treason. And once the restraining influence of Hezekiah and Isaiah was no longer at work, Judah's spiritual and moral life declined even more rapidly.

Manasseh of Judah

The decline of Judah is seen most clearly in the person of Hezekiah's son Manasseh, who came to the throne as sole regent in 686 and remained in power until 642.[1] That he ruled for fifty-five years implies that he shared regal responsibility with Hezekiah from about 696 to 686. Why his father promoted Manasseh to this place of authority at the tender age of twelve must remain a matter of speculation. It is possible, of course, that Hezekiah's near-fatal illness (ca. 702) prompted him, as soon as his son reached a suitable age, to take measures insuring the dynastic succession.[2]

Equally mysterious is Hezekiah's inability to communicate something of his own godliness to his son, for Manasseh proved to be the antithesis of everything for which Hezekiah stood. After Manasseh came into his own, he reverted to the Canaanite cults which had held sway in the land before the conquest; and, like Ahab of Israel, he erected altars to the Baals and images of Asherah. He went as far as to engage in human sacrifice, offering his own sons in the Valley of Ben Hinnom. Practitioners of every kind of pagan religious art—sorcerers, diviners, witches, mediums, and spiritists—were reinstated. The ultimate blasphemy, however, was the installation of an image of Asherah within the holy temple itself, the place where Yahweh had said he would place his own name forever (2 Kings 21:2–7).

The result of this wholesale abandonment of righteousness was the word of Yahweh through his prophets that Judah would suffer the same fate as Israel. The same criteria by which Samaria had been judged would be applied to Jerusalem, and the verdict of guilt would

1. Unless otherwise noted, the regnal dates in this chapter are those of Edwin R. Thiele, *The Mysterious Numbers of the Hebrew Kings* (Grand Rapids: Eerdmans, 1965), p. 161. The chronology of Judah's latter years is not without its problems in details—a matter that cannot be addressed here—as one can see, for example, in Alberto R. Green, "The Chronology of the Last Days of Judah: Two Apparent Discrepancies," *JBL* 101 (1982): 57–73.

2. Thiele, *Mysterious Numbers*, pp. 157–58.

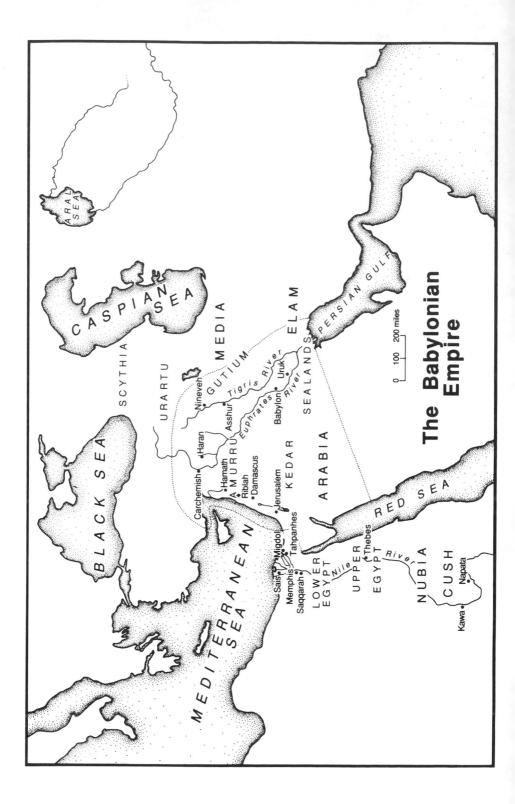

The Babylonian Empire

0 100 200 miles

ARAL SEA

CASPIAN SEA

BLACK SEA

MEDITERRANEAN SEA

RED SEA

PERSIAN GULF

SCYTHIA

URARTU

GUTIUM

MEDIA

ELAM

SEALANDS

ARABIA

KEDAR

AMURRU

NUBIA

CUSH

LOWER EGYPT

UPPER EGYPT

Nineveh

Asshur

Haran

Carchemish

Hamath

Riblah

Damascus

Jerusalem

Uruk

Babylon

Tigris River

Euphrates River

Nile River

Migdol

Tahpanhes

Sais

Memphis

Saqqarah

Thebes

Napata

Kawa

be self-evident. Then Judah, the remaining element of the people of God, would be led away in chains of slavery.

The chronicler relates that Manasseh's stubborn refusal to heed the warning of the prophets led to his being deported to Babylon by the Assyrians (2 Chron. 33:10–13). The Assyrian monarch responsible must surely have been Ashurbanipal (668–627), son and successor to Esarhaddon.[3] The reference to Babylon as Manasseh's destination provides a helpful chronological clue since Ashurbanipal did not bring Babylon under his control until 648.[4] Manasseh could not have been taken there earlier than that. More information may be gained from Ashurbanipal's annals, which recount an invasion of Egypt in 667 in which he eventually took the city of Thebes with material assistance from Manasseh.[5] The Assyrian text clearly shows that Manasseh was a vassal of Ashurbanipal as early as 667.[6] His removal to Babylon in 648 or shortly thereafter suggests that Manasseh had violated his arrangement with Ashurbanipal.

How long the king of Judah was in Babylon is unknown, but presumably he was moved to repentance and faith at a very early point in his captivity. The Lord heard his earnest prayer and graciously brought about his return to Jerusalem and restoration to the throne of David. Upon his return Manasseh demolished the accoutrements of paganism which he had set up and restored the worship of the true God. The people continued to gather at the high places, the chronicler observes, but only to serve Yahweh (2 Chron. 33:17). Manasseh also refortified Jerusalem and the outposts, a task necessitated by the possibility of further Assyrian involvement in the west, or perhaps actually required by the Assyrians, who still regarded Manasseh as a vassal.[7]

The chronicler's inclusion of Manasseh's sin, deportation, repentance, and restoration is most instructive for it serves as a foreshadowing in microcosm of the Judean captivity itself. The nation would

---

3. John Bright theorizes that Manasseh may have been deported for abetting the rebellion of Šamaš-šum-ukīn (652–648), Ashurbanipal's brother and viceroy of Babylon (*A History of Israel*, 3d ed. [Philadelphia: Westminster, 1981], p. 311). Many scholars, however, deny the historicity of the deportation account, attributing it to poetic fancy or an attempt at edification. See, for example, J. Alberto Soggin, *A History of Ancient Israel* (Philadelphia: Westminster, 1984), p. 239.

4. B. Oded, "Judah and the Exile," in *Israelite and Judaean History*, ed. John H. Hayes and J. Maxwell Miller (Philadelphia: Westminster, 1977), p. 445.

5. James B. Pritchard, *Ancient Near Eastern Texts Relating to the Old Testament*, 2d ed. (Princeton: Princeton University Press, 1955), p. 294.

6. Hanoch Reviv, "The History of Judah from Hezekiah to Josiah," in *World History of the Jewish People*, vol. 4, part 1, *The Age of the Monarchies: Political History*, ed. Abraham Malamat (Jerusalem: Massada, 1979), p. 200.

7. Ibid.

sin and be carried off to Babylonian exile. There the captives would repent and in the providence of the covenant-keeping God would eventually be restored. The prophets of the time must certainly have taken note of Manasseh's experience and have used it heuristically to point to the pattern of Judah's national life and its inevitable outcome.

Amon of Judah

Amon, Manasseh's son, seems not to have heard or heeded the lesson, however, for he reversed the pattern his repentant father had established and revived the paganism that had characterized Manasseh's earlier years (2 Kings 21:19–24; 2 Chron. 33:21–25). This may be at least partially blamed on baneful parental influences on the young prince in his impressionable years, for he was born at least sixteen years before his father's repentance and return to Jerusalem (see 2 Kings 21:19). It is also likely that there were in the kingdom vested religious and political interests that disapproved of Manasseh's reforms and wished to restore the old order. Part of their strategy was to induce the young king to abandon his father's policies and cast his lot with them.

It is also reasonable to assume that Manasseh's return home was purchased at the price of a pledge of loyalty to the Assyrian government and that Amon, ever wary of Ashurbanipal, attempted to remain in his good graces. Amon's assassination within two years, then, may well have been at the hands of a party of anti-Assyrians (2 Kings 21:23). These rebels were in turn killed by a counterrevolutionary movement that placed Amon's eight-year-old son Josiah on the throne (2 Kings 21:24).[8] Whether this scenario is correct in detail or not, we do know that Josiah eventually turned against Assyria, for he met his death in an effort to assist a Medo-Chaldean alliance whose aim was the destruction of Assyria.

The International Scene: Assyria and Egypt

It will be instructive at this point to look at the international scene in the seventh century, particularly as the world was dominated by Assyria and Egypt at first and then by Babylonia.[9] Within eight years

---

8. Bright, *History*, pp. 316–17.

9. For the following discussion see especially the Esarhaddon texts published by Rykle Borger, *Die Inschriften Asarhaddons, Königs von Assyrien*, AfO supplement 9 (1956); Pritchard, *Ancient Near Eastern Texts*, pp. 289–91.

of his incorporation of Babylonia into the Assyrian orbit in 689, Sennacherib was murdered while at worship in Nineveh. His son Esarhaddon, who had been serving as his father's representative in Babylonia, returned at once to Nineveh, restored order, and seized the Assyrian throne. Meanwhile, the assassins, two of Sennacherib's own sons, had fled to Urartu and from that base continued to harass Assyria for many years.

The Sealands dynasty took advantage of the turmoil engendered by this series of events and asserted its independence in Babylonia once again. The rebels had hoped to gain Elamite support in this action, but it was not forthcoming, so Esarhaddon was able to put down the revolt and appoint a ruler of his own choice.[10]

Another source of trouble arose in the northwest in the form of a series of skirmishes initiated by the Asguzaya, a people who later became known as Scythians. This was settled by an alliance involving a royal marriage but cost Assyria considerable border territories. Also in the west the Sidonians fomented a rebellion against Assyrian authority; only after Esarhaddon sacked the city (677) was he able to bring stability to that region once again.[11]

Then, to the east, Esarhaddon arranged a series of treaties with the Medes, perennial foes of the Mesopotamian states. These treaties, many of which have survived, are of particular interest because they provide information not only about matters of history, but about the structure of Neo-Assyrian texts of this type.[12] The alliance to which they attest was extremely fragile, however, and within ten years Media and Assyria were locked in bitter conflict.

Once more Esarhaddon addressed Assyria's most perplexing and insoluble problem, that of the Sealands people who doggedly persisted in their struggle to make Babylonia a kingdom separate from Assyria.[13] He had been forced to put down rebellion at the very beginning of his reign, but it seems that nothing short of total removal of the Chaldean power base and its replacement by his own royal house would bring about any kind of permanent stability. He therefore hit upon the notion of a sort of dual monarchy in which his son Ashurbanipal would rule as prince over Assyria and a second son, Šamaš-

10. For Esarhaddon's conciliatory policy toward Babylonia see J. A. Brinkman, "Through a Glass Darkly: Esarhaddon's Retrospects on the Downfall of Babylon," *JAOS* 103 (1983): 35–42.

11. H. Jacob Katzenstein, *The History of Tyre* (Jerusalem: Schocken Institute for Jewish Research, 1973), p. 259.

12. D. J. Wiseman, *The Vassal Treaties of Esarhaddon* (London: British School of Archaeology in Iraq, 1958).

13. A. T. Olmstead, *History of Assyria* (Chicago: University of Chicago Press, 1975 reprint), pp. 350–52.

šum-ukīn, would function similarly in Babylonia.[14] This would pander to the pride of the peoples to the south by placing them on an equal footing with Assyria and would also allow the Assyrians to exercise control over all of Mesopotamia. Though this arrangement appeared to work for a time, it overlooked the almost fanatical determination of the Chaldean princes to dominate Babylonia at any cost.

With the Babylonian problem thus resolved, at least for a time, Esarhaddon undertook his most successful expedition of all—the conquest of Egypt.[15] The kingdom of the Nile was then (671 B.C.) under the rule of the Nubian king Tirhakah, but he was preoccupied with other problems and so lost Memphis and all of Lower Egypt to the Assyrians.[16] He recovered, however, and regained Lower Egypt by 669. While en route to deal with this emergency Esarhaddon died.[17] It is quite likely that Manasseh of Judah became an Assyrian vassal in connection with Esarhaddon's successful campaign against Egypt in 671.

Tirhakah had become king of the illustrious Nubian Dynasty 25 upon the death of his brother Shebitku in 690. As a young military officer of about twenty years of age he had participated in the unsuccessful effort by Egypt and her allies to repel Sennacherib from Judah in 701. When at last he became pharaoh, he ruled in peace for the first half of his twenty-six-year reign. By 674, however, Assyria began to make her presence felt in a threatening way; and though Esarhaddon was initially repulsed from Egypt's borders, he managed, by 671, to seize Memphis. Even Esarhaddon's death in 669 gave Tirhakah little respite, for Ashurbanipal, the next king of Assyria, commenced his own military operations against Egypt in 667.[18] This resulted not only in the fall of Memphis once more, but the penetration of Assyrian forces to Thebes itself, in the very heart of Egypt. Tirhakah was forced even farther south, to Napata, and within three years (664) died there.

In Assyria Ashurbanipal (668–627)[19] had taken immediate steps to secure himself as undisputed monarch following his father's death.[20]

14. Ibid., pp. 396–97.

15. Kenneth A. Kitchen, *The Third Intermediate Period in Egypt (1100–650 B.C.)* (Warminster: Aris and Phillips, 1973), pp. 391–92.

16. For the Assyrian text documenting this conquest see Albert Kirk Grayson, *Assyrian and Babylonian Chronicles* (Locust Valley, N.Y.: J. J. Augustin, 1975), p. 85, Chronicle 1.4. 23–27.

17. Ibid., ll. 30–33.

18. Kitchen, *Third Intermediate Period*, pp. 392–93.

19. The chronology of the last half century of Assyrian history is extremely problematic. The system accepted here is that of Joan Oates, "Assyrian Chronology, 631–612 B.C.," *Iraq* 27 (1965): 135–59.

20. The primary sources for Ashurbanipal can be found in Robert S. Lau, *The Annals of Ashurbanipal*, Semitic Study Series 2 (Leiden: E. J. Brill, 1903); M. Streck,

He first had to deal with the Medes, who not only had violated the treaties they had forged with Esarhaddon, but had begun to cut off vital trade routes to the Iranian interior. His own brother Šamaš-šum-ukīn, who was ruler of the Babylonian provinces, also became restless under Ashurbanipal's leadership and made plans to create a more important niche for himself.

Of greatest concern to Ashurbanipal, however, was the perilous situation in Egypt.[21] As soon as it was feasible, therefore, he resumed his father's imperialistic designs on Egypt. He retook Memphis and, after Tirhakah's death, responded to an attempt at Egyptian countermeasures. He then appointed Psammetichus, son of Neco I of Sais, as ruler in Egypt, thus introducing a new dynasty, the twenty-sixth.[22]

The Egyptian countermeasures just mentioned were undertaken by Tirhakah's nephew Tantamani (664–656), who was able to retake Memphis temporarily, kill Neco I, the last ruler of the twenty-fourth (Saite) dynasty, and gain recognition throughout Egypt as the next king. But Ashurbanipal's campaign of 663 drove Tantamani out of the north, though he continued to be regarded as king at Thebes.

Meanwhile, Psammetichus (663–610) had been appointed ruler of Egypt by Ashurbanipal and, as a loyal vassal, was aided by the Assyrians in gaining control of the Delta, Middle Egypt, and Thebes by 656. He removed Tantamani from his throne, and thus, by about 655, Egypt was united from Nubia to the Mediterranean under one ruler. Emboldened by his success in bringing all Egypt under his domination and also, no doubt, by the troubles Ashurbanipal was having elsewhere, Psammetichus refused to continue payment of tribute to Assyria by 656, though Egypt remained more or less an ally of Assyria until his death and even beyond.

The difficulties Ashurbanipal faced were partly at the hands of the Elamites, but primarily from his own brother Šamaš-šum-ukīn, who still held sway in Babylonia.[23] The reasons for the conflict were deep-rooted and complex, but a crisis was reached when Šamaš-šum-ukīn began to differ publicly with his brother over policy decisions Ashurbanipal had made, particularly in his selection of local rulers who

---

Ashurbanipal, 3 vols. (Leipzig: J. C. Hinrichs, 1916); R. C. Thompson, *The Prisms of Esarhaddon and of Ashurbanipal* (London: Oxford University Press, 1931); Arthur C. Piepkorn, *Historical Prism Inscriptions of Ashurbanipal* (Chicago: University of Chicago Press, 1933); Mordechai Cogan, "Ashurbanipal Prism F: Notes on Scribal Techniques and Editorial Procedures," *JCS* 29 (1977): 97–107. See also note 26.

21. The complex dealings of Ashurbanipal with Egypt are brilliantly explicated by Anthony J. Spalinger, "Assurbanipal and Egypt: A Source Study," *JAOS* 94 (1974): 316–28.

22. Kitchen, *Third Intermediate Period*, pp. 394–95.

23. Olmstead, *History of Assyria*, pp. 440–52.

circumvented Šamaš-šum-ukīn's authority.[24] This precipitated the formation of a coalition of Elam, Guti, Amurru, Arabia, certain Aramean states, and Babylonia itself; their combined forces attacked Assyria as early as 652.[25] Ashurbanipal managed to withstand this revolt, however, and Šamaš-šum-ukīn, thoroughly defeated and demoralized, committed suicide.[26] Ashurbanipal then punished Elam savagely and defeated the Aramean princes who had participated in the attempted coup against him. These retaliatory strikes were delayed for various reasons until the years 642–639. After that the annals of Ashurbanipal cease, and consequently his last thirteen years are very obscure.[27]

We do know that Ashurbanipal was succeeded by his son Ashur-etil-ilāni (627–623). By now the handwriting was clearly on the wall, and insightful observers must have known that Assyria's days were numbered. Ashur-etil-ilāni did manage to suppress at least two uprisings in his brief reign, but Babylonia, Media, Phoenicia, and Judah itself openly repudiated his authority.

After a brief rebellion by Sin-šum-lišir, a second son of Ashurbanipal, the kingship of Ashur-etil-ilāni was brought to an end by yet a third son, Sin-šar-iškun (623–612). This took place in the third year of Nabopolassar, the Babylonian successor to the Assyrian appointee Kandalanu.[28] Sin-šar-iškun commenced hostile actions against Nabopolassar with the intention of regathering Babylonia to the Assyrian fold, but Nabopolassar proved to be more than capable of resisting these efforts and undertook offensive measures of his own.

Gradually the Assyrian territory was whittled away, and Sin-šar-iškun was powerless to reverse the process. By 614 the ancient city of Asshur was lost to the Medes, and only two years later Nineveh itself fell to these same irresistible foes. Nabopolassar relates, in the best surviving historiographical document of the time—the "Babylonian Chronicle"—that he had intended to join Cyaxares the Median king in the conquest of Asshur, but was detained at Babylon.[29]

With the fall of Nineveh and Sin-šar-iškun, the last king of Assyria

24. Sami S. Ahmed, "Causes of Shamash-shum-ukin's Uprising, 652–651 B.C.," *ZAW* 79 (1967): 1–13. For other possibilities see G. Frame, "Another Babylonian Eponym," *RA* 76 (1982): 166.

25. J. A. Brinkman, "Foreign Relations of Babylonia from 1600 to 625 B.C.: The Documentary Evidence," *AJA* 76 (1972): 279.

26. Olmstead, *History of Assyria*, p. 475. Ashurbanipal's achievement is now convincingly documented in Mordechai Cogan and Hayim Tadmor, "Ashurbanipal's Conquest of Babylon: The First Official Report—Prism K," *Or* 50 (1981): 229–40.

27. Olmstead, *History of Assyria*, pp. 627–28.

28. Oates, "Assyrian Chronology," *Iraq* 27 (1965): 146–48.

29. B. M. 21901, 11. 28–29, published in D. J. Wiseman, *Chronicles of Chaldaean Kings (625–556 B.C.) in the British Museum* (London: Trustees of the British Museum, 1961), p. 59.

came to the throne. Aššur-uballiṭ II (612–609) was an army officer who regrouped the Assyrian forces at Haran, but he had to abandon the city when it came under fierce attack from the Babylonians.[30] Neco II of Egypt made a valiant attempt to come to the aid of Assyria, obviously fearing the growing might of the Medo-Babylonian axis. The Egyptian army was intercepted by the little host of Josiah of Judah, however, and might well have been detained long enough to ensure the Babylonian victory.[31]

Forced to abandon Haran, Aššur-uballiṭ moved west once more, this time to the important city of Carchemish on the upper Euphrates. Relentlessly the Babylonian armies took up the pursuit and in 605, under their brilliant commander and crown prince Nebuchadnezzar, crushed the Assyrian remnant once and for all.[32] Again Egypt had sent reinforcements, but they too were defeated and driven out of Syria and Palestine altogether. And so Assyria passed off the stage of world history after more than twelve hundred years of national existence. The rod of Yahweh had accomplished his purposes and now was laid to rest.

Josiah of Judah

Relations with Assyria

Against this backdrop the biblical account of the reign of Josiah takes on fuller meaning, for, as has been stressed repeatedly, biblical history did not transpire in a vacuum. This was particularly true once international trade began to be routed through Palestine. Thereafter that little land could hardly expect to sit on the sidelines as a spectator. Inevitably it was drawn time and again into the swirling currents of world events as a tiny boat is involuntarily dragged into the vortex of a great maelstrom.

At no time was this more the case than in the days of Josiah, for during his reign (640–609) the whole balance of power in the Near Eastern world shifted radically from what it had been for almost three hundred years. Assyria was in its death throes, and Egypt, though more stable than it had been for centuries, was still a mere shadow of its former self. On the other hand, the Medes and their cousins the Persians were beginning to move out from their isolation in the high-

---

30. B. M. 21901, 11. 58–62.
31. For the background to and strategy of the battle at Megiddo see Abraham Malamat, "Josiah's Bid for Armageddon," *JANES* 5 (1973): 267–79.
32. B. M. 21946, 11. 1–7.

lands of Iran and were giving strong signals that they in time would be a factor to be reckoned with. Most dramatic of all, however, was the meteoric rise of the Neo-Babylonian Empire on the foundation of the Chaldean kingdoms. Surely it was manifest to all the world that Babylon was now the seat of awesome power and that she would dictate the course of human events for a long time to come.

Such was the world situation when Josiah succeeded Amon. We previously proposed that Amon, like his father Manasseh, had remained loyal to the Assyrians and that he was slain by an element that was under the mistaken impression that Assyria's collapse was imminent. The fact that Egypt, Judah's giant neighbor to the south, was paying at least lip service to Assyrian sovereignty seemed to make no difference to these rebels. The majority in Judah did not share their sentiment, apparently, for Amon's killers were themselves slain, and a pro-Assyrian group placed Josiah, then only eight years old, on the throne.[33] Since everything we know of Josiah's politics indicates that he was opposed to Assyria, it is safe to assume that his initial position changed within a few years and he became vehemently antagonistic to Assyria.

In the past the prophets had warned against affiliation with the Assyrians, but those who ministered in the days of Josiah—Jeremiah, Habakkuk, and Zephaniah—are relatively silent about the Assyrians. Nahum is an exception; in fact, his entire book is about the coming destruction of Nineveh. Yet there is no word even in Nahum against the formation of Judean-Assyrian ties. The attention of the prophets of Josiah's time is, rather, riveted on Babylonia, for by the beginning of the reign of Josiah in 640 it was obvious that Judah's judgment was to come not from Assyria but Babylonia. Unlike Assyria, however, Babylonia was not to be resisted. In fact, as Jeremiah repeatedly argues, Judah must submit to Babylonia, not in a sense of servile vassalage, but in recognition of the inexorable fact that Babylonia was the agent by which Yahweh would discipline his people in exile.

The point here is that the sources tell us very little about Josiah's relationship with Assyria. As a matter of fact, Assyria seems to be overlooked almost entirely by the contemporary biblical records until the very end, when Josiah, by forestalling the Egyptian forces at Megiddo, cooperated with the Babylonian-Median onslaught at Haran, the aim of which was the utter destruction of Assyria.

33. One must also not slight the religious motivations of Josiah's supporters, however, for, as Carl D. Evans points out, the "people of the land" placed Josiah on the throne "in order to safeguard the Davidic succession" ("Judah's Foreign Policy from Hezekiah to Josiah," in *Scripture in Context*, ed. Carl D. Evans et al. [Pittsburgh: Pickwick, 1980], p. 170).

Religious Reformation

Josiah's real interests lay in reformation.[34] As early as his eighth regnal year (632), when he was only sixteen years old, he turned his heart to the things of God and four years later undertook a systematic purge of every vestige of paganism (2 Chron. 34:3).[35] This had been achieved to a great extent by Manasseh upon his return from Assyrian deportation, but Amon had undone his father's work completely and had in his brief two years managed to reinstate the Canaanite cults. Josiah not only removed these abominations from Judah in a more thorough manner than had ever been the case before, but he included the regions to the north as far as Naphtali in his reformation.[36] Of particular interest are his destruction of the altar and high place at Bethel and his burning of the bones of the priests who had officiated there long ago in the days of Jeroboam I (2 Kings 23:15–20). At long last the prophetic word came to pass that Josiah would once and for all remove the syncretistic cult of Bethel from the land (1 Kings 13:1–2).

The excision of idolatry from Judah was only one side of the coin of reformation, however. It now was necessary for Josiah to lead the nation back to Yahweh and to restore the structures of worship and service according to Mosaic prescription. This work commenced in the king's eighteenth year (622) with his edict to repair the temple, which had deteriorated greatly since the days of Hezekiah sixty years before (2 Kings 22:5–6). Having raised large sums of money from the popu-

34. The cynical suggestion of some scholars (e.g., W. Eugene Claburn, "The Fiscal Basis of Josiah's Reforms," *JBL* 92 [1973]: 11–22) that Josiah's motives or methods were other than religious finds absolutely no support in the text itself.

35. The author of Kings makes no reference to any date earlier than Josiah's eighteenth year (622), the year of the discovery of the Torah scroll, the reformation, and the great Passover (2 Kings 22:3; 23:23). What his account appears to compress into one year actually must have occupied several years, commencing, as the chronicler says, with Josiah's eighth year. John Gray suggests that the compiler of Kings probably telescoped these three stages of the reformation (*I & II Kings* [Philadelphia: Westminster, 1970], p. 725). Mordechai Cogan, on the other hand, views the account in Chronicles as an example of dating major royal achievements to a king's first or early years, in this case to "show the earliness and self-motivation of the king's piety" ("The Chronicler's Use of Chronology as Illuminated by Neo-Assyrian Royal Inscriptions," in *Empirical Models for Biblical Criticism*, ed. Jeffrey H. Tigay [Philadelphia: University of Pennsylvania Press, 1985], pp. 204–5). While the theory has much to commend it elsewhere, this is hardly a suitable example. Frank M. Cross and David Noel Freedman have attempted to connect the events of Josiah's eighth, twelfth, and eighteenth years to major crises in Assyrian history, but this seems unlikely. See "Josiah's Revolt Against Assyria," *JNES* 12 (1953): 56–58, and the response of Evans, "Judah's Foreign Policy," in *Scripture in Context*, p. 171.

36. As Reviv, "History of Judah," in *World History of the Jewish People*, vol. 4, part 1, pp. 203–4, points out, this implies that Josiah's political influence extended far beyond the limited borders of Judah proper.

lace, Josiah commissioned Hilkiah the priest to see that it was used to hire workmen to undertake the project. In the process of bringing the money out from the temple treasury Hilkiah happened upon a copy of the Book of the Law of Moses, which he immediately delivered over to Shaphan the scribe. Shaphan took it to the king and proceeded to read it to him. At once Josiah, in deepest contrition and fear, tore his clothing at hearing the word of God concerning wrath and judgment.

It is not possible to enter into the debate about the precise contents of the scroll found by Hilkiah. It clearly consisted of at least Deuteronomy and likely the entire Pentateuch, for some of the policies which Josiah proceeded to implement presuppose the teachings of Moses.[37] A more baffling question is, How could the Torah have been lost for decades, not to be recovered until 622 and even then only by accident? Liberal scholarship argues that the document in question was the Book of Deuteronomy and that it had never been lost at all. It was, rather, a piece composed by a prophetic circle interested in bringing about reform. In order to give it canonical authority it was attributed to Moses. It may, in fact, have drawn upon authentic Mosaic tradition. In any case, it was not a product of the hand of Moses but of anonymous scribes of the seventh century. Perhaps, it is proposed, it was drafted by an underground movement in the days of Manasseh and placed in the temple in the hope that it might be found and might inspire Manasseh to seek after Yahweh. It was not discovered in his day, however, and only by chance finally surfaced in 622.[38]

This reconstruction disregards universal Jewish tradition about the authorship of Deuteronomy and also fails to explain how it is possible that no one in Josiah's time, including the priests and scribes, questioned the alleged Mosaic authorship of a document about which there was, supposedly, not one shred of tradition. Moreover, those aspects of Josiah's reformation which appear to be based uniquely on the teaching of Deuteronomy are attested to in Israel's religious life long before Josiah. The critic must concede that the major prescriptions of Deuteronomy were known long before the discovery of the scroll in the temple. This being so, is it really incredible that Deuteronomy had long existed and had simply been suppressed until its providential discovery by Hilkiah?

In the era of the printing press and the dissemination of the printed page in multiplied millions of copies it is difficult to appreciate the

37. See especially Oswald T. Allis, *The Five Books of Moses* (Philadelphia: Presbyterian and Reformed, 1949), pp. 178–84.

38. This view is conveniently summarized but not completely accepted by Ernest W. Nicholson, *Deuteronomy and Tradition* (Philadelphia: Fortress, 1967), pp. 1–17.

scarcity of written texts in the ancient world. But even some of the most important works composed on durable clay tablets are known only in single copies despite the recovery of some of the great libraries of the ancient past. What, then, must be said of those Old Testament writings which were penned on fragile and perishable materials such as papyrus, leather, and parchment? Furthermore, it is most unlikely that the Scriptures at any time in Old Testament Israel existed in more than a few dozen copies at the very most. Unless scrupulous care were taken to preserve them, they would be subject to the ravages of war and natural disaster or simply disintegrate with time. There is no reason, then, why a diabolical, despotic ruler such as Manasseh could not have seized virtually all the copies of the Torah and destroyed them in order to advance his own apostate ends. Somehow in the providence of God a pious priest or scribe managed to safeguard a copy in a hiding place in the temple and prayed that it might not perish until it could once more take its position as the bedrock of Israel's life.

This undoubtedly is what happened. Josiah, knowing full well that the document he had heard was the very word of God, inquired of the Lord as to its implications for the present situation. The answer came through Huldah the prophetess that the judgments contained in the scroll would surely come to pass. Josiah himself would be spared, however, for he had sought the Lord with all his heart. Josiah did not respond to this word with smug self-satisfaction, but showed his intense love for his people by leading them in covenant renewal with their God. He gathered the leaders of Judah and the people of Jerusalem at the temple. And there, after publicly reading the covenant statutes, Josiah affirmed his personal commitment to them and enjoined them upon his hearers as well (2 Kings 23:1–3).

The ceremony of covenant renewal was followed by the celebration of the greatest Passover feast in the history of Israel since Moses and Samuel (2 Chron. 35:1–19). This likewise was conducted with strict adherence to the ceremonial code of the newly discovered scroll, which required meticulous attention to the organization and preparation of the priests and Levites, the handling of the sacred ark, and the ritual of sacrifice. The king himself provided thirty thousand sheep and goats and three thousand cattle for the use of the people. Other leaders, inspired by this example, made their own lavish contributions. When all was ready, the slaughter began and the blood was sprinkled as prescribed in the Mosaic regulations. The temple musicians joined in the service, and the gatekeepers carried out their responsibilities to the letter. Finally the laity, from Samaria as well as Judah, bore witness in their worship to the redemptive grace of God, who once more had delivered them from bondage to paganism and unbelief and had made them his own special people in all the earth.

Even all this, however, was not sufficient to stave off the judgment of God. The sin of Manasseh in leading the nation to repudiate the covenant had planted the seeds of inevitable destruction for Judah, Manasseh's repentance and Josiah's reformation notwithstanding. Both the repentance and the reformation were, from the divine viewpoint, inadequate because both were only superficial; neither penetrated to the level of permanent life-changing renewal (2 Kings 23:26–27). The unavoidable consequence was defeat and deportation, from which a godly remnant would someday emerge as the instrument through whom the Lord would continue his redemptive purposes.

The Fall of Jerusalem

The Debacle at Megiddo

The sources are silent about the next thirteen years, but in 609 Neco II of Egypt, in response to an urgent appeal from Aššur-uballiṭ of Assyria, marched north through Palestine on his way to Haran to deliver his friend from an approaching Babylonian military force. Josiah, loyal to the Babylonians, learned of Neco's plans and so took measures to intercept the Egyptian troops in the hope of defeating them or at least impeding their progress to Haran (2 Kings 23:29). Though Judah no doubt by then had recovered much of her strength and territory, she was no match for the mighty Egyptian juggernaut. Courageously Josiah engaged Neco at Megiddo, though the chronicler intimates that Josiah's actions were contrary to the will of God (2 Chron. 35:22).[39] The result was a devastating defeat for Judah and the untimely death of Josiah at thirty-nine years of age. What motivated him to such rashness and disobedience may never be known,[40] but to his contemporaries Josiah stood apart as a man of singular devotion to his people and his God. Jeremiah the prophet composed laments in his honor, and the chronicler says that they were sung by the people even down to his own time (2 Chron. 35:25).

39. Stanley Brice Frost describes the "deuteronomist's" omission of this detail as a "conspiracy of silence": it was difficult for him to square it with his picture of Josiah. The chronicler, however, was not averse to attributing Josiah's death to personal sin ("The Death of Josiah: A Conspiracy of Silence," *JBL* 87 [1968]: 369–82). If there were an attempt at cover-up or whitewash, however, why has the death narrative been retained in Kings at all?

40. For possible explanations see Abraham Malamat, "The Last Kings of Judah and the Fall of Jerusalem," *IEJ* 18 (1968): 137, n. 1.

Jehoahaz of Judah

The death of Josiah must have dealt a shattering blow to the aspirations of the pious of Judah, who were hoping for continuation of the peace, prosperity, and religious devotion that he had introduced. It also revealed just how shallow the national commitment to the covenant was, for almost overnight the nation plunged back into evil.

Josiah's successor was his son Jehoahaz,[41] an evil king whose reign of only three months was terminated by Neco II of Egypt (2 Kings 23:31–33). Neco's army, though forced back south and west of the Euphrates by the Babylonians after the battle of Haran, was able to retain at least some measure of hegemony in lower Syria and Palestine. The Babylonians' preoccupation with the last remnants of Assyrian resistance precluded their undertaking any steps to claim those areas for themselves until after the fall of Carchemish in 605.

Egypt's dominance in Palestine is clearly seen in Neco's treatment of Jehoahaz. He was removed from Judah's throne and sent to Riblah in central Syria where he remained under Egyptian detention. Neco then set Jehoiakim, Jehoahaz's older brother, in his place and as a sign of Egyptian sovereignty required Judah to pay tribute of a hundred talents of silver and a talent of gold. Jehoahaz was then removed from Riblah and exiled to Egypt where he lived out the remainder of his days.

Jehoiakim of Judah

Meanwhile Jehoiakim, finding himself with the terrible burden of raising the tribute Egypt demanded, had to resort to the only means of raising revenues that was available to him—taxation of his people (2 Kings 23:35). This obviously unpopular measure could not have endeared him to his subjects, but as long as Egypt was in control there was little else Jehoiakim could do. Liberation from Egyptian bondage came in 605, when Nebuchadnezzar, commander of Babylonia's armies, crossed the Euphrates, expelled the Egyptians from Palestine, and brought Jehoiakim under Babylonian protection. It was soon evident, however, that this protection was nothing more than continued slavery under a new master.

The Neo-Babylonian Empire

Historical background

The Neo-Babylonian Empire played a crucial role in Judah's history from 609 to 539 B.C. For this period historical documents of remark-

---

41. Malamat suggests that Jehoahaz's appointment by "the people of the land" (2 Kings 23:30), even though he was not the eldest son, implies a coup to install an anti-Egyptian on the throne of Judah ("Last Kings," p. 140).

able objectivity and detail supplement the Old Testament sources and provide unusual insight into the complex factors which combined to bring about Judah's fall and restoration.[42] But first a brief look at the historical background is in order.[43]

Following the collapse of Kassite domination in the mid-twelfth century, the northern part of Mesopotamia fell to Assyria and the southern part to the second Isin dynasty, which held sway until about 1027. This in turn was succeeded by three minor dynasties (1026–980), the first of which was the so-called Second Sealands Dynasty, named thus because it extended all the way to the marshy coastal regions of the Persian Gulf. Then a native Babylonian, Nabu-mukin-apli (979–944), seized control of the Sealands area. By around 890 Assyria had defeated Babylonia. Until Assyria's final overthrow, a process which began in 626, she maintained domination of central and southern Mesopotamia, though there were, of course, sporadic rebellions against Assyria and a few times when she completely lost dominion there.

Table 8   **The Neo-Babylonian Kings**

Nabopolassar	626–605
Nebuchadnezzar II	605–562
Evil-Merodach	562–560
Neriglissar	560–556
Labaši-Marduk	556
Nabonidus	555–539

In the meantime Aramean migrants had been gradually pushing their way into the Tigris-Euphrates basin. There they began to coexist with such ethnic groups as the Kaldu (or Chaldeans), first attested in a document from the reign of Aššur-naṣirpal II of Assyria (ca. 878).[44] The three major Chaldean tribes—Bit-Yakin, Bit-Dakkuri, and Bit Amukani—first appear in texts from the era of Shalmaneser III (ca. 850). Eventually becoming the dominant political element in the south, they were the forerunners of the Neo-Babylonian Empire founded by Nabopolassar in 626. It is accurate to say, then, that "Chaldean" and "Neo-Babylonian" are interchangeable terms to describe a people or peoples who occupied central and lower Mesopotamia in post-Kassite times. Though their ancient roots might be found in Sumero-

42. A fundamental bibliographical and documentary resource for this period is Rykle Borger, "Der Aufstieg des neubabylonischen Reiches," *JCS* 19 (1965): 59–78.

43. For the following see especially J. A. Brinkman, *A Political History of Post-Kassite Babylonia, 1158–722 B.C.*, Analecta Orientalia 43 (Rome: Pontifical Institute, 1968).

44. Ibid., p. 260.

Akkadian stock, by the first millennium they had assimilated other ethnic elements, most notably various Aramean tribes.

Nabopolassar

The final move toward a lasting Babylonian independence of Assyria began, ironically, under the rule of Šamaš-šum-ukīn (668–648), a son of Esarhaddon of Assyria and viceroy of Babylon. His brother, Ashurbanipal (668–627), opposed him because of suspicions that he had separatist ambitions. After Šamaš-šum-ukīn's abortive rebellion, Ashurbanipal reigned over a unified Assyria and Babylonia. It is possible that the records which attest a Babylonian ruler named Kandalanu are in fact referring to Ashurbanipal under an alias.[45] Ashurbanipal was succeeded in Assyria by Ashur-eṭil-ilāni (627–623); another son, Sin-šum-lišir, took over for a few months in Babylonia (623). Sin-šar-iškun then seized power in Assyria (623–612) and attempted to succeed Sin-šum-lišir in the south. He was prevented from doing so, however, by Nabopolassar, a Chaldean who, ironically, may have been appointed governor of the Sealand three years earlier by Sin-šar-iškun himself, who was then the Assyrian general in charge of the armies in Babylonia.[46]

According to the Babylonian Chronicle, Nabopolassar engaged Sin-šar-iškun in battle at Uruk and prevailed decisively.[47] He then formally ascended the throne of Babylon on November 23, 626, though obviously this move was not accepted nor recognized by the Assyrians. For three years Nabopolassar defended his new realm against Assyrian efforts to retake it; finally, he drove Sin-šar-iškun, who had just become king, out of the land entirely in 623.[48]

Nine years later, in 614, Nabopolassar took the ancient sacred city of Asshur after it had already been sacked by the Medes.[49] He then made an alliance with the Median king Cyaxares, a relationship which may have been confirmed by a marriage linking their families.[50] Then, in 612, Nabopolassar captured Nineveh,[51] with the aid of the Umman-Manda (perhaps the Scythians)[52] and the Medes. The Assyrians shifted

45. Oates, "Assyrian Chronology," *Iraq* 27 (1965): 159; see also Julian Reade, "The Accession of Sinsharishkun," *JCS* 23 (1970): 1.

46. Oates, "Assyrian Chronology," *Iraq* 27 (1965): 143.

47. Wiseman, *Chronicles*, p. 51 (B. M. 25127).

48. Reade, "Accession," *JCS* 23 (1970): 5.

49. Grayson, *Assyrian and Babylonian Chronicles*, p. 93, Fall of Nineveh Chronicle 24–30.

50. Wiseman, *Chronicles*, p. 14.

51. Grayson, *Assyrian and Babylonian Chronicles*, p. 94, Fall of Nineveh Chronicle 38–49.

52. Wiseman, *Chronicles*, p. 16.

their seat of government to Haran, but Nabopolassar, with the support once more of the Umman-Manda,[53] took the city, occupied it for a year, and then in 609 repelled the Assyrians and their Egyptian allies who attempted to recapture Haran, and drove them west across the Euphrates River.[54] For the next three years the Babylonians were preoccupied with the task of dealing with Urartu in order to open trade routes and secure the northern frontiers. At last Nabopolassar turned to the only remaining Assyrian stronghold, Carchemish, and in 605 defeated Assyria once and for all and forced Egypt to withdraw from north Syria.

This major blow at Carchemish was struck not by Nabopolassar personally, but by his young son and commander in chief, Nebuchadnezzar. Not satisfied with the defeat of Neco and his Egyptian hosts, the energetic prince pursued them across the Euphrates and all the way to Hamath. In fact, the Old Testament suggests that Nebuchadnezzar followed them as far south as Egypt and that he forced Jerusalem to pay tribute and yield prisoners, including Daniel the prophet.[55]

The succession of Nebuchadnezzar

When Nabopolassar died unexpectedly, Nebuchadnezzar left off his pursuit of Neco to return to Babylon to secure his succession. He did so on September 7, 605, and remained in Babylon until the turn of the year, when once more he set his sights on western domination.

Jehoiakim, it will be recalled, was an appointee of Neco of Egypt, who occupied Palestine and southern Syria between the years 609 and 605. Jehoiakim like his brother Jehoahaz was evil and for his sin was visited with the judgment of Yahweh. Until Egypt was permanently expelled from Palestine by Nebuchadnezzar following the battle of Carchemish, Judah was an Egyptian vassal state obligated to pay heavy tribute. Nebuchadnezzar not only drove Egypt out of the land but immediately incorporated Judah into the Babylonian Empire and demanded that the tribute which had been paid to Egypt be given to Babylonia instead.

Careful attention to all the sources indicates that Nebuchadnezzar penetrated deeply into Syro-Palestine after the fall of Carchemish, some of his troops having moved as far as Jerusalem itself. With lightninglike action he ridded the land of the Egyptians, made Jehoiakim

53. William F. Albright identified these Umman-Manda as Medes rather than Scythians, a view that appears to be correct ("The Seal of Eliakim and the Latest Pre-exilic History of Judah, with Some Observations on Ezekiel," *JBL* 51 [1932]: 86–87).

54. Grayson, *Assyrian and Babylonian Chronicles*, p. 96, Fall of Nineveh Chronicle 66–72.

55. Wiseman, *Chronicles*, p. 26, citing 2 Kings 24:7 and Josephus *Antiquities of the Jews* 10.6.

swear allegiance, and sent a number of Jewish captives back to his capital. All this took place in a matter of a few weeks, for by August 15, 605, Nabopolassar had died and Nebuchadnezzar had to return at once to Babylon.

As the author of Kings indicates, Jehoiakim remained a loyal subject to the Babylonians for the next three years (605–602). He then rebelled for some unexpressed reason;[56] retribution was swift and sure (2 Kings 24:1–2). Nebuchadnezzar sent troops from Babylonia and from some of his western vassal states such as Aram, Moab, and Ammon, and forced Jehoiakim to submit.[57] The chronicler says that Nebuchadnezzar went as far as to bind Jehoiakim with shackles in order to take him as a prisoner of war to Babylon (2 Chron. 36:6). Apparently he relented but as punishment stripped the temple of many of its sacred articles and took them to his own pagan temples in Babylon. Thereafter until his death in 598 Jehoiakim remained in subservience to the Babylonian overlord.

Meanwhile Nebuchadnezzar had undertaken several western campaigns against Judah's neighbors. It may have been his preoccupation with these states, in fact, that gave Jehoiakim the courage to break his alliance with Nebuchadnezzar. The chronicles in any case reveal that Nebuchadnezzar's first campaign after succeeding his father was in his first regnal year (604). At that time he plunged deep into Palestine and took the Philistine city of Ashkelon. In year four (601) he engaged Neco II in a great battle near the border of Egypt, a contest which evidently ended in a draw. Perhaps the Babylonian was not altogether unsuccessful, however, for he may have brought Judah back under his control in the course of this campaign.

Jehoiachin and Zedekiah of Judah

In his sixth year (599–598) Nebuchadnezzar marched into north Syria and in his seventh (598–597) took Jerusalem from Jehoiachin, son and successor of Jehoiakim (2 Kings 24:10–17). On March 15/16,

---

56. Malamat, "Last Kings," *IEJ* 18 (1968): 142–43, associates Jehoiakim's rebellion with the Babylonian conflict with Egypt in the winter of 601/600 B.C., which is attested to by a letter written in Aramaic from the town of Saqqarah. For the letter see William H. Shea, "Adon's Letter and the Babylonian Chronicle," *BASOR* 223 (1976): 61–64.

57. Wiseman, *Chronicles*, p. 31, points out that the campaign against Jehoiakim is not mentioned in the Babylonian records (B. M. 21946, reverse 5–7) because Nebuchadnezzar's main objective was Egypt and not Judah. See John R. Bartlett, "Edom and the Fall of Jerusalem, 587 B.C.," *PEQ* 114 (1982): 16, for the view that "Aramean" should be retained in 2 Kings 24:2 and not replaced with "Edomite," as some scholars argue. The Edomite hostility against Arad which is described in letters of the period could, as Yohanan Aharoni suggests, refer as well to 587–586 as to 600–598 ("Three Hebrew Ostraca from Arad," *BASOR* 197 [1970]: 28).

597, he set up as king still another son of Josiah, namely, Zedekiah.[58] The last exploit of Nebuchadnezzar which is recorded in the Babylonian Chronicle is a campaign against the Elamites. Unfortunately the chronicle breaks off at 594–593, and nothing more is known from Babylonian sources until 557–556. The Old Testament speaks of such momentous accomplishments as his capture of Jerusalem in 587–586, but the extrabiblical texts are silent on the whole matter.

After replacing his father on the throne of David, Jehoiachin evidently maintained an anti-Babylonian posture that immediately brought Nebuchadnezzar's stern reaction. After only three months in power Jehoiachin found his city surrounded by the Babylonian hosts and he quickly capitulated.[59] This time the royal family was deported along with other leading citizens including Ezekiel the prophet. The cream of Judah's military force and her most skillful craftsmen also had to abandon their land and homes to go into exile. Finally, Nebuchadnezzar helped himself once more to the temple treasures and carried them back to Babylon as a sign of his complete success.

Though Zedekiah, Jehoiachin's uncle and Josiah's son, was left as puppet ruler of Judah, it is clear that the Jewish people regarded Jehoiachin as the true scion of David until the day of his death.[60] He never returned to Jerusalem, it is true, but after long years as a political prisoner in Babylon he was placed on a government pension and apparently was treated more as an honored guest of Babylon than as her prisoner (2 Kings 25:27–30). It must have seemed to the exilic Jewish community that the time would surely come when Jehoiachin would lead them back triumphantly to Jerusalem and restore the former glory of the house of David.[61]

Zedekiah was, however, king *de facto* of whatever was left of Judah in 597. Evil like his brothers, he paid no attention to the admonishings of Jeremiah the prophet to accept Babylonian suzerainty as the will of God. Rather, he rebelled against Nebuchadnezzar, thus inviting sure and swift disaster.[62] The date of this rebellion cannot be determined (see Ezek. 17:11–18), but by 588 Nebuchadnezzar advanced upon Jerusalem and commenced a siege which resulted in the fall of the city

58. B. M. 21946, reverse 11–13.

59. Malamat, "Last Kings," *IEJ* 18 (1968): 144, concludes that the siege lasted one month at most.

60. Albright, "Seal of Eliakim," *JBL* 51 (1932): 91–92. For the ambivalence created by the existence of two kings of Judah in her last decade see Martin Noth, "The Jerusalem Catastrophe of 587 B.C. and Its Significance for Israel," in *The Laws in the Pentateuch and Other Essays* (Edinburgh: Oliver and Boyd, 1966), pp. 266–80.

61. Jon D. Levenson suggests that the historian holds out hope even in the face of apparent despair ("The Last Four Verses in Kings," *JBL* 103 [1984]: 361).

62. Malamat, "Last Kings," *IEJ* 18 (1968): 151, associates this rebellion with the accession of Hophra of Egypt in February, 589, an event that encouraged Zedekiah to break with Babylonia.

and the end of the Judean monarchy in July of 586 (2 Kings 25:1–7).[63] Zedekiah escaped through an opening in the city wall and fled to the region of Jericho. He was soon overtaken, however, and brought before Nebuchadnezzar at his Syrian headquarters in Riblah. There he was forced to witness the execution of his sons before he himself was blinded and taken to Babylon.

The Aftermath

The major public buildings and the residences of Jerusalem were set afire and leveled to the ground by Babylonian troops commanded by Nebuzaradan. They then reduced the great defensive walls to rubble, so that the once magnificent city lay as a smoldering ruin unable to protect the rabble who still resided there.

Whatever of value remained in the temple was appropriated by the Babylonians and carried triumphantly back to Babylon as the spoils of war. The population itself, except for the very poorest and least influential, was deported en masse. Only a few, among them Jeremiah, were allowed to remain behind. The principal leaders, including the high priest Seraiah and his assistants, were brought before Nebuchadnezzar at Riblah and there were mercilessly executed. Thus Judah and Jerusalem ceased to be the focus of divine covenant activity on earth. The burden of covenant continuity now rested upon the exiles scattered throughout the eastern Mediterranean world from Egypt to the Persian Gulf. Yahweh would work with them to effect his immutable promise of redemption and reconciliation. And to this all the prophets of the time testified.

The chronicler, as usual, makes a statement about the theological meaning of these awful events. Jerusalem fell, he says, despite the patient efforts of Yahweh, through his prophets, to bring the people to their senses. They mocked these messengers until there was no remedy but destruction and deportation (2 Chron. 36:15–16). Having refused to be the covenant sons and servants of Yahweh, the community in exile now had to fulfil the role of slave to a pagan despot. Only when the appointed time of discipline was over could they expect to return to their native land and there resume their responsibility as the elect people of God.

The Prophetic Witness

Our discussion of the last century of Judah's history has been so far a chronicling of political and military events from a more or less de-

---

63. Abraham Malamat, "The Last Years of the Kingdom of Judah," in *World History of the Jewish People*, vol. 4, part 1, pp. 218–20.

tached point of view. At this time, then, we must get beyond objective history into its deeper meanings. Of course, the biblical historians have done this to a certain extent by their very selection of the events they have preserved in writing for the modern reader and by occasional theological judgments. Our account cannot be complete, however, until the prophets of the period are allowed to have their say.

Nahum

One of the earliest of these prophets is Nahum the Elkoshite, whose message in its entirety antedates the closing days of Assyria.[64] Little is known of the man himself, for he does not refer to himself except in the introduction nor is he mentioned elsewhere in the Old Testament. His oracle against Nineveh is of special interest because only he and Jonah were preoccupied with Assyria. Unlike the Book of Jonah, however, which presents Nineveh as an illustration of God's universal redemptive concern, the burden of Nahum is the judgment of God upon her.

After an introductory hymn describing Yahweh's avenging majesty (1:2–8),[65] the prophet addresses both Judah and Nineveh with the message that Nineveh is on the verge of destruction because of her vile idolatry and cruel treatment of God's chosen people. Like Thebes she will utterly fall and become a spectacle before all the world. No amount of defensive preparation will avail, for Assyria's tragic end is a foregone conclusion. And once she falls, she will never rise again, for her wound will be fatal and forever.

Though one cannot date this anti-Assyria diatribe precisely, it is clear that forces were already at work on the world scene that portended no good for Assyria. Nineveh eventually fell to Babylonia in 612, but the lack of reference to the Babylonians in the oracle would suggest that Nahum is speaking from a much earlier vantage-point. Thebes had fallen in 663, on the other hand, an event that seems to be somewhat remote from Nahum's present. It seems best to propose that the prophet was viewing the beginnings of Assyria's decline before it became obvious that Nabopolassar of Babylonia would be the agent of Assyria's demise. A setting in the last third of Ashurbanipal's reign (640–627) would not be at all unreasonable.

By then Josiah, the fiercely anti-Assyrian king of Judah, had come

64. For a succinct discussion of introductory matters see Roland K. Harrison, *Introduction to the Old Testament* (Grand Rapids: Eerdmans, 1969), pp. 926–30.

65. Ralph L. Smith, *Micah-Malachi*, Word Biblical Commentary (Waco: Word, 1984), pp. 72–73. Other scholars, on the basis of an alleged acrostic pattern, view the hymn as extending through 2:3. See, for example, George Buchanan Gray, *The Forms of Hebrew Poetry* (London: Hodder and Stoughton, 1915), pp. 243–63. This, however, requires too much imaginative emendation to be seriously entertained.

to power. Judah had experienced tremendous suffering at Assyrian hands during the reign of his grandfather Manasseh, suffering to which Nahum refers (2:11–13); and one may be sure that Josiah's own policies had resulted in Assyrian reprisal or at least threats. The word of comfort offered by Nahum to Judah would have been singularly appropriate and encouraging to the godly King Josiah, who must have felt some measure of insecurity in the face of a still very powerful Assyria. There is a possibility that Nahum played a significant role in the earliest stirrings of reformation in Judah in 632, the eighth year of the young monarch.

Habakkuk

Less still is known of Habakkuk.[66] What is known is that he was a gifted composer of music (see 3:19) as well as a prophet and that he prophesied of the closing days of Judah's history. His reference to the Babylonians indicates that they had already become an independent and terrifying presence, a state of affairs which surely presupposes the accession of Nabopolassar to Babylonian kingship in 626 (1:6–11). A *terminus ad quem* of 605 is virtually certain since the judgment upon Judah appears to be totally in the future.[67] On the other hand, Judah is in such a perilous state—injustice abounds and there is no redress— that one can hardly envision Josiah in power any longer. The description of moral and civil anarchy fits very well the early years of Jehoiakim (608–605) just before the evils of Judah brought divine intervention in the form of Nebuchadnezzar.

Habakkuk's description of the Babylonian hordes is graphic in the extreme (1:5–11). They have begun to overwhelm the nations in a manner that the world has never seen before. Nothing can stand in their way as they seek universal domination. Moreover, they do so in proud self-sufficiency. Habakkuk finds it difficult to reconcile the Babylonians' arrogant ungodliness with God's use of them as his means of chastening Judah and the nations (1:13).

The response of the Lord is to concur with the prophet's assessment that the Babylonians are a wicked people who, in greedy pursuit of the wealth of the nations, have covered their garments with blood. Though Yahweh has permitted them to succeed and prosper, the Babylonians will at length drink of the cup of his judgment. All appeals to their lifeless gods will be in vain in that day, for only Yahweh is God.

---

66. Harrison, *Introduction*, pp. 931–38.
67. Harrison, *Introduction*, p. 936, with most scholars, dates the book after 605. Gleason L. Archer, Jr.'s, date of "somewhere around 607 or 606 B.C." seems most satisfying, however (*A Survey of Old Testament Introduction* [Chicago: Moody, 1964], p. 344).

Satisfied, Habukkuk composed a prayer in which he celebrates the awesome person of the Lord and his works in history.[68] From the exodus to the conquest Yahweh had bared his mighty arm against his foes and had brought his redeemed people victory and salvation (3:1–15). In light of the past, then, Judah can take confidence in what Yahweh will do for his people as they await the coming of the Babylonian hosts. No matter what happens, the prophet sings, all will be well, for Yahweh is sovereign.

Zephaniah

The setting of the message of the third prophet of Judah's final years—Zephaniah—is much more easily determined, as is the identity of the man himself. He relates that he was of royal blood, the great-great-grandson of King Hezekiah,[69] and that he prophesied during the reign of Josiah (1:1). Lack of any reference to the reformation of Josiah suggests a date early in Josiah's reign rather than after the cleansing of the temple (622).[70] This suggestion finds support in the description of Judah's spiritual and moral decay. The people worship the starry host and swear by Molech,[71] as we know they did in the times of Manasseh and Amon and even in Josiah's childhood years (1:4–6). All this, the Lord says, he will punish in the great day of his judgment, a day which is imminent and inevitable.

Judah will not be alone in that time of wrath, however, for other nations also have spurned Yahweh's overtures of grace and must suffer the consequences. The Philistines are listed first (2:4–7), and they indeed experienced the awful might of Nebuchadnezzar in his very first campaign (604).[72] Moab and Ammon, the kin of Judah who had proved to be filled with hate toward her, would also fall (2:8–11). Though explicit evidence is lacking in the sources to confirm that this came to pass, there is no good reason to believe otherwise.[73]

The oracle concerning the Cushites (2:12) has to do with the defeat

68. See especially William F. Albright, "The Psalm of Habakkuk," in *Studies of Old Testament Prophecy*, ed. H. H. Rowley (Edinburgh: T. & T. Clark, 1950), pp. 1–18.

69. See, however, Smith, *Micah-Malachi*, p. 125, who argues that this could not be a reference to King Hezekiah since he had no son named Amariah. The objection rests on the assumption that if Hezekiah had a son named Amariah, he would be mentioned elsewhere, a gratuitous assumption to say the least.

70. Harrison, *Introduction*, p. 940.

71. For a possible archaeological confirmation of Molech worship from precisely this period see Randall W. Younker, "Israel, Judah, and Ammon and the Motifs on the Baalis Seal from Tell el-'Umeiri," *BA* 48 (1985): 173–80.

72. Wiseman, *Chronicles*, p. 69 (B. M. 29146, 1. 18).

73. John R. Bartlett, "The Moabites and Edomites," in *Peoples of Old Testament Times*, ed. D. J. Wiseman (Oxford: Clarendon, 1973), pp. 242–43.

of the Nubian dynasty which ruled over Upper Egypt from Thebes. The precise fulfilment of this prophecy is difficult to ascertain; but inasmuch as the oracles concerning the other nations deal with punishment which would someday be inflicted by Babylonia, it is possible that Nebuchadnezzar's attempted conquest of Egypt in 567 is in view.[74]

Assyria's doom at Babylonian hands is the last in the list of foreign nations which have incurred the wrath of Judah's God because of their mistreatment of his people (2:13–15). At the time of the oracle Nineveh was still standing, an indication that Zephaniah's ministry preceded the fall of that city in 612. This confirms the impression that the prophet flourished early in Josiah's reign and also suggests that the other oracles of the series antedate Nineveh's destruction. That great city, Zephaniah proclaimed, would be utterly devastated and left bare of human habitation. And indeed the very location of Nineveh was forgotten by the world until the excavators of Kuyunjik discovered it to be the site of ancient Nineveh.[75]

Finally, Zephaniah spoke once more to his own city and nation, castigating rulers, prophets, and priests alike for their utter disregard of Yahweh's covenant principles (3:1–7). In spite of his frequent and dramatic deliverances of Judah from hostile powers, his people had refused to fear him and mend their ways. Yahweh therefore would assemble the nations to judgment, and Judah too would feel his fury. But from both the pagan world and Judah would emerge a godly remnant who would bless his name and make him known in all the earth. Even those scattered to the ends of the earth would return and be restored to the favor of the Lord (3:14–20).

The line between historical and eschatological fulfilment is often a very fine one and difficult to discern. Here in Zephaniah, as in all the prophets, that demarcation is blurry. It is clear, however, that God's judgment on Judah and the nations took place more than once in Old Testament times and that there always emerged from it a purified people who embraced his covenant terms of salvation. It is equally true that the judgments and restorations of historical times did not exhaust what the prophets had in view, but that there yet remains a climactic and final encounter between the Lord and all humankind in which judgment and salvation will find ultimate expression.

Jeremiah

By far the greatest and most informative voice of Judah's final preexilic generation was that of Jeremiah, who is significant both as

---

74. For the text see Pritchard, *Ancient Near Eastern Texts*, p. 308; see also Alan Gardiner, *Egypt of the Pharaohs* (London: Oxford University Press, 1961), pp. 361–62.

75. André Parrot, *Nineveh and the Old Testament* (New York: Philosophical Library, 1955), pp. 16–17.

historical source[76] and theological interpreter. He introduces his work by identifying himself as the son of Hilkiah and a citizen of the priestly community of Anathoth (Râs el-Kharrûbeh), a Levitical town on the northern slopes of the Mount of Olives. This suggests that Jeremiah filled a dual role, that of priest, for which he was qualified by birth and training, and that of prophet, for which he was qualified by virtue of the divine call. Of this fact we should make nothing more than that a member of a priestly family was called to prophesy as well. Certainly there is nothing in Jeremiah's own writings to suggest that he was a cultic prophet or that he had any interest in the temple beyond that of any other prophet.[77]

Fortunately, Jeremiah dates many of his oracles, though the order of his book is not strictly chronological. To avoid sheer speculation, then, as we attempt to reconstruct Judah's history from the Jeremianic perspective, we will not rely too heavily on those passages which offer no chronological clues. Nonetheless, since the undated sections are helpful for an understanding of the milieu in which Jeremiah lived and worked, we will give them brief attention.

With unusual precision Jeremiah at the very beginning lays out the chronological boundaries of his ministry. The word of God came to him, he says, in the thirteenth year of Josiah, that is, in 627 (1:2). His public ministry then continued throughout the reigns of Jehoahaz, Jehoiakim, Jehoiachin, and Zedekiah, right to the end of the kingdom in 586 and even beyond. Thus he witnessed the major events of Judah's final forty years. We know that Jeremiah continued to prophesy past the date of Jerusalem's cataclysmic judgment, for he was offered, and he accepted, the option of remaining in Judah rather than going with the captives into Babylonian exile. Having remained in Jerusalem for a while, he went to Egypt, undoubtedly against his will. The last event in his book is the account of the release of Jehoiachin from prison by Evil-Merodach of Babylonia in 562. Though Jeremiah would have been eighty-five or ninety years old by then, there is no good reason to deny that he personally recorded in his memoirs this rise in the fortunes of Jehoiachin.

The call of Jeremiah to the prophetic ministry came, as we have seen, in 627, well after Josiah's initial attempts at reformation, but five years before the discovery of the Torah scroll in the temple and the great religious revival which immediately followed. This explains why Jeremiah's earliest messages to Judah are words of condemna-

76. For an appreciation of Jeremiah as historical source see F. Charles Fensham, "Nebukadrezzar in the Book of Jeremiah," *JNSL* 10 (1982): 53–65.

77. Georg Fohrer, *History of Israelite Religion*, trans. David E. Green (Nashville: Abingdon, 1972), pp. 261–62.

tion. He was called to speak of the uprooting and destruction of nations, including Judah, and their eventual rebuilding and replanting (1:10). The chosen people must be told that their sins would incur the chastisement of Yahweh, a message they would not want to hear, but Jeremiah the messenger would be protected from any violent reaction on their part.

The essence of Judah's sin was her disloyalty to Yahweh her God, who had brought her up out of Egypt into the land of promise. She had abandoned him in pursuit of other gods, or, as Jeremiah phrases it:

> My people have committed two sins:
> They have forsaken me,
>   the spring of living water,
> and have dug their own cisterns,
>   broken cisterns that cannot hold water. [2:13]

All the discipline that the Lord had already brought upon them by the agency of Assyria and Egypt had been to no avail. The people still shamelessly denied their God. Like an unfaithful wife they had joined themselves to other lovers (3:1).

But Yahweh still loved his people and desired their reconciliation. He therefore commanded Jeremiah to send a word of hope to them— not only to those in Judah but to those in Israel as well. This word might well have prompted Josiah to invite the inhabitants of the north to attend his great Passover of 622. But Jeremiah saw a contradiction between the message of optimism and the very evident threat from the enemy that loomed on the horizon.[78] Jerusalem would soon be under siege; and though the prophets and priests were preaching peace, there was no real peace at all (8:11). Instead the snorting of the enemy's horses could be plainly heard by the prophet (8:16).

This did not necessarily mean complete annihilation, however, for the Lord would graciously forgive and would maintain his promises to those who repented and renewed their covenant commitment. This remnant would someday be restored to the land Yahweh had given their ancestors (16:14–15). Captivity was a foregone conclusion, however, and there would be disasters and destruction of every kind. As a sign of the uncertain times Jeremiah was told by the Lord to remain unmarried, for any children born to the prophet would surely perish in the catastrophes which awaited the nation (16:1–4). Even so, there

---

78. Edwin M. Yamauchi identifies the foe from the north as a combination of Chaldeans and Scythians, the presence of the latter being suggested by characteristically Scythian artifacts found in Palestine ("The Scythians: Invading Hordes from the Russian Steppes," *BA* 46 [1983]: 90–99).

was hope for the man who trusted in the Lord. He would survive and stand in the day of wrath and judgment (17:7–8).

The greater part of chapters 1–17 of Jeremiah is set in the reign of Josiah, probably before the restoration of the temple and the discovery of the Torah scroll in 622.[79] The message is almost totally one of condemnation and judgment, thus suggesting that no national repentance of any kind has taken place. It is reasonable to assume that Jeremiah's stern warning of impending disaster made an impact on the young ruler Josiah and that the king, acting on the counsel of the prophet, took the measures toward reformation recorded in the historical sources. While this reformation was not as pervasive nor its results as enduring as the public celebrations seem to indicate, it nonetheless shows that Jeremiah's ministry was not entirely in vain in its early years.

Since there are no specific chronological guidelines, there is no way to determine whether any of Jeremiah's utterances between 622 and Jehoiakim's succession in 608 found their way into the book. We have already argued that chapters 1–17 are from Josiah's early days. It should also be pointed out that nearly all the remaining chapters can be assigned to some period after 609. This strongly suggests that the years between 622 and 608 were a period of such relative stability, peace, and spiritual renewal that no prophetic word, particularly of judgment, was needed.

The situation was radically different after 609, however, for the wicked son of Josiah, Jehoiakim, had come to power. Almost at once there was a resumption of Jeremiah's public ministry. The earliest evidence is in chapter 26 where Jeremiah receives a word from Yahweh "early in the reign of Jehoiakim." It had not taken long for Jehoahaz and Jehoiakim to lead Judah away from whatever measure of godliness she had known under Josiah. Jeremiah responded by warning Jerusalem that she, like Shiloh of old, would be totally destroyed if she did not heed the word of Yahweh through his prophets (26:9). Some of the people demanded that Jeremiah be executed then and there for his unpopular accusatory message. Others urged that he be spared as Micah was in the days of Hezekiah, and that his message be heeded as the very word of God. Though the second group prevailed and Jeremiah was set free, another prophet, Uriah, was not so fortunate and paid for his bold witness with his life (26:20–24).

In the year that Nebuchadnezzar first came to Jerusalem and placed Jehoiakim under tribute (605) Jeremiah recorded several significant

---

79. This is not to suggest that chapters 1–17 constitute an independent literary unit. On the complex matter of the arrangement of the Book of Jeremiah see John Bright, *Jeremiah*, Anchor Bible (Garden City, N.Y.: Doubleday, 1965), pp. lv–lxxxv.

events. The precise chronological data which the prophet supplies indicate that the city had already capitulated and that Jehoiakim was therefore technically under Babylonian suzerainty. And yet the city remained intact and its population suffered very little. There was cause for optimism and a concomitant disregard of the warning signals that this first Babylonian incursion should have communicated.

Jeremiah therefore pronounced a word of greater judgment (ch. 25). He had announced the word of God to Judah for twenty-three years, all in vain, so now Nebuchadnezzar would come and completely destroy the nation and take its people into a seventy-year captivity (25:11). And Judah would not be alone in experiencing divine wrath. All the nations of the Near Eastern world would suffer the crushing blows of the mighty Babylonian war machine. Details of these conquests are found in chapters 46–49. Egypt, mentioned first (46:2–28), had just suffered a humiliating defeat at Carchemish. This, however, was just the beginning of her problems. Nebuchadnezzar would not be content until Memphis itself was laid waste and Thebes brought under Babylonian control. All this was achieved by 567.

The Philistines also would know the wrath of the God of Israel (47:1–7). Even before Neco II of Egypt had attacked Gaza in his campaign of 609, Jeremiah had prophesied that the Philistine pentapolis would be victims of military conquest from a totally unexpected source: from the north. This was fulfilled in the campaign of Nebuchadnezzar in his first regnal year, 604.

Moab (48:1–47), Ammon (49:1–6), and Edom (49:7–22), though related to Judah by common ancestry, would not escape. The Babylonian eagle would swoop down upon them and pick their bones clean of all flesh. Yet the Lord would not make an end of Moab and Ammon but would restore their fortune in days to come. Edom, however, would never recover and, like Sodom and Gomorrah, would forfeit human habitation.

Finally, Damascus, Kedar, and Hazor would know the crushing heel of Babylonian imperialism (49:23–33). The cities would be laid in the dust and their populations scattered to the four winds. Their refusal to know and serve the God of Israel in spite of the mediation of his grace through his chosen people must result in certain and irremediable judgment.

Also in Jehoiakim's fourth year the Lord commanded Jeremiah to write down all the judgments he had earlier uttered concerning Judah and the nations. Accordingly, Jeremiah dictated and Baruch recorded his words on a scroll (ch. 36). This must have taken place after Nebuchadnezzar's subjugation of Jerusalem, for the scroll contained the judgments which Jeremiah delivered after Jehoiakim's capitulation. The first of these—upon Egypt—was, as we saw, delivered after the battle of Carchemish. Baruch took the completed scroll and read it before the temple in the ninth month of Jehoiakim's fifth year, which had been proclaimed a time of fasting (Jer. 36:9–10).[80]

The contents of the scroll so disturbed the king when he heard it read that he cut it into pieces which he then burned in the brazier before which he was sitting. Yet Jehoiakim showed no fear, no sense of impending doom. The reason quite likely lay in the fact that he had not been unduly punished by the Babylonians, though heavy tribute had been levied and a number of important prisoners had been taken away. In fact, he now enjoyed the benefits of Babylonian protection by virtue of his role as Nebuchadnezzar's vassal.

And yet the prophetic word was insistent: Jerusalem would fall under divine judgment and her people would be scattered to the ends of the earth. As evidence that that word could not fail though the king might burn it up, Jeremiah laboriously dictated its contents once more to Baruch. This time the message was directly aimed at Jehoiakim. His family would no longer sit on the throne of David, and he himself in death would lie exposed to the elements for his sinful disobedience (36:30).

The only message of Jeremiah clearly addressed to Jehoiachin, son of Jehoiakim, is that of chapter 22, which develops the judgment on Jehoiakim and his line which we have just mentioned. The date of the oracle is 597, shortly after Jehoiakim's death. After an introductory word in which he appeals to the young king to turn to Yahweh, Jeremiah reminds him that the greedy and self-aggrandizing policies of his uncle Jehoahaz and his father Jehoiakim had resulted in banishment and gruesome death respectively. Should he do no better—and Jeremiah surely is pessimistic about the matter —Jehoiachin can also expect an awful end. He will go to Babylon as a trophy of war, never to return to his homeland. Worse still, none of his offspring will ever sit on the Davidic throne (22:24–30). History attests to the fulfilment of this word of the prophet. But the Davidic dynasty did not lack a legitimate occupant after all, for God, true to his immutable and unconditional promise, provided a scion of David through another line, that of Nathan rather than Solomon.[81] Jesus, foster son of Joseph, descendant of Jehoiakim, was conceived in the womb of Mary, who

80. Bright, *Jeremiah*, p. 182, points out that this was the very month in which the Babylonian army sacked the city of Ashkelon. Judah's fasting may well have been prompted by that attack.

81. Marshall D. Johnson, *The Purpose of Biblical Genealogies* (Cambridge: Cambridge University Press, 1969), pp. 243–49. I owe this reference and insight to my colleague Darrell Bock. See also Eugene H. Merrill, "1 Chronicles," in *The Bible Knowledge Commentary*, ed. John F. Walvoord and Roy B. Zuck (Wheaton, Ill.: Victor, 1985), vol. 1, p. 595.

was every bit as much a descendant of David, but not of the kings of Judah who succeeded him.

Early in the reign of Zedekiah, in the year 593 (27:1; cf. 28:1), Jeremiah reiterated the message of judgment to Judah and her neighbors (chs. 27–28) that Nebuchadnezzar was coming and that it was useless to resist. The only sensible course of action would be capitulation and submission. But conflicting prophetic voices were at the same time predicting that the exile would soon be over and that Jehoiachin would return and bring with him the temple articles which the Babylonians had stolen away in 605 and again in 597. One of these in particular, Hananiah ben Azzur, confidently asserted that all this would happen within two years (28:3–4)! Before the end of that year Hananiah was dead, and two years later it was clear that he had spoken a lying word and that Jeremiah's prediction of seventy years still stood.

At about the same time Jeremiah wrote two letters, one addressed to the captives in Babylon (29:4–23) and the other composed in the form of a long prophetic oracle concerning the Babylonians themselves (chs. 50–51). The first was delivered by a delegation of Jews sent by Zedekiah to Babylon for an audience with Nebuchadnezzar; the second was delivered by a member of a delegation that included Zedekiah himself. The reason for these journeys is not related, but it is altogether possible that they had to do with the annual presentation of tribute.[82]

In any event, the letter addressed to the exiles instructs them to settle down in the land of their captors and to await patiently the passing of the seventy years, after which (and only after which) they will return home. The generally favorable conditions of their existence in Babylon are already evident, for the prophet tells his people to marry, have families, build houses and businesses, and be supportive of the Babylonian authorities. He is hardly addressing prisoners of war languishing in concentration camps. He informs them that hopes of returning soon are fruitless, for Zedekiah, the present occupant of Judah's throne, will shortly be unseated and the last vestiges of the kingdom will be cruelly eroded away. Their future for now lies in Babylon, not Jerusalem. But this will not be the case forever. In God's good time he will bring his chosen people back to their land that they might once more be planted there in accordance with his purposes for them as a redemptive people.

The Babylonian judgment (chs. 50–51) describes in graphic terms the meteoric collapse of that magnificent empire beneath the hammer blows of a northern foe. This will make possible the restoration of the exiles, who then will see that Babylonia, like Assyria, had been merely a pawn in the hands of the Almighty. The Medes and their allies will

---

82. Bright, *Jeremiah*, p. 211.

reduce the golden city to ashes, and her very location will be forgotten. To symbolize this fact Jeremiah ordered the courier who delivered the written text of the oracle to read it publicly in Babylon. Having done that, he must tie a stone to it and throw it into the Euphrates. As it sank beneath the murky waters, so Babylon itself would disappear amongst the sea of nations (51:63–64).

The rise of Egyptian might and influence in the first decade of the sixth century began to cause a shift in the balance of power in the Near Eastern world. Zedekiah, a reluctant vassal of Babylonia, broke his treaty with Nebuchadnezzar in 588 and thus invited instant retaliation. Even while the Babylonian westward march was under way, Jeremiah proclaimed, in the parables of the potter's shop (ch. 18) and the broken jar (ch. 19), that Judah's end was near. Like the vessel Jerusalem would soon be shattered and become a refuse dump.

Jeremiah's boldness and apparent attempt to undermine Judean morale landed him in the stocks (ch. 20). Even though he was released the next day, the price he was beginning to pay in terms of psychological stress and physical abuse caused the prophet to question his call and message. Why should the Lord lead him to preach submission when the traditional word from the prophets in an hour of dire need was to rely upon the strong arm of God who could and certainly would deliver? The king and people were also asking this question. If indeed the Babylonians were coming, should not Jeremiah rally them to resistance in the power of God rather than undermine them with what appeared to be treasonous cries for capitulation? When Zedekiah sought his counsel, all Jeremiah could advocate was surrender. The reason was simple, the prophet said: God had determined the destruction of the city and nothing could be done to change that. Human opposition to the decreed purposes of God must inevitably lead to tragic consequences.

In the midst of the siege of Jerusalem it seemed for a time as though the false prophets were right and Jeremiah wrong, for Hophra of Egypt arrived in the land, forcing Nebuchadnezzar to look to his rear flanks (37:11).[83] With the Babylonians temporarily withdrawn, the city gained a badly needed respite. Even Jeremiah took advantage of the situation and sought to leave the capital long enough to attend to business at his home in Benjamin. He was intercepted, however, and being accused of desertion to the Babylonians was thrown into a dungeon (37:15). Bad soon became worse: the rumors of Jeremiah's ostensibly treasonous attitudes and actions resulted in his incarceration in a wa-

---

83. Malamat, "Last Kings," *IEJ* 18 (1968): 152, dates this episode in the spring of 587.

tery pit where he surely would have perished had it not been for the intercession of Ebed-Melech the Cushite (38:7–13).

Still under arrest, Jeremiah offered one last word of advice to Zedekiah—surrender and you, your family, and the city will be spared death and devastation (38:17–23). Zedekiah was nearly persuaded. Only his pride of position and need to maintain a face of courage in the midst of certain calamity prevented him from acceding to the word of the man of God. That stubbornness against the truth proved to be the undoing of the king and all his people with him.

In 587, the year before Jerusalem fell, Hanamel, Jeremiah's cousin, came to him in his place of confinement and urged Jeremiah to buy from him a field at Anathoth (32:6–15). Hanamel obviously believed that, whereas he would soon be exiled, Jeremiah would be left behind and, hence, in a position to care for the estate. Jeremiah, in response to the direction of the Lord, complied and ordered Baruch to take the scroll on which the transaction was recorded and place it in a clay jar to preserve it till the exile would be over and Jeremiah's heirs could reclaim their lands and properties.

Jeremiah's action was a testimony to the promise of Yahweh that he would bring his people back to the land and would make with them a new covenant (32:37–41). Yahweh would take the initiative himself to create within his people a new heart, a new disposition to love and obey him. The land once more would enjoy bounty and blessing. Out of the death and debris of the ruined city would spring new life and hope. The ancient messianic promises of Yahweh would find fulfilment when an heir of David would sit on his throne forever (33:14–18). The present indeed was bleak beyond description, but in the day of restoration Yahweh would bring to pass the fullness of his redemptive, saving plan for Israel and all the nations of the earth.

At last the day of judgment predicted by Jeremiah and his fellow prophets came to pass. Jerusalem's walls were breached, the Babylonians occupied the city, and Zedekiah fled for his life. He was apprehended, however, blinded, and taken in shackles to Babylon. Jerusalem was then looted of its treasure and burned to the ground (39:1–10). Meanwhile, Jeremiah was freed from the procession of Judeans who were on their way to Babylonian exile and was given a choice by Nebuzaradan, the Babylonian commander: he could go on to Babylon or he could remain in Judah. Deciding on the latter, he was to witness yet another series of tragic events in which he would be personally caught up.

Before the Babylonians left the region, they selected the pro-Babylonian Jew Gedaliah to serve as governor of the peasants left in the land (40:7). He made his headquarters at Mizpah and from there administered the affairs of Judah in keeping with the wishes of his Babylonian masters. Not everyone was pleased with this arrangement, however, and within a short time a conspiracy was hatched by Ishmael ben Nethaniah to get rid of Gedaliah. Ishmael was representing the interests of Baalis, king of Ammon,[84] who apparently was envious or perhaps fearful of the prospects of an ongoing semi-independent Judah that was already beginning to attract Jewish refugees from surrounding states including his own.[85]

When word of the plot came to Johanan ben Kareah, a Jewish army officer, he proposed to Gedaliah that he be allowed to kill Ishmael before the conspiracy proceeded further (40:13–15). Not believing the report, Gedaliah refused. A few months later Gedaliah was entertaining Ishmael and a group of his comrades at Mizpah when suddenly they rose up against the governor and murdered him, a number of his officials, and the Babylonian soldiers who were there (41:1–3). Ishmael then took prisoners and headed toward Ammon. Before he could get beyond Gibeon, however, he was intercepted by Johanan and his followers. The prisoners were freed by Johanan, but Ishmael and eight of his men managed to escape to Ammon. Johanan headed south to Egypt, fearful that the Babylonians would consider him and his party responsible for the assassination of Gedaliah (41:16–18).

On their way Johanan's party came across Jeremiah and pleaded with him to intercede with Yahweh in their behalf. Jeremiah's response was that they ought not to go to Egypt but remain in the land. The Babylonians would not trouble them, he said, for Yahweh would be with them. Should they go to Egypt, they would suffer sword and famine (ch. 42).

Johanan nonetheless disregarded the prophet's word and made his way to Egypt, taking with him those members of the royal family whom the Babylonians had left in the care of Gedaliah. Even Jeremiah and Baruch were coerced into going and eventually found themselves at Tahpanhes (Tell Dafanneh) in the northeast Delta (43:1–7).[86] There Yahweh spoke to the prophet and revealed that Nebuchadnezzar would someday build a royal canopy over the very place the Jews were using as refuge. His destruction of Egypt would include destruction of the Jewish refugees who had sought asylum there.

Jeremiah therefore prepared a message to be circulated to the Jew-

---

84. For an important new confirmation of this name see Larry G. Herr, "The Servant of Baalis," *BA* 48 (1985): 169–72. Henry O. Thompson and Fawzi Zayadine had previously identified Baalis (correctly) as the son of Amminadab mentioned in a bottle inscription from Tell Siran ("The Works of Amminadab," *BA* 37 [1974]: 13–19).

85. Bartlett, "Edom and the Fall of Jerusalem," *PEQ* 114 (1982): 18–19.

86. For confirmation of Jeremiah's historical and geographical descriptions of Jewish settlement in Egypt see Eliezer D. Oren, "Migdol: A New Fortress on the Edge of the Eastern Nile Delta," *BASOR* 256 (1984): 31–32.

ish Diaspora that had settled throughout the length of Egypt. They had largely embraced the Egyptian way of life, including the religious systems, and so had denied their identity and role as children of the covenant. For this they would suffer the chastisement of the Lord as their ancestors had before them. The Jewish community of Egypt would be destroyed except for a remnant that would return to their homeland (44:1–14).

Again the word of warning fell on deaf ears. Rather than turn to the Lord the Jews of Egypt vowed to continue their pagan ways and to trust the gods of Egypt for blessing and protection (44:15–19). In resignation Jeremiah could only reaffirm his message of divine judgment and deliver the word that Egypt would suffer the wrath of God for her sins. Hophra (= Apries), who was then reigning (589–570), would be given over to his enemies, and thus the pagan shelter in which the disobedient Jews of Egypt sought security would come crashing to the ground (44:30).

Jeremiah's history ends at this point (ca. 585), except for his note concerning the release of Jehoiachin from Babylonian incarceration in 562. In the absence of documentation to the contrary, it is likely that Jeremiah spent his remaining days in Egypt, living among and ministering to the exilic community there. Why he failed to record events after 585 cannot be known, of course. It is certain that he kept in touch with Jewish life throughout the world, however, as his reference to the release of Jehoiachin attests.

13 The Exile and the First Return

An Introductory Overview

The Course of the Deportations

The first submission of Jerusalem to the Babylonians in 605 B.C. ushered in the period described by Jeremiah as the seventy-year captivity, a period that began in that year and ended with the overthrow of Babylon in 539.[1] Those long years in which the élite of Judean social

1. John Bright, *Jeremiah*, Anchor Bible (Garden City, N.Y.: Doubleday, 1965), pp. 160–61. This is obviously a round number since the captivity was only sixty-six

469

and religious life were absent from the homeland are more popularly called the exile in modern literature, a singularly appropriate term since it not only suggests the forced removal of the Jewish population to Babylon, but also poignantly communicates the absence of Yahweh as well. The real tragedy of the exile was not the removal of the people nor even the utter destruction of the city and temple. It was the departure of their God from their midst, an absence symbolized in one of Ezekiel's visions by the movement of the Shekinah from the temple to the summit of the Mount of Olives (Ezek. 11:23). In a certain sense, therefore, the end of the Jewish captivity in 539–538 was not synonymous with the end of the exile, for Yahweh did not return at that time to inhabit a new temple. Rather, the prophets predicted that he would return only in the eschatological age when Messiah himself will be the glory of the Lord (e.g., Hag. 2:7–9).

The first phase of Judah's exile was approximately coincident with the accession of Nebuchadnezzar (605–562) to the throne of Babylon. The young prince, having engaged the Egyptians in battle at Carchemish in 605 and having defeated them there, was, by the untimely death of his father, deflected from his further objective of removing them from Palestine. He did succeed, however, in sacking Jerusalem and in taking Jewish prisoners back to his capital.[2] He left Jehoiakim as king of Judah, a move that proved unwise, for Jehoiakim rebelled against Babylonian overlordship and Nebuchadnezzar found it necessary to return in about 601. He returned again in 597, after Jehoiachin, son of Jehoiakim, came to the throne. Nebuchadnezzar sent the young king into exile where he remained until his death. Meanwhile, Nebuchadnezzar placed Zedekiah, brother of Jehoiakim, on the throne. This arrangement, too, proved to be politically unsound because of Zedekiah's refractoriness, so Nebuchadnezzar came once more, this time utterly demolishing Jerusalem and the temple and carrying the upper strata of Israelite society into exile (586).

Life in the Diaspora

This state of affairs lasted until the first return of exiles shortly after Cyrus's decree of liberation in 538.[3] The exile period, then, was in the

years in fact, but the figure is close enough for Daniel to use it (Dan. 9:1–2). The reference to seventy years in Zechariah 1:12 and 7:5 applies to a different period, that between the destruction of the temple (586) and its rebuilding (515). See David L. Petersen, *Haggai and Zechariah 1–8* (Philadelphia: Westminster, 1984), p. 149; Petersen, however, prefers the dates 590–520.

2. The silence of the Babylonian records concerning a siege of Jerusalem in 605 (see Dan. 1:1) is not sufficient to prove it did not occur. See D. J. Wiseman, "Some Historical Problems in the Book of Daniel," in *Notes on Some Problems in the Book of Daniel*, ed. D. J. Wiseman et al. (London: Tyndale, 1965), p. 18.

3. For the conquest of Babylon and the events leading up to it see A. T. Olmstead, *History of the Persian Empire* (Chicago: University of Chicago Press, 1948), pp. 49–58.

main from 586 to 538. As to conditions in Palestine during this time, little is known from either biblical or extrabiblical sources, though the evidence indicates a rather pessimistic situation overall.[4] Those Jewish exiles who, either before or during the deportations of Nebuchadnezzar, had gone to Egypt appear to have fared much better, though, again, our sources are meager—they are almost completely confined to one site, Elephantine.[5]

Concerning Jewish life in Babylon we are, however, much better informed. The biblical literature offers hints here and there that life on the whole was pleasant and that the people adjusted remarkably well to their new locale.[6] This judgment is confirmed by the few cuneiform records which testify to Jewish life.[7] Yehezkel Kaufmann argues that there is no evidence of anti-Semitism among the Babylonians and that, in fact, the Jews frequently enjoyed economic well-being and even rose to high political office.[8]

In any case it is clear that by the time of the decree of Cyrus most of the exiled Jews were of a generation that had never known the motherland firsthand. That is, they had been born in exile; and though they thought and dreamed of Jerusalem, they were very much people of Babylon. The older generation and the idealists among them longed

---

4. See William F. Albright, *The Biblical Period from Abraham to Ezra* (New York: Harper, 1963), pp. 84–87. For suggestions as to political organization see Sean E. McEvenue, "The Political Structure in Judah from Cyrus to Nehemiah," *CBQ* 43 (1981): 353–64.

5. Bezalel Porten, *Archives from Elephantine: The Life of an Ancient Jewish Military Colony* (Berkeley: University of California Press, 1968). For settlements elsewhere in Egypt see Eliezer D. Oren, "Migdol: A New Fortress on the Edge of the Eastern Nile Delta," *BASOR* 256 (1984): 35–56.

6. For example, Jeremiah 29:4–7; Ezekiel 33:30–32. For a contrary view see J. M. Wilkie, "Nabonidus and the Later Jewish Exiles," *JTS* 2 (1951): 36–44.

7. These consist of the Murashu documents and other materials discussed in Michael D. Coogan, "Life in the Diaspora: Jews at Nippur in the Fifth Century B.C.," *BA* 37 (1974): 6–12. These materials were originally published by Hermann V. Hilprecht and Albert T. Clay, *Business Documents of Murashu Sons of Nippur Dated in the Reign of Artaxerxes I (464–424 B.C.)*, Babylonian Expedition 9 (Philadelphia: University of Pennsylvania, 1898).

8. Yehezkel Kaufmann, *History of the Religion of Israel*, vol. 4, chs. 1–2, *The Babylonian Captivity and Deutero-Isaiah* (New York: Union of American Hebrew Congregations, 1970), pp. 9–11; see also Julian Morgenstern, "The Message of Deutero-Isaiah in Its Sequential Unfolding," *HUCA* 29 (1958): 5–6. Evidence of even preferential treatment of the Jews is seen in the case of Jehoiachin, who was put on a royal pension by Evil-Merodach; see William F. Albright, "King Jehoiachin in Exile," in *The Biblical Archaeologist Reader*, ed. David Noel Freedman and G. Ernest Wright (Garden City, N.Y.: Doubleday, 1961), vol. 1, pp. 106–7. Coogan, "Life in the Diaspora," *BA* 37 (1974): 9–10, suggests that there is "no hint of discrimination or of restriction on religious or ethnic grounds. Jews are engaged in the same types of contractual relationships, at the same interest rates, as their non-Jewish contemporaries at Nippur." Though the circumstances Coogan describes are a century later than the exile proper, there is no reason to feel that there were appreciable differences in treatment in the sixth century.

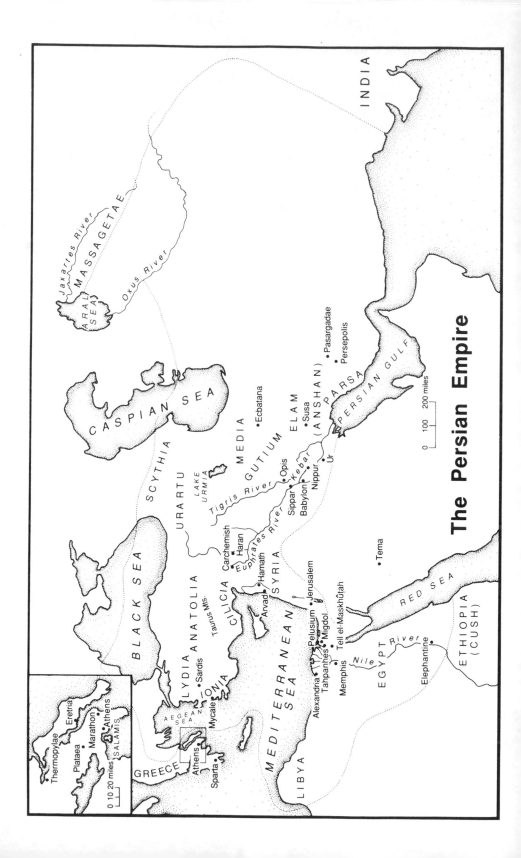

The Persian Empire

INDIA

MASSAGETAE

Jaxartes River

Oxus River

ARAL SEA

CASPIAN SEA

SCYTHIA

URARTU

Pasargadae
Persepolis

PARSA (ANSHAN)

PERSIAN GULF

0   100   200 miles

Ecbatana

MEDIA

GUTIUM

ELAM

Susa

LAKE URMIA

Tigris River

Opis
Sippar *Kebar*
Babylon
Nippur
Ur

BLACK SEA

Carchemish
Haran

Euphrates River

ANATOLIA

LYDIA

Sardis

Taurus Mts.

CILICIA

Hamath

SYRIA

Arvad

Jerusalem

Tema

RED SEA

ETHIOPIA (CUSH)

Pelusium
Migdol
Alexandria
Tahpanhes
Memphis
Tell el-Maskhūtah

EGYPT

Nile River

Elephantine

MEDITERRANEAN SEA

LIBYA

IONIA

Mycale

AEGEAN SEA

Athens
Sparta

GREECE

Thermopylae
Eretria
Plataea   Marathon   Athens
SALAMIS

0 10 20 miles

for home, to be sure, but it is a striking fact that Sheshbazzar, Zerubbabel, and the other leaders of the first return apparently were unable to recruit a majority of the Jews to accompany them back to Judah. This, of course, is understandable given the relatively hospitable way of life in Babylon and the grim prospects of beginning life again in a land of death and ashes. But the real point to be made here is the adaptability, the assimilability of the people by and large. Like countless other refugee or displaced peoples before and after them, they demonstrated the flexibility of the human psyche by not only remaining in the land, but allowing the land to penetrate and remain in them.

To argue that the Jews, as committed as they were (and are) to community and tradition, could live under the relatively favorable conditions of Babylonian exile and not absorb them in large measure is naively to assume a stubborn tenacity or rigid isolationism alien to what little is known about Judah in exile. The Jews, ever an adaptable and yet cohesive people, have historically demonstrated a desire and an ability to be good citizens of whatever land they inhabit. This extends to military service, education, culture, and, not least, language. It is unreasonable as well as contrary to the evidence to assume that the Jews of Babylonian exile were isolated by either coercion or choice, physically or intellectually. They imbibed deeply of the society in which they lived and yet retained the cherished faith, life, and traditions of their ancestors.[9] Most particularly the prophets Isaiah and Ezekiel reveal an acute awareness of the two—the ancient ways of their ancestors and a new world in which they participated and whose images, metaphors, and whole pattern of life they could bend to their holy purposes.[10] They spoke to a people who were immersed in the culture of their time and place. How better to communicate the eternal purposes of God for his people as well as for Babylon than in the idiom with which they had become so intimately familiar? Should we, indeed, expect anything less of the prophets than that they were men of their times who spoke to and about their community in words and language the people could understand? The language certainly was Hebrew throughout, but it was Hebrew everywhere imbued with lexical and literary nuances whose source cannot be doubted—Babylonia and her rich inventory of cultural and religious expression.

9. Arthur J. Zuckerman, "The Coincidence of Centers of Jewry with Centers of Western Civilization," in *Shiv'im: Essays and Studies in Honor of Ira Eisenstein*, ed. Ronald A. Brauner (New York: Ktav, 1977), pp. 99–116.

10. Ezekiel's awareness of Babylon came, of course, from his being an eyewitness and actual participant, while Isaiah prophesied of such things, especially in chapters 40–55; see Eugene H. Merrill, "The Language and Literary Characteristics of Isaiah 40–55 as Anti-Babylonian Polemic," Ph.D. diss., Columbia University, 1984.

The Return from Exile

In God's time the exile ended and a return was undertaken, albeit
not without difficulty. Nebuchadnezzar had died in 562, an event that
precipitated the rapid demise of the Neo-Babylonian Empire and paved
the way for its replacement by Cyrus and the Persians. Nebuchadnezzar's son and successor, the ineffectual Evil-Merodach (562–560),[11] is
known primarily as the ruler who released Jehoiachin of Judah from
confinement and provided him with a royal pension until his death.
Next to rule was Neriglissar (560–556), brother-in-law of Evil-Merodach, who did nothing to forestall the collapse of the empire, nor did
his ill-fated son Labaši-Marduk. The latter was murdered by forces
determined to reduce the power of the god Marduk. They in turn
seated Nabonidus (555–539) on the throne.[12] His devotion to the moon
god Sin, whose cult centers were at Ur and Haran, alienated him from
both the clergy and populace of Babylon where Marduk worship was
centralized. And, of course, Marduk himself was displeased, as various
inscriptions inform us, and began to seek a means of dispossessing
Nabonidus and finding a "shepherd" who more faithfully would tend
the Babylonian flock.[13]

Such a shepherd was Cyrus of Anshan, who, having subdued the
Medes and all other rivals,[14] had created the most powerful political
and military force the world had seen up to that time. After a succession of lightninglike strokes against enemies far and near Cyrus was
able, in 539, to encircle and take Babylon with virtually no resistance.
Nabonidus had made a habit of absenting himself from the capital;
he did so even (or especially) at New Year's when it was customary
for the king to participate as a principal in traditional rites. These
absences were so frequent and long-lasting that *de facto* control was

11. The authoritative treatment of his reign is Ronald H. Sack, *Amel-Marduk,
562–560 B.C.: A Study Based on Cuneiform, Old Testament, Greek, Latin and Rabbinical
Sources* (Neukirchen-Vluyn: Butzon und Bercker Kevelaer, 1972).

12. This series of events is documented in Sidney Smith, *Babylonian Historical
Texts Relating to the Capture and Downfall of Babylon* (London: Methuen, 1924). See
also Raymond P. Dougherty, *Nabonidus and Belshazzar*, Yale Oriental Series 15 (New
Haven: Yale University Press, 1929); Olmstead, *History*, pp. 34–38.

13. A propaganda piece (the so-called Persian Verse Account of Nabonidus) which
details the sins of Nabonidus and rehearses Cyrus's appointment by Marduk may be
found in Smith, *Babylonian Historical Texts*, pp. 82–97; and in A. Leo Oppenheim,
"Babylonian and Assyrian Historical Texts," in James B. Pritchard, *Ancient Near Eastern Texts Relating to the Old Testament*, 2d ed. (Princeton: Princeton University Press,
1955), pp. 312–15. The famous Cylinder of Cyrus also makes this point (pp. 315–16).
For the transliteration of the text see F. H. Weissbach, *Die Keilinschriften der Achä-
meniden*, Vorderasiatische Bibliothek 3 (Leipzig: J. C. Hinrichs, 1911), pp. 2–7.

14. Stephen Langdon, *Die neubabylonischen Königsinschriften*, Vorderasiatische
Bibliothek 4 (Leipzig: J. C. Hinrichs, 1912), pp. 252–61, n. 6 (Nabon), esp. 1.29–35.

placed in the hands of his son Belshazzar. It was this unfortunate vice-regent who presided over the collapse of his city and nation upon the arrival of Gubaru, the Persian commander and governor of Gutium. Belshazzar apparently died during or shortly after this conflict,[15] while Nabonidus was captured and immediately thereafter paroled. Some two weeks later Cyrus himself triumphantly marched into the city to celebrate the final step in his attainment of virtually universal hegemony.[16]

Cyrus had the enlightened and beneficent policy of permitting all captive peoples to return to their homes. The Jews, of course, were included and saw in this decree the blessing of God in fulfilling his prophetic word. The deliverance was to them no less meaningful and miraculous than was the exodus from Egypt under Moses; indeed, the language of the prophets, for example, in Isaiah 40–66, is filled with motifs reminiscent of the exodus. The majority of the exilic community may have settled in comfortably in Babylon, but those with an eye to the eternal purposes of God saw in the captivity a judgment and in the prospects of return a sure sign that God was not through with his people; they had a redemptive role yet to play.

The World Situation During the Exile

The Decline and Fall of Babylonia

Within a year of the conquest of Jerusalem Nebuchadnezzar laid siege to the island portion of Tyre, having already brought Sidon, Arvad, and the mainland portion of Tyre under his control.[17] The siege lasted for thirteen years, but even after the island finally surrendered in about 573, the Babylonians had little profit to show for their efforts. As a kind of compensation Nebuchadnezzar moved south into Egypt in 568 and laid waste a great part of the Nile valley. Only the western Delta seems to have emerged unscathed.[18]

The remaining years of Nebuchadnezzar's life are shrouded in mystery as far as the extrabiblical sources are concerned. It is clear that he died in 562 and was succeeded by his son Evil-Merodach. As we have noted, this king was responsible for the release of Jehoiachin from imprisonment. Otherwise the record of his reign is cast in a rather

15. Dougherty, *Nabonidus and Belshazzar*, pp. 174–75.

16. Olmstead, *History*, pp. 38–51.

17. H. Jacob Katzenstein, *The History of Tyre* (Jerusalem: Schocken Institute for Jewish Research, 1973), pp. 330–31.

18. Ibid., pp. 338–39.

negative light, and in 560 he was assassinated by Neriglissar, his sister's husband.

Neriglissar managed to undertake at least one major campaign across the Taurus mountain range, an action taken perhaps to counteract a Median advance into central Anatolia, and also completed some impressive building projects. His tenure was brief, however (560–556). His young son Labaši–Marduk, who succeeded him, had reigned only one month when he was beaten to death.

The role that Nabonidus played in the death of Labaši-Marduk is not clear, but in any event he found himself on Babylon's throne in succession to the dynasty of Nabopolassar, which had lasted for exactly seventy years.[19] Nabonidus was the son of a nobleman named Nabu-balatṣu-iqbi and Adda-guppi, a high priestess of the moon god. This influential cultic leader, who lived to the great age of over one hundred, made a profound impact on the religious life of her son and for that reason played a crucial role in the eventual fall of Babylon itself.[20]

If Nabonidus is the same as a high official of that name in Nebuchadnezzar's eighth year (597), he himself must have been advanced in years by 555.[21] This is entirely possible in light of the fact that his mother, who died in 547, was born in 650.[22] Some scholars also equate Nabonidus with Labynetus, who mediated a dispute between the Lydians and Medes in 585.[23]

Nabonidus, influenced by his mother, was a pious devotee of the moon god Sin. As long as he was a mere citizen, even if an important one, this caused no particular difficulty. When he became king of Babylonia, however, the situation radically changed, for Babylon was a city dedicated to the worship of Marduk, chief deity of the Babylonian pantheon. At once, therefore, a conflict arose that would spell the disastrous ruin not only of Nabonidus but of the entire Babylonian Empire.

A crisis was not long in coming, for in his very accession year Nabonidus claimed to have had a dream in which Marduk told him to rebuild the decrepit temple of Sin, the so-called E-ḫul-ḫul.[24] Clearly

19. Olmstead, *History*, pp. 35–36.
20. Peter R. Ackroyd, *Exile and Restoration* (Philadelphia: Westminster, 1968), pp. 19–20.
21. Dougherty, *Nabonidus and Belshazzar*, p. 31.
22. Albert Kirk Grayson, *Assyrian and Babylonian Chronicles* (Locust Valley, N.Y.: J. J. Augustin, 1975), p. 107, Nabonidus Chronicle 2.13–14; see also Oppenheim, "Historical Texts," in Pritchard, *Ancient Near Eastern Texts*, pp. 311–12, for the so-called Family of Nabonidus text, which traces her life from the twenty-first year of Ashurbanipal through the ninth of Nabonidus.
23. D. J. Wiseman, *Chronicles of Chaldaean Kings (626–556 B.C.) in the British Museum* (London: Trustees of the British Museum, 1961), p. 39.
24. Oppenheim, "Historical Texts," in Pritchard, *Ancient Near Eastern Texts*, p. 310.

this was an attempt by the new king to justify the introduction of the worship of Sin into the religious jurisdiction of Marduk and to allay the suspicions of both priests and people as to its impropriety.

In his first full year, 555, Nabonidus, having at least temporarily pacified his critics, undertook his first campaign, a move to the northwest which resulted in the conquest of Hamath and Haran. In his third year he was again in Syria and succeeded in taking other cities in that region. Of particular interest to him was Haran, which, along with the ancient city of Ur, was a center of the worship of Sin. He had previously forged a treaty with Cyrus against the Medes, who were then in possession of Haran. The Medes had thereupon vacated the city to engage the Persians in battle, thus providing Nabonidus an opportunity to move in and claim it for himself.[25]

At once Nabonidus commenced the restoration of Haran as a cult center. He erected a great statue of the moon god and rebuilt the E-ḫul-ḫul temple. This only exacerbated the suspicions and hostilities of the Babylonian clergy, for it had become apparent to them that Nabonidus was not attempting just to elevate Sin to a higher rank, but was intent on substituting him for Marduk altogether.[26] The situation became so uncomfortable for Nabonidus that in his sixth year (550) he went into a ten year self imposed exile at Tema, the great oasis of the Syro-Arabian desert east of the Red Sea.[27]

Nabonidus did not abdicate by any means, however, but left the everyday affairs of government in the hands of his son Bel-šar-uṣur (= Belshazzar). Documentation is limited for the period as a whole.[28] It is clear, however, that Nabonidus occupied himself in military activity in his years away from Babylon, particularly against Arabian tribes which were becoming increasingly visible and troublesome. But he also cultivated an interest in antiquities, collecting and restoring objets d'art and rebuilding fallen temples and other ancient structures.[29] As for Belshazzar, virtually nothing is known of him until that

---

25. Sidney Smith, *Isaiah, Chapters XL–LV* (London: Oxford University Press, 1944), p. 33.

26. This is spelled out in the so-called Persian Verse Account of Nabonidus. See Smith, *Babylonian Historical Texts*, p. 88, Persian Verse Account 2.10–17; Oppenheim, "Historical Texts," in Pritchard, *Ancient Near Eastern Texts*, pp. 312–15.

27. This may be assumed from the fact that while silent on the matter for the sixth year, the Nabonidus Chronicle places him in Tema in his seventh year (549). See Grayson, *Assyrian and Babylonian Chronicles*, p. 106, Nabonidus Chronicle 2.5.

28. See, however, Dougherty, *Nabonidus and Belshazzar*, pp. 96–97, 133; Gerhard F. Hasel, "The Book of Daniel: Evidences Relating to Persons and Chronology," *AUSS* 19 (1981): 42–45; A. R. Millard, "Daniel 1–6 and History," *EQ* 49 (1977): 71–72.

29. William L. Reed, "Nabonidus, Babylonian Reformer or Renegade?" *LexTQ* 12 (1977): 24.

fateful night in 539 when he read the handwriting on the wall which predicted his imminent downfall.

While Nabonidus spent ten years in Tema, Cyrus was busily occupied in amassing an empire. Soon all that was left to incorporate into his vast realm was Babylon, and so he set his sights upon that prize. In the fall of 539 he took the city of Opis on the Tigris. A few days later, on October 10, he took Sippar without opposition. Nabonidus meanwhile had returned to Babylon just in time to witness the collapse of his glorious city and its capture, without resistance, by Gubaru, governor of Gutium and commander of the Persian army. This took place on October 12; two weeks later, on October 29, 539, Cyrus himself entered the city in peace. He forbade destruction, appointed Gubaru governor, and left the religious and civil administration of Babylon unchanged.[30]

The Origins of the Persian Empire

Cyrus traced his roots back to both the Medes and the Persians. Both were descendants of Aryan tribal folk who had moved south to the Urartian plateau from Russia and who, by 1000 B.C., had settled in the vicinity of Lake Urmia in what is now extreme northwestern Iran. Gradually the Medes moved east and occupied west Iran south of the Caspian Sea, while the Persians migrated far to the southeast and settled in southwest Iran toward the Persian Gulf.[31]

Table 9   **The Persian Kings**

Cyrus II	559–530
Cambyses II	530–522
Gaumata	522
Darius Hystaspes	522–486
Xerxes	486–465
Artaxerxes I	464–424
Darius II	423–404
Artaxerxes II	404–358

The royal line of which Cyrus was a part was founded by Achaemenes, who ruled from about 700 to 675.[32] It was he who gave his name to the Achaemenid dynasty. His son Teispes (675–640) extended the boundaries of Parsa (Persia) as far south as Pasargadae. Because his realm was now so greatly stretched out, Teispes divided it between

30. Grayson, *Assyrian and Babylonian Chronicles*, pp. 109–11, Nabonidus Chronicle 3.12–28.

31. Roman Ghirshman, *Iran* (Hammondsworth: Penguin, 1954), pp. 90–96.

32. For the following sketch down to Cyrus II see Ghirshman, *Iran*, pp. 95–126.

his two sons, Ariaramnes in the south and Cyrus I in the north. He also regained his independence from the Medes, who had made Parsa a vassal state in about 670.

The line of Ariaramnes (640–615) included Arsames, Hystaspes, and Darius Hystaspes, while that of Cyrus I (640–600) produced Cambyses I (600–559) and Cyrus II (559–530), the Cyrus who created the empire. Cambyses, who was placed over Persia after Persia once more became a Median province, married the daughter of the Median king Astyages. Cyrus II, being the offspring of that marriage, united in himself the royal houses of Media and Persia.

The Median contemporary of the Persian Achaemenes was Deioces, about whom little is known. Phraortes (675–653) his son made Parsa a vassal, as we saw, but his death in battle against the Assyrians in 653 helped Teispes regain independence. The Median throne remained vacant from 653 to 625 because of Scythian domination of northwest Iran, but in time Cyaxares (625–585) overthrew the Scythians and the Assyrians, establishing Median control over all of northern Mesopotamia and Iran. He also reduced Persia to submission, setting up Cambyses as governor over that province. Cyaxares was succeeded by his son Astyages (585–550), whose daughter would be the mother of the great Cyrus II.

Cyrus himself was a vassal of his grandfather, ruling a region known as Anshan.[33] He did take the liberty of locating his capital at Pasargadae and began the process of unifying several Persian tribes which hitherto had resisted consolidation. He also made an alliance with Nabonidus of Babylonia, an arrangement which was tantamount to rebelling against Astyages since the Babylonians now were Media's bitter foes. Summoned to the imperial capital at Ecbatana, Cyrus refused to go. Astyages therefore launched an attack upon his willful grandson, but the old king's army defected. In a masterful stroke Cyrus marched against Ecbatana, took Astyages prisoner, and made Media itself a Persian province.

Cyrus at once laid claim to all Median territories, a claim which led to immediate confrontation with Lydia. A powerful kingdom on the Aegean Sea in western Asia Minor, Lydia was then under the leadership of Croesus, a monarch of almost legendary status in Greek classical literature. Croesus anticipated the world-conquering aspirations of the far-famed Persian and so marched east to prevent his arrival in the Hellenic sphere of influence. Cyrus forced him back to his capital Sardis, however, and there defeated him (547). Cyrus then formed Croesus's kingdom into a new Persian satrapy, Saparda, and estab-

---

33. Olmstead, *History*, pp. 34–51; Smith, *Isaiah*, pp. 35–48.

lished friendly ties with the Greeks of the region, who would later serve him as allies and mercenaries.

Meanwhile Babylonia, because of the absence of Nabonidus in Tema, began to deteriorate internally and externally under the incompetent Belshazzar. Many Babylonian provinces such as Elam fell away to Persia, and in 539 Cyrus sent an army under his general Gubaru to invest Babylon itself.[34] The city fell without a struggle, and Cyrus immediately made it the capital of yet another Persian satrapy, Babirus, which included Syria, Phoenicia, and Palestine within its jurisdiction.

One reason for the ready capitulation of Babylon to Cyrus was the bitter antagonism that the Babylonians felt toward Nabonidus and his son for their anti-Marduk religious posture. Cyrus had already gained a reputation as an enlightened ruler who was extremely lenient and eclectic in his viewpoint. He maintained the status quo in lands which fell to his control, at least as much as he could without jeopardizing his sovereignty. One feature of his policy was to recognize the claims of native gods over their followers and to make no effort to supplant them with gods of his own. In fact, he came to Babylon at the express wishes of Marduk himself, since Marduk had become angry at Nabonidus's irreverence and wished to replace him with another king, a shepherd who would more faithfully tend Marduk's human flock. That shepherd, of course, was Cyrus.

Cyrus's enlightened policy also had direct bearing on the plight of the exilic Jewish community in Babylonia, for Cyrus accorded to Yahweh, their God, the same deference he paid to Marduk and all other deities. A logical outgrowth of this policy was his decree that the Jews be allowed to return to their homeland. Only in a restored temple in Jerusalem could Yahweh function effectively as the God of Judah. And so, in eager solicitation of the favor of Yahweh, Cyrus repatriated the Jewish people and provided them with the authorization and wherewithal to rebuild their city and temple as a fitting place for their God.

Following this decree in 538 Cyrus continued to maintain and even expand his magnificent empire. He died in 530 in combat against the Massagetae in the Jaxartes River valley in central Asia.

---

34. The Nabonidus Chronicle states that on the sixteenth day of Tashritu "Ugbaru, governor of the Guti, and the army of Cyrus entered Babylon without a battle" (3.15–16). It goes on to relate that "Gubaru, his district officer, appointed the district officers in Babylon" (3.20) and that "on the night of the eleventh of the month Marchesvan Ugbaru died" (3.22). William H. Shea argues (correctly in our opinion) that Ugbaru and Gubaru are one and the same and that both are to be distinguished from the Gubaru who was made satrap by Cyrus some time later ("Darius the Mede: An Update," *AUSS* 20 [1982]: 245).

The Jewish People During the Exile

In Judah

In the midst of these earthshaking events in the world of nations God's elect people continued to maintain their identity though no longer as one nation in one place. The miserable remnant that had evaded the three deportations to Babylon in 605, 597, and 586 as well as the flight to Egypt under Johanan numbered perhaps no more than twenty thousand souls.[35] With Jerusalem and all the major towns in ruins, these peasants eked out a subsistence as small farmers and raisers of livestock. Some idea of their wretched lot may be gathered from the Lamentations of Jeremiah, which, though poetic, capture very realistically what life must have been like not only for the prophet but for the average citizen (see also Ezek. 33:21–29).

One must not conclude, however, that there was no sense of community in Judah anymore.[36] There surely were efforts to rebuild not only houses and towns but the infrastructures of social life. And within the provincial structures imposed upon the land by the Babylonians there emerged some kind of local government. Moreover, the cult did not disappear, although with the destruction of the temple it must have taken a different shape from that known previously. Very likely something akin to the synagogues which arose elsewhere in the later Diaspora must have arisen in Judah to meet the needs of the people for corporate worship and study of Torah.[37] On the whole, however, the biblical texts are silent concerning the nature and activities of the nonexilic community.

In Babylon

Ironically, though Judah remained the geographical locus of the covenant race, Babylon became its historical and intellectual home. And this was true not only in the years of the exile per se, but for centuries to come. In fact, in the first several centuries of the Christian Era, Babylon was the center of a thriving religious community that

35. Albright, *Biblical Period*, p. 87.
36. A good assessment of the situation in Judah in exilic times may be found in Ackroyd, *Exile and Restoration*, pp. 20–31.
37. For various suggestions see Solomon Zeitlin, "The Origin of the Synagogue," in *The Synagogue: Studies in Origins, Archaeology, and Architecture*, ed. Joseph Gutmann (New York: Ktav, 1975), pp. 14–26; Martin Noth, "The Jerusalem Catastrophe of 587 B.C. and Its Significance for Israel," in *The Laws in the Pentateuch and Other Essays* (Edinburgh: Oliver and Boyd, 1966), pp. 263–64; Peter R. Ackroyd, *Israel Under Babylon and Persia* (London: Oxford University Press, 1970), pp. 27–28.

had generated its own Jewish tradition separate from Jerusalem and Alexandria. There devout scribes and scholars created a Babylonian Talmud, and a Babylonian Masoretic school produced its own families of biblical texts and manuscripts.[38]

This is not particularly surprising, for the exiles, though they must not have been numerous, were the very cream of Jewish political, intellectual, and religious life. They began to live in their own ghettoes. Once it was evident that they would be there for a long time they began to settle down, purchase property, and engage in business. There is evidence that some of them attempted resistance early on, but they eventually came to see that peaceful coexistence was the only practical course.[39] In fact they became so comfortable that the majority did not return to Judah once the way had been cleared by the decree of Cyrus.

The view of Ezekiel

The best insight into exilic life in Babylonia is provided by the prophet Ezekiel, who spent all his years of public ministry there. Like Jeremiah, Ezekiel was a priest, as is clear from his express testimony (1:3) and his great interest in matters of the cult. His writings are particularly helpful to our investigation because they are for the most part in chronological order and are unusually replete with chronological and historical data.[40]

The prophet begins his account by establishing the setting—he was with the exiles by the Kebar River in the thirtieth year. The Kebar is the *nār kabari* mentioned in Babylonian records, a canal that forms an extension of the Euphrates River.[41] By "thirtieth year" Ezekiel most likely is referring to his own thirtieth year.[42] This was 593 B.C., the fifth year of the exile of Jehoiachin, as the prophet himself states (1:2). His habit of dating events in terms of the exile of Jehoiachin substantiates our point (p. 452) that Jehoiachin, not Zedekiah, was considered the true Davidic heir.[43]

38. Shmuel Safrai, "The Era of the Mishnah and Talmud (70–640)," in *A History of the Jewish People*, ed. Haim H. Ben-Sasson (Cambridge: Harvard University Press, 1976), pp. 373–82. For the Babylonian exile as a setting for Jewish florescence, see D. Winton Thomas, "The Sixth Century B.C.: A Creative Epoch in the History of Israel," *JSS* 6 (1961): 33–46.

39. John Bright, *A History of Israel*, 3d ed. (Philadelphia: Westminster, 1981), p. 346; William H. Shea, "Daniel 3: Extra-Biblical Texts and the Convocation on the Plain of Dura," *AUSS* 20 (1982): 30–32.

40. For a thorough review of all the dates see K. S. Freedy and Donald B. Redford, "The Dates in Ezekiel in Relation to Biblical, Babylonian and Egyptian Sources," *JAOS* 90 (1970): 462–85.

41. It is now known as the *šaṭṭ en-nîl*; see Walther Zimmerli, *Ezekiel: A Commentary on the Book of the Prophet Ezekiel* (Philadelphia: Fortress, 1979), vol. 1, p. 112.

42. Walther Eichrodt, *Ezekiel* (Philadelphia: Westminster, 1970), p. 52.

43. Zimmerli, *Ezekiel*, vol. 1, pp. 114–15.

Ezekiel was commissioned by the Lord to minister to the exile community which lived near the Kebar, particularly to those in the settlement of Tel Abib (3:15). His message to the exiles had to do with the imminent destruction of Jerusalem. They undoubtedly thought that the holy city would survive even though they had been carried away from it. They had to be made to understand, however, that Jerusalem was invincible only as long as God's people were true to him. As matters stood, they had failed to remain loyal; in fact, the situation back in Jerusalem was worse than it had ever been before. The result would be imminent and irremediable judgment. Through a series of graphic illustrations—drawing a picture of the city under siege (4:1–3), shaving his hair (5:1–4), and preparing chains of slavery (7:23–27)—Ezekiel proclaimed the impending doom of Zion.

In the sixth year, 592, Ezekiel was sitting in his own house with the council of Jewish elders when the Lord suddenly took him in vision to Jerusalem where he witnessed a series of abominable religious perversions perpetrated by the leaders of Judah in the holy temple itself (ch. 8). The result was the departure of the cherubim and the glory of God from the temple and their suspension over the Mount of Olives. This signified that the annihilation of the city and temple was a foregone conclusion. But before he saw the divine glory depart, Ezekiel heard the same promise that all his prophetic forebears had heard: God's people might go into bitter captivity and bondage for their sin, but he would give them a new heart to love and serve him and would bring them back once again to their land. Like dry bones brought back to life, they would be rejuvenated and reunited, Israel with Judah, and David himself would be king over them (11:14–21; ch. 37).

The view of Daniel

Daniel is the second major source of information for the life of the exiles in Babylonia prior to Cyrus's decree. In fact, Daniel lived beyond that era and provides invaluable documentation for the Persian rule in Babylon under Darius the Mede and Cyrus. It is impossible here to enter the debate concerning the historicity of either Daniel or the events he describes.[44] All that need be said is that his account has not been shown to be contrary to what is known from extrabiblical texts

44. See, for example, Arthur J. Ferch, "The Book of Daniel and the 'Maccabean Thesis,'" *AUSS* 21 (1983): 129–41; John Goldingay, "The Book of Daniel: Three Issues," *Themelios* 2 (1977): 45–49; Gerhard F. Hasel, "The Book of Daniel and Matters of Language: Evidences Relating to Names, Words, and the Aramaic Language," *AUSS* 19 (1981): 211–25; Millard, "Daniel 1–6 and History," *EQ* 49 (1977): 67–73; Gordon J. Wenham, "Daniel: The Basic Issues," *Themelios* 2 (1977): 49–52; Edwin M. Yamauchi, "Daniel and Contacts Between the Aegean and the Near East Before Alexander," *EQ* 53 (1981): 37–47.

and that his rhetoric and language are eminently at home in the sixth century, the era in which the book purports to have been written. It is only on the most subjective and circular lines of evidence that the man and his writing have been denied historicity.

According to his own account Daniel was among the nobility taken prisoner by Nebuchadnezzar in the course of his first conquest of Jerusalem (605). Soon after arriving in Babylon Daniel and some of his young comrades were selected by Ashpenaz, a court official, to be trained in the arts and sciences of Babylonia. The apparent goal was to prepare them to be members of the diplomatic corps who could someday represent Babylonia's interests, perhaps in Palestine itself. They were apt students, but they refused to violate their own religious convictions in order to conform to Babylonian custom.

In Nebuchadnezzar's second year he had a dream which greatly disturbed him (Dan. 2). He then demanded of his diviners that they should reveal both the dream and its meaning under penalty of death. When none could do so, Daniel offered his good offices. Informing the king that he spoke only as the emissary of the true God, Daniel revealed not only the dream but its interpretation. Convinced that Daniel spoke truth, Nebuchadnezzar acknowledged the power of Yahweh and promoted Daniel and his three friends to positions of great authority in the province of Babylon. Though neither Daniel nor any of his fellows can be identified in the extrabiblical texts, there is abundant evidence that foreigners, including Jews, rose through the ranks of Babylonian government and occasionally reached the highest echelons.[45]

Some time later Nebuchadnezzar had another dream, which Daniel interpreted to mean that the king, because of his hubris in refusing to acknowledge the sovereignty of the Most High, would be reduced to a bestial existence: for seven years he would be insane and unable to rule (Dan. 4). At the end of the seven years he would be restored and would resume his regency. All things came to pass as the prophet predicted, and Nebuchadnezzar at last acknowledged that he was but a pawn in the hand of a heavenly King.

Skeptical scholars deny that Nebuchadnezzar ever suffered the malady described by Daniel, but their argument is extremely shaky.[46] Though, indeed, the king's insanity has yet to be corroborated by extrabiblical documentation, it is important to note that the Babylonian records are almost totally silent on those years when such a thing is most likely to have happened—the last decade of his life. Efforts to

45. Shea, "Daniel 3," *AUSS* 20 (1982): 46–47.
46. See, for example, Louis F. Hartman and Alexander A. Di Lella, *The Book of Daniel*, Anchor Bible (Garden City, N.Y.: Doubleday, 1978), pp. 178–79.

salvage some credibility for the story by suggesting that Daniel was referring to Nabonidus rather than Nebuchadnezzar[47] are totally unsatisfying, for not only do they vitiate the reliability of Daniel as source material, but the alleged insanity of Nabonidus bears little resemblance to the state of affairs recounted in Daniel.[48]

For reasons altogether unclear Daniel says nothing of the period between the reign of Nebuchadnezzar and that of Belshazzar. When next he takes up his pen, he recalls the momentous night in 539 when Belshazzar, in a drunken orgy, received a word from the God of heaven that the Medes and Persians were on their way to bring an end to his reign and seize his kingdom for themselves. Realizing perhaps the inevitability of his judgment Belshazzar, in perhaps his finest hour, honored the man who brought him the fateful message by making him third ruler in the kingdom. This implies that Nabonidus was first, his son Belshazzar second, and Daniel third.[49]

This arrangement was no sooner made than it came to a tragic end, for Nabonidus was taken prisoner by Gubaru, the Persian general, Belshazzar was slain, and Babylon became just another one of the satrapies of the Persian Empire. Daniel's references to "Darius the Mede" (Dan. 5:31; 6:1) and "Darius son of Xerxes" (Dan. 9:1) appear to be his way of describing this general Gubaru. It was he who "was made ruler over the Babylonian kingdom" by Cyrus (Dan. 9:1). This change in rulership over Babylon only enhanced Daniel's opportunities for statesmanship, for Cyrus soon saw in him an able administrator who had distinguished himself in Babylonian public service for over sixty years. Darius the Mede therefore appointed him to be one of three supervisors over the whole provincial system of the empire.[50] So capable was Daniel that Darius planned to elevate him to the very top of his government. But Daniel's peers, filled with envy, concocted a scheme which obliged the king to sentence Daniel to death. Daniel was delivered, however, and by that miracle caused Darius, like Nebuchadnezzar before him, to confess the superiority of Daniel's God.

47. Ackroyd, *Exile and Restoration*, p. 37.

48. Hasel, "The Book of Daniel," *AUSS* 19 (1981): 38–42.

49. William H. Shea, "Nabonidus, Belshazzar, and the Book of Daniel: An Update," *AUSS* 20 (1982): 133–49.

50. The appointment, though certainly issuing from Cyrus, was actually made by "Darius the Mede" (Dan. 5:31; 6:1; cf. 6:28). It seems best, without going into the debate here, to accept Shea's identification of Darius the Mede with Gubaru, governor of Gutium, who as the head of the Persian army conquered Babylon ("Darius the Mede," *AUSS* 20 [1982]: 234–47). For the view that Darius was the second Gubaru (cf. n. 34) see John C. Whitcomb, Jr., *Darius the Mede* (Philadelphia: Presbyterian and Reformed, 1963). For an identification with Cyrus himself see Wiseman, "Some Historical Problems," in *Notes on Some Problems*, pp. 9–16.

It was in the first year of "Darius the Mede" (i.e., 539) that Daniel came to understand that the seventy years of which Jeremiah had spoken were about to expire and that his compatriots would soon return to rebuild the temple, which still lay in ruins (Dan. 9:1–2). The decree of Cyrus was about to be issued, and thousands of Jews would return to Jerusalem to reestablish the covenant community on its sacred soil. Daniel quite rightly, however, saw the exile still in force as long as the temple remained unrestored. His prayer was that God should look with favor upon his desolate sanctuary (9:17) and cause his holy name to dwell there once again (9:19). The answer to that prayer came to pass in a remarkable way when Haggai and Zechariah inspired the people to build the dwelling-place of Yahweh once again.

But there was an even greater response to Daniel's fervent prayer. Building on the idea of the seventy years of exile, Yahweh promised that at the end of "seventy 'sevens' " ("seventy weeks of years," RSV) he would do something far more wonderful than rebuild his temple. He would send the Anointed One, the messianic Savior who would die for his people and thereby put an end to the ages-long opposition to the purposes of God (Dan. 9:24–27).[51]

In Egypt

The third main center of Jewish population following the collapse of Judah was Egypt. The land of the Nile had always been a favorite place of refuge for the people of Israel. Abraham had gone there in a time of famine, Joseph and later Jacob and his family settled there, and there Jeroboam sought and found asylum. This was because of Egypt's physical proximity to Palestine and also because of a certain sense of affinity which existed between the two peoples. Though Egypt, to be sure, had enslaved the Israelites and thereafter symbolized or typified bondage, she nonetheless was viewed with special favor by the Lord. Many of the eschatological promises of blessing for Israel include special benefits for Egypt as well (Isa. 19:24–25).

It is not surprising, then, that Israelite and Judean refugees fled to Egypt again and again in biblical times. Almost certainly they did so at the time of the conquest of Samaria by the Assyrians in 722, and Jeremiah reports that he himself participated in a move to Egypt after Jerusalem had fallen to Nebuchadnezzar. This contingent consisted of the principal military officers, members of the royal family, and Jews who had recently returned to Judah from neighboring lands following

51. J. Dwight Pentecost, "Daniel," in *The Bible Knowledge Commentary*, ed. John F. Walvoord and Roy B. Zuck (Wheaton, Ill.: Victor, 1985), vol. 1, pp. 1361–65.

the appointment of Gedaliah as governor (Jer. 43:4–7). Their immediate destination was Tahpanhes (Tell Dafanneh) in the eastern Delta
(Jer. 43:8), but they eventually settled also in Migdol (Tell el-Heir) in
the northeast Delta, and in Memphis. As early as Jeremiah's time they
filtered south to Upper Egypt, either creating new settlements there
or joining those already in existence (Jer. 44:1).

It is clear that this migration to Egypt was looked upon with disfavor by the Lord (Jer. 42:15–17), for it left the pitiful remnant in
Judah with only a very fragile base. Besides, the Jews already in Egypt
had begun to abandon Yahwistic faith and to worship the gods of their
adopted land. The result would be the judgment of the Lord upon
Egypt at the hand of Nebuchadnezzar, and with it would come the
decimation of the Jewish community that had settled there.

The Babylonian conquest came, indeed, and brought about the devastation prophesied by Jeremiah. But not all the Jews of Egypt perished, for at least one colony—that at Elephantine in Upper Egypt—
survived and in postexilic times became the center not only of Jewish
political life, but of a cult associated with a rival temple.[52] Even later
than that, in the fourth century Alexander encouraged the relocation
of thousands of Jews from Palestine to his new city of Alexandria.
Within a few generations that community became perhaps the most
vibrant and creative focus of Jewish life and thought in the entire
world.

The World Situation During the Period of Restoration

Lest we get too far ahead in our story, it is important now to examine the historical and cultural context in which the exilic com-
munities, particularly those of Babylonia, returned to the land of
promise and undertook the restoration predicted by all the prophets.
The biblical sources, particularly Ezra and Nehemiah, provide a rich
fund of information for the period from the decree of Cyrus (538) to
the governorship of Nehemiah (ca. 430), but even that information
must be fleshed out by a careful reconstruction of contemporary Persian history.

Cambyses II of Persia

In 530 Cyrus went to the Jaxartes River area in central Asia to put
down an impending infraction of his northeast border by the Massa-

---

52. Porten, *Archives from Elephantine*.

getae. He was mortally wounded in the conflict, however, and expired within three days. Cambyses his son, whom he had left in charge at home, brought his father's body back to Pasargadae for burial and then assumed the Achaemenid throne.

Cambyses II (530–522) had held important posts in the Persian government for many years and as early as 538 had been designated by Cyrus as his heir apparent.[53] At the time of his accession he was governor of the important district around Sippar, north of Babylon, and even bore the title "King of Babylon," indicating clearly the prestige he enjoyed. Upon taking the throne he sought to enhance that prestige and secure his succession by marrying his sisters and slaying his full brother Bardiya, a deed he concealed from the public.

The first major action of the new king was the invasion of Egypt, the only one of the four major pre-Persian kingdoms (Media, Lydia, Babylonia, Egypt) remaining to be conquered.[54] With Phoenician allies he attacked Amasis II (570–526) and followed up with a victory over Psamtik III (526–525) at Pelusium. After executing Psamtik, Cambyses marched south all the way to the Ethiopian border, annexing the Ethiopian territories lying nearby. He then organized all of Egypt into a satrapy called Mudraya, with Memphis as its capital. He named his kinsman Aryandes as satrap over this new jurisdiction and then headed back to Persia.

Cambyses had no sooner started out than he learned that a usurper claiming to be Bardiya, his murdered brother, had seized power. This impostor, probably either Smerdis or Gaumata, first gained a following in Babylon; on July 1, 522, he was acclaimed king throughout the entire empire. When Cambyses saw that all was lost, he committed suicide.

Darius Hystaspes of Persia

Gaumata's success, ironically, lay in the fact that Cambyses had concealed Bardiya's death and so had no way now to prove it. One may assume that Bardiya had achieved great popularity with certain elements that resented Cambyses' succession. Not everyone was fooled by Gaumata, however, so a plot was soon under way to remove the usurper and restore legitimate government to Persia. The leadership of this coup was in the hands of Darius Hystaspes, who, with six collaborators, assassinated Gaumata on September 29, 522, and placed himself in power.[55]

53. Olmstead, *History*, pp. 86–93, 107–8.
54. Ibid., pp. 88–92.
55. Ibid., pp. 107–16.

This coup was not a particularly popular move, for Darius, though of royal blood by virtue of his descent from Teispes through Ariaramnes, was not of the immediate family of Cyrus. In order to forestall further opposition he prepared a lengthy inscription in which he revealed in detail the murder of Bardiya by Cambyses and the fact that Gaumata was not Bardiya after all but an impostor. Though these efforts managed to quell the uneasiness of the Persian leaders themselves, rebellions nevertheless erupted throughout the empire. Babylonia, because of its size and importance, was of particular concern to Darius. Too weak at first to bring this major satrapy under control militarily, Darius worked through diplomatic channels and by 520 was able to reassert Persian authority in Babylon. With Babylon back in line, the rest of the rebel states soon reaffirmed their loyalty.

With peace and stability once more a reality, Darius proceeded to implement far-reaching administrative reforms. Of no little importance was the continuing development of a legal system that had already become famous for the unalterability of the king's edicts. Both Daniel (6:8, 12, 15) and Esther (1:19) show an awareness of this feature of Persian jurisprudence. Founded no doubt on ancient legal precedent such as the code of Hammurabi, law under Darius was administered with at least a theoretical concern for justice.[56]

Another accomplishment was the introduction of a completely revised fiscal policy.[57] Darius led the way in standardizing coinage and weights and measures, thus facilitating trade and commerce. Unfortunately these reforms were accompanied by a drastic inflationary spiral which in turn brought further governmental intervention and control in the private sector. This proved to be extremely unpopular throughout the empire and before long caused severe repercussions which nearly brought Darius to ruin.

A third area of intense activity was that of massive building projects. By 521 Darius had removed the capital to Susa, in old Elam three hundred miles northwest of Pasargadae, and there erected a magnificent palace.[58] It is this structure that is referred to in both Esther and Nehemiah as the "citadel of Susa" ("Shushan the palace," kjv). Later in his reign Darius undertook the construction of a whole new city named Persepolis where he hoped to locate the capital permanently. He was able only to begin the project, however, so his son and successor Xerxes carried it through to completion. Susa seems to have continued as the real center of government, however, while Persepolis

56. Ibid., pp. 119–34.
57. Ibid., pp. 186–94.
58. William Culican, *The Medes and Persians* (New York: Praeger, 1965), pp. 87–89.

was more or less a showplace, a tourist attraction to which successive generations of Persian kings took important guests to impress them.[59]

The only significant area of the empire that remained intractable in 520 was the satrapy of Mudraya, that is, Egypt.[60] Darius set out for that distant land in 519, passing, as caravans and armies had for millennia, through Syria and Palestine. These lands on the Mediterranean littoral were then part of the Babylonian satrapy, but because of their distance from both Babylon and Susa were less susceptible to supervision. As a result there was turmoil there incessantly, and only when the Persian kings intervened directly could some measure of order be established.

This was the case in 520 in Judah. The Jews had begun the reconstruction of Jerusalem and the temple and had immediately encountered opposition from both the Samaritans and Tattenai, the satrap of the province. Darius was told by the Jewish leaders that Cyrus himself had authorized their building projects. When he researched the royal archives and discovered this indeed was true, he ordered the hostilities against the Jews to cease at once. No doubt his itinerary through Palestine had something to do with the alacrity with which his wishes were implemented.

Having entered Egypt in 519, Darius marched unimpeded all the way to Memphis. The city readily submitted to him because of his sympathy for the local cult, but before he could consolidate his holdings there, he had to return to Susa to deal with an attempted usurpation.[61]

Darius remained in Susa for the next several years but eventually resumed his expansionism. By about 516 he had pressed east as far as India and then returned to Africa to deal with the Libyans. His northward penetrations were not so successful, however, for he met stiff resistance from the Scythians and was forced to retreat. Still unsatisfied he set his sights on Europe. His first attempt to bring the independent Aegean states under his control failed when the Ionian states which were already under Persian suzerainty broke free to assist their harassed kinfolk. He eventually prevailed, however, and incorporated all of western Asia into his realm.[62]

Flushed with success Darius made an ill-advised sweep across the

59. Ibid., pp. 89–90. For an excellent survey of Persian art and architecture see Denise Schmandt-Besserat, *Ancient Persia: The Art of an Empire* (Austin: University of Texas, 1978).

60. Olmstead, *History*, pp. 141–44.

61. G. B. Gray and M. Cary, "The Reign of Darius," in *Cambridge Ancient History*, 2d ed., ed. J. B. Bury et al. (Cambridge: Cambridge University Press, 1939), vol. 4, pp. 182–84, 212–14.

62. Ibid., pp. 214–28.

Aegean Sea in the year 490 with the intent of conquering Athens and the other city-states of the Greek peninsula.[63] The city of Eretria suffered destruction and enslavement. Aroused, the Athenians met Darius head-on. In the decisive battle at Marathon the Persians underwent a humiliating defeat and were forced to retreat to the Asian mainland. Convinced that victory had eluded him only because of insufficient manpower, Darius resolved to return once more to Greece to finish what he had begun. A revolt in Egypt preempted this action, however. Before Darius could completely resolve his new problem and resume his European operations, he died, leaving his grand design to his son Xerxes (486–465).

Though Darius suffered from the same character defects which afflict most powerful rulers—overweening pride, selfish ambition, and an unrealistic overestimation of his capabilities—he was relatively farsighted, cultured, and benign. As we have noted, he designed and commenced the construction of the magnificent city of Persepolis, to this day regarded as one of the wonders of the ancient world. He also sponsored the digging of a canal between the Nile and the Red Sea. Of more significance than either of these, however, was his establishment of a highway network that laced his vast empire together and a postal system that permitted rapid communication on a scale undreamed of before his time. And most important of all, he provided a secure milieu in which the newly returned and struggling Jewish community could once more sink roots into the soil of the Holy Land. Under his sovereignty they were free from the threat of everything but petty annoyance from hostile neighbors.

The First Return

Cyrus as the Agent of Yahweh

In the nineteenth century a barrel-shaped inscription which records Cyrus the Great's decree authorizing captive peoples in Babylonia to return to their places of origin was discovered. This inscription was primarily a propaganda piece designed to demonstrate that Cyrus had been called by Marduk, god of Babylon, and that his rule there and over all the earth was at the behest of the gods. One cannot deny the political and psychological genius of the man; indeed, his policy of permitting aliens to return to their homelands and to establish self-rule within the larger structure of the empire was nothing short of brilliant.[64]

---

63. Ibid., pp. 233–68.

64. That this policy also had its negative side should not be overlooked. See Amelie Kuhrt, "The Cyrus Cylinder and Achaemenid Imperial Policy," *JSOT* 25 (1983): 83–97.

The biblical historians and prophets recognized Cyrus's genius, of course, but they also saw that it was Yahweh, not Marduk, who had called and gifted Cyrus. Isaiah spoke of Cyrus as the "shepherd" of Yahweh (44:28), "his anointed" whose right hand he held in order to empower him to subdue nations (45:1). It was he whom the Lord would use to authorize and facilitate the return of his people and the rebuilding of his city and temple.

What role Daniel may have played in all this is unclear, but one cannot help feeling that it was major. In any case the Jewish exiles understood Cyrus's decree to be the doing of Yahweh himself. Both the chronicler (2 Chron. 36:22–23) and Ezra (1:1–4) interpreted the decree to be a fulfilment of the word of Jeremiah and maintained that it was Yahweh and not Marduk who had inspired Cyrus to such a noble course of action. But one should not read into the accounts that Cyrus had become a worshiper of Yahweh; he was no more a worshiper of Yahweh than Nebuchadnezzar had been when he extolled Yahweh before Daniel. Both were syncretists who were willing for reasons of politics to welcome any new god into their respective pantheons. One cannot deny, however, that both were under the control of the sovereign God of heaven and earth who used them, witting or not, to achieve his holy purposes.[65]

Sheshbazzar, the Leader of the Return

The principal source of information about the first return from exile is Ezra, a Zadokite priest (7:1–5) and professional scribe and teacher of Torah. Though he himself did not return to Jerusalem until 458, eighty years after the decree, he obviously possessed excellent sources, including both written memoranda and word of mouth, and provides remarkable detail.

According to Ezra, Cyrus not only gave his permission for the Jews to go home, but stipulated that they must be assisted in every possible way by the peoples among whom they were living (1:3–4). Moreover, all of the temple treasures that Nebuchadnezzar had looted years before and placed in Babylonian shrines were turned over to Sheshbazzar, the prince of Judah, Jehoiachin likely having died by then. Having been appointed governor of the reconstituted state by Cyrus (5:14), Sheshbazzar led the exiles back to Jerusalem (1:11), where he proceeded to lay the foundations of the temple (5:16). Since he is not mentioned again, the identity of Sheshbazzar has become a matter of

65. Eugene H. Merrill, "Daniel as a Contribution to Kingdom Theology," in *Essays in Honor of J. Dwight Pentecost*, ed. Stanley D. Toussaint and Charles H. Dyer (Chicago: Moody, 1986), pp. 211–25.

debate. Many scholars allege that he is none other than Zerubbabel,[66] the major political figure of the first few decades back in Judah. But this is impossible because Zerubbabel is never called prince and, in addition, is not the son of Jehoiachin but of Shealtiel (Ezra 3:8). It is most likely that Sheshbazzar is the same as Shenazzar, one of the sons of Jehoiachin mentioned in 1 Chronicles 3:18.[67] In the next verse Zerubbabel is listed as the son of Pedaiah, another one of Jehoiachin's sons as is Shealtiel. Whether the son of Shealtiel or Pedaiah, Zerubbabel would be Shenazzar's (i.e., Sheshbazzar's) nephew. It is very possible that Sheshbazzar died early after his return and that Zerubbabel succeeded him as leader.

The Number of Returnees

The total number of returnees was 42,360 in addition to 7,337 slaves and 200 singers (Ezra 2:64–65). These appear to have been primarily Judeans though one cannot rule out the possibility of Israelites as well.[68] Nehemiah (7:4–5) notes that in his day, almost a hundred years later, Jerusalem was very sparsely populated; and so he searched the genealogical lists to determine, no doubt, if any of the early returnees by virtue of their lineage should have taken up residence in Jerusalem rather than in the surrounding countryside. This corroborates the impression that only a very small percentage of the Jews who came back were descendants of Jerusalemites. When one remembers, however, that Jerusalem bore the brunt of the Babylonian assaults of 605, 597, and 586, and that only about twenty-five thousand went into exile, it is not difficult to believe that the Jerusalemites were greatly diminished in number. Furthermore, the descendants of the urbane, creative, and successful Jerusalemites were undoubtedly the most inclined to remain in Babylon rather than return to what most surely would have been a radically inferior lifestyle.

Problems Following the Return

It must have taken quite some time for the return to be organized and for the journey itself to be completed. When Ezra refers to the

66. For example, Carl F. Keil, *The Books of Ezra, Nehemiah, and Esther* (Grand Rapids: Eerdmans, 1950 reprint), p. 27.

67. Bright, *History*, p. 362; Hayim Tadmor, "The Babylonian Exile and the Restoration," in *A History of the Jewish People*, ed. Haim H. Ben-Sasson (Cambridge: Harvard University Press, 1976), p. 168.

68. Captive peoples in Babylonia maintained their homogeneity and identity throughout this period and so would have had no problem in returning to their homelands en bloc. See I. Eph'al, "The Western Minorities in Babylonia in the 6th–5th Centuries b.c.: Maintenance and Cohesion," *Or* 47 (1978): 74–90, esp. p. 83.

seventh month (3:1), he means the seventh month of the first year back. This must be 537 since the decree of Cyrus was issued in 538.[69] By that time the people had begun to settle in. In the seventh month, under the inspiring leadership of Joshua the priest and Zerubbabel, they built an altar on the ruins of the old one on the temple mount and celebrated the first Feast of Tabernacles since the exile. Then, as Solomon had done centuries before, the people ordered building materials from Sidon and Tyre and commenced the construction of the house of the Lord. The foundations were laid in the second month of the following year, 536, all under priestly supervision. This done, the assembly burst out in praise to Yahweh, singing the very hymn that David had composed on the occasion of the housing of the ark of the covenant in his new tabernacle on Mount Zion (1 Chron. 16:34). The joy was not unanimous, however, for the foundations of this new temple bespoke a building that paled into insignificance when compared to that of Solomon. The mixed feelings of the elders who remembered the first temple (Ezra 3:12–13) were one of the major problems addressed a few years later by the prophet Haggai (2:3).

The weeping of the elders must have demoralized Zerubbabel and his colleagues, but it was not by any means the only problem they faced. The Samaritans, that mixture of nonexiled Israelites and peoples transplanted in the north by the Assyrian kings, had developed a syncretistic cult that had a patina of Yahwism but was essentially pagan in nature. Hearing about the temple project in Jerusalem, they wished to participate in it and align themselves with the covenant community of Judah. Recognizing the impurity of the Samaritan religious system, and perhaps motivated also by no little sense of petty exclusivity, the Judean leaders declined the overture. Thus spurned, the Samaritans set about to impede the work on the temple, a harassment they continued for sixteen years (536–520).

A change in Jewish fortunes came after the accession of Darius Hystaspes to Persia's throne in 522. Having been occupied for his first two years with securing his succession, he was able by 520 to give attention to matters affecting the farther reaches of the empire, including the problem of Samaritan-Judean antagonism. This had only intensified after Haggai and Zechariah lent their encouragement to the rebuilding efforts in Darius's second year. As a result, the Samaritans appealed to Tattenai, the satrap of the whole region west of the Euphrates. He and his subordinates, having investigated the situation, challenged the authority by which the Jews claimed the right to build.

---

69. F. Charles Fensham, *The Books of Ezra and Nehemiah*, New International Commentary (Grand Rapids: Eerdmans, 1982), pp. 58–59.

Unsatisfied with the Jews' response, Tattenai composed a letter to Darius which questioned the legality of the Jewish activity (Ezra 5).

Since the Jews had made an appeal to the decree of Cyrus, Darius initiated a search of the Babylonian archives to determine if in fact such a document really existed. A copy turned up in Ecbatana, the old Median capital where Cyrus had been in residence at the time of the decree.[70] Completely persuaded of the justness of the Jewish cause, Darius issued an edict in behalf of the beleaguered state: he commanded Tattenai and his cronies not only to cease and desist from their interdiction of the Jewish cause, but to pay whatever expenses might be accrued both in building and in the maintenance of public worship (Ezra 6:6–12). Failure to comply, Darius ominously threatened, would result in the direst reprisals. Since Darius only a few months later undertook his Egyptian campaigns, it is more than likely that he stopped at Jerusalem along the way to see that everything was carried out as he had ordered.

Encouragement from the Prophets

Haggai

As we have suggested, Haggai and Zechariah had a great deal to do with lifting the morale of the people and enabling them to get on with construction of the temple. For sixteen long years little had been done except to lay the foundations. On the other hand, the people had provided suitable housing for themselves and had begun to develop a rather prosperous way of life. But Yahweh's house lay in ruins as the people procrastinated in the face of relentless Samaritan opposition.

The prophet Haggai, about whom virtually nothing of a personal nature is known, spoke first. Aware perhaps that Darius had established himself at Susa and would soon be in a position to support the Jewish cause, Haggai urged the people to put aside their own selfish interests and to undertake the work on the temple without further ado (1:4–9). Within three weeks Zerubbabel and Joshua had marshaled a labor force to set about the work with renewed enthusiasm. As the building began to take shape, it was obvious that it would never match the temple of Solomon for immensity and beauty. But that was not the important thing, Haggai reminded the people. What truly mattered was the fact that the day would come when Yahweh would fill the humble structure with his glory (2:6–9). Then and only then would the temple begin to fulfil its true function.

70. Olmstead, *History*, p. 57.

Zechariah

Two months after Haggai's first oracle the prophet Zechariah called for repentance. The work on the temple was then under way once more, but the mere construction of a house of worship would hardly suffice for the people's basic need, that of being restored to fellowship with their God and entering once more into covenant relationship with him (1:2–6). Three months later, still in Darius's second year, Zechariah had the first in a series of visions. Among their messages was that the temple would be completed. They also predicted in apocalyptic fashion the victory of Judah over all enemy nations and the gathering of all repentant people to Yahweh through the testimony of his obedient covenant people. Zerubbabel and Joshua, representing civil and ecclesiastical authority respectively, would be greatly elevated and would stand before the Messiah in the eschatological day (chs. 3–4). Then, in a remarkable act, Zechariah drew near to Joshua and this time, viewing him as a messianic prototype, crowned him with a royal diadem (6:9–15). By doing so Zechariah joined regal and cultic privilege in one man, just as David had experienced it; Joshua somehow symbolized the Davidic line revived all over again.

The temple was completed in 515, the sixth year of Darius, which was twenty years after its foundations were laid (Ezra 6:15). This date marks the end of Jeremiah's "seventy years" in a cultic sense, for as long as Yahweh had no earthly dwelling-place in Jerusalem, his people also could never truly be at home. Though the Shekinah, being a feature reserved for the end of the age, did not come into evidence again with the completion of the temple, the people nevertheless rejoiced in God's goodness and dedicated the temple with effusive praise and a generous offering. Jew and proselyte alike celebrated the following Passover with special understanding; for just as God had brought his people out of Egypt nine hundred years earlier and marked the occasion with the Passover feast, so now he had redeemed them from Babylonian bondage and brought them once more into the Promised Land.

With the completion of this festivity a pall of silence falls over the land of Judah as far as historical documentation is concerned. We next pick up the threads of the story shortly after Xerxes (486–465) took the throne of Persia. The beautiful Jewish maiden Esther, by winning his heart, would change the course of Jewish life in exile.

14 Restoration and New Hope

The Persian Influence
Xerxes
Artaxerxes I
Esther
Subsequent Returns: Ezra and Nehemiah
The Problem of Priority
Ezra the Priest and Scribe
Nehemiah the Governor
Malachi the Prophet

The history of Old Testament Israel came to an end within one hundred years of the completion of the second temple. Little is known from the biblical documents about the years from 515 to approximately 474, so the content of this chapter must be limited almost exclusively to the middle half of the fifth century.[1] The major biblical sources for these years are Ezra and Nehemiah, though Esther and Malachi also make important contributions to our understanding of specific problems confronting the remaining exilic community and the Judean state respectively.

The Persian Influence

Persia remained the dominant world power throughout Judah's final biblical era and, in fact, would continue as such until the rise of

---

1. An excellent bibliographical resource for this period can be found in Menachem Mor and Uriel Rappaport, "A Survey of 25 Years (1960–1985) of Israeli Scholarship on Jewish History in the Second Temple Period (539 B.C.E.–135 C.E.)," *BTB* 16 (1986): 56–58. The difficulties of reconstructing the history of a period for which there are few biblical texts are described well by Peter R. Ackroyd, "Faith and Its Reformulation in the Post-exilic Period: Sources," *TD* 27 (1979): 323–34.

Alexander in 333 B.C. and his conquest of Persepolis in 330. It is important, then, that the course of Persian history be reviewed at least briefly so that the biblical story, which everywhere presupposes the Persian influence, may be more fully appreciated.

Xerxes

Darius Hystaspes, under whose auspices the Jewish temple was rebuilt, died in 486 and was succeeded by his son Xerxes, the Old Testament Ahasuerus.[2] He had for some years been designated heir by his father, so the change in leadership was without contention. By virtue of his governorship of Babylon, Xerxes was admirably prepared to undertake the formidable responsibilities of his new office.

Xerxes' first interest lay in the completion of the royal palace at Susa and the further aggrandizement of Persepolis, the latter project occupying him on and off for the twenty-one years of his reign (486–465). A more pressing concern, however, was with Egypt, which rebelled at once upon his accession. In less than two years he was able to resolve this problem, but by his suppression of the Egyptian religion he alienated the priests, without whose support he could not reasonably expect Egyptian subservience.

Like his father, Xerxes seemed irresistibly drawn to the west and the conquest of Greece, so after reorganizing his armies and navies, he moved west in 481. The badly divided Greek states were unable to achieve an effective coalition and at first were badly mauled by the superior Persian forces. Even the redoubtable Spartans were defeated at Thermopylae though they fought to the last man. At Salamis, however, the tide changed. Having trapped thousands of Greek warriors at Salamis, Xerxes underestimated their almost fanatical courage and as a result lost more than two hundred Persian ships. He at once sought for a scapegoat and found one in his Phoenician and Egyptian mercenaries, whom he accused of cowardice. They therefore abandoned him and returned to their own countries.

Xerxes then left for Persia, having placed his general Mardonius in command of the Persian troops still remaining in Greece. Because of a series of tactical blunders, Mardonius suffered one setback after another until he lost his life in the battle of Plataea. The final blow ending Xerxes' aspirations to conquer Greece was administered at Mycale in

2. For the course of Persian history under Xerxes see A. T. Olmstead, *History of the Persian Empire* (Chicago: University of Chicago Press, 1948), pp. 230–88. Robert Dick Wilson, *A Scientific Investigation of the Old Testament* (Chicago: Moody, 1959), p. 69, n. 25, has shown conclusively that "Ahasuerus" is the Hebrew rendering of the Greek "Xerxes."

479. The Greeks had now destroyed two of the Persian armies and forced a third to return to Asia. While this was a shattering blow to Persia, it enabled the Greeks to see what a united front could accomplish. They therefore formed the Delian League in 478 with Athens as the dominant partner. The implications of this for the creation of a Greek nation are obvious.

Meanwhile Xerxes had become completely discredited and so turned to a life of licentious indulgence. He dallied with the most beautiful women of the court, including the wives of some of his chief officials, and thereby sowed the seeds of irreparable dissension.[3] At last his dissipation was rewarded by assassination at the hands of a palace official or jealous husband.

Artaxerxes I

The reins of government should have then been handed over to Darius, the eldest son of Xerxes, but instead Artaxerxes his brother murdered him, with the encouragement of Artabanus, captain of the guard, and took his place as king.[4] Artaxerxes tried to restore the credibility of the central government by a reorganization of the satrapies and reduction of some of the taxation which his father had imposed. This had little effect, however, and private lands began to fall to the crown because of unpaid taxes. The result was widespread unrest and even revolt, particularly in the more remote provinces. By 460 Egypt refused to pay further tribute and solicited and received support from the Delian League in this bold act of defiance. Persia undercut this arrangement by bribing Sparta to go to war with Athens, a move that neutralized the league and jeopardized not only Egypt but Athens.

Athens managed to survive alone and in fact formed something of an empire itself.[5] This provoked further Persian hostility, and from 450 until the beginning of the Peloponnesian Wars (431) territorial control on both sides of the Aegean seesawed between Athens and Persia with neither gaining permanent advantage. The orator-statesman Pericles had begun to lead Athens to a position of dominance amongst all the Greek states by 458, a situation that the latter feared and resented. The civil wars which then broke out freed Artaxerxes of further concern for his western Asia provinces, allowing him to attend to matters closer to home including the ongoing unrest in Judah over the rebuilding of the walls of Jerusalem. His death in 424 was ap-

---

3. Some of this is graphically narrated by Herodotus in *History* 9.109–13.
4. Olmstead, *History,* pp. 289–90.
5. J. B. Bury, *A History of Greece* (London: Macmillan, 1963), pp. 346–425.

proximately coincident with the end of the Old Testament period and is therefore an appropriate place to conclude our review of Persian history.

Esther

The only biblical witness to the reign of Xerxes is the Book of Esther, a document whose historicity is denied by practically all critical scholars.[6] This is not because the book contradicts anything that is known of that period from Persian, Greek, or other extrabiblical sources—for it surely does not[7]—but because these sources do not explicitly corroborate such details as the Feast of Purim or even the existence of Esther and her cousin Mordecai.[8] But an *argumentum e silentio* should never be used in serious historiography. Unless irrefutable evidence to the contrary surfaces, one must on principle assume that Esther is a reliable historical document originating in and faithfully recounting the era it professes to record.

The Book of Esther begins in the third year of Xerxes (ca. 483). The king was then at Susa presiding over a lavish banquet in honor of his subordinates from all over the empire—from India to Cush, as the narrator puts it. For six months Xerxes had exhibited the splendor of his court and now was capping it all off with a seven-day banquet.[9] After a week of reveling and drunkenness the king demanded that his queen Vashti be brought before the assembly so that he might parade her beauty before them as further evidence of his splendor (Esth.

6. For a typical view see J. Alberto Soggin, *Introduction to the Old Testament*, trans. John Bowden (Philadelphia: Westminster, 1980), p. 404, who summarizes, "What we have is not details of events which actually took place, but a historical novel." For a strong defense of the book's historicity see Gleason L. Archer, Jr., *A Survey of Old Testament Introduction* (Chicago: Moody, 1964), pp. 404–6; and J. Stafford Wright, "The Historicity of the Book of Esther," in *New Perspectives on the Old Testament*, ed. J. Barton Payne (Waco: Word, 1970), pp. 37–47.

7. As Robert Gordis points out, "Whatever his date, the author of Esther has an excellent familiarity with Persian law, custom, and languages in the Achaemenid period" ("Studies in the Esther Narrative," *JBL* 95 [1976]: 44). For a similar view see A. R. Millard, "The Persian Names in Esther and the Reliability of the Hebrew Text," *JBL* 96 (1977): 481–88.

8. An undated Persian text does, however, mention a certain Marduka (the Babylonian equivalent of the Hebrew name *Mordecai*) who was a high official under Darius Hystaspes or Xerxes. Carey A. Moore argues that "this Marduka could be the biblical Mordechai" ("Archaeology and the Book of Esther," *BA* 38 [1975]: 74).

9. There is thus a distinction between the six months of celebration and the one week of banqueting that followed. Carey A. Moore suggests that the affair was a celebration of victory over Egypt and a show of confidence in preparation for his Greek campaigns (*Esther*, Anchor Bible [Garden City, N.Y.: Doubleday, 1971], p. 12; see also Wright, "Historicity," in *New Perspectives*, p. 37).

1:10–12). When she refused to come, Xerxes deposed her and sought for another to take her place as his principal queen (Esth. 2:1–4).[10]

Thus the narrator paves the way for the introduction of Esther, a young Jewess living at Susa with her older cousin Mordecai. Their presence there suggests both the wide distribution of the Jewish Diaspora a century after the fall of Jerusalem and the fact, already emphasized, that the majority of the exiled Jews remained in the lands of their captivity even when they had the opportunity to leave. Their assimilation into their new world is also clear from the very names of the principal protagonists in this story.[11] "Mordecai" is a Hebrew transliteration of the Babylonian divine name *Marduk*. Why a pious Jew should bear such a name is not easy to answer.[12] His cousin's name is similarly pagan in its overtones. "Esther" is a form of Ishtar, the Babylonian goddess of love and war. She also bore a Hebrew name, Hadassah, by which she probably was known to the Jewish community.

Mordecai's prominence in the Persian court attests, moreover, that Jews could rise to the highest levels of government and society.[13] One must not make too much of this, however, in the case of Mordecai, since he forbade his cousin to disclose her Jewish identity and so most likely hid his own as well. This may, in fact, help to explain why both he and Esther chose non-Hebrew personal names in the first place.

After the requisite time of preparation, Esther was made queen in Xerxes' seventh year (479). By then he had brought both Egypt and Babylonia under control and had launched his unsuccessful campaign against the Greek states. It will be recalled that Xerxes had returned from the west by 479, leaving Mardonius to suffer defeat in the battle of Plataea. It seems clear that Esther became queen shortly after Xerxes retired from his Greek adventures.

Xerxes' humiliating setback may account for the conspiracy which Mordecai uncovered, a plot by two palace officials to assassinate the king (Esth. 2:19–23). His disclosure of the treachery was duly noted in the archives and would prove later on to be of crucial importance in gaining royal favor. The need for such favor came about when Xerxes promoted Haman to be prime minister and Haman then required all other officials to kneel in his presence. Mordecai refused to do so; when asked about the matter, he stated that such behavior was contrary to

10. Wright, "Historicity," in *New Perspectives*, pp. 40–43, presents some rather cogent arguments to show that Vashti of the Book of Esther is none other than Amestris of the classical texts.

11. Moore, *Esther*, pp. 19–20.

12. For suggestions see Michael D. Coogan, "Life in the Diaspora: Jews at Nippur in the Fifth Century B.C.," *BA* 37 (1974): 10–11.

13. Ibid., p. 10; Bezalel Porten, *Archives from Elephantine: The Life of an Ancient Jewish Military Colony* (Berkeley: University of California Press, 1968), pp. 279–80.

his convictions as a Jew. Haman then hit upon the idea of getting rid of Mordecai and at the same time initiating a pogrom against the Jews in general. Xerxes by then had given up any notion of conquering Greece and was looking for someone he could blame. Haman's suggestion that the Jews would make an ideal target appealed to the king immensely, so an edict of annihilation was issued. This was to be carried out in the twelfth year of Xerxes, 474.

Meanwhile the king had been researching the archives and came across the record of Mordecai's part in foiling the assassination plot (Esth. 6:1–3). He therefore decided to promote Mordecai to high office. He also invited Esther to make any request she might have. Boldly revealing her Jewish identity for the first time, Esther told the king all that Haman had plotted against Mordecai and her people. Xerxes immediately put Haman to death and issued a countermanding decree which authorized the Jews throughout the empire to protect themselves against Haman's evil purge. When the local officials everywhere understood that Xerxes was now in support of the Jews, they joined in the effort to put down the anti-Jewish campaign. And so once more the God of Israel, though never mentioned by name in the Book of Esther, bared his mighty arm in behalf of his people.

To commemorate this miraculous deliverance the Feast of Purim was instituted, a festive occasion to mark the turning of sorrow into joy (Esth. 9:26–28). Along with the Mosaic festivals it must be celebrated without fail by every generation as a commemoration of God's faithful preservation of Israel.

Subsequent Returns: Ezra and Nehemiah

The Problem of Priority

About sixteen years after the institution of Purim in Susa, Ezra the scribe and priest made his way from Babylon to Jerusalem as the head of a contingent of Jewish returnees. He dates his journey specifically in the seventh year of Artaxerxes, that is, 458 (Ezra 7:8). Not only was his return permitted by the Persian king, but Artaxerxes issued a decree—the text of which Ezra has preserved—to the effect that whatever silver and gold Ezra received from the king, Babylonian sources, and Jews elsewhere should be taken back to Jerusalem and used for the purchase of sacrificial animals for the temple of Yahweh. If that was not enough, more could be requested from the royal treasury. If there was a surplus of funds, it could be used in any way Ezra and his people wished. Finally, Ezra was authorized to appoint public officials throughout the trans-Euphratean satrapy. These were to be men who were expert in and would enforce the Torah.

A problem that must be addressed at this juncture concerns the identity of the Artaxerxes who issued the decree. Dependent on the answer to this problem are the date of Ezra's return and, hence, the chronological sequence of Ezra and Nehemiah. Traditional scholarship has maintained that it was under Artaxerxes I (464–424) that Ezra went to Jerusalem and that Nehemiah did so under the same king thirteen years later.[14] Ezra's pilgrimage was in Artaxerxes' seventh year (458) and Nehemiah's in his twentieth year (445).

An alternative view that has gained considerable following argues that Nehemiah indeed returned to Jerusalem in 445 under Artaxerxes I, but that Ezra did not return until the seventh year of Artaxerxes II, who reigned from 404 to 358.[15] This would place Ezra's return in 398 and give Nehemiah chronological priority by more than forty-five years. The position of John Bright, on the other hand, is that Ezra arrived in 428. This is based on the assumption that "seventh year" in Ezra 7:7–8 is an error for "thirty-seventh year," an assumption that is purely gratuitous.[16]

There are four arguments for the nontraditional sequence:

1. *Nehemiah returned to Jerusalem to rebuild its walls; yet it seems that when Ezra returned, the walls were standing.*[17] But Ezra's words "God . . . has given us a wall of protection in Judah and Jerusalem" (9:9) can hardly be taken literally, since there was no wall around Judah. In addition, Ezra employs the word *gādēr* for "wall," whereas the usual word to describe Jerusalem's walls is *ḥômâ*.[18] There is, however, every reason to believe that some kind of literal wall had indeed existed in Jerusalem just before Nehemiah's return, for he is surprised to learn that it has been destroyed (Neh. 1:3–4).[19] Why would he have been upset to learn, 140 years after the event, that Nebuchadnezzar had broken down the city walls? In fact, it is inconceivable that Ne-

14. A detailed discussion of the problem may be found in John Bright, *A History of Israel*, 3d ed. (Philadelphia: Westminster, 1981), pp. 391–402.

15. Otto Eissfeldt, *The Old Testament: An Introduction*, trans. Peter R. Ackroyd (New York: Harper and Row, 1965), p. 554; Norman H. Snaith, "The Date of Ezra's Arrival in Jerusalem," *ZAW* 63 (1951): 62–63.

16. Bright, *History*, p. 400.

17. Ibid., p. 393.

18. F. Charles Fensham, *The Books of Ezra and Nehemiah*, New International Commentary (Grand Rapids: Eerdmans, 1982), pp. 130–31; I. H. Eybers, "Chronological Problems in Ezra-Nehemiah," *Die Ou-Testamentiese Werkgemeenskap in Suid-Africa* 19 (1979): 12.

19. Peter R. Ackroyd, *Israel Under Babylon and Persia* (London: Oxford University Press, 1970), pp. 174–75. Ezra 5:3 may indicate that Zerubbabel had undertaken some reconstruction of the wall. The meaning of the Aramaic *'uššarnā'* is, however, unclear, though the Vulgate and Syriac understand it to mean "wall." See Carl F. Keil, *The Books of Ezra, Nehemiah, and Esther* (Grand Rapids: Eerdmans, 1950 reprint), p. 27; Snaith, "Date of Ezra's Arrival," *ZAW* 63 (1951): 58–59; Eybers, "Chronological Problems," *Die Ou-Testamentiese Werkgemeenskap in Suid-Africa* 19 (1979): 10, 12.

hemiah knew nothing of this. The wall he mentions must be a wall that he thought was standing in his own day.

2. *Ezra and Nehemiah seem not to be aware of each other's existence and certainly give no evidence of being contemporaries. The three passages where they do appear together—Nehemiah 8:9; 12:26, 36—are merely later glosses.*[20] The latter part of the argument is without textual support whatsoever and is a classic instance of begging the question. The former part, then, no longer has any force, since Nehemiah does in fact mention Ezra. Ezra's failure to mention Nehemiah is clearly because he had completed most of his major tasks in the thirteen years before Nehemiah arrived. Besides, it was common for contemporaries not to speak of one another. This can be illustrated by Haggai and Zechariah, Isaiah and Micah, and a host of other examples.

Wishing to respect the texts in Nehemiah which refer to Ezra, Bright concedes that the two were contemporaries but still maintains that Nehemiah was earlier. He also proposes a chronological rearrangement of the historical material. In the traditional interpretation Ezra returned in 458 (Ezra 7–8). When informed that many members of the holy race had intermarried with their pagan neighbors, Ezra led his people in a prayer of confession (Ezra 9–10). Then in 445, after Nehemiah had returned and rebuilt the walls of Jerusalem, Ezra read the law to the Israelites (Neh. 8), who thereupon confessed their sins and promised to obey the commands of God (Neh. 9–10). Bright counters that since Ezra was commissioned by Artaxerxes to teach the law (Ezra 7:25), the reading of the law must have occurred soon after Ezra's arrival. Moreover, "the tractability of the people when confronted with their mixed marriages (Ezra 10:1–4), and their readiness to conform to the law (v. 3), suggests that its public reading had already taken place."[21] Accordingly, Bright suggests that upon arrival in Jerusalem in 428 (Ezra 7–8), Ezra proceeded to read the law (Neh. 8). He then confronted the people on the issue of mixed marriages (Ezra 9–10), and they confessed their sin and swore obedience to the covenant (Neh. 9–10).

Bright's proposal would be attractive except that it requires adding the number "thirty" to both verse 7 and verse 8 of Ezra 7. It is argued that the passage originally read that Ezra came up to Jerusalem in the thirty-seventh year of Artaxerxes, that is, in 428. According to this chronology, Nehemiah first arrived in 445, went back to Susa in 433, and then, on his return to Jerusalem a few years later, met Ezra for the first time. As much as one might wish for such a solution, one

20. Eissfeldt, *Old Testament*, p. 552.
21. Bright, *History*, p. 396.

must find a way to achieve it other than arbitrary manipulation of the text.

3. *Ezra appears to have dealt with the intermarriage problem with much greater severity and finality than did Nehemiah.* It is alleged that Nehemiah had been too lenient, demanding only that in the future the Jews not give their children in marriage to foreigners (13:25), while Ezra insisted that the marriages already entered upon be terminated (10:10–14).[22] This, however, is extremely tenuous evidence. If, as the traditional view maintains, Ezra's reform occurred in about 457 and Nehemiah's in about 430, after his return from Susa, the twenty-five years between them would have been ample time for mixed marriages to have become a problem all over again. Furthermore, it is arbitrary indeed to argue that one measure was more stern or decisive than the other. Ezra and Nehemiah each responded to the peculiar situations they faced with measures appropriate to them and to the problem as they perceived it.[23]

4. *The high priest contemporary with Nehemiah was Eliashib (Neh. 3:1, 20–21; 13:28), but Ezra retired to the chambers of Jehohanan, the son of Eliashib (Ezra 10:6).* How could Ezra have preceded Nehemiah when he found abode with the son of the priest of Nehemiah's day?[24] This argument draws upon Nehemiah 12:10–11, 22, where the priestly line is listed as Jeshua, Joiakim, Eliashib, Joiada, Jonathan (a variation of Jehohanan, as is Johanan), and Jaddua. Here it is clear that Johanan is actually the grandson of Eliashib, not the son, which only exacerbates the problem. Furthermore, Johanan appears in the Elephantine papyri as the high priest of Jerusalem in the seventeenth year of Darius II.[25] This would be 407, fifty years after the traditional date of Ezra's arrival in Jerusalem and his reformation. He must, therefore, have returned in the seventh year of Artaxerxes II (ca. 398) and not the seventh year of Artaxerxes I.

In response, one should note that the Eliashib of Ezra 10:6 is not called a priest and so may not be the Eliashib of Nehemiah's time.[26] Also, Johanan is the son of Eliashib in Ezra, but the grandson in Nehemiah. Josephus reports that this grandson of Eliashib slew his own brother Jeshua when Bigvai, Nehemiah's successor as governor, tried

22. J. Maxwell Miller and John H. Hayes, *A History of Ancient Israel and Judah* (Philadelphia: Westminster, 1986), pp. 473–74; Snaith, "Date of Ezra's Arrival," *ZAW* 63 (1951): 61.

23. Eybers, "Chronological Problems," *Die Ou-Testamentiese Werkgemeenskap in Suid-Africa* 19 (1979): 14.

24. Ackroyd, *Israel Under Babylon and Persia*, p. 193.

25. Miller and Hayes, *History*, p. 469.

26. Fensham, *Ezra and Nehemiah*, p. 136.

to install him as high priest.[27] It is difficult to believe that Ezra felt comfortable enough with this character to share quarters with him.

One attractive proposal to harmonize the evidence is that of Frank Cross, who suggests that there is a haplography in the priestly genealogies in Nehemiah 12.[28] He posits an original list in which there were two Eliashibs and two Johanans, one pair in Ezra's time and another in Nehemiah's. The problem with this suggestion is that there is no manuscript support for it at all and therefore it is pure conjecture. Although it would alleviate the problem of the sequence of Ezra and Nehemiah, one cannot reconstruct texts on the basis of what would support a historical hypothesis.

In light of this lengthy examination of the evidence it seems clear that the traditional view that Ezra preceded Nehemiah has the most to commend it. It is not without its problems, to be sure, but it provides a comfortable structure against which the narrative of both books may be understood.

Ezra the Priest and Scribe

Ezra received permission from Artaxerxes I to lead an exilic band back to Jerusalem. The Persian king authorized him to do virtually whatever he desired in the trans-Euphratean provinces, including Judah. It will be helpful to see if there were any political factors that motivated Artaxerxes to this beneficent policy, for, try as we might, it is difficult to believe that the king was operating out of purely charitable motives.

We have already suggested that the neutralization of the Delian League after 460 left Artaxerxes free to deal with matters closer to home. He instructed Megabyzus, an official who had bribed Sparta to attack Athens and had then been made governor of the satrapy of Syria, to lead Persian troops south from Cilicia to wage war on Egypt, the ally of Athens. After defeating Athenian troops at Prosopitus (an island in the Nile Delta), Megabyzus brought Egypt itself to submission in 456.[29] Very possibly, then, in 458 Artaxerxes viewed a loyal Judean province as an important asset for his anticipated disciplinary action against Egypt.[30] And what better way to ensure Judean loyalty than to allow Ezra, no doubt a highly popular and powerful Jewish

27. Frank M. Cross, "A Reconstruction of the Judean Restoration," *Interp.* 29 (1975): 188–89 (published also in *JBL* 94 [1975]: 4–18).

28. Ibid., pp. 189–90.

29. Olmstead, *History*, p. 308.

30. Carl Schultz, "The Political Tensions Reflected in Ezra-Nehemiah," in *Scripture in Context*, ed. Carl D. Evans et al. (Pittsburgh: Pickwick, 1980), pp. 233–34.

leader, to reestablish Jewish life and culture in that little land that was so crucial to Persian success?

Having assembled at the Ahava Canal the caravan of those making the long journey to Jerusalem, Ezra led them in fasting and prayer and then distributed among the leading priests and Levites the treasures he had collected from the king and the Jewish community (Ezra 8:15–30). When they arrived at the holy city, they offered burnt offerings to Yahweh and proceeded to the task of rebuilding and reformation. The temple had been completed fifty-eight years before, but since that time spiritual and moral declension had set in. Ezra was confronted with the need for immediate major steps to purify the religious and social life of the young community.

The first item on the agenda was the question of intermarriage. Ezra learned that the people, priests and Levites included, had engaged in mixed marriages with the surrounding pagan peoples, an act that squarely contradicted Mosaic teaching. So distraught was he that he went into deep grief and mourning and sought the face of God (Ezra 9:3–15). God had been faithful in preserving a little remnant from the judgment of destruction and captivity. But now, Ezra lamented, the remnant itself was in danger of forfeiting its privileges as the people of God. Like their ancestors under Joshua almost a millennium before, they were entering unholy alliances with the people of the land. If the Lord did not forgive them this sin, there would be no hope of their continuing as the covenant nation before him.

The popular response was as Ezra had prayed. The people repented, and the priests and the other leaders with them reaffirmed their commitment to the covenant pledge to be a pure and holy people (Ezra 10:1–8). Three days later all the men of the nation gathered at Jerusalem and there received instruction about dissolving their illegal marriages. Though the record is unclear on the matter, we must assume that the individuals guilty of intermarriage divorced their foreign mates. Yet the need for similar action twenty-five years later under Nehemiah suggests quite the contrary.

Nehemiah the Governor

Nothing more is known of the ministry of Ezra after his first year in Judah until the arrival of Nehemiah in 445, thirteen years later. These were no doubt difficult years for Ezra, both from internal, domestic causes and from the unremitting harassment of the Samaritans and others who opposed the privileged status of the Jewish state. The situation that prompted Nehemiah to go to Jerusalem testifies eloquently to Ezra's problems, and what Nehemiah found when he got there only confirms them.

After Megabyzus, the Syrian governor, had subdued Egypt, he took the Greek and Egyptian commanders with him to Susa under promise of protection there. For several years the promise was kept, but in 449 Amestris, the widow of Xerxes and queen mother, demanded their execution. The fulfilment of her demands so infuriated Megabyzus that he fled Susa, returned to Syria, and from there declared the independence of the trans-Euphratean satrapy. He had sufficient following to repel at least two campaigns against him; but then, having made his point, he returned to Susa and declared his fealty once more to the Persian crown.[31]

The relevance of all this to the narrative of Nehemiah's journey to Jerusalem is that the Syro-Palestinian satrapy was in a very precarious position as far as Artaxerxes was concerned. He knew full well that what had happened once could happen again and that he might be unable to recover his rebellious territories the next time. Clearly he was willing to do anything that might consolidate his position and ensure continued loyalty from his volatile subjects. When Nehemiah volunteered to go to Jerusalem to stabilize the situation there, Artaxerxes saw in the request not only a way to accede to the heartfelt burden of his beloved cupbearer for his Jewish kinfolk, but a way to place someone over Judah whom he could trust to remain loyal to Persia and to achieve a climate of tranquility and order.[32]

Megabyzus had revolted in 449 and reasserted his loyalty about two years later. According to Nehemiah, he requested permission to go to Jerusalem in 445, the twentieth year of Artaxerxes (2:1). One may assume that conditions throughout Syro-Palestine were chaotic after 449 and that there was desperate need for strong leadership there. Particularly hard hit was Judah, for not only must it have suffered the ravages of rebellion and counterrebellion, but it was constantly under attack, verbally if not physically, from the Samaritans and their allies. The report of the broken walls of Jerusalem may, in fact, reflect something of the devastation that the city suffered during those chaotic years.

Nehemiah is one of the most inspiring figures of biblical history. As was the case with many talented and ambitious Jews of the Diaspora, he had risen through the ranks of government; eventually he achieved the position of cupbearer to the king.[33] There had to be an implicit trust between the two, for the cupbearer could be bribed to slip poison into the king's goblet or do him other harm. Yet, in spite of his intense

31. Olmstead, *History*, pp. 312–13.
32. John M. Cook, *The Persian Empire* (New York: Schocken, 1983), p. 128.
33. For the significance of the cupbearer in the Persian court see Olmstead, *History*, p. 217: "Behind Xerxes stands the cupbearer, who in later Achaemenid times was to exercise even more influence than the commander-in-chief."

loyalty to his king, Nehemiah had a higher loyalty—that to his God. Though he had never been to Jerusalem, his heart was there, and like Daniel he must have prayed every day with his face toward Zion.

In the year 445 Nehemiah's brother Hanani and several other travelers returned from a journey to Jerusalem (Neh. 1:1–3). Whether they had been on an inspection tour for the king cannot be determined, but in any case they reported to Nehemiah the wreckage and despair they saw everywhere in the holy city. This so heavily weighed on the pious zealot that he fasted and prayed for many days. Reminding the Lord of his promises to restore and prosper his dispersed people, Nehemiah asked that he might find favor in the eyes of the king and be allowed to participate in Jerusalem's renewal in some way.

Artaxerxes soon noticed Nehemiah's crestfallen condition and inquired as to its cause. When he found out, he at once authorized Nehemiah to return to Jerusalem and gave him royal letters granting him safe conduct and whatever materials were necessary to the task of rebuilding (Neh. 2:7–8). When he arrived, Nehemiah found the situation even worse than he had imagined. The walls and other structures lay in ruins, and the rulers of the adjacent districts were adamantly opposed to their reconstruction.

One of these rulers, Sanballat the Horonite, is attested to in the Aramaic papyri of Elephantine as having been governor of Samaria in the seventeenth year of Darius II, that is, in 407.[34] Since by then he had adult sons, it is certainly reasonable that he had been governor forty years earlier. Tobiah, governor of Ammon, is less well known.[35] Geshem the Arab, the third principal antagonist, is documented outside the Bible, however. The primary source of information is a silver bowl discovered in 1947 at Tell el-Maskhûṭah in Lower Egypt.[36] Like three other such bowls it has a dedicatory inscription to the goddess Han'-Ilat; in addition, it has the line, "that which Qaynu, son of Gašmu, king of Qedar, brought in offering to Han-'Ilat." Gašmu is the biblical Geshem. On the basis of the particular Aramaic writing, the nature of the bowl, and Athenian coins discovered at the same site, this inscription has been dated around 400.

The major resistance of these antagonists was not to the establish-

---

34. H. L. Ginsberg, "Aramaic Letters," in James B. Pritchard, *Ancient Near Eastern Texts Relating to the Old Testament*, 2d ed. (Princeton: Princeton University Press, 1955), p. 492; Porten, *Archives*, pp. 289–93. The Sanballat family is well known from the Samaria papyri; see Frank M. Cross, "Papyri of the Fourth Century B.C. from Dâliyeh," in *New Directions in Biblical Archaeology*, ed. David Noel Freedman and Jonas C. Greenfield (Garden City, N.Y.: Doubleday, 1971), pp. 47–48, 59–63.

35. See, however, Benjamin Mazar, "The Tobiads," in *IEJ* 7 (1957): 137–45.

36. William J. Dumbrell, "The Tell el-Maskhuta Bowls and the 'Kingdom' of Qedar in the Persian Period," *BASOR* 203 (1971): 33–44.

ment of the cult of Yahweh, the reason for the opposition by these same peoples seventy-five years earlier (Ezra 5:3), but to the reestablishment of Judah as a viable and powerful rival to their own principalities. They had no doubt sided with Megabyzus in his rebellion and now correctly saw Nehemiah as a strong pro-Persian sent among them to police the region as the henchman of Artaxerxes himself. That they dared to interfere with Nehemiah's project shows a certain residue of independence from Persia, especially since the content of Artaxerxes' letter of authorization was well known to them.[37]

Nehemiah wasted no time: within three days he undertook a complete survey of the perimeter of the city to determine the course of the walls and the steps necessary to their reconstruction. At once the Jewish leaders concurred with Nehemiah as to what had to be done, so the task commenced without further ado. Sanballat, Tobiah, and Geshem, after a futile attempt to impede the work by mockery, suggested that the Jews were being disloyal to the king, an absurd charge in light of Artaxerxes' memorandum. As the work proceeded apace, they became alarmed, for the closing up of the city walls meant that Jerusalem soon would be impregnable to military threat. A defensible Jewish capital to them was an ominous sign of Jewish independence and eventual Jewish domination of the entire region. Perhaps a revival of the Davidic empire was not far-fetched after all. It certainly was in line with Jewish prophetic expectation. Nehemiah therefore was forced to defend the work from interruption even as the building continued.

When taunting and ridicule failed, the opposition resorted to pleas for negotiations, during the course of which they would assassinate Nehemiah. Sanballat and Geshem particularly were intent on persuading Nehemiah to meet with them on the plain of Ono (Kafr 'Anā),[38] just ten miles east of Joppa.[39] Five times they communicated with him. The fifth time took the form of a letter from Sanballat which accused Nehemiah of having monarchical ambitions in violation of his commitment to Artaxerxes (Neh. 6:5-7). Sanballat then dropped a hint that he would not disclose such treachery to the Persian king if Nehemiah would agree to meet with him and work out an accommodation.

Nehemiah firmly rejected this overture as a fabrication designed to lure him from the city and expose him to assassination. But the in-

37. J. Alberto Soggin, A History of Ancient Israel (Philadelphia: Westminster, 1984), pp. 273-74.

38. Yohanan Aharoni, The Land of the Bible (Philadelphia: Westminster, 1979), p. 440.

39. This was probably regarded as a neutral place, lying between Ashdod and Samaria and outside the borders of Judah; see Jacob M. Myers, Ezra-Nehemiah, Anchor Bible (Garden City, N.Y.: Doubleday, 1965), p. 138.

trigue was not yet over. Shemaiah ben Delaiah, a fifth columnist hired by Tobiah and Sanballat, pleaded with Nehemiah to seek sanctuary in the temple to protect himself against a supposed band of thugs who were intent on murdering him (Neh. 6:10–14). Nehemiah at once realized that such a display of cowardice would undermine Jewish morale and discredit him in the eyes of his people. He therefore rejected that option as well and cast himself upon the Lord for encouragement and strength.

After only fifty-two days the walls were completed. Their course and the extent of urban area they enclosed cannot be determined today because of archaeological inaccessibility, but the best interpretation of the data provided by Nehemiah is that postexilic Jerusalem was very small, even smaller than the preexilic city.[40] It was only after the Maccabean enlargement of the city in the second century B.C. that it approached its earlier size. Nevertheless, the completion of the project completely demoralized the enemies of the Jews, for they saw in it the handiwork of God (Neh. 6:16).

Once the city was secure, Nehemiah set about the even more important task of reorganizing the government and effecting a sorely needed spiritual and moral reformation.[41] He first appointed doorkeepers, singers, and other Levitical personnel and designated his brother Hanani as mayor of the city. He then began to address economic problems (Neh. 5:1–5). The prophet Haggai had pointed out an acquisitive mentality among some of the people, a selfish attention to their own enhancement at the expense of the temple and the poor (Hag. 1:2–6). This same spirit prevailed throughout the years of Ezra's leadership and now confronted Nehemiah as well. The problem had been exacerbated by both the civil war instigated by Megabyzus and the constant interference of the Samaritans and their allies. Certainly the near siege of Jerusalem during the weeks of construction only added to the misery, for food was running low and those in a position to supply it were holding out for exorbitant prices.

Some of the Jews had had to mortgage their properties to purchase food, while others had borrowed to pay the Persian taxes. Unable to repay what they had borrowed, they had been forced to deliver their sons and daughters over to their creditors as indentured slaves. The shameful thing about all this was that those who were profiting at the expense of the poor were not the heathen of the land but wealthy Jews! They were enslaving their own brothers and sisters at the same time

40. Kathleen Kenyon, *Jerusalem* (New York: McGraw-Hill, 1967), pp. 105–11.

41. For the scope of the reform see Edwin M. Yamauchi, "Two Reformers Compared: Solon of Athens and Nehemiah of Jerusalem," in *The Bible World*, ed. Gary Rendsburg et al. (New York: Ktav, 1980), pp. 269–92.

that community funds were being used to redeem Jews from indenture to Gentiles (Neh. 5:6–8). Infuriated, Nehemiah demanded that these usurious practices cease and that all persons and properties be released at once.

Nehemiah next attempted to distribute the population more evenly throughout the land. Apparently most of the returnees had settled in the villages and towns where the Babylonian destruction had been minimal. Jerusalem was virtually abandoned because of the massive devastation there (Neh. 7:4). Now that the temple and the walls had been restored, it was necessary for private housing to be built and for the sparsely populated city to be settled. The plan devised by Nehemiah was to research the genealogical records and require those who were of Jerusalemite descent to move there.

Finally, when the seventh month of the year arrived, Nehemiah assembled all the people in Jerusalem to celebrate the autumn festivals. On the first day of the month, New Year's Day, Ezra stood to read the Torah to the masses gathered before him (Neh. 7:73–8:3). When some began to weep, Nehemiah urged them rather to rejoice for this was a day holy to Yahweh. They then began to build booths in accordance with the instructions for the Feast of Tabernacles. When the fifteenth day of the month arrived, they entered the week-long celebration commemorating God's wondrous provision for his people in the wilderness as he led them to the Promised Land. All the while Ezra read from the sacred scrolls, and the people rejoiced in their new exodus and preservation.

On the twenty-fourth day of the seventh month Nehemiah called a special assembly devoted to covenant reaffirmation (Neh. 9:1). The covenant text itself is in the form of a prayer which begins by extolling Yahweh as the Creator: he alone is God.[42] It next addresses him as the God of history who elected Abraham and the fathers and promised them the land of Canaan as their inheritance. He redeemed his oppressed people from Egyptian slavery by mighty deeds, gave them law at Sinai, and after chastening them for their disobedience in the wilderness, at last brought them into the land he had promised to give them. Yet they continued to sin until they were uprooted from the land and taken captive by foreign nations. But God was gracious and merciful and restored them once more to the land. Finally, the prayer petitions him to regard their contrition and respond to their need. They are back in the land, indeed, but they remain a vassal people to an alien king (Neh. 9:32–38).

With the commitment solemnly recited, the leaders put it in writing

---

42. For Nehemiah 8–10 as covenant material see Dennis J. McCarthy, "Covenant and Law in Chronicles-Nehemiah," *CBQ* 44 (1982): 34–35.

and set their signatures to the document. Binding themselves with a curse and an oath, all the people likewise affirmed their intentions to observe the covenant requirements. Specifically they pledged to avoid intermarriage with pagans, to observe the Sabbaths, to pay the temple taxes, to follow the regulations concerning tithing and the offering of the firstborn, and to be faithful to the ministry of the temple of God.

All the preceding events appear to have transpired in one year, 445, the first year Nehemiah was in Jerusalem. He remained there for twelve years and then returned to Susa for a brief period (Neh. 5:14; 13:6–7). It was evidently during those years of absence (ca. 433–430) that the population redistribution that Nehemiah had authorized was carried out. This may have been the occasion on which the priest Eliashib moved into Jerusalem.[43] In any event, when Nehemiah returned from Susa, he found Eliashib there and, much to his disgust, his old foe Tobiah as well. Tobiah was related by marriage to some of Jerusalem's leading citizens (Neh. 6:17–18) and somehow had managed to take advantage of those connections to move right into the temple precincts themselves. Nehemiah's reaction is predictable—he ordered Tobiah thrown out and the chambers where he had been staying to be purified.

It is not possible to know what pressing business called Nehemiah back to Susa in 433. It may be simply that his leave of absence had expired and he returned to renew it. In any case he did not remain there very long, though long enough to permit all kinds of problems to reappear. We have already mentioned the harboring of Tobiah in Eliashib's temple quarters. Nehemiah also found that the Levites had been neglected, the Sabbath was being violated, and the old nemesis of intermarriage was once more in full vogue. Even one of the sons of Joiada the priest had married the daughter of Sanballat (Neh. 13:28)!

Nehemiah once more was forced to effect sweeping changes. He dedicated the wall[44]—probably on the anniversary of its construction—and took the occasion as an opportunity to establish a system which would provide for the Levites out of the offerings of the people as the law required. He also had the Mosaic stipulation read concerning the exclusion of foreigners, particularly Ammonites and Moabites,

43. Fensham, *Ezra and Nehemiah*, p. 260. Fensham points out, correctly in our opinion, that this Eliashib must not be confused with Eliashib the high priest, since the latter would hardly be identified as the overseer of the storerooms (Neh. 13:4).

44. Though most scholars connect Nehemiah 12:27–47 with 6:15 (e.g., Myers, *Ezra-Nehemiah*, p. 202), there is nothing implicit in "dedication" to limit it to an initial act of commitment. Bright (*History*, p. 383) proposes that the initial dedication took place some years after the construction. The phrases "at that time" in Nehemiah 12:44 and "on that day" in 13:1 and the unity of 12:27–13:3 make it clear that all the events recorded therein took place after Nehemiah's return to Jerusalem in about 430.

from the sacred assembly of Israel (Neh. 13:1–3; cf. Deut. 23:3–6). This no doubt was in response to the presence of Tobiah the Ammonite in the temple courts. Nehemiah then addressed the matter of Sabbath breaking and laid out strict guidelines that were to be followed by Jew and Gentile alike if they wished to avoid divine judgment and his personal wrath. Finally Nehemiah rebuked those guilty of improper marriage, even lashing out at them physically and warning them that continuation of this practice would invite his further displeasure and that of the Lord.

Malachi the Prophet

The final source of Old Testament historical information from a contemporary is the prophet Malachi. Little is known of him—even his name, perhaps[45]—but it does seem clear that his ministry coincided with some part of the governorship of Nehemiah. The lack of reference to Nehemiah and the fact that Malachi inveighed against the very abuses in religious and social life that Nehemiah corrected upon his second arrival in Jerusalem suggest that Malachi uttered his oracles in precisely that period when Nehemiah was back in Susa. A date of from 433 to 425 is, therefore, quite likely.[46]

Like Nehemiah, Ezra does not appear in Malachi's writings. Some scholars believe that Ezra had died before 432.[47] This might account for the deterioration of state and cult in Judah during Nehemiah's absence, a condition that prompted Malachi's calls to repentance and Nehemiah's subsequent reform. The great burden of the prophet is covenant violation. God had loved his people, Malachi said, but they failed to apprehend that love and, indeed, rewarded it with dishonor and disobedience (Mal. 1:6–14). This was manifested in their hypocritical offering of maimed and diseased animals to the Lord while their priests turned from the teaching of Torah and violated the covenant of Levi (Mal. 2:8). Moreover, many of the Jews, disregarding their marriage vows, had divorced their legitimate wives, thus signaling their utter contempt for the covenant whereby God had married them

---

45. "Malachi" (Heb., *mal'ākî*) means "my messenger" and so may be a nom de plume for an otherwise anonymous prophet; see Joyce G. Baldwin, *Haggai, Zechariah, Malachi* (Downers Grove, Ill.: Inter-Varsity, 1972), p. 211.

46. Walter C. Kaiser, Jr., *Malachi: God's Unchanging Love* (Grand Rapids: Baker, 1984), p. 17.

47. For example, Eybers, "Chronological Problems," *Die Ou-Testamentiese Werkgemeenskap in Suid-Africa* 19 (1979): 15. If Ezra died before 432, of course, the dedication of the walls must have been celebrated before Nehemiah returned to Susa, for Ezra is listed as a participant (Neh. 12:36).

to himself (Mal. 2:10–16). As a result the Lord would send his messianic messenger both to purge the evil from the covenant people and to purify a remnant that would walk before him in truth. In that day, Malachi asserts, "the sun of righteousness will rise with healing in its wings" (Mal. 4:2), and the Lord "will turn the hearts of the fathers to their children, and the hearts of the children to their fathers" (Mal. 4:6). Thus will be achieved the eternal purposes of God, who will bring history to its consummation by that great climactic act of redemption and restoration in his beloved Son.

The history of Old Testament Israel closes with the last chapter of the last book of the Old Testament canon. But the history of Israel as a kingdom of priests does not end there. In this respect the Old Testament is not a closed book but one that is open-ended to the purposes of God as reflected in the New Testament, purposes to be realized in the church and in eschatological Israel.

Our account has attempted to view the history of Israel not just as a socio-political phenomenon, but as an outworking of the redemptive plan of the Lord, that is, as a theological message. The world of humanity, alienated from God by the fall, is still the object of his love and grace. The Old Testament tells the story of the implementation of that grace through the vehicle of an elect man (Abraham) who gave rise to an elect nation (Israel), a kingdom of priests whose task was to demonstrate microcosmically what it means to be the redeemed people of God and to be the mediator to the world of his saving revelation.

The nation failed miserably in Old Testament times, but a remnant continued and still continues to bear witness to the unfailing covenant commitment of the Lord to seek out a people for his name. The kingdom of priests, then, is not a relic of ancient times and distant places, but is an ongoing manifestation in the earth of the gracious purposes of the King of kings and Lord of lords.

Bibliography

This bibliography contains only full-length treatments of the history and civilization of the ancient Near East and of Israel. The massive volume of literature in these disciplines requires that our lists be highly selective. For journal articles on more specific topics see the footnotes throughout the book.

The Ancient Near East

Albrektson, Bertil. *History and the Gods: An Essay on the Idea of Historical Events as Divine Manifestations in the Ancient Near East and in Israel.* Coniectanea Biblica, Old Testament Series 1. Lund: Gleerup, 1967.

Bottéro, Jean; Elena Cassin; and Jean Vercoutter, eds. *The Near East: The Early Civilizations.* New York: Delacorte; London: Weidenfeld and Nicolson, 1967.

Burney, Charles A. *The Ancient Near East.* Ithaca, N.Y.: Cornell University Press, 1977.

Cambridge Ancient History. Vols. 1–2, 3d ed., edited by I. E. S. Edwards et al.; vol. 3, 2d ed., edited by John Boardman et al. Cambridge: Cambridge University Press, 1970–1982.

Childe, V. Gordon. *New Light on the Most Ancient East.* New York: Norton, 1969.

Dentan, Robert C., ed. *The Idea of History in the Ancient Near East.* American Oriental Series 38. New Haven: Yale University Press, 1955.

Finegan, Jack. *Archaeological History of the Ancient Middle East.* Boulder, Col.: Westview, 1979.

Frankfort, Henri. *The Birth of Civilization in the Near East.* Bloomington, Ind.: Indiana University Press; Garden City, N.Y.: Doubleday, 1950.

Hallo, William W., and William K. Simpson. *The Ancient Near East.* New York: Harcourt Brace Jovanovich, 1971.

Hawkes, Jacquetta. *The First Great Civilizations.* New York: Knopf, 1973; Harmondsworth: Penguin, 1977.

Kitchen, Kenneth A. *Ancient Orient and Old Testament.* London: Tyndale; Chicago: Inter-Varsity, 1966.

—————. *The Bible in Its World: The Bible and Archaeology Today.* Exeter: Paternoster; Downers Grove, Ill.: Inter-Varsity, 1977.

Kupper, J.-R. *Les nomades en Mésopotamie au temps des rois de Mari.* Paris: Société d'édition "Les Belles Lettres," 1957.

Mellaart, James. *Earliest Civilizations of the Near East.* New York: McGraw-Hill, 1965.

Moscati, Sabatino. *Ancient Semitic Civilizations.* New York: Putnam; London: Elek, 1957.

—————. *The Face of the Ancient Orient: A Panorama of Near Eastern Civilizations in Pre-Classical Times.* Chicago: Quadrangle, 1960; New York: Doubleday, 1962.

Schwantes, Siegfried J. *A Short History of the Ancient Near East.* Grand Rapids: Baker, 1965.

Van Seters, John. *In Search of History.* New Haven: Yale University Press, 1983.

Wiseman, D. J., ed. *Peoples of Old Testament Times.* Oxford: Clarendon, 1973.

Israel

Ackroyd, Peter R. *Israel Under Babylon and Persia.* London: Oxford University Press, 1970.

Albright, William F. *From the Stone Age to Christianity.* Garden City, N.Y.: Doubleday, 1957.

Ben-Sasson, Haim H., ed. *A History of the Jewish People.* Cambridge: Harvard University Press, 1976.

Bright, John. *Early Israel in Recent History Writing.* Studies in Biblical Theology 19. London: SCM; Chicago: Alec R. Allenson, 1956.

—————. *A History of Israel.* 3d ed. Philadelphia: Westminster, 1981.

Bruce, F. F. *Israel and the Nations: From the Exodus to the Fall of the Second Temple.* London: Paternoster; Grand Rapids: Eerdmans, 1963.

Davies, W. D., and Louis Finkelstein, eds. *The Cambridge History of Judaism.* Vol. 1, *Introduction: The Persian Period.* Cambridge: Cambridge University Press, 1984.

de Vaux, Roland. *The Early History of Israel.* Translated by David Smith. Philadelphia: Westminster, 1978.

Fohrer, Georg. *Geschichte Israels: Von den Anfängen bis zur Gegenwart.* 3d ed. Heidelberg: Quelle und Meyer, 1982.

Gottwald, Norman K. *The Tribes of Yahweh.* Maryknoll, N.Y.: Orbis, 1979.

Grant, Michael. *The History of Ancient Israel.* New York: Scribner, 1984.

Greenberg, Moshe. *The Hab/piru.* New Haven: American Oriental Society, 1955.

Harrison, Roland K. *A History of Old Testament Times.* London: Marshall, Morgan and Scott; Grand Rapids: Zondervan, 1957.

Hayes, John H., and J. Maxwell Miller, eds. *Israelite and Judaean History.* Philadelphia: Westminster, 1977.

Herrmann, Siegfried. *A History of Israel in Old Testament Times.* Translated by John Bowden. Philadelphia: Fortress, 1975. Rev. ed., 1981.

Jagersma, H. *A History of Israel in the Old Testament Period.* Translated by John Bowden. Philadelphia: Fortress, 1983.

Kenyon, Kathleen. *Amorites and Canaanites.* London: Oxford University Press, 1966.

_____. *Archaeology in the Holy Land.* New York: Praeger, 1960.

Kitchen, Kenneth A. *Ancient Orient and Old Testament.* London: Tyndale; Chicago: Inter-Varsity, 1966.

_____. *The Bible in Its World: The Bible and Archaeology Today.* Exeter: Paternoster; Downers Grove, Ill.: Inter-Varsity, 1977.

Mayes, A. D. H. *Israel in the Period of the Judges.* Naperville, Ill.: Alec R. Allenson, 1974.

Miller, J. Maxwell, and John H. Hayes. *A History of Ancient Israel and Judah.* Philadelphia: Westminster, 1986.

Noth, Martin. *The History of Israel.* 2d ed New York: Harper and Row, 1960.

_____ *History of Pentateuchal Traditions.* Translated by Bernhard W. Anderson. Englewood Cliffs, N.J.: Prentice-Hall, 1972.

Oesterley, W. O. E. *A History of Israel.* Vol. 2, *From the Fall of Jerusalem, 586 B.C., to the Bar-Kokhba Revolt, A.D. 135.* Oxford: Clarendon Press, 1932.

Orlinsky, Harry M. *Ancient Israel.* 2d ed. Ithaca, N.Y.: Cornell University Press, 1960.

Pfeiffer, Charles F. *Old Testament History.* Grand Rapids: Baker, 1973.

Ricciotti, Giuseppe. *The History of Israel.* Translated by Clement Della Penta and Richard T. A. Murphy. 2 vols. 2d ed. Milwaukee: Bruce, 1958.

Soggin, J. Alberto. *A History of Ancient Israel.* Translated by John Bowden. Philadelphia: Westminster, 1984.

Thiele, Edwin R. *The Mysterious Numbers of the Hebrew Kings.* Grand Rapids: Eerdmans, 1965.

Van Seters, John. *In Search of History: Historiography in the Ancient World and the Origins of Biblical History.* New Haven: Yale University Press, 1983 (esp. chs. 7–10).

Weippert, Manfred. *The Settlement of the Israelite Tribes in Palestine.* Studies in Biblical Theology, 2d ser., vol. 21. London: SCM; Naperville, Ill.: Alec R. Allenson, 1971.

Wood, Leon J. *A Survey of Israel's History.* Grand Rapids: Zondervan, 1970.

Scripture Index

Subject Index